ZECHARIAH
9–14

VOLUME 25C

THE ANCHOR BIBLE is a fresh approach to the world's greatest classic. Its object is to make the Bible accessible to the modern reader; its method is to arrive at the meaning of biblical literature through exact translation and extended exposition, and to reconstruct the ancient setting of the biblical story, as well as the circumstances of its transcription and the characteristics of its transcribers.

THE ANCHOR BIBLE is a project of international and interfaith scope. Protestant, Catholic, and Jewish scholars from many countries contribute individual volumes. The project is not sponsored by any ecclesiastical organization and is not intended to reflect any particular theological doctrine. Prepared under our joint supervision, THE ANCHOR BIBLE is an effort to make available all the significant historical and linguistic knowledge which bears on the interpretation of the biblical record.

THE ANCHOR BIBLE is aimed at the general reader with no special formal training in biblical studies; yet, it is written with the most exacting standards of scholarship, reflecting the highest technical accomplishment.

This project marks the beginning of a new era of cooperation among scholars in biblical research, thus forming a common body of knowledge to be shared by all.

William Foxwell Albright
David Noel Freedman
GENERAL EDITORS

THE ANCHOR BIBLE

ZECHARIAH 9–14

◆

A New Translation
with
Introduction and Commentary

CAROL L. MEYERS
AND ERIC M. MEYERS

THE ANCHOR BIBLE

Doubleday

New York   London   Toronto   Sydney   Auckland

THE ANCHOR BIBLE
PUBLISHED BY DOUBLEDAY
a division of Bantam Doubleday Dell Publishing Group, Inc.
1540 Broadway, New York, New York 10036

THE ANCHOR BIBLE, DOUBLEDAY, and the portrayal of an anchor with the letters A and B are
trademarks of Doubleday, a division of Bantam Doubleday Dell Publishing Group, Inc.

Cartography copyright © 1993 Martie Holmer

Library of Congress Cataloging-in-Publication Data

Bible. O. T. Zechariah 9–14. English. Meyers. 1993.
  Zechariah 9–14: a new translation with introduction and commentary /
Carol L. Meyers and Eric M. Meyers. — 1st ed.
     p.   cm. — (The Anchor Bible; v. 25C)
  Includes bibliographical references and index.
  1. Bible. O. T. Zechariah 9–14—Commentaries.   I. Meyers, Carol L.
II. Meyers, Eric M.   III. Title.   IV. Series: Bible. English. Anchor
Bible. 1964; v. 25C.
BS192.2.A1   1964.G3   vol. 25C
[BS1663]
220.7'7 s—dc20   92-34535
[224'.98077]   CIP

ISBN 0-385-14483-0

Printed in the United States of America
November 1993

First Edition

10 9 8 7 6 5 4 3 2 1

CONTENTS

♦

Contents

PREFACE

♦

The completion of this volume on Second Zechariah marks for us the end of more than a decade of work on late biblical prophecy. We began with our study of Haggai in the early 1980s and then continued immediately with First Zechariah; our work on those two prophets of the late sixth century appeared in an earlier Anchor Bible volume (25B). Our exegetical efforts dealing with that era of biblical prophecy are now brought to a conclusion with this volume on Second Zechariah (Zechariah 9–14). As the reader will see, we believe that the final form of Zechariah 9–14 postdates that of Haggai and Zechariah 1–8 by well over half a century. Nonetheless, there is a certain logic to the fact that our work on Haggai and First Zechariah was not truly completed until we studied Second Zechariah. After all, chapters 9–14 of Zechariah belong to the same canonical book as chapters 1–8, which in turn are integrally related to the Book of Haggai.

In examining Second Zechariah, we have thus had to grapple constantly with the agonizingly difficult question of how the Book of Zechariah in its entirety entered the canon of the Hebrew Bible in the form in which we now have it. Although we have hardly resolved this issue, our awareness of the problem and our attention to it has, we hope, allowed us to glimpse aspects of the canonical process that shaped the traditions of the Second Temple period and that produced the Hebrew Bible and the New Testament. Related to this matter of canon formation and tradition transmission is the striking fact that the author(s) of Second Zechariah draws extensively, perhaps more than the author of any other biblical book, from the range of existing authoritative texts. Hence we have also been keenly aware of the complexity of this work in its connection to other parts of the Hebrew Scripture. For all these reasons, we have been alternately exhilarated as we explored the literary richness of the text and frustrated as we attempted to penetrate its many enigmatic passages.

In our exegetical NOTES, as well as in the COMMENT to each chapter, we present some of the discoveries we made as we explored the language and world of Second Zechariah. The NOTES in particular are meant to explain the words and syntax as well as the imaginative sweep of the metaphor. We have included extensive philological and grammatical discussions as well as interpretive conclusions. In so doing, we have sought relevant information from many Near Eastern languages and literatures and from the material culture, as retrieved through archaeology and survey, of the region, especially of Syro-Palestine itself.

The COMMENT to each chapter provides a more general and less technical analysis of the chapter as a whole and of its subunits. Because of the very obscure nature of some of the passages, we have taken extra effort in several of the COMMENT sections to summarize not only our conclusions but also the interpretations or reading strategies proposed by other scholars. Thus it might be helpful for some readers, after beginning with our Translation of the text, to turn next to the COMMENT, as an overview of the chapter, before looking at the NOTES for a detailed exegesis.

The Introduction contains an indication of the major results of our work on Second Zechariah. A brief résumé of the historical situation of the first century of Persian rule in the Levant, which we believe represents the historical setting for this composite work, is followed by a discussion of how we believe this work responds to the exigencies of that setting, and then by an overview of the unique literary character of Zechariah 9–14, in which inner biblical exegesis, intertextuality, and innertextuality reach unprecedented levels of sophistication and creativity.

Many people have asked us how we have managed to work together on such a large project over so many years. It is not easy to answer such a question. But at the very least, we would stress that we were able to sustain the tedium and difficulty often encountered along the way because we both found the biblical materials themselves so compelling in all their powerful intricacy of language and meaning. We hope that our efforts to understand this prophetic book of such diversity and eloquence will make it more accessible to serious readers of the Bible.

The task of preparing this volume has been facilitated by several institutions and by more people than we could possibly name in these few paragraphs. Little could have been achieved without the support of Duke University, or of our colleagues and staff in the Department of Religion. We are particularly grateful to the departmental administrator, Wanda Camp, for overseeing the preparation of the manuscript of this book; to Sondra Thompson, who typed the first draft; to Christie Tyson, who saw the manuscript through countless revisions and adjustments; and to Jane Kuenz and Darleen Hatherly, who helped us with a final series of corrections and additions. They all provided great skill and unfailing patience.

Most of the research for and writing of this book took place during the sabbatical leave awarded to each of us by Duke in 1990–1991. We spent that year as visiting faculty in the Department of Religion at Princeton University and as resident members of the Center of Theological Inquiry in Princeton. We are greatly appreciative of having had access to the resources as well as the collegiality of both institutions. We would especially like to thank the director of the Center of Theological Inquiry, Daniel W. Hardy, for his encouragement and support during our stay in Princeton.

Any number of graduate students, over the past decade or more, have assisted us in our research and in our consideration of the scholarly issues involved in this project. For the actual preparation of the manuscript, two students, Karla

Shargent and Barry Jones, have provided critical readings and useful comments. A third student, John Jorgensen, provided invaluable assistance through his preparation of the indexes. We are indebted to all of them for their willingness to help, especially at a time when they were in the midst of preparing for their own professional careers in biblical studies. We can only hope that their experience in working on this project will have contributed to their development as scholars.

We dedicated our first Anchor Bible volume to our daughters, Julie and Dina, who at that time had endured nearly five years of life with parents struggling to understand Haggai and First Zechariah. Their forbearance again, as we prepared this volume and as they reached college age and beyond, has been gratifying. Never did they make us feel that they were competing with Second Zechariah for our attention. In supporting our involvement with this project, they understood that our parental dedication to them would never be threatened or diminished by our scholarly commitments.

No one has made this task more challenging and worthwhile than David Noel Freedman—as friend, mentor, colleague, and editor par excellence. Thus it is to him that we dedicate this volume and to him that we offer our profound gratitude. He gave encouragement when it was needed, understanding when it was required, and criticism when it was warranted. The shortcomings of this volume remain the authors' sole responsibility; many of its strengths are the result of David Noel Freedman's painstaking and brilliantly perceptive encounters with the Masoretic Text of the Hebrew Bible, as communicated to the authors in lengthy and penetrating critiques of an earlier version of this work. It is our hope that the results of this exchange between authors and editor will benefit all who seek to understand Second Zechariah.

Carol L. Meyers
Eric M. Meyers

August 1992
Duke University
Durham, North Carolina

LIST OF CHARTS AND MAPS

◆

Abbreviations and Signs

♦

AAR	American Academy of Religion
AB	Anchor Bible
ABD	*Anchor Bible Dictionary*. New York: Doubleday, 1992
AfO	*Archiv für Orientforschung*
AH	*Akkadische Handwörterbuch*, ed. W. van Soden. 3 vols. Wiesbaden: Otto Harrassowitz, 1965–81
AJSLL	*American Journal of Semitic Languages and Literatures*
Akk	Akkadian
ANEP	*Ancient Near East in Pictures Relating to the Old Testament*, ed. J. B. Pritchard. Princeton: Princeton University Press, 1954
ANET	*Ancient Near Eastern Texts Relating to the Old Testament*, ed. J. B. Pritchard. Princeton: Princeton University Press, 1954
AOAT	Alter Orient und Altes Testament
ARM	Archives royales de Mari
ASOR	American Schools of Oriental Research
ATD	Das Alte Testament Deutsch
BA	*Biblical Archaeologist*
BAR	*Biblical Archaeology Review*
BASOR	*Bulletin of the American Schools of Oriental Research*
B.C.E.	Before the Common Era
BDB	F. Brown, S. R. Driver, and C. A. Briggs, *Hebrew and English Lexicon of the Old Testament*. Oxford: Oxford University Press, 1907, 1955
BHS	*Biblia Hebraica Stuttgartensia*. Stuttgart, 1977
BJRL	*Bulletin of the John Rylands Library*
BWANT	Beiträge zur Wissenschaft vom alten und neuen Testament
BZAW	Beihefte zur Zeitschrift für die Alttestamentliche Wissenschaft
CAD	*Chicago Assyrian Dictionary*, ed. L. Oppenheim. Chicago: University of Chicago Press, 1956–
CBQ	*Catholic Biblical Quarterly*
C.E.	Common Era
CTQ	*Concordia Theological Quarterly*
CurTM	*Currents in Theology and Mission*
EI	*Eretz Israel*

ET	*Expository Times*
ÉTR	*Études théologiques et religieuses*
EvQ	*Evangelical Quarterly*
FRLANT	Forschungen zur Religion und Literatur des Alten und Neuen Testaments
GKC	*Gesenius' Hebrew Grammar*, ed. E. Kautzsch, trans. A. E. Cowley. 2d Eng. ed. Oxford: Clarendon Press, 1910
HAR	*Hebrew Annual Review*
HAT	Handbuch zum Alten Testament
HBD	*Harper's Bible Dictionary.* San Francisco: Harper & Row, 1985
HTR	*Harvard Theological Review*
HUCA	*Hebrew Union College Annual*
IB	*Interpreter's Bible.* Nashville: Abingdon
IDB	*Interpreter's Dictionary of the Bible.* Nashville: Abingdon
IEJ	*Israel Exploration Journal*
JB	*Jerusalem Bible*
JBL	*Journal of Biblical Literature*
JETS	*Journal of the Evangelical Theological Society*
JNES	*Journal of Near Eastern Studies*
JNWSL	*Journal of Northwest Semitic Languages*
JPS	Jewish Publication Society
JQR	*Jewish Quarterly Review*
JSJ	*Journal for the Study of Judaism in the Persian, Hellenistic, and Roman Periods*
JSOT	*Journal for the Study of the Old Testament*
JSS	*Journal of Semitic Studies*
JTC	*Journal for Theology and the Church*
JTS	*Journal of Theological Studies*
KAI	*Kanaanäische und aramäische Inschriften*, ed. H. Donner and W. Röllig. 3 vols. Wiesbaden: Otto Harrassowitz, 1974
KAT	*Kommentar zum Alten Testament*, ed. E. Sellin, continued by J. Herrmann
KTU	*Die Keilalphabetischen Texte aus Ugarit*, I, ed. M. Dieterich, O. Loretz, and J. Sammartin. AOAT 24 (1976)
LXX	Septuagint
MT	Masoretic Text
NEB	*New English Bible.* Oxford and Cambridge, 1970
NJB	*New Jerusalem Bible*
NJPS	The *New Jewish Publication Society* of America Translation of the Holy Scriptures:
	The Torah, 2d ed., Philadelphia, 1967
	The Prophets: Neviʾim, Philadelphia, 1978
	The Writings: Kethubim, Philadelphia, 1970
NRSV	*New Revised Standard Version.* New York: Oxford, 1989
NT	New Testament

OA	*Oriens Antiquus*
OT	Old Testament
OTL	Old Testament Library
OTS	*Oudtestamentische Studiën*
RA	*Revue d'assyriologie et d'archéologie orientale*
RB	*Revue biblique*
RHR	*Revue de l'histoire des religions*
RSR	*Recherches de science religieuse*
RSV	*The Holy Bible, Revised Standard Version.* New York: Nelson, 1952
RTR	*Reformed Theological Review*
SBL	Society of Biblical Literature
SH	*Scripta Hierosolymitana*
SJT	*Scottish Journal of Theology*
Syr	Syriac
Targ	Targum
TDOT	*Theological Dictionary of the Old Testament,* ed. G. J. Botterweck, H. Ringgren, and H. J. Fabry. 6 vols. Grand Rapids: Eerdmans, 1974–
ThWAT	*Theologisches Wörterbuch zum Alten Testament,* ed. G. J. Botterweck, H. Ringgren, and H. J. Fabry. 6 vols. Stuttgart: Kohlhammer, 1970–
Tos	Tosefta
Ugar	Ugaritic
UT	C. H. Gordon, *Ugaritic Textbook.* Rome, 1965; Supplement 1967
VT	*Vetus Testamentum*
VTSup	Vetus Testamentum, Supplements
Vulg	Vulgate
ZAW	*Zeitschrift für die Alttestamentliche Wissenschaft*
ZTK	*Zeitschrift für Theologie und Kirche*
*	Unattested form.
2, 3	Supralinear number after a biblical reference (e.g., Zech 11:13^2, 14:6^3) indicates that the word or form being discussed appears twice or three times in that verse.

Note on the Translation

◆

Every work of translation must repeatedly come to grips with the necessity of making a decision between a smooth and artful style in the language to which the text is being translated, and a translation that may appear awkward or stilted but that remains as faithful as possible to the original. The variations in convention, syntax, and structure between any two languages render this task formidable if not insurmountable at times. Furthermore, the vocabulary of one language rarely admits of a one-to-one correspondence with words of another. Nuanced terms have no close parallels, and some words have not even a remote equivalent. Idiomatic expressions are notoriously difficult to render into another language in a way that provides their meaning and, at the same time, gives a sense of how the idiomatic language has been used in the original.

In the face of such problems, our guiding principle has been to remain as faithful as possible to the Hebrew syntax, to provide to the best of our ability an arrangement of words and a rhythm of language that characterizes the Hebrew original. To do so has meant, more often than we had anticipated, that the English does not read smoothly. The artistry of the Hebrew in such cases can be recovered for the non-Hebrew reader only by reference to the NOTES, where the reasons for the apparently awkward English renderings are laid forth.

Much of our analysis of this prophetic work involves awareness of literary features such as the repetition of key words and phrases, envelope constructions, chiasms, and the use of formulaic or stereotyped expressions. Transferring these features into English often produces a repetitious or stilted text, usually unacceptable in a language such as English, which has a rich vocabulary and in which the conscious varying of words and phrases is as much a stylistic feature as is the repetition of words and phrases in Hebrew. To provide a varied diction in English would be to misrepresent the artful arrangement of words in the Hebrew text. To create a smooth word order in English would be to destroy the conscious balancing of terms and parts of speech in the Hebrew.

The places in the translation that appear flawed are, for the most part, the result of our attempts to be consistent in rendering a given Hebrew root by the same English word, at least where the context is approximately the same, and by our efforts to respect the structure and integrity of the Hebrew sentence, whether it be poetic, prosaic, or somewhere in between. Because the vague last-mentioned category is a prominent feature of this prophetic book, we have deemed it especially important to refrain as much as possible from tampering with the Hebrew word order and from using more or fewer words for a given Hebrew word or phrase than appear in the original. It has not been possible in every case to follow these self-imposed guidelines, but the effort has been made.

Finally, the reader should realize that the arrangement of some lines of Hebrew text into poetic form is the result of our analysis of the structure of the Hebrew line, the relative paucity of particles associated with prose, and the presence of parallelism (see our discussion Form: Prose and Poetry in the Introduction). Many lines were difficult to characterize, as they could be said to partake of both prose and poetry. In such cases our decision to arrange some of these lines as poetry and others as prose was meant to create a variation, and so to indicate that Zechariah 9–14 contains a fair amount of such language, which can be termed oracular or elevated prose.

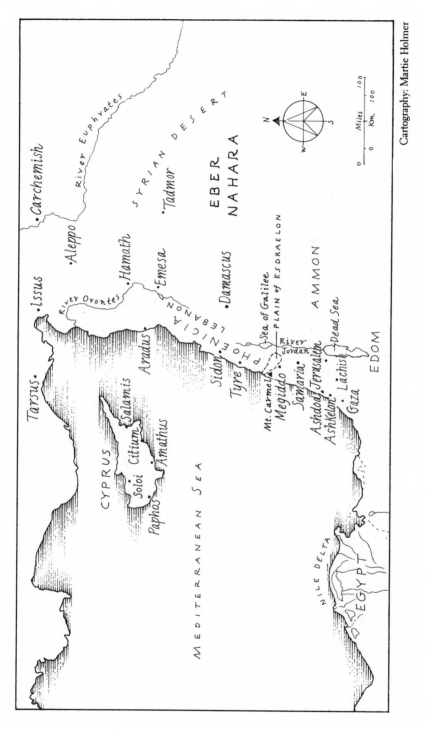

Cartography: Martie Holmer

MAP 1 SATRAPY OF BEYOND-THE-RIVER (EBER NAHARA)

xxi

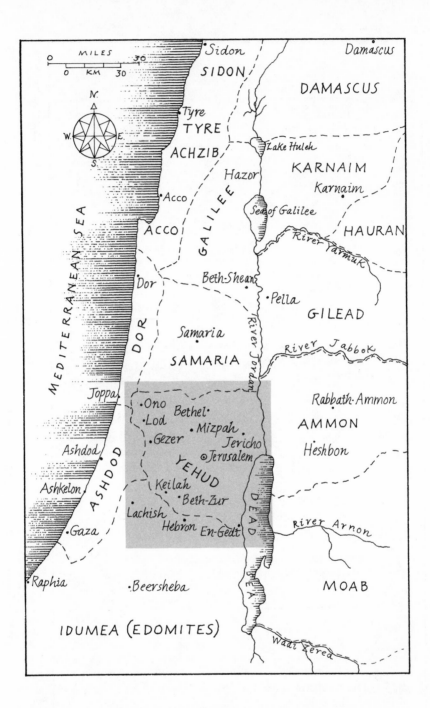

Map 2 Yehud and Other Persian Provinces in the Satrapy of Beyond-the-River

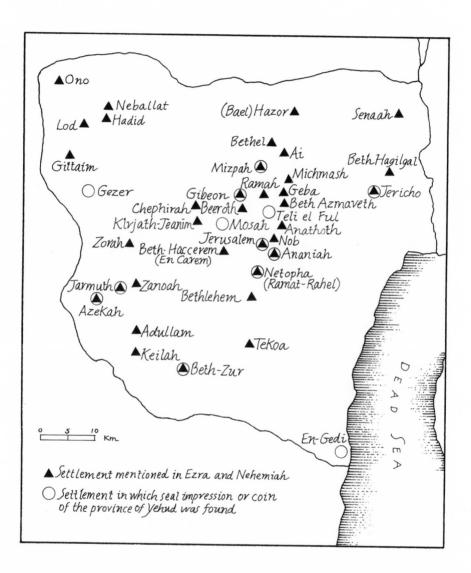

MAP 3   PROVINCE OF YEHUD, WITH SOME OF THE MAJOR SETTLEMENTS (adapted from Stern 1982)

The results of surveys in the past few decades suggest a somewhat smaller territorial extent. Moreover, it is important to note that not all these sites were occupied throughout the entire Persian period (cf. Introduction, pp. 15–59).

THE BOOK OF SECOND ZECHARIAH

TRANSLATION

◆

ZECHARIAH 9–14: TRANSLATION

◆

PART ONE: CHAPTERS 9, 10, 11

Zechariah 9

Restoration of the Land of Israel (9:1–8)

9   ¹An oracle: the word of Yahweh in the land of Hadrach;
        and Damascus is its resting place.
    For to Yahweh is the eye of the people
        and all the tribes of Israel;
    ²And also Hamath—which borders on it—
        Tyre and Sidon, for they're shrewd indeed.
    ³Tyre has built herself a bulwark;
        she has piled up silver like dust
        and gold like the mud of the streets.
    ⁴Surely the Lord will impoverish her
        and slam her wealth into the sea,
        and she will be consumed by fire.
    ⁵Ashkelon will see and be afraid,
        and Gaza too will agonize greatly,
        and Ekron, for he will dash her hopes.
    The king will perish from Gaza,
        and Ashkelon will not be ruled.
        ⁶and a villain will rule in Ashdod.
    For I will destroy the Philistines' pride;
        ⁷I will remove its blood from his mouth
        and his abominations from between his teeth.
    But there will remain also one for our God;
        He will be like a clan in Judah,
        and Ekron like a Jebusite.

⁸I will encamp at my House,
     a garrison against invaders;
An oppressor will not overrun them again,
     for now I'm watching with my eyes.

The King's Entry into Jerusalem (9:9–10)

⁹Exult greatly, O Daughter Zion!
     Shout aloud, O Daughter Jerusalem!
Behold, your king is coming to you,
     righteous and saved is he;
     humble and riding on an ass—
     on a young ass, a foal of a she-ass.
¹⁰I will cut off the chariot from Ephraim
     and the horse from Jerusalem,
     and the bow of war will be cut off.
He will promise peace to the nations;
     his rule will be from sea to sea,
     from the river to the ends of the earth.

Restoration of the People Through Yahweh's Intervention (9:11–17)

¹¹As for you, by the blood of your covenant
     I have set your prisoners free from a pit with no water in it.
¹²Return to a stronghold, O prisoners of hope;
     today too I announce I'm restoring to you double.
¹³For I have bent Judah to me;
     I have set Ephraim as a bow.
I will rouse your sons, O Zion,
     against your sons, O Greece;
And I will make you like a warrior's sword.
¹⁴Then Yahweh will appear above them;
     his arrow will go forth like lightning.
Lord Yahweh will sound the horn
     and advance with the southern storms.
¹⁵Yahweh of Hosts will protect them;
     they will consume and will conquer with sling stones;
     they will drink and be rowdy, as with wine;
     they will be full like the basin, like
     [the ones at] the corners of the altar.
¹⁶Yahweh their God will rescue them;
     on that day his people will be like sheep;

4

For like gemstones of a crown
    they will shine on his land.
[17]Then how good and how lovely!
    Grain will make the young men flourish,
      and new wine the maidens.

Zechariah 10

Yahweh Empowers Judah and Rescues Ephraim (10:1–12)

10   [1]Ask of Yahweh rain at the time of the spring-rains,
    of Yahweh, the lightning maker;
and rainstorms may he give to them,
    to each one grain in the field.

[2]For the teraphim have spoken deception,
    and the diviners have seen falsity.
They speak worthless dreams
    and give vain comfort.
Therefore they have set forth like sheep;
    they're humble without a shepherd.
[3]My anger has flared against the shepherds,
    and I will attend to the he-goats.
For Yahweh of Hosts has attended to his flock, the House of Judah,
    and will make them like his mighty horse in battle.
[4]From them will come the cornerstone,
    from them the tent peg,
    from them the bow of war,
    from them every overseer—together.
[5]They will be like heroes in battle,
    trampling in muddy places.
They'll fight because Yahweh is with them;
    they will confound those mounted on horses.
[6]I will make the House of Judah mighty,
    the House of Joseph I will save.
I will restore them because I had compassion on them;
    for they will be as though I had not rejected them.
For I am Yahweh their God,
    and I will respond to them.
[7]Ephraim will be like a hero;
    their heart rejoices as with wine.
Their children will see and rejoice—
    let their heart exult in Yahweh.
[8]I will whistle to them and gather them in,
    for I have redeemed them.

They will multiply as before.
⁹Though I sowed them among the peoples,
in remote places they'll remember me.
They'll give life to their children,
and they will return.
¹⁰I will bring them back from the land of Egypt;
and from Assyria I will gather them.
To the land of Gilead and to Lebanon I will bring them,
till no room is found for them.
¹¹He will traverse the sea of stress,
he will smite the rolling sea,
and all the depths of the stream will dry up.
The splendor of Assyria will be brought low,
and the scepter of Egypt will pass away.
¹²I will make them mighty in Yahweh;
in his name they will go about—utterance of Yahweh.

Zechariah 11

Opening Oracle: The Cry of Trees, Shepherds, and Lions (11:1–3)

11 ¹Open your doors, O Lebanon!
Let fire consume your cedars.
²Wail, O cypress! for the cedar has fallen,
the mighty ones destroyed.
Wail, O oaks of Bashan! for the dense forest is brought low.
³Hark: the wail of the shepherds,
for their wealth is destroyed.
Hark: the roar of the lions,
for the pride of the Jordan is destroyed.

The Shepherd Narrative (11:4–16)

⁴Thus spoke Yahweh my God, "Shepherd the flock to be slaughtered. ⁵Those who buy them will slaughter them, and they will not be held guilty; and those who sell them will say, 'Blessed is Yahweh, for I have become rich.' For their shepherd will not pity them. ⁶For I will not again pity the inhabitants of the land"—utterance of Yahweh. "I will indeed deliver every person to the hand of his neighbor and to the hand of his king; they will crush the land and I will not rescue [any] from their hand."

⁷So I shepherded the flock to be slaughtered, for the merchants of the flock. I took for myself two staffs: one I called Delight and the other I called Bonds.

Thus I shepherded the flock. ⁸I got rid of the three shepherds in one month; for I became impatient with them and also they felt loathing toward me. ⁹Then I said, "I will not shepherd you. Whoever is to die shall die. Whoever is to be destroyed shall be destroyed. And whoever is left shall devour each other's flesh."

¹⁰Then I took my staff Delight, and severed it, to break my covenant, which I made with all the peoples. ¹¹And so it was broken on that day. The merchants of the flock, who were watching over me, thus knew that this was the word of Yahweh. ¹²Then I said to them, "If this seems good to you, give me my wage; but if not, withhold it." So they weighed out my wage, thirty pieces of silver. ¹³Then Yahweh said to me, "Cast it into the treasury," this worthy sum at which I was valued by them. So I took the thirty pieces of silver, and I cast it into the treasury, at the House of Yahweh.

¹⁴Then I severed my second staff, Bonds, to break the kinship between Judah and Israel.

¹⁵Then Yahweh said to me, "Again, take for yourself the gear of a foolish shepherd. ¹⁶For I will indeed raise up a shepherd in the land:

> Those to be destroyed he will not attend to,
>> the one who wanders he will not seek;
>> the injured one he will not heal,
>> the one who stands firm he will not sustain.
> But the flesh of the fatted he will devour,
>> and their hooves he will tear off."

Woe Oracle to the Worthless Shepherd (11:17)

¹⁷Woe O worthless shepherd,
>> the one who abandons the flock!
May a sword be against his arm,
>> and against his right eye.
His arm will surely wither,
>> and his right eye will surely go blind.

PART TWO: CHAPTERS 12, 13, 14

Zechariah 12

Introduction: Yahweh as Creator (12:1)

12   ¹An oracle: the word of Yahweh concerning Israel—utterance of Yahweh,

> The one who stretched out the heavens and founded the earth,
> Who fashioned the breath of humankind within.

Oracles Concerning the Nations and Judah (12:2–11)

2"Behold, I am making Jerusalem a cup of reeling for all the peoples around, for [they] will be in the siege against Judah, and against Jerusalem. 3On that day I will make Jerusalem a burdensome stone for all the peoples. All who carry it will surely cut themselves, for all the nations of the earth will be gathered against her. 4On that day"—utterance of Yahweh—"I will smite every horse with panic and its rider with wildness. But on the House of Judah I will open my eyes, while every horse of the peoples I will smite with blindness. 5Then the clans of Judah will say in their hearts: 'There is strength for the leaders of Jerusalem in Yahweh of Hosts their God.' 6On that day, I will make the clans of Judah like a fire pot amid trees and like a fire torch amid sheaves. Then they will consume, on the right and on the left, all the peoples around. Jerusalem will dwell again in her place, in Jerusalem."

7Yahweh will save the tents of Judah first, so that the glory of the house of David and the glory of the leaders of Jerusalem will not be greater than Judah's. 8On that day, Yahweh will protect the leaders of Jerusalem so that the weak one among them on that day will be like David, and the house of David will be like God, like the Angel of Yahweh before them.

9"On that day I will seek to annihilate all the nations that come against Jerusalem. 10Then I will pour out on the house of David and on the leaders of Jerusalem a spirit of favor and supplication, so that they will look to me concerning the one they have stabbed."

They will mourn for him as one mourns for the only child and grieve for him as one grieves for the firstborn. 11On that day the mourning in Jerusalem will be as great as the mourning of Hadad-Rimmon in the plain of Megiddo.

Catalog of Mourners (12:12–14)

12The land shall mourn, all the families by themselves:
The family of the house of David by themselves,
and their women by themselves;
The family of the house of Nathan by themselves,
and their women by themselves;
13The family of the house of Levi by themselves,
and their women by themselves;
The family of the Shimeites by themselves,
and their women by themselves;
14All the remaining families, all the families by themselves,
and their women by themselves.

Zechariah 13

Oracle: Cleansing of the Leadership (13:1)

13 1"On that day a fountain will be opened for the house of David and the leaders of Jerusalem, for cleansing [sin] and for [cleansing] defilement."

Oracles on the End of False Prophecy (13:2–6)

²"On that day"—utterance of Yahweh of Hosts—"I will cut off the names of the idols from the land, so that they shall not be mentioned again; and I will also remove the prophets and the spirit of impurity from the land. ³If anyone still prophesies, his father and his mother who bore him will say to him, 'You will not live, for you have spoken falsity in the name of Yahweh.' Then his father and his mother who bore him will stab him when he prophesies.

⁴"On that day, the prophets will be ashamed, each one of his vision when he prophesies. They will not put on a hairy mantle in order to deceive. ⁵Rather, he will say, 'I am not a prophet. I am a tiller of the soil, for the soil has been my possession since my youth.' ⁶If someone says to him, 'What are these bruises between your shoulders?' he will say 'I was bruised in the house of my friends.' "

Devastation for Many, Survival for Some (13:7–9)

⁷O sword, arise against my shepherd,
    against one intimate with me—utterance of Yahweh of Hosts.
Slay the shepherd, that the flock may be scattered;
    I will turn my hand against the least.
⁸And in all the land—utterance of Yahweh—
    two parts in it will be cut off and perish,
    and the third will remain in it.
⁹Then I will bring the third to the fire;
    I will refine them as one refines silver,
    and I will assay them as one assays gold.
They will call upon my name,
    and I will answer them;
I will say, "That is my people,"
    and they will say, "Yahweh is my God."

Zechariah 14

Jerusalem's Devastation and Rescue (14:1–5)

14   ¹Behold a day of Yahweh is coming:
    Your spoil will be divided in your midst,
    ²for I will gather all the nations
    to Jerusalem, for war.
Then the city will be captured,
    the houses will be plundered,
    and the women will be ravished;

Half the city will go into exile,
      but the rest of the people will not be cut off from the city.

³Yahweh will go forth and fight against those nations as when he fights on the day of battle. ⁴His feet will stand, on that day, on the Mount of Olives, which is facing Jerusalem from the east. The Mount of Olives will be split in half from east to west by a very great valley. Half of the mountain will recede northward and half southward. ⁵You will flee [by] the valley of the mountains, for the valley of the mountains will reach to Azel. Thus you shall flee as you fled because of the earthquake in the days of Uzziah, king of Judah. Then Yahweh my God will come; and all the holy ones will be with you.

Jerusalem Restored (14:6–11)

⁶It will be on that day: there will no longer be cold or frost. ⁷One day, that will be known to Yahweh, there will be neither day nor night, for at evening time it will be light.
      ⁸On that day, the living waters will go forth from Jerusalem, half of them to the eastern sea and half of them to the western sea. This will be so in summer and in winter.

⁹Yahweh will be king over all the earth;
      and on that day Yahweh will be one, and his name one.

¹⁰All the land will stretch around like the plain from Geba to Rimmon, south of Jerusalem, which will stand high and dwell in her place—from the Gate of Benjamin to the place of the first gate, to the Corner Gate and the Tower of Hananel to the king's wine-presses. ¹¹They will dwell in it, and there never again will be a total destruction. Jerusalem will dwell in security.

The Fate of Jerusalem's Foes (14:12–15)

¹²This will be the plague with which Yahweh will smite all the peoples who have waged war against Jerusalem: each one's flesh will rot away while he is standing on his feet; his eyes will rot away in their sockets; and his tongue will rot away in his mouth. ¹³On that day a great panic of Yahweh will be upon them. Everyone will seize his neighbor's hand, and his hand will be raised against his neighbor's hand. ¹⁴Judah also will fight in Jerusalem. The wealth of all the surrounding nations—gold, silver, and garments—will be gathered in great abundance. ¹⁵Such will be the plague on the horse, the mule, the camel, and the ass, and every animal that is in those camps during this plague.

The Future for Jerusalem/Judah and the Nations (14:16–21)

¹⁶Then every survivor from all the nations that had come against Jerusalem will go up every year to bow down to King Yahweh of Hosts and to celebrate the

10

Feast of Booths. [17]Should any of the families of the land not go up to Jerusalem to bow down to King Yahweh of Hosts, then there will be no rain for them. [18]And if the family of Egypt does not go up and does not come in, then no [rain will be] for them; there will be the plague with which Yahweh smites the nations that do not go up to celebrate the Feast of Booths. [19]Such will be the sin of Egypt and the sin of all the nations that do not go up to celebrate the Feast of Booths.

[20]On that day, "Holy to Yahweh" will be on the horse's bells. The pots in the House of Yahweh will be like the basins before the altar. [21]Every pot in Jerusalem and in Judah will be holy to Yahweh of Hosts. And all who sacrifice will come and take from them and cook in them. No longer will there be a Canaanite in the House of Yahweh of Hosts on that day.

THE BOOK OF SECOND ZECHARIAH

INTRODUCTION

◆

THE HISTORICAL CONTEXT

The canonical Book of Zechariah, according to virtually all scholarly appraisals, consists of two separate prophetic works: Zechariah 1–8, or First Zechariah, which is treated in another AB volume (Meyers and Meyers 1987); and Zechariah 9–14, or Second Zechariah. It is nearly axiomatic in recent studies of the latter to claim that neither the historical setting nor the social context of chapters 9–14 can be recovered (e.g., Childs 1979: 474–76) and perhaps should not even be sought (Mason 1982c: 343–44). The historico-critical method that has been so successfully applied to other biblical materials has surely faltered in its application to this book, as revealed by the widely divergent conclusions briefly reviewed below (see Review of Previous Research). Even more sophisticated attempts to ferret out the complex social dynamic supposedly underlying the text are noteworthy for creating hypothetical factions without any sound verification from explicit textual references or from external data.

The difficulty in contextualizing Second Zechariah is made all the more frustrating by this work's juxtaposition with Haggai and Zechariah 1–8, both of which manifest an opposite extreme with respect to the availability in a prophetic text of much historical and sociopolitical information. Those two books, canonically linked to Second Zechariah, provide specific data, mention Yehudite leaders and Persian rulers by name, refer to some concrete challenges of the restoration community, and relate in both specific and symbolic language the response of these prophets and some of their constituency to the issues of the day.

Not so for Second Zechariah, hence the flourishing of alternative and of more comprehensive methodologies in dealing with this book. These other approaches are to be applauded, and their contribution to an understanding of late biblical prophecy heralded. Yet the emergence of new analytical processes, such as the application of critical theory, and the perceived impasse in historical analysis should not signal an end to contextualizing approaches concerned with the sociopolitical reality of the prophet's world. At present, sophisticated new ways to use archaeological data from the territory of Yehud (the name of the small Persian province occupying some of the territory known as Judah in the

15

preexilic period), as well as the application of social-scientific modes of inquiry (as developed for the early centuries of the biblical period) to the concluding centuries of the period of the Hebrew Bible, make a renewed consideration of Second Zechariah in the postexilic world possible. Our examination of the "historical context" thus introduces some fresh elements to the ongoing discussion of this critical epoch—as formative in its way, if not more so, as the Exodus event at the outset of Israelite national existence—in the history of Israel and of postbiblical Western religion.

The Sixth Century

In our commentary on the combined works of Haggai and First Zechariah (chapters 1–8) (Meyers and Meyers 1987), we dealt with the prophetic response to the events in Palestine and Babylonia that occurred in the seventy years between the destruction of the Jerusalem Temple in 587/586 B.C.E. and the dedication of the Second Temple in 516/515. We attempted to understand those two prophetic works within the context of socioeconomic and political developments in the Persian Empire and in light of the cultural tradition of Israel to which those prophets were heir. In an examination of Haggai and Zechariah 1–8 it became clear that the experience of the Exile definitively shaped the subsequent destiny of the Jewish people. It was in the crucible of that era that the remnant of Judah learned to pray without a temple, collected their sacred writings for posterity in the form of the Primary History (Genesis through Kings), and articulated a policy of accommodation to Persian imperial rule. Those achievements rank among the most important in all of Jewish history. Most of them, moreover, were accomplished before the return to Eretz Israel, a process that began after Cyrus the Great's momentous edict in 538 B.C.E.

Still, as chart 1 shows, the last third of the sixth century was also marked by the impressive and significant adaptations of the community in Yehud. The experience of the return to the land and the rebuilding of the destroyed Temple, despite the small numbers of people involved, was to have a powerful influence within the Yehudite community and upon its relations with the diaspora communities in the postexilic period and for centuries thereafter. A relatively small population in a much-reduced version of the preexilic kingdom of Judah successfully reestablished the Jerusalem Temple with its complex religious, economic, and political functions, apparently through the encouragement and support of the Persian overseers. Haggai and Zechariah 1–8 give eloquent testimony to the mood of hope in those days of the return immediately preceding the completion of the rebuilding of the Temple.

In responding to the profound social and political changes that impacted the world order in the sixth century, the postexilic community was faced with challenges that would affect their domestic and external affairs for approximately two hundred years. At the end of this time Alexander the Great would implant a new order, which was to survive in a variety of forms for about a millennium, through the Byzantine era, in southwest Asia. Perhaps the most striking aspect

CHART 1
CHRONOLOGICAL DATA RELEVANT TO ZECHARIAH 9–14

587/586	Destruction of Jerusalem and the Temple; mass deportation of Judeans to Babylon
538	Edict of Cyrus; first return under Sheshbazzar
522	Darius I (reign 522–486) takes office, organizes empire into satrapies
522/521	Zerubbabel appointed governor in Yehud; second return
520	Second Temple refoundation ceremony
516/515	Second Temple dedication
486	Xerxes I (reign 486–465) takes office; Greco-Persian wars begin
480	Persians defeated by Greeks at Battle of Salamis
478	Delian League formed to liberate Greek cities from Persians
465	Artaxerxes I Longimanus (reign 465–424) takes office
460–450	Egyptian satrapal revolt(s)
458	Mission of Ezra (?)
449	Peace of Callias between Persia and Athens
445–433	Nehemiah's mission as governor; sent in 445 to refortify Jerusalem
424	Darius II (reign 424–405) takes office
419	Hananiah, governor of Yehud (?), writes to Jews of Elephantine regarding Passover

of life in the early postexilic period was the surprising measure of autonomy in internal affairs granted by the Persians to inhabitants of the various provinces of the empire. In the sixth century the Persians in general followed a policy of allowing ethnic populations to govern themselves and to maintain their own cultural traditions. After the reorganization of the empire in about 522 and the consolidation of power at the beginning of his reign, Darius I installed his major supporters in key positions of leadership as a kind of reward for their loyalty. He placed them as governors in his satrapies, as advisers at court, and as intelligence inspectors throughout the kingdom. In some lands, such as Egypt and Yehud, that were especially important for strategic or other reasons, Darius installed local leaders who were loyal to him and who could further Persian imperial aims. In Egypt he installed Ujahorresne, and in Yehud Zerubbabel, in positions of religious and political leadership.

The beginning of the Second Temple period in 515 B.C.E. has all too frequently been viewed as a period of decline in Israelite religion. It is a period that has been said to have encompassed the demise of prophecy, as well as a narrowing of religious concerns and a concomitant overemphasis on the Temple and its ritual. This assessment of the late biblical period arose mainly from the classic nineteenth-century work of Wellhausen (1957) on the history of Israel and its denigration of Israel's supposedly ever-increasing commitment to law, narrowly conceived after the Exile, in contrast to the prominence of prophecy

17

as the supposed high point of all biblical religion in the preexilic and exilic periods. Recent scholarship on the postexilic era, however, has made great strides in acknowledging the enormous creativity of this period and in rescuing Second Temple Judaism from the often unwarranted and frequently harsh charges of exclusivism, ritualism, or legalism to which it has been subjected. Still, there persists a tendency to identify certain prophetic views, characterized as "visionary," as being more authentic than the Temple-oriented culture, supported by some prophets, that was renewed in the late sixth century (P. D. Hanson 1975: passim).

One example of evidence that the sixth century was a remarkably creative and fruitful period is the apparent existence of extensive protocanonical activities, which led to the publication of the Primary History at midcentury (see Freedman 1991: 1–40) and perhaps a revised edition later in the century. In addition, with the prophetic corpus nearing completion, efforts had surely begun to ensure its proper transmission and safekeeping. As the "last" of the writing prophets uttered their words in the next century, that segment of the Hebrew Bible was also completed. In short, the sixth century was a period of unparalleled importance for Israel. It was a period that witnessed the death and rebirth of a nation, and that was marked by the emergence of an unprecedented spirit of renewal as expressed in literary activity, which continued unabated in the fifth century until the time of Ezra.

The Fifth Century: Political Developments

The modus operandi established by the leaders of Yehud by 515, by which a series of governors and high priests successfully managed the secular and political affairs of Yehud along with its cultural and religious traditions, did not last more than a generation and a half, possibly two. The governorship was linked at first with the descendants of the Davidic dynasty. But the last Davidide to serve in a public office after the return was Shelomith, ʾāmâ of the governor Elnathan (E. M. Meyers 1985; Meyers and Meyers 1987: 12–13), at the very end of the sixth century or the beginning of the fifth century. The termination of her position and the apparent disappearance of the Davidic family from public life in the early fifth century were perhaps indicative of a general deterioration in the internal affairs of Yehud, such as is reflected in the prophetic books of Second Zechariah and Malachi and in the historical reportage of the books of Ezra and Nehemiah. Chart 2, adapted from a chart in our commentary on Haggai and Zechariah 1–8 (Meyers and Meyers 1987: 14), presents information about the leadership in Yehud from 538 to 433 B.C.E.

There is no doubt that the fairly stable situation achieved in late sixth-century Yehud was badly shaken by the significant world events that were taking place around it in the fifth century (see chart 1). Chief among those were the Greco-Persian wars, which undoubtedly preoccupied the very regime that had given the postexilic community its relative independence within the overall structure of Achaemenid imperial rule. The onset of these wars, at the end of

CHART 2
GOVERNORS, DAVIDIDES, AND HIGH PRIESTS OF YEHUD IN THE PERSIAN PERIOD (538–433 B.C.E.)

Dates	*Governors*	*Davidides*	*High Priests*
538	Sheshbazzar (*phh*, Ezra 5:14; "prince," Ezra 1:8)	Sheshbazzar b. before 592 (uncle of)	Jehozadak b. before 587 (father of)
520–510?	Zerubbabel (*pht yhwdh*, Hag 1:1, 14)	Zerubbabel b. 558–556 (?)	Joshua b. ca. 570
510–490?	Elnathan (*phwᵓ*, bulla and seal)	Shelomith (*ᵓāmāh* of Elnathan) b. ca. 540	
		Hananiah b. ca. 545	Joiakim b. ca. 545 (brother of)
490–470?	Yehoᶜezer (*phwᵓ*, jar impression)		Eliashib I b. ca. 545
		Shecaniah b. ca. 520 (father of)	Johanan I b. ca. 520 (father of)
470–	Ahzai (*phwᵓ*, jar impression)	Hattush b. ca. 495 (father of)	Eliashib II b. ca. 495 (father of)
445–433	Nehemiah (*hphh*, Neh 5:14; 12:26)	ᵓElioenai b. ca. 470	Joiada I b. ca. 470

the sixth century, placed the imperial aims of the Indo-European Persians in direct conflict with those of the Greeks. Darius I crossed the Bosporus in 512 B.C.E. in an attempt to extend his power as far north as the mouth of the Danube (Herodotus 4.83–144). As a result, the Greek cities of Ionia and Cyprus declared open rebellion against the Persians in 499. They were joined by Athens in this endeavor. Once begun, hostilities lasted for generations and pitted east again west, Asia against Europe. The Greco-Persian conflict was a struggle whose outcome in the fifth century, with Persia holding onto many of its territories in eastern Mediterranean lands, would be reversed in the fourth century by Alexander of Macedon, when Asia was unable to repel the European armies any longer. Still, even by the mid-fifth century, Persian domination was not completely reestablished or maintained.

The superior mobility of Athens, because of its great navy, led to what was probably Darius's most humiliating defeat, in 490 B.C.E., at the Battle of Marathon. His son Xerxes I (486–465) carried on the struggle against Greece but suffered great defeats at Artemisium, Thermopylae, and Salamis; and the Greek allies succeeded in expelling the Persians from Asia Minor and Cyprus through major victories at Plataea in Thessaly, at Mykale in Ionia, and at Eurymedon in Pamphylia.

Given this struggle between the two superpowers in the first three decades of the fifth century, it is not surprising that both Babylon and Egypt sought to take advantage of the situation of international hostility and unrest by attempting to carve out a much greater degree of independence for their respective territories. By 481, Xerxes ceased to be called king of Babylon; and Babylonia probably became an independent satrapy discrete from the province of Beyond-the-River (Miller and Hayes 1986: 464).

The achievement of Babylonia's independence from Persia during this period must have had immediate repercussions in Palestine. Such was the hypothesis about a response in Yehud proposed by Morgenstern decades ago (1956; 1957). Morgenstern argued that the first effect in Yehud was an attempt to install a new Judean king on the throne, whom he identified as Menahem (see Isa 51:12–13; 1957: 17–18). According to Morgenstern's theory, Xerxes thereupon urged the surrounding nations to form a coalition and attack Jerusalem, which was destroyed along with the Temple. It was into such a setting that Ezra was then sent—to rebuild the destroyed Temple and to reestablish the cult. Nehemiah came shortly later to restore completely the city walls and prevent interference from the authorities in Samaria. The missions of both Ezra and Nehemiah, therefore, in Morgenstern's view, were inspired by the events of the 480s, notably the Babylonian revolt. Although his views have never received much acceptance in the field of biblical studies or Near Eastern history, his insights into the broader implications of the Greco-Persian wars for Palestinian history deserve serious attention.

In his recent and significant work on this subject, Hoglund (1989; 1992) shares with Morgenstern the assessment that the Persian wars with the West had a major influence on Persian provinces as well as on Babylon, although the specific assessment of how that influence was manifest diverges from Morgenstern's theory. In analyzing the archaeological remains of various fifth-century Palestinian sites, Hoglund casts doubt on the view held by numerous archaeologists and biblical scholars that there were wholesale disturbances in Yehud at about 475 B.C.E. (so Wright 1965: 167; Stern 1982: 253–54; Williamson 1985: 60; and Aharoni 1979: 358). Individual scholars did not directly attribute their views to the influence of Morgenstern's theory about the Babylonian revolt. Yet their ideas indirectly contributed to supporting his assertion that in the second and third decades of the fifth century (ca. 485–475) there were widespread disturbances in Palestine and that those events are reflected in the archaeological remains of sites up and down the Levantine coast. Hoglund has convincingly shown (1989; 1992), however, that much of the evidence for those disturbances has been incorrectly dated and that the dates should be later, that is, at about 450.

In addition, Hoglund has demonstrated that, in the mid-fifth century, the Persians took extraordinary measures to tighten their administrative control over their Levantine territories by constructing a series of distinctive fortresses on both sides of the Jordan River, on the coastal plain, and throughout the hill country of Palestine (1989: 446ff. and illustrations). These fortresses were no doubt manned by imperial garrisons whose distinct charge was to maintain strict control of the empire in local affairs and to prevent local populations from aligning themselves with the Greek forces that threatened Persia.

That such measures came in response to increased instability, if not rebellion, in the provinces seems clear. Because the fortresses were probably constructed in about 450 or slightly later, we suggest that the specific historical context for such measures lies in the aftermath of the Egyptian, rather than the Babylonian, response to the Greco-Persian wars. That is, it was the Persian actions following an Egyptian satrapal revolt in the 450s, when the Egyptians sensed a weakening grip by the Persians on the far-flung empire and so attempted to throw off Achaemenid domination, rather than, or perhaps in addition to, the earlier events in Babylonia, that led to a strengthening of Persian control of its territories and a concomitant decrease in autonomy in those holdings.

In any case, to understand events in Palestine in the fifth century it must be recognized that the three decades leading up to the mission of Nehemiah in 445 had a profound impact on the internal affairs of Yehud. Although particulars may be lacking, the overall picture is surely one of international strife and accompanying restrictions. It is no wonder that as the political picture muddied at home and abroad and as the reins of Persian control became tighter than they had ever been, the Yehudites turned increasingly to eschatological thinking in their attempts to cope with the present world order.

Some echoes of Israel's responses to these earthshaking events are surely preserved in the compendium of prophetic oracles we call Second Zechariah, which are the focus of this commentary. To be sure, Persia is nowhere explicitly mentioned in Zechariah 9–14. However, this situation can be understood as a function of the apocalyptic, or heightened eschatological, mode of the oracles. They move to the transhistorical realm precisely because of the apparently hopeless nature of the present reality. But other literary responses mentioning Persia do exist, including that of the great Greek tragedian Aeschylus, who has captured the essence of these times in his play *The Persians*. The following excerpt poignantly preserves a universal perspective on the Greco-Persian conflict:

> Nations wail their native sons,
> Who by Xerxes stuffed up hell;
> Many heroes, Persia's bloom,
> Archers, thick array of men,
> Myriads have perished. Woe, O King of noble strength
> Cruel! Cruel! Asia kneels.
> (Grene and Lattimore 1959–60: 252)

Although the details of the Egyptian revolt are complex and so are difficult to reconstruct, many of its major events can be established. The rough outlines of the revolt are worth reviewing. In all probability it began in 464 at the beginning of the reign of Artaxerxes I. Artaxerxes had just assumed power at the

Persian court, where his father, Xerxes I, had been killed by his vizier, when the Egyptian Inaros, son of a nonroyal official Psammetichus, organized the revolt (Cook 1983: 99; Hoglund 1989: 256). Inaros was probably the leader of a non-Egyptian ethnic community in the western Delta. His leadership of the revolt reflected a growing dissatisfaction with regional administrators and represented a major challenge to Persian claims to be the legitimate successors of the pharaohs. The satrap of Egypt, Achaemenes, suffered a major setback at Papremis, after which the Athenians joined the revolt and provided greatly needed naval forces to attack the Persian garrisons from the Nile River. Although preoccupied with the effort to recapture Cyprus, the Athenians looked upon the Egyptian revolt as a unique opportunity to assert their dominance in the eastern Mediterranean. Their first efforts to defeat the Persians failed, however, for troubles in the Delian League contributed to the weakness of Athens. Indeed, by 455 the Athenian fleet and Egyptian rebels were soundly defeated by the Persians, who were led by Arsames, satrap of Egypt, and Megabyzos, satrap of Beyond-the-River. The Peace of Callias (449) succeeded for a limited while in keeping Athens out of Egypt and Cyprus in exchange for leaving the western coast of Asia Minor free of Persian interference (Miller and Hayes 1986: 464).

The Egyptian revolt and the doomed entry of the Greek military on the side of the Egyptians represented the most serious challenge to imperial power the Persians were to suffer in the fifth century. Had Inaros and his Greek allies succeeded in overthrowing Persian control, Persian holdings in all the eastern Mediterranean and Levant undoubtedly would have been threatened. To safeguard against such a possibility in the future, from 460 onward the Achaemenid Empire was constantly undertaking new ways to exercise greater control over its western provinces. Some measures were directed against the continuing Greek threat. Others were directed largely at other local populations of the empire, especially those bordering on the area of unrest, for during the 450s such others must have entertained a thought or two about embarking on a similar course of action or about joining the Egypto-Greek insurrection. The result, as we have already mentioned, was an effective network of Persian fortresses in the Levant and the installation of garrisons that controlled the major roads and arteries linking the Persian capital with the Mediterranean Sea. The many grain pits of the Persian period discovered at sites such as Tell el-Hesi or Tell Jemmeh also witness these events: they served the Persian soldiers while they patrolled strategic roadways (Betlyon 1991; van Beek 1983).

The Fifth Century:
Economic and Demographic Conditions

The political developments of the first half of the fifth century surely point to a change from the conditions of the late sixth century, when Achaemenid policies contributed to the optimism and hope, attending restoration activities, that characterize Haggai and First Zechariah. It is no wonder, then, that the oracles of Second Zechariah, coming decades if not a half-century or more later, reflect a more lachrymose view of reality, which is manifest both in the reworking of the meaning of destruction and exile and in the heightened eschatological thrust of many of the statements of Zechariah 9–14.

These features of Second Zechariah must be seen not only in light of the political currents but also against the economic background, and the related demographic situation, of the fifth century. Recent archaeological work and analysis—particularly the compendious work of Stern (1982), the thorough surveys in Galilee, Ephraim, Judah, and Benjamin (Kokhavi 1972; Finkelstein 1988–89; Magen and Finkelstein forthcoming; Ofer forthcoming), and several doctoral dissertations (Hoglund 1989; Carter 1991)—make it possible now to examine the material conditions of Yehud in a way hitherto not possible. The Persian period has long been considered one of the most obscure eras in ancient Palestinian history during biblical times. Now, at last, many details of its cultural history are emerging from the mists of the past.

Perhaps the most important development in the overview of this period (538–332 B.C.E.), because of its great significance for assessing changes that occurred over time within the Persian period as a whole, is the refinement of its chronology. Rather than lump all sites with Persian-period remains into a single cultural unit termed "Persian," it is now possible to identify changes in the ceramic repertoire during the course of the centuries of Achaemenid hegemony over Palestine and hence to subdivide this time span into two epochs: Persian I (538–ca. 450) and Persian II (ca. 450–332). This refinement in periodization (see Carter 1991: 93–96) makes it possible to identify changes in settlement patterns and density, that is, to discern population growth and some increase in prosperity, during the two centuries of Yehud's existence under Persian domination.

Now that sites of the late sixth and first half of the fifth centuries can be considered separately from all other sites with Persian-period remains, it becomes clear that Yehud in the first century or so of the postexilic period was considerably less settled and less populous than it was in the period taken as a whole. To put it another way, there was a significant increase in the number and size of Persian-period sites in the second part of the Persian period as opposed to the first part. Chart 3, adapted from Carter (1991: 162, Table 3, and Appendix 2), shows an increase after the mid-fifth century in the total number of inhabited sites, in the approximate area of actual settlements, and in the estimated population. It should be noted that in assigning sites to Yehud for this chart, a conservative approach seemed most appropriate. The complex issues of the boundaries of the province have achieved no scholarly consensus, so an appraisal that takes geographical and environmental as well as historical factors into account seemed more useful than one that relies chiefly on textual sources.

It is clear from the data in chart 3 that Yehud did not flourish, if the number and size of sites can be taken as some measure of prosperity, in the earlier part of the postexilic era. A comparison with settlement patterns in the hill country in the preceding (Iron II) period confirms the sense of dramatic population decrease that characterized Persian I. In the late preexilic period, 21 percent of

CHART 3
SIZE AND POPULATION OF YEHUD IN THE POSTEXILIC PERIOD

	Persian I	Persian II
Number of sites[a]	92	114
Settled area[b] (in dunams)	434	678
Approximate population[c]	10,850	17,000

[a]Includes both excavated sites and sites identified in survey; omits caves and tomb sites with Persian remains. (The figures are tentative, because distinctions between Persian I and II are very difficult when it comes to evaluating survey data.)

[b]Includes both excavated and surveyed sites, and a 10 percent correction factor for estimated sites as yet undiscovered. One dunam = about .25 acre or .1 hectare (one hectare = 10,000 square meters or 2.47 acres).

[c]Using a population coefficient of 25 persons per dunam, which takes into account the variation in density among the various ecological niches of Yehud.

all hill-country sites were located in Judah and Benjamin; in the Persian period as a whole, that percentage dropped to 11 (B. A. Jones 1991, based on Kokhavi 1972; Finkelstein 1988–89; and Zertal 1986). In comparison with the preceding and following epochs, the late sixth and first half of the fifth centuries represented a low point in the demographic history of ancient Israel.

The demographic situation in Jerusalem, which became a focus of Second Zechariah's eschatology, is perhaps even more dramatic, considering how swollen the capital city had become in the late eighth century (until the 587 destruction), probably because of the influx of refugees from the north after the Assyrian conquest of the Northern Kingdom in 721. After the Exile, however, despite the rebuilding of the Temple and presumably also of the associated administrative complex, Jerusalem remained a rather tiny community, as chart 4 indicates (based on Carter 1991: 109–20, 159–62; cf. Avigad 1954; Broshi 1978; Bahat 1990: 34–36). As evident in chart 4, it was only after the mission of Nehemiah (in the Persian II period) and the accompanying efforts, perhaps initiated by the Persians, to repopulate Jerusalem and rebuild its walls, that this city began to recover some of its former extent and importance.

The failure of Yehud to recover quickly, in terms of population and material gains, from the devastation of the Babylonian conquest can also be seen in the disparity between the type of sites in Yehud in comparison with those in the adjacent regions. Very few of the Persian period sites in Yehud could be characterized as urban settlements, whereas sizable urban centers flourished, for example, along the coastal plain and in the adjacent Shephelah during the same time period. The extensive occupation and well-planned character of many of these sites (e.g., Dor, Jaffa, and Shiqmona, and perhaps also the Philistine cities) in areas bordering on Yehud are testimony to the way those cities were brought into the orbit of eastern Mediterranean trade. Linked to the Phoenician

CHART 4

SIZE AND POPULATION OF JERUSALEM
IN THE POSTEXILIC PERIOD

	Persian I	*Persian II*
Occupied area[a]	15–20	50–60
Public area[b]	70–80	70–80
Approximate population[c]	475–500	1,750

[a]Residential sectors, in dunams
[b]Temple Mount and administrative complex, in dunams
[c]Using a population coefficient of 25 persons per dunam

centers to the north, these coastal cities of Palestine, in contrast to the inland sites of Yehud, shared in the prosperity of the thriving commercial activity of the Persian I period.

Not only the size and nature of the sites, but also other aspects of their material culture, attest to the differential in material prosperity between coastal and Shephelah sites and their inland neighbors. The flourishing sea trade, notably with Greece, and the commercial development of the age can be discerned mainly in the repertoire of artifacts recovered from the former group of sites. The excavated remains from those sites include imported ceramics of the Persian period. These ceramics are dominated by fine wares from the Aegean, notably of east Greek and Attic origin, and are indicative of trade with the West. The East Greek wares (mainly from Chios, Lesbos, Rhodes, and Samos), not attested at sites in Yehud, appear in the neo-Babylonian and Persian I periods. Only the Attic wares that dominate in the fifth and fourth centuries are found in Yehudite territory as well as in coastal and Shephelah sites, and these seem to come mainly from the Persian II period. The inland Palestinian sites clearly did not participate as soon, or as fully, in the fruits of the extensive commercial connections that the Persian domination of the eastern Mediterranean fostered (B. A. Jones 1991). Perhaps the less-than-bountiful agricultural foundations of the hill country economy were taxed to their limit by Achaemenid policies and were slow to reach the point of surplus necessary for participation in the international markets.

Whatever the reason, the settlements of Yehud did not immediately share in the prosperity brought about by the new ties between east and west under Persian imperialism. Consequently, the expectations of the restoration community, in economic as well as political terms, were not met during the first epoch (Persian I) of postexilic life. The great concern in Second Zechariah with the gathering of the dispersed, the repopulation of the greater land of Israel, the restoration of its former extent, and the full inhabitation and flourishing of Jerusalem reflects the anguish of a prophetic mind or minds steeped in the perspectives of earlier prophetic voices and so unable to bring present fifth-century conditions into alignment with what early generations had envisioned. These visions are not lost, however, in the treatment of Second Zechariah. Rather, they are given vivid expression in the intensely eschatological oracles of Zechariah 9–14.

PROPHETIC RESPONSE

In our volume on Haggai and Zechariah 1–8 (Meyers and Meyers 1987: xl–xlviii), we argued that those two works were redacted and organized into a composite work for publication and presentation in time for the dedication of the Second Temple. Our reasons for such a claim were based on both literary and historical features of Haggai and First Zechariah. Especially significant are the data preserved in the chronological headings, which span the period from August 29, 520 B.C.E. (Hag 1:1) to December 7, 518 B.C.E. (Zech 7:1). The latter date is the last such piece of information to be preserved in the prophetic corpus. No such chronological details are provided in Second Zechariah. Nonetheless, as the preceding historical résumé indicates, we can reconstruct some of the significant world events for the second seventy-year period after the Exile, from the dedication of the Second Temple (515 B.C.E.) to the Mission of Nehemiah (445 B.C.E.). It is within this period, particularly toward its end, that we assign the collection of oracles and utterances that constitute Zechariah 9–14.

Unlike the prophecies of Haggai–Zechariah 1–8, which were elicited by a specific set of historical circumstances concentrated in a very brief period and identified within the prophetic books themselves, the materials that constitute Second Zechariah were probably composed, uttered, collected, and arranged over a much longer period. In the course of the events of the first half of the fifth century, the relatively secure and somewhat autonomous situation of the early restoration era was replaced by the less stable circumstances that emerged from the Greco-Persian (and Egypto-Persian) struggles that preoccupied the eastern Mediterranean and Levant for virtually the entire fifth century. Thus the themes, as well as the intensely retrospective and eschatological interests, of much of the Second Zechariah collection must have been directly affected by the political currents of the early to mid-fifth century, and especially by Persia's efforts to strengthen control over its western provinces.

Many scholars have proposed that the sociopolitical setting for Zechariah 9–14, and the supposed impact of tumultuous world events in the prophecies of Second Zechariah, are to be found in the period of Alexander the Great or in the Hellenistic world of the third century (see, e.g., Delcor 1951a). Others would assign a much earlier date, whereas a more cautious group sees too little reference to political reality in Zechariah 9–14 to justify any close dating or assigning of historical context or even authorship. Although we resonate with the group that urges caution in seeing any historical milieu, we have a more optimistic stance in light of what we have set forth above (cf. various NOTES and COMMENTS that follow). We believe that assigning Second Zechariah to pre-fifth-century periods or to the Hellenistic world is unwarranted. Instead, the nature of the responses contained in Zechariah 9–14 is comprehensible in light of the situation in the first half of the fifth century, as best we can comprehend it, even though some earlier form of chapter 9 might have been appropriated and only refined at that time. Earlier materials may also be embedded in other sections of Second Zechariah; see also the discussion below, in Literary Considerations, Intertextuality of Zechariah 9–14.

The social setting for the language of power also contributes to the case for a mid-fifth-century date for the canonical form of Second Zechariah. Such language appears prominently in Second Zechariah, especially in the military (or divine warrior) imagery of chapters 9, 10, 12, and 14. The extensive and vivid depictions of violent militant actions are in striking contrast to the restraint of First Zechariah (4:6ff. and 6:11ff.), the peaceful scene of Zech 9:9 notwithstanding. The emergence of the language of power in Second Zechariah can best be understood as characterizing a period in which there had been a collapse of the possibility of realizing the expectations of national restoration that were part of the message of exilic prophecy. With the glorious hopes foreclosed in social and political reality, the continued validity of the expectation for restoration involved its transfer to the eschatological realm. Only by supernatural and transhistorical means, through divine intervention, could a restoration be envisioned (see D. L. Smith 1989: 85).

The Persian military activities in response to the problems with Greece and Egypt reduced the potential of provincial autonomy. At the same time, the Persian empowerment of Ezra and Nehemiah in leadership roles in Yehud foreclosed any possibility of significant royal involvement in leadership. Thus Second Zechariah's oracles, with their strong images of divine action, make the most sense against the backdrop of the fifth century, when circumstances had changed for the worse. Yehud was in a recession, both politically and socioeconomically, or perhaps even in a depression. The context thus would have been one of lowered expectations, by the people of Yehud, for any change in their political or economic status. They could hardly have sensed an imminent realization in history of Yahweh's promise.

Chapters 9–14 probably do not represent the sayings of a single prophet in response to a specific event or series of historical events. Rather, they represent the collected sayings of one or more individuals, who spoke within the framework of earlier prophecy as it had been transmitted at that time (cf. Freedman 1991: 66–73). More specifically, the author or authors of Second Zechariah were undoubtedly individuals who emerged in the shadow of Zechariah, the prophet of the restoration, inasmuch as the language and themes of First Zechariah played a definitive role in shaping chapters 9–14. Some might characterize the author(s) of these chapters as belonging to a circle of prophets among whom the words of the earlier prophets were preserved and expanded upon, but among whom the words of Zechariah ben-Berechiah ben-Iddo (Zech 1:1) were especially revered. It was within such a group that "canonical intentionality" (Childs 1979: 482) was achieved, whereby chapters 9–14 were attached to chapters 1–8

27

of Zechariah, which had already been attached to and circulated with the Book of Haggai (see Meyers and Meyers 1987: lxii–lxiii).

In short, the impetus for such change and revision, i.e., the expansion of the existing Book of Zechariah, was undoubtedly a combination of factors: (1) the general impact of the Greco-Egyptian rebellion and its aftermath; (2) the greater control exerted by the Persians on their Levantine holdings, especially Yehud; (3) an awareness that a significant repopulation of Jerusalem and Yehud, and attendant economic prosperity—both of which should have followed upon Temple restoration—had not materialized; and, perhaps, (4) the perception that prophecy in its traditional form was at an end and that the authoritative prophetic works and words of the past needed to be collected for posterity. The Book of the Twelve Minor Prophets was ultimately the result of such factors.

Whether or not the closing of the Book of the Twelve Minor Prophets represents the unique perspective of the canonical process in the time of Ezra or earlier, or even possibly later in light of the data from Qumran (see The Text of Second Zechariah, later in this Introduction), the writing down of God's words (Jer 15:16 and 36:20ff.) and their transmission in written form greatly affected the last years of biblical prophecy. First Zechariah's visionary depiction (5:1–4) of a "flying scroll" is an unusual and striking testimony to the centrality of a recognized body of an official and authoritative literature operating in the restoration community. The airborne roll of parchment signifies a codification of legal materials, all of which have the authority of divine covenant (see Meyers and Meyers 1987: 277–93).

One implication of such a prophetic vision is surely that, by the late sixth century and during the fifth century, prophecy was shifting away from the oral medium of communication to the written medium (cf. Davis 1989 and Utz-schneider 1989). The dramatic change in prophetic speech patterns, as evident, for example, in the marked increase in the use of transmission formulas to establish the authority of the prophetic word, suggests such a transformation. Indeed, the heightened layering of formulaic language and the clustering of introductory terms before oracular materials may have been a means of aug-menting the authority of these works by authors who were aware of the canon-formation activities of the sixth and fifth centuries and who hoped that their works would be assured a place in the emerging canon.

The decline of poetic speech in favor of oracular prose also points toward such an interpretation. Dependence on the written word, therefore, whether it be the words of "former prophets" (Zech 1:4) or quotations or reinterpretations of other materials from the Torah, was a feature (see Literary Considerations, Intertextuality of Zechariah 9–14, later in this Introduction) of late biblical prophecy that not only marked new directions in prophetic activity but also contributed to the need to preserve the works of early authoritative materials more permanently and systematically. This impetus to preserve and transmit sacred writings must also be seen, of course, within its functional context of sustaining communal traditions and values and thereby maintaining community identity under the dramatically altered social, economic, and political conditions of the exilic and postexilic periods among both the exiles and those remaining in their ancestral homeland.

Combining chapters 1–8 and 9–14 of what was to become the canonical Book of Zechariah must surely have been part of the overall process of preserving and building on sacred traditions. The theme of the centrality of the Temple, so essential to First Zechariah, is restated and supplemented in Second Zechariah, along with a much expanded eschatology, well beyond the limited articulation of chapters 7–8. Zechariah 1–8 envisions a future rooted in the return from Babylonian exile and the reorganization of Judean life around the Temple. Chapters 9–14 anticipate the ultimate, full restoration of Israel, the return of all the exiles, and the final participation of all the nations in recognizing Yahweh's sovereignty (14:16–19), as human history comes to a climax and is transformed into a truly sacred society (14:20–21), again with the center of the new order being Jerusalem and its Temple.

Second Zechariah therefore may not be an individual personality whose life and motivation can be discerned and described, although in the discussion of the literary aspect of Zechariah 9–14 (later in this Introduction), the possibility of single authorship of these chapters is entertained. "Second Zechariah" in this commentary is the nomenclature used to characterize a grouping of prophetic materials that have a consistency of language, a coherence of ideas, and a congruence with First Zechariah, whether they are the result of the work of one or many prophets and/or redactional hands.

FORM: PROSE AND POETRY

In our previous discussion of the character and texture of the language of Haggai and Zechariah 1–8, we concluded that most of it could be considered prose, or oracular prose, by any means of measure or analysis (Meyers and Meyers 1987: lxiii–lxvii). Despite the fact that printed editions of the Masoretic Text set off much of the text as poetry, we resisted the temptation to describe it as poetic or even as "poetic prose." Applying the Andersen-Freedman method (1980: 57–66) of statistical analysis of the prose particles *ʾšr*, *ʾt*, and *h* to Haggai–Zechariah 1–8, we observed that the text fell well within the percentages of oracular prose: it exhibits an average of 18.7 percent for Haggai and 15.8 percent for Zechariah 1–8.

Among many others, Hoftijzer (1965: 50) admits that it is extremely difficult to delimit the boundaries between prose and poetry, and that it is especially difficult to characterize the essence of ancient Hebrew poetry. Nevertheless, it is important to note that in his study of the density of *ʾet syntagmemes* (i.e., the particle *ʾet* and the word or words following it) he reaches the conclusion that all the Book of Zechariah, except chapter 9, is narrative prose material (1965: 52). Hill, when applying the Andersen-Freedman prose-particle system of counting, similarly concludes that all of Zechariah except chapter 9 falls squarely within the range of prose; that is, in statistical terms, the frequency of prose particles is about 15 percent (1982: 108). He contends that the same holds true for Haggai and Malachi. Although our statistics (see chart 5) vary slightly from those of Hill, they nonetheless accord well with his observations.

It is significant that in Hoftijzer's and Hill's studies and in our analysis, chapter 9, with a prose-particle density of 1.4 percent, aligns clearly with blocks of poetic material. The fact that there is such a striking difference between chapter 9 and the rest of Zechariah raises the possibility that its transmission history is also distinctive and that its present position in the canonical book is the result of editorial placement. Taken at face value, the headings (*maśśāʾ*) of chapters 9 and 12 are intended to make parallel two distinct units, chapters 9–11 and chapters 12–14, the first consisting of 642 words and the latter of 751 words. Our exegetical treatment of chapter 9, however, indicates not only that its canonical placement is logical but also that it connects with the texts that follow it (chapters 10–14). Furthermore, we remain unconvinced that the strikingly poetic character of chapter 9 in and of itself constitutes evidence that the entire chapter must predate the rest of Second Zechariah. For further discussion of the place of chapter 9 in Second Zechariah, we refer the reader to its treatment in Literary Considerations (see especially charts 6 and 7 and the discussion of what is presented in those charts).

Despite the fact that the Book of Second Zechariah exhibits an inner canonical logic and even elaborates on many of the themes of First Zechariah, we hold to the consensus view that Zechariah 1–8 has an authorship completely separate from that of Zechariah 9–14. The statistical treatments of Radday and Wickmann, which attempt to demonstrate the authorial unity of all of Zechariah based on statistical linguistics and word-frequency profile (1975) must be rejected. The criticism by Portnoy and Petersen (1984) of those works seems amply justified. Among other things, they conclude that on statistical grounds

CHART 5
PERCENTAGE DISTRIBUTION OF PROSE PARTICLES
IN ZECHARIAH 9–14

Chapters/Verses	Words	ʾšr	ʾt	hᶜ	Totals	Percentageᶜ
9:1–17[a]	222	0	0	3/4	3/4	1.4/1.8
10:1–12	166	1	6	5	12	7.2
11:1–17	254	4	18	31/32	53/54	20.9/21.3
12:1–14[b]	227	1	8	22/28	31/37	13.8/16.3
13:1–9	152	1	8	19/22	28/31	18.4/20.4
14:1–21	372	9	6	53/64	68/78	8.8/21.5
Total	1383	16	48	133/155	195/216	13.4/14.7

[a]Average for Zechariah 9–11 is 9.8 percent, excluding nonconsonantals.
[b]Average for Zechariah 12–14 is 16.9 percent, excluding nonconsonantals.
[c]The second number includes nonconsonantals.

Zechariah 1–8 may be distinguished from 9–11 and 12–14, and that Zechariah
9–11 and 12–14 may be distinguished from each other (1984: 12). In other
words, they make a strong case for multiple authorship. Given that chapter 9 is
not treated by Hill because it has a unique poetic character, a fact with which
we agree, it would seem appropriate to leave the matter of the exact date of its
original composition open for the time being, despite the fact that its subsequent
canonical revision and placement quite suits its present context in Second
Zechariah.

It is not at all unusual for a prophetic work to be as variegated as Zechariah
in terms of the variety of its literary styles. Indeed, Hebrew literature, as well as
the literature of other parts of the world, is replete with the mixing of various
genres within a common setting or work. In theory, at least, when so pure a
form of poetry as chapter 9 stands out as it does from the surrounding material,
it need not necessarily be the result of independent origin and authorship.
Because the overall statistical profile of the Haggai–Zechariah–Malachi corpus
is so similar except for chapter 9, it is at least feasible though not necessary that
the history of that chapter is more complex than other portions of those three
prophetic works.

One final observation may be made about the statistical analysis of chapters
9–14. Although the overall average of the distribution of prose particles for these
chapters is 13.4 or 14.7 percent (cf. 15.8 percent for Zechariah 1–8), the
percentage for chapter 10—7.2—is quite low and perhaps signifies something
about the evolution of what most commentators call Part One of Second
Zechariah (chapters 9–11). A sample of five thousand prose words from the
Pentateuch and Former Prophets yields about 17 percent; thus 7.2 percent is
much closer to poetry than to prose. The reader is referred to the NOTES section
of the commentary for a more detailed discussion of this and related issues. The
point suggested by this profile is that some of the material in Second Zechariah,
especially chapter 9 and possibly chapter 10 as well, is quite complex and may
bespeak, as we suggest in Literary Considerations, a new literary strategy by a
fifth-century hand rather than a random mix of older (poetic) materials with
later prose. Such variation in texture contributes to our understanding of
chapters 9–14 as a grouping of utterances and sayings that achieves a compelling
inner coherence. This view comports well with Hill's linguistic examination of
Zechariah 10–14, which he places in the pre-Ezra period of the decline in
Hebrew, or the first half of the fifth century B.C.E. (1982: 130–32). This dating
on linguistic grounds, it should be noted, is in complete agreement with our
conclusions about dating based on sociopolitical and economic factors.

The reader may observe that in our translation a number of subunits that are
fully within the prose range have nonetheless not been set off as narrative prose.
These sections (11:1–3, 17; 12:1, 12–14; 13:7–9; 14:1–2) represent distinct
variations from the surrounding prose subunits. Although not poetic in a
technical sense, their nonnarrative character makes at least some of them quasi-
poetic. More important, they contribute to the variegated composition of the
work (chapters 9–14) as a whole. Consequently, our decision not to set all the

31

subunits with prose-particle counts that place them in the prose category as conventional prose is meant to indicate the richness of texture in Second Zechariah.

LITERARY CONSIDERATIONS

With so little concrete historical or social information evident in Second Zechariah, attention to its literary features becomes a critical matter. This is true not only because the issue of how and why this work departs from earlier prophetic writings has not been well understood, nor only because its use of figurative language is often so difficult to penetrate. The need to consider its idiosyncratic blend of materials and its complex relationship to the emerging canon arises from the way in which these prophetic chapters are part of the agonizing social drama of the postexilic period and of the transformative process of that era—a process that rescued a battered and disrupted community from the dangers of dissolution and disappearance. In this respect these texts, no less than other sacred writings and perhaps even more so in light of the relative dearth of contextualizing information, must be viewed as a nexus of social reality, literary expression, and conceptualizations of God's will (cf. the introductory chapter of Craig 1992).

Much of our exploration of the literary aspects of this prophet are embedded in our exegetical NOTES, as well as in the COMMENT following each chapter. Indeed, the very convergence of the literary dimension of the text with the issues of society and of beliefs mandated that we take into account the literary articulation of these six biblical chapters in our attempt to comprehend their meaning and functions. We direct readers to those discussions as they appear. Here, rather than attempt to summarize the different literary features and strategies that we discovered in the text, it is our intention to deal with some overall patterns discernible within Zechariah 9–14 as a whole and to identify and explore the interface between this prophetic work and the authoritative texts hovering in the background.

Integrity of Zechariah 9–14

At first perusal, and even at subsequent serious readings, the materials of Zechariah 9–14 seem to be a bewildering hodgepodge of disparate forms and divergent foci. This very feature of these chapters provides perhaps the strongest justification for the theory that the various components of Second Zechariah are from different hands and/or from distinct chronological or social settings. The apparently composite nature of the text has meant that it has frequently been characterized as an anthology (see Lacocque 1981: 138–39).

Although we have no quarrel with identifying Zechariah 9–14 as a work with variegated components, and indeed believe it is important to highlight that feature, we resist the notion that this characteristic implies a random or even an agglutinative process of collection. Rather, two important and interrelated points emerge from the composite quality of this prophetic work. One concerns the way the work coheres despite the appearance that its parts are relatively unconnected. The second is the possible symbolic meaning and functional role of a prophetic work that brings together such a variety of genres and issues. Each of these points will be examined, the first in this section and the second in Form and Function in Second Zechariah's Oracles.

The case for the unity of Second Zechariah on the basis of a perceived chiastic arrangement (as made especially by Lamarche 1961 and Baldwin 1972) surely overmanipulates the materials to achieve its purpose. Nevertheless, there are indications of a structural arrangement that may be distinct from that which a redactional hand may have wrought. It has long been noticed that the word "oracle" (*maśśāʾ*) has been placed as part of a messenger formula at the opening of both chapters 9 and 12 and at the beginning of Malachi, apparently to mark three large blocks of material (9–11; 12–14; and Malachi) and give them a kind of parallel status. The existence of these markers has led us to subdivide the six chapters of Second Zechariah into Part One (chapters 9–11) and Part Two (chapters 12–14). In addition, the way "on that day" punctuates the material of chapters 12 to 14 (appearing seven times in chapter 12, three times in chapter 13, and seven times again in chapter 14) but is totally absent from 9–11 serves to separate the six chapters of Second Zechariah into two parts of three chapters each.

In accepting such a division, however, we were guided by more than the presence, possibly through redactional activity, of "an oracle" in 9:1 and 12:1. The attention in our NOTES to lexical and thematic interconnections led us to recognize how the opening line(s) or subunits of chapters 10 and 11, and then of chapters 13 and 14, each echo the language and/or message of the concluding verse(s) of the preceding chapter. Chapter 12 does not share in this feature; like chapter 9, it initiates a subdivision of the six-chapter prophetic work. Chart 6 shows the relationship of ending and beginning texts.

This structural indication of cohesion among the diverse materials of Zechariah 9–14, in and of itself, might still be interpreted as evidence of skilled redactional work. However, other aspects of interconnection of the materials in these chapters must be taken into account. More specifically the "innertextual-

CHART 6
CONNECTIONS OF CHAPTER ENDINGS WITH BEGINNINGS OF CONTIGUOUS CHAPTERS

	9:17	10:1	
Chapters 9–11		10:10–12	11:1 (2, 3)
	12:12–14	13:1	
Chapters 12–14		13:8–9	14:1–2

ity" of chapters 9–14—the way various thematic and lexical features of the text cohere (Utzschneider [1989: 31] calls this "innere Kontextualität")—seems to indicate an overall integrity to these six chapters. In chart 7 the instances of internal cross-referencing and repetition of allusions are laid out in graphic form. Items present in the chapter number in the left column are noted, under the horizontal chapter designations, according to where they recur. The items are not exact quotations in most cases but rather, especially when words are linked with slashes, are meant to indicate idiosyncratic clusterings of themes as well as of individual terms.

The chart portrays the manifold instances of self-referencing in chapters 9–14, and several other points emerge. For one thing, there is a linkage in every chapter with every other chapter of this prophetic work. Moreover, the most intense internal connecting occurs between chapters 9 and 14. The beginning and ending of Second Zechariah thus constitute an envelope that sets off the whole of chapters 9–14, despite the variety of materials within, as a discrete prophetic work. This innertextuality of Second Zechariah, as well as its intertextuality (considered below), lends support to the thesis of the integrity of the work. It also suggests that the prophetic oracular discourse of this work (and perhaps of other prophetic books) may be closer to an origin in written composition than in oral speech.

Before we turn to Second Zechariah's linkage with other biblical materials, several other aspects that may signify its integrity should be noted—aspects that are noticeable in looking at Zechariah 9–14 within the Haggai–Zechariah–Malachi corpus of the Twelve Minor Prophets, the grouping that constitutes its canonical setting. One of the most prominent literary strategies of the other three books (Haggai, First Zechariah, and Malachi) of the Haggai–Zechariah–Malachi corpus is the frequent use of interrogatives (cf. Pierce 1984a: 283–85). Chart 8 enumerates, for the four components of the Haggai–Zechariah–Malachi section of the Twelve, the many instances in which questions appear as rhetorical devices and/or as part of a dialogic format.

The frequent use of the interrogative mode in Haggai, Zechariah 1–8, and Malachi is readily apparent. Especially in the latter two, the presence of questions is essential: formulaic questions (with answers) frame the visionary sections of First Zechariah, and the disputations of Malachi consist of responses to posed questions. In these books, and in Haggai too, the rhetorical use of questions is integral to the messages being delivered. Clearly, the dialogic mode created by the use of questions is essential to the discursive plan of all three works. This striking feature of the Haggai–Zechariah–Malachi corpus, taken as a whole, may represent an early stage of the characteristic dialectic strategy of rabbinic discourse.

Yet despite the overwhelming presence of interrogation in these three canonical books, the discrete section of Zechariah known as Second Zechariah stands quite apart. Only in one instance in Second Zechariah does a question appear. That text (13:6), however, is in fact an indirect use of a question, which comes in the hypothetical reporting of someone else's query, and so perhaps should be discounted as an example of interrogation in Second Zechariah. With or without Zech 13:6, the absence of the use of questions as a literary strategy in this prophetic work is striking. This absence finds congruence with the dearth of information about the prophet-narrator and the lack of a sense of his (their) interaction with others, the possible identification of prophet with shepherd in certain aspects of the retrospective shepherd narrative notwithstanding (but see NOTES and COMMENT to 11:4–16). The prophet, by being excluded from most of the material of chapters 9–14, does not figure as an actor in the events recounted or projected. This invisibility contributes to the sense of the prophet's omniscience and thus helps to establish the authority of the oracular material.

Intertextuality of Zechariah 9–14

The linkage of Second Zechariah with other scriptural texts has long been noticed (e.g., by Delcor 1952, Mason 1973 and 1982a and c; Lacocque 1981; Pierce 1984a; see discussion below in Review of Previous Research). In this respect, Zechariah 9–14 is no different from the bulk of biblical materials. Indeed, as the recent attention to "inner-biblical exegesis" (notably by Fishbane 1985; cf. his earlier works, e.g., 1977, 1979, 1980) has shown, virtually no part of the canon is free from signs of reformulation and response in the transmission of authoritative tradition. The Hebrew Bible, "the repository of a vast store of hermeneutical techniques" (Fishbane 1985: 14), provides testimony to the extraordinary vitality of received tradition in generating additional authoritative materials.

Yet Second Zechariah seems to stand apart even from the wealth of examples of intertextuality in the Hebrew Bible. In the range of type and function of both allusions and citations, these six prophetic chapters abound in references to other biblical works. It may not be an exaggeration to suggest that Zechariah 9–14 surpasses any other biblical work in the way it draws from existing tradition. These interconnections between this book and other parts of the canon can be subdivided into two major groups: links with First Zechariah, and links with other biblical sources.

The first group of associations has already been mentioned above in this Introduction in the section Prophetic Response, wherein we discuss briefly the canonical joining of First and Second Zechariah. It is also addressed in our review of the scholarly literature, in which the work of Mason in particular is noted (especially 1976). Mason argues for a series of similar features between the two parts of the canonical Book of Zechariah. Drawing attention to a plethora of lexical and thematic congruences, he posits a series of shared emphases. Not everyone accepts Mason's conclusions. Childs (1979: 482–85), for example, is suspicious of the supposed direct literary connections, be they lexical or exegetical. Yet even Childs sees relational elements uniting the two parts of the canonical book.

Because the matter of Second Zechariah's connections with First Zechariah has been so thoroughly investigated by Mason and has evoked important and

CHART 7
INNERTEXTUALITY IN SECOND ZECHARIAH:
THEMATIC AND LEXICAL CONNECTIONS WITHIN CHAPTERS 9–14

Chapter	9	10	11	12	13	14
9	╳	horse/chariot/ bow/war grain flourishing return people as sheep	people as sheep fire consumes	clans in Judah fire consumes	people as sheep silver/gold imagery	Yahweh in Jerusalem, against invaders basin at altar nation/ universality battle/warrior motif gold/silver/ wealth horse
10	horse/chariot/ bow/war grain flourishing return people as sheep	╳	Lebanon/ Gilead Bashan filled people as sheep	horse (rider) bulwarked siege	false prophecy people as sheep	battle/warrior motif horse wealth gathering

11	people as sheep / fire consumes	Lebanon/Gilead Bashan filled	blindness	people as sheep	neighbor's hand image
12	clans of Judah / fire consumes	horse/(rider) bulwark/siege	X	leaders of Jerusalem/ house of David stabbing	nations gathered / nations annihilated / Jerusalem inhabited
13	people as sheep / silver/gold imagery	false prophecy / people as sheep	borders of Jerusalem/ house of David stabbing	X	exile/devastation / sin/cleansing sin / fountains/waters of Jerusalem
14	Yahweh in Jerusalem, against invaders / nations/universality / basin at altar / battle/warrior motif / gold/silver/ wealth / horse	battle/warrior motif / horse / wealth / gathering	nations gathered / nations annihilated / Jerusalem inhabited	exile/devastation / sin/cleansing sin / fountain/water of Jerusalem	X

CHART 8

INTERROGATIONS IN THE HAGGAI–ZECHARIAH–MALACHI
CORPUS

Book	Texts	Total
Haggai	1:4, 9; 2:3, 12, 13, 15, 19	10
Zechariah 1–8 oracles and other materials visions (seven visions plus prophetic vision)	1:5, 6; 4:7; 7:3, 5, 6, 7 (8) 1:9, 12, 19, 21; 2:2; 3:2 4:2, 4, 5, 11, 12, 13; 5:2, 5, 6, 10; 6:4 (17)	25
Zechariah 9–14	13:6?	1?
Malachi	1:2, 6, 7, 8, 9, 13; 2:10 2:10, 14, 15, 17; 3:2, 7, 8, 13, 14	23

balancing responses in the scholarly community, we will refrain here from collecting all the congruities. Attention is drawn to them in the NOTES, and some of the major ones appear below in our treatment of Second Zechariah in relation to other biblical sources in general. We have no doubt about the validity of seeing the two parts of the canonical Zechariah in close relationship. Yet, in light of the extraordinarily numerous instances in which Zechariah 9–14 draws upon many other authoritative texts, the question ought to be raised as to whether the First–Second Zechariah interplay is remarkable on its own, or whether it is simply one of many instances of Second Zechariah's referential treatment of his scriptural forebears, notably prophets but not limited to them.

Those scholars who have argued for Second Zechariah's linkage to other biblical books have tended to focus on the connections with other prophets. There is some consensus that the three Major Prophets (Isaiah, Jeremiah, and Ezekiel) are particularly prominent in this respect. Several scholars would highlight Second Isaiah within that corpus (e.g., Lamarche 1961: 124–47, in his attention to the servant passages). Others would add one or other of the Twelve; Lacocque, for example, mentions Joel and would emphasize congruities with so-called Third, rather than First or Second, Isaiah (1981: 139).

The identifying and tallying of instances of intertextuality is to some extent subjective, but nonetheless we have decided to lay out for the reader in charts 9 and 10 some of the major instances in which the text of Zechariah 9–14 relates to other biblical texts. The grouping of references in these charts is in no way meant to imply that all the references operate in the same way, when in fact the modes of interrelationship are quite varied. In some (relatively few) cases, there seems to be direct echo or citation. More often, the Zecharianic allusions serve to expand, modify, or even subvert the texts from which they draw. At this point, lumping together a significant number of examples of intertextuality should not blur the nuanced ways in which they operate to both validate and transform received materials.

As previously noted, all three of the Major Prophets apparently figure prominently in Second Zechariah. So do a fair number of other texts, which will soon become apparent. Yet, among the Major Prophets, the role of Jeremiah deserves special consideration. That prophetic work should be a focus of the analysis of intertextuality not so much for the oracular material in it that is usually identified as Jeremianic, but rather for its overall role as a Deuteronomic work with strong evidences of a redaction by a Deuteronomic editor (see, e.g., Hyatt 1942 and 1951; Cazelles 1951; Nicholson 1970). Taking into account the existence of certain phrases, lexical choices, toponyms, temporal markers, and concepts (mainly as established by Weinfeld 1972) that can be identified as Deuteronomic, a special relationship between Second Zechariah and Jeremiah as part of Deuteronomic tradition can be established.

The recent dissertation by Person (1991 [cf. forthcoming]) "The Deuteronomic Redaction of the Book of Zechariah," may, as suggested below, go too far in positing a pivotal editing role for a Deuteronomic hand in establishing the final form of Zechariah 9–14. We would prefer to see the evidences of Jeremiah (Jer-D) and Deuteronomic tradition (DtrH) in Second Zechariah within the context of the broader and more inclusive intertextuality of that prophet. Still, Person's painstaking perusal of Deuteronomic language visible in Second Zechariah has provided a convincing case for Second Zechariah's being steeped in Deuteronomic tradition. Chart 9 is only a very selected sampling of dozens of words, phrases, and concepts that run through Jer-D and DtrH and that appear in Second Zechariah.

It is apparent from chart 9 that the combination of Jeremianic and Deuteronomic texts that show evidence of congruity with texts of Second Zechariah constitutes a significant number of cross-references. Because, according to text-critical and thematic analysis, Deuteronomic activity apparently continued well into the postexilic period (as argued by Person 1991), or at least a Deuteronomic "school" continued to be part of the Yehudite community after the Exile, these congruities would seem to indicate, at the very least, that Second Zechariah was steeped in the literature and worldview of that school. By the postexilic period, however, Deuteronomic literature was surely already merged with other authoritative texts; thus the using of correspondences to suggest a Deuteronomic redaction to Second Zechariah may be unwarranted. If, as we discuss below, one of the factors involved in Second Zechariah's intertextuality is the need to cope with unactualized revelatory texts, Jeremianic material would certainly rank high among them and would surely attract the exegetical attention of a figure (or figures) such as Second Zechariah.

Be that as it may, the presence of the widespread connections of Second Zechariah beyond Jer, Jer-D, Dtr, and DtrH must not be overlooked. For that reason, we have collected in chart 10 a list of correspondences between

CHART 9
SECOND ZECHARIAH AND DEUTERONOMIC LITERATURE:
SELECTED EXAMPLES OF CORRESPONDENCES

	Zech 9–14	Dtr/DtrH[a]	Jer[b]	Other[c]
Yahweh is one	14:9	Deut 6:4 + 5×	———	———
Covenant relationship (people/God)	13:9	6×	8×	Lev, Ezek (5×), First Zech
"Name" of Yahweh	10:12; 13:3; 13:9b; 14:9	20×	10×	Lev, Isa, Zeph, Ps, Prov
dwell securely	14:11	4×	4×	Ezek (8×)
false prophecy (šqr + dbr/nbʾ)	13:3	1× (cf. Deut 13:2–12)	21×	Mic, Ps, Isa
devouring flesh (in curses)	11:9, 16	3×	1×	Lev, Lam (2×)
covenant breaking	11:10	1×	2×	Ezek
splitting mountains/ earth	14:4	2×	———	Isa, Hab
peoples/nations around (sbyb)	12:2, 6; 14:14	1×	1×	———
House of Joseph	10:6	7×	———	Amos, Obad
Booths	14:16, 18, 19	3×	———	Ezek (2×)
Philistine cities in same order	9:5–6	———	1×	———

[a]Includes materials from the Book of Deuteronomy and also from the books comprising the Deuteronomic history.

[b]This includes materials from both Jeremianic oracles and the Deuteronomic redaction of Jeremiah.

[c]The books listed represent single instances unless otherwise noted.

Zechariah 9–14 and other biblical texts. These references are not necessarily comprehensive; if anything, we have been conservative in our selection, omitting any terms or words, even if rather rare, that might be attributed to the use of a general shared vocabulary rather than to a conscious interconnecting. Even so, the list is striking in its extent and in the wide spectrum of materials that appear.

How can one understand this plethora of intertextuality? We consider below

CHART 10
INTERTEXTUALITY IN SECOND ZECHARIAH:
PROMINENT EXAMPLES, BY CHAPTER

Second Zechariah	*Language or Theme*	*Other Biblical Texts*
9		
9:2–3	shrewdness/wealth of Tyre/Sidon	Ezek 26–28
9:3	mud of the streets	Ps 10:43; 2 Sam 22:43
9:4	consumed by fire	Amos 1:4, 7, 10; Zeph 1:18; 3:8; Ezek 23:25
9:5–6	Philistine cities	Amos 1:7–8; Zeph 2:4; Jer 25:20
9:9	daughter of Jerusalem	Isa 37:22; 2 Kgs 19:21; Mic 4:8; Zeph 2:14; Lam 2:15
9:9	come/ass	Gen 49:10–11
9:9	righteous ruler	Jer 23:5; 33:5; Isa 11:4
9:10	rule/sea to sea/ends of earth	Ps 72:8 (cf. Amos 8:12)
9:11	blood of the covenant	Exod 24:3ff.
9:11	waterless pit	Gen 37:24; Jer 38:6
9:12	restoring double	Isa 61:1, 7
9:14	God's appearance/glory over the people	Isa 66:2
9:14	God from the south	Hab 3:3
9:16	people like sheep	(see Zech 11:4)
9:17	how good and lovely	Isa 62:3; Ps 133:1; Cant 4:10; 7:2, 7
10		
10:2	deception of diviners	Deut 18:10–11; 2 Kgs 17:17; Jer 14:14; 27:9–10; 29:9–10
10:2–3	shepherd imagery	(cf. Zech 11:4–21)
10:4	cornerstone	Ps 118:22; Isa 22:23ff.
10:6	Yahweh answers	Isa 41:17
10:8	people multiply	Jer 23:3; Ezek 36:1
10:9	scattering of people	Ezek 5:2, 10, 12; 6:18
10:10	no room . . .	Josh 17:16
10:11	smiting sea	Ps 74:13–17
11		
11:1	opening of doors (imperative)	Ps 24:7

CHART 10 (continued)

Second Zechariah	Language or Theme	Other Biblical Texts
11:1	fire consumes	(see Zech 9:4)
11:3	hark/wail/shepherds	Jer 25:3
11:4	shepherd imagery	1 Kgs 22:17; Jer 23:1–4; 25:34–38; Ezek 34:1–23; 37:25–27
11:7, 10, 14	two staffs	Ezek 37:15–23
11:9	whoever/die/destroyed	Jer 15:2
11:16	shepherd's failings	Ezek 37:16
11:17	withered arm	1 Kgs 13
12		
12:1	creation	Gen 1:1; 2:7; Isa 42:5; 44:24; 45:12; 51:13, 16; Amos 4:13; Jer 10:12; 51:15; Pss 18:10; 104:2
12:2	cup imagery	Jer 25:15–31; 49:12; Isa 51:17, 22; Ps 75:9 (NRSV 75:8); Lam 4:21
12:4	smite/panic/wilderness/blindness	Deut 28:28
12:6	fire consumes	(see Zech 9:4)
12:8	angel going before	Exod 13:21; 14:19
12:10	mourn an only child	Amos 8:10; Jer 6:26
12:13	plain of Megiddo	2 Chron 35:22 (cf. 2 Kgs 23:29–30)
13		
13:1	fountain/cleansing sin/defilement	Num 8:7; 19:9–31; 31:23
13:2	purging idolatry	Deut 12:2–3; Ezek 14:1–8
13:3	lying in Yahweh's name (as false prophecy)	Deut 18:20–22; Jer 20:9; 26:16; 29:23; 44:16; Ezek 14:9–10
13:3	parental responsibility	Deut 13:6–10; 21:18–21
13:4	shame of prophetic behavior	Mic 3:5–8
13:4	hairy mantle	Gen 25:25; 1 Kgs 19:13, 19; 2 Kgs 2:8, 13, 14
13:5	denial of being prophet	Amos 7:14
13:6	prophet's bruises	1 Kgs 20:35 (cf. 1 Kgs 18:19; Deut 14:1)

CHART 10 (continued)

Second Zechariah	Language or Theme	Other Biblical Texts
13:7	shepherd imagery	(see Zech 11:4)
13:8	threefold fate of conquered	Ezek 5:12 (cf. 1 Kgs 19:1–18)
13:9	purifying in fire	Num 31:23 (later—Mal 3:2)
13:9	call and answer	Exod 6:7; Lev 26:12; Deut 26:17–18; Hos 1:8; 2:21–23; Jer 7:23; 31:33; Ezek 37:22
14		
14:1, 3	plunder/spoil	Ezek 38:12–13
14:2	nations against Jerusalem	Jer 4:5–8; 25:1–21; etc.; Ezek 38:1–6
14:2	spoil	Deut 13:12–16
14:2	houses plundered/women ravished	Isa 13:16
14:4	feet will stand	Micah 1:24; Amos 4:13; 9:15
14:4	Mount of Olives	Ezek 11:23
14:5	mountains moved	Ezek 38:19–21
14:5	former earthquake	Amos 1:1; Isa 6:4
14:6–7	new creation	Gen 1:3–5
14:8	cosmic waters	Gen 2:6, 10–14; Ezek 17:5–8; 31:5, 7; 47:1–12; Joel 4:18 (NRSV 3:18); Jer 8:13
14:9	Yahweh is one	Deut 4:6 (Shema), etc.
14:9	Yahweh's name	Deut 12:14, and many times in Dtr literature
14:13	panic of Yahweh	Deut 7:23; 1 Sam 4:5; Isa 22:5
14:13	enemies kill each other	Ezek 38:21
14:14	silver/gold/garments	2 Kgs 7:8
14:15	horse . . . ass	(later [?]–Ezra 2:66–67; Neh 7:68)
14:16	King Yahweh	Ps 24:10; 98:6
14:16	Booths	Deut 16:13–15; 31:9–13; Ezek 20:32
14:20	"Holy to Yahweh"	Exod 28:36 (= 39:30)

the collective role of the frequency with which passages in Second Zechariah echo traditional language, images, or concepts. For now, it is important to point to several other aspects of the extensive use of existing materials that this listing reveals. For one thing, this phenomenon is fairly evenly distributed among the book's six chapters and all their subunits. Although these materials contain rather diverse, though perhaps not so discrete as has been generally supposed, literary genres, they clearly share a tendency to respond to existing sources.

Another significant and related feature is the fact that chapter 9 and chapter 10, one or both of which (because of their poetic character as well as their use of divine-warrior imagery) are thought by many to be considerably earlier than the other chapters of Second Zechariah, do not differ from the other chapters in their frequent use of preexisting sources. Furthermore, chapters 9 and 10, like the others, include allusions to a broad range of texts, including Deuteronomic texts and preexilic prophets (as perhaps expected), and examples of language found in exilic or postexilic prophetic works. This in and of itself could be argued the other way—that allusions to aspects of later prophetic works in Zechariah 9 (or 10) represent either (1) the common use of independently circulating and nonextant materials available to both the Zechariah 9 (and 10) author and the hands responsible for Jeremiah, Ezekiel, and Third Isaiah, or (2) instances of later canonical prophets drawing upon early Zecharianic materials.

The frequent use of references to other texts in Zechariah 9 (and 10), however, cannot be considered apart from the fact that the phenomenon of intertextuality, though probably present throughout Scripture, is especially prominent in postexilic texts. This is true not only of prophetic books. Surely late biblical historiography, for example, is heavily informed by early biblical history writing. And postexilic psalms, it seems, often draw extensively from existing literature of a variety of genres (Brettler forthcoming). If the density of intertextuality is considered a distinctive feature of postexilic literature (see Petersen 1977: 15–16 and sources cited), then Zechariah 9 (and 10) would seem to share in that dimension of late biblical literature. As we indicate in the NOTES to those chapters, the presence of pure poetry and the nature of the toponyms and of the mythic motifs do not necessarily, in and of themselves, mandate an early date for this material. Rather, in light of the other evidence presented above for the cohering of the six chapters of Second Zechariah, the so-called early features of chapter 9 (and 10) can equally be attributed to the impulse toward intertextuality that so dominates all the sections of Second Zechariah.

One other aspect of chart 10 must be noted, and that is the way it lumps together a great variety of exegetical strategies employed by the prophet(s) in the allusions to earlier materials. The reader will have to go to our NOTES, one by one, to see how each instance of intertextuality deals uniquely with the referent at issue. Nearly always, the Zecharianic usage represents a transformation of genres: for example, a Pentateuchal curse or blessing emerges in an oracular statement, or a legal prescription is reworked into an eschatological forecast. The range and creativity of the intertextual process are striking. For this reason, the notion of late biblical prophecy as derivative or dependent, as somehow secondary to the great prophetic voices of the Exile and earlier, misses the extraordinary skill of figures such as "Second Zechariah," who managed to set forth an eloquent and hopeful message to a beleaguered community while holding fast to the revelatory authority of his forebears.

One extreme, though not isolated, example of such a negative evaluation of late biblical prophecy is worth citing: "Second Zechariah does not 'act like a prophet' in the sense of making independent and original oracles of his own. Instead he seems concerned with gathering up expectations of earlier prophets and interpreting them or showing how they are to be fulfilled" (North 1972: 51). The use of references to earlier materials is mistakenly labeled "dependence" (cf. Petersen 1977: 15–16), a term that gives the impression of slavish adherence or copying and of lack of originality. What an erroneous impression that is! Indeed, the responses in late canonical works to earlier ones may represent in some ways an even greater degree of creativity and sensitivity, in both a literary and an ideological sense, than do the texts to which they refer. Furthermore, later biblical writers had an extraordinary advantage in their literary task. They had available a remarkably diverse range of authoritative materials from which to draw, and from which they felt compelled to draw. The very heterogeneity and multivocality of the biblical corpus in its protocanonical status in the postexilic era provided—even demanded—that it generate new forms and meanings highly original in their own way, in the radically different sociopolitical milieu of Yehud (cf. Boyarin 1990: 39).

In the postexilic period, especially after the flush of expectation and hope of the early restoration era had faded and the realities of Persian dominance and of economic stagnation had become painfully clear, original minds responded to the profound tension between past and present. They transformed existing authoritative predictive prophecies, without negating their sanctity or validity, into equally valid formulations that could erase the prevailing sense of hopelessness and powerlessness while simultaneously sustaining traditional community values and beliefs.

Form and Function in Second Zechariah's Oracles

In the preceding sections, a number of specific characteristics of Second Zechariah have been presented. These can now contribute to a more general evaluation of this prophetic work's place in biblical tradition. Such an evaluation is linked to the question of the prophetic status of this work. Clearly it is included, in terms of canon formation, within that section of Hebrew Scripture designated "Prophets." Yet, like the three other late biblical prophets with which it is grouped, as well as other postexilic works such as Third Isaiah and possibly Joel, it stands apart in significant ways from the great prophetic works of the Exile and of earlier times. Some would even call them "deutero-prophetic" (see Petersen 1977) and claim that classical Hebraic prophecy had ceased by the waning decades of the sixth century B.C.E.

Such theories are part of a larger discussion about what constitutes a prophet, how one identified a true messenger of God in ancient Israel, and how one evaluates the apparent and inevitable tension among all those claiming to dispense revelatory communications from the Israelite deity. In various NOTES to chapter 13 and in the COMMENT to that chapter, as well as in several other places, these difficult issues are considered. Chapter 13 in particular raises vexing questions about the place of prophecy within society and within authoritative literature, and about the very vocabulary used in the Hebrew Bible for prophets of all kinds and for their distinctive activities and discourse.

Such profound issues and questions, needless to say, have evoked a voluminous literature and a multitude of theories, some well reasoned and compelling, others wildly speculative, and still many others occupying the long continuum between those two poles. This is hardly the place to review that literature. We simply note that it can readily be accessed through the leading biblical handbooks and introductions. We also draw attention to one recent and stimulating set of papers (by Auld, Carroll, and Overholt), in *JSOT* 48 (1990), as a good example of the lively and sophisticated nature of the contemporary discussion of prophecy as well as of the disparate and even contradictory proposals competing for scholarly consensus. Both the biblical sources and the current analytical tools are so varied and complex that the prospect of unanimity in appraisal of the critical questions would seem precluded.

In not reviewing the literature on the phenomenon of Hebrew prophecy, we hardly mean to downplay its importance. We have learned much from many colleagues, past and present. What we offer in this commentary by way of a perspective on Second Zechariah as prophet(s), or on Zechariah 9-14 as prophetic literature, is indebted to the insightful suggestions and formulations of others. Having said all this, we nonetheless venture now to comment on how the information provided in this discussion of the literary features of Second Zechariah contributes to an understanding of the place of these six chapters in Hebraic tradition.

Many of the features described above can be comprehended as playing a role in establishing the prophetic authority of the author(s) of Zechariah 9-14. Some of these features this book shares with other postexilic prophetic works, whereas others may be unique to it. All told, they lead to the conclusion that Second Zechariah represents a highly creative prophetic work. That it differs from preexilic models cannot be contested. (But do not those preexilic exemplars also differ in fundamental ways, theologically and stylistically, despite commonalities, from each other?) Yet the differences should not lead to a denigration of the worth of Second Zechariah. Resounding calls for justice and righteousness, such as appear in exilic and earlier prophets, should not be the only benchmarks of prophetic value. We return to this point after summarizing briefly the literary features that indicate authoritative prophetic status for this work, whatever formal title one would or would not give to the individual(s) responsible.

First, the matter of Zechariah 9-14 being anthology-like in its bringing together a number of different traditional prophetic genres should no longer be regarded necessarily as evidence of multiple authorship and/or redactions. It appears, at first, to be a loose collection of invectives, threats, heraldic odes, promises, extended metaphors, symbolic actions, and perhaps even allegories or parables (although, as explained in the COMMENT to chapter 11, such categories do not seem applicable). It concerns remnants of the Northern Kingdom Israel as well as of Judah; it deals with specific geopolitical entities, near and far; it foresees a sacred altar in Jerusalem and its Temple but does not separate national interests from universal concerns. It does all this in language that ranges from some of the purest poetry in all the Hebrew Bible to passages that contain a denser clustering of prose elements than do average portions of the Pentateuch or Former Prophets (see the previous section Form: Prose or Poetry).

This complexity of genre, content, and style, which in the past tended rather strongly to suggest a multiplicity of hands, need no longer be so regarded. Only rather rigid Western expectations about how a text should proceed—in some logical, externally coherent progression—finds a lack of unity or coherence in an intensely composite work. The point made by Long (1984) about the Deuteronomistic history—that it is a collection of paratactic texts creatively brought together through the use of metaphors, thematic patterns, and cultural referents rather than a poorly organized collection of historical dramas—is equally, if not more, applicable to Second Temple prophetic texts. The latter need no longer be deemed loose collections by disparate hands (see Craig 1992: 5). We have not pressed this point too strongly and have consistently referred to the "author or authors," or the "author(s)," of Second Zechariah. Yet the unifying elements identified above should allow the possibility to be entertained, however remote, that a single author is responsible for the entire work, with only minor redactional additions or alterations.

The composite nature of the material functions in much the same way as its intertextuality. It acknowledges the varying forms of authoritative literature, especially but not exclusively prophetic literature, with which the prophet (now to be referred to, tentatively, in the singular) is wrestling as he tries to make sense of his world and give hope to his community. Again, like the intertextuality, the presence of a rich variety of genres drawn from traditional modes contributes to the dynamics of communication between the prophet and his readers/listeners. The diversity of forms symbolizes the fullness of an authoritative cultural tradition only because the prophet shares that tradition with his audience. The composite nature of the work bridges two gaps. One is the gap between past texts and the present one, for although the new oracles transform the old ones, they do not reject their authenticity (cf. Fishbane 1980: 354–55); the shared multiplicity of genres serves to sustain the authority of the older texts. The other gap is that between prophet and audience, because the former claims to be speaking Yahweh's message to people warned to be suspicious of those making such claims. Therefore, the audience's awareness of the prophet's appropriation of the wider sort of recognized revelatory materials serves to authenticate his position and give validity to his message.

The second feature to be reconsidered, the intertextuality of Second Zechariah, shares many functions with the literary richness of these chapters, as the previous discussion has indicated. It cannot function without what Fishbane calls "canonical consciousness" (1980: 360). That is, the citations of and allusions to earlier biblical materials depend on both prophet and audience being aware of those materials. Although the canon was not yet complete in the fifth century, there was surely an impressive collection of Pentateuchal and Prophetic (former and latter) materials, as well as significant parts of the Writings, that the community recognized as being authoritative and sacred revelation (see Freedman 1991). Furthermore, the probability that many in the community were more than passingly familiar with the contexts of the authoritative texts seems strong. Thus the rhetorical success of Second Zechariah, in composing a text replete with instances of intertextuality, depends on the audience's ability to bridge the gap between old and new texts. This in turn authenticates the new text, leading it to partake of the revelatory qualities of the old and thus to validate both the message and the messenger who addresses the fifth-century world in Yehud.

The flourishing of intertextuality is, after all, virtually inescapable if the vitality of an old, extensive, sometimes obsolete, and often unactualized—but unfalteringly seen as divine revelation—literature is to be sustained. Second Zechariah thus can be viewed as a kind of proto-midrash, a composite work that simultaneously absorbs and heralds tradition while also transforming it. Thus many of the astute observations of Boyarin (1990) and others in establishing a theory of midrash, with its dialectic of intertextuality, elucidate the dynamics of Second Zechariah. The intertextuality promotes continuity of a fixed, received tradition without freezing it; it generates flexibility and adaptability and so sustains the life and creativity of that tradition.

Although our discussion has repeatedly mentioned the prophet's past and present, it must be emphasized that his prophetic intertextuality is driven by an orientation to the future (see Boyarin 1990: 22). Second Zechariah wanted his community to overcome the sense of hopelessness and powerlessness, in light of the sociopolitical reality, that their reading of previous predictive prophecies could only have exacerbated. The eschatological solution, with future divine intervention finally bringing fulfillment to the divine promises of the old texts, both upholds and denies the received tradition. This "exegetical consciousness" (Fishbane 1980: 360–61), by changing the authoritative source, would seem to be destructive of tradition. Yet by invoking it in order to transform it, it also reasserts that source's authority and constructs a new authority that will both signify and serve a resoundingly positive future.

The eschatological solution should not, however, be the only focus of this discussion of the dynamics of Second Zechariah's use of intertextuality. In reaching into sacred tradition to affirm his status as messenger and to assert a reading of that tradition that will open up the future, it establishes an all-encompassing validation of the tradition. The very breadth of the intertextual referents, from virtually every corner of the existing protocanonical documents (see chart 10), serves to authenticate the entire corpus of these documents.

That corpus might be considered a mosaic carpet. Second Zechariah has pulled tesserae from every element of that carpet's design and created a new mosaic. Yet the distinctive color of each tile brings with it the way it fit into the old pattern, even as it helps create a new pattern. Thus the viewer's perception is enriched by the layers of signification in the new carpet. He or she sees the fresh design and also the original design from which it is recomposed. The new design bears within it all of the old, the nonreproduced tesserae as well as those used anew. So it is with the new text—all the parts not explicitly referenced are nonetheless present because of the broad selection of those that are.

Consequently, all of existing Scripture, including the texts that convey most directly or eloquently the social and moral values of ancient Israel, even though unspecified, do become reaffirmed as part of the dynamics of intertextuality. All of tradition, with the referred-to texts constituting a synechdoche for the entire body of material from which they are drawn, thus reemerge in the prophet's present world and become refocused as essential revelation to carry the community toward the eschatological future. Although Second Zechariah's use of a selection of older texts in a sense disrupts their original integrity, it also sustains that integrity.

The presence of this dynamic, given the richness of Second Zechariah's mosaic of ancient tiles rearranged, means that this prophetic book can hardly be considered devoid of moral content or thrust. The prophet's explicit allusions are selective in a way that meets his purposes in addressing the particular needs of his day. But the whole piece from which they are taken is simultaneously reactivated. The ability of Second Zechariah to do this, to reactivate the past, to engage a community aware of the past and accepting of its traditions, and thereby in despair, is surely the mark of a highly creative process. It is also the mark, in establishing continuity and enabling the survival of identity and values, of a successful culture (cf. Boyarin 1990: 22).

The composite nature and intertextuality of Second Zechariah as a work of the Second Temple period having been discussed at considerable length, it remains to reiterate briefly one other feature that also contributes to the way this prophet claims revelatory authority and so participates in the prophetic tradition. We refer here to the absence of the interrogative mode, as described above. Although intertextuality and a text composed of genres known from earlier authoritative sources serve, as we have shown, to create a dialogue between past and present and to engage the prophet with his audience, the direct use of interrogation in forming a dialogic dynamic in the new text itself is omitted. Were questioning not so prominent in the contiguous prophetic texts in the Book of the Twelve, this fact might seem unremarkable. However, Zechariah 9–14 is notable in its canonical context as lacking this feature. As such, its discursive style becomes fully assertive; nothing is left open to question. What is proclaimed in the oracles is a reality to be unquestionably actualized in the future. The authority of the message and the messenger, devoid of the explicit give-and-take of interrogation, even though the answer in such instances may well be predetermined, is communicated to the audience. The interactive process inherent in the intertextuality of Second Zechariah and in its richly genred composite nature is not extended to the declarative mode of this work. Its oracles proclaim quite directly, even though their meanings may be difficult for us to comprehend several millennia later, God's intention to intervene on behalf of the people.

The many modes in which Second Zechariah establishes itself within authoritative tradition surely place these chapters within the prophetic genre. Although they may diverge in both style and overt content from earlier prophetic works, they quite emphatically continue many aspects of the message and form of those works. In drawing upon the language and imagery of prophetic eschatology, they contribute to the transformation of that eschatology into the kind of apocalyptic literature that becomes characteristic of much of the late Second Temple period. If they differ, they do so not because the author(s) of Second Zechariah is (are) any less creative or any less possessed of a heightened moral consciousness, but rather because the world of the fifth century posed its own unique set of circumstances to which he was responding. Insofar as Zechariah 9-14 represents an extraordinary concentration of inner biblical exegesis, it both demonstrates the vitality of biblical prophecy in its own time and, as a kind of proto-midrash, provides a prototype for the flourishing of cultural modes that were to sustain the spiritual and moral life of the community into the postbiblical period. The kind of prophetic energy concentrated in Second Zechariah, rather than marking the end of biblical prophecy, assured its continuity—albeit under a new nomenclature and through altered literary forms.

THE TEXT OF SECOND ZECHARIAH

The vocalized Hebrew text as edited by Elliger and printed in the *Biblica Hebraica Stuttgartensia* (1977) has provided the basis for this work, as it did for our volume on Haggai and Zechariah 1-8 (1987). *BHS* is based on a manuscript approximately a thousand years old that was found in Leningrad. A leather scroll from the Judean desert of the twelve Minor Prophets, published in 1961 (Milik) and dated to the second century C.E., has supported the high standing and reliability of the MT, as the scholarly analyses in the years since that publication have shown. Despite a somewhat more complex textual transmission than that of First Zechariah, the MT of Second Zechariah has proved to be far more reliable than anticipated.

We have been privileged to consult the unpublished dissertation of Fuller (1988) on the Hebrew manuscripts of the Minor Prophets from Qumran Cave 4. Six of a total of seven separate manuscripts are presented and analyzed in his work. Only three of the texts (4QXII^a, 4QXII^c, and 4QXII^e), however, are well enough preserved to allow any analysis of their textual affinities. Text "a" dates to ca. 125–50 B.C.E., text "c" dates to ca. 75 B.C.E., and text "e" dates to ca. 50 B.C.E. These scrolls contain virtually no evidence to support the hypothesis that there is a textual tradition other than the one that underlies the MT. Comparing these texts with the MT reveals only three variations between the MT and the Qumran Hebrew versions; all other differences are minor and reflect alternative spelling traditions, harmonizing tendencies, and occasional expansions. In no single instance in Second Zechariah has any ancient Hebrew version proved superior to the traditional MT.

However, of the ancient Hebrew versions of the Minor Prophets, 4QXII[a] provides startling information on another level. Dated to the middle of the second century B.C.E., it uniquely places Jonah after Malachi in the Book of the Twelve. There is little doubt of the genuineness of this ordering (Fuller 1988: 151), which suggests that the final order in the collection of the scroll of the Minor Prophets was fluid for some time after 150 B.C.E. The usual opinion, however, is that the reference in Sir 49:10 to the Twelve Prophets suggests that the order was fixed by the beginning of the second century B.C.E. Still, it cannot be doubted that the Qumran evidence is of significance to the larger issue of how the canonical process was concluded in the last century and a half of the Second Temple period.

Sasson (1990: 15), citing a rabbinic midrash to the Book of Numbers, notes the tradition of eleven minor prophets; the Book of Jonah, which was treated separately, was excluded in that tradition, which perhaps reflects the changing place of Jonah in Jewish theology in late antiquity. Blenkinsopp, in considering Jonah's unique position among the minor prophets, notes that the prophetic word in Jonah does not impair the freedom of God to repent even after the prophet had spoken (1983: 271). For such an important theological reason, it is not surprising to find Jonah placed last.

The publication of the Greek Minor Prophets scroll of the second century C.E. from Nahal Hever (Tov et al. 1990) completes a very positive picture of the MT, one based on new material relating to the minor prophets. Although there are minor variations that suggest a pre-MT *Vorlage* against which the Greek scroll was revised, that *Vorlage* and the MT are closer to one another than is the Greek text that underlies this new scroll to the Septuagint itself. The several extant variant readings for Second Zechariah are of no significance whatever for our study.

The remarkable accuracy and readability of the MT is reflected in the critical apparatus to our translation. Of the sixteen instances in which we have sensed minor corruption and so chosen to alter the text, only two (13:7 and 14:5) favor readings of the versions. In all other cases we have been able to make sense of the MT through either modest alterations in the consonants or through minor changes in pointing. These cases include the following: 9:15; 10:9; 11:2, 5, 7, 13[2], 16; 12:5, 7, 8; 13:5, 7; 14:5, 6[3], 12. (For a full discussion of these emendations the reader is referred to these verses as they appear in the NOTES.) The general picture of the reliability of the MT accords well with the situation for First Zechariah and for the Hebrew text of the Minor Prophets in general.

REVIEW OF PREVIOUS RESEARCH

The history of research on chapters 9–14 of the Book of Zechariah reflects deep scholarly dissension about the character of this work. Much of the disagreement concerns the relationship between chapters 1–8, so-called First or Proto-Zechariah, and chapters 9–14, so-called Second or Deutero-Zechariah. More specifically, the issues that have aroused scholarly discussion and debate include the problem of the unity of the canonical book (chapters 1–14), the question of unity in chapters 9–14, the dating of all or portions of chapters 9–14, and the nature and circumstances of the supposed editorial and redactional activity that was brought to bear on chapters 9–14 both before and after the appearance of all fourteen chapters as a single work.

It is standard practice in presenting a *Forschungsbericht*, or summary of previous research, to attempt to identify what might qualify as a consensus view. The overwhelmingly various and wildly contradictory views concerning the date and nature of the material in Second Zechariah make such a goal difficult, if not impossible, to attain. Nonetheless, in a consideration of how other exegetes have approached this material, some noteworthy points of congruence in recent studies of this material emerge. These points are evident in two major areas: in recognizing a postexilic date for Second Zechariah, and in calling attention to the instances and fact of intertextuality in those chapters, that is, the frequent use of earlier biblical materials in many aspects of the prophet's language and message.

Neither of these trends came easily or early in the history of interpretation, although some attention to use of earlier biblical material in Second Zechariah does appear in the works of past generations of biblical scholars. Still, both tendencies are prominent mainly in more recent scholarship. Greater attention in the last decade or so to the later Minor Prophets, despite the long delays in publishing both the Hebrew and Greek texts from the Judean wilderness that would facilitate the study of these books, is in part responsible for these trends. Continuing and renewed interest in the Book of Second Zechariah, especially chapters 9–14, is certainly also due in no small measure to the role of material from these chapters in the New Testament. Passages from Second Zechariah are quoted more frequently in the Passion narratives of the gospels than are any other group of sayings from the prophets. In addition, Second Zechariah apparently had a marked impact on the author of the Book of Revelation (Mason 1977: 77).

Prior to a consideration of these trends, a brief overview of scholarship is in order. In reflecting on the earliest treatments of Second Zechariah, one can see how the New Testament connections stimulated research. It was the quotation in Matt 27:9–10, incorrectly attributed to Jeremiah (see NOTES to Zech 11:13), that attracted the attention of the seventeenth-century English scholar John Mede (quoted by Mitchell 1912: 232). Mede sensed in the attribution to Jeremiah a better tradition than that of the Masoretes; in fact, he suggested that the Holy Spirit through Matthew claimed three chapters of Zechariah (9–11) for their real author, Jeremiah. Otherwise, a major step in Second Zechariah scholarship occurred in 1785, when William Newcome proposed that chapters 9–11 were written before 722 B.C.E. and that chapters 12–14 were written after the destruction of Jerusalem in 587–86 B.C.E. (*apud* R. L. Smith 1984: 243; P. D. Hanson 1975: 288). In addition, Newcome convincingly argued that chapters 1–8 differed so significantly in form and content from 9–14 that they had to emanate from another hand. By the end of the eighteenth century, therefore, the view that there were multiple authors of the canonical Book of Zechariah took hold. Save for the computer study of Radday and Wickman (1975), which we deal with in our discussion of the prose and poetry of the book (see above), there have been only a few scholars since that time who have argued for unity of authorship in all fourteen chapters. These include C. H. H. Wright in 1879, E. B. Pusey in 1885, G. L. Robinson in 1896, A. Van Hoonacker in 1902, and more recently E. S. Young in 1950 and R. K. Harrison in 1970 (cf. R. L. Smith 1984: 243–44).

A rather complex reconstruction of the various literary units of chapters 9–14 was proposed at the beginning of the nineteenth century by L. Bertholdt in 1814 and B. Flugge slightly earlier (so P. D. Hanson 1975: 288 and R. L. Smith 1984: 243). Not only did these interpretations posit different authors for various parts of Second Zechariah, but also they proposed any number of historical settings for them. Those settings ranged from the eighth century, the time of Amos and Isaiah, to about 520 B.C.E., the time of First Zechariah. The first major change away from such approaches came in 1824, when J. G. Eichhorn argued for a postexilic date for all of chapters 9–14, which he argued should be dated to slightly later than Alexander the Great's conquest of the Levant (i.e., the late fourth century B.C.E.), with Zech 13:7–14:21 dating to Maccabean times (Eichhorn 1824: 455ff.). The results of his suggestions have been far-reaching, and similar views are held by many scholars to this day. The suggested dates for Second Zechariah, in short, range from about 750 to 150 B.C.E.

Eichhorn's proposals for a late dating of individual units, as well as of the entire composite of Zechariah 9–14, did not gain much popularity until B. Stade greatly elaborated upon them in his seminal work, published in 1881 and 1882 in the prominent journal *Zeitschrift für die alttestamentliche Wissenschaft* (ZAW), of which he was the first editor. Stade's articles remain to this day among the most influential in Zechariah studies; and his insistence on setting Second Zechariah within the broad continuum of prophecy in general, from Jeremiah to Ezekiel, finds many resonances in the secondary literature today. In the end, however, Stade, like the majority of scholars, succumbed to the temptation to see in some of the so-called historical allusions (e.g., 9:1–8; 9:13; 10:10; 11:1–3; etc.) reflections of the Hellenistic era in Palestine.

More than any other scholars working in late prophecy, Mason and P. D. Hanson have urged readers to disavow the tendency that took firm roots in the nineteenth century and came to full bloom in the twentieth, namely, to read the text of Second Zechariah with the expressed intention of seeking to identify historical events in the words of the prophet(s). Both have correctly urged caution in dealing in such a manner with texts that are by their very nature complex, elusive, elliptical, and perhaps apocalyptic (P. D. Hanson 1975: 280ff.; Mason 1973; 1976). Moreover, in view of the fact that Second Zechariah uses or alludes to so many older biblical materials, they seek to understand how these materials were reworked to deal with issues that arose in Second Zechariah's day.

Surely one must be cautious and refrain from assigning too narrow a range for the utterance and transmission of the sayings. The first priority in all exegetical inquiry should be to allow the texts to speak for themselves. However, as readers of this commentary will see, the idea that the historical setting cannot be recovered can no longer be maintained. Although the specific dynamics of Yehudite leadership and tensions defy reconstruction, sensitivity to demographic, economic, and political trends in the late sixth and the fifth centuries allow us to provide a more nuanced picture of Second Zechariah's world, and what evoked the oracles of chapters 9–14, than has hitherto been possible (earlier in this Introduction, see The Historical Context).

Despite the above-mentioned trends, the wide gap in scholarly opinions has continued throughout this century. Hanson follows in Stade's footsteps and identifies as the consensus the view assigning Zech 9:1–8 to the period of Alexander the Great. The list of other distinguished scholars who begin their discussion of Second Zechariah with such a chronological framework for chapter 9 includes Eissfeldt, Elliger, Dentan, and Delcor, to name but a few of the major figures (listed in P. D. Hanson 1975: 290; see also Otzen 1964: 11–34 and Eissfeldt 1964: 434–40). Those who today still argue for an eighth-century setting for Zech 9:1–8 include Kraeling, Horst and Robinson, and Malamat. Such luminaries as Marti, Mitchell, Duhm, Sellin, Bewer, and Oesterley have opted for a Maccabean or late Hellenistic setting for the entire work.

Among the many scholarly voices claiming diversity for Second Zechariah, perhaps the most articulate proponent of a unified literary structure for Zechariah 9–14 has been Lamarche (1961). Discerning in these six chapters, which he dates to about 500–480 although not completely rejecting the possibility of an Alexandrine setting for the whole (1961: 146), the organizing principle of chiasm, Lamarche identifies twelve units in chapters 9–14 in which a chiastic pattern operates. For example, he claims that Zech 9:1–8 has its counterpart in 14:16–21, and 10:2–3 its counterpart in 13:2–6 (Lamarche 1961: 112–13). Lamarche's most outspoken follower has been Baldwin (1972: 75–81). In addition to making a case for the inherent unity of Second Zechariah, Lamarche has also asserted that the messianism of Second Zechariah was developed as a kind of commentary on Isaiah 40–55. In this respect, he anticipated the work of Mason, who has provided a compendious and valuable analysis of how the language of Second Zechariah draws from earlier biblical texts.

We remarked above that the main trends in the contemporary scholarship of Second Zechariah are two: first, a consensus that the material comes from the postexilic, or Persian, period; and second, the recognition of a marked presence of intertextuality. The convergence on the Persian period can be found in the works of a number of scholars, including the authors, who approach the material from different perspectives. It is in this connection that we commend the linguistic work of Hill (1982). Developing the typological approach of R. Polzin (1976), Hill expands and refines nineteen of the grammatical and syntactic categories used by Polzin with the purpose of distinguishing the relative chronology of early and late biblical Hebrew prose. Because the methodology developed by Hill involves only prose, Zechariah 9 is excluded from his study. The main result of his study is that Zechariah 10–14 may be dated on linguistic grounds to between 520 B.C.E. and 458 B.C.E. In reaching this conclusion, Hill notes (1982: 130) that his results coincide with the date proposed by P. D. Hanson (1975: 280–481) and by Kirkpatrick (1915: 442–56) and are relatively close to that of Freedman (1976; 1991), who places the composition of the postexilic prophets and their incorporation into the unofficial canon at about 500 B.C.E.

Hill's impressive work at the very least suggests that Zechariah 10–14 was extensively edited or redacted in the early fifth century. Our research also narrows the date to the early to mid-fifth century. Not only was the editing, if any, done in this period, but it was apparently also at this time that the main composition was done. The reader is referred to NOTES and COMMENT for our views on chapter 9.

It is unfortunate that we have been unable to consult the commentary of D. L. Petersen, who has been laboring on late biblical prophecy during the very same years as have we. Readers of our works on First Zechariah will note many similarities of approach in his work (1984). Anticipating his forthcoming commentary on Zechariah 9–14, we can refer to his refutation of the unity theory of Second Zechariah based on statistical analysis (Portnoy and Petersen 1984). In so arguing, he posits three distinct parts to the Book of Zechariah: chapters 1–8, 9–11, and 12–14. Zechariah 9–11, he contends, is slightly earlier than chapters 12–14, the latter being middle and late apocalyptic, the former early apocalyptic. His characterization of chapters 9–11 as poetic, however, is one with which we cannot fully agree. As we have previously indicated, only chapter 9 qualifies as true poetry, although chapter 10 is close to poetry. Petersen's consideration of chapters 9–11 and 12–14 as distinct booklets derives from the common headings *maśśā'* in 9:1 and 12:1, which may have been added to create the appearance of greater unity but which may not have much to do with the original shape of Second Zechariah.

The bewildering array of commentaries on Second Zechariah and the range of interpretive options they provide in approaching the text is challenge enough for anyone contemplating research in the Minor Prophets. Indeed, a truly significant number of commentaries provide solid philological and text-critical data that are indispensable for working with the material. Given the far-ranging parameters sketched above for dating the origin or editing of the material of Second Zechariah, the following commentaries are among the most thorough and helpful: Mitchell (1912), Otzen (1964), Saebø (1969), Chary (1969), and Rudolph (1976). These works, together with Jansma's useful text-critical guide to the versions (1950), to be used now with information from the new scrolls from Qumran and the Judean wilderness (Fuller 1988; Tov et al. 1990), provide an invaluable resource for the continuing exegetical study of Second Zechariah.

In concluding this short survey, which in its brevity has drawn attention to only some of the many fine studies of all or parts of Second Zechariah, we single out for mention several works so innovative that it is readily apparent, after considering them, that scholarship in later biblical prophecy is clearly at a turning point.

Paul Hanson's work, *The Dawn of Apocalyptic* (1975), certainly ushered in a new era in the study of the literature of the postexilic period. Approximately half of the book is devoted to Haggai and First and Second Zechariah, and the final third devoted solely to a detailed treatment of Second Zechariah. Building on the sociological insights of Weber and Durkheim, and in many ways reflecting the *Zeitgeist* of the 1960s, Hanson sees in Zechariah 9–14 the literature of a group of dissident and dissatisfied followers of Isaiah of the Exile (Second Isaiah). He suggests that these followers, whom he labels "visionaries," together with a group of disenfranchised Levites, vied for control of Israel's leadership in the early postexilic era. In elaborating on this hypothetical schism within Israel, he calls the prophets Haggai and Zechariah 1–8 "hierocrats" and accuses them and their followers of selling out to the Persian-supported government. Moreover, he claims that their platform is devoid of eschatology.

In challenging the pro-Temple hierocratic leadership, Hanson argues, the visionaries borrowed the language of the old Canaanite warrior myth and combined it with Israel's own conquest language, as handed down from the tribal league and traditions of the royal cult (1975: 285). The prophecies of Second Zechariah thus represent, in his estimation, a repository of dissident utterances from 550–475 B.C.E. that changed the shape of Second Temple Judaism. In them, Hanson discerned the voice of apocalyptic, with its recrudescent Canaanite myth and heightened eschatology, which was soon to go underground until Maccabean times.

The interest in the Second Temple period that Hanson's work aroused has given momentum to new work in late biblical prophecy, an area of study that, in America at least, had languished for quite a long time. At the same time, the criticisms of Hanson's work have been very serious and have been sustained over the years since its publication. In general, scholars have resisted his rather oversimplified and polarized division of postexilic Israel into two "parties," visionaries and hierocrats. They have noted that his sociological reconstruction of these two competing groups is not supported by any externally verifiable criteria. They have questioned the assumption of a straightforward relationship between text and social context and thus have raised serious doubts about the connection P. D. Hanson makes between ideology and social status (see especially Kovacs 1976). His definitions of prophetic and apocalyptic eschatology, moreover, have not won broad acceptance. Finally, his explanation of Haggai and Zechariah 1–8 within such an interpretive framework has led him to a very negative reading, perhaps unjustifiably so, of those texts.

A more positive and promising approach to the study of late biblical prophecy has been undertaken by Rex Mason in many of his publications. Unfortunately, his only detailed study of Zechariah 9–14 remains his unpublished 1973 University of London Ph.D. dissertation: "The Use of Earlier Biblical Material in Zechariah 9–14: A Study in Inner Biblical Exegesis." A brief summary of this study appeared in 1976 (227–39), and highlights from it may be gleaned in Mason's 1977 Cambridge University Press commentary, *The Books of Haggai, Zechariah, and Malachi* and in his 1982 article in *Studia Evangelica*. Apparently influenced by the work of M. Delcor (1952), who had noted that the various sections of Second Zechariah seemed to be heavily dependent on earlier biblical material, especially the prophets Ezekiel, Jeremiah, and Second Isaiah (chapters 40–55), as well as by the so-called Third Isaiah (chapters 56–66), Mason amplified those observations and established a solid case for the literary dependence of all of Zechariah 9–14 on earlier materials.

Although Mason is imprecise about the date of composition, which he believes would be the fifth century or later (1977: 90), he characterizes the work of Second Zechariah "as a kind of eschatological 'hymn-book' for the community" (1977: 81). Because of such extensive use and reinterpretation of earlier prophetic materials, he, like Delcor, understands Zechariah 9–14 either as the work of a single prophet or as the work of a *traditio* circle, or circle of followers of the prophet, who interpreted events in their own day in light of the earlier sayings of Zechariah or the major prophets, which they reworked to make those sayings more cogent and compelling to a later generation. In this respect, Second Zechariah is surprisingly similar to some of the writings of Qumran, especially the *pesharim*.

In regard to the general social setting of postexilic Jewish thought, Mason in his most recent work (1990) has argued that there was great variety in the leadership, which included prophets, preachers, teachers, and rhetors, all of whom shared a discernible theological unity expressed in such thematic elements as the Temple and its cult and the continuing influence of the Davidic covenant and legacy (p. 143). Taken together, Mason's works have had a major impact on the study of postexilic prophecy and have contributed to a more positive evaluation of the origins of Second Temple Judaism.

Person's work (1991; forthcoming) should also be noted as a study introducing a new perspective on an old problem. Person suggests that Second Zechariah's frequent dependence on earlier biblical materials reflects the activity of one who is most at home in the Deuteronomic literature. Indeed, he identifies an enormous overlap between Second Zechariah and Jeremiah and the Deuteronomic history, accepting the idea that the Book of Jeremiah was redacted by the same school that redacted and promulgated the Primary History. By identifying phrases, language, and readings in Zechariah that are Deuteronomistic (see chart 9 and discussion in Literary Considerations), he argues that the so-called Deuteronomic school was active until the time of Ezra, incorporating three main elements in its theology: a high eschatology, a strict view of false prophecy, and a specific notion about the "end" of prophecy. Although we do not agree with all of Person's conclusions, especially the way they fail to give sufficient recognition to the prominent connection between Ezekiel and Second Zechariah, we expect that his work will have much to contribute to Second Temple period studies.

Finally, the perspective of canonical criticism should be considered, inasmuch as the Book of Zechariah consists of fourteen chapters in all the versions. Childs's *Introduction to the Old Testament as Scripture* (1979), though taking into account only Mason's 1976 essay on the relation between Zechariah 1-8 and Zechariah 9-14, makes a series of important observations about the canonical shape of the entire book. For example, like Mason, he sees numerous thematic and theological points of congruence between the two parts of Zechariah; indeed, he argues for a greater compatibility than is usually acknowledged, except by scholars such as Mason and Delcor, between chapters 1-8 and 9-14 (pp. 480, 482). Moreover, the very fact that such compatibility exists suggests that, whatever the original setting of certain sections of the text may have been, their present canonical ordering demands its own reading and consideration. If, for example, Zech 9:1-8 had a specific (and early) historical mooring at one time, just as chapters 1-8 did in the time of Darius I (so Meyers and Meyers 1987), their canonical positioning allows those texts to refer to the future as well as the past (pp. 471-81). Childs accepts the idea that chapters 9-14 come from another and later hand; and he dates parts of chapters 1-8 to before 538 B.C.E., in the reign of Cyrus, a suggestion we find completely unreasonable. Nonetheless, his plea for a holistic reading of the texts strikes a sympathetic chord in us as it has in others (R. L. Smith 1984: 249; Coggins 1987: 68).

In any exegetical examination of Second Zechariah, an awareness of and openness to the canonical form of the whole Book of Zechariah surely allows the reader a kind of flexibility in interpretation that the final author or redactor of the book perhaps had in mind when setting out to "publish" this work. Such an openness makes it virtually impossible to consider that chapters 1-8 stemmed from a narrow-minded hierocratic group and chapters 9-14 from a high-minded visionary and apocalyptic group. Whether or not we accept Childs's specific suggestions, his impassioned call for a unified reading should be heard:

> It is important to recognize that the editorial joining of the two parts of Zechariah not only serves to alter the reading of the first chapters in terms of the last, but the reverse dynamic is also set in motion. The presence of Proto-Zechariah significantly affected how the community heard the message of the last chapters. To suggest that the late apocalyptic writers had lost interest in the everyday ethical responsibilities of the covenant because of a fixation on the coming age fails to reckon with the canonical shape of the book as a whole. The strong imperatives of ch. 8 which the editors link inextricably with the coming age serve as a constant warning against misunderstanding the nature of the coming kingdom. Judah's repentance is described in 13.9 by a repetition of the same ancient covenant formula found explicitly in 8.8. Thus ch. 8

provides the content to the imperatives which ch. 13 signals and links the two parts of the book closely together (pp. 484–85).

For additional information on the secondary literature the reader is referred to the Bibliography and NOTES, as well as to the bibliographies in the existing commentaries and special studies noted therein.

BIBLIOGRAPHY

♦

Aalen, S.
  1974 "ʾôr." *TDOT* 1.147–67.
Abel, F.-M.
  1936 Asal dans Zacharie XIV, 5. *RB* 45:385–400.
Ackroyd, P. R.
  1962 Zechariah. In *Peake's Commentary on the Bible*. Ed. M. Black, 646–
    55. London: Nelson.
  1979 The History of Israel in the Exilic and Post-Exilic Periods. In *Tradition
    and Interpretation: Essays by Members of the Society for Old Testament
    Study*. Ed. G. W. Anderson, 320–50. Oxford: Clarendon; New York:
    Oxford.
Aharoni, Y.
  1979 *Land of the Bible*. 2d ed. Philadelphia: Westminster.
Albright, W. F.
  1940 *From the Stone Age to Christianity: Monotheism and the Historical
    Process*. Baltimore: Johns Hopkins University.
Alt, A.
  1953–59 *Kleine Schriften zur Geschichte des Volkes Israel*. Vols. 1–3. Mu-
    nich: Beck.
Alter, R.
  1981 *The Art of Biblical Narrative*. New York: Basic Books.
Amiran, R.
  1970 *Ancient Pottery of the Holy Land: From Its Beginnings in the Neolithic
    Period to the End of the Iron Age*. New Brunswick, N.J.: Rutgers
    University.
Amsler, S.
  1972 Zacharie et l'origine de l'apocalyptique. VTSup 22. Leiden: Brill.
Andersen, F. I., and D. N. Freedman.
  1980 *Hosea*. 24. Garden City, N.Y.: Doubleday.
  1989 *Amos*. 24A. New York: Doubleday.
Anderson, G. A.
  1992 Sacrifice and Sacrificial Offerings: Old Testament. *ABD* 5.870–76.
Auld, A. G.
  1990 Prophecy in Books: A Rejoinder. *JSOT* 48:31–32.

Avigad, N.
  1954   Seven Ancient Hebrew Seals. *Bulletin of the Israel Exploration Society* 18:147–53 (Hebrew).
  1987   The Contribution of Hebrew Seals to an Understanding of Israelite Religion and Society. In *Ancient Israelite Religion: Essays in Honor of Frank Moore Cross*. Ed. P. D. Miller, Jr., P. D. Hanson, and S. D. McBride, 195–208. Philadelphia: Fortress.
  1976   *Bullae and Seals from a Post-Exilic Judean Archive. Qedem*, vol. 4. Jerusalem: Hebrew University Institute of Archaeology.
Avi-Yonah, M.
  1954   The Walls of Jeremiah—A Minimalist View. *IEJ* 4:239–48.
Bahat, D.
  1990   *The Illustrated Atlas of Jerusalem*. New York: Simon & Schuster.
Baldwin, J.
  1972   *Haggai, Zechariah, Malachi*. Tyndale Old Testament Commentaries. Downers Grove, Ill.: Inter-Varsity.
Baly, D.
  1957   *The Geography of the Bible*. New York: Harper & Row.
  1963   *The Land of the Bible*. London: Lutterworth.
Barkay, G.
  1990   A Bowl with the Hebrew Inscription QDŠ. *IEJ* 40:124–29.
Barker, M.
  1978   The Evil in Zechariah. *Heythrop Journal* 19:12–27.
Barth, C., J. Bergman, and H. Ringgren
  1975   "*gyl; gîlāh.*" *TDOT* 2.469–75.
Bartnicki, R.
  1976   Das Zitat von Zach. IX, 9–10 und die Tiere im Bericht von Mattäus über dem Einzug Jesu in Jerusalem (MT XXI, 1–11). *Novum Testamentum* 18:161–66.
Baumann, A.
  1978   "*deleth; dal.*" *TDOT* 3.330–33.
  1990   "*yll; yᵉlēl; yᵉlālâ.*" *TDOT* 6.82–87.
Bergman, J., M. Ottosson, and G. J. Botterweck
  1980   "*chālam.*" *TDOT* 4.421–32.
Bergman, J., H. Ringgren, and B. Lang
  1980   "*zabach.*" *TDOT* 4.8–29.
Bernhardt, K.-H.
  1974   "*ʾāven.*" *TDOT* 1.140–47.
Bernhardt, K.-H., J. Bergman, and H. Ringgren
  1978   "*hāyāh.*" *TDOT* 3.369–81.
Betlyon, J. W.
  1991   Archaeological Evidence of Military Operations in Southern Judah during the Early Hellenistic Period. *BA* 54:36–43.
Bewer, J. A.
  1922   *The Literature of the Old Testament*. New York: Columbia University.

Blenkinsopp, J.
1981   Interpretation and the Tendency to Sectarianism: An Aspect of Second
       Temple History. In *Jewish and Christian Self-Definition*. Ed. E. P.
       Sanders, 1–26. Philadelphia: Fortress.
1983   *A History of Prophecy in Israel from the Settlement in the Land to the
       Hellenistic Period*. Philadelphia: Westminster.
Boer, P. A. H. de
1948   An Enquiry into the Meaning of the Term "massāʾ". *OTS* 5:197–214.
Borowski, O.
1987   *Agriculture in Iron Age Israel*. Winona Lake, Ind.: Eisenbrauns.
Botha, F. J.
1955   Zechariah 10:11a. *ET* 66:177.
Boyarin, D.
1990   *Intertextuality and the Reading of Midrash*. Bloomington: Indiana
       University.
Bratsiosis, N. P.
1975   "*bāśār*." *TDOT* 2.317–32.
Brettler, M.
1989   *God Is King: Understanding an Israelite Metaphor*. JSOT Supplement
       Series 76. Sheffield: JSOT.
forthcoming   Images of YHWH the Warrier in Psalms. In *Women, War, and
       Metaphor*. Ed. C. Camp and C. Fontaine. *Semeia* 61.
Bright, J.
1981   *A History of Israel*. 3d ed. Philadelphia: Westminster.
Broshi, M.
1978   Estimating the Population of Ancient Jerusalem. *BAR* 4:10–15.
1990   Methodology of Population Estimates: The Roman Period as a Case
       Study. Paper delivered at the Second International Congress on
       Biblical Archaeology, Jerusalem.
Broshi, M., and R. Gophna
1984   The Settlements and Population of Palestine During the Early Bronze
       Age II–III. *BASOR* 253:41–53.
Brouwer, C.
1949   *Wachter en Herder*. Wageningen.
Browning, D. C.
1988   The Textile Industry of Iron Age Timnah and Its Regional and
       Socioeconomic Contexts: A Literary and Artifactual Analysis. Ph.D.
       diss., Southwestern Baptist Theological Seminary.
Bruce, F. F.
1961   The Book of Zechariah and the Passion Narrative. *BJRL* 43:336–53.
1972   The Earliest Old Testament Interpretation. *OTS* 17:37–52.
Burger, J. A.
1981   Tradition and Interpretation in Zechariah 9–14. Master's thesis, Uni-
       versity of Pretoria.

Caquot, A.
1985   Brèves Remarques sur l'Allégorie des Pasteurs en Zacharie 11. In *Mélanges bibliques et orientaux en l'honneur de M. Mathias Delcor.* Ed. A. Caquot, S. Légasse, and M. Tardieu, 45–55. Kevelaer: Butzon & Baker; Neukirchen-Vluyn: Neukirchener Verlag.

Carroll, R. P.
1979   Twilight of Prophecy or Dawn of Apocalyptic? *JSOT* 14:3–35.
1990   Whose Prophet? Whose History? Whose Social Reality? Troubling the Interpretative Community Again: Notes Towards a Response to T. W. Overholt's Critique. *JSOT* 48:33–49.

Carter, C.
1990   Ethnoarchaeology and the Province of Yehud—Some Thoughts on Population, Demographics, and Economy. Paper delivered at the AAR/SBL Constructions of Ancient History and Religion Group, New Orleans.
1991   A Social and Demographic Study of Post-Exilic Judah. Ph.D. diss., Duke University.

Cazelles, H.
1951   Jérémie et le Deutérome. *RSR* 38:5–36.

Chary, T.
1969   *Aggée–Zacharie–Malachie.* Paris: Gabalda.

Childs, B. S.
1959   The Enemy from the North and the Chaos Tradition. *JBL* 78:187–98.
1978   The Canonical Shape of the Prophetic Literature. *Interpretation* 32:46–55.
1979   *Introduction to the Old Testament as Scripture.* Philadelphia: Fortress.

Clements, R. E.
1977   Patterns in the Prophetic Canon. In *Canon and Authority.* Ed. G. W. Coats and B. O. Long, 42–55. Philadelphia: Fortress.

Clements, R. E. and G. J. Botterweck
1975   "*gôy.*" *TDOT* 2.426–32.

Clifford, R. J.
1966   The Use of *Hôy* in the Prophets. *CBQ* 28:458–64.
1972   *The Cosmic Mountain in Canaan and the Old Testament.* Harvard Semitic Monographs, vol. 4. Cambridge: Harvard University.

Coggins, R. J.
1975   *Samaritans and Jews: The Origins of Samaritanism Reconsidered.* Oxford: Basil Blackwell; Atlanta: John Knox.
1987   *Haggai, Zechariah, Malachi.* Sheffield: *JSOT.*

Cohen, A., ed.
1948   *The Twelve Prophets.* Bournemouth: Soncino.

Cook, J. M.
1983   *The Persian Empire.* London: Dent.

Craig, T.
1992   Metaphor and Social Drama in Second Temple Prophetic Texts. Ph.D. diss., Vanderbilt University.

Cross, F. M., Jr.
  1969 New Directions in the Study of Apocalyptic. In *Apocalypticism*, ed.
        R. Funk, 157–65. *JTC* 6. New York: Herder & Herder.
  1973 *Canaanite Myth and Hebrew Epic.* Cambridge: Harvard University.
  1981 The Priestly Tabernacle in the Light of Recent Research. In *Temples
        and High Places in Biblical Times.* Ed. A. Biran, 169–80. Jerusalem:
        Hebrew Union College.
Cross, F. M., Jr., and D. N. Freedman
  1955 The Song of Miriam. *JNES* 14:237–50.
Crossan, J. D.
  1985 Parables. *HBD*, 747–49. San Francisco: Harper.
Crotty, R. B.
  1982 The Suffering Moses of Deutero-Zechariah. *Colloquium* 14:43–50.
Curtis, J. B.
  1957 An Investigation of the Mount of Olives in the Judaeo-Christian
        Tradition. *HUCA* 28:137–80.
Dahood, M.
  1963 Zacharia 9, 1, ʿÊN ʾĀDĀM. *CBQ* 25:123–24.
  1965, 1968, 1970 *Psalms I, II, III.* AB 16, 17, 17A. Garden City, N.Y.:
        Doubleday.
Davis, E. F.
  1989 *Swallowing the Scroll: Textuality and the Dynamics of Discourse in
        Ezekiel's Prophecy.* *JSOT* Supplement Series, no. 78. Bible and Liter-
        ature Series, 21. Sheffield: Almond.
Delcor, M.
  1951a Les Allusions à Alexandre le Grand dans Zach. 9:1–8. *VT* 1:110–24.
  1951b Un Problème de Critique Textuelle et d'Exégèse: Zach. 12:10. *RB*
        58:189–99.
  1952 Les Sources du Deutéro-Zacharie et ses Procédés d'Emprunt. *RB*
        59:385–411.
  1953 Deux Passages Difficiles: Zach. 12:11 et 11:13. *VT* 3:67–77.
Demsky, A.
  1981 The Temple Steward Josiah ben Zephaniah. *IEJ* 31:100–3.
Dentan, R.
  1956 Zechariah 9–14. *IB* 6.1089–114.
Dever, W. D.
  1992 A Case-Study in Biblical Archaeology: The Earthquake of CA. 760
        BCE. *EI* 23:27–35.
Dick, M. B.
  1984 Prophetic Poiēsis and the Verbal Icon. *CBQ* 46:226–46.
Dion, P. E., and R. Pummer
  1980 A Note on the "Samaritan-Christian Synagogue" in Ramat-Aviv. *JSJ*
        11:217–22.
Dodd, C. H.
  1953 *According to the Scriptures.* New York: Scribners.

Donner, H. R., and W. Röllig
1964–68   *Kanaanäische und Aramäische Inschriften*. Wiesbaden: Otto Harrassowitz.

Dothan, T.
1982   *The Philistines and Their Material Culture*. New Haven and London: Yale University; Jerusalem: Israel Exploration Society.

Dothan, T., and S. Gitin
1987   The Rise and Fall of Ekron of the Philistines: Recent Excavations at an Urban Border Site. *BA* 50:197–222.

Driver, G. R.
1938   Linguistic and Textual Problems: Minor Prophets. *JTS* 39:393–405.

Duhm, B.
1910   *Die zwölf Propheten: In den Versmassen der Urschrift übersetst*. Tübingen: J. C. B. Mohr.

Dumbrell, W. J.
1978   Kingship and Temple in the Post-Exilic Period. *RTR* 37:33–42.

Eichhorn, J. G.
1824   *Einleitung in das Alte Testament*. Vol. 4. Göttingen: C. E. Rosenbusch.

Eisenbeis, W.
1969   Die Wurzel šlm im Alten Testament. BZAW 113. Berlin: De Gruyter.

Eising, H.
1980   *"zākhar." TDOT* 4.64–82.

Eissfeldt, O.
1947   "My God" in the Old Testament. *EvQ* 19:7–20.
1964   *Einleitung in das Alte Testament*. Tübingen: J. C. B. Mohr.
1974   *"ʾadhôn." TDOT* 1.59–72.

Elayi, J.
1982   Studies in Phoenician Geography During the Persian Period. *JNES* 41:83–110.

Eliade, M.
1961   *The Sacred and the Profane*. Trans. W. R. Trask. New York: Harper & Row.

Elliger, K.
1949–50   Ein Zeugnis aus der jüdischen Gemeinde im Alexanderjahr 332 V. Chr.: Eine Territoralgeschichtliche Studie zu Sach 9:1–8. *ZAW* 62:63–115.
1975   *Das Buch der zwölf kleinen Propheten II: Die Propheten Nahum, Habakuk, Zephanja, Haggai, Zacharja, Maleachi*. ATD 25. Göttingen: Vandenhoeck & Ruprecht.

Ellul, D.
1981   Variations sur le Theme de la Guerre Sainte dans le Deutero-Zacharie. *ÉTR* 56:55–71.

Ephꜥal, I.
1979   Assyrian Dominion in Palestine. In *The World History of the Jewish*

People: The Age of the Monarchies—Political History. Ed. A. Malamat, 276–89. Jerusalem: Massada.

Farbridge, M.
1970   *Studies in Biblical and Semitic Symbolism.* New York: KTAV.

Feigin, S.
1925   Some Notes on Zechariah 11, 4–17. *JBL* 44:203–13.
1944   Babylonian Parallels to the Hebrew Phrase "Lowly, and Riding Upon an Ass." In *Studies in Memory of Moses Schorr 1874–1941.* Ed. L. Ginzberg and A. Weiss, 227–40. New York: The Professor Moses Schorr Memorial Committee (Hebrew).

Finkel, I. L.
1983–84   Necromancy in Ancient Mesopotamia. *AfO* 29–30:1–17.

Finkelstein, I.
1988   The Value of Demographic Data from Recent Generations for Environmental Archaeology and Historical Research. Paper delivered at the International SBL Meetings, Sheffield.
1988–89   The Land of Ephraim Survey 1980–1987: Preliminary Report. *Tel Aviv* 15–16:117–83.

Finley, T. J.
1982   The Sheep Merchants of Zechariah 11. *Grace Theological Journal* 3:51–65.

Fishbane, M.
1977   The Qumran Pesher and Traits of Ancient Hermeneutics. In *Proceedings of the Sixth World Congress of Jewish Studies.* Ed. A. Shinan, 97–114. Jerusalem: World Union of Jewish Studies.
1979   *Text and Texture.* New York: Schocken.
1980   Revelation and Tradition: Aspects of Inner-Biblical Exegesis. *JBL* 99:343–61.
1985   *Biblical Interpretation in Ancient Israel.* Oxford: Clarendon.

Fohrer, G.
1965   *Einleitung in das Alte Testament.* Heidelberg: Quelle und Meyer.

Forbes, R. J.
1955–64   *Studies in Ancient Technology.* 9 vols. Leiden: Brill.

Freedman, D. N.
1963   The Law and the Prophets. *VTSup* 9. Leiden: Brill.
1972   Acrostics and Metrics in Hebrew Poetry. *HTR* 65:367–92.
1976   Canon of the Old Testament. *IDB* Supplement. 130–36.
1980   *Pottery, Poetry and Prophecy.* Winona Lake, Ind.: Eisenbrauns.
1981   Temple Without Hands. In *Temples and High Places in Biblical Times.* Ed. A. Biran, 21–30. Jerusalem: Hebrew Union College.
1990   Formation of the Canon of the Old Testament. In *Religion and Law.* Ed. E. B. Firmage, 315–31. Winona Lake, Ind.: Eisenbrauns.
1991   *The Unity of the Hebrew Bible.* Ann Arbor: University of Michigan.

Freedman, D. N., J. R. Lundblom and G. J. Botterweck
1986   "*hārâ.*" *TDOT* 5.171–76.

Frick, F. S.
1985   *The Formation of the State in Ancient Israel.* Social World of Biblical Antiquity Series, vol. 4. Decatur, Ga.: Almond.

Friedman, R. E.
1983   The Prophet and the Historian: The Acquisition of Historical Information from Literary Sources. In *The Poet and the Historian.* Ed. R. E. Friedman, 1–12. Harvard Semitic Series, vol. 26. Chico, Calif.: Scholars.

Frymer-Kensky, T.
1977   The Atrahasis Epic and Its Significance for Our Understanding of Genesis 1–9. *BA* 40:147–55.

1983   Pollution, Purification, and Purgation in Biblical Israel. In *The Word of the Lord Shall Go Forth: Essays in Honor of David Noel Freedman in Celebration of His Sixtieth Birthday.* Ed. C. L. Meyers and M. O'Connor, 399–414. Winona Lake, Ind.: Eisenbrauns/ASOR.

Fuggian, H. J.
1951   The Messianic Teachings of Zechariah 9–14. Ph.D. diss., Southern Baptist Theological Seminary.

Fuhs, H. F.
1978   *"gāʿal."* TDOT 3.45–48.

Fuller, R. E.
1988   The Minor Prophets Manuscripts from Qumrân, Cave IV. Ph.D. diss., Harvard University.

Galling, K.
1952   Die Exilswende in der Sicht des Propheten Sacharja. *VT* 2:18–36.

Gamberoni, J.
1974   Die Geistbegabung in Alten Testament, besonders nach Joel 3:1–5. In *Die Gabe Gottes.* Ed. P. Nordhues, 9–32.

Gaster, T. H.
1961   *Thespis: Ritual, Myth, and Drama in the Ancient Near East.* Rev. ed. Garden City, N.Y.: Doubleday.

Gelb, I. J.
1973   Prisoners of War in Early Mesopotamia. *JNES* 32:70–98.

Gelin, A.
1951   La Question des "Relectures" Bibliques a l'Intérieur d'Une Tradition Vivante. In *Sacra Pagina* 1. Ed. J. Coppens, A. Descamps, and E. Massaux, 303–15. Gambloux: J. Duculot.

Gerstenberger, G.
1962   The Woe-Oracles of the Prophets. *JBL* 81:249–63.

Gese, H.
1973   Anfang und Ende der Apokalyptic, dargestellt am Sacharjahrbuch. *ZTK* 70:20–49.

1974   Nachtrag: Die Deutung der Hirtenallegorie Sach 11, 4ff. In *Vom Sinai zum Zion,* 231–38. Beiträge zur evangelischen Theologie, vol. 64. München: Kaiser.

Gevaryahu, H. M. I.
  1975   Biblical Colophons: A Source for the "Biography" of Authors, Texts
         and Books. In VTSup 28, 42–59. Leiden: Brill.
Ginsberg, H. L.
  1953   The Oldest Interpretation of the Suffering Servant. VT 3: 400–4.
  1978   The Oldest Record of Hysteria with Physical Stigmata: Zech. 13:2–6.
         In Studies in the Bible and Ancient Near East, Samuel E. Loewen-
         stamm Festschrift. Ed. Y. Avishur and J. Blau, 23–27. Jerusalem: E.
         Rubinstein's Publishing House.
Gitin, S.
  1987   Urban Growth and Decline at Ekron in the Iron II Period. BA 50:206–
         22.
Godelier, M.
  1980   Processes of the Formation, Diversity, and Bases of the State. Inter-
         national Social Science Journal 32:609–23.
Goodenough, E. R.
  1964   Jewish Symbols in the Greco-Roman Period. Bollingen Series, vols. 10
         and 11. New York: Pantheon.
Gordis, R.
  1930   Midrash in the Prophets. JBL 49:417–22.
  1949   Quotations as a Literary Usage in Biblical, Oriental and Rabbinic
         Literature. HUCA 22:157–219.
Gordon, R. P.
  1975   Targum Variant Agrees with Wellhausen! ZAW 87:218–19.
Gottwald, N. K.
  1979   The Tribes of Yahweh. Maryknoll, N.Y.: Orbis.
Goudoever, J. van
  1961   Biblical Calendars. 2d rev. ed. Leiden: Brill.
Grech, P.
  1969   Interprophetic Re-Interpretation and Old Testament Eschatology. Au-
         gustinianum 9:235–65.
Greenberg, M.
  1983   Ezekiel 1–20. AB 22. Garden City, N.Y.: Doubleday.
Greenfield, J. C.
  1976   The Aramean God Rammān/Rimmōn. IEJ 26:195–98.
Greenspahn, F. E.
  1989   Why Prophecy Ceased. JBL 108:37–49.
Grene, D., and R. Lattimore, eds.
  1959–60   The Complete Greek Tragedies. Chicago: University of Chicago.
Grigsby, B. H.
  1986   "If Any Man Thirsts . . .": Observations on the Rabbinic Background
         of John 7, 37–39. Biblica 67:101–8.
Gross, A.
  1984   R. Abraham Saba's Abbreviated Messianic Commentary on Haggai

and Zechariah. In *Studies in Medieval Jewish History and Literature,* vol. 2. Ed. I. Twersky, 389–401. Cambridge and London: Harvard University.

Gundry, R. H.
1967 *The Use of the Old Testament in St. Matthew's Gospel.* Leiden: Brill.

Gutwirth, E.
1981 The "World Upside Down" in Hebrew. *Orientalia Suecana* 30:141–47.

Haag, H.
1975 *"bath."* TDOT 2.332–38.

Halpern, B.
1978 The Ritual Background of Zechariah's Temple Song. *CBQ* 40:167–90.

Hanson, P. D.
1973 Zechariah 9 and the Recapitulation of an Ancient Ritual Pattern. *JBL* 92:37–59.
1975 *The Dawn of Apocalyptic.* Philadelphia: Fortress.

Hanson, R. S.
1980 *Tyrian Influence in the Upper Galilee.* Meiron Excavation Project, num. 2. Cambridge, Mass.: ASOR.

Haran, M.
1978 *Temples and Temple-Service in Ancient Israel.* Oxford: Clarendon.

Har-El, M.
1984 The "Pride of the Jordan." *EI* 17:181–87 (Hebrew).

Hareuveni, N.
1980 *Nature in Our Biblical Heritage.* Trans. H. Frenkley. Kiryat Ono, Israel: Neot Kedumim.

Harrelson, W.
1962 Nonroyal Motifs in the Royal Eschatology (Is 8; Mic 4; Zech 9). In *Israel's Prophetic Heritage: Essays in Honor of James Muilenburg.* Ed. B. W. Anderson and W. Harrelson, 147–65. New York: Harper.
1968 The Celebration of the Feast of Booths According to Zech XIV 16–21. In *Religions in Antiquity,* 88–96. Studies in the History of Religions (Supplements to Numen), vol. 14. Leiden: Brill.
1990 Inclusive Language in the New Revised Standard Version. *The Princeton Seminary Bulletin* 11:224–31.

Herr, M. D.
1971 The Historical Significance of the Dialogues between Jewish Sages and Roman Dignitaries. *SH* 22:123–50.

Hill, A. E.
1982 Dating Second Zechariah: A Linguistic Reexamination. *HAR* 6:105–34.

Hoffner, M. A., and G. J. Botterweck
1986 *"ḥēṣ."* TDOT 5.118–24.

Hoftijzer, J.
1953 A Propos d'Une Interpretation Recente de Deux Passages Difficiles: Zach. 12.11 et Zach. 11.13. VT 3:407–9.
1965 Remarks Concerning the Use of the Particle ʾt in Classical Hebrew. OTS 14:1–99.

Hoglund, K.
1989 Achaemenid Imperial Administration in Syria–Palestine and the Missions of Ezra and Nehemiah. Ph.D. diss., Duke University.
1992 Achaemenid Imperial Administration in Syria–Palestine and the Missions of Ezra and Nehemiah. SBL Dissertation Series, no. 125. Atlanta: Scholars Press.

Hopkins, D.
1985 The Highlands of Canaan. Social World of Biblical Antiquity Series, vol. 3. Decatur, Ga.: Almond.

Horst, F., and T. H. Robinson.
1964 Die zwölf kleinen Propheten—Nahum bis Maleachi. 3d ed. HAT 14. Tübingen: J. C. B. Mohr.

Höver-Johag, I.
1986 "tôb." TDOT 5.296–317.

Hummel, H. D.
1964 The Old Testament Basis of Typological Interpretation. Biblical Research 9:38–50.

Hurowitz, V. (A.)
Forthcoming Solomon's Golden Vessels (1 Kings 7:48–50) and the Cult of the First Temple. ʿAl Shulei Ha-Meʿil: Studies in Biblical, Jewish, and Near Eastern Ritual, Law, and Literature in Honor of Jacob Milgrom. Ed. D. P. Wright and D. N. Freedman. Winona Lake, Ind.: Eisenbrauns.

Hyatt, J. P.
1942 Jeremiah and Deuteronomy. JNES 1:156–73.
1951 The Deuteronomic Edition of Jeremiah. In Vanderbilt Studies in the Humanities, vol. 1. Ed. R. C. Beatty, J. P. Hyatt, and M. K. Spears, 71–95. Nashville: Vanderbilt University.

In der Smitten, W. T.
1980 "chᵃmôr." TDOT 4.465–70.

Izard, M.
1975 Le royaume du Yatenga. In Éléments d'ethnologie, vol. 1. Ed. R. Cresswell, 216–48. Paris: A. Colin.

James, F.
1934 Thoughts on Haggai and Zechariah. JBL 53:229–35.

Jansma, T.
1950 Inquiry into the Hebrew Text and the Ancient Versions of Zech. 9–14. OTS 7:1–142.

Janssen, E.
1956 Juda in der Exilszeit: ein Beitrag zur Fraga der Entstehung des Judentums. FRLANT 51. Göttingen: Vandenhoeck & Ruprecht.

Janzen, W.
1972 *Mourning Cry and Woe Oracle.* BZAW 125. New York and Berlin: De Gruyter.

Japhet, S.
1982 Sheshbazzar and Zerubbabel: Against the Background of the Historical and Religious Tendencies of Ezra-Nehemiah. ZAW 94:66–99.

Jepsen, A.
1980 *"chāzāh."* TDOT 4.280–90.

Jidejian, N.
1969 *Tyre Through the Ages.* Beirut: Dar El-Mashreq.

Johnson, A. R.
1967 *Sacral Kingship in Ancient Israel.* Cardiff: University of Wales.

Jones, B. A.
1991 Résumé of the Persian Period. Unpublished seminar paper, Duke University.

Jones, D. R.
1962 A Fresh Interpretation of Zechariah IX–XI. VT 12:241–59.

Kallai, Z.
1960 *The Northern Boundaries of Judah from the Settlement of the Tribes Until the Beginning of the Hasmonaean Period.* Jerusalem: Magnes Press (Hebrew).

Kedar-Kopfstein, B.
1978 *"dām."* TDOT 3.234–50.
1980a *"zāhābh."* TDOT 4.32–40.
1980b *"chagh; hgg."* TDOT 4.201–13.

Kedar-Kopfstein, B., and J. Bergman
1978 *"dām."* TDOT 3.234–50.

Kelso, J. L.
1948 *The Ceramic Vocabulary of the Old Testament.* BASOR Supplementary Studies, nos. 5–6. New Haven, Conn.: ASOR.

Kennett, R. H.
1927 Zech. XII–XIII.i. Notes and Studies. JTS 28:1–9.

Kimhi, D.
1837 *Commentary upon the Prophecies of Zechariah.* Trans. Rev. A. M'Caul. London: J. Duncan.

King, P. J.
1991 Bible Lands: Exploring the Valleys of Jerusalem. *Bible Review* 7:28–33, 52.

Kirkpatrick, A. F.
1915 *The Doctrine of the Prophets.* London: Macmillan.

Kitchen, K. G.
1973 The Philistines. In *Peoples of Old Testament Times.* Ed. D. J. Wiseman, 53–78. Oxford: Clarendon.

Knibb, M. A.
1982 Prophecy and the Emergence of the Jewish Apocalypses. In *Israel's*

Prophetic Tradition: Essays in Honour of Peter R. Ackroyd. Ed. R. Coggins, A. Phillips, and M. Knibb, 155–80. Cambridge and New York: Cambridge University.

Knudtzon, J. A.
1915 Die el-Amarna Tafeln. Leipzig: J. C. Hinrichs.

Koch, K.
1962 Der Spruch "Sein Blut bleibe auf seinem Haupt" und die Israelitische Auffassung vom Vergossenen Blut. VT 12:396–416.
1974 Ezra and the Origins of Judaism. JSS 19:173–97.

Koenig, J.
1962 L'activité herméneutique des scribes dans la transmission du texte de l'Ancien Testament. I. RHR 161:141–74.

Kokhavi, M., ed.
1972 Judea, Samaria and the Golan: Archaeological Survey 1967–1968. Jerusalem: The Archaeological Survey of Israel (Hebrew).

Kosmala, H.
1969 The Term geber in the Old Testament and in the Scrolls. VTSup 17, 159–69. Leiden: Brill.
1975 "gābhar." TDOT 2.367–82.

Kovacs, B. W.
1976 Contributions of Sociology to the Study of the Development of Apocalypticism: A Theoretical Survey. Paper given at SBL Consultation on the Social World of Ancient Israel, St. Louis.

Kraeling, E. G. H.
1918 Aram and Israel. New York: Columbia University.
1924 The Historical Situation in Zech. 9:1–10. AJSLL 41:24–53.
1940 The Meaning of the Ezekiel Panel in the Synagogue at Dura. BASOR 78:12–18.

Kraus, H. J.
1966 Worship in Israel. Trans. G. Buswell. Richmond, Va.: John Knox.

Kronholm, T.
1990 "yātar I." TDOT 6.482–91.

Krueger, R. R.
1983 The Fifth Sunday After Pentecost: Zech. 12:7–10—A Homiletic Study. CTQ 47:45.

Kuhrt, A.
1983 The Cyrus Cylinder and Achaemenid Imperial Policy. JSOT 25:83–97.

Kutsch, E.
1973 Das sogennante "Bundesblut" in Ex. 24:8 und Sach. 9:11. VT 23:25–30.

Lacocque, A.
1981 Zacharie 9–14. In Agée, Zacharie, Malachie, by S. Amsler, A.

Lacocoque, and R. Vuilleumier. Commentaire de l'Ancien Testament 11c. Neuchâtel-Paris: Delachaux & Niestlé.

Lamarche, P.
1961 *Zacharie IX–XIV. Structure Littéraire et Messianisme.* Paris: Gabalda.

Lang, B.
1983 *Monotheism and the Prophetic Minority: An Essay in Biblical History and Sociology.* Sheffield: Almond.

Lemche, N. P.
1991 *The Canaanites and Their Land: The Tradition of the Canaanites.* JSOT Supplement Series, vol. 110. Sheffield: JSOT.

Leupold, H. C.
1956 *Exposition of Zechariah.* Columbus, Ohio: Wartburg.

Levenson, J. D.
1985 *Sinai and Zion: An Entry into the Jewish Bible.* Minneapolis: Winston.

Levine, B.
1968 On the Presence of God in Biblical Religion. In *Religions in Antiquity,* 71–87. Studies in the History of Religions (Supplements to Numen), vol. 14. Leiden: Brill.
1989 *Leviticus.* The JPS Torah Commentary. Philadelphia: Jewish Publication Society.

Lipiński, E., ed.
1979 *State and Temple Economy in the Ancient Near East.* Leuven: Departement Oriëntalistiek.

Lohfink, N.
1986 "*ḥāram.*" TDOT 5.180–99.

Lohfink, N., and J. Bergman
1974 "*ᵓechādh.*" TDOT 1.193–201.

Long, B. O.
1984 *1 Kings, with an Introduction to the Historical Literature.* Grand Rapids, Mich.: Eerdmans.

Longman, T.
1987 *Literary Approaches to Biblical Interpretation.* Foundations of Contemporary Interpretation, vol. 3. Grand Rapids, Mich.: Academie Books.

Lucas, A.
1962 *Ancient Egyptian Materials and Industries.* 4th ed., rev. and enl. by J. R. Harris. London: E. Arnold.

Luckenbill, D. D.
1926–27 *Ancient Records of Assyria and Babylonia.* 2 Vols. Chicago: University of Chicago.

Lundquist, J. M.
1984 The Common Temple Ideology of the Ancient Near East. In *The Temple in Antiquity.* Ed. T. G. Madsen, 53–76. Religious Monograph Series, vol. 9. Provo: Brigham Young.

Luria, B.-Z.
  1981a And a Fountain Shall Come Forth from the House of the Lord. *Dor le Dor* 10:48–58.
  1981b The Jewish *Yetur. HUCA* 52:11–32.
McCall, D. K.
  1942 The Date and Authorship of Zechariah 9–14. Ph.D. diss., Southern Baptist Theological Seminary.
McCarter, P. K.
  1980 *I Samuel.* AB 8. Garden City, N.Y.: Doubleday.
McCarthy, D. J.
  1980 The Uses of "wᵉhinnēh" in Biblical Hebrew. *Biblica* 61:330–42.
McKane, W.
  1986 A *Critical and Exegetical Commentary on Jeremiah.* International Critical Commentary. Edinburgh: Clark.
McNeill, W. H.
  1976 *Plagues and Peoples.* Garden City, N.Y.: Anchor Press/Doubleday.
Maass, F.
  1974 "ʾādhām." *TDOT* 1.75–87.
Mackay, C.
  1968 Zechariah in Relation to Ezekiel 40–48. *EvQ* 40:197–210.
Magen, I., and I. Finkelstein
  forthcoming *Archaeological Survey in the Hill Country of Benjamin.*
Malamat, A.
  1950–51 The Historical Setting of Two Biblical Prophecies on the Nations. *IEJ* 1:149–59.
  1991 The Secret Council and Prophetic Involvement in Mari and Israel. In *Prophetie und geschichtliche Wirklichkeit im alten Israel: Festschrift für Siegfried Herrman zum G5. Geburtstag,* 231–36. Stuttgart: W. Kohlhammer GmbH.
Mantel, H. D.
  1973 The Dichotomy of Judaism During the Second Temple. *HUCA* 44:55–87.
Marti, K.
  1904 *Das Dodekapropheton.* Kurzer Handkommentar zum alten Testament. Tübingen: J. C. B. Mohr.
Mason, R. A.
  1973 The Use of Earlier Biblical Material in Zechariah 9–14: A Study in Inner Biblical Exegesis. Ph.D. diss., University of London.
  1976 The Relation of Zech. 9–14 to Proto-Zechariah. *ZAW* 88:227–39.
  1977 *The Books of Haggai, Zechariah, and Malachi.* Cambridge Commentary on the *NEB.* Cambridge: Cambridge University.
  1982a Inner Biblical Exegesis in Zech. 9–14. *Grace Theological Journal* 3:51–65.
  1982b The Prophets of the Restoration. In *Israel's Prophetic Tradition.* Ed.

R. Coggins, A. Phillips, and M. Knibb, 137–54. Cambridge: Cambridge University.

1982c Some Examples of Inner Biblical Exegesis in Zechariah 9–14. *Studia Evangelica* 7:343–54.

1990 *Preaching the Tradition: Homily and Hermeneutics after the Exile.* Cambridge: Cambridge University.

Mateos, P. C.

1972 Uso e interpretación de Zacarías 9, 9–10 en el Nuevo Testamento. *Estudio Agustiniano* 7:471–93.

1973 Uso e interpretación de Zacarías 9, 9–10 en el Nuevo Testamento. *Estudio Agustiniano* 8:3–29.

May, H. G.

1955 Some Cosmic Connotations of *Mayim Rabbîm*, "Many Waters." *JBL* 74:9–21.

Mayer, G.

1990 *"yārad." TDOT* 6.315–22.

Mello, A.

1984 Prigionieri della speranza. *Parola Spirito et Vita* 9:69–81.

Mendels, D.

1983 Hecataeus of Abdera and a Jewish "patrios politeia" of the Persian Period (Diodorus Siculus XL, 3). ZAW 95:96–110.

Mettinger, T. N. D.

1982 The Dethronement of Sabaoth. *Coniectanea Biblica.* Old Testament Series, vol. 18. Lund: Gleerup.

Meyer, L. V.

1972 The Messianic Metaphors in Deutero-Zechariah. Ph.D. diss., University of Chicago.

1977 Allegory Concerning the Monarchy: Zech. 11:4–17, 13:7–9. In *Scripture in History and Theology: Essays in Honor of J. Coert Rylaarsdam.* Ed. A. L. Merrill and T. W. Overholt, 225–40. Pittsburgh: Pickwick.

Meyers, C. L.

1976 *The Tabernacle Menorah.* ASOR Dissertation Series, no. 2. Missoula: Scholars.

1983a Jachin and Boaz in Religious and Political Perspective. *CBQ* 45:167–78.

1983b Of Seasons and Soldiers: A Topological Appraisal of the Premonarchic Tribes of Galilee. *BASOR* 252:47–59.

1985 "altar." *HBD* 22–24.

1986 *"sap"* (threshold). *ThWAT* 5.898–902.

1987 David as Temple Builder. In *Ancient Israelite Religion: Essays in Honor of Frank Moore Cross.* Ed. P. D. Miller, Jr., P. D. Hanson, and S. D. McBride, 357–76. Philadelphia: Fortress.

1988 *Discovering Eve: Ancient Israelite Women in Context.* New York: Oxford University.

1989 Recovering Eve: Biblical Woman Without Postbiblical Dogma. In

Women and a New Academy: Gender and Cultural Contexts. Ed. J. F. O'Barr, 62–80. Madison, Wis.: University of Wisconsin.

1992 Temple, Jerusalem. *ABD* 6.350–69.

forthcoming Realms of Sanctity: The Case of the "Misplaced" Incense Altar in the Tabernacle Texts of Exodus. *Festschrift for Menahem Haran.*

Meyers, C. L., and E. M. Meyers

1987 *Haggai, Zechariah 1–8.* AB 25B. Garden City, N.Y.: Doubleday.

1992 Jerusalem and Zion After the Exile: The Evidence of First Zechariah. In *"Sha'arei Talmon": Studies in the Bible, Qumran, and the Ancient Near East Presented to Shemaryahu Talmon.* Ed. M. Fishbane and E. Tov, 121–35. Winona Lake, Ind.: Eisenbrauns.

Meyers, E. M.

1983 The Use of *Tora* in Haggai 2:11 and the Role of the Prophet in the Restoration Community. In *The Word of the Lord Shall Go Forth: Essays in Honor of David Noel Freedman in Celebration of His Sixtieth Birthday.* Ed. C. L. Meyers and M. O'Connor, 69–76. Winona Lake, Ind.: Eisenbrauns/ASOR.

1985 The Shelomith Seal and Aspects of the Judean Restoration: Some Additional Reconsiderations. *EI* 17:33–38.

1987 The Persian Period and the Judean Restoration: from Zerubbabel to Nehemiah. In *Ancient Israelite Religion: Essays in Honor of Frank Moore Cross.* Ed. P. D. Miller, Jr., P. D. Hanson, and S. D. McBride, 509–21. Philadelphia: Fortress.

forthcoming Messianism in First and Second Zechariah and the "End" of Biblical Prophecy. *Dwight Young Festschrift.* Winona Lake, Ind.: Eisenbrauns.

Milgrom, J.

1971 Sin-Offering or Purification-Offering? *VT* 21:237–39.

1976a Two Kinds of *ḥaṭṭā'␣t. VT* 26:333–37.

1976b *Cult and Conscience: The Asham and the Priestly Doctrine of Repentance.* Leiden: Brill.

1981 The Paradox of the Red Cow (Num 19). *VT* 31:62–72.

1983 *Studies in Cultic Theology and Terminology.* Leiden: Brill.

1991a *Leviticus.* AB 3, New York: Doubleday.

1991b The *ḤAṬṬĀ'T*: A Rite of Passage? *RB* 98:120–24.

Milik, J. T.

1961 Textes Hébreux et Araméens. In *Les Grottes de Murabba'ât.* Ed. P. Benoît et al., 67–205. Discoveries in the Judaean Desert, vol. 2. Oxford: Clarendon.

Miller, J. H.

1979 Haggai–Zechariah: Prophets of the Now and Future. *CurTM* 6:99–104.

Miller, J. M., and J. H. Hayes

1986 *A History of Ancient Israel and Judah.* Philadelphia: Westminster.

Miller, P. D., Jr.
1970   Animal Names as Designations in Ugaritic and Hebrew. *Ugarit-Forschungen* 2:177–86.

Mitchell, H.
1912   A *Critical and Exegetical Commentary on Haggai, Zechariah, Malachi, and Jonah.* International Critical Commentary. Edinburgh: Clark.

Morgenstern, J.
1956   Jerusalem—485 B.C. *HUCA* 27:101–79.
1957   Jerusalem—485 B.C. (Continued). *HUCA* 28:15–47.
1961   The Suffering Servant—A New Solution. III. *VT* 11:406–9.

Mowinckel, S.
1962   *The Psalms in Israel's Worship.* 2 Vols. Trans. D. R. Ap-Thomas. Oxford: Basil Blackwell.

Müller, H.-P.
1978   "*hmm; hwm; mᵉhûmāh.*" *TDOT* 3.419–22.

Müller, H.-P., and M. Krause
1980   "*chākham.*" *TDOT* 4.364–85.

Naveh, J.
1958   Khirbet al-Muqannaᶜ—Ekron: An Archaeological Survey—I. *IEJ* 8:87–100, 165–70.

Nicholson, E. W.
1970   *Preaching to the Exiles: A Study of the Prose Tradition in the Book of Jeremiah.* Oxford: Basil Blackwell.

Nobile, M.
1984   Ez 37, 1–14 come constitutivo di uno schema cultuale. *Biblica* 65:476–89.

North, R.
1972   Prophecy to Apocalyptic via Zechariah. VTSup 22. Leiden: Brill.

Noth, M.
1966   *The Laws in the Pentateuch and Other Studies.* Trans. D. R. Ap-Thomas. London: Oliver and Boyd.
1981   *The Deuteronomistic History.* JSOT Supplement Series, no. 15. Sheffield: JSOT.

Oded, B.
1979   *Mass Deportation and Deportees in the Neo-Assyrian Empire.* Wiesbaden: Dr Ludwig Reichert Verlag.

Oesterley, W. O. E. and T. H. Robinson
1934   *Introduction to the Books of the Old Testament.* New York: Macmillan.

Ofer, A.
forthcoming   *The Judean Mountains During the Biblical Period.*

Ollenburger, B. C.
1987   *Zion, the City of the Great King: A Theological Symbol of the Jerusalem Cult.* JSOT Supplement Series, no. 41. Sheffield: JSOT.

Opelt, I.
  1984   Der "Hebestein" Jerusalem und eine Hebekugel auf der Akropolis von
         Athen in der Deutung des Hieronymus von Sach. 12, 1–3. In
         Vivarium, Festschrift Theodor Klauser zum 90. Geburtstag. Ed. E.
         Dassmann and K. Thraede. Jahrbuch für Antike und Christentum,
         Ergänzungsband 11. Münster Westfalen: Aschendorffsche Verlags-
         buchhandlung.
Oppenheim, A. L.
  1956   *The Interpretation of Dreams in the Ancient Near East, with a
         Translation of an Assyrian Dream-Book.* Philadelphia: American Phil-
         osophical Society.
Orlinsky, H. M.
  1965   The Seer in Ancient Israel. OA 4:153–74.
Ottosson, M.
  1974   "ʾerets." TDOT 1.390–405.
Otzen, B.
  1964   *Studien über Deuterosacharja.* Copenhagen: Prostant Apud Munks-
         gaard.
Overholt, T. W.
  1988   The End of Prophecy: No Players Without a Program. JSOT 42:103–
         15.
  1989   *Channels of Prophecy: The Social Dynamics of Prophetic Activity.*
         Minneapolis: Fortress.
  1990a Prophecy in History: The Social Reality of Intermediation. JSOT
         48:3–29.
  1990b "It Is Difficult to Read." JSOT 48:51–54.
Patterson, O.
  1982   *Slavery and Social Death: A Comparative Study.* Cambridge: Harvard
         University.
Paul, S.
  1989   A Technical Expression from Archery in Zechariah IX 13. VT 39:495–
         97.
  1992   Polysensuous Polyvalency in Poetic Parallelism. In *"Shʿarei Talmon":
         Studies in the Bible Qumran, and the Ancient Near East Presented to
         Shemaryahu Talmon.* Ed. M. Fishbane and E. Tov, 147–63. Winona
         Lake, Ind.: Eisenbrauns.
Peoples, J., and G. Bailey
  1988   *Humanity: An Introduction to Cultural Anthropology.* St. Paul: West.
Person, R.
  1991   Deuteronomic Redaction in the Post-Exilic Period: A Study of Second
         Zechariah. Ph.D. diss., Duke University.
  forthcoming   *Deuteronomic Redaction in the Post-Exilic Period: A Study of
                Second Zechariah.* JSOT Supplement Series. Sheffield: JSOT.
Petersen, D. L.
  1977   *Late Israelite Prophecy: Studies in Deutero-Prophetic Literature and in
         Chronicles.* SBL Monograph Series, no. 23. Missoula: Scholars.

1984   Zechariah's Visions: A Theological Perspective. *VT* 34:195–206.
1984   *Haggai and Zechariah 1–8: A Commentary.* OTL. Philadelphia: Westminster.

Petitjean, A.
1969   *Les Oracles du Proto-Zacharie.* Paris: Gabalda; Louvain: Editions Imprimerie Orientaliste.

Pierce, R. W.
1984a   Literary Connectors and a Haggai/Zechariah/Malachi Corpus. *JETS* 27:277–89.
1984b   A Thematic Development of the Haggai/Zechariah/Malachi Corpus. *JETS* 27:401–11.

Plöger, O.
1968   Trito-Zechariah. In *Theocracy and Eschatology.* Trans. S. Rudman, 78–96. Oxford: Basil Blackwell.

Polzin, R.
1976   *Late Biblical Hebrew: Toward an Historical Typology of Biblical Hebrew Prose.* Harvard Semitic Monographs, no. 12. Missoula: Scholars.

Pope, M.
1962   Number, Numbering, Numbers. *IDB* 3.561–67.

Porten, B.
1968   *Archives from Elephantine.* Berkeley: University of California.

Porteous, N.
1961   Jerusalem-Zion: The Growth of a Symbol. In *Verbannung und Heimkehr. Wilhelm Rudolph Festschrift.* Ed. A. Kuschke, 235–52. Tübingen: J. C. B. Mohr.

Portnoy, S. L., and D. L. Petersen
1984   Biblical Texts and Statistical Analysis: Zechariah and Beyond. *JBL* 103:11–21.

Preuss, H. D.
1974   "ʾĕlîl." *TDOT* 1.285–87.
1975   "bôʾ." *TDOT* 2.20–50.
1976   *Deuterojesaja.* Neukirchen-Vloyn: Neukirchener Verlag.
1978   "gillûlîm." *TDOT* 3.1–5.
1990   "yāṣāʾ." *TDOT* 6.225–50.

Rabin, C.
1954   *The Zadokite Documents.* Oxford: Clarendon.

Radday, Y. T. and M. A. Pollatschek
1980   Vocabulary Richness in Post-Exilic Prophetic Books. *ZAW* 92:333–46.

Radday, Y. T., and D. Wickmann
1975   The Unity of Zechariah Examined in the Light of Statistical Linguistics. *ZAW* 87:30–55.

Rainey, A. F.
1975   The Identification of Philistine Gath. *EI* 12:63–76.

Reynolds, S. C.
1966   Man, Incarnation, and Trinity in the Commentary on Zechariah of Didymus the Blind of Alexandria. Ph.D. diss., Harvard University.

Ricoeur, P.
1977   *The Rule of Metaphor: Multi-Disciplinary Studies of the Creation of Meaning in Language.* Trans. R. Czerny, K. McLaughlin, and J. Costello. Toronto: University of Toronto.

Ringgren, H.
1974a   *"ʾāch."* TDOT 1.188–93.
1974b   Behold Your King Comes. VT 24:207–11.
1974c   *"ʾelōhîm."* TDOT 1.267–84.

Rohland, E.
1956   Die Bedeutung der Erwällungst tradition Israels für die Eschatologie de alttestamentlischen Propheten. Ph.D. diss., University of Heidelberg.

Rost, L.
1938   *Die Vorstufen von Kirche und Synagoge in Alten Testament.* BWANT 4/24. Stuttgart: W. Kohlhammer.

Rudolph, W.
1976   *Haggai; Sacharja 1–8; Sacharja 9–14; Maleachai.* KAT 13/4. Gütersloh: Gütersloher Verlagshaus Gerd Mohn.

Ruffin, M. L.
1986   Symbolism in Zechariah: A Study in Functional Unity. Ph.D. diss., Southern Baptist Theological Seminary.

Saebø, M.
1969   *Sacharja 9–14. Untersuchungen von Text und Form.* Neukirchen-Vluyn: Neukirchener Verlag.
1978   Vom Grossreich zum Weltreich: Erwägungen zu Pss. 72:8, 89:26; Sach. 9:10b. VT 28:83–91.

Sage, E. C.
1890   The Hebrew Syntax of Haggai, Zechariah, and Malachi with Special Reference to Its Bearing upon the Difficult Questions Connected with These Prophecies. Ph.D. diss., Yale University.

Sancisi-Weerdenburg, H., ed.
1987   *Achaemenid History I: Sources, Structures, and Synthesis.* Leiden: Nederlands Instituut voor het Nabije Oosten.

Sant'Anna, Z.
1973   The Restoration Venture: A Study of Haggai and Zechariah. Th.D. thesis, Union Theological Seminary in Virginia.

Sasson, J.
1976   Ass. *IDB* Supplement:72–73.
1990   *Jonah.* AB 24B. New York: Doubleday.

Scharbert, J.
1975   *"brk."* TDOT 2.279–308.

Schnackenberg, R.
1972   Das Schriftzitat in Joh 19, 37. In *Wort, Lied und Gottesspruch: Beiträge zu Psalmen und Propheten, Festschrift für Joseph Ziegler.* Ed. J. Schreiner, 239–47. Echter Verlag: Katholisches Bibelwerk.

Sellin, E.
1930   *Das Zwölfprophetenbuch übersetzt und erklärt.* KAT 12/2 (3d ed.). Leipzig: Scholl.
Sendrey, A.
1969   *Music in Ancient Israel.* New York: Philosophical Library.
Seybold, K.
1973   Spaetprophetische Hoffnungen auf die Wiederkunft des davidischen Zeitalters in Sach 9–14. *Judaica* 29:99–111.
1978   *"hebhel." TDOT* 3.313–20.
Shargent, K.
forthcoming   "With Her Hands on the Threshold": The Cultural Meaning of Space for the Daughters of Ancient Israel. Ph.D. diss., Duke University.
Shiloh, Y.
1980   The Population of Iron Age Palestine in the Light of a Sample Analysis of Urban Plans, Areas, and Population Density. *BASOR* 239:25–35.
Smith, D. L.
1989   *The Religion of the Landless: The Social Context of the Babylonian Exile.* Bloomington, Ind.: Meyer-Stone.
Smith, M.
1971   *Palestinian Parties and Politics That Shaped the Old Testament.* New York: Columbia University.
1972   Pseudepigraphy in the Israelite Tradition. *Pseudepigrapha.* I. Geneva: Foundation Hardt, 191–215.
1989   Hellenization. In *Emerging Judaism.* Ed. M. E. Stone and D. Satran, 103–28. Minneapolis: Fortress.
Smith, M. S.
1990   *The Early History of God.* San Francisco: Harper & Row.
Smith, R. L.
1984   *Michah-Malachi.* Word Biblical Commentary, vol. 32. Waco, Tex.: Word Books.
Speiser, E. A.
1967   The Rivers of Paradise. In *Oriental and Biblical Studies.* Ed. J. J. Finkelstein and M. Greenberg, 23–34. Philadelphia: University of Pennsylvania.
Stade, B.
1881   Deuterozacharja: Eine Kritische Studie. ZAW 1:1–96.
1882a   Deuterozacharja: Eine Kritische Studie. ZAW 2:157–72.
1882b   Deuterozacharja: Eine Kritische Studie. ZAW 2:275–309.
Stern, E.
1982   *Material Culture of the Land of the Bible in the Persian Period, 538–332 B.C.* Warminster, England: Aris & Phillips.
Steuernagel, C.
1912   *Lehrbuch der Einleitung in das Alte Testament.* Tübingen: J. C. B. Mohr.

Stieglitz, R. R.
1990 The Geopolitics of the Phoenician Littoral in the Early Iron Age. *BASOR* 279:9–12.
Stinespring, W. F.
1965 No Daughter of Zion: A Study of the Appositional Genitive in Hebrew Grammar. *Encounter* 26:133–41.
Sweet, J. P.
1981 Maintaining the Testimony of Jesus: The Suffering of Christians in the Revelation of John and Use of Zech. 12–14 in the NT. In *Suffering and Martyrdom in the New Testament: Studies Presented to G. M. Styler.* Ed. W. Horbury and B. McNeil, 101–17. Cambridge and New York: Cambridge University.
Tadmor, H.
1961 Azriyau of Yaudi. In *Studies in the Bible.* Ed. C. Rabin, 232–71. *SH* 8. Jerusalem: Magnes Press.
1984 *The World History of the Jewish People: The Restoration—The Persian Period.* Jerusalem: ʿAm Oved (Hebrew).
1987 The Origins of Israel as Seen in the Exilic and Post-Exilic Ages. In *Convegno Sul Fema, Il Origni di Israeli,* 15–27. Roma: Accademia nazionale dei Lincei.
Thompson, J. A.
1962 Horse. *IBD* 2.646–48.
Thomson, J. G. S. S.
1955 The Shepherd-Ruler Concept in the OT and Its Application in the NT. *SJT* 8:406–18.
Thureau-Dangin, F.
1933 La Stèle d'Asharné. *RA* 30:53–56.
Torrey, C. C.
1936 The Foundry of the Second Temple at Jerusalem. *JBL* 55:247–60.
Tournay, R.
1974 Zacharie XII–XIV et L'Histoire D'Israel. *RB* 81:355–74.
Tov, E., et al.
1990 *The Greek Minor Prophets Scroll from Nahal Hever: 8 Hev XII gr.* Discoveries in the Judean Desert, vol. 8. Oxford: Clarendon.
Treves, M.
1963 Conjectures Concerning the Date and Authorship of Zechariah IX–XIV. *VT* 13:196–207.
Tsevat, M.
1980a *"chālaq" II. TDOT* 4.448–51.
1980b *"chāmal." TDOT* 4.470–72.
Tsumura, D. T.
1981 Two-Fold Image of Wine in Psalm 46:4–5. *JQR* 71:167–75.
Tucker, G. M.
1977 Prophetic Superscriptions and the Growth of a Canon. In *Canon and Authority.* Ed. G. W. Coats and B. O. Long, 56–70. Philadelphia: Fortress.

Utzschneider, H.
1989 *Kunder oder Schreiber? Eine These zum Problem der "Schriftprophetie" auf Grund von Maleachi 1, 6–2, 9.* Beiträge zur Erforschung des Alten Testaments und des Antiken Judentums 19. Frankfort am Main, Bern, New York, Paris: Peter Lang.

van Beek, G. W.
1983 Digging Up Tell Jemmeh. *Archaeology* 36:12–19.

van der Toorn, K.
1990 The Nature of the Biblical Teraphim in the Light of the Cuneiform Evidence. *CBQ* 52:203–22.

van Dijk, H. J.
1968 A Neglected Connotation of Three Hebrew Verbs. *VT* 18:16–30.

de Vaux, R.
1961 *Ancient Israel.* Trans. J. McHugh. London: Darton, Longman, & Todd.

Vermes, G.
1970 Bible and Midrash: Early Old Testament Exegesis. In *The Cambridge History of the Bible*, vol 1. Ed. P. R. Ackroyd and C. F. Evans, 199–231. Cambridge: Cambridge University.

Vicent Saera, R.
1984 Tradiciones targúmicas de Zacarías 9–14 en Juan 12. In *Simposio Bíblico Español.* Ed. N. F. Marcos, J. T. Barrera, and J. F. Vallina, 495–511. Madrid: Universidad Complutense.

von Soden, W., J. Bergman, and M. Saebø
1990 *"yôm; yômām; yôm YHWH." TDOT* 6.7–32.

Wagner, S.
1975 *"biqqēsh." TDOT* 2.229–41.

Waldman, N. M.
1978 The Breaking of the Bow. *JQR* 69:82–88.

Wanke, G.
1984 Prophecy and Psalms in the Persian Period. In *The Cambridge History of Judaism.* Ed. W. D. Davies and L. Finkelstein, 162–88. Cambridge and New York: Cambridge University.

Warmuth, G.
1978 *"hôdh." TDOT* 3.352–56.

Waterman, L.
1954 The Camouflaged Purge of Three Messianic Conspirators. *JNES* 13:73–78.

Weinberg, J. P.
1973 Das Bēit ʾĀbōt im 6–4. Jh. V. U. Z. *VT* 23:400–14.
1974 Die Agrarverhältnisse in der Bürger-Tempel-Gemeinde der Achämenidenzeit. *Acta Antiqua* 22:473–86.

Weinfeld, M.
1972 *Deuteronomy and the Deuteronomic School.* Oxford: Clarendon.
1975 *"bĕrîth." TDOT* 2.253–79.

Weingreen, J.
1963   Exposition in the Old Testament and in Rabbinical Literature. In *Promise and Fulfillment*. Ed. F. F. Bruce, 187–201. Edinburgh: Clark.

Wellhausen, J.
1898   *Die Kleinen Propheten*. Berlin.
1957   *Prolegomena to the History of Ancient Israel*. New York: Meridian (o.d.p., 1883).

Wevers, J. W.
1962   Chariot. *IDB* 1.552–54.

Willi-Plein, I.
1973   hn: Ein Übersetzungsproblem—Gedanken zu Sach. 12:10. *VT* 23:90–99.

Williamson, H. G. M.
1985   *Ezra, Nehemiah*. Word Biblical Commentary, vol. 16. Waco, Tex.: Word Books.

Wilson, B. R.
1973   *Magic and the Millennium*. New York: Harper & Row.

Wilson, R. R.
1980   *Prophecy and Society in Ancient Israel*. Philadelphia: Fortress.
1985   The Family. *HBD* 302–3.

Wolfe, R. E.
1935   The Editing of the Book of the Twelve. *ZAW* 53:90–129.

Wolff, H. W.
1964   Der Aufruf zur Volksklage. *ZAW* 76:48–56.

Woude, A. S. van der
1984   Die Hirtenallegorie von Sacharja XI. *JNWSL* 12:139–49.
1985   Sacharja 14:18. *ZAW* 97:254–55.

Wright, G. E.
1965   *Shechem: The Biography of a Biblical City*. New York: McGraw-Hill.
1967   The Provinces of Solomon (1 Kings 4:7–19). *EI* 8:58–68.

Würthwein, E.
1950   Amos-Studien. *ZAW* 62:10–52.

Yadin, Y.
1963   *The Art of Warfare in Biblical Lands*. 2 vols. New York: McGraw-Hill.
Zertal, A.
1986   The Israelite Settlement in the Hill Country of Manasseh. Ph.D. diss., Tel Aviv University (Hebrew).

Zijl, P. J.
1971   A Possible Interpretation of Zech. 9:11 and the Function of "The Eye" (ʿAyin) in Zechariah. *JNWSL* 1:59–67.

Zobel, H.-J.
1978   "*hôy*." *TDOT* 3.359–63.
1990   "*yiśrāʾēl*." *TDOT* 6.397–420.

Zolli, E.
1955   "*ʿeyn ʾadām*" (Zach 9:1). *VT* 5:90–92.

PART ONE

ZECHARIAH 9–11

◆

ZECHARIAH 9

◆

Restoration of the Land of Israel

9 ¹An oracle: the word of Yahweh in the land of Hadrach;
    and Damascus is its resting place.
For to Yahweh is the eye of the people
    and all the tribes of Israel;
²And also Hamath—which borders on it—
    Tyre and Sidon, for they're shrewd indeed.
³Tyre has built herself a bulwark;
    she has piled up silver like dust
    and gold like the mud of the streets.
⁴Surely the Lord will impoverish her
    and slam her wealth into the sea,
    and she will be consumed by fire.
⁵Ashkelon will see and be afraid,
    and Gaza too will agonize greatly,
    and Ekron, for he will dash her hope.
The king will perish from Gaza,
    and Ashkelon will not be ruled.
    ⁶and a villain will rule in Ashdod.
For I will destroy the Philistines' pride;
    ⁷I will remove its blood from his mouth
    and his abominations from between his teeth.
But there will remain also one for our God;
    He will be like a clan in Judah,
    and Ekron like a Jebusite.
⁸I will encamp at my House,
    a garrison against invaders;
An oppressor will not overrun them again,
    for now I'm watching with my eyes.

The King's Entry into Jerusalem

⁹Exult greatly, O Daughter Zion!
    Shout aloud, O Daughter Jerusalem!

Behold, your king is coming to you,
    righteous and saved is he;
      humble and riding on an ass—
      on a young ass, a foal of a she-ass.
[10]I will cut off the chariot from Ephraim
    and the horse from Jerusalem,
      and the bow of war will be cut off.
He will promise peace to the nations;
    his rule will be from sea to sea,
    from the river to the ends of the earth.

Restoration of the People Through Yahweh's Intervention

[11]As for you, by the blood of your covenant
    I have set your prisoners free from a pit with no water in it.
[12]Return to a stronghold, O prisoners of hope;
    today too I announce I'm restoring to you double.
[13]For I have bent Judah to me;
    I have set Ephraim as a bow.
I will rouse your sons, O Zion,
    against your sons, O Greece;
And I will make you like a warrior's sword.
[14]Then Yahweh will appear above them;
    his arrow will go forth like lightning.
Lord Yahweh will sound the horn
    and advance with the southern storms.
[15]Yahweh of Hosts will protect them;
    they will consume and will conquer with sling stones;
    they will drink and be rowdy,[a] as with wine;
    they will be full like the basin, like
    [the ones at] the corners of the altar.
[16]Yahweh their God will rescue them;
    on that day his people will be like sheep;
For like gemstones of a crown
    they will shine on his land.
[17]Then how good and how lovely!
Grain will make the young men flourish,
    and new wine the maidens.

NOTES

9:1. *An oracle.* This word, *maśśāʾ* in Hebrew, is a technical term derived from the root *nśʾ*, meaning "to bear," "carry," or "lift up." Modeled on the

[a]Adding *waw* and reading *whmw*, third-person plural perfect.

Arabic *maqtal* form (*GKC* §45c; de Boer 1948: 197), the usual sense of the word in prophetic speech is "that which is lifted up" or "oracle" or even "pronouncement." The intent of the term is clearly to give authority to the words of Yahweh that follow. It occurs frequently as a heading or title for oracles directed at specific audiences, e.g., Babylon (Isa 13:1), Moab (Isa 15:1), Damascus (Isa 17:1), Egypt (Isa 19:1), Nineveh (Nah 1:1). It can also simply identify the nature of the divine communication at the beginning of a biblical book, as in "the oracle that the prophet Habakkuk saw" (Hab 1:1). The opening words of Nahum (1:1) also imply that the "oracle" was communicated with a prophetic vision.

The prophetic passage, Jer 23:33–40, most often cited in reference to this one contains Jeremiah's negative and mocking usage of *maśśāʾ* as a "burden." Inasmuch as Zechariah 9–14 clearly draws upon Jeremiah in many instances (especially in 11:4ff. and 13:2ff.; cf. NOTES and COMMENTS for these passages), there may be some justification for translating the term "burden" in Zechariah. However, Second Zechariah's extensive use of earlier prophetic materials (see chart 9, p. 40) tends to involve a shift in meaning or a reworking of earlier materials. Thus, even if Zechariah 9 is drawing upon the language of Jeremiah 23, the intent may differ. Such seems to be the case here. The message of the oracles of Second Zechariah do not have the same focus as those of Jeremiah.

There is no doubt that in Jeremiah 23 *maśśāʾ* means "burden" or "burdensome word" (McKane 1986: 547) and that it involves a wordplay on the literal meaning of the root. In fact, Jer 23:33 may also refer satirically to Jeremiah himself (ibid. 1986: 599), whose words were so ladened with doom. The possibility that doom is appropriate here (and in Zech 12:1 where it recurs; see below and NOTE to 12:1) arises because of the destruction proclaimed for Israel's enemies. Yet the overall message in Second Zechariah is positive for God's people, unlike that in Jeremiah 23; hence it seems that "doom" may be too restrictive a translation. Moreover, that "doom" in Jeremiah may be related to the problem of false prophecy does not necessarily mean that it is to be similarly construed here. False prophecy is indeed an issue in Zechariah 9–14, but it emerges in later chapters and is not the focus of either chapter 11 or 12, the two chapters that begin with *maśśāʾ*.

The Masoretic notation, or conjunctive accent mark, of *mappaḥ* under the *sin* might indicate a construct chain, which would be translated "the oracle of the word of Yahweh." Some commentators who accept the opening of Zechariah 9 as a construct chain have been struck with what they believe to be a resulting disturbance of meter in Zech 9:1. Hence they restore a second "Yahweh" before "in the land of Hadrach." For example, although there is no support in the versions for a second "Yahweh," P. D. Hanson (1975: 294–96) restores it, explaining its loss as being due to haplography. His translation reads: "The oracle of Yahweh's word: Yahweh is against Hadrach." Such an emendation, however, does not solve any metrical problem. The first two verses, consisting of two bicola (v 1) and one bicolon (v 2), form a very symmetrical unit. The syllable count is as follows:

verse 1a $10 + 7 = 17$
verse 1b $7 + 7 = 14$
verse 2 $7 + 10 = 17$

The total number of syllables is forty-eight, which provides an average of eight syllables per colon, the standard for most poetry in the Hebrew Bible. Thus the addition of "Yahweh" *metri causa*, i.e., on metrical grounds, is to be questioned.

Without a second "Yahweh," the understanding of *maśśā' dĕbar-YHWH* as a construct chain becomes less compelling. The relationship of "oracle" to "word of Yahweh" seems to be one of equivalence rather than of possession; thus "the word of Yahweh" is set off in our translation to indicate its appositional function. That yet a third indicator of a divine message ("utterance of Yahweh") appears after "oracle" and "the word of Yahweh" in 12:1 adds to the sense that these multiple proclamations of divine message are part of a strong prophetic intention to establish authority for the oracular material being introduced. Thus *maśśā'* followed by "word of Yahweh" is in keeping with the general practice of late biblical prophecy to provide additional terms of authority to the divine word and to give the impression of verbatim transmission (Meyers and Meyers 1987: 91).

The heading of the beginning of Second Zechariah is parallel to the headings of Zech 12:1 and Mal 1:1. Although "word of Yahweh" occurs a total of nineteen times in the Haggai–Zechariah–Malachi corpus, it is found in only these three places together with "oracle" *(maśśā')*. Hence this combination serves to create three subsections (Zechariah 9–11; Zechariah 12–14; and Malachi) of the second part of the Haggai–Zechariah–Malachi corpus (see Introduction, chart 5 and p. 33).

We suggest that the heading does double duty, functioning as a title or introduction to Zechariah 9–11 and serving as part of the message of the first oracular statement. In this sense, the opening words of Zech 9:1 diverge from those of Zech 12:1 and Mal 1:1. In each of the latter two instances, with the addition of further introductory words or equivalences, the heading stands alone and does not become part of the ensuing oracle. At the beginning of Part Two of Second Zechariah (chapters 12–14) "utterance of Yahweh" appears after "An oracle: the word of Yahweh." And Mal 1:1 supplies the idiomatic phrase "by the hand of Malachi," which copies the transmission style of the beginning of Hag 1:1 to form an envelope construction that brings together the Books of Haggai, Zechariah, and Malachi. Although the headings for Zech 9:1, 12:1, and Mal 1:1 lack the extensive additional chronological information provided in the Haggai–Zechariah 1–8 corpus (Meyers and Meyers 1987: xlvi), they do nonetheless provide the basic literary framework for Second Zechariah and Malachi and, because of the additional words in Mal 1:1, appear to be the work of a redactor or group responsible for bringing the last three prophetic books into their canonical arrangement.

The heading, "An oracle: the word of Yahweh," concludes with the preposition *b*, "in" ("in the land of Hadrach"). In Zech 12:1 the equivalent preposition is ʿal, meaning "concerning"; in Mal 1:1 it is ʾel, meaning "to," In the latter instances the additional phrases follow the preposition.

the word of Yahweh. The frequency with which this expression occurs in Haggai and First Zechariah exemplifies the way the language of Zechariah 9–14 provides continuity between Second Zechariah and its immediate predecessors in the canon. The first four appearances of the expression in Haggai–First Zechariah (Hag 1:1, 3; 2:1, 10) occur with the words "by the hand of," whereas eleven of the remaining usages are followed by the preposition "to." The presence of the phrase is intended to show that the recipient of the "word of Yahweh" is legitimate and, consequently, that the word itself (that is, the prophetic statements) is authoritative. Linking "an oracle" with "the word of Yahweh" serves to strengthen the force and validity of the prophetic words at a time when such speech was rare. It also helps to distinguish the prophecies that follow from the sayings of earlier prophets, who clearly influenced their successors. As we explain in the previous NOTE, the combination of *maśśāʾ* with *dĕbar-YHWH* here, and in 12:1 and Mal 1:1, is apparently distinctive to late biblical prophecy.

The preference for the formula dĕbar-YHWH over more anthropomorphic formulas such as "Yahweh spoke" (e.g., Zech 2:12 [NRSV 2:8]; 8:3, 4, 6, etc.) emphasizes the prophet's role as mediator of God's authoritative communications to the people. Because Second Zechariah is from an age when classical prophecy was coming to an end, the attachment of this phrase to another familiar oracular designation, *maśśāʾ*, may reflect a concern to validate the prophet's message. Both NRSV and NJB have followed BHS in setting off "oracle" (or "proclamation" in NJB) from "the word of Yahweh," in disservice to the structure of intensification of prophetic authority.

Hadrach. This geographical term, found only here in the Hebrew Bible, refers to a district in Syria. Known as *Hatarikka* or *Hatari(k)ka* in Assyrian sources (see *ANET*: 282, 283), it was apparently created following Tiglath-Pileser III's advance toward Damascus, Samaria, and other Syro-Palestinian territories in 738 B.C.E. As a district name, the term may have been derived from a major city of the same name in that district, just as the newly created district of Kallania (Calneh) was named for its capital in 738. As a city, it is probably to be identified with Umm-esh-Shershuh, a site on the Orontes River northwest of Tel Bire (Kraeling 1918: 98). A stele erected to celebrate the 720 B.C.E. victory of Sargon II at Karkar also mentions Hadrach as a city, along with Hamath (Thureau-Dangin 1933). In this verse, because it is found with ʾereṣ as part of the phrase "land of Hadrach," the likelihood is that it represents the district.

The appearance of Hadrach in Assyrian sources, along with most of the other places named in Zech 9:1–6, has led many scholars to suppose that the first six verses of Second Zechariah address the particular political situation of the late eighth century, when the Assyrians were advancing to the west. Malamat (1950–51), e.g., relates Zech 9:1–6 to the 720 B.C.E. campaign of Sargon II. Kraeling earlier (1924) proposed that these verses represent a sequence of events between 739 and 720 B.C.E., and Steurnagel (1912) suggested a date in the reign of Tiglath–Pileser III. These particular historical readings of the text, however, are not compelling when the overall contents and context of Zechariah 9 are considered (see COMMENT); nor are readings, such as those by Elliger (1949–50) and Delcor (1951), that suggest a later (Hellenistic) setting. To be sure, the particular sites and districts mentioned in Zechariah 9 do not reflect the geopolitics of the late sixth or fifth century. Yet, insofar as Second Zechariah is drawing upon earlier materials and reworking them for his largely eschatological purposes, the ideal future represented by the toponymic specificity of Zechariah 9 is based on expectations shaped by tradition rather than by contemporary reality.

The mention of Hadrach is notable in several ways. First, it is the northernmost of the geographical entities that appear in Zechariah 9 and thus is a suitable beginning to the set of place names, with their overall north-to-south organization, of verses 1–6. Second, situated between Aleppo (in the district of Arpad) to the north and Hamath to its south, Hadrach lay well beyond the greatest extent of the Davidic–Solomonic kingdom and thus was not within either the historical or ideal borders of the Israelite kingdom. Third, like Damascus and Hamath, it was not subjected to the violent action of Yahweh; rather, again like Damascus and Hamath, it is presented as having accepted Yahweh's dominion. Finally, whether a district or a city, Hadrach—like its two Syrian counterparts—represents an inland, not a coastal, territory.

Damascus. This major Aramaean city, mentioned nearly fifty times in the Hebrew Bible (e.g., 1 Kgs 15:18; 20:34; Isa 7:8), is located at the western edge of the Syrian desert. The name "Damascus" also can indicate the territory around the city, that is, the Aramaean kingdom that had Damascus as its capital (see Ezek 47:16, 17; 48:1; cf. 1 Kgs 19:15). In this instance, the territorial meaning is to be preferred because of its parallel relation to Hadrach and because exilic sources such as Ezekiel (cf. 2 Chron 28:23) use it in that way. Such an understanding of Damascus would be supported by taking the term "land" (ʾereṣ) before "Hadrach" as doing double duty, so that "land" governs both Hadrach and Damascus.

Like Hadrach and Hamath, Damascus is an inland area, probably outside the traditional real or ideal border of Israel (see COMMENT below). Again like these two areas, Damascus is presented as one already acknowledging Yahweh's sovereignty and thus not subject to violent action.

its resting place. That is, its "place of repose," from the root *nwḥ* (cf. LXX and Syr, which incorrectly read *minḥâ*, "sacrifice"). Although many commentators have been loath to accept the true import of this oracle, namely, that God's word extends beyond the actual boundaries of Israelite territory, its universalistic intent is quite clear. Syria was always viewed as a place of hostility by Israelites, and the popular emendation (as by Mitchell 1912: 270) of "eye of the people" in the next line (see NOTE) to "cities of Aram" is intended to support such an interpretation. So too is the understanding of the preposition *b* before

"Hadrach" in the preceding line in an adversative sense, i.e., "against Hadrach" instead of "in the land of Hadrach," as we have translated.

P. D. Hanson's suggestion (1975: 286–87) that the term *měnūḥātô* reflects the language of holy war and hence should be translated "throne dais" (as in 1 Chron 28:2; Isa 66:1; Ps 132:8, 14), although having some merit, does not sufficiently suit the present context to warrant its use. Irrespective of whether all or portions of chapter 9 are viewed as representative of the divine warrior genre, it should be recognized that the exegetical thrust of the text is complex and contains elements other than that genre. To be sure, ancient cosmic imagery, which can be traced back to Ugaritic literature, is an appropriate and effective medium for communicating a message of Yahweh's universal power and dominion. The use of "repose" or "resting place," however, is an example of how the author/editor/redactor of Second Zechariah has made lexical choices that connect this prophetic unit with the ideas and language of First Zechariah.

That God's presence can be transported to the north is the subject of Zechariah's Seventh Vision (6:1–8), and the word used to indicate that God's spirit has been placed "in the northland" is the Hiphil of *nwḥ*, the same root found here (Meyers and Meyers 1987: 329–31; cf. also the use of *nwḥ* in Zech 5:11). Thus, while the notion of "throne dais" may well be part of the imagery of *měnūḥātô*, other considerations mandate a translation that takes into account the literary cross-referencing of Second Zechariah with Zechariah 1–8; hence our preference for "resting place." Note also that "I will encamp" below, in verse 8, although it comes from the root *ḥnh*, is similar in Hebrew. Its usage at the end of the 9:1–8 subunit constitutes a purposeful wordplay, i.e., the use of two different roots that sound similar and also have similar meaning ("to encamp" and "to repose" or "rest"). Because verse 8 closes the first subunit of chapter 9, its usage at that point can hardly be coincidental.

the eye of the people. There has been a great deal of scholarly discussion about the meaning of the Hebrew *ꜥên ꜣādām,* literally "the eye of the man," which seems awkward. Many would emend one or both of these words. The first word is changed variously to *ꜥam,* "people" (e.g., P. D. Hanson 1973: 42), *ꜥārê,* "cities of" (Mitchell 1912: 263; and others), or even to *ꜥiyôn,* "Ijon," a city in the territory of Naphtali mentioned in 1 Kgs 15:20, 2 Kgs 15:29, and 2 Chron 16:4. All of these emendations entail changing the second word to *ꜣărām.* The appeal of such a change is clear: it requires only that the Hebrew letter *resh* be substituted for *dalet,* which is very similar in appearance. The resulting "Aram" seems to fit the context—a series of Syrian–Aramaean place names—quite well. These suggested emendations provide renderings such as "people of Aram" or "cities of Aram." Another possibility involves the fact that in several places *ꜥyn* has an extended image as "territory" or "area" (Exod 10:5, 15; Num 22:5, 11) and so does not need emendation, and that *ꜣādām* may be a masculine form of *ꜣădāmâ,* "earth." The resulting "surface of the earth" (Dahood 1963), however, does not fit the context nearly so well as do the other proposals. Another possibility is that *ꜥyn ꜣadm* is a place name that is simply not known to us from the Bible or from Assyrian inscriptions.

Despite the difficulty of "the eye of the people" and the apparent suitability of "cities [or people] of Aram" or a toponym not elsewhere attested, the need to emend the Hebrew is questionable. For one thing, there is no support in the versions for any emendation. Moreover, changing "eye" means losing the inclusion formed by the use of "eyes" at the end of 9:8, at the close of the first subunit of Part One of Second Zechariah (see Introduction for a discussion of the division of the book). Furthermore, the use of "eye," although somewhat unusual, makes sense in light of the lexical connections between Zechariah 9 and Zechariah 1-8 (see Introduction for our analysis of the overall lexical and thematic relationships between First and Second Zechariah). The noun "eye" or "eyes" appears a dozen times in First Zechariah as part of the visionary language, and its position at the beginning and end of this opening section of Zechariah 9-14 echoes its prominence in Zechariah 1-8. Finally, ʾādām at the outset of chapter 9 has a parallel use in 12:1, the opening verse of Part Two of Second Zechariah.

Thus the reasons for retaining the MT are compelling, and understanding the meaning of the phrase is not beset with any particular difficulties despite the rather infelicitous ring of our suggested translation. "Eye" is a versatile word in most languages, and its range of metaphorical usages is considerable. It is used figuratively for various mental or spiritual faculties. Consider Ps 123:1-2, for example, in which the psalmist and others lift their eyes to God, who is enthroned in heaven, in acknowledgement of divine sovereignty.

The fact that "eye" is in the singular (construct) and not in the more usual dual form poses no particular problems (cf. Ps 33:18), especially because the second word (ʾādām) of the phrase is a singular noun used collectively. The word ʾādām is found frequently in the Bible. It can denote individuals but is most prominently used as a collective singular indicating a class or group (Maass 1974: 75) referred to as "man" or "mankind" in most English translations until recently, when the need for inclusive language has brought about a shift to such terms as "humankind" (as in the NRSV's rendering of Gen 1:27) or "people."

"The eye of the people" here thus means the inclination of the inhabitants of the territories north of Israel, whether in its real or ideal extent, toward Yahweh. These people were the traditional enemies of Israel, the threat from the north; hence it is fitting for them to symbolize the expected attitude of all peoples (cf. Zech 8:20-23) in acknowledging Yahweh's sovereignty.

tribes of Israel. As a meaningful territorial and political entity arising in earliest Israel, the "tribe" (šēbeṭ) did not fare well under the monarchy. The nation-state replaced the tribal unit as the primary level of sociopolitical organization, and the redistricting policies of Solomon, in many cases, paid no heed to the traditional tribal boundaries (see 1 Kgs 4:7-19 and Wright 1967). The dissolution of the united monarchy contributed further to the meaninglessness of the notion of an entity composed of all the tribes, and the Babylonian conquest dealt a final blow to whatever modicum of reality may have been retained in the concept of a confederation of tribes.

Nonetheless, the idea of the tribe and the collective notion of the "tribes of

Israel," representing both the people and the territory of Israel, proved to be extremely tenacious. The tribe had been the primary unit of social organization during Israel's formative period (Gottwald 1979). As such it was determinative in establishing the family-oriented lineage system as a major symbolic expression of Israelite self-understanding. Thus, although the term "tribe" appears with decreasing frequency in biblical texts dealing with the monarchy, and then with the Exile and the Restoration, it never disappears. Indeed, in the exilic and postexilic periods it takes on new meaning, especially in its plural form and in construct with "Israel," to represent the ideal of the people restored in their land. Most notable in this regard is the vision of the restored land in Ezekiel (see Ezek 47:13, 21, 22; 48:19, 29, 31), with Jerusalem and the Temple at its center and with the twelve gates to the city named for the "tribes of Israel." The tribal ideal thus becomes part of the vocabulary of self-description that enables both the exiles and those remaining in Judah to retain their corporate identity despite the loss of political autonomy and in the face of domination by an external power. Such appeal to historical terminology is one example of the mechanisms of survival that emerged during the Babylonian and Persian periods in both Yehud and the diaspora.

In this passage, the phrase "all the tribes" represents Yahweh's earthly inheritance (cf. Isa 63:17), the heartland of the future age in which all humanity turns to the one God. Yahweh's presence in lands beyond the historical and traditional tribal allotments, as expressed in the first three lines of 9:1, is unthinkable without the reestablishment of Israel in its paradigmatic tribal form, with "all" the tribes themselves turning toward Yahweh. This language of Israel's earliest sociopolitical structure is found again below, in the use of "clan" (see NOTES to 9:7). Furthermore, the use of this designation for Israel, along with the careful delineation of Israelite and non-Israelite territories in this subunit, represents one of the ways Second Zechariah departs from patterns of the preexilic and exilic prophets (see discussion that follows in COMMENT, pp. 167–68).

A final important point about this phrase is that it can be connected with the imagery of gemstones of a crown mentioned at the end of this chapter (see NOTE to "For like gemstones of a crown," v 16). That phrase can denote the Israelite tribes, in which case the beginning and end of this chapter are linked.

2. *Hamath.* A major city on the Orontes River, Hamath figured prominently in the campaigns of Tiglath-Pileser III and Sargon II. Its role in these Assyrian advances on the west has led some to conclude that this prophecy should be dated to that period (see above, NOTE to "Hadrach," 9:1). However, the importance of Hamath in Near Eastern history and its significance in biblical geography is hardly limited to the eighth century.

Like Hadrach and Damascus, Hamath can refer to either the city of that name or the territory of which the city served as center or capital. In the latter instance the area is known as the "land of Hamath" (e.g., 2 Kgs 23:33; 25:21; Jer 39:5). Perhaps most relevant to this appearance of the name Hamath is the frequent use of the phrase *lĕbōʾ ḥămāt*, "the entrance to Hamath," "approach to Hamath," or "Lebo-Hamath." This phrase is typically used to denote a site on the northern boundary of the ideal tribal territory (as in Josh 13:5; Num 13:21; 34:8; see also Ezek 47:15, 20 and 48:1). Lebo-Hamath can probably be identified with Lebwah, which is in the northern part of the Beka^c Valley. A related phrase, "border (gĕbûl) of Hamath" is used in Ezek 47:16 and 17, along with "border of Damascus," again in reference to Ezekiel's visionary perspective of the returned tribal lands.

Although Hamath is third in the list of Aramaean city-states or districts, it actually lies between Hadrach and Damascus, south of the former and north of the latter. This may seem to be a problem to those who are concerned about geographical matters such as caravan itineraries or routes of military campaigns. Yet there is actually no difficulty when one recognizes the real purpose of the list, which is to typify the Aramaean territories as they impinged on Israel or represented the territory north and east of Israel. Perhaps Hadrach, and certainly Damascus (see Ezek 47:18), pertain to the eastern border, whereas Hamath relates to the northern extent of the Israelite tribes.

which borders on it. The verb *gbl*, a relatively rare denominative from the word "border, boundary," appropriately here describes the relationship between the "tribes of Israel" and the territory beyond—in this case, Hamath. The noun is commonly used to denote the extent of territories or peoples, especially of Israel or of its subdivisions, and it appears frequently in the territorial description of Ezekiel 45–48 (e.g., 45:1, 7).

The Hebrew lacks a relative pronoun—a common phenomenon in poetry—but "which" can be supplied (see *GKC* §155.2(b)(1)), with the verb referring to Hamath. Somewhat more troublesome is the preposition *b* with the singular object ("on it"). The antecedent of "it" is problematic. Perhaps it is to be understood as one of the feminine city or territorial names mentioned above, or it may refer to the collective *ʾereṣ* ("land") of verse 1a.

Tyre and Sidon. These Phoenician cities on the Lebanese coast are regularly paired, as, e.g., in Jer 27:3, Ezek 27:8, and Joel 4:4 (NRSV 3:4), and hence can be taken to represent all of Phoenicia. Along with Byblos and Arwad, these two cities were prominent in the biblical period. Not all of the Phoenician cities, however, were of equal power throughout the Iron Age and into the Persian and later periods. Sidon apparently achieved hegemony over the northern coast early in the Iron Age, with the consequence that "Sidonian" became practically synonymous with "Phoenician" (Stieglitz 1990: 10). The Table of Nations in Genesis lists Sidon as the firstborn of Canaan and does not mention Tyre or Byblos, though Arwad is listed (10:15–19; see also 1 Chron 1:13); and when Solomon contracts with the Tyrians for labor and materials for the Temple, the timber cutters are called "Sidonians" (1 Kgs 5:20 [NRSV 5:6]).

Phoenician supremacy also lay with Sidon in the Persian period and later (Elayi 1982: 93–7). Classical historians, who normally list Sidon before Tyre, may be reflecting that reality (Jidejian 1969: 59); in the Roman period, the notion that Sidon is the primary Phoenician center was perpetuated in the coinage.

The use of "Sidon" or "Sidonians" to represent Tyre or Phoenicia in various periods notwithstanding, Sidon was in fact eclipsed by Tyre during the Iron II period, especially from the tenth to eighth centuries B.C.E. during the reign of Hiram and his successors. It was at the beginning of that epoch that Solomon formed his alliance with Tyre's king, that skilled (see next NOTE) Tyrian artisans were employed to make the bronze vessels for the Temple (1 Kgs 7:13–47), and that part of the territory of Asher was given over to Tyre. Moreover, later in the Iron Age Tyre withstood an extended, five-year siege by the Assyrians and then a thirteen-year siege when the Babylonian king Nebuchadnezzar, following his successful advance upon Jerusalem (587–86), attempted to capture Tyre. As an off-shore island with a mainland settlement, it was uniquely able to maintain its economic might and political independence. Thus, despite the dominance of Sidon in the premonarchic era, and again in the Persian period and later, Tyre held a special significance in Israelite history, especially with regard to its territorial limits (see COMMENT below). It is not surprising, therefore, to find that Tyre dominates in this passage of Second Zechariah. Tyre is mentioned first, and the next two verses depict its fate, which may in fact reflect the fate of all the Phoenicians.

Scholarly discussion of Tyre and Sidon in this verse has tended to suggest removing one or the other of these city names, partly because the term that follows ("shrewd") is in the singular. The Greek and Latin translators, also bothered by the singular verb, rendered it in the plural. Metric considerations, along with the sense that Tyre is secondary here because of its prominence in the next verse, have led P. D. Hanson (1975: 298; cf. Mitchell 1912: 264 and others) to regard its presence in verse 2 as secondary and so to delete it. The syllable count, however, argues against emendation; the range of 22 to 26 syllables per line, based on the Masoretic pointing, falls well within the normal range (for the approach adopted here see the bibliography cited in Andersen and Freedman 1980: 77 and, especially, in Freedman's essay [1972] on acrostics and metrics). Using both form and content as criteria for scansion, verses 3–8 may be arranged as tricola as follows, with alternate countings indicated with slashes:

Syllable Count for Zechariah 9:3–8		
verse 3	6 + 7 + 7 =	20
4	8/9 + 7 + 7 =	22/23
5	8 + 8 + 9 + 7 + 7 =	39
6	8 + 9 =	17
7	9 + 8 + 9/10 + 9/10 + 6/7 =	41/44
8	10 + 6 + 10 + 9 =	35

Taking into account the syllable count for verses 1–2 (see NOTE to "An oracle" in v 1), the totals for verses 1–8 are 222/226 for twenty-eight cola. If eight is taken as the average number of syllables per cola, there would be 224 syllables in these verses ($8 \times 28 = 224$). Thus, with 222/226 syllables, the character of this unit falls squarely within the parameters of Hebrew poetry.

they're shrewd. Taking "Tyre and Sidon" together as collectively representing Phoenicia, the Hebrew uses the singular verb. The root *ḥkm* is most often associated with sagacity or "wisdom" in the sapiential biblical books—Job, Proverbs, and Ecclesiastes. The term "wisdom," however, encompasses a broad range of meanings, including technical skill, as that of an artisan, political or economic diplomacy or shrewdness, and even everyday pragmatism or cleverness (Müller and Krause 1980: 373, 378). In this text, the cleverness associated with achieving economic success is clearly the appropriate nuance, given the reference in the next two verses to the wealth of Tyre, characterized as its silver and gold. This association of skill or cleverness—"wisdom"—with the accumulation of wealth is found in several other instances in the Hebrew Bible. Noteworthy among them is a passage in Ezekiel, for it also involves Tyre. In Ezek 28:3–5 the prince of Tyre is considered "wiser," that is, more shrewd, than Daniel, the legendary figure in Ugaritic literature, because he amassed great wealth in silver and gold (v 4) and was skilled in trade (v 5). Note also the reference in Ezek 27:8 to "your skilled ones, O Tyre." Other explicit associations between the amassing of wealth (gold and silver) and wisdom or shrewdness (*ḥokmâ*) occur in Prov 3:13–14, 8:10, and 16:16, although in the latter two instances the acquisition of wealth is contrasted with the gaining of wisdom. The meaning of the term in Zechariah 9 either makes use of Ezekiel, or, along with Ezekiel, draws upon a well-attested use of *ḥkm*. Its message is clear: the Phoenician cities of Tyre and Sidon are adept at international trade and hence have accumulated considerable wealth.

3. *Tyre has built herself a bulwark*. The Hebrew text, *wattiben ṣōr māṣôr lāh*, uses paronomasia effectively to emphasize the most prominent feature of Tyre, i.e., its fortification or "bulwark"; it probably chooses *māṣôr* over *meṣûrâ*, which also can refer to defense works, for poetic considerations (cf. the use of *māṣôr* in 12:2). The singling out of Tyre to represent Phoenicia (see NOTE to "Tyre and Sidon" in v 2) reflects Tyre's dominance during the time of Israel's monarchy. In addition, this is one of the many instances in which Second Zechariah echoes earlier prophetic material. Other prophetic oracles, such as those of Isaiah 23 and Amos 1, were directed against the Phoenicians; but chapters 26–28 of Ezekiel are most directly evoked and reworked here. Those chapters contain the descriptions of Tyre's sins, which occasioned the prophecy that Nebuchadnezzar would besiege and destroy the city: first, that it rejoiced at Jerusalem's destruction in 587–86 (26:2); second, that it placed false confidence in the wealth and resources it had accumulated (27:2ff.); and third, that the king of Tyre was arrogant, prideful, and represented the unacceptable Canaanite concept of divine kingship (28:2ff.).

Many scholars have seen in this mention of Tyre's fortifications reference to a specific historical event. One possibility is that it refers to one of the sieges by the Assyrians or Babylonians (see NOTE to "Tyre and Sidon" in v 2). It is important, however, to note that Tyre did not fall to the Babylonians as predicted by Ezekiel; and Ezekiel 28 (e.g., vv 4–5) is replete with images of Tyre's wealth, images that recur in Zech 9:2–4. The other frequently mentioned suggestion

involves the Hellenistic period. Because of the well-known confrontation between Alexander the Great and the city of Tyre in the fourth century, many, if
not a majority, of commentators have seen these passages as referring to that
period and, hence, date all of Second Zechariah to the Greek period. Typical
of such views is this comment: "This prophecy was, no doubt, so designed by
divine providence as to cover the victorious progress of Alexander the Great, for
the order of the towns mentioned is identical with Alexander's line of march
after the battle of Issus . . . a word portraying in colors taken from Alexander's
conquests the downfall of Gentile power and the conquests achieved by Israel's
king" (Leupold 1956: 165). Noteworthy among the major commentators who
hold similar views are Delcor (1951a), Elliger (1975), Eissfeldt (1964), Oesterly
and Robinson (1934), Chary (1969), Dentan (1956), Fohrer (1965), Mitchell
(1912), etc.

Attempting to relate the verses about Tyre in Zechariah to a specific historical
event, however, means taking them out of their overall context in this carefully
constructed configuration of places in Zechariah 9 (see COMMENT for a
discussion of the import of the various toponyms). Such an approach should be
reconsidered in light of the overall thrust of this chapter. Rather than reflecting
a specific event, Zech 9:1–8 deals with a catalog of Israel's archetypal enemies,
listed in an order that has its own logic. Recognizing that the text is rooted in
history but transcends a narrow historical focus allows for an awareness of how it
presents Yahweh's far-reaching concerns for people beyond the historical borders
of Israel.

Verses 3 and 4, each consisting of one tricolon, are elegantly organized to
represent the full range of images that are appropriate to Tyre, which stands for
all of Phoenicia. The image of "bulwark" in 3a, which opens the sequence, is a
military one, as is the image of destruction by fire presented in the concluding
line, verse 4c. The four remaining, interior, images are all economic and are
bracketed by the military images—bulwark and fiery destruction—which together form an inclusion. The pattern is as follows:

verse 3a	"bulwark"	military
b	" silver/dust"	economic
c	"gold/mud"	economic
verse 4a	"impoverish"	economic
b	"slam wealth"	economic
c	"fire"	military

The argument for the inclusion between verses 3a and 4c is further strengthened by the chiastic use of verbs. Verse 3a begins with a verb, and verse 4c ends
with one. Note also that there is a chiasm in verses 4a and b, with verbs at the
end and at the beginning of succeeding cola. Clearly, these verses have been
carefully crafted.

she has piled up silver. The use of the root *ṣbr* ("to heap up"), which is found
only several times in the Bible, with "silver" is unique. Although clearly familiar

with and drawing upon the language of Ezekiel, the prophet does not slavishly copy Ezekiel's words. Rather, he asserts his own literary identity in referring to Israel's northern neighbor, whose wealth is legendary.

"Piled up silver" is an explicit reference to the accumulation of great wealth by Tyre, which was the principal maritime power in the Mediterranean for much of the Iron II period (see NOTE to "Tyre and Sidon," 9:2), and echoes very closely verse 4 of Ezekiel 28: "You have amassed great wealth for yourself, and have gathered gold and silver in your treasuries." In Zechariah, however, the order of the precious metals has been reversed, i.e., silver comes before gold; in addition, Zechariah has used a relatively rare word for "gold" (see NOTE below in this verse to "gold") instead of the more familiar zāhāb.

Several comments about the traditional ordering of silver and gold may help to explain why silver normally comes first (see Meyers and Meyers 1987: 348–49). The priority of silver over gold suggests that silver was more valuable than gold until later periods, especially during the Persian period when access to new sources of silver increased the relative value of gold objects as they became relatively more scarce. That shift may have begun earlier, however, inasmuch as Assyrian tribute lists suggest that vassal kings such as Hezekiah paid far more tribute in silver than in gold (ANET: 288; 2 Kgs 18:14). Still, the rarity of silver objects found in Palestinian excavations of strata dating from before the Persian period attests to silver's scarcity in the early biblical period. The traditional ordering of "silver" and "gold" here is thus not unexpected, although late biblical texts nearly always list gold before silver, as in Chronicles, Esther, and Daniel. In the Haggai–Zechariah–Malachi corpus, both orderings are found. Gold precedes silver in Zech 14:14 and Mal 3:3, whereas two other occurrences in Haggai and Zechariah (Hag 2:8; Zech 6:11) reflect the older situation. That both arrangements are attested in the corpus of the last of the prophets seems to strengthen the argument for a Persian-period date for the redaction of the Book of the Twelve, and especially for Haggai, Zechariah, and Malachi, because this was a period when the relative value of these precious commodities was changing.

Another factor that may contribute to the inconsistency of late biblical texts in their ordering of silver and gold is the apparent use of silver to supplement the circulation of Persian gold (so M. Smith 1989: 123). Furthermore, if the Phoenicians were responsible for disseminating pre-Hellenistic Greek influence in Palestine (ibid: 124), that might account for the listing of silver first here, since silver was so valued in Phoenicia, where "pure" silver was readily available and important in Phoenicia's commercial activities (R. S. Hanson 1980: 19).

like dust. Although the simple meaing in this verse is "piled up as much silver as possible," i.e., as much as there is dust, there is also a hint of irony here in anticipation of verse 4 that follows, where removal of Tyre's wealth becomes the vehicle for dispossessing her from her traditional locale and inheritance, i.e., Phoenicia. Perhaps alluding to the Song of Hannah (1 Sam 2:7–8), where the Hiphil *yrš* means "to impoverish" or "to make poor" (v 7), the prophet in the present instance adds "like dust" with the intent of evoking the poignant image of 1 Sam 2:8: "He raises up the poor from the dust." At the same time, the use of "dust" with a precious metal as a hyperbolic expression of its plentitude is a standard combination in other Semitic languages, although it is normally found in reference to gold. See the next NOTE for a discussion of the apparent shift from "gold" to "silver" as accompanied by the "dust" imagery.

Although the terminology here is explicitly concerned with Tyre's economic life, as distinct from the military focus of the opening and closing lines of this Tyre pericope (9:3–4), the use of "dust" (and "mud"; see NOTE below in this verse) may also be an allusion to the military action that will reverse Tyre's fortunes. "Dust" is parallel to "mud" in a Davidic psalm within a context celebrating David's victory over his enemies, whom he reduces to a status compared to dust and mud (Ps 18:42 = 2 Sam 22:43). That both aspects of Tyre's existence are involved in the terminology—its wealth explicitly and its political fate indirectly—indicates the interrelatedness of the economic and political aspects of this, or any, polity.

gold. The Hebrew word here, *ḥārûṣ*, is a term for "gold" used only rarely in the Hebrew Bible: here, once in Psalms (68:14 [*NRSV* 68:13]), and five times in Proverbs. Compare the more common *zāhāb*, which is used 385 times, and the several other synonyms—*ketem, paz, sĕgôr*, and perhaps *beṣer*—none of which occurs more than nine times. The variety of terms for "gold" is probably a function of technical differences in the kind of gold indicated or of geographical differences in the source of gold. It is not always possible, however, to understand the exact meaning of the terms for "gold," especially because they often seem to be used elliptically for phrases that denote certain qualities or points of origin of the gold.

Nonetheless, because the Akkadian cognate *ḥurāṣu* (cf. Ugaritic *ḥrṣ*) apparently can refer to gold recovered from either one of the two forms in which gold was available in Near Eastern antiquity—alluvial or placer gold (*ḥurāṣu ša maʾî* [*šu*], gold from water [*AH* 2: 664]) or gold ore (*ḥurāṣu ša abnišu*, gold from stone [*CAD* 1: 55])—it seems unlikely that *ḥārûṣ* indicates an aspect of gold technology. Rather, like the Akkadian and Ugaritic equivalents, it may have originally been a color term (cf. Arabic *ḥarida*, "to be yellow"), especially since in Akkadian it is often modified by various color terms (see C. L. Meyers 1976: 51, n. 94). Whatever its origin, the fact that the cognate in Ugaritic is the usual term for "gold" (as is *zāhāb* in Hebrew) would make the choice of *ḥārûṣ* here seem suitable to the context: a passage dealing with the Canaanite coasts, along with other terms (such as "shrewd") that have an association with that geopolitical area.

Furthermore, *ḥārûṣ* is always found paired with *kesep* ("silver"), which is not the case with the other biblical terms for "gold." This pairing is undoubtedly related to a stock phrase in both Akkadian (*kaspu uḫurāṣu* [*AH* 1: 454b]) and Ugaritic (*ksp . . . ḥrṣ* [e.g., *KAI* 13.4f.]), which perhaps has been borrowed here (as suggested by Kedar-Kopfstein 1980a: 34). The order of the stereotyped Semitic phrase is "silver" before "gold," a sequence that is atypical of late biblical texts (e.g., Chronicles, Esther, Daniel), which tend to list gold (*zāhāb*) before silver (cf. Meyers and Meyers 1987: 347–48 and preceding NOTE), but is echoed in the sequence here. The phrase accompanying "silver" in Zech 9:3, "like dust," however, is usually found with "gold" in Semitic texts (see previous and following NOTES).

The close connection of *ḥārūṣ* with the Canaanite world in this passage is also indicated in light of the other biblical passages containing this word for "gold." The Proverbs passages (e.g., 3:13–14; 16:16) find wisdom (*ḥōkmâ*) better than wealth, as signified by silver and gold, and wisdom (meaning "skill, cleverness, shrewdness") is part of the language associated here with Tyre and Sidon (as well as Byblos; cf. Ezek 27:8–9). And the Psalms usage (68:14 [NRSV 68:13]) is in a passage filled with language strongly influenced by Ugaritic.

mud of the streets. This phrase continues the imagery of uncountable quantities suggested by the phrase "like dust" used in reference to silver in the preceding tricolon. Because of the stock phraseology in other Semitic languages connecting dust rather than mud with gold (*ḥārūṣ*), the switch here is unexpected. Yet the sequence—silver followed by gold—is expected. The reversal of the accompanying descriptive phrase may be the result of silver/gold being paired with what was apparently another well-known combination. Psalm 18:43, with a parallel in 2 Sam 22:43, describes David's victory over his enemies, whom he made like "dust" and whom he cast out like the "mud of the streets." In the dust/mud combination "dust" precedes "mud," hence the linkage with the silver/gold pair meant a change in the conventional order, "gold [is as plentiful] as the dust [of the earth]" (*ḥurāṣe ki-i e-be-ri* in Amarna letters 16:14, 19:61, 27:106, and 29:164; see Knudtzon 1915: *ad loc.*). The dust/mud pair, in being linked chiastically with silver and gold as representative of wealth in Zechariah 9, thus not only intensifies the image of the economic success of the Phoenician cities but also, in light of the military imagery associated with the pair in Psalm 18 and in the Song of David in 2 Samuel 22, subtly hints at the military opening and closing to these two verses (9:3–4) dealing with Tyre (see chart and discussion in our NOTE to the beginning of 9:3).

4. *will impoverish her.* The literal meaning of the Hiphil *yrš* is "to dispossess" or "to disinherit," as is the case in the majority of its biblical attestations. In an attempt to see a reflection of holy-war language, P. D. Hanson translates, "will capture" (1975: 294). His selection of such a loaded verb clearly implies a view that Yahweh intends to impose divine sovereignty even in foreign lands. However, Yahweh is making Tyre weak through removal of its wealth (v 4b following). Because of the imagery of Tyre's wealth in verse 3 and in the following tricolon, we render the verb in English with the appropriate nuance of removal of wealth—"impoverish"—which also occurs at 1 Sam 2:7: "Yahweh makes poor (*môrîš*) and makes rich." In addition, as the first of a set of three parts that constitute the tricolon of verse 4, the verb begins a set of three statements of increasing force. To understand it as something other than "impoverish" would be to violate the intensification established by the parallelism of this tricolon.

slam her wealth into the sea. Most commentators take this idiom as presented in BDB (298), "to destroy the sea defenses" or "ramparts" (*ḥêl*) of Tyre. Consequently, they see in this verse a further support for assigning a date for

Second Zechariah to the period of Alexander the Great, who was the first conqueror of Tyre to capture the city, a feat he accomplished by building a mole, or stone causeway, to connect the mainland with the offshore city (see first NOTE to 9:3). Previous attackers such as the Assyrians and Babylonians had besieged the city to weaken it but had not succeeded in conquering it. All such interpretations, however, depend on understanding *ḥêl* to mean "rampart."

Another well-attested meaning of *ḥêl*, however, is "wealth," as in Zech 14:14 and in many other prophetic passages (e.g., Isa 8:4; 10:14; 30:6; 60:5, 11; 61:6; Mic 4:13; Jer 15:13; 17:3; Zeph 1:13; and Ezek 26:12). Because this is one of four consecutive references to the economy of Tyre, the more appropriate meaning relates to the destruction of the very foundation of Tyre's existence as a powerful city, to wit, its economy or "wealth." Nothing in this verse need refer to the destruction of a rampart or defense system. Indeed, this second tricolon of verse 4 intensifies and specifies the somewhat more abstract notion of impoverishment that the first tricolon presents. Like "impoverish," it deals with the economic life of Tyre as do the second and third tricola of the preceding verse (see chart in first NOTE to 9:3). By referring to the wealth of Tyre, it helps form the poetic structure and the artful arrangement of content in this oracle concerning Tyre in verses 3 and 4. Still, the nuance of *ḥêl* as "rampart" may lurk in the background, making this word function as a double entendre. Similarly, the verb *hikkâ*, a Hiphil from the root *nkh*, meaning "to strike, knock down," bespeaks violence. In short, if Tyre is losing her economic viability, it is through the violence that will befall her.

she will be consumed by fire. The Hebrew is straightforward, conjuring up a picture of the city of Tyre burning to the ground. The Hebrew phrase *bᵉš ᵓkl* is an idiom that poetically characterizes the destruction of war: cities were plundered and "consumed by fire." Although "Lord" is the subject of the first two tricola of this verse, and of the closely related passages dealing with consuming fire in Amos (1:4, 7, 10), the phrase here is in the Niphal, which keeps it somewhat distant from the holy-war imagery connected with Yahweh's instrumentality in bringing fire to the cities to be destroyed. The fact that the preposition *b* ("by") appears with "fire" implies human instrumentality, inasmuch as when God is the agent of fiery disaster the preposition is omitted (Andersen and Freedman 1989: 239). Still, the use of the passive no doubt is meant to indicate that Yahweh is ultimately responsible for what happens.

The military image completes the envelope construction that begins in verse 3a (see first NOTE to that verse) and effectively ends the prophetic treatment of Phoenicia. It also is the strongest of the three statements in this verse concerning the fate of Tyre. This city will lose its wealth presumably forever, for the city itself—not just its economy—will be destroyed. Thus the last colon of this tricolon has a political dimension, which suits the prophet's concern to have, in his eschatological perspective, the lands belonging to Israel's allotted territory restored to their rightful owner Israel (see COMMENT).

The destruction of Tyre by fire is featured in the dramatic climax of the oracle against Tyre in Amos 1:9–10 (cf. also the destruction by fire in Zeph

1:18; 3:8; and Ezek 23:25). The oracles in Amos 1, as we have noted, seem to have been influential in shaping those of Zech 9:1–8, the tendency to refer to or rework older biblical materials being one of the salient features of late biblical prophecy. Such a relationship to authoritative literature, evident in marked intertextuality, is at the core of First and Second Zechariah (Mason 1976: 233–38; see below, NOTE to "will remain," 9:7). This ancient image of Israel's enemies being consumed by fire recurs in Second Zechariah in 12:6 (cf. NOTES to "like a fire pot" and "consume").

5. *Ashkelon.* Mention of this city initiates the third, or Philistine, group of this first section, 9:1–8, of Part One of Second Zechariah. Ashkelon was one of the five cities—Gaza, Ashkelon, Ashdod, Gath, and Ekron—that constituted the so-called Philistine Pentapolis and the only one of these cities to be situated directly on the coast. With its small harbor and its position on a major north–south highway, the Via Maris, Ashkelon was an important Canaanite city-state even before becoming part of Philistia. During the period of the Philistines' greatest power (twelfth to tenth centuries), Ashkelon was their leading maritime city.

Although five cities constituted the Philistine confederation, only four of them appear in this passage; Gath is omitted. In listing only four of the five cities, the prophet here seems to be following the treatment accorded to Philistia by other prophets: Amos, Jeremiah, and Zephaniah (see chart 12 in our COMMENT) all list four of the five Philistine cities, omitting only Gath. The oracles of Amos 1, which are related to this passage in many ways (see, e.g., NOTE to "Tyre . . ." in 9:3, as well as Introduction), include three verses (1:6–8) dealing with Philistia: Gaza (which Amos singles out for special attention), Ashdod, Ashkelon, and Ekron. Gath is missing from this listing, although it is clear that Amos knows of its existence because of the reference to "Gath and the Philistines" in 6:2. Jeremiah 25 lists all the nations that will be forced to drink the cup of divine wrath; included in this group are "all the kings of the land of the Philistines—Ashkelon, Gaza, Ekron, and the remnant of Ashdod" (25:20), but not Gath. Elsewhere, in his oracle concerning the Philistines (chapter 47), Jeremiah singles out Gaza and Ashkelon, apparently in response to the contemporary historical situation, in which Egyptian troops were menacing those two cities. Finally, Zephaniah 2 recounts the devastation of Philistia, especially the cities of Gaza, Ashkelon, Ashdod, and Ekron (Zeph 2:4), but not Gath. In Zephaniah, Ashkelon is the one city accorded additional mention (2:7).

The omission of Gath from all of these prophetic threats (although it does appear elsewhere in Amos, in 6:2) directed to the Philistine cities is curious, especially in light of the fact that Gath is mentioned in the Bible considerably more often than any other of the Philistine cities. Second Zechariah may be following prophetic tradition in directing his prophecies toward the same four cities, but the prior question as to why just those four appear in all these prophetic lists needs to be addressed. Two possibilities can be entertained.

The first concerns the identity of the site. Gath is the only one of the cities of the Philistine Pentapolis that lacks relatively secure geographic identification.

Neither archaeologists nor historical geographers have been able to establish conclusively which of several candidates, Tell es Safi perhaps being the most prominent (see Rainey 1975; but cf. Kitchen 1973: 62), is actually Gath. This situation possibly reflects a lack of continuity in the history of the site, which may be the result of its being somewhat less prominent, politically and economically, than its four sister cities. In the periods following the Philistine heyday of the early Iron Age, Gath as an inland site may not have been able to sustain the same level of economic development possible when it was closely allied with the maritime-oriented economy of at least three of the other Philistine sites. The Shephelah perhaps could support, in the heartland of Philistia, only one urban center, Ekron, which itself suffered a decline in the tenth to eighth centuries (Gitin 1987: 214).

The second possibility, which may be not unrelated to the first, concerns the history of the relationship between this particular Philistine city and the Israelites. Surely in the era of the Philistines' greatest strength Gath shared in the enmity that existed between the Philistines and the tribal league. The captured "ark of God" was held for a time in Gath (1 Sam 5:8). However, the pattern of hostility between Israel and the Philistines took a different course for Gath. During the period of David's social banditry, he and his six hundred men and their households found refuge in Gath (1 Sam 27:1–7), for David was a formal vassal of Achish, king of Gath. For sixteen months, David and this sizable entourage dwelled in one of Gath's satellite towns; so secure were they there that Saul, upon hearing that David was in Gath, ceased to pursue him. Clearly the Gittites and David's group were on good terms. Indeed, six hundred Gittites eventually followed David to Jerusalem, one of them, Ittai, swearing fealty to David and to Yahweh (2 Sam 15:18–22). Thus it was no accident that when David feared to bring the ark to Jerusalem, he gave it to a Gittite, Obed-edom, for safekeeping. The ark remained there safely for three months, and Obed-edom and all that was his received Yahweh's blessing (2 Sam 6:9–12).

Although enmity with some Gittites continued—witness the account of Goliath the Gittite and the other giants of Gath (2 Sam 21:19–22)—there can be no question that David's early connection with this one Philistine city initiated a relationship between Gath and Israel that differed from the hostile relationship of the other Pentapolis cities to Israel. By the time of Rehoboam, Gath alone among the Philistine cities was reckoned as a Judean city (2 Chron 11:5–12). This history of partial rapport with one part of a group that in many ways was Israel's enemy *par excellence* did not escape notice of the four Israelite prophets whose oracles against the nations included threats to the Philistines. Gath was spared because its citizens and King David had been on good terms and perhaps, therefore, because the city itself, unlike the others of the Pentapolis, had indeed been incorporated into Judah by the time of the divided monarchy.

Zechariah 9, in mentioning only four of the Philistine cities, is in agreement with the other three prophetic texts that list them. Yet it diverges from the other two poetic contexts of these names, Amos 1 and Zephaniah 2, in the order in which the names are given. And although the order of the cities is the same here as in Jeremiah 25, Zechariah 9 repeats two of the names, thus disrupting the Jeremianic sequence. Chart 11 in our NOTES to "Ekron," below, shows the divergent patterns. The arrangement of the names of the cities in Zechariah thus should not be considered a simple or random or stereotyped list, particularly because it differs from the other prophetic lists. Only three of the four city names appear in verse 5, which begins and ends with Ashkelon. Gaza comes second and Ekron third; then Gaza too is repeated before the second mention of Ashkelon. This arrangement (Ashkelon/Gaza/Ekron/Gaza/Ashkelon) serves to create a focus on Ekron, which is in the center (cf. NOTES to "Ekron" below, in this verse and in v 7).

Although the placement of Ekron in the center of verse 5 has much to commend it in light of the return to Ekron in verse 7, such an understanding of this sequence of Philistine cities is dependent upon the versification of the MT. Because the next verse (9:6) contains only two lines, the first of which seems to go better with verse 5 and the second with verse 7, many commentators (e.g., Mitchell 1912; P. D. Hanson 1973; and others) would see "a villain will rule in Ashdod" (9:6a) as completing the poetic subunit begun with 9:5d ("the king will perish from Gaza"). In this way, all of verse 5 plus the first line of verse 6 produce the first of two six-line Philistine sections. If this be the case, Ashkelon and Gaza are the first two cities mentioned, followed by Ekron; then Ashkelon and Gaza recur, but in reverse order, and Ashdod completes the section. This arrangement can still be seen as calling attention to Ekron, for only Ekron is not depicted as having its leadership revoked in some way (as is the leadership of Ashkelon, Gaza, and Ashdod; see NOTES to "will perish" and "not be ruled" in v 5 and to "villain" and "will rule" in v 6).

see . . . be afraid. The English translation does not do justice to the Hebrew for these verbs, whose assonance—*tēreʾ . . . tîrāʾ*—contributes to the poetic effect. The verb ("agonize") in the next colon is related to these two verbs, so that all three verbs are to be understood in relation to both Gaza and Ashkelon. The prophet has distributed the terms poetically to enhance their effect.

This line concerns Ashkelon's awareness of something that evokes fear; the assumption is that the tragedy befalling Tyre described in the previous verse is what is provoking Ashkelon's agitation. That the cities of Philistia would be both aware of and alarmed by events in Phoenicia fits the situation in the Persian period, when there were especially close connections between the Phoenician cities and those on the southern coast of Palestine. The Persians sought to foster Phoenician trade in competition with Greek maritime activity (Aharoni 1979: 415). To this end, the Persians evidently gave some Palestinian coastal cities the status of colonies, of either Tyre or Sidon (see the early fifth-century sarcophagus inscription of Eshmunʾazar of Sidon, *ANET*: 662). With their economic livelihood thus dependent on one of the Phoenician maritime powers, it is no wonder that the economic and political decimation of those cities would cause considerable anguish for the colonies in Philistia.

Gaza . . . Gaza. As the southernmost city on the Palestinian coast, Gaza was a regional center during many periods of its history. During the time of

Egypt's domination of Canaan in the Late Bronze Age, it served as the capital of the Egyptian province in southern Canaan. Although Sir Flinders Petrie identified ancient Gaza with Tell el ʿAjjul, most archaeologists now would consider Tell Harube, which lies in the northeastern part of the modern city of Gaza, about five kilometers from the coast, to be the site of the Canaanite and Philistine city (Dothan 1982: 35). From the perspective of biblical sources relating to the period of Philistine domination, Gaza may have been the chief of the five cities; in the Samson stories, Gaza was apparently the place where the Philistine lords *(sĕrānîm)* gathered to offer sacrifices at the temple of their god Dagon (Judg 16:23, 27).

Like Ashkelon, Gaza appears twice in this verse: first in reference to the city's awareness of impending disaster, and then in announcing that its political life has been disrupted.

agonize. The verb, from the root *ḥwl*, meaning "to dance" or "to writhe" (in pain or anguish), echoes in its Hebrew form *(tāḥîl)* the sound of a word in the previous verse, where Tyre's wealth *(ḥêlâ)* is cast into the sea. This is one of the aspects of Tyre's fate that is causing Gaza to experience anguish. The frequent figurative use of *ḥwl* to indicate mental or spiritual agony as opposed to physical pain is found mainly in biblical poetry or elevated prose. For example, the army that comes on the day of Yahweh is preceded by a devouring fire, before which peoples are "in agony" (Joel 2:6).

Ekron. The central line of this five-line verse concerns Ekron, the only one of the Philistine cities mentioned in this verse to which the prophet returns (see below, NOTE to "Ekron" in 9:7) in this section (vv 1–8) dealing with Aram, Phoenicia, and Philistia. The focus on Ekron is achieved not only by the prophet's mentioning it again in a separate context but also by the way it is placed in the central position in this verse. As we pointed out in our NOTE to "Ashkelon" (v 5), the list of four of the Philistine cities bears certain similarities to the passages in Jeremiah, Amos, and Zephaniah containing the prophetic threats against those cities. As can be seen in chart 11, Zechariah departs from

CHART 11
LISTINGS OF PHILISTINE CITIES IN AMOS, ZEPHANIAH, JEREMIAH, AND ZECHARIAH

Amos (1:7–8)	Zephaniah (2:4)	Jeremiah (25:20)	Zechariah (9:5, 6)
Gaza	Gaza	Ashkelon	Ashkelon
Ashdod	Ashkelon	Gaza	Gaza
Ashkelon	Ashdod	Ekron	Ekron
Ekron	Ekron	Ashdod	Gaza
			Ashkelon
			Ashdod

the order of Amos and Zephaniah, both of which begin with Gaza and end with Ekron. Those two lists begin with the three coastal cities of Philistia (except that their ordering of Ashkelon and Ashdod is not the same) and then add Ekron, one of the two interior cities of the Philistine Pentapolis (see our NOTE to "Ashkelon," v 5, for a discussion of the omission of Gath). Jeremiah's list, the only one in prose, seems to set the pattern for Second Zechariah—except that Zechariah disrupts the pattern by repeating "Ashkelon" and "Gaza," in reverse order, so as to frame "Ekron."

Ekron is the only one of the cities of the Philistine Pentapolis that is not mentioned in ancient written sources that predate the Philistine control of the city. Hence, many scholars supposed Ekron to be the only Philistine city in southeast Palestine actually founded by the Philistines themselves. However, the identification of Ekron with Tel Miqne, or Khirbet el-Muqannaᶜ (see Naveh 1958), and the recent excavations at that site, have demonstrated that, like the other chief Philistine settlements, Ekron has a history that extends back into the Late Bronze Age if not earlier (Dothan and Gitin 1987).

The northernmost of the cities of the Philistine group, and located only twenty-two miles southwest of Jerusalem, Ekron controlled territory that had been allotted to the tribe of Dan (Josh 19:43). According to the biblical account, however, Dan could not acquire this territory and instead settled in the north, leaving Judah as the tribe that would have to contend with the Philistine territory of Ekron, the eastern border of which formed the western limit of Judah. Thus it was indeed fitting for Judah to be the tribe mentioned along with Ekron in the conclusion of the Philistine section of Second Zechariah in verse 7 (see NOTES to "like a clan in Judah" at 9:7). Like the Jebusites on the border of Benjamin and Judah and with whom Ekron is compared, Ekron also is associated with two tribes.

her hope. Derived from the root *nbṭ*, which means "to look" or "to look toward," often with the expectation of something positive (as in Zech 12:10) the noun *mebbāṭāh* ("hope") apparently expresses Ekron's confidence that allies will come to her aid. Such is the case in the only other place where this word occurs: in Isa 20:5 and 6, where it refers to the vain hope of the inhabitants of the coastland—the Ashdodites—that the Ethiopians or Egyptians would rescue them from the advancing armies of the Assyrians under Sargon II. Because of its rarity, the text is sometimes emended, with several Greek manuscripts, to *mibṭāḥâ*, "her confidence." Although such an emendation is not impossible, the text as it stands fits the context quite well.

The source of Ekron's expectation of help is not directly specified. However, because Ashkelon, in the first line of this verse, is said to have seen something that causes her to be afraid—namely, the destruction of Tyre—it stands to reason that Tyre is the source of Ekron's hope. This makes sense in light of the close commercial, and sometimes political, ties between the urban centers of the Phoenician coast, especially Tyre, and the Philistine cities (see NOTE to "Ashkelon" at the beginning of this verse).

he will dash. It is difficult to determine whether the Hiphil *hōbîš* is from the root *bwš*, meaning "to be ashamed, put to shame," or from *ybš*, "to dry up, wither." Either meaning fits the context here, namely, that Ekron's hope is for naught. However, the MT *hbyš* is the Hiphil of *bwš*, not *ybš*. Further, *bwš* in the Qal, followed by *min* ("from, by"), normally indicates "to be disappointed in," as in Isa 20:5 (cited also in preceding NOTE) where the people are "disappointed in Ethiopia," the object of the preposition there being in apposition with "hope," the same word as the object of "he will dash" in this line. Perhaps the use of the Hiphil rather than the Qal is deliberate, intended to anticipate the use of forms of both *bwš* ("be confounded," 10:5) and *ybš* ("dry up," 10:11; cf. also "wither" in Zech 11:17) in the next chapter. The subject of the third-person masculine singular verb must be Yahweh, whose actions will certainly affect Ashkelon and Gaza as well as Ekron.

king. The use of *melek*, "king," is often cited in an attempt to establish an exact historical reference for this Philistine passage. However, it is not clear that the use of this title can be attributed to a given historical period. Nor can its use be precluded even in the period of Persian rule; note that in the fifth century Eshmunʾazar, in his own inscription, retains the title "king," as does Tabnit of Sidon (*ANET*: 662). The Hebrew *melek* appears here without the definite article. The omission of the *heh* ("the") is probably a function of the poetic character of Zechariah 9, which is characterized by the virtual absence of prose particles such as the definite article. The same is true in verse 10 below, where "chariot" and "horse" appear without the definite article (see NOTE to "chariot . . . horse").

will perish. The first three lines anticipate disaster in expressing the fear, agitation, and lost hope of Ashkelon, Gaza, and Ekron, respectively. Now those emotions are shown to be justified, at least for Gaza in this line and Ashkelon in the next. The death of the king of Gaza will symbolize the end of Gaza, or, rather, the end of its current political status. The verb "perish" (*ʾbd*) is used in the related oracle in Amos to refer to the death of all the Philistine remnant rather than of an individual ruler or the population of one of the cities. The use of *ʾbd* in relation to individuals tends to be characteristic of Late Biblical Hebrew (*BDB*: 1). The shift in its appearance with the Philistines to its use with a single king in Zech 9:5 may be the result of this tendency or simply an instance of the author of the Zechariah passage dealing creatively with a former prophecy. Yet it may just as well mean that the Philistine city and its inhabitants will not be destroyed, for they are about to become Israelites; only the political autonomy of the city, marked by the death of its ruler, will come to an end.

not be ruled. Most translations render the Hebrew *lōʾtēšēb*, "to be uninhabited" (as NRSV) or "to be without inhabitant" (*NJPS*), because the verbal root (*yšb*, "to sit, dwell"), when used in relation to a city or land, has a figurative meaning: "to be peopled, inhabited." Indeed, most occurrences in the Hebrew Bible of the participial form (*yōšĕbîm*) of the verb indicates "inhabitants" or "residents." However, a case can be made for a specialized meaning, perhaps derived from the idiom *yōšēb ʿal hakkisseʾ*, "the one who sits on a throne," that is, "ruler" (so Cross and Freedman 1955: 248–49, in reference to several poetic passages, including Zech 9:5–6; see also Alt 1953: 196 and the extensive discussion in Gottwald 1979: 511–34). As a development from this idiomatic usage, the finite verb, as is the case here in Zech 9:5 and in the next verse (see NOTE to "will rule," 9:6) can mean "to rule."

The use of the participle *yōšēb* to mean "ruler" or "leader" and the verbal form to mean "rule" is attested in a number of places in Hebrew prophecy, including in the oracle against the Aramaeans (1:5) and the Philistines (1:8) in Amos (see Andersen and Freedman 1989: 229, 253–255, 258, who translate "sovereign"), in First Zechariah (8:20–21; see Meyers and Meyers 1987: 437–38), and below in 12:5 (see NOTE to "for the leaders of Jerusalem"). It also appears several times in Hebrew prose. In addition, the title *yšb* is found in the Tell Fekherye bilingual and in the Sefire texts in reference to Aramaean rulers. Whether it is synonymous with "king" or represents some variant of dynastic political authority cannot be determined. In either case, however, the term clearly designates a hierarchical political figure.

Rendering the verb, with the negative particle, in this specialized sense in Zech 9:5 allows this poetic line—"Ashkelon will not be ruled"—to fit its context more appropriately. The preceding line mentions a king who is removed by death, and the next line also involves a problem with the leadership of a Philistine city. Thus to talk of a city uninhabited would not be logical in this sequence of verses dealing with situations of crisis in the exercise of human political authority. Ashkelon, like Gaza and Ashdod, will be bereft of viable leadership.

6. *villain.* This word *(mamzēr)* appears only twice in the Hebrew Bible, here and in Deut 23:3 (NRSV 23:2). The meaning of the Hebrew is uncertain; an unattested verbal root, *mzr*, is perhaps related to the Aramaic "be bad" or the Arabic "be foul, corrupt." Because postbiblical Hebrew and Aramaic have related nouns that denote the offspring of incest or adultery, the meaning "bastard" is often suggested for the verse in Deuteronomy (e.g., RSV) as well as for this Zechariah usage. Some take the word collectively (again, NRSV; cf. Lacocque 1981: 147) and render "a mongrel people." That development of *mamzēr*, however, probably should not be read back into biblical texts. In this instance, the reign of a man of illegitimate birth, or the presence of a mixed people, would not be a suitably negative image unless the term is being used very colloquially—to denote a real scoundrel. Consequently, "villain," as denoting someone repulsive or corrupt and thus a person who will cause as much harm to Ashdod as does the loss of leadership in Ashkelon or the death of the king in Gaza (in the preceding three lines in 9:5; see various NOTES to that verse), seems more appropriate.

Although physical destruction is proclaimed for Phoenicia, Philistia's fate is more insidious. Its cities lose their viability in one of two ways: a city can lose its ruler, as is the case in Ashkelon and Gaza, or, as in the case of Ashdod, it can become ruled by someone corrupt, with the implication also being that the city cannot survive as an independent political entity under such conditions. The author of Second Zechariah thus indicates the end of Philistia in a political sense but not, as for Phoenicia, with its physical destruction.

will rule. In Hebrew, the verb begins the line. The verb *yšb* is the same as in the last line of the preceding verse. In both places, it means "rule" rather than the more common "to inhabit, dwell" (see NOTE to "not be ruled" in 9:5).

Ashdod. The fourth of the four Philistine cities to appear in this passage, Ashdod was (and still is) situated on the Via Maris north of Ashkelon. Although not actually on the coast itself, it was considered a coastal town rather than an inland city like Gath or Ekron. It had a small adjunct harbor town (Tel Mor, or Ashdod-Yam) for most of its history, but it never became the maritime power that Ashkelon did. Nonetheless, it clearly was a major urban center and perhaps even the leading Philistine city by the late premonarchic period, inasmuch as it was to Ashdod that the ark was transported after it was captured at Ebenezer (1 Sam 5:1). Ashdod also had a temple to Dagon during the period when it was a Philistine city. In the postexilic period, it is linked with Ammon and Moab as an example of a place whose women married Jews, with the result that half the children of those liaisons, in the case of Ashdod, could speak only "Ashdodite" and not the language of Yehud (Neh 13:23–24). In this Nehemiah reference, the name "Ashdod" probably refers to the district or province rather than to the city itself (see Aharoni 1979: map 34).

Neither of these aspects of its role in biblical texts explains why Ashdod is the only one of the four Philistine cities figuring in this passage to be mentioned only once. Perhaps the prophet intends to cite a total number of seven Philistine cities and thus can mention one, Ashdod, only once because the other three are mentioned twice. We can only note that what is omitted is mention of this city's awareness of any impending problems. Rather, it suffers a traumatic shift in political fortunes without first witnessing Phoenicia's fate. It can also be noted, however, that in Amos 1:6–8, which deals with Philistia, Ashdod (1:8) is said to be "cut off" or "destroyed" just as is Philistia, mentioned in the next line, which may thus contain an indirect second reference to Ashdod.

I will destroy. These words begin the second half of verse 6, which seems to fit better with the following verse than it does as part of verse 6, composed of just this colon and the preceding one (see NOTE to "Ashkelon," 9:5). This colon also marks a shift to the first person, with Yahweh announcing what will happen to the Philistines. Note also that the same verb (translated "cut off") is used below in verse 10, thus providing a lexical connection between the 1–8 and 10–11 subunits of Zechariah 9.

The verb *krt* in the Hiphil, literally meaning "to cut, cut off," is often used in the sense of destroying (killing) animals or people. In this instance, in its use with *gāʾôn* ("pride"), which itself is ambivalent, the more extensive and inclusive sense "destroy" seems justified. The use of *krt* represents another connection of Zechariah 9 with Amos, where 1:8 describes the cutting off of the "inhabitants" (or "rulers") from Ashdod. The Amos passage provides support (see next NOTE) for the idea that "pride" is meant to refer specifically to the leader of Ashdod.

The use of *krt* also provides a wordplay in Hebrew. The object of the destruction is the "pride of the Philistines," and an alternative name for Philistines is *kĕrētîm* (Cherethites). The Hiphil of *krt*, *hikrattî* would conjure up the collective *hakrētî*.

pride. The word "pride" (*gā'ôn*) can have, as it does here, the negative sense of arrogance, or, in other instances, the positive sense of deserved pride. It can also refer to that which might cause either pride or arrogance, namely, a nation's wealth, power, and/or material magnificence. In prophetic oracles, the word appears in contexts in which Yahweh is depicted as bringing to an end the sovereignty of one or another of Israel's traditional enemies: Egypt (Ezek 32:12), Babylon (Isa 13:11, 19), Assyria (Zech 10:11). However, because the verb *hkryt* (see previous NOTE) usually indicates the cutting down of real things, such as people, rather than abstract ideas, *gā'ôn* is probably used in both ways in this verse: to represent abstract pride or wealth as well as the ruler amassing such aspects of power. Indeed, in Amos 1:8, which is closely related to this verse, it is the "ruler of Ashdod" (*yôšēb mē'ašdôd*) whom Yahweh strikes (turns his hand against).

The use of *gā'ôn* here in reference to the leader(s) of the Philistines is part of this set of prophetic occurrences. However, unlike the Phoenicians discussed above, the Philistines have not been specifically accused of amassing material wealth. Yet their very independence as political entities is at stake, presumably because they occupy territory assigned to Yahweh's people. In this sense political power is the cause of the "pride" that Yahweh is bringing to an end. The people of Philistia will not cease to exist; but their political autonomy, in the form in which it has been manifest, will be terminated.

7. *I will remove*. The Hiphil of *swr* ("to turn aside, be removed") provides a strong link with First Zechariah, where it is used in a similar sense in connection with the investiture of Joshua, the high priest: " 'Take (*hāsîrû*) the filthy garments off him'; and to him he said, 'Look, I have removed your iniquity from you and I have clothed you in pure vestments' " (3:4; see Meyers and Meyers 1987: 178). Joshua's filthiness is contrasted with the state of purity he is to obtain when he is ultimately garbed in new vestments. His uncleanness is perhaps related to his having lived formerly in Babylon, an unclean land where sinful and impure people live (Meyers and Meyers 1987: 187–88, 218–19). The appearance of "remove" in Zechariah 9 thus evokes thematic congruence with First Zechariah through strong verbal correspondence. Whereas the more limited purpose of Joshua's divestment and investiture is access to the Heavenly Council, here the purification of Philistia enables the Philistines access to the holy, that is, makes them part of Israel (see NOTES below to "Ekron" and "like a Jebusite"). In a broader sense, the cleansing of Joshua represents the cleansing of the entire Jewish community, a theme that also unites large portions of First Zechariah with this and other sections of Second Zechariah (Mason 1976: 231–32).

its blood. The masculine singular suffix is attached to "blood," hence the term literally reads "his blood." Consequently, the Greek, Syriac, and Targum all translate the suffix: "I will take the blood out of their mouth." The antecedent of the suffix is clearly *gā'ôn* ("pride," or "leader"; see last NOTE to v 6) of the preceding verse. However, the blood is not to be taken as the Philistines' own blood but rather the blood of other living things taken into the mouth of the Philistine ruler, who here may represent all Philistines.

The word for "blood" *(dmyw)* is plural here (cf. some Greek manuscripts, which render it in the singular, *dmw*), a fact that is relevant to this context. The word for "blood" *(dām)* occurs hundreds of times in the Hebrew Bible, only seventy of those instances in the plural. The plural form seems to have a peculiar semantic force (see Koch 1962) indicating two aspects of its nature: the plural is used when the blood of a living being is separate from its system and appears as spurts, pools, or drops; and the plural is used when wrongful blood has been spilled and somehow haunts the one who spilled it. Both of these aspects are suitable to this context, which negates the core of Philistine sacral practice— namely, eating the blood of sacrificial animals—as antithetical to Hebraic practice and indicates that those who perform such deeds will cease to do so.

Although this is the only instance of the plural of "blood" used in regard to animals, the fact that it is linked with "mouth" in this line and "abominations" in the next (see following NOTES) surely points to Philistine sacrificial practices, which God is about to abrogate. Blood occupies a prominent role in the belief systems and practices of many cultures (see Kedar-Kopfstein [with Bergman] 1978: 237–39 and bibliography, 234). As a fluid that appears to originate in the body and move through it, in a way that was inexplicable to ancient people, blood was viewed as mysterious, magic, and imbued with the very essence of life. The ancient Israelites were not unique in treating the blood of humans and animals in special ways and in viewing the blood as the essence of life of an individual, whether of human or beast.

The Israelites' attitude to blood, however, was characterized by a concern that it not be consumed, a concern that underlies this appearance of "blood" in association with "mouth." The prohibition against eating blood appears in many different parts of the Bible (e.g., Lev 17:10ff.; 1 Sam 14:32ff.; Deut 12:23; Ezek 33:25). The fact that the first of the Noahite laws (Gen 9:4) bans the eating of the lifeblood of animals indicates the biblical view that this prohibition goes back to earliest times. The strong and oft-repeated biblical injunction not to eat the blood of slaughtered animals, but rather first to drain it out, seems to underlie this Zechariah passage. The polemic of many biblical passages against pagan use of blood seems to be more against the consuming of animal flesh with the blood still in it rather than against the practice of drinking blood as such, which was apparently not a ritual practice among the people surrounding ancient Israel. Indeed, in Ezekiel (33:25), eating blood with flesh is listed first, followed by idolatry and murder, as the sins of the nations that will cause Yahweh to dispossess them.

The emphasis on eating blood (with flesh) that appears in this passage (as well as in Ezekiel) as a mark of unacceptable behavior of non-Israelites should be viewed especially in relationship to the literature of the exilic and postexilic periods. As D. L. Smith has demonstrated (1989: 139–49), the intensified attention to cultic law in this period must be viewed not only as an attempt to establish (or reestablish) purity after the sins that brought about defeat and exile. It must also be seen as a means to help preserve identity in the face of Israel's becoming, whether in exile or in Yehud, a community without political independence, that is, without the boundaries that normally separate one people from another. In the late biblical period, the emphasis on and development of purity laws—including those governing what can or cannot be eaten—was one of the mechanisms for social survival that characterize the adaptations of both the Yehudites and the exiles to their radically altered status.

Thus, the removal of the blood from the mouths of the Philistines—along with the "abominations"—is as powerful an image as any biblical author could conjure up. Certainly it carries more than the mere nuance of consuming the lifeblood of animals. It is also a matter of Israelite identity. If this quintessentially non-Israelite mode of behavior is being removed from the Philistines, then the result will be a group of people who, "like the Jebusites," become part of God's people.

his mouth. Again, the antecedent of "his," as for "its blood," is the Philistines of the previous verse, as represented by "pride" (see NOTE to this word in v 6), i.e., "leader." The use of "mouth" along with "blood" leaves little doubt that the offense is the consuming of blood. Together with "abominations" (unclean foods; see next NOTE) that are in the Philistine "teeth" (in the next line), the unacceptable cultic behavior of the Philistines is set forth. The obverse of this situation—the removal of blood and abominations—means the purification of the Philistines and their becoming Israelites, as exemplified by the status of Ekron (see NOTE below to "Ekron," as it appears in the last line of 9:7), which is incorporated into the kinship genealogies that function to express the unity of all Israel.

abominations. The Hebrew word *šiqqûṣ* (and especially the related *šeqeṣ*, which would appear almost the same in the plural), refers to the "detested things," that is, animals forbidden as food. Although *šiqqûṣ* can indicate other detested items or behaviors, the fact that it is linked here with something put into the mouth (between or in their "teeth") argues for the more limited meaning here, forbidden food. In Leviticus (7:21 and 11:10, 11, 12, 20, 23), the creatures prohibited from the Israelite list are specified, with the use of the term *šeqeṣ*. However, by not using exactly the same word as in the Leviticus legal materials, the author of Second Zechariah perhaps wishes not only to invoke the dietary prohibitions demanded by the parallelism (see "its blood from his mouth" as discussed in the previous two NOTES) but also to suggest that those detested things stand for all pagan behaviors, especially idolatry, which were anathema to the Israelites, as expressed by many prophets (e.g., Jer 4:1; Isa 66:3; Ezek 5:11; cf. Deut 29:16 [NRSV 29:17] and 2 Kgs 23:13, 24).

As we have suggested in the second NOTE (to "its blood") to verse 7, the denunciation of the Philistines is symbolized by an announcement that their eating practices and associated idolatrous behaviors will be changed and brought into alignment with those of Israel; they will thus become Israelites. Why does dietary purity, of all things, represent here the aspects of non-Israelite behavior that will have to cease in order for God's will, in restoring Israel, to be accomplished? The answer to this probably lies in the social dynamics of the postexilic period, when the concern for cultic purity was a reflection of the need for "identity-markers" (D. L. Smith 1989: 145) in a world where the existing boundaries between peoples had been dissolved by imperial conquest and the resettling of peoples. Food behaviors, which are part of daily life for all human beings, are thus the most representative of religious-ethnic practices that can be used to define one group as opposed to another.

Once the Philistines cease consuming blood with meat and stop eating unclean animals, their identity as Philistines will dissolve. As their cities are restored to their rightful place as part of the ideal Israel, they will merely become a legitimate part of the Israelite tribes (see also NOTES below to "Ekron" and "like the Jebusites" in 9:7e). As the historic enemies of Israel, they nonetheless occupy a special place in this eschatological vision. They will not suffer material devastation; rather, they will lose their political identity as their rulers are removed, and their religious-ethnic identity as they cease following their own cultic practices. God's mercy extends, in achieving the ultimate aims of restoring Israel, even to Israel's traditional nemesis, the Philistines.

his teeth. The removal of "abominations" from the Philistines' "teeth" complements the parallel removal of the "blood" from "his mouth." The dual plural "teeth" is used quite rarely in this connection, although it is sometimes found in reference to Israel's oppressors or the wicked (Pss 3:8 [NRSV 3:7]; 58:7 [NRSV 58:6]; 124:6). Such an unusual usage here makes even more vivid the picture of the consuming of forbidden food. The import of this imagery, in reference to Philistine identity and autonomy, is explained in the preceding NOTES to "its blood," "his mouth," and "abominations;" see also the NOTES below to "Ekron," "Judah," and "like a Jebusite."

will remain. The leadership of the Philistines will be destroyed, yet here the singular Niphal of *š'r* refers to the survival of one individual Philistine leader. The choice of the verb is noteworthy because its derivative noun, "remnant," is frequently associated with the beloved and righteous of Israel, as is notably the case in Zech 8:6, 11, 12; Isa 37:4; 2 Kgs 19:4; Mic 2:12; 5:6–7; 7:18; Jer 23:3; 31:7; Zeph 2:7, 9; etc. The prophecy regarding the Philistines seems quite aware of the antithetical prophecy of doom in Amos 1:8 in which the "remnant" of the Philistines perishes (cf. Jer 25:20, where we read "remnant of Ashdod"). If this is a reworking or reflection of an older prophecy, a process that is characteristic of both First and Second Zechariah, the reordering of the cities and reversal of the fortunes of the cities indicates a purposeful shift on the part of the editor(s), redactor(s), or prophet(s) in the school or tradition of Zechariah.

our God. The use of *'ĕlōhîm*, a word for God that appears thousands of times (2,570; see Ringgren 1974c: 272) in the Hebrew Bible, is somewhat unusual in its occurrence here with the first-person plural suffix "our." "Your/our/my God," following the name of God—Yahweh—is a stereotyped formula, occurring hundreds of times. But a pronominal suffix with "God" outside that formula is less common and expresses something intentional about God. In this case, and especially in Second Isaiah, "our God" represents an awareness that the God of

Israel is not the god of other peoples but that other nations will one day recognize Israel's deity. Isaiah 52:10, e.g., proclaims that all the "ends of the earth" will recognize what "our God" does. The personal suffix thus highlights, in Zech 9:7, Israel's relationship to God and in so doing emphasizes the notion that the Philistines are to become part of the group that participates in that relationship. The Philistines will become like Israelites, part of the "family" of Israel (see next NOTE and preceding NOTES in this verse), unlike the other nations outside Israel who, in the universal scheme of Zechariah, acknowledge Yahweh while retaining their own national and cultural identity.

like a clan in Judah. Many commentators accept the reading of "leader" or *ʾelep* for the MT *ʾallūp*, as proposed in *BHS* and as understood in some of the versions, such as the Greek and Latin, which read "leader of a thousand." Mason also sees the term as referring to an individual, although he understands *ʾallūp* in the sense of "intimate" or "friend" (1973: 25), which normally occurs as an adjective (Ps 55:14 [*NRSV* 55:13]; Mi 7:5; Prov 16:28; 17:9; Jer 13:21; etc.).

Yet here, as in Gen 36:15–30 and also in Zech 12:5, 6 (see NOTES below) the MT *ʾallūp* has a collective sense and clearly refers to a group or social unit. Indeed, Gottwald adopted such an interpretation of this text (1979: 277) and Mitchell (1912: 269) was among the earliest exegetes to offer such a view, translating *ʾallūp* as "family." Gottwald also contends that *ʾelep* ("leader") would not be used as a military term except in the context of a monarchical society and that *ʾallūp*, connoting a social group, is most appropriate in an archaizing poetic context such as Zech 9:7 (1979: 278).

The significance of the phrase "like a clan in Judah" is clear: the surviving leader is about to become part of Judah in the most inclusive way. As we have indicated in our NOTES to the Philistine cities in verses 5 and 6 above, Philistia is to be distinguished from the other territories mentioned in verses 1–3, namely Phoenicia and Aram or Syria, in that it was situated at the periphery of Judah and in what was to have been the territorial allotment of Dan and especially Judah. Thus the fate of the Philistines was to differ from that of Phoenicia or Aram. The Philistines occupied the tribal lands of Israel; and as these lands are to be restored to Israel, so will the leaders of those cities be incorporated into Israel, as if they were a "clan," i.e., part of the lineage terminology that linked together all those considered to be Israelites. Why were the Philistines not to be destroyed in the process? The answer may lie in the way Ekron (see next NOTE) was representative of the Philistines and what this may tell us of the makeup of the Philistine cities.

The comparison of an individual surviving leader to a corporate entity ("clan") may seem strange; but this comparison balances the subsequent one, in which a corporate entity (the city of Ekron) is compared to an individual ("Jebusite"). This chiastic arrangement of individual and group terms perhaps serves to indicate the totality of the future incorporation of Philistia—of both its leaders and its populace—into the restored people of Yahweh.

Ekron. Also known as Tel Miqne, or Khirbet el-Muqannaʿ, Ekron is approximately fifty acres in size and is the largest site associated with the inner coastal plain. It lies on the western edge of the border between Philistia and

Judah, in territory originally assigned to Dan, and its selection to be compared to the Jebusites surely derives in part from its location so close to the heartland of Judah. Extensive new excavations (Dothan and Gitin 1987) now make it possible to reconstruct more of the site's history and ethnic makeup, factors that can illuminate its role in Second Zechariah's attitude toward the Philistines. As we pointed out in our NOTE to Ekron in 9:5, Tel Miqne was the site of a Canaanite city-state in the Late Bronze Age. By the beginning of the Iron Age (twelfth century) the Philistines had turned it into a large fortified city, which shrank from fifty acres to ten acres on the upper tell by the tenth century. The last prior expansion occurred some time after 732 B.C.E., slightly earlier than reported by Gitin (1987: 206–7), according to B. M. Gittlen (oral communication), director of Field II excavations. This expansion is critical for a consideration of the ethnic composition of the site's population in the late Iron Age. The site was destroyed in 603 B.C.E., probably by Nebuchadnezzar, and a much more modest occupation was erected over its ruins in the sixth century. After the 1990 excavation season, it still could not be determined how long the settlement had lasted, although it is unlikely that habitation continued into the fifth century.

Regarding its ethnic makeup, it is fairly clear that Ekron, like all the Philistine cities, was originally Canaanite and then Philistine in the Iron Age, at least until the late eighth century B.C.E. After the Assyrian deportations from Israel in the north at the end of the century, however, it is likely that some Israelites settled in Ekron (Gitin 1987: 216; Ephʿal 1979). The Assyrians, in their massive efforts to relocate the population of the Northern Kingdom, may well have sent captives to Philistia. Evidence for this is provided by the many four-horned altars, which are typologically similar to those made in the Northern Kingdom and so appear to be the work of Israelite craftsmen, and the presence of many ostraca in Hebrew-Phoenician script that are to all intents and purposes Hebrew in content. These artifactual remains indicate that Ekron, as the Philistine border city closest to Judah, had a population with an Israelite component in the seventh and sixth centuries or, at the very least, had absorbed some aspects of Israelite culture by that time.

Furthermore, there is good reason to believe that other Philistine cities had a mixed population that included Israelites or Judeans, either through Assyrian resettlement policies or because of certain events. Uzziah, earlier in the eighth century, conquered Gath and Ashdod (2 Chron 26:6). Surely that conquest involved the stationing of Judean officers in those cities. In addition, Uzziah built settlements in Ashdod's territory and elsewhere in Philistia, again bringing a Judean population to the area. Similarly, the discovery of a late seventh-century Hebrew inscription at Meṣad Ḥashavyahu, just north of Ashdod, indicates a Judean presence in the vicinity in the time of Josiah. Finally, Nehemiah's concern that Jews were marrying Ashdodites clearly reflects a situation in which there were cultural, if not kinship, connections between Ashdod and Yehud that facilitated such liaisons.

These data suggest that at the end of the preexilic period, and perhaps into the Persian period, Ekron and some parts of Philistia had mixed populations that included Israelites and/or Judeans. This fact, coupled with the historical understanding of Philistia to be part of Israel's territorial heritage, gave Ekron and the other Philistine cities a special role in the oracles of Zech 9:1–8. The restoration of Israel's territory would involve not only Philistia but also its inhabitants. The southern coast, both geographically and demographically, would become part of Israel.

like a Jebusite. Just as the Jebusites were absorbed into the population of Jerusalem after David established his capital there, so too would the Philistines become part of Judah. The Philistines are represented by Ekron, the closest border city and perhaps also the one with the closest ties to the population of Yehud (see previous NOTE). Ekron also shared with Jebus the status of being located in territory associated with two tribes: Jebus with Judah and Benjamin, Ekron with Judah and Dan. Second Zechariah holds a different view of the Philistines than do the other prophets—Amos, Jeremiah, and Zephaniah (see NOTES to "Ashkelon," 9:5a, and "Ekron," 9:5b)—who included the Philistine cities in their oracles against the nations. Although the author of Second Zechariah may be drawing on the imagery of the earlier prophets, he alters the existing view of the Philistines' fate. Their leadership will be damaged; and the cities themselves—population plus land—will become absorbed into the tribe of Judah in the restored Israel in the new age, just as Jebusites had been incorporated into Israel at the time of David. The mention of the Jebusites also draws attention to Jerusalem, to which the prophet turns in the next verse.

8. *I will encamp.* It is significant that this last verse of the first part of chapter 9 begins with this verb, *ḥnh*, especially because its use with *l* meaning "at" is quite rare, occurring elsewhere only in Num 2:34. Although 9:1–8 begins with Damascus as the "resting place" (*mĕnūḥātô*, 9:1) of "the word of Yahweh," the only and true permanent center of God's earthly presence, or "encampment," is in the Temple at Jerusalem. There is a clever wordplay here, in 9:1 and 8, in which two different roots that sound alike and have similar meanings frame this subunit of the first section of Second Zechariah, Part One (chapters 9–11). Similarly, the use of "eye/eyes" in verses 1 and 8 (see NOTES to "eye of the people," v 1, and, below, to "I am watching with my eyes" in this verse) also serves to frame verses 1–8 and separate them from the next subunit, which deals with the royal entry to Jerusalem (vv 9–10).

The idea of God's "encamping" at the Temple is very similar to the idea of "dwelling" there (see Meyers and Meyers 1987: 168), which is more commonly expressed by the root *škn*, sometimes translated "to tabernacle," or "to indwell," because of its associations with the period of the Tabernacle in Israel's early history (Cross 1981). The Targum not surprisingly translates *ḥnh* as *škn* and adds "like a wall of fire," obviously conscious of the thematic connection between this verse and Zech 2:14 (NRSV 2:10). The unique metaphoric usage of "I will encamp," chosen to provide a literary connection with verse 1, is also evocative of the oracular Expansion on the Themes of the First Three Visions in First Zechariah, especially of Zech 2:14 (NRSV 2:10)—"Shout and rejoice, O daughter of Zion, for indeed I am coming to dwell *(škn)* in your midst" (cf. Zech 8:3)—which involves both the image of God's dwelling and that of Zion as daughter. It is no coincidence that Zech 9:9 opens with an apostrophe to "Daughter Zion." The author or redactor of 9:8 has clearly used language and themes that link this verse with Zech 9:1 and also Zech 2:14 (NRSV 2:10).

at my House. That is, at my Temple. For a full discussion of the symbolism and typology of temple ideology in Israel, see the NOTE to "House of Yahweh" in Hag 1:2 in Meyers and Meyers 1987: 21–23. Not only is the Temple of Yahweh the place where God "dwells" or "camps," it is also the symbol par excellence of the deity's sovereignty and earthly presence in Jerusalem, the center from which emanate God's power and sanctity. Moreover, it is the emblem of the Second Jewish Commonwealth, without which neither the religion of Judaism nor the Jewish people would have survived. Temple rebuilding is the central focus of the Book of Haggai. Refounding the Temple is the central theme of First Zechariah, and purifying the Temple cult is a central thrust of the Book of Malachi. Second Zechariah, although not temple-centered in the same way, does touch on these themes at various points, and its climax at 14:20–21 partakes of all of them.

a garrison. The MT reading *(miṣṣābâ)* is fairly close to the Greek "defense" or "bulwark," to the Syriac, and possibly even to the Latin, which may be translated "standing pillar" *(maṣṣēbâ)*. The root is *nṣb*, "to take a stand" or "to be stationed at," and the feminine noun is attested only in the present verse as pointed in the MT. The related masculine noun *maṣṣab* is normally translated "garrison" or "outpost," whereas the feminine is rendered as "guard" or "watch" by *BDB* (663). The sense is clear, and hence there is no need to emend.

against invaders. That is, "so that no one shall march to and fro," as translated by NRSV. The MT is identical to Zech 7:14 and the suggestions to delete this phrase as a gloss (*BHS*; P. D. Hanson 1975: 298; Jansma 1950: 69) or textual variant (Mason 1976: 228) are unfounded. The idea is that Yahweh's presence in Jerusalem at the Temple, the divine dwelling place on earth, will provide a protective shield against any hostile force. That this phrase is the same as in Zech 7:14, where its meaning is negative and applied to the past, may be another instance in which Second Zechariah draws on an earlier passage and gives it new meaning. The context here demands a positive interpretation because God's intention is protective. In evoking the past by way of a quotation of 7:14, the author/redactor may be attempting to emphasize the contrast between the past, when the land was left wasted so that it was not safe to "move about" or "come and go," and the present or future, when the threat of "invaders" is removed because of God's presence in the Temple (see NOTES and COMMENT to Zech 7:14 in Meyers and Meyers 1987: 405–8).

The idea that Jerusalem will be protected because of God's presence is expressed also in Zech 2:8–9 (NRSV 2:4–5), where the image is of a "wall of fire," and God's presence is called "Glory." In addition, it is somewhat similar to the concept in Zech 1:16, as pointed out by Saebø (1969: 159b). These notions are deeply entrenched in First Zechariah, and their appearance in Second Zechariah is a sign of the ties between chapters 1–8 and 9–14.

oppressor. As in Zech 10:4. God will provide protection against all who would "oppress" the people. The word for "oppressor," *nôgēś*, can refer to foreigners or overlords who exact tribute (Dan 11:20) or to a severe taskmaster, as was the case with the Egyptians who "oppressed" the Israelites (Exod 3:7; 5:6, 10, 13, 14; Job 3:18). It can occasionally even be applied to an Israelite, as is the case when Jehoiakim exacted *(ngś)* silver and gold from the people to pay Pharaoh Neco (2 Kgs 23:35). The use of such a term for a potential enemy of Israel is quite appropriate here, for God's presence in the Temple will guard against such political or economic domination by non-Israelites.

will not overrun them again. That is, no enemy or attacker will be free again to impose harm on God's people, i.e., the Israelites, *ʿălêhem* ("them"); hence we do not accept the suggestion of *BHS* to delete. This expression is nearly identical with Joel 3:17, where instead of "oppressor," it is *zārîm*, or "foreigners" or "strangers," who will never again pass through the holy city of Jerusalem. It may well be that the author/editor has intentionally reworked the Joel passage to be sure that his audience will attach the nuance of "foreigner" to "oppressor."

I'm watching with my eyes. Many commentators are uncomfortable with this expression and, like *BHS*, want to emend it to "I saw their (his) affliction," *rāʾîtî beʿēynô*, possibly having in mind Exod 3:7: "I looked upon the affliction of my people." As we observed above (see NOTE to "the eye of the people" in 9:1), the people of Aram were looking to Yahweh. A fitting counterpart exists here, with an emphasis on God's watching the people serving to close this first subunit of Second Zechariah. That God watches over the people of Israel is the focus of all of verse 8 and forms an envelope construction with verse 1.

Saebø (1969: 161ff.) has emphasized the importance of the theme of "the eye of Yahweh" in First Zechariah, citing Zech 2:12 (NRSV 2:8); 3:9; 4:10; and 8:6. The use of "eye"/"eyes" in 9:1 and 8 thus constitutes an important correspondence between First and Second Zechariah. In addition, the verb "watching," from *rʾh*, "to see," has probably been used here deliberately to help establish ties to First Zechariah, which is noteworthy for its frequency of the use *rʾh* (eighteen times) as well as *ʿyn* (twelve times). Furthermore, the idiom "to lift one's eyes" appears repeatedly in connection with the visions of First Zechariah (on these idioms, see Meyers and Meyers 1987 *ad loc.*). Thus the concluding phrase of verses 1–8 is most appropriate in terms of the language of this subunit and also of First Zechariah. It separates these verses from the next subunit (vv 9–10) dramatically, echoing words and themes of First Zechariah.

Despite the ways in which the language of verse 8 links with that of verse 1 to set off verses 1–8 as the first subunit of Zechariah 9, verse 8 at the same time is transitional to verse 9 and the succeeding verses. The shift from the third to the first person for Yahweh, beginning in verse 6 and appearing also in verse 7 and this verse ("I will encamp") serves to connect the first subunit with the next two subunits of Zechariah.

9. *Exult.* The use of the feminine imperative of *gyl* to begin the proclama-

tion unit (vv 9–10) is typical of the way this verb functions in the Hebrew Bible. Used only in the Qal, it indicates present or future action and is often used in the imperative (as here) or in the jussive or cohortative. Furthermore, it frequently stands by itself in a sentence, unaccompanied by any direct reference to what causes the exultation. This verb is frequently paired with another term for rejoicing, as it is here with *rw*ᶜ ("shout aloud"; see third NOTE to this verse). The term probably refers to the spontaneous shouting, without specific sung or spoken words, that expresses great joy (Barth, Bergman, and Ringgren 1975: 471). Found only in the poetic books of the Bible, it typically involves the exultation in Yahweh that accompanies God's extraordinary acts on behalf of those desperately in need of divine intervention. Thus, although the cause of rejoicing is not found in the same sentence as the verb here, the second part of the verse resoundingly proclaims the reason for the emotional outbursts represented by "exult" and "shout aloud."

The presence of "exult" in Zech 9:9 evokes the earlier daughter-of-Zion passage in First Zechariah at 2:14 (NRSV 2:10), where a pair of imperatives ("shout" and "rejoice") creates the image of joyous excitement among those who behold God's great presence. It also echoes Zeph 3:14, which invokes "Daughter Zion" and which has in its call to rejoice a pairing with *rnn*, a verb that appears frequently in Psalms (Pss 84:3 [NRSV 84:2]; 98:4, 8). The coupling of imperatives followed by an exhortation to "Daughter Zion" also occurs at Mic 4:10. The use of a verb such as *gyl* or *rw*ᶜ ("exult"; "shout aloud") followed by a proclamation of someone coming (with the verb *bw*ʾ, "to come") creates a great sense of expectation and provides assurance that what had been predicted is indeed going to take place, as in Zech 2:14 (NRSV 2:10) and Ps 98:8.

O Daughter Zion. In Hebrew poetry, "daughter" *(bat)* plus a toponym is commonly used. It is thought to designate the inhabitants of a particular place (Haag 1975: 334) or to indicate the place itself and thus, collectively, its population. However, close attention to the grammar of the expression indicates a more specific usage. Although "daughter" *(bat)* plus a place name is frequently translated "daughter of [place]," thereby implying that the place has a daughter, it is clear that such a translation is erroneous. The idiom refers to the place itself, personified as a daughter. The phrase *bat-ṣîyyôn* is an example of the appositional genitive (Stinespring 1965; cf. GKC §128k and 122h, i, the latter in error, as Stinespring shows). The specific daughter-Zion combination appears twenty-six times in the Hebrew Bible.

The frequent use of "daughter" or daughters" in Scripture to personify a place and to enhance its role in a poetic text is imperfectly understood. Perhaps because place names are normally feminine, this female kinship term came to designate various locales and their inhabitants. The suitability of "daughter" here is probably related to the dependent status of daughters. Just as unmarried daughters cannot act independently of their parents, so Yahweh's people must rely on God and on the king who is coming for their future to be arranged. For other aspects of daughter imagery, see NOTE below to "As for you," 9:11 (cf. Shargent forthcoming).

"Daughter Zion" in this verse is parallel to "Daughter Jerusalem," the two expressions together signifying the holy city. Although these exhortations at the beginning of verse 9 apparently draw upon Zeph 3:14 (see previous NOTE), they do not include "Israel," which accompanies "Zion" and "Jerusalem" in Zephaniah. Zechariah 9, in contrast, focuses especially on Jerusalem. This attention to Zion/Jerusalem is appropriate at this point because it directly follows the announcement in verse 8 that God will be in the Temple in Jerusalem (see NOTES to "I will encamp" and "a garrison," v 8). Just as this verse echoes the language of the oracular expansion of Zechariah 2 (especially 2:14 [NRSV 2:10]), so too the previous verse uses images associated with that chapter of First Zechariah, again 2:14 (NRSV 2:10) in particular. The fact that both verses 8 and 9 connect with First Zechariah, along with their common concern for Jerusalem, provides continuity between the first and second subunits of chapter 9. The theme of Jerusalem as a sacred city where the future king will rule (v 10) is thus a natural sequel to the theme of reestablishing God's presence in the Temple. Thus, although the second subunit (9:9–10) of this chapter in many ways stands apart from verses 1–8 and 11–17, it nonetheless is thematically connected to its context (see also NOTE below to "stronghold," v 12).

The call to Zion as witness and celebrant of a new world order, characterized by stability (worldwide peace), is part of Zion's traditional role in the expectation for Yahweh to overcome Israel's enemies and establish Israelite/Davidic/divine sovereignty in Jerusalem. This role for Zion is part of the "Zion tradition," in which a number of motifs accrue to the depiction of Zion, especially in Psalms (see Rohland 1956 and Ollenburger 1987). These motifs are part of a general Near Eastern typology of royal accession (see below in this verse, NOTE to "your king").

It should also be noted that "Daughter" appears twice here, thus prefiguring the double use of "sons" in verse 13 (see NOTE there to "your sons, O Zion"). This is another of the ways in which the subunits of Zechariah 9 are interconnected.

Shout aloud, O Daughter Jerusalem. "Daughter Jerusalem," which occurs only five other times in the Bible (Isa 37:22; 2 Kgs 19:21; Zeph 3:14; Lam 2:15; Mic 4:8), serves to narrow the scope of "Daughter Zion" of the previous bicolon, which can be used to connote a broader audience than merely Jerusalem (cf. Lam 2:1 and Zeph 3:14), as is the case with "Zion" in Zech 2:11 (NRSV 2:7; see Meyers and Meyers 1987: 164). Still, the two terms together serve to focus attention on Jerusalem and on its sacred precinct, the Temple Mount.

The verb *rwᶜ* literally means "to shout out," as in a war cry, and can also connote the blowing or sounding of the shofar or battle horn. It is often used in parallel with "exult," or similar terms; thus it is difficult to tell whether it represents a unique cry or is a synonymous term. The latter may be the case, because there seems to be an increase in the synonymity of such verbs in the postexilic era (Barth, Bergman, and Ringgren 1975: 471). Just as Daughter Zion and Daughter Jerusalem are complementary images, so too "exult" and "shout aloud" represent activities attributed to both Zion and Jerusalem. This passage may evoke Isa 40:9, where "Zion the Herald" and "Jerusalem the Herald" are the equivalent of "Daughter Jerusalem" and "Daughter Zion."

Behold . . . is coming. The use of the interjection "behold" *(hinnēh)* plus the imperfect of *bw* heralds the imminence of the royal figure. This verse differs from Zech 2:14 (NRSV 2:10) and Zeph 3:14ff., which are similar to this passage but which focus on the presence of Yahweh, rather than the king, in the holy city. For Zephaniah it is Yahweh the warrior (v 17) who is the "king of Israel" (v 15) and who will bring victory and, ultimately, a gathering together of the people (v 20). In Zech 2:14–15 (NRSV 2:10–11) Yahweh's presence in Jerusalem is reestablished, thereby sanctifying the land of Judah. Here, the excitement generated by the two imperatives ("exult," "shout") and the two apostrophic phrases is directed toward "your king."

your king. First, it is important to note the possessive-feminine suffix on the word "king"—the king hereby announced is the king of Zion and Jerusalem, whose attention is evoked by the female idioms "Daughter Zion" and "Daughter Jerusalem" (see NOTES above). The term *melek* ("king") itself is a loaded one in the present context, which is unmistakably eschatological and which foreshadows the emergence of messianic language in intertestamental literature and the New Testament. Although the royal aspect of the term is clear, the tone of this verse markedly diverges from the military language of the preceding and succeeding verses (especially vv 13–15; see E. M. Meyers forthcoming). The attitudes toward kingship in late biblical prophecy must be seen against the backdrop of the political status of the province of Yehud in the postexilic period under Persian rule. Among the final three canonical books of prophecy, Haggai, Zechariah, and Malachi, the most heightened royal eschatological passage is in Haggai (2:20–23), which focuses on a historical figure, Zerubbabel, to express its support of the Davidic dynasty. Although Zerubbabel is usually addressed as *pehâ*, or governor, in recognition of his civil leadership, in Hag 2:23 he is called "servant" and "signet," terms used to describe the ideal role of an Israelite ruler in special relationship to Yahweh and normally reserved for David (see Meyers and Meyers 1987: 68–70).

The nonmilitary tone of this verse is similar to that of the royal passages of Zechariah 1–8, where royal language is used (3:8; 4:6–10; 6:12) but is quite muted, especially in the so-called Zerubbabel Insertion of 4:6–10: "Not by might and not by power; but with my spirit, said Yahweh of Hosts" (v 6). At 6:11, leaving the plural "crowns" intact, and at 6:14, reading the singular "crown" or *hā'aṭeret*, the royal figure, or Davidic scion, is relegated to being a symbol of the future (Meyers and Meyers 1987: 349–54, 362–64, 366ff.). The pragmatic tone of First Zechariah indicates that it was in the best interests of the restoration community to support the Achaemenid-sponsored theocracy of Yehud as the only viable way of securely establishing the Jewish community of returnees in the Holy Land. The Persians, however, could not allow a monarchy to exist in Yehud when the satrapal organization was being imposed throughout the empire, a system which presupposed local rule through rulers (governors and satraps) loyal to them, yet who supported their own indigenous cultures.

Thus the language in First Zechariah partakes of the idea of royalty but omits the power imagery that would normally accompany the notion of political autonomy or a sovereign state.

Having a governor such as Zerubbabel who was of the Davidic line surely kept monarchist feelings alive for a time in Yehud, although they seem to have been focused on a future time. When Zerubbabel's tenure as governor ended about the end of the sixth century, there appears to have been one last gasp of Davidic leadership. This was the joint leadership of Elnathan, governor, and Shelomith, his ʾāmâ, presumably Zerubbabel's daughter (1 Chron 3:19; E. M. Meyers 1985). Chart 2, summarizing this data, appears in the Introduction, p. 19.

Precisely how long Shelomith and Elnathan ruled together is not certain, since the chronology depends on Avigad's paleographic analysis of the bullae (1976; cf. the discussion in Meyers and Meyers 1987: 11–16). Nor are the circumstances surrounding the transfer of power from governor to governor at all clear. Furthermore, the question of what happened to the Davidic family and its quest for leadership cannot be resolved, despite the many theories that there was a struggle for leadership (see COMMENT to chapter 12 below). The succession in the high priesthood was also quite complex. Judging from the attacks on the Temple cult in Malachi and in Isaiah 56–66, corruption of priestly high office came fairly soon after the disassociation of the royal family from the governorship. In any event, the nonmilitary tone of the present passage about a future king may be a reflection of the political realities that impacted on the "end" of prophecy, as well as the desire of the compiler of Second Zechariah to bring his eschatalogical prophecies into closer alignment with the restoration era of First Zechariah.

Even in light of the preceding discussion, it is still worth noting that this passage partakes of a more general Near Eastern typology, whereby the accession of a new ruler is viewed as the inaugural event in a new era characterized by peace and well-being (Ollenburger 1987: 143). This new period is often depicted as having been secured through the military might of the ascendent king, whose victory in battle has succeeded in subduing opposition and in securing political and social stability. A case in point is Ashurbanipal's declaration of the worldwide peace following his installation as king:

> At the proclamation of my honored name, the four regions of the world were glad and rejoiced. . . . The hurled weapons of the enemy sank to the ground. The well-organized enemy broke their battle line. Their sharp lances came to a stop, they brought their drawn bows to rest. . . . In city and in homes, a man took nothing from his neighbor by force. . . . No deed of violence was committed. The lands were quiet. The four regions of the world were in perfect order, like the finest oil (Luckenbill 1927: n. 987, cited in Ollenburger 1987: 143–44).

The image of the accession of the royal figure here, and the ensuing peace, is limited to the concept of the cessation of war following the destruction of Israel's enemies. The language of the next verse, about the termination of horse-and-chariot combat and bow-and-arrow weaponry (see NOTES below; cf. NOTE to "set . . . as a bow" in v 13), completes the imagery of the end of violent confrontation that accompanies a new king and of the associated peace. And the language of the preceding verse, in involving personified Zion as celebrant to the heralded event of kingship restored, builds on the role of Zion in Yahweh's defeat of chaos. Psalm 76 provides another example of this imagery. There, Yahweh establishes his abode "in Zion" (v 2), having broken "the flashing arrows, the shield, the sword, and the weapons of war" (v 3), while also stunning the "horse and rider" (v 6).

righteous. This is the first of four attributes that the future ruler will bear. In addition to being "righteous" (*ṣaddîq*), he will be "saved," "humble," and "riding on an ass." Other translations prefer to understand *ṣaddîq* in a more military sense: e.g., *NEB*, "his cause won;" *NRSV* and P. D. Hanson (1975: 294), "triumphant;" *NJPS*, "victorious." Mitchell (1912: 273), however, translates "just," which is in accord with the exegetical view adopted here. Because this passage is so central to the entire Book of Zechariah and in many ways the centerpiece of its future vision, our interpretation is not only important for understanding Second Zechariah but also for comprehending the process by which separate blocks of literary material were transmitted and incorporated into the canonical book. We have already rejected (see various NOTES to vv 1–8) the idea of a divine-warrior context for the present form of chapter 9, although certain verses suggest such a setting in an earlier stage in the redaction history of this chapter.

BDB lists "victorious" as the first meaning of *ṣaddîq*, giving 2 Sam 23:3 and Jer 23:5 along with this verse as examples of such a nuance. Mason (1973: 46) cites Isa 41:2, where the word *ṣedeq* is used in reference to Cyrus, as a major justification for such an interpretation; he also gives as parallels the occurrences in Isa 45:8 and 51:5, where the root *ṣdq* appears together with the root *yšʿ* as it does here (see next NOTE). Normally, however, *ṣaddîq* simply means "just" or "correct," i.e., "righteous." Thus it seems difficult to yield priority to the military nuance, given its semantic field. Two parallels that are more appropriate are Jer 23:5 and 33:15. Jeremiah 23:5 reads: "Behold the days are coming— utterance of Yahweh—when I will raise up for David a righteous shoot (*ṣemaḥ ṣaddîq*), and he shall reign as a king and deal wisely, and shall execute justice and righteousness in the land." The term in Jer 33:15 for "righteous shoot" is *ṣemaḥ ṣĕdaqâ*. Two passages in First Zechariah (3:8 and 6:12) inform our understanding of the Jeremiah passages, because they use "shoot" (*ṣemaḥ*). Both of these First Zechariah passages have royalist associations but do not mention Zerubbabel (who is explicitly named in 4:6). For a full discussion of the meaning of *ṣemaḥ*, see our previous discussion (Meyers and Meyers 1987: 202). In brief, however, *ṣemaḥ* in First Zechariah connotes dynastic legitimacy, and the combination of this meaning with the agricultural origin of the word is common in the prophetic literature (C. L. Meyers 1976: 151–53).

The metaphoric use of the term *ṣemaḥ* to present dynastic legitimacy is also documented in an early third-century B.C.E. Phoenician inscription from Lapethos in Cyprus, where it occurs with the term *ṣdq*, the two words together meaning "legitimate heir" (Donner and Röllig 1968: n. 43, 1.11). Originally discussed in 1893, the text is sixteen lines long and is incised into a partially carved door molding. The relevant line follows the mention of a King Ptolemy, without year designation, and the act of bringing dedicatory sacrifices to the altar of Melkart: ". . . for my life and the life of my offspring forever, and the legitimate heir or seed (*ṣmḥ ṣdq*) and his wife and his blood." This inscription is widely cited in support of the interpretation of Jer 23:5 and 33:15, where the "Shoot" is understood to be the Davidic scion. Similarly, a fifth-century B.C.E. Phoenician inscription from Sidon (Donner and Röllig 1968: n. 16) conveys the legitimacy of the dynastic heir, *Bōd ʿaštart*, *Ytnmlk*, by the expression *bn ṣdq*. The term *ṣdq* alone, meaning "legitimate heir," also occurs at Ugarit but is more relevant to the Jeremianic passages cited than to this one. For a review of the literature on the subject, see Petitjean (1969: 199–202).

In view of these parallels, the term *ṣaddîq* as it is applied in a royal context represents the king as not only the ideal king (e.g., Isa 11:4) but as the legitimate, correct, dynastic, "rightful" heir as well. The term "righteous" in English speaks more to the character of the scion than of his legitimacy, but in any case, those two aspects are intended to be conveyed here. In Zech 3:8 *ṣemaḥ* is linked to the royalist term *ʿebed*, as also in Hag 2:23. In Zech 6:12 the role of the "Shoot" is tied to dynastic continuity in the pun on *ṣemaḥ/yiṣmaḥ* and Temple building. The future Davidide is relegated to the eschatological future both here and in First Zechariah; yet the present reality recedes here in a way that it does not in First Zechariah. Still, this prophecy accords well with the earlier ones in First Zechariah; and the fact that they mesh so well may be evidence of redactional or editorial skill, or of the author's intentional utilization of themes and language of his immediate predecessor.

saved. Our rendering differs from the standard English ones, which favor "victorious" (NRSV; cf. P. D. Hanson 1975), "his victory gained" (NEB), or "triumphant" (NJPS). These translations probably derive from the battle context of the surrounding material. Yet "saved" is close to "having salvation," which the great twelfth-century Hebraist and grammarian David Kimhi proposed in his commentary on the prophecies of Zechariah (1837: 87). The Hebrew form as pointed in the MT is *wĕnôšāʿ*, which is a Niphal participle from *yšʿ* meaning "to be saved" or "delivered." Because Kimhi's suggestion is based on understanding the MT *nôšaʿ* as a perfect, i.e., *nôšaʿ*, repointing with *pathach* under the *šin*, the nuance of "having salvation" is not compelling.

The ancient versions also had difficulty in understanding this word. The Greek reads "savior" (*sōzōn*), which might better be derived from the Hiphil participle *mōšîaʿ*, appearing together with *ṣaddîq* in Isa 45:21, which may have influenced the Versions. The Latin similarly translates as *salvator*, and the

Targum and Syriac have the active noun forms *pārēq* ("redeemer") and *prwqʾ* ("savior"), respectively *(BHS)*. Medieval Jewish scholars have, in fact, accused Christians of tampering with the text of the versions. Kimhi, who flourished and wrote his commentary on Zechariah 9 in 1190 C.E., during the time of the Third Crusade, pointed out that Jews made such accusations because they believed that Christians changed the text to provide additional proof of their Christian faith (Kimhi 1837: 98). Yet all of the ancient versions except the Latin are Jewish, and they uniformly support an understanding of the noun as active, which in Hebrew is probably the Hiphil. Thus medieval Jews were simply in error when they supposed *sōzōn* to be a Christian interpolation. Moreover, given the mood of the times, at least some Hellenistic Jews would have been more comfortable with an active designation for the messiah. The Aramaic Targumim, which may reflect the reality that the Septuagint and Vulgate were the most prevalent translations of the text in the early church, would have found the idea of an active redeemer figure quite congenial.

Two other biblical texts, Deut 33:29 and Ps 33:16, contain the Niphal of *yšʿ* and so can assist in determining more precisely what the Niphal participle means. In the Deuteronomy passage, the people are "saved" by Yahweh's power: "Happy are you, O Israel! Who is like you, a people *saved* by Yahweh . . . the shield of your help, and the sword of your triumph!" [italics added]. Psalm 33:16 is even more illuminating, because *melek* ("king") occurs together with *nôšāʿ*: "A *king* is not *saved* by his great army; a warrior is not delivered by his great strength" [italics added] *(NRSV)*. The king does not bring about a victory—victory is God's doing, as in the Deuteronomic text, where the people are "saved" *(nôšāʿ)* because Yahweh is their "help" (or "shield") and "sword." Note also that this root, albeit not in the Niphal, describes God's rescue of the House of Joseph in Zech 10:6. In short, the king will be restored only because God will have intervened, rescuing him from his captivity or enemies, and allowing him to return to the capital Jerusalem (Zion) from whence his eschatological rule will be worldwide. Yahweh is victorious over the enemies, with the result that the king is "saved," thereby enabled to assume power (cf. NOTE above to "your king").

The first image of this bicolon, "righteous" (see NOTE above in this verse) presents the royal legitimacy of the king and also implies that his character is suitable for the high position he will hold. The second term, "saved," emphasizes that the king's status is dependent upon divine action. Without Yahweh's power, the reestablishment of monarchic rule in Israel could not be accomplished. The next two images ("humble" and "riding on an ass"; see following NOTES) delineate the status and royal position of the king.

humble. Although the sense of "lowly" or "humble" is not widely attested for the root ʿnh, it does occur with this sense six other times in the Bible, twice in Psalms in the first person (25:16; 86:1), and four times as an attribute of the "people" *(ʿam)* of Israel (2 Sam 22:28 = Ps 18:28 [NRSV 18:27]; Isa 66:2; Zeph 3:12). It occurs frequently with *ʾebyôn* ("poor," as in Jer 22:16; Ezek 16:49; 18:12), and in Zech 7:10 it is found with *gēr* and conveys the idea of low economic status. That sense is surely a reflection of the tremendous disruptions in Judean life in the late preexilic period, for the category of "poor" lies at the very heart of prophetic concern and Deuteronomic emphasis. The related meaning of "humble" or "lowly" finds support in northwest Semitic epigraphy in the eighth-century B.C.E. ZKR inscription, where the term is attested with such a meaning (Rudolph 1976: 180; ANET: 501–2) and in the versions.

In addition, the closely related or equivalent term ʿānāw, which also means "humble," appears in a variety of other passages (Prov 3:34; 16:19 with the Qere and frequently on the Psalter). The most relevant passage of all, however, is Num 12:3, where it is applied to Moses himself, who is described as the most humble person on the earth. The sense of this term seems to derive from the ancient Near Eastern virtue of humility, attributed to good leaders and rulers. Although kings hardly exhibited humility toward their subjects or enemies, they were expected to be pious and humble to their god, upon whom they depended for victory in battle. This king's ability to ascend the throne and claim dominion over his (and other) people is the direct result of his having been "saved" (see previous NOTE) by Yahweh, and so he must surely act humble and subservient to God.

Many commentators see in the term ʿānî an attribute of the suffering servant, namely, "affliction," as in Isa 14:32, 51:21, 54:11, and especially 53:4, "Yet we accounted him stricken, struck down by God, and afflicted (mĕʿūneh)" (NRSV). Although NEB and NRSV have adopted the translation "humble" at Zech 9:9, Mason in his commentaries (1977: 89 and 1973: 51–52) supports the idea of wrongful affliction. The "humble" character of the royal figure before his god, however, is what is indicated here. Furthermore, it may help to modify, as does "riding on an ass" below, the normal imagery of royalty. "Saved" indicates the dependence of the future king on Yahweh in a political sense—the king would not be empowered to rule without divine help; so too will the king not benefit socially or economically by his position.

This idea of the future king apart from the trappings of privilege normally associated with monarchic rule is quite comprehensible when viewed from the perspective of how situations of dominance are sustained and accepted by those being dominated. The existence of the kingship model as the program for Israel's future, as drawn from the historical fact of the Davidic monarchy, involves a structure whereby one part of society—the king and his bureaucracy—exists at the summit of that society and dominates the rest of the members of society. This inherently inegalitarian arrangement is established through the violence of the dominating party and/or the consent of the dominated groups (Godelier 1980: 609). The latter is probably the more powerful of the two components of domination, and the agreement of the ruled to submit to such a position is better sustained by ideological (religious) conviction, i.e., consent and thus cooperation, than by violent oppression. Indeed, religious beliefs are ideal in creating the sense of legitimacy necessary to establish and maintain a system of dominance.

One way to ensure the dominated population's integration into the ideological structure that maintains a relationship of dominance and privilege over a serving citizenry, in archaic societies, as is the case in a monarchic polity, is to have the people identify with the elite or ruling class. This can be accomplished in various ritual and symbolic ways. A classic example is for an ascendant ruler to dress poorly and live abstemiously for a time, while establishing acceptance by and thus control over the occupants of his territory. One ethnographic account of such a process relates how "the new chief . . . appears alone, humbly, before the oldest occupants of the country, to ask them to accept his authority and accord him the legitimacy that only the land can confer. He offers or promises them presents." Thus a ritual drama is enacted, whereby the new ruler is "humiliated" and subsequently acknowledged as rightful king (Izard 1975: 234).

The idea of humility, therefore, along with the other attributes mentioned in this passage (notably "saved"; see previous NOTE), and also the presence of mundane animals emphasized in the succeeding phrases (see next three NOTES), can be seen as functioning to mitigate the inequitable relationship that characterizes a monarchic system. The ruler takes on, symbolically at the outset of his reign, the qualities of those who must consent to his rule, thereby blurring the marked distinctions between ruler and ruled. That the future ruler is portrayed in this way thus may constitute a compensating factor in the otherwise negative aspects of the monarchic model for the eschatological future. Domination, which should belong only to God, nonetheless exists for God's appointed one, who is one of the people but yet must exhibit godlike attributes of dominance and power if he is to establish justice and peace.

riding on an ass. The image of a royal figure mounted on an ass rather than on a horse derives from a rather well-established Near Eastern practice of royalty in procession on a mule (Feigin 1944; Sasson 1976: 72–73). The description here is perhaps a reapplication of the text of Gen 49:10ff., where in Jacob's blessing of Judah the dynastic promise is related to an action involving donkeys (Fishbane 1980: 355 and 1985: 501–2). Fishbane suggests that the postexilic setting of Zechariah 9 is propitious for reworking an older text that foresees a future that has not been realized since the Exile. An ancient blessing is reworked into this striking oracle, giving authority to what it envisions. The New Testament (Matt 21:5 and John 12:15) is quite comfortable with the imagery of this passage; in adhering to its peaceful tone, it remains faithful to the original intent of Zechariah.

What does the "ass" imagery represent, in light of the frequent emphasis on kings in relation to horses and chariots in the Bible, especially in First Zechariah (1:8; 6:2, 3, 6; cf. Hag 2:22)? Horses and chariots represent the military, or power, aspects of political domination. "Riding on an ass" is a royal image that does not partake of that dimension of dynastic authority. Elliger (1975: 149), in pointing to numerous ancient rituals for kings on mules, may be correct in emphasizing that the present setting, by signaling a postvictory scene, is intended to repudiate warfare of any kind. By substituting nonmilitary animals for horses, the prophet is reversing the power imagery associated with a king's rule. In the eschatological future, the restoration of the Davidic monarchy will radically alter the notion of kingship—the future king will not exert exploitative domination or foster socioeconomic elitism (cf. the way "humble" functions: see previous NOTE). Indeed, the beginning of verse 10 (wĕhikrattî), "I will cut off," makes it clear that the future king will not need to depend on force in the eschatological future (see below, NOTE to "chariot . . . horse"). It is difficult to determine whether this altered perspective of the royal figure can be related to the political realities in Yehud in the time of Second Zechariah, by which time any realistic expectation of full political power being restored to Yehud would have dissipated. The presence in First Zechariah of God's spirit, rather than political force, as the theme for the future may have been based on political pragmatism. Such may also be the case here, with the Near Eastern ideology of stability and world order accompanying a new ruler involved to further strengthen the eschatological imagery of a restored Davidide (see above, NOTE to "your king" in this verse). In any case, it would be overburdening the text to see it as a reflection of conflicting royal ideologies (as P. D. Hanson 1973: 43–44 and Mason 1976: 237).

The word ḥămôr, "ass," indicating the king's mount, is the first of three animal terms used in this passage. Its commonplace usage in the Bible signifies a beast of burden (e.g., Gen 42:26; 44:13; 45:23; 1 Sam 16:20; 2 Sam 16:1; etc.). However, cognate terms at Ugarit and Mari were used for animals that a deity rides or that draw a chariot in a ritual festival. In contrast to the horse, the mule was evidently a symbol of peace (In der Smitten 1980: 466, 469). Although a lowly beast (Gen 49:14ff.), it also could signify royalty. The story of Saul retrieving asses may be an allusion to his future office, and the succession story of Solomon has him on a mule rather than a horse (although the word there is pered rather than ḥămôr [1 Kgs 1:33, 38]). The range of images attached to ḥămôr is striking, and they all may contribute to the message of this passage— that the king represents peace, that his humble beast is suitable for his role in submitting to divine power while exerting his own royal dominion, and that he is a legitimate monarch. The use of a lowly animal is one of the ways in which a royal figure partakes of the life-style of the people he dominates. In this way he bridges the structural gap between those in power and those subjugated and thereby helps to win the cooperation of people dominated by a royal elite (see NOTE to "humble" in this verse).

young ass. That is, a young, male, and vigorous ass (ʿayir), rather than a "colt" (young horse), as it is sometimes translated (e.g., NRSV). Although it is used seven other times in the Bible, the occurrence in Gen 49:11 is the only one that involves a context related to its usage in Zech 9:9, for the Genesis passage deals with Judah's royal destiny. Hence the use of ʿayir in both places is hardly coincidental; and it is interesting that both Matthew and John adopt the Septuagint's use of pōlon in the Zechariah passage, which is also the Greek at Gen 49:11. The New Testament writers, in being faithful to a common translation of "young ass," have correctly preserved part of the ancient Near Eastern tradition of a sacred ass associated with a royal procession. They have chosen to use the term pōlon because of the Septuagint's translation of Gen

49:11, which also explains their inconsistencies in translating *ḥămôr* (see Mitchell 1912: 276). Justin Martyr seems to be the first ancient author to link this passage (Zech 9:9 and its New Testament quotations, Matt 21:5 and John 12:15) with Gen 49:11 (*Dialogue with Trypho* 53).

The contrast between "young ass" and "horse" is as great as between "ass" (see previous NOTE) and "horse" in denoting a nonmilitary animal. The force of the *waw* on the second *ᶜal* before "young ass" is probably that of *waw copulativum* (GKC §154a), i.e., the equivalent of "namely." The king is obviously not riding on two asses, but rather on a particular kind of ass, and the second term for "ass"—"young ass"—is introduced to emphasize the precise character of the beast. Two unusual and technical terms are therefore used in parallel to make an important point.

The combination of "young ass" together with "a foal of a she-ass" (see following NOTE) occurs at Mari in connection with making a covenant while slaughtering an ass (In der Smitten 1980: 468). In that context the combination may signify a purebred ass in contrast to the mixed offspring of a female horse and a male ass. In any case, this animal, like the others mentioned here, is a nonelite beast and as such fosters the image of the royal figure as one of the people. Despite his actual position of domination, he is portrayed as being no different in some, though not all, ways from those he dominates (see above, NOTE to "humble").

a foal of a she-ass. Lit., "a son of she-asses," *ben-ᵓătōnôt.* Because of the parallelism between "ass" and "colt," either would come from a "she-ass," a beast of burden, as is *ḥămôr* (on the lowly aspect of these animals, see above in this verse, NOTE to "humble"). Most attestations of this term occur in Numbers 22, however, where the "she-ass" is none other than Balaam's talking mule (v 30). Of the total thirty-four occurrences of the term "she-ass" in the Hebrew Bible, however, only two mention that such a beast could be ridden. The first is Num 22:22, where Balaam "rides upon a she-ass with two youths alongside." The other is the Song of Deborah (Judg 5:10), where "those who ride on white she-asses" are addressed. This third variety of donkey thus has some special associations, which make it suited to the royal context here. The use of the plural is a bit troublesome for translators and commentators; the singular is used only in the Balaam story. The plural "she-asses" perhaps better conveys the notion of a lowly beast of burden that underlies all three words associated with the royal mount. These three animal terms together represent the condition of royalty minus military power that characterizes the portrayal of the monarchic figure of Zech 9:9–10.

10. *I will cut off.* The Hebrew (*hikrattî*) repeats exactly the first word of verse 6b, where the root *krt* is used in a more expanded sense to indicate destruction (see NOTE to "I will destroy," 9:6). Here, and below in this verse, the basic meaning, "cut off," fits the military context. The use of "cut off" specifically with horses and chariots echoes the language of Mic 5:9 (NRSV 5:10), except that in Micah "horses" precedes "chariots." Indeed, the verb *hikrattî* appears four times in Micah (5:9–12; NRSV 5:10–13) to indicate God's

violent destruction of military installations and forces, as well as the objects of idolatry. In Second Zechariah, Yahweh is destroying instruments of war—horse, chariot, and bow; the king of the previous verse will thus be able to rule in peace. This imagery of divine destruction of military arsenals and of subsequent stability is part of biblical Zion traditions and of Near Eastern motifs surrounding the ideology of kingship, especially at the time of the accession of a new monarch to the throne (see above, NOTES to "O Daughter Zion" and "your king" in v 9).

Yahweh is the speaker here, as has been the case since verse 6b above, and continues as speaker through verse 13. The preceding verse, however, does not have Yahweh speaking in the first person; and the resumption in verse 10 of the first person with "cut off" has apparently been of concern to the versions. Both the Greek and Syriac read "he will cut off." Such a change is unnecessary, although many commentators accept it, inasmuch as the context allows for Yahweh to be the speaker; and it is unwarranted in that it would remove the notion of divine agency in eliminating instruments of war. If Ephraim and Jerusalem (Judah) are to be militarily activated, as they are below in 9:13, it is Yahweh who is responsible. Similarly, the military rescue of Ephraim and Jerusalem, by virtue of God's destruction of the invading armies, is Yahweh's doing and thus is the divinely ordained precursor of the king's proclamation of peace.

chariot . . . horse. Neither of these nouns is preceded in Hebrew by the definite article *(heh)*, nor is the next one ("bow"). The omission of the article is surely an aspect of the poetic character of Zechariah 9 (see, in the Introduction, our discussion of the poetic structure of this chapter). That these nouns are all in the singular is also somewhat unusual but can similarly be attributed to the use of poetic language. A single chariot or horse would be meaningless as an instrument of war; rather, the chariot and horse here must stand collectively for all the chariots and horses that constitute a military assault on Yahweh's people.

Because the verb "cut off" does double duty in these two poetic lines, the objects of the verb, as well as the geographic locales that follow, are brought together to form a unity. Yahweh will terminate the use of chariotry (composed of "horses" and "chariots"), which represents the political sovereignty of Ephraim and Jerusalem (see following NOTE).

In Near Eastern antiquity, beginning in the second millennium, chariot warfare was the key to military dominance and, hence, political sovereignty. The prominence of the chariot in the tribute lists of Assyrian and Egyptian kings attests to its critical role in warfare. The very emergence of nation-states with imperial holdings in the ancient world was possible in part because of the development of horse-drawn chariots as a striking force (Wevers 1962: 553; Yadin 1963: 74, 86–90, 297–99).

The military aspect of horse-and-chariot warfare, as the key to political domination, figures prominently in biblical language relating both to foreign rulers and to Israelites. Indeed, the very resistance of Samuel to the establishment of a monarchic government is expressed by the warning that, first and foremost, a king will draft Israelites for his chariot forces (1 Sam 8:11). Such forces represent the absolute control of a political entity that can exercise dominion through the effective use of military power. It is no wonder, then, that the image of chariots is used as a metaphor for Yahweh's sovereignty (as Isa 66:15 and Hab 3:8, where the word for "chariot" is *merkebâ*). Horses and chariots (*markĕbôt*) represent divine omnipotence in the final vision of First Zechariah (Zech 6:1–8; see Meyers and Meyers 1987: 317–19). Furthermore, they appear in prophetic visions of the future—either as the enemy force that will be overthrown (as *merkābâ* in Hag 2:22; see Meyers and Meyers 1987: 67, 82–84) or as the transport of kings who will enter Jerusalem and the Davidic palace riding in chariots and on horses (Jer 17:25; 22:4).

Against this backdrop of biblical and Near Eastern function and imagery, the appearance of "horse" and "chariot" in this focal unit of Zechariah 9 plays a distinct role. The use of these military terms echoes the words of both Haggai and First Zechariah, and in that sense sustains the connections of Second Zechariah to the Haggai–Zechariah 1–8 corpus. However, Zech 9:10 uses a somewhat different word for "chariot"—*rekeb*—and in this way constitutes a departure from the terminology of Haggai and First Zechariah. Perhaps in shifting to *rekeb* the prophet is echoing the language of Jer 17:25 and 22:4, which also use *rekeb* and which apparently have affected the imagery of the previous verse, where the restored Davidide enters Jerusalem "riding" on an animal (see various NOTES above to 9:9). In any case, the divine violence involved in eliminating the chariot armies and weaponries is presented as leading to universal peace, when the restored king, although he may possess arsenals and fighting forces, will not have to use them (see NOTE to "your king" in v 9).

Just as the king is "humble," yet still a royal figure, so too will he rule without activating the military aspects of political power that had long signified the ability of any monarch to achieve and sustain sovereignty. The eschatological vision here proclaims "peace to the nations" without the notion of accompanying conquest or power; the military violence on the part of Yahweh will precede peace. The new king will accede to the throne, and perfect political stability will become a reality.

Ephraim . . . Jerusalem. Just as "chariot" and "horse" are paired in these two lines of Zech 9:10 as objects of a single verb ("cut off") that does double duty, so Ephraim and Jerusalem are linked to form a whole, an entity that equals all Israel.

Ephraim, the largest of the northern tribes, occupied the central position in the northern hill country and became the most powerful of the tribal groups that constituted the Northern Kingdom. Consequently, the name "Ephraim" became virtually synonymous with "Israel" as the name of the Northern Kingdom. This is particularly true in the eighth-century prophecies of Isaiah of Jerusalem (e.g., Isa 7:2, 8, 9, 17) and of Hosea (as Hos 5:3, 11–14, etc.), although the equation of Ephraim with the North also occurs in later biblical texts (e.g., Jer 7:15; 2 Chron 25:7, 10). "Ephraim" as a term for the Northern Kingdom may derive from the historical parameters of the Northern Kingdom after the Galilean and Transjordanian tribes were torn away by Tiglath-Pileser; that is, in the eighth century and later the Kingdom of Israel was little more than the size of the tribe of Ephraim. For this reason, beginning with eighth-century prophets, this term becomes a common designation for the Northern Kingdom. Similarly, Jerusalem alone, because of the way it dominated Judah, stands for the Southern Kingdom (Noth 1966: 138); the capital represents the entire realm, frequently in Isaiah, Jeremiah, and elsewhere. In First Zechariah, "Jerusalem" with the additional phrase "and the cities of Judah," represents the postexilic province of Yehud.

The combination of Ephraim and Jerusalem, which stand for the Kingdoms of Israel and Judah, thus represents all Israel. This perspective is similar to that of the first eight verses of Second Zechariah (9:1–8), where the complex set of geographical references involves a conception of the ideal boundaries of the united kingdom.

bow of war. This phrase continues the military imagery of "horse . . . chariot." Here it refers to part of the weaponry of the restored kingdom, weaponry that is cut off in this vision, for the royal sovereignty that is being established is one of peace rather than war. The word "bow" appears alone in the next section of Zechariah 9, where Judah (rather than Jerusalem, as in this verse) and Ephraim are again mentioned, this time as instruments of Yahweh's military power (see first NOTE to 9:13). In addition, the phrase "bow of war" appears in the military language of Zech 10:4.

It should be noted that along with the "lance," the "bow" is the instrument of war mentioned in Ashurbanipal's accession account. It functions there as part of the language pointing to the utter cessation of violence and military strife when the powerful new ruler ascends the throne (cf. NOTE to "your king" in v 9) and an era of worldwide peace is to be expected.

promise. This word literally means "speak," but when followed by *l* ("to") it often has the meaning of promising to a person or group that the thing which is promised will surely come to pass. In Genesis, for example, Abraham recalls that Yahweh "spoke to" him and swore that his descendants would posses the land of Canaan (Gen 24:7). In other words, that of which God speaks will in fact become a reality; whatever is spoken will assuredly occur. If the king here speaks of peace, there can be no question that peace will be established. After victory in battle, the winner dictates terms of peace to those who have been overcome by Yahweh's intervention. The word for promise or speak *(dbr)* can have juridical overtones, thus underscoring the king's mandate in imposing his peaceful sovereignty. Moreover, the proclamation of the king's rule, in Near Eastern typology, implies the establishment of world order: *dbr* as "proclaim" is linked with stability.

The use of *dbr*, meaning to "speak" or "promise," is followed in the next line by a description of the king's rule. This combination of terms is reminiscent of the Davidic psalm near the end of 2 Samuel, where David, at the end of his life, recalls what Yahweh has said/promised to him regarding his own sovereignty over Israel.

peace. The word *šālôm* has many nuances, a number of which are appropriate to this passage. Given the fact that the three preceding clauses all deal with the removal of instruments of military power, the notion of "peace" as cessation from war is certainly a primary meaning of this usage.

The establishment of peace is also part of biblical royal imagery, as found in Isa 9:5–6 (*NRSV* 9:6–7), where the rule of the one who will sit on the Davidic throne is one of peace, where this future ruler is called the "prince *(śar)* of peace," and where his eternal authority is predicated upon the end of military violence as expressed by the destruction of the boots and clothing of soldiers. Similarly, Mic 5:4 (*NRSV* 5:5) anticipates a Davidic ruler who will be known "to the ends of the earth," just as will the restored king here in the last line of this verse, and who will be the "one of peace." Here, as in First Isaiah and Micah, peace is established by the final defeat of all the nations that come against Yahweh's people. After a great last future battle, the enormous power of Yahweh as delegated to his anointed one constitutes the backdrop for the king's ability to dictate terms of peace and thereby establish a stable world order.

The language of peace is thus part of the universal language of prophetic eschatology. "Peace" at the end of First Zechariah (8:19) is coupled with truth; these two qualities, having been established in Judah, mean that the other nations of the world will then acknowledge Yahweh's sovereignty. It should also be noted that "peace" in association with "righteousness," which appears in the preceding verse (see NOTE to "righteous" in 9:9), is a combination often linked with the city of Jerusalem (Porteous 1961: 239ff.). As the city of righteousness and peace, Jerusalem with the king restored will assume its eschatological role. This language of peace and universality need not be construed as arising from a specific historical period (as it is by Eisenbeis 1969: 215–21); rather, it can be seen as part of the ongoing development of the eschatological idea. Similar ideas are found together in Psalm 72, a royal psalm attributed to Solomon, which uses quite archaic language and contains the same universal language as does the end of this verse (see NOTE to "sea . . . sea" below).

This is the only usage of *šālôm* in Second Zechariah, whereas it is found six times in the Haggai–First Zechariah corpus. Four of those occurrences come in Zechariah 8 (vv 10, 12, 16, 19), the last one involving the universalistic theme mentioned above.

nations. The identity of "nations" *(gôyîm)* seems clear: all the other political entities in the world. The universalistic theme is inclusive, in that the Davidide in Jerusalem will be acknowledged by lands beyond Israel. Much the same notion is expressed by the "many nations" and "mighty nations" of Zech 2:15 (*NRSV* 2:11) and 8:22. In all these places, the word for "nations" has a more political than cultural dimension, although the latter is not altogether absent in Zech 8:23. The meaning in Second Zechariah, however, seems to be entirely political, considering the use of "rule" in the next line. Yet although the language is derived from the political world, the image transcends political reality and looks toward a future time in which the experiences and events that characterize political history give way to the universal events of Yahweh's sovereignty, which emanates, in this case, from Jerusalem and the restored royal figure presented in 9:9.

rule. The root *mšl,* "to rule, have dominion," occurs frequently in the Hebrew Bible. Appearing in more than eighty places, its specific nuances are often difficult to sort out, especially as they may be distinct from the closely related *mlk,* "to rule, reign." Nonetheless, an interesting pattern in the occurrence of the verb can be discerned. Of all the times it refers to the reign of Davidic kings, the verb *mšl* is used only in regard to David, Solomon, and Hezekiah. These are precisely the monarchs whose realms went beyond the borders of Judah and/or Israel. David subdued neighboring lands by military conquest, and Solomon continued Israelite imperial domination over these territories. Several centuries later, Hezekiah briefly held sway over Philistine territory. Otherwise, monarchic rule in Judah is never expressed by this verb, even though several kings other than these three had managed to acquire territory outside Judah and Israel. Perhaps David, Solomon, and Hezekiah were the only ones to have succeeded in imposing an international political and economic structure on the acquired territories, thereby justifying the use of *mšl.* The verb thus has only limited use for Judean or Israelite monarchs. In contrast, God's rule over all kingdoms of the world is often expressed by *mšl* (e.g., Isa 40:10; Ps 22:29 [NRSV 22:28]; 59:14 [NRSV 59:13]; 1 Chron 29:12; etc.). In addition, this verb also signifies the imperial domination of other nations over Israel— notably, in relation to this verse, the Philistines (Judg 14:4 and 15:11), but also the Egyptians (Ps 105:20), Babylon (Isa 14:5 and Jer 51:46), and the nations (Ps 106:41).

Used in this way, *mšl* indicates the rule or dominion of one group over one or more other distinct groups—that is, over a group of which the ruler is not intrinsically a part. Thus *mšl* is particularly suited to express the idea of imperial dominion or international rule, whereby an emperor rules *(mlk)* over his own group or territory and exerts dominion *(mšl)* over territory and/or peoples not his own. The notion of Yahweh's universal reign is an apt extension of such a concept as it is found in political, rather than sapiential, contexts in the Bible, for it has a more figurative dimension in wisdom literature. It is not surprising, therefore, to find *mšl* in eschatological prophecy that envisions the rule of a royal figure who will represent on earth the universal sovereignty of Yahweh. Such is the case in the Crowning passage of First Zechariah, where the "shoot," who builds Yahweh's temple in Jerusalem, will occupy the throne and "rule" (6:13). The extent of this rule is what sets the shoot apart from the associated, enthroned priest. In this case, in Second Zechariah, the worldwide domain of the king in Jerusalem is explicitly set forth in this last bicolon of 9:10.

In introducing the ensuing delineation of the "nations," the universal extent of the king's rule, the verb *mšl* represents the one difference between these two poetic lines and two otherwise identical lines in Psalm 72, where verse 8 reads "May he rule from sea to sea, /and from the River to the ends of the earth." In the Psalm passage, "rule" translates *yērd* (from *rdh,* "to rule"), a word choice that may have been dictated by a desire to recall the first word of verse 6, *yērēd* (see Dahood 1968: 182).

sea to sea. This phrase occurs several times in Hebrew poetry, notably in Amos 8:12 and in Ps 72:8 (as mentioned in the previous NOTE). Micah 7:12 has a very similar phrase, in which "sea" appears twice but with a different preposition as the connector. The notion of great expanse between two seas also appears in Zech 14:8 and Joel 2:20, which mention the "eastern sea" on the one hand and the "western sea" on the other, although in both these passages, despite the eschatological setting, the territory indicated is probably a limited one (see NOTE to "eastern sea . . . western sea," 14:8). In Amos, and perhaps also in Zechariah 14 and Joel, the twofold use of "sea" seems to have specific directional meanings. The Amos passage involves four compass directions, two of which are specified as north and east, leaving one "sea" to represent west, undoubtedly thus referring to the Mediterranean, as *yām* ("sea") often does, and the other "sea" to represent south. The identity of a southern sea is less clear, but it could refer either to the Dead Sea or to the Gulf of Eilat/Aqaba (Andersen and Freedman 1989: 825). Yet even with the seas representing compass directions and not specific bodies of water, the fact that they are part of a set of four compass directions means that all four together represent the whole earth, as fits the context in Amos, where 8:11a mentions all the earth.

That global directions are implied even when specific seas are the reference points surely indicates that "sea to sea" lends a dimension of universality in Zech 9:10 that is quite consonant with its eschatological perspective. Furthermore, the oppositional structure "sea to sea" partakes of cosmic imagery, as it does more overtly in Zech 14:8, where Yahweh's worldwide rule is related to the flow of cosmic waters from Jerusalem. Indeed, the appearance of "sea" in 9:10 in parallel with "river" in the last line of this verse adds to the sense of the global extent of the king's rule. The pair *yām/nāhār*, sea/river, reflects a combination in Northwest Semitic in which *ym* and *nhr* are synonyms rather than meaning two different or specific bodies of water (see UT 68: 19–20 and Dahood 1968: 120–21, in reference to Ps 66:6). In sum, the "sea to sea" combination, intensified by the imagery of the next line ("river to the ends of the earth"), constitutes language that conveys the universality of the king's domain. The directional imagery functions as a kind of merism: all points and thus everything in between.

river. No definite article precedes *nāhār*, "river," no doubt because of the poetic context, as is the case for "chariot" and "horse" at the beginning of this verse. "River" is often rendered with a capital *R* in English translations, probably to indicate an identification of the river with a specific river, in this case the Euphrates. However, given that "sea to sea" (see previous NOTE) above probably does not represent specific bodies of water and that *yām* and *nāhār* seem to be a poetic pair, "river" here should be seen as part of the vocabulary representing the global extent of the king's rule. The fact that "river" in Near Eastern mythology refers to the primordial river from which the four rivers of paradise flow, comparable to the freshwater ocean of Sumero–Akkadian myth, supports the understanding of "river" here as a term designating global rule.

ends of the earth. This poetic phrase represents the extreme limits of the earth. The noun *ʾepes*, "end, extremity," is coupled with "earth" more than a dozen times in Hebrew poetry (e.g., Deut 33:17; 1 Sam 2:10; Jer 16:19; Isa 45:22). The Jeremiah example is particularly interesting in that it involves the ends of the earth as the house of "nations" that turn to Yahweh and forsake their own traditional gods. The universality of Yahweh's rule, through a Davidic sovereign at Jerusalem, is suggested by "ends of the earth." The last words of this verse, and this second section of Zechariah 9, thus portray once more the universal aspect of the future hope.

11. *As for you.* Literally "and also you," this phrase echoes the use of *gam*, "also," in verse 2 above. "You" here is feminine singular, thus anticipating and emphasizing the feminine singular suffix of "covenant" in this line and also of "prisoners" in the next line. However, the identity of the "you" is not specified, even though this verse seems to begin a new subunit of Zechariah 9 and to have been composed independently of the preceding two sections. Even if that be the case, verses 11–14 are meant to be taken with verses 1–8 and 9–10, as they represent another important group, the exiles, in the overall message of Zechariah 9. Hence, the feminine-singular pronoun would appear to pick up on the last-mentioned female character in these oracles, specified as both Daughter Zion and Daughter Jerusalem in 9:9. The prophet is thus addressing Zion/Jerusalem, which represents all Israel in the sense that the covenant involved in this line is the agreement between Yahweh and all the people. Yet, although the prophet is speaking to Zion/Jerusalem, he is beginning an oracle that concerns a specific group of Yahweh's people—those who have been removed from their homeland. Thus, if "Zion/Jerusalem" is the referent of "you," its role as a place name is as relevant here as is its value in signifying the people of the covenant with Yahweh. The function of "Zion/Jerusalem" as the antecedent of "as for you" also serves to connect this third subunit with the previous one.

The use of the feminine singular, particularly if it indeed is meant to refer to the "Daughter" of verse 9a and b, is particularly suggestive of helplessness and dependency, with respect to the status of prisoners, especially in contrast to the masculine and military imagery below in verse 13, which speaks of Zion's sons. Although women at various stages in life possessed considerable social power, the status of unmarried daughters was probably the one of least independence for women. Hence, daughter imagery suits the context of an oracle dealing with exiles, who, of course, lack independence. Furthermore, the idea that "you" refers to Daughter Zion would make this passage reminiscent of the language of Ezekiel 16, which concerns God's relationship with the people of Jerusalem, Samaria, and Sodom—depicted as mother and daughters—and which contains the only other place in the Hebrew Bible, besides this line, in which "covenant" appears with the feminine singular suffix.

A point of additional interest in this address, presumably to Daughter Zion, is the difficult word at the beginning of the next verse. The prisoners are called upon to return to a "stronghold" (*biṣṣārôn*, a word that occurs nowhere else in the Hebrew Bible). For a discussion of that term, see the NOTE below; meanwhile, note that some exegetes (as *BHS:* 1074) suggest emending it to *bat-ṣîyyôn*, "Daughter Zion."

by the blood of your covenant. This unusual phrase is introduced by the preposition *b*, which acts as *b-instrument*, showing the means by which something is done (GKC §119.o and p). Yahweh's action in the next line—the freeing of captives—is in this way linked to the existence of a covenant that mandates such action.

The association of "blood" with "covenant" occurs elsewhere only in Exod 24:3–8, which describes the covenant ceremony that took place at Sinai. The making of the covenant between Yahweh and the people was accompanied by a ceremony, which, along with swearing an oath, was important in the ancient Near East for validating the terms of a covenantal agreement. The covenant ceremonies in the ancient world were of various kinds, with the offering of a sacrifice as a common aspect (see Ps 50:5). Indeed, the cutting of animals in association with covenant making, as in Genesis 15, Jeremiah 34, and in various ancient Semitic texts, may have served to make the parties aware of the fate that would befall the violator of the agreement; but this cutting also should be considered a sacrificial ritual (Weinfeld 1975: 262–63).

The covenant sacrifice of Exodus 24 involved the setting up of pillars to represent the twelve Israelite tribes, which in itself constituted a symbolic act to remind the covenanting group of its obligations (cf. Josh 24:26ff.). Moses then arranged for animals to be sacrificed by the young men. Finally, as a prelude to reading aloud the covenant document (*sēper habbĕrît*), Moses is said to have divided in half the blood of the sacrificial offerings: he put half in basins, and the other half he threw against the altar. After the reading of the document and its acceptance by the people, Moses took the blood—presumably the half from the basin, threw it upon the people, and declared it to be the "blood of the covenant" (*dam-habbĕrît*). As a result of the redactional process, this covenant ceremony comes immediately after the Decalogue and the Covenant Law of Exodus 20–23. Consequently, the "blood of the covenant" becomes associated with the stipulations in those chapters (Kedar-Kopfstein 1978: 249), which end with God's promise to establish the Israelites in their land. This aspect of the Sinai covenant is particularly relevant to Second Zechariah's use of covenant language to emphasize the inevitability of God's restoring all the people to the land. Jewish tradition and some scholars would relate "blood of the covenant" to circumcision, because of the association of "blood" with circumcision in Exod 4:26. However, the lack of the word "covenant" in that passage on the one hand, and the contextual suitability of the Sinai covenant as the relevant reference on the other hand, make that suggested association implausible. The allusion to the Sinai ceremony is likewise supported by the language of verse 15 below, which refers to the sacrificial altar and a basin.

The actual form of the phrase "blood of the covenant" is slightly different in Zech 9:11 than in Exod 24:8, which reads, "Behold the blood of the covenant

139

that Yahweh has cut with you. . . ." The Zechariah passage, which is a shortened form of the Exodus one, has a suffix ("your") attached to "covenant." This feminine-singular ending, anticipated by "you" (fem. sing.; see preceding NOTE), emphasizes (Daughter) Zion as the one to be affected by God's covenant allegiance. Insofar as all covenants must involve two parties, and because God is the speaker here, there is no need to render it "blood of my covenant with you" (as NRSV and others); "your covenant" implies that it is also God's covenant. Note a similar construction in Ezek 16:61, a passage cited in the preceding NOTE because of its similarity in invoking the image of Israel (Jerusalem) as daughter and in which God refers to "your (fem. sing.) covenant." See also the next verse in Ezekiel (16:62), which reads, "I will establish my covenant with you. . . ."

set . . . free. The common Hebrew root *šlḥ*, "to send," in the Piel means "to send out, away" and so can refer specifically to the sending out of someone from captivity. Animals, for example, are "set free" or "let loose" so that they can return to their natural habitat (e.g., Gen 8:7, 8; Lev 14:7, 53). Most prominent among such uses of *šlḥ* are the many passages in Exodus (5:1, 2, etc.) in which Moses calls upon the pharaoh to let his people go, i.e., to set them free or send them out from their bondage in Egypt. The verb appears here in the perfect tense, thereby indicating that the act of liberation has truly begun.

your prisoners. The possessive suffix, as for "covenant" in the preceding line (see NOTE above), is feminine singular, as is also the pronoun "you" at the beginning of this verse. As explained in the NOTE to "As for you," the referent for the "you" and "your" is Zion/Jerusalem, which stands for all Israel, including those of her number who are not present in the ancestral land and thus are in need of being allowed to return.

The noun *ʾāsîr*, "prisoner," from the root *ʾsr*, "to bind, tie, imprison," is used mainly in poetic contexts: as in Isa 14:17, in reference to the prisoners held by the king of Babylon; in Job 3:18 in a group of references to people who suffer or are not free; in Lam 3:34 in reference to those imprisoned following the conquest of Zion; and several times in Psalms (68:7 [NRSV 68:6]; 79:11; 102:21 [NRSV 102:20]; 107:10), all in reference to God's mercy for those who suffer greatly, namely, prisoners. Otherwise, the term occurs only in the Joseph story, or Gen 39:20 and 22, where the verbal form also is found several times.

The occurrence of "prisoners" twice in this subunit of Zechariah 9 (in this verse and in the next), along with another phrase—"pit with no water in it" (see following two NOTES)—involves language referring to the condition of exile. The use of prison imagery throughout the Bible has probably been conditioned by the Israelite experience of exile as a kind of political imprisonment (D. L. Smith 1989: 171–74). Prisons as a means of formal punishment were not part of the judicial system of ancient Israel nor probably of Near Eastern jurisprudence, although people could be held in custody until their cases were adjudicated (as Num 15:34; 1 Kgs 22:27). Thus the language of imprisonment conveys the idea of confinement, or lack of freedom—more often than not at the hands of a foreign political power—rather than punishment. Under these circumstances, prisoners tend to be people who are innocent and therefore suffering unjustly as they wait to be restored to their homes or for their fates to be otherwise decided.

This nonpunitive nature of imprisonment thus lent to the image of internment a particular suitability to the experience of exile, in which large numbers of Judeans were held against their will. Although they were not bound physically and had, in fact, some freedom to move about within their new places of residence, their existence as a people within the Babylonian system was that of a landless group and, as such, social outsiders at the lowest levels of the hierarchical structure of Babylonian society. Indeed, although the exiles were not technically slaves in Mesopotamia, many of the psychological and social conditions of exile must be seen as constituting the same kind of traumatic situation as that effected by the enslavement of persons. This conception of the harsh state of exile (examined in D. L. Smith 1989) gives new understanding to the biblical imagery of imprisonment, in passages such as Zech 9:11–12 and in some of the "diaspora hero" stories—of which the Joseph story is exemplary—that arose as part of the folklore of hope. This folklore was one of the several coping mechanisms that emerged among the exiled Judeans and helped them to maintain their identity, their attachment to their homeland, and their ability to look toward a better future despite the alienation—the imprisonment—of exile.

pit. The noun *bôr* usually means "cistern" or "well." People could also be cast into such an installation to be held prisoner (as Jer 37:16; 38:6). As an extension of its usage to denote a water installation, i.e., an enclosed, watertight space, it is found with "house" (*bêt habôr,* Exod 12:29 and Jer 37:16) to indicate a dungeon or prison. Just as water cannot escape from a cistern or well, unless someone comes to draw it up, so a person or persons can be confined in a space until someone from the outside releases them. A further extension of that meaning involves the use of the word for the ultimate enclosure, the tomb or grave (as Isa 14:19) or even Sheol (as Ps 30:4 [NRSV 30:3]; cf. Lam 3:55).

In this particular case, the prison imagery seems clear, especially because the word "prisoners" appears in this verse and the next. Zechariah 9:11 uses "pit" in reference to the catastrophe of exile in much the same way that the author of Lamentations, in 3:53 and 55, compares the helplessness and pain of the destruction to that of being thrown into a pit. Furthermore, the next phrase, whether original to the text or not (see next NOTE), in its present form connects the image of "pit" as prison to the stories of the imprisonments of Joseph and Jeremiah.

with no water in it. Some would translate the Hebrew phrase, which consists of three words, by the single English word "waterless" (NRSV) or even "dry" (NJPS). There is nothing intrinsically wrong with such renderings, except that they give no indication of the way the Hebrew presents a negative attribute, to wit, by 'yn ("it is not") followed by a noun ("water") and, in this case, by a preposition with suffix ("in it"). More important than the way the negative is expressed here is the question of whether this entire phrase is a gloss, as has long been supposed (as by Mitchell 1912: 282; P. D. Hanson 1975: 298; Mason 1977: 92). The additional words might better be explained as an attempt to draw a connection between this passage and the Joseph and Jeremiah stories (Gen 37:24; Jer 38:6), the two other places where "with no water in it" occurs. Indeed, there is no versional support for this being a later addition. Furthermore, the quality of "having no water in it" may be considered an essential part of the imagery. A pit that does contain water implies death for anyone who is cast into it, whereas a pit without water is unmistakenly akin to a prison, from which hope for removal is possible. This possibility fits precisely the general theme of deliverance of Zech 9:11–17 as well as the specific mention of hope in the next verse (see NOTE to "hope," 9:12).

12. Return. Some manuscripts have a form of the verb yšb ("to dwell, inhabit") rather than of šwb, "to return." Although the Greek and Syriac both may have been influenced by such a tradition, the context certainly favors the MT, which has the verb in the imperative commanding the prisoners to return, that is, the exiles to go back to their ancestral homes.

to a stronghold. Because the word for "stronghold" is a hapax legomenon, many exegetes have been reluctant to accept it in its existing form. The suggestions for emendation include treating it as a gloss and excising it entirely, moving it to the next line, or changing the word itself (to either ṣiyyôn, "Zion"; bat-ṣiyyôn, "Daughter Zion"; or ṣārâ, "trouble"). However, the idea of the exiles returning to their homeland to occupy a "fortress" or "stronghold," a term that would characterize Jerusalem and Yehud in the mid-fifth century when the Persian government erected a whole string of fortresses in its western provinces to guard against Greek expansion (Hoglund 1989), fits the historical context and provides a link with the military language of the next three verses of Zechariah 9. The ostensible reason for the erection of these fortresses in Yehud was so that the Persians could exercise greater control over the local populations, which may have grown weary of their lack of autonomy and eager for self-rule. Yehud (with Jerusalem) was indeed a "stronghold" by the mid-fifth century B.C.E., and hence there may be a measure of irony in the use of this word.

The term for "stronghold," biṣṣārôn, may be rare in biblical Hebrew, but its choice is appropriate to its setting in this passage. Its root is bṣr, meaning "to cut off, enclose," and a related noun from that root means "sheepfold" (Mic 2:12). If the word for "stronghold" conjures up the image of an enclosure for sheep, then it suits the prophet's fondness, in verse 16 below and again in chapters 10 and 11, for such imagery. Furthermore, it is a word that, in providing a similarity in sound to "Daughter Zion" and "Zion," helps to connect this verse with verse 9 above and verse 13 following. Finally, it may suggest a play on the word "Tyre" (ṣûr in Hebrew), which figures prominently in the first subunit of Zechariah 9.

All of these possibilities of wordplay thus make it compelling to retain the existing text. One might wonder why the related term mibṣār, "fortification," would not have been suitable. But that word would not have provided the same sound connection. In addition, mibṣār may, at a technical level, indicate walled cities (as Num 32:17, 36; Josh 10:20) or city walls (Num 13:19), military architecture that differs from the kind of forts that were part of the Persian line of defense against Greece.

Retaining "to a stronghold" in its MT form need not be seen as disruptive to the metric form, as long as the full text of the next line is retained (see NOTE below to "today too I announce"). Then, verse 12 would consist of two rather short but reasonably balanced bicola, or four cola:

	syllables	*accents*
šubw lbṣrwn	6	2
ʾsyry htqwh	6	2
gm hyywm	3	1
mgyd mšnh ʾšyb lk	7	4

Verse 12, in fact, is part of a larger unit, verses 11–13, inasmuch as verse 14 shifts abruptly from the first person, for Yahweh, to the third person. The dominant form in verses 11–13 is the use of the second-person feminine singular, "as for you" *(gm-ʾt)* in verse 11 being the key to all of the subsequent second-person suffixes, effectively strengthening them: 11a *(bnyk)*, 11b *(ʾsyryk)*, 12d *(1k)*, 13d *(bnyk)*, and 13e *(wśmtyk)*. Structurally, verse 11a and verse 13e form an envelope because of their common emphasis on the second person, each matching the other with seven syllables.

prisoners. See NOTE to "your prisoners" above, 9:11.

hope. The connection of this word with "prisoners," which, with "pit," is part of the imagery of exile (see NOTES to "your prisoners" and "pit," v 11), contributes to the message that the exiles will be restored. The ability of an exiled group to sustain its identity amidst the adverse conditions of separation from homeland and minority status in a foreign country, depended on the emergence of various survival mechanisms. Such mechanisms included adaptation in social structure and mode of leadership. They also involved the strengthening of socioreligious forms (e.g., ritual) and the emergence of a folklore that emphasized hope for deliverance. This latter aspect of survival during exile gave rise to the "diaspora novella" (D. L. Smith 1989: 153ff.) with its use of prison as a symbol of exile. The result of such literary developments, as well as sociopolitical and cultural adaptations, allowed the exiles to maintain their identity, a major component of which was the tie to the ancestral homeland, and thus to foster the hope for return. "Hope" here thus conveys more than a vague belief that the future will somehow be better; it involves the specific form of release from confinement or prison: it implies return to Zion. Just as Jeremiah (29:11; 31:17) linked the future hope with the return of the exiles to their land, so Second Zechariah's use of the imagery of prison and of hope evokes the expectation of restoration.

The word for "hope" in Hebrew has a *heh*, which is a vocative particle rather than the definite article. The poetic nature of this chapter means that the use of such prose particles as "the" is minimal. However, it is possible that the Masoretes thought it was the definite article.

today too I announce. These words are taken as secondary by many critics because of metric imbalance or because they seem to be an explanatory aside. If "to a stronghold" is retained, however, as we have suggested it should be, the problem of balance is less acute. The "too" *(gam)* echoes the *gam* in "As for you" in the preceding verse, where *gam* both links this part of Zechariah 9 to the first subunit (v 2) and emphasizes the "you" (Zion) that God is addressing. Here the "too" signals an addition to the expected, hoped-for restoration as well as being part of the linkage created by the repetition of this particle. The participle "announce" parallels the verbal form in the last bicolon, "I'm restoring." The pronoun "I" must be supplied with "announce," whereas it is included with "restoring" as well as with the previous verb that has Yahweh as the subject, "set . . . free" in verse 11, where the imminence of divine action is expressed by the use of the perfect (see NOTE to "set . . . free," 9:11). A slight shift to the future is implied by the use of the imperfect in "restoring." Thus "announce," in the middle of this sequence of three verbal forms in verses 11–12 involving Yahweh's action, focuses on the present moment with the use of *hayyôm*, "today." This series can be summed up as follows:

> I have set   perfect   = immediate past (i.e., imminent)
> [I] announce   participle = present: "today"
> I'm restoring   imperfect = immediate future

Seen in this way, "today too" is not extraneous but rather part of a verbal sequence and a component of the linkage of the subunits of this chapter. Similarly, the verb "announce" (the root *ngd* in the Hiphil, meaning "to declare, announce, proclaim") can be seen as an integral part of the divine message. The idea of God's announcing or proclaiming divine intention or requirement is not unusual; e.g., Yahweh tells Pharaoh what will happen (see Gen 41:25) and tells David (through the prophet Nathan in 2 Sam 7:11) that he will found a dynasty.

restoring to you double. The use of *šwb* in the Hiphil, followed by the preposition "to" and a noun or pronoun, means to "give back, bring back, restore, recompense." All of these nuances of meaning are possible in the context of this verse. That it refers to the exiles, who are to return to their land, is indicated by the use of "return" at the beginning of this verse (see NOTE above), where the prisoners are told to return to the "stronghold," i.e., Jerusalem and/or Yehud. Thus the idea of restoration is prominent. At the same time, the addition of "double" *(mšnh)* adds the dimension of recompense. Those in exile in the Persian period are not those who had originally been sent into exile. The sins of earlier generations may have caused the destruction and dispersal of Yahweh's people. But subsequent generations of exiled Judeans do not share in the responsibility for bringing about the punitive aspects of the Babylonian conquest. As "prisoners," they are innocent, since the imagery of imprisonment does not have a punitive dimension (see NOTE to "your prisoners" in the previous verse). Their restoration to Zion should thus involve some recompense for the undeserved suffering involved in the condition of exile. Surely the thoughts of the prophet here are akin to those of Third Isaiah, in chapter 61, who likewise proclaims liberty for prisoners (v 1) and the establishment of a double portion for those whose suffering was double (*mšnh*, v 7).

13. *bent . . . to me*. The imagery of the "bow of war" (see NOTE to 9:10) is resumed through use of language that reflects a technical knowledge of the bow and arrow. The use of *drk* meaning "to bend (the bow)" is relatively rare (cf. Jer 51:3; Ps 7:13 [NRSV 7:12]; 11:2; 37:14; Lam 2:4; 3:12; 1 Chron 5:18; 8:40; Isa 5:28; 21:15; etc.)—the root normally means "to tread," "march," or "walk upon." The use of a root meaning "to tread" for readying a bow is comprehensible in light of the way a bow is prepared for shooting. It involves two actions. First the bow is strung, a movement that requires the archer to step (i.e., "tread") down on one end of it so he can bend it sufficiently to attach the cord that is connected to both ends of the bow. Then the bow is set; that is, the arrow is laid across the cord so that it is ready to be aimed and released. The bending (or treading) plus setting (see NOTE below to "set . . . as a bow") together constitute the whole activity required to prepare a bow for shooting. Thus Ephraim and Judah together also constitute the "bow", i.e., the divine weaponry about to be released as God prepares for battle.

In most instances the "bow of war" is directed against Israelites who did not repent (Ps 7:13 [NRSV 7:12]) or whose sins were deserving such punishment (Lam 2:4). The usage in verse 13 indicates the opposite situation: the bow is represented by Judah and Ephraim, who together (see next NOTE) represent the entire nation, and is used against the enemies of Israel.

The bow in 9:10 is part of the arsenal of human weaponry. Here, however, it is associated with God's military activity, that is, divine power expressed metaphorically via images of war. The bow and/or arrow symbolized various deities in the ancient world, and Yahweh's might vis à vis enemies is similarly portrayed in the Bible (see below, NOTE to "his arrow will go forth," 9:14). Still, the use of this weaponry is associated with God's people; God will not be fighting this final battle alone but through the weaponry of Judah/Ephraim.

Judah . . . Ephraim. The pairing of these two tribes is meant to convey all Israel, just as in verse 10 (see above, NOTE to "Ephraim . . . Jerusalem"), where Ephraim and Jerusalem are combined to stand for the entire nation, and in 10:6 (see below, NOTES to "House of Judah" and "House of Joseph"), where Judah and Joseph are paired to indicate all Israel. The use of "Judah" rather than "Jerusalem" as in 9:10, and the reversal of the order, seem to bear no significance other than a poetic variation of phrasing in expressing the all-embracing nature of God's plan for Israel. Yet the use of "Judah" rather than "Jerusalem" may be related to the apostrophe to "Zion" (= Jerusalem) in the next line of this verse.

set . . . as a bow. The use of *ml* ("to fill, fulfill") with "bow" (*qešet*) is unusual and appears to be technical; it is discussed as such at the end of this

NOTE. Our translation adheres closely to the Hebrew, as does *NJPS*, although other translators have a tendency to add words that are not in the Hebrew: "For I have bent Judah as my bow; I have made Ephraim its arrow" (NRSV; NEB; P. D. Hanson 1975; etc.). The poetic structure certainly allows *qešet* ("bow") to do double duty and serve both bicola of the line. Such a claim is supported by the fact that *qešet*, which occurs above in 9:10 and below in 10:4 as "bow of war" (see NOTES to this phrase at 9:10 and 10:4), never means "arrow," although it can be used for the whole shooting apparatus and thus might include "arrow." Such is the case in 2 Kgs 9:24, where *mlʾ* is used with *qešet*: "And Jehu filled his hand with the bow *(wyhwʾ mlʾ ydw bqšt)* and he smote Jehoram between his shoulders, and the arrow went out from his heart." Clearly Jehu's actions in filling his hand with the bow, i.e., setting the bow, involve pulling back the cord with the arrow in place, inasmuch as the result is that the fleeing King Jehoram is struck with such force in the back ("between the shoulders") that the arrow pierces his heart. In short, "bow" here is surely a *pars pro toto* for bow-and-arrow; the imagery of setting, or nocking, a bow unquestionably involves the use of an arrow.

The fact that "arrow" appears in the next verse (14) may have caused some confusion. Perhaps the similarity in content with Isa 49:2, where the servant of Yahweh is referred to as a "polished arrow" *(ḥēṣ)*, has also influenced this tendency to read "arrow" into this bicolon. Indeed, Mason turns to that verse and other servant passages to explain the broadening purview of the oracle: "We seem to have here, then, something of a similar reinterpretation of Second Isaiah to that found in Trito-Isaiah, an interpretation and application of his teaching which is fully in line with the thought of proto-Zechariah" (Mason 1973: 77). The similarities between Zechariah 9 and the servant passages of Second Isaiah are rather vague and are not closely tied to verbal congruencies. Hence, although we agree with Mason about some possible thematic influence, the intent of this verse seems quite different.

To return to our statement above that the Hebrew *milleʾ qešet* ("fill the bow") is technical, we find corroborating evidence in Akkadian literature. The text from the Annals of Ashurbanipal cited above in the NOTE to "your king" (v 9) contains the phrase "drawn bows" (Akk. *qašātēšunu malâti*). It also appears in the *Assyrian Dream Book*: "if (a man in his dream) nocks [*qaštu umalli*, i.e., fits an arrow on the string of . . .] a bow" (329. ii. 12; Oppenheim 1956: 286, n. 132), among other Assyrian texts. Thus Akkadian *qašta mullû* surely is "the interdialectical etymological and cognate equivalent of the Hebrew *hapax legmenon*, *milleʾ qešet*" (Paul 1989). Filling the bow means to "nock" it, to fit the arrow into the already "bent" (see first NOTE to this verse) bow. This explanation about the technical language of preparing to shoot a bow contributes to our assessment that *qešet* does double duty—that it is the central, pivotal word in a skillfully constructed poetic line. This feature of Hebrew poetics—pivotal polysemy or Janus parallelism—has only recently been recognized in biblical scholarship (Paul 1992).

The fact that one of the Akkadian parallels to this Hebrew idea occurs in the text from the Annals of Ashurbanipal that inform our discussion of "king" in verse 9 contributes to our understanding of this chapter of Zechariah as drawing upon Near Eastern accession ideology. The idea of stability in the eschatological future uses the language depicting the peace and quiet that will ensue with all weaponry being laid aside, when a new ruler is enthroned. Here, in the third subunit of chapter 9, the details of the divine exercise of military might that will accompany (or precede?) the return of a king to Jerusalem uses the "drawn bow" terminology of a royal accession text.

rouse . . . against. This Polel verb from ʿwr ʿal means "to arouse" or "to incite to activity against" (cf. Zech 13:7 where the Qal is used with ʿal).

your sons, O Zion. "Zion" here stands for all Israel: for Ephraim and Jerusalem (v 10; cf. NOTES), who will both be rid of invading foes. "Sons" appears also in the next line with "Greece" (see NOTE below) to denote the enemy. The double use of "sons" in this verse functions in some interesting ways. For one thing, it may echo the double use of "Daughter" in verse 9, thus connecting the language of the second and third subunits of this chapter. "Daughter" in verse 9 is used there with "Zion" and with "Jerusalem" (see NOTES), both terms referring to Israel, whereas here "sons" is linked with Israel and the enemy, as befitting the more overtly military context, with Yahweh attacking the foe.

In addition, there is a play on words between "sons" *(bānîm)*, used twice here, and "stones" *(ʾăbānîm)*, used twice below ("sling stones" of v 15 and "gemstones of a crown" of v 16; see NOTES). Not only do these two words sound alike (surprisingly, in English as well as in Hebrew), but they may also have some other features in common. That is, stones and children are mentioned together elsewhere in the Bible—in Isaiah 54, which lists various stones *(ʾăbānîm)* in verses 11–12 and then mentions children *(bānîm)* twice in verse 13. In this connection, the New Testament has a similar linkage of sons and stones: "God is able from these stones to raise up children to Abraham" (Matt 3:9 = Luke 3:8). Such wordplays between sons and stones suggest that both usages of "stones" in Zechariah 9 have figurative overtones representing people, as we explain in our NOTES in both instances.

your sons, O Greece. Many commentators would like to delete this phrase, which is the object of the preposition "against" *(ʿal)*, because it appears to intrude on the metric structure of this line (P. D. Hanson 1975: 298; Mitchell 1912: 285) and so must be an error stemming from dittography. Although opposing the deletion of this phrase on metric grounds, Rudolph (1976: 184) emends it to *hnyky ywn*, i.e., "warriors of Greece," basing it on Gen 14:14 and a double haplography. Perhaps he does so in part because of the unique pairing of direct address to Greece and Zion (discussed at the end of this NOTE). Neither the deletion nor emendation is convincing, however. Removal of the phrase, although creating closer parallelism, eliminates the central object of Yahweh's anger, Greece, which appears in nearly all the major textual traditions. Most exegetes have, in fact, argued for a Maccabean or Hellenistic date for the redaction precisely because of this reference to the Greeks and the putative mention above to the siege of Tyre by the Greeks (see NOTE to "Tyre . . ." at Zech 9:3). Others have interpreted the appearance of "Greece" as a gloss meant to apply an existing prophecy to a later circumstance (Ackroyd 1962: 652). At the same time, it could be a gloss on Gen 10:4 or other passages where the term *ywn* occurs (Ezek 27:13, 19; Dan 8:21; 10:20; 11:2).

The fact of the matter is that "sons of Greece" is quite appropriate to the mid-fifth century B.C.E., when the Greeks and the Persians were locked in a historic struggle for control of the eastern Mediterranean and the Syro-Palestinian land mass (cf. the discussion in the Introduction, pp. 18–22). This crisis came to a head between 460 and 450 B.C.E., when the Egyptian satrapal revolt encouraged the Athenian navy to insert itself more directly into the region in order to gain direct control over places that had been so strategically important to the Persians until then (Hoglund 1989: 303–4; E. M. Meyers forthcoming). The struggle between Persia and Greece is memorialized in Aeschylus's play *The Persians*, which celebrates Greece's ultimate victory over Persia in the Aegean world.

The degree to which, or indeed whether, Israel viewed Greece's involvement in regional affairs negatively is not at all clear from the sources. What is clear is that as a result of these tensions, Persia began to tighten its control over its holdings in the region, and especially in Yehud (E. M. Meyers 1987). Hoglund's study (1989) of this period has demonstrated convincingly that Nehemiah's activities in Jerusalem came directly in response to such tensions. We have already commented in the NOTE to "stronghold" (v 12) that Persia's construction of forts at this time was also connected to the escalation of tension in the region. The text of Zech 9:13, if it dates to the fifth century as proposed above, suggests that Greece might have been perceived as a threat to both Persia and Yehud. In light of the longstanding Persian policy of allowing indigenous peoples to govern their own affairs (Meyers and Meyers 1987: xxxvii–xl), albeit within a restricted environment, Persia by midcentury might have been considered the lesser of two evils (cf. the depiction of Judah and Jerusalem held captive by the Greeks in Joel 4:6 [NRSV 3:6]). At the same time, the increased Persian military presence in Palestine in the mid-fifth century could hardly have been conducive to Yehudite hopes of national autonomy.

The involvement of the great powers of the day in portentous events such as the Egyptian satrapal revolt (460–50 B.C.E.), the involvement of the Athenian navy in the related unrest in Cyprus and Phoenicia, and Persian efforts in establishing a series of fortifications along the main roadways of Palestine, as is also contended by Hoglund (1989), undoubtedly created a feeling of great insecurity in Yehud. World events surely left their impression on the literary world of the fifth-century prophets, and the choice of the expression "sons of Greece" seems certainly to be an authentic echo of those times. Despite the eschatological context here, *yāwān* ("Greece") reflects an immediate reality and need not be understood as alluding to "distant, unknown peoples on the edge of civilization" (Baldwin 1972: 169). Our English translation has smoothed out the metrical problems; by splitting the object of the verb and the object of the preposition that goes with the verb into two bicola, we have sought to retain its poetic integrity. There is no semantic problem with a verb's taking both a direct object, namely, *bny ṣywn*, "sons of Zion," and an object of a preposition, namely, *bny ywn*, "sons of Greece." Such constructions are attested in poetry (Isa 10:26; 14:9) and in those instances do not disturb the parallel structure or meter.

Although the text as it stands has no blatant metrical or grammatical problems, it does contain the anomaly of using direct address to two different peoples at the same time. This unusual sequence involves Yahweh first addressing Zion, then addressing Greece, and finally going back to the first group in midsentence; surely it is Zion, not Greece, that is made a warrior's sword in verse 13e. This irregularity may stretch the constraints of prose usage, but as part of its poetic originality, it surely heightens the dramatic effect of this verse. In addition, it allows for the double usage of "son," thus contributing to the wordplay with "stones" (*ʾbny qlʿ/nzr*, "sling stones" and "stones of the crown"), which also appears twice (see previous NOTE).

warrior's sword. This simile is also drawn from a stock of military images and is appropriately applied to all Israel, i.e., Judah and Ephraim (see second NOTE to v 13). Similar language appears in the next chapter: "bow of war" (10:4); "heroes [= warriors] in battle" (10:5); "Ephraim will be like a hero [= warrior]" (10:7). In chapter 10 the notion of all Israel is indicated by the phrases "House of Judah" and "House of Joseph" (v 6; see NOTES). P. D. Hanson suggests that chapter 10 is an acknowledgement of Yahweh's providing fertility after a battle against the forces of chaos (= unfaithful leaders) and that the divine-warrior language has been adapted to other purposes (1975: 325). Although we are not convinced by this interpretation, we agree that the continuity in the imagery between these two chapters is unmistakable. See also the use of "sword" in Zech 11:17 and 13:7.

14. *Yahweh will appear above them.* This expression has close affinities with First Zechariah in that it draws on the language of theophany to convey the idea of God's presence, as is also the case in 9:8 ("I will encamp at my House;" see NOTES above). Although the Niphal of *rʾh* is common in the Bible, its usage with *ʿal* is not. The closest parallel is Isa 60:2, which states that God's glory "will appear over you." Moreover, the image of God's glory appearing to the people of Israel in the wilderness "in a cloud," in Num 14:14, uses the Niphal plus the preposition *b*, "in." By using a theophany image in the first bicolon of this line and linking it with the military images of the second, the previous verses are brought into close alignment with the final ones of this chapter.

It should be noted that with "Yahweh" here as subject of the verb, there is a sharp shift from first and second person to the use of third person for God. Similarly, the apostrophe (second person) of the previous verse gives way here to third person for "them." Presumably the prophet/poet is now speaking in his own voice.

his arrow will go forth. As indicated in the NOTES to verse 13 above, the word "arrow" was missing there, although its presence was surely implied by the use of "bow." Its inclusion here propels the divine-warrior image forward and connects verses 10–13 with verse 14 and the following verses. God's "arrow" will be a source of protection (v 15) for the people as it "goes forth like lightning." Linking Yahweh's presence with this military imagery enhances the theophanous tone of the first half of the poetic line; God's presence implies power and, hence, divine protection for the people (Levine 1968; see next two NOTES).

With "bow" (see above, 9:13, and below, 10:4) "arrow" (Heb ḥēṣ) is used metaphorically for Yahweh's power over enemies. The bow and arrow symbolized various deities in the ancient Near East (e.g., Erra, Ninurta, Nergal, ʿAnat, Reshep; so Hoffner and Botterweck 1986: 118–24); and biblical images of divine action, either on behalf of Israel (Num 24:8; Deut 32:42) or in punishment of Israel (e.g., Deut 32:23; cf. Ps 7:14 [NRSV 7:7]), repeatedly partake of such imagery. The association of God's arrows with "lightning" (see next NOTE) continues the imagery, which connotes divine theophany along with the vanquishing of enemies (see 2 Sam 22:7–16 = Ps 18:6–15). Furthermore, the idea of an "arrow" going forth "like lightning" involves the assigning of the use of human weaponry to Yahweh as well as Yahweh's use of metereological phenomena as implements of war (cf. Brettler forthcoming). These two aspects combine, the metaphoric value of each intensifying the other.

like lightning. The metaphor continues to derive from the world of myth, "the cosmic realm of the God of the storm, of Marduk rushing forth to duel Tiamat with his arrows and his storm chariot, of Baal the cloud rider marching out to vanquish Yamm" (P. D. Hanson 1975: 322; cf. Psalms 29 and 68 and previous NOTE). Chapter 9 reflects many ancient mythic elements. But such echoes of mythic or divine-warrior language, which appears in earlier biblical materials, should be viewed as part of Second Zechariah's general tendency to echo the language of authoritative literature. Second Zechariah or his redactors were not waging a propaganda war against a rival group (so P. D. Hanson 1975: 292ff.) but rather expressing a mythic-prophetic worldview that suited the times and was deeply rooted in Israel's past experience. Because Second Zechariah's era was full of changes that were to impact not only on the history of Israel but on the very fabric of world history, such cosmic language was quite appropriate. At the same time, its mythic character has been transformed in being put into the service of prophetic speech. Lightning is part of the visual component of theophanous imagery, and it is complemented by the sound images of the succeeding line (see next NOTE).

sound the horn. This is the only instance in the Bible where Yahweh sounds the horn. The horn or shophar (šôpār) was an important instrument in the musical repertoire of ancient Israel. Indeed, it is mentioned in the Bible more often than any other instrument. It belongs to the category of aerophones, instruments in which sound is produced by blowing air through them (Sendrey 1969: 262). The shophar, like the other "horns" in the Bible—designated by the words qeren and yôbēl—was made from the horn of an animal, usually a ram. It thus differed from the trumpet (ḥăṣōṣĕrâ), which was made of metal, silver, or bronze (see, e.g., Num 10:2–10), and was used chiefly in cultic contexts. The shophar was used for signaling, sometimes for occasions of celebration (as in 1 Kgs 1:34 and 2 Kgs 9:13) or for festal events (e.g., Ps 81:3 [*NRSV* 81:4]; Joel 2:15), but mostly as a call to arms. The military aspects of the shophar thus figure prominently in this passage, in which the sound of the horn is part of the language portraying divine might. Yahweh as warrior defeats the enemies of Israel (see two previous NOTES). As in the parallel bicolon, where "storms" appears, the horn imagery calls upon the sense of sound to depict God's activity, thus complementing the first two lines of the verse, where visual imagery conveys divine movement on behalf of the people.

Lord Yahweh. "Lord Yahweh" (*ʾadōnāy yhwh*), not "Yahweh" alone, sounds the trumpet. Although the two epithets for God seemingly intrude into the metrical scheme, thereby encouraging commentators like Mitchell (1912: 284) and *BHS* to delete one of them, the presence of both adds drama to the verse. Furthermore, the double name fits well with the expanded title for God, "Yahweh of Hosts," at the beginning of the next verse. It is also noteworthy that of nearly two hundred instances of the expression "Lord Yahweh" in the Bible, the vast majority of them occur in the Book of Ezekiel, a book that has had a significant influence on both First and Second Zechariah. Thus, although the language (see other NOTES to this verse) draws from Near Eastern mythology, the creative hand(s) of the prophet(s) or his (their) disciple(s), in adapting the mythic imagery to its present context, may be noted.

The double subject in this poetic line presents a contrast to the absence of a subject in the parallel line, "advance with the southern storms." "Lord Yahweh" thus does double duty, serving as subject for both of these lines. Because the second line does not have a subject, there is room in it for the object of the verb, "storms," to be enhanced with another word, "southern," that adds to the presentation of the storm imagery.

An examination of the occurrences of the divine name in chapter 9 reveals that it appears in two sections, verses 1–7, and verses 14–16, a total of ten times. Its absence from verses 8–13 arises from the fact that Yahweh is speaking in the first person in those verses. The distribution of divine names in chapter 9 is as follows:

verse 1	*yhwh*	verse 14	*wyhwh*
	lyhwh		*wᵓdny yhwh*
verse 4	*ᵓdny*	verse 15	*yhwh* (*ṣbᵓwt*)
verse 7	*lᵓlhynw*	verse 16	*yhwh ᵓlhym*

There is considerable symmetry here. This suggests that the placement and distribution of the divine names are deliberate, because the use of a particular name and its use at all are usually authorial options. This pattern of names for God thus contributes to the notion of the poetic design and integrity of the chapter as a whole.

the southern storms. The idea of Yahweh's using a storm or tempest (*śĕʿārâ*) as a vehicle of divine action is rare but not unique in the Hebrew Bible. Most well known are the cases of Elijah (2 Kgs 2:1, 11), who ascends to heaven in a "storm"; the opening vision, of a chariot, of Ezekiel (1:4), who beholds a "storm" in the north with four living creatures in it; and God's appearance to Job out of a whirlwind, i.e., a "storm" (Job 38:1; 40:6). That God appears to his people in the south *(tēmān)* is also rare but finds expression in the term "Teman" in Hab 3:3. The usage in Habakkuk apparently derives from southern-sanctuary tradition existing in Israel (Freedman 1981) but not in Canaan. In this tradition, Yahweh's southern locale is known as Sinai (Deut 33:2; Judg 5:5; Ps 68:9), Paran (Deut 33:2; Hab 3:3), Edom (Judg 5:4; M. S. Smith 1990: 3), or Seir (Deut 33:2). The association of Yahweh with Teman is also attested at the end of the ninth century in the Kuntillet ʿAjrud inscriptions, where Yahweh is known as "Yahweh of Teman" (M. S. Smith 1990: 50 and 87). The present idiom thus draws upon Israel's own past, which in turn is indebted to Canaanite myth and language. The language here is striking in that it suggests a creative literary spirit.

We use "southern" here to translate *tēmān*, although it might literally be rendered "storms of the south," because "storms" is a construct.

15. *Yahweh of Hosts.* The full designation of the divine name, although used less frequently in Second Zechariah than elsewhere in First Zechariah, Malachi, or Haggai, is not unexpected, and "of Hosts" should not be deleted as frequently suggested (e.g., Mitchell 1912: 284; P. D. Hanson 1975: 295; and others). It occurs again in Zech 10:3 and in chapter 12 (v 5), chapter 13 (vv 2, 7), and chapter 14 (vv 16, 17, 21); see also the NOTE to "Lord Yahweh," 9:14. The full term is particularly appropriate here because of the battle scene it introduces: "Yahweh of Hosts" signifies the leader of heavenly armies.

will protect them. Although the noun *māgēn* (shield) is fairly common in the Hebrew Bible, the root *gnn* ("to surround, defend, protect") is found only eight times. Most of these occurrences express God's protection of Jerusalem against the Assyrians in the eighth century (Isa 37:35; 38:6; 2 Kgs 19:34; 20:6; cf. Isa 31:5). Elsewhere, it is found only in Second Zechariah—in this verse and in 12:8, where it also refers to the defense of Jerusalem. This verse is somewhat vague with respect to the antecedent of "them." It is probably the same "them" as in verse 14a, where it refers to Zion. But, as a masculine plural pronoun, it probably also, here and in verse 14, goes all the way back to verse 1 and the reference to "tribes (masc. pl.) of Israel." In light of the other uses of *gnn* and because of the reference above in verse 13 to "sons, O Zion" as representatives of God's military minions, we can also assume that divine protection here is being bestowed specifically upon Jerusalem, which represents all Israel.

The theophanous appearance of Yahweh (9:14; see NOTE above) is accompanied by expressions of divine power, the point of which is to secure protection for the people. This combination—divine presence, power, and protection—recurs in the Hebrew Bible as an expression of Israel's conception of Yahweh (Levine 1968).

they will consume and . . . conquer. The Hebrew text of this verse is complicated and so is often construed as being corrupt. The ancient versions reflect these difficulties and provide a variety of readings (Jansma 1950: 76ff.). The first portion of the Hebrew text, however, can be translated and understood without resorting to wholesale emendation. The meaning is clear: Yahweh's minions will be drawn into the eschatological struggle. God's involvement in the struggle against Israel's enemies may echo divine-warrior language; but, as in verse 13, it is the people who are the instruments of victory.

The common suggestion to delete "they will consume" is based on the fact that a second verb seems redundant in the poetic structure of the colon. It is also argued that *ʾkl* ("eat, consume") has been attracted or added to the original text by the influence of the verb "to drink" *(šth)* in the second half of the verse (cf. Isa 22:13 and Ezek 39:17). P. D. Hanson (1975: 298) proposes that something has been lost and restores it to "they will consume their flesh like bread." However, such a restoration would still require the addition of "like" *(k)* before "sling stones." Nonetheless, "consume" is appropriate to the context; it may be elliptical for "consume with fire," which is used in 9:4 (see NOTE) in relationship to the destruction of Tyre. At the same time, it begins a set—the first verbs in 14bc and the only verb in 14d—that portrays eating, drinking, and being full. Thus there seems to be a complicated pattern of interwoven imagery here, involving the violence and tumult of battle with the tumultuous restoring of victory. "Conquer" *(kbš)* may be understood as governing "sling stones" (see next NOTE), which represents the enemy.

with sling stones. Many translations accept the proposed emendation *ʾbny qlʿ*, i.e., "slingers," or "sons of the sling." For example, NRSV reads: "They shall devour and tread down the slingers." A similar understanding can be achieved without emendation, simply by assuming that "sling stones" is a synecdoche or metonymy for "slingers of the stones." In support of such an understanding are other instances in the Bible of tools of war standing for those who use them. For example, at the end of his lament over Saul and Jonathan, David cries out, "How the mighty have fallen, and the weapons of war have perished!" (2 Sam 1:27); clearly he is referring to the loss of two great warriors, represented by their weaponry. Furthermore, *ʾbny qlʿ* ("sling stones") is otherwise attested, in Job 41:20 (NRSV 41:28) and 2 Chron 26:14 (in the pl.), whereas "slingers" does not appear elsewhere.

Another possibility would be to supply the comparative particle *k* ("like") before *ʾbny qlʿ*. Perhaps *k* fell out by haplography with *kî ʾăbnê-nēzer* in verse 16b, where *kî* ("like") functions as a conjunction before "gemstones." The possibility that *k* is original is increased by the appearance of several phrases beginning with "like" or "as" in the next colon ("as with wine," "like the basin," "like [the ones at] the corners of the altar"). Or *k* may not even be required for "like" because of the poetic context.

The verb ("conquer") used here with *ʾbny qlʿ*, however, refers to military action and not to the activities of the celebrants. Hence supplying *k*, in keeping with what appears in 15c and d, would be making this colon more like the next one than it should be. That is, 15b describes violent action, even if "consume" does do double duty and introduce a sequence of celebrating actions in addition to describing the overthrow of the enemy (see previous NOTE). Furthermore, the term *ʾbny qlᶜ*, like *ᶜbny-nzr* in the next verse, is unusual. The fact that one echoes the other suggests that both are correct in the MT and should not be emended.

Having said all this, we suggest that the best way to resolve the question of what *ʾbny qlᶜ* means here is to point out that this colon is transitional between the action of verse 14, in which Yahweh exhibits cosmic force and weapons in advance of the battle, and verse 15c and d, in which there is tempestuous celebration by the victors. The first verb in 15b may refer to both those momentous activities, but "conquer" refers only to the military actions. Thus "sling stones" would be the last in the series of weapons mentioned in this passage: "conquer with sling stones." Although the preposition *bĕ* ("with") does not appear in this verse, it is found twice in the preceding verse. "With" can be supplied here, even without the *bĕ*, because in poetic contexts prepositions such as this are often omitted in places where ordinary prose would have them. Clearly, the poetry does not prevent the use of *be* ("above") or *kĕ* ("below"). The desire to have *ʾbny-nzr* echo *ʾbny qlᶜ*, however, may have kept the prophet/poet from supplying the preposition in this instance.

One further argument in favor of reading "sling stones" is the way this term and "gemstones of a crown" constitute a double use of "stones." Taken together they function as a wordplay on "sons," which appears twice in verse 13 (see NOTE to "your sons, O Zion"), thereby echoing the double appearance of "Daughter" in verse 9 (see NOTE to "O Daughter Zion").

Finally, we note that both "sling stones" and "gemstones of a crown" represent people as well as objects in this passage. Yahweh's arsenal of weapons is linked to Judah and Ephraim in verse 13a and b (see NOTES); and Zion is linked with the sword in 13c and e. Thus the sling stones of this verse, as part of Yahweh's weaponry, must surely also be equated with Zion (or perhaps Zion's sons, as in 13c). The image of Yahweh using sling stones against Israel's enemies is vividly presented in Josh 10:11, which recounts how "Yahweh threw down huge stones from heaven." These stones are represented by "hailstones" in Joshua 10, much as God's arrows are metaphorically linked with lightning in verse 14 (see NOTE) of this chapter.

they will drink and be rowdy. The Hebrew text is difficult, and the MT vocalization of *hāmū* has evoked a number of suggestions. Some identify *hāmû* as a third-person plural pronoun, *hēmmâ* (Hebrew) or *himmô* (Aramaic), or *šĕtîmû*, an old third-person plural ending added to *štw*. Some Greek uncials apparently read "their blood" *(to haima auton = dāmām* for *hmw)*, providing the possibility of crude holy-war imagery, "they will drink their blood like wine" *(NRSV)*. An alternative is to take *hmw* as the perfect third-person plural of the verb *hmh*, "to murmur" or "to growl," which would indicate tumultuous behavior (cf. Prov 20:1) as befits deliverance in battle. Although there is no *waw* to connect the two verbs, it could have fallen out by haplography because of the *waw* in the previous word *(wštw)*, "they will drink." Such an emendation makes sense of the Hebrew text, especially given the otherwise enigmatic "as with wine" that follows. Becoming "rowdy," as if the subjects have had too much wine, conveys the emotional state attendant upon the plenitude only divine intervention can secure. Indeed, the availability of enough wine to allow people to drink and become cheerful (or rowdy), to gladden people's hearts, was a sign of prosperity; and the presence of some wine but not sufficient to allow merriment, indicates that the full sustenance accompanying God's protective presence is not yet at hand (see Hag 1:6 and Meyers and Meyers 1987: 25–26).

full like the basin. The children of Israel will be so filled in the day of Yahweh's victory that they will be "full like the basin" of the Temple. The term for "basin" is *mizrāq* here and below in 14:20, which refers to "basins before the altar." The cultic setting of the term is clear in all attested instances except in Amos 6:6, where the well-to-do are accused of lying on "beds of ivory" (v 5) and drinking wine from "bowls" or "basins." The Amos passage, however, is similar to this one in combining drinking imagery with "basins." Elsewhere (as in Exod 27:3; 38:3; Num 4:14; 2 Kgs 12:14 [NRSV 12:13]), *mizrāq* denotes a bronze Tabernacle and Temple vessel to be used at the outer altar. It is also the term used to designate the golden basins, probably associated with the golden table in the First Temple (1 Kgs 7:50; cf. 1 Chron 28:17 and see Hurowitz forthcoming) and the large quantities of golden basins contributed to the Second Temple (Neh 7:70). In addition, a large silver basin holding a grain offering is mentioned in Num 7:13. The differences among these basins is discussed in our NOTE to "basins of the altar" in 14:20. In this text, the nature of the basin as a sacred vessel, usually for holding liquids, is the main point of its usage.

The use of the singular for "basin" is curious insofar as it is followed by the plural "the corners of the altar." Hence, many commentators have deleted "corners" and translate "they will be full like an altar bowl." Although neither the Tabernacle nor Temple texts specify what the "basins" associated with the altar were used for, the description of the tribal offerings in Numbers 7 (vv 13, 19, and ten others) indicates that some basins were used for grain offerings (of flour plus oil). If this is the allusion, then we have reference here to both wine and grain. Yahweh's presence is protective (see above, NOTE to "will protect them"); it also means that God will provide, that is, sustain the people with food and drink. The comparison of the people to sacral vessels, which presumably will be regularly filled, suggests that those about to be rescued (see next verse) will be safe and, moreover, assured of sustenance. The wine and grain allusions thus anticipate the sentiments of the last verse of this chapter, which celebrates the benefits of wine and grain.

corners of the altar. The description of the bronze Tabernacle altar (Exod 27:2; 38:2) specifies that there will be horns at its four "corners." The word for "corners" in the Tabernacle texts, however, is the plural of *pinnâ*, whereas this verse uses *zāwît*, a word found elsewhere in the Bible only in Ps 144:12, where it apparently represents the corner pillars of a building. Although the Hebrew word is not the same as that in the sacral Pentateuchal passages, it undoubtedly refers to the same feature of one of the sacrificial appurtenances, the term *zāwît* being a late equivalent, perhaps as a loan-word from Aramaic, of *pinnâ*.

The bronze altar of sacrifice involved an elaborate set of tools and vessels, including "basins." The function of the basins is not specified in the Tabernacle texts of Exodus. Elsewhere, however, priestly texts indicate that they were receptacles for blood gathered from sacrifices at the outer altar. Yet, as we have suggested in the previous NOTE, their association with the tribal offerings of Numbers 7 indicates that at least in some instances they were filled with grain offerings. Thus grain, indirectly, and wine appear together in this verse to convey the idea of the satiety that will accompany Yahweh's saving of the people and to anticipate the image of plenty in verse 17, which concludes this first section of Part One of Zechariah 9-14.

Second Zechariah, like First Zechariah, uses cultic imagery in his oracular portrayal of God's role in bringing about Israel's restoration. Zechariah 9-14 does not employ the vivid, visionary symbols of his predecessor, for whom Temple restoration was central. Indeed, the centerpiece vision (Zechariah 4) involves the golden lampstand of the Temple. Yet Second Zechariah draws upon the language of the Temple and its service in his portrayal of the eschatological future. In the material that constitutes Second Zechariah, this attention to Temple culminates in chapter 14, which heralds the celebration of the Feast of Booths (14:16) and the time when all the Temple vessels, like the "basins before the altar" (14:20; see NOTE), will be holy.

16. *Yahweh their God.* Frequently considered redundant or an expansion of the divine name, "their God" (*ʾĕlōhēhem*) is often deleted. Only some of the Greek uncials omit it, however, and it is attested in all the main witnesses to the MT. It should also be noted that *ʾlhyhm* balances *ʾlhynw* in verse 7 and adds to the array of divine names in that chapter (see NOTE to "Lord Yahweh," 9:14). Moreover, it occurs in Hag 1:12², Zech 6:15 (although with a second-person suffix), and Zech 10:6. Expanded designations of Yahweh, as in verse 14 ("Lord Yahweh") or in verse 15 ("Yahweh of Hosts"), are well attested in both First and Second Zechariah and are another indication of continuity of style.

will rescue them. That is, "will save them," from the root *yšʿ*, meaning "to achieve victory in battle"; see the NOTE to "saved" in 9:9. The eschatological context of this oracle is made clear by the familiar expression "on that day," although many commentators want to delete it. It occurs in a similar context at the end of First Zechariah (8:7, 13), in Zech 10:6, and in Zech 12:7 with the sense "to be victorious." The Hiphil form used here states God's deliverance in an emphatic way. It is thus the culmination or summary of what the preceding verses portray: "I'm restoring to you double" (v 12), "Yahweh of Hosts will protect them" (v 15), etc. The language of deliverance is thus sustained and intensified; it is part of the language of hope developed in exile (see NOTE to "your prisoners," 9:11).

on that day. Although the MT puts this phrase in the first colon, for metrical reasons it seems better to assign it to the second. This phrase is standard prophetic language for future time, as indicated in the previous NOTE. It occurs at a key point in Haggai (2:23), where it connotes the future day in which the Yehudites will achieve political independence and self-rule under Davidic leadership. It occurs also in First Zechariah to punctuate key moments of Israel's future: 2:15 (NRSV 2:11), when God's presence will return to Zion; 3:10, when every person will live peacefully with every other; 6:10, when the crowning of the future leaders will occur. Each of these instances is an oracle. That the expression occurs eighteen times in Second Zechariah (see especially NOTES to this phrase at 12:3 and 13:1) indicates the heightened eschatological nature of those oracles and of the collection as a whole. Its role here is integral to the scenario of God's future deliverance of the people.

his people will be like sheep. Just as a shepherd rescues lost sheep, so will Yahweh save Israel. Because of metrical considerations (see previous NOTE), we assign this phrase to the second colon, unlike the Masoretes, who placed the *athnach*, the equivalent of a semicolon, after "his people" and hence understood this phrase to belong in verse 16a. If it is to be understood as a construct chain, the text literally reads "like the sheep of his people," which is how the Greek understands it. However, it does not have to be a construct chain. The term *kṣ'n* ("like sheep") actually constitutes one phrase in a predicate relationship to *'mw* ("his people"), which is independent of *kṣ'n*. Literally, these words together read: "like (a) sheep (is) his people."

The use of the term "sheep" (*ṣō'n*) to symbolize the people Israel is well attested in the Hebrew Bible. It frequently signifies the multitude of Israel (Ezek 36:37, 38; 2 Sam 24:17 = 1 Chron 21:17; Jer 23:1, 2, 3; Ezek 24:5; etc.), and it is an important image in Second Zechariah (10:2; 11:4, 7³, 11, 17; 13:7; see NOTES below for a further discussion of the images). With Israel so frequently depicted as God's flock, it is no wonder that God is frequently known as "the one who shepherds" the flock (as in Gen 48:15; Hos 4:16; Isa 40:11; Mic 7:14; Ezek 34:14, 15; Ps 79:13; 95:7). Similar imagery of Israel's being lost and restored to its "pasture" occurs in Jer 50:6–7, 19.

The closest parallel to the present expression comes from Ezekiel (36:38), who likens Israel to the "flock of holy things" and the "flock at Jerusalem," both expressions using constructs, *kĕṣ'ōn qādāšîm* and *kĕṣō'n yĕrūšālayim* (v 38). In verses 37 and 38 of Ezekiel 36, however, we find the expression *(ka)ṣō'n 'ādām*, i.e., the flock of people. God is called upon to increase the population of Israel like the flocks of sheep that people tend. Although some would delete the expression in Zechariah, it is meaningful in this context. It draws upon familiar imagery, as in Ezekiel (cf. also Mic 2:12; Ps 44:12, 23 [NRSV 44:11, 22]) and resonates with many other biblical texts. Furthermore, in suggesting population growth, it adumbrates the flourishing of young people—the next generation—in the next verse and in the passage dealing with the restoration of Ephraim in chapter 10 (see NOTES to vv 8 and 10).

For like gemstones of a crown. The shift in imagery between the pastoral scene of a shepherd with sheep to gemstones is abrupt. The use of *kî* as a conjunction, rendered in our translation as "for," which could also be translated "because," facilitates this transition. The common suggestion to join the comparative adjective *k* to *'abnê-nēzer*, to mean "like gemstones of a crown," is therefore unnecessary, although such an interpretation would not significantly alter the meaning. The Masoretic notation, especially the placement of the *athnach* after "his people," supports the case for understanding *kî* as a conjunction in Hebrew. Furthermore, having *ᵓbny-nzr* appear in just this form indicates a connection with or echo of *ᵓbny qlᶜ* ("sling stones") of verse 15 (see NOTE). Nonetheless, the comparative "like" can be supplied in such poetic contexts as this.

The expression "gemstones of a crown" (*ᵓabnē-nēzer*), literally "stones of a crown," combines two kinds of images into a simple construct. Stones of all kind figure prominently in First Zechariah: the engraved stone with seven facets set before Joshua the high priest (3:9); "the premier stone" of the Temple of Zerubbabel (4:7); the "tin stone" or foundation stone of that Temple (4:10); "the lead stone weight" of the Ephah vision (5:8)— all of these provide dramatic and symbolic power to Temple imagery in First Zechariah (see Meyers and Meyers 1987: *ad loc.*). The image of Israel as a crown has perhaps also been influenced by Isa 62:3: "You shall be a crown of beauty in the hand of Yahweh, and a royal diadem in the hand of your God." But surely the most direct source of crown imagery would be Zech 6:11 and 14, where two crowns are prepared, one for Joshua and the other set aside for the future royal descendant of David, although the word for "crown" used there is *ᶜăṭārâ*. Because the use of technical terms relating to the Temple or its leaders, however, is very subtle and highly selective, the use of *nēzer* in this verse is not accidental and undoubtedly informs us about aspects of the imagery not readily apparent in English translation.

When Joshua the high priest is invested (Zech 3:1–10) and cleansed in preparation for his new duties, he receives a "clean turban" (*ṣānîp ṭāhôr*) to place on his head. The meaning of "clean" in that context is ritual purity and does not have a hygienic sense. The word *ṭāhôr* in other contexts can also mean "shining," as is the case with gemstones such as sapphire (Exod 24:10). It can also depict the brightness of other shining stones as well. According to Exod 29:6 and Lev 8:9, a *nēzer* can be added to the turban, which may have shining stones or metal on it, as is the case with *ṣîṣ* ("metal plate"). The shining component relates to the priest's functions, which is the import of the stone set before Joshua in Zech 3:9. The use of terminology associated more with royalty than with the priesthood in the investiture scene emphasizes the fact of Joshua's newly expanded powers (Meyers and Meyers 1987: 192).

The term *nēzer* can also convey the insignia of royal power, as it does in reference to David (2 Kgs 11:12 = 2 Chron 23:11) and Saul (2 Sam 1:10; see also Ps 89:40 [NRSV 89:39]). Its usage here, therefore, in conjunction with "stones" and coming right after the cultic imagery in verses 15 and 16 expresses both a cultic or priestly image as well as a royal one, the latter suiting the presence of a royal figure in verse 9, above. Because Israel has now become the object of Yahweh's saving actions, its ultimate deliverance is appropriately expressed in language that has both royal and priestly nuances. Whereas the English translation may seem slightly awkward, the Hebrew text is subtly nuanced in its hopeful view of the future. Such a view will embrace a royal figure with his special responsibilities and at the same time preserve a priestly figure with his prerogatives and assigned areas of responsibility.

That this view is present and is in harmony with First Zechariah has been difficult to recognize because of the extensive holy-war imagery in the present context. Mason (1973: 86) has sought to understand the crown imagery as a reinterpretation "of the specific promise of proto-Zechariah at the time of the joint ministry of Joshua and Zerubbabel. For this would mean that it is the community of which the prophet speaks who are to become what Joshua and Zerubbabel had been." The historical circumstances in which chapter 9 was written or promulgated were surely different from the era of the early restoration. Yet, despite great change, the prophetic belief in a better future instigated by Yahweh and realized through both royal and priestly leadership remained firm throughout the Persian era.

One further aspect of this phrase deserves mention. Just as "sling stones" in verse 15 is used metaphorically for Zion or Israel, as the forces that Yahweh will use in the cosmic attack upon the enemy, so too does "gemstones of a crown" function to symbolize people. In this case, the referrent may be the "stones" that figure in the priestly garb in the Tabernacle texts of Exodus. There are to be "two onyx stones" engraved with the names of the "sons of Israel" (Exod 28:9); this may be another instance of a "stone"/"sons" connection (see NOTE in v 13 to "your sons, O Zion"). These stones are part of the ephod's shoulder pieces. In addition, the breastpiece is to have twelve stones, representing the "twelve sons" and also the "twelve tribes" (Exod 28:17–21). The linkage of "stones" with "sons" is augmented with specific reference to "tribes." This language, in contributing to the imagery of Zech 9:16, provides a connection with the "tribes of Israel" of 9:1. The ending of Zechariah 9 in this way echoes its beginning.

will shine. Most commentators want to derive this meaning from the root *nss,* "to sparkle" or "to glitter." The textual witnesses here are divided. The Septuagint has "rolled" *(kyliontai),* apparently taking the root to be *nws.* The Hebrew, however, transmits *mitnôsĕsôt,* i.e., a Hithpoel feminine plural from *nss* (or possibly *nws*), which is probably derived from *nēs* ("standard" or "ensign"). The D-stem reflexive verb occurs only here and in Ps 60:6 [NRSV 60:4] with any meaning resembling the present text, which could be rendered more literally as "for gemstones of a crown will be raised up (or unfurled) in the land," i.e., flashing back and forth as the stones reflect the sunlight. The most famous passages using the noun form are undoubtedly those in Isa 5:26, 11:12, and 49:22, where Israel is heralded as a "beacon" or "signal" to the nations. The Latin reflects such an understanding by translating "will be elevated." Rudolph (1976: 185) accepts the etymology from *nēs* as appropriate, but with the meaning "to shine." Others see the possible influence of Lam 4:1 where "sacred stones" *(ʾabnê qōdeš)* are "scattered about," and indeed the Syriac translates *nss* in that way. The general sense of the verb seems clear, whatever the precise meaning may be: the "gemstones" (see previous NOTE) will become highly visible to the people in the land.

his land. The word for land is *ʾădāmâ,* a term that is widely used in the Hebrew Bible. It frequently, as here, refers to Israel's territory, the promised land, which was not originally Israel's possession. The land in fact was Yahweh's; Yahweh is the one who bestows it upon Israel (e.g., Exod 20:12; Lev 20:24; Deut 21:1; 1 Kgs 9:7; Jer 24:10; Ezek 28:25). Israel in turn takes it as an inheritance. This view of the land is present in this text, where the third-person suffix "his," referring to Yahweh, is attached to "land." The use of *ʾădāmâ* rather than other possible terms for "land" (such as *ʾereṣ*) may be related to the fact that *ʾădāmâ* is the preferred term for arable land that is cultivated by humans (see Zech 13:5). Such a nuance would be meaningful in light of the emphasis on agrarian prosperity in the verses preceding and following this one (see NOTES). At the same time, the presence of royal-cultic language ("gemstones of a crown") perhaps suggests that "land" here is also elliptical for "holy land," which occurs in the Bible only in First Zechariah (Zech 2:16 [NRSV 2:12]; see Meyers and Meyers 1987: 170–71).

17. *how good and how lovely!* This elegant exclamation announces the dawning of a new age of prosperity that will soon overtake the land and its people. A similar juxtaposition of two adjectives occurs in Ps 133:1 ("How good and pleasant it is for kindred to live together"); and in Canticles (4:10²; 7:2, 7 [NRSV 7:1, 6]), the interrogative "how" *(mah)* is used frequently in an exclamatory sense to call attention to the beauty of the beloved. Even the tents of Jacob are praised in such poetic terms: "How goodly are your tents, O Jacob, your dwelling places, O Israel" (Num 24:5).

grain . . . new wine. The two commodities "grain" *(dāgān)* and "new wine" *(tîrôš)* are regularly used together to express the bounty of the land (e.g., Gen 27:28, 37; Deut 11:14; 2 Kgs 18:32, etc.). When enemies and foreigners possess them (Isa 62:8), the absolute antithesis of the condition envisioned here obtains. These two commodities echo those of verse 15 above (see NOTES to "drink and be rowdy" and "full like the basin"). A third commodity listed in Hag 1:11, "fresh oil" *(yiṣhār)*, is probably omitted here because the poetic structure demands only two items.

The eschatological setting of this oracle, announced in verse 16 with the expression "on that day," makes it clear that ample "grain" and "new wine" will be present when God restores Israel. This concept is similar to themes found in Haggai, where the rebuilding and refounding of the Temple were occasions for prophetic expressions of the agricultural plenitude that would accompany God's renewed favor for Israel. For example, in Hag 2:19 the terms "seed" and "vine" represent "grain" and "wine." In that text, God's renewed blessing comes as the result of the Temple's refoundation (Meyers and Meyers 1987: 65–66). Here, although the context is eschatological, the Temple imagery is indirectly present in the expression "gemstones of a crown" in the previous verse (see NOTE above). The ending of this verse is similar in tone to the oracular conclusion to the crowning of Joshua in Zech 3:10.

young men . . . maidens. This familiar pair of designations occurs in both the singular (Deut 32:25; 2 Chron 36:17; Jer 51:22; Ezek 9:6) and the plural in the order in which it appears here, i.e., "men" before "maidens." It also occurs in many parallel constructions in that order (e.g., Ps 78:63; 148:12; Isa 23:4;

etc.). The term *bāḥûr*, "young man," connotes someone in the prime of manhood. Its companion term, *bĕtūlâ*, means "virgin," which perhaps indicates the prime of womanhood, the promise of female fertility. The pair of terms connotes vigor and youth (cf. the pair *ʾiš/ʾiššâ*, in Jer 51:22, which connotes a mature age). The emphasis on youth is part of a future orientation of these oracles, and the mention of flourishing young men and women anticipates the "children" of 10:7 and 9 (see NOTES below) and the demographic expansion of 10:10.

In this text "grain" goes with "young man" and "new wine" with "maiden." Although men might well have worked longer hours in the fields tilling the ground, women also participated in such activities, especially during labor-intensive periods of the growing seasons (cf. Ruth 2:3, 17). And although women did work in the vineyards and are associated with wine making (Judg 21:21), men also had responsibilities in wine production. The division of labor between men and women was not sufficiently rigid with respect to these particular tasks to warrant any special significance here. The absence of a second verb supports the case for a situation of complementarity between men and women. Although some would restore a verb to go with "young man" ("Grain will make fat *(dšn)* young men, wine will make the maidens flourish"; see P. D. Hanson 1975: 296), adding *dšn* to bring the last two cola into closer balance is unnecessary inasmuch as "to flourish" can surely do double duty. That is, it can work forward and backward, governing both cola, thereby intensifying the complementary pairing of men and maidens. Both products (grain and wine) will make both groups flourish.

flourish. The root *nwb*, used here in the Polel, is very rare. It occurs only in this verse and in Psalms (62:11 [NRSV 10]; 92:15 [NRSV 14]) and Proverbs (10:31). A noun form meaning "fruit" occurs at Isa 57:19. The versions have difficulty with the verb and translate it as a participle. Rudolph (1976: 185) suggests the Hiphil of *nwn*, "to propagate" or "increase," although it occurs only once, in Ps 72:17 [NRSV 72:16]. The masculine singular of the verb, *yĕnôbēb*, agrees with its two masculine subjects, "grain" and "new wine." Because the verb does retrospective double duty, i.e., refers back to both *tyrwš* and *dgn* and thus reflects the normal practice in Hebrew of connecting the verb with the first subject, the singular form of the verb is used.

COMMENT

Late biblical prophecy in many ways epitomizes the biblical process—existing authoritative material influencing the formation of new sacred literature. Of all the oracles and narratives that are grouped together to form Second Zechariah, Zechariah 9 perhaps is the best example of the ongoing vitality of the prophetic tradition even as that tradition was, in terms of its canonical shape, drawing to a close. The poetic form of this chapter, as well as its thematic and literary contacts with earlier biblical prophecy, have produced a prophetic unit that beautifully represents the creative continuity characterizing many of the later books of the Hebrew canon.

Although the material that constitutes each of its three subunits is quite varied, the overall result is a chapter that is resoundingly universal in its scope while never losing sight of the special concern of Yahweh for Israel that is at the core of the worldwide purview. The chapter thus begins with a focus on restoring the historical homeland, the land of Israel. It ends with a concern for the Israelites who have been removed from their homeland, namely, the exiles. These two components of Yahweh's concern for Israel are linked by the central subunit (vv 9–10), which announces the arrival of the royal figure who will rule over the restored land and people as well as all the nations.

Thematically and structurally, this chapter has been carefully shaped. It stands as a unity, albeit one that is linked with the succeeding chapters. It may indeed contain earlier materials, but it has been put together in a deliberate fashion by someone, perhaps the very prophet/poet responsible for all of Second Zechariah (see section on Literary Considerations in the Introduction), who intended chapters 9–14 to cohere in the form and order in which we have them.

This chapter contains an abundance of references to particular places, and it makes prominent use of concrete imagery drawn from the realia of military activity. These features create a strong sense of the prophet's moorings in historical times. Yet the prophet's words are not directed toward specific or expected events of his immediate present but, rather, are all projected into the eschatological future. In addition, although the language of violence is present in each of the subunits, such language is present in each case only to be negated, to give way to the cessation of aggressive behavior by both God and humanity and the concomitant establishment of peace.

Restoration of the Land of Israel, 9:1–8.

Following the oracular heading, the first seven verses of this subunit contain a carefully arranged sequence of oracular statements, together proclaiming that God will restore the land that was promised to the twelve tribes of Israel. The prophet accomplishes this by providing three groupings of geographical references, each of which contributes an essential dimension to the overall territorial orientation of 9:1–8. These groups are:

Syria/Aram	9:1–2a
Phoenicia	9:2b–4
Philistia	9:5–7

The subunit is then concluded by a verse (9:8) that indicates the center, the Temple in Jerusalem, from which Yahweh will recover for Israel its historic geographical heritage.

The material that constitutes these groupings plus the conclusion forms a literary subunit, not only because of the territorial theme that it develops but also because of the appearance of a term—"eye"/"eyes" in verse 1 and again in verse 8–that frames these eight verses. Indeed, the use of "eye" in verse 1 (see NOTE) is so unusual that its intentional selection as part of an inclusion seems to be the best way to understand why it appears there. "Eye"/"eyes" apparently also functions, as does so much in Second Zechariah, to link these last six chapters of the Book of Zechariah with the visionary material of First Zechariah, where "eyes" figures so prominently (see NOTES to "eye(s)" in vv 1 and 8). In addition to the "eye"/"eyes" usage, the appearance of "word of Yahweh" at the beginning of verse 1 and God's "eyes" at the end of verse 8 form an inclusion of a slightly different kind: this section opens and concludes with distinctive features of Yahweh.

The geographical focus of 9:1–8 has both territorial and political signifi-cance. It begins, appropriately, with that group that is not construed to be part of Israel's geographical extent. The three Syrian cities, or, more likely, districts—Hadrach, Damascus, and Hamath—that appear in verses 1–2 are all inland cities. Together they represent the eastern sector of the Lebanon—the territory east of the coastal area (Phoenicia). Each of these sites, however, had a different status with respect to the traditional, biblical boundaries of the land of Israel. Hadrach, the northernmost of the three, was apparently part of Syria but never part of the northern lands that were reckoned as part of Canaanite territory and, hence, as lands that somehow ought to be considered Israelite. The northern border of such lands—part of "the land that still remains" to be conquered (Josh 13:1–7)—was the entrance to the Hamath district, marked by Lebo-Hamath. The mention of Hamath in verse 2, as a city/district bordering on the Israelite tribes, clearly reflects this conceptualization of the ideal land of Israel. Thus the Syrian districts represented by both Hadrach and Hamath were external to the territory of the Israelite tribes even from the most inclusive viewpoint.

The case of Damascus and its relationship to the ideal land of Israel is less clear. It is located considerably south—almost fifty miles—of the border of the Hamath district and thus, from the perspective of northern extent, it would be within the greater land of Canaan allotted to Israel (see Aharoni 1979: map 17). Damascus the city, or the district also called by that name, however, is notable for lying at the western edge of the Syrian desert, a location that led to the great strength, longevity, and prominence of Damascus as a commercial center in antiquity. As such, it probably should be considered on the eastern border of the northern sector of the land unconquered by Joshua but still to be included in the greater Israel. Even if this is not the case, it should be emphasized that Damascus would have been within territory that, although perhaps part of an ideal Israel, was not given as a specific tribal apportionment (Aharoni 1979: 237) and thus would have been, at best, only quasi-Israelite territory.

The presence of Damascus in this group of Syrian territories thus probably represents the northeast edge of greater Israel. Moreover, Damascus also had great political significance. Appearing as cruel and domineering in earlier Israelite prophecy (as Amos 1:3–5), it was virtually a permanent threat to the northern border of Israel throughout most of the period of the monarchy. Damascus is consequently more than a territorial marker; with the other two northern areas mentioned in Zech 9:1 and 2, it may also be representative of the foe or threat from the north, a motif occurring time after time in Israelite prophecy (notably Jer 3:18; 23:8; cf. Zech 6:8; see Childs 1959 and Meyers and Meyers 1987: 324–25, 330–31), even though the mention of these northern territories is devoid of the chaos language that normally accompanies the appearance of the northern threat in postexilic prophecy.

Whether construed in the territorial or political sense, or both, these three toponyms are significant in that they represent areas over which the Israelite tribes had no claim but which traditionally posed grave dangers to the territorial integrity of the tribal portions and thus to the Northern Kingdom. The threat to territorial claims is characteristic of all three groups—Phoenicia, Philistia, and Syria/Aram as well. The northern group, however, never was seen as needing to be reclaimed or acquired. Thus it is appropriate that of the three groups in Zech 9:1–8, it is the only one for which violent activity is not indicated. The inhabitants of Syria/Aram are truly outside Israel. Whatever enmity existed between them and the Israelites in historical times will dissipate in the approaching eschatological age. Hence those areas, which stand for nearly all nations extraterritorial to Israel (those holding Israelites captive being the exception; see Zech 9:11–17) will automatically be among those with which peace will be established. Damascus, the epitome of enmity, will be a "resting place" for Yahweh's word. Indeed, all the people of the north are acknowledging Yahweh, with their "eye" to Yahweh and with Yahweh's word present. The eschatological age in the north, involving no shift in territorial hegemony, begins without tumult or strife.

Not so for the next group of non-Israelites in the geographical configuration of Zech 9:1–8. Phoenicia is represented in 9:2–4 by its two most prominent cities, Tyre and Sidon. Both sites are mentioned, unless one emends the text, as some are wont to do (see NOTE to "Tyre and Sidon," v 2), to remove one or the other of these place names. The text as it stands seems acceptable, however; and the appearance of the names of both these major cities, even though the focus of the oracular pronouncement is on only one of them—Tyre—contributes to the way in which the configuration of sites mentioned in all three groupings conveys the prophetic message about the restoration of Israel's territory. The fact is that the two cities balanced each other throughout much of their history, with one alternately stronger than the other, and with the name of one sometimes standing for both. Against that peculiarity of their historical relationship, the pair of names takes on the nuance, critical to the prophet's aim in this passage, of representing all of Phoenicia.

Whereas the Syrian territory of the first grouping is unambiguously external to the tribal apportionment, even though the case of Damascus is somewhat borderline, as discussed above, the Phoenician territory occupies a much different role in the biblical conception of the full extent of the land of Israel. Although all the border markers (Josh 13:4–5) are difficult to identify (see

Aharoni 1979: 237–38), it seems clear that a major segment of "the land that still remains" consisted of Phoenician territory. The northern extent of this territory was probably somewhere north of Byblos. The southern extent is more difficult to comprehend: the Litani River may have been part of the border, except that Tyre—or at least its hinterland (recalling that Tyre was an offshore island until the Hellenistic period)—which is south of the Litani, should probably be included.

Part of the Phoenician sector of the land not immediately acquired as tribal territory, unlike the portion bordering on Syria, did, for a brief time at least, become part of the tribal allotment. The tribe of Asher, which was situated along the coast from the Carmel range northward, is associated with "Sidonian" lands, at least as far north as Sidon and including Tyre's mainland fortified city (Josh 19:28–30; cf. Judg 1:32). However, the extent of Asher's actual control of these lands is questionable, because the Phoenician coast stands out, in the period of Davidic–Solomonic expansion and imperial control, as the one area virtually within the land of Israel that remained external to Israelite domination. David may have been able to exert pressure on Tyre, but he chose to have a profitable economic alliance with her rather than to subjugate her. Indeed, Tyre's strength and independence are reflected in certain events of the Solomonic era, when a significant section of Asher's territory—twenty Galilean sites—was never regained. The integrity of Asher was severely affected by this action; and the Israelite identity of this Galilean tribe was probably permanently damaged as its major sites were now reckoned, perhaps more appropriately from a socioeconomic perspective, with the Phoenician territory and its maritime orientation (C. L. Meyers 1983b: 56–57).

Whatever sense the cession of the northwestern fringe of Israelite territory to Phoenicia may have made in political, social, and economic terms, it was never forgotten in Israel's ongoing nationalistic self-conception. Although all of Phoenicia may have been beyond the expectations of territorial restoration, certainly those parts of it that had at one time been under Israelite tribal control were considered part of what had been allotted to Israel and, hence, were expected to be restored to her national extent. Yet the prophecies at the end of Ezekiel would include all of Phoenicia, in that the western boundary is given as the Mediterranean coast as far north as a point "opposite Lebo-Hamath" (Ezek 47:20). Because Second Zechariah's oracles indicate a familiarity with Ezekiel, the Phoenician grouping of Zech 9:2–4 is likely to reflect the maximum perspective on Phoenicia, as part of the promised territory, whether or not it had all, at any time, come under Israelite political control.

The language used to describe the fate of Tyre (and thus of all Phoenicia) reflects acknowledgment of both her political and economic strength. It mentions her fortification system, and it uses ancient poetic imagery involving the plentitude of silver and gold to convey her economic success. Then the prophet reverses these aspects of Tyrian might as, with her wealth ceasing and her political existence terminated, she is utterly destroyed ("consumed by fire," 9:4c). Although Yahweh is clearly the agent of Tyre's demise, the language here does not invoke the divine-warrior imagery that becomes explicit in the third subunit of Zechariah 9 (especially in v 14). Even the common biblical notion of the divine consuming fire is presented somewhat indirectly with respect to Yahweh's role in Phoenicia's fate. One has the sense that Yahweh's eschatological intervention to restore Phoenicia and, in the next verse, Philistia to Israel is somehow to take place through the due course of human military and political exploits. The situation is strikingly different in the 9:11–17 subunit dealing with exiles.

The third grouping of place names in Zech 9:1–8 involves Philistia. Although there were five cities in the Philistine league, only four of them appear in this grouping, which deals with the last of the three major areas not acquired by the tribes but considered in some way part of Israel. As the listing in chart 12 shows, Second Zechariah was not alone in expressing hostility toward the cities of Philistia.

Chart 12 reveals two anomalies: the absence of prophetic tirade against Gath and the association of Ekron with more than one tribe. In our NOTES to "Ashkelon" in 9:5 we explore in considerable detail the reasons for the omission of Gath by all the prophets who mention Philistine cities. The status of Gath in terms of its relationship to Israel diverged from that of the other Philistine cities, going back to the time of David's accord with that city. Indeed, it may well have been considered part of Judah by the time of the Divided Monarchy and hence not an enemy city; thus it could hardly be included in a list of places that would be subjected to drastic upheaval. As for Ekron, its association with two tribes rather than one, along with its proximity to the heartland of Judah, makes it stand out among the Philistine cities. In the restored land of Israel, its population can be compared to the Jebusites. If Jebus, on the border of Judah and Benjamin, can be identified with Jerusalem, then Ekron would share Jebus's connection with two tribes and thus make the comparison especially apt.

The four Philistine cities presumably represent the whole of Philistine territory that remained distinct from Judah during the monarchy. Although the Syrian territory represented by Hadrach, Damascus, and Hamath was considered

CHART 12
CITIES OF THE PHILISTINE PENTAPOLIS:
TRIBAL TERRITORIES AND PROPHETIC THREATS

City	Tribal Territory	Prophetic Threats
Ashdod	Judah	Amos, Jer, Zeph, Zech
Ashkelon	Judah	Amos, Jer, Zeph, Zech
Ekron	Judah/Dan	Amos, Jer, Zeph, Zech
Gath	Judah	(Amos*)
Gaza	Judah	Amos, Jer, Zeph, Zech

*Gath appears in Amos 6:2 but not in the listing of Philistine cities in Zech 1:7–8.

external to the tribal territories, and the Phoenician lands represented by Tyre and Sidon are somewhat ambiguous in their status with respect to an ideal Israel, there can be no doubt that the Philistine domination over the southern coast of Palestine, as well as Philistine expansion into the Shephelah, was at the expense of Israelite tribal claims.

Accordingly, the Philistine cities are depicted as facing a different fate from that of the Phoenician and Syrian territories. Syria, in fact, faces no threat—the area in the north has its own integrity, looks toward Yahweh, and enjoys peace. Phoenicia, in contrast, will have its fortunes reversed; it will lose its economic vitality and will suffer catastrophic destruction. If at least parts of Phoenicia were included in Israelite territorial claims, the recovery of those parts would mean that they would be free from the perennial threat of control by the coastal powers.

The fate of Philistia would be considerably different. The Philistine cities, which enjoyed close economic and sometimes also political ties with the Phoenician maritime powers, would be greatly alarmed in witnessing the fate of Sidon and Tyre, their allies and sometimes their colonial rulers. However, their fears would not be fully realized, for what lay in store for them was not economic crisis or physical devastation. Rather, only the political leadership of the Philistine cities would be curtailed—either by complete loss of leadership or by having a corrupt ruler take over. In this way, the cities would all have lost viable leadership and thus be ripe for incorporation into the polity, Israel, that all along had claim on their territories. Gath, perceived as already part of Israel (Judah), even with its Philistine population, is not specified here, but the others are enumerated. With their leadership gone, Yahweh will destroy their positive self-conception and identity—the "pride" that accompanies political and economic success as well as the individual ruler responsible for those achievements—and their unacceptable cultic orientation so that they can be part of the traditional inheritance of Israel. The Philistines would surely suffer great trauma in such political upheaval, which might in fact have economic ramifications; yet they would survive and merge with Israel, as already may have been the case for Ekron (see NOTE in v 5).

The Philistines, unlike the Syrians or even the Phoenicians, are thus seen as having an internal connection with Israel. As their cities are reclaimed for Israel, their people will be counted among the Israelites. The same kind of family-based language ("clan," 9:7) that is used to represent the various social units of Israel below the tribal level will be applied to the Philistines. Furthermore, just as the Jebusites became assimilated into Israel once David subdued Jebus, so too will the Ekronites become fully integrated into the restored people of Israel.

It is indeed fitting that the last geographical term mentioned in the first subunit of Zechariah 9 is "Jebusite," referring to the pre-Davidic inhabitants of Jerusalem. This reference subtly leads into the last verse of this subunit, which announces Yahweh's residence in the Temple ("my House," v 8) in Jerusalem. David had acquired some property from the Jebusite Araunah in order to build an altar there and so forestall an advancing outbreak of pestilential disease and, thus, the loss of human life. David's dealings with this Jebusite were extremely cordial. Furthermore, according to the Chronicler's account (1 Chron 22:1; 2 Chron 3:1) of this pivotal episode in Jerusalem's history, this Jebusite plot of land with its altar to Yahweh becomes the site of God's house in Jerusalem. There is much to commend the Chronicler's report (see C. L. Meyers 1987: 358, 373 n. 8); and the link between the Jebusites and Yahweh's Temple thus forms a suitable background for the connection between the mention of Jebusites, as examples of non-Yahwists who become part of Israel, as will Ekron–Philistia, and the holy center of God's universal reign from which divine protection over all Israel will be restored.

The appearance of "Jebusite," in addition, serves to connect thematically the first subunit of Zechariah 9 with the second one, which announces the restoration of a royal figure to reign in Jerusalem. The Jebusites are associated with David, the chief dynastic figure in ancient Israel. Consequently, the mention of this group, the conquest of which led to the establishment of a royal capital in Jerusalem and eventually to the erection of Yahweh's house there, provides transition to verses 9–10, which concern the arrival of the eschatological king in Jerusalem and the accompanying new order of universal well-being and peace.

The first subunit of Second Zechariah draws upon the historical and literary heritage of Israel to present a carefully constructed depiction of restored Israel. The configuration of geopolitical terms reflects an acute awareness of the historical role of Israel's neighbors in limiting its freedom and its territorial integrity. Yet in the presentation of this array of place names, the overall conception of the ideal borders of Israel dominates. Thus, the prophet transcends attention to any specific historical developments and portrays an eschatological future of the tribal allotments realized, as they never had been before. Only divine intervention will secure that condition. By ending this subunit with reference to God in the divine residence on earth, Second Zechariah also echoes the notions of Haggai and First Zechariah—that the rebuilt Temple will bring about peace (i.e., protection for Israel), prosperity, and the acclaim of the nations for Jerusalem's sovereignty.

In delineating the future Israel in terms of a historical understanding of its territorial allotments, Second Zechariah represents something of a departure from the expectations of other Israelite prophets. For them, the ideal future arrangement was apparently that Israel would occupy the entire region between Assyria and Egypt. That is, they would be willing to share the future world with those two superpowers but not with any of the lesser political entities in between. This perspective, although it may be prefigured in preexilic prophets (as in Amos 9), tends to appear in prophecies coming from the end of the sixth century: Micah 4–5, Joel 4, and the last section of Jeremiah. However, it must be remembered that those prophecies, if they are indeed of the late sixth century, are coming from the period in which, with the beginnings of Persian hegemony, the idea of an expanded Israel, beyond its historical ideal borders, would have been most possible.

But Second Zechariah comes from a different time, when real historical restoration seems virtually impossible. The oracles of Zechariah 9–14, although partaking of specific historical data, are consistently eschatological. At the same time, they reflect an awareness of the Exile, an experience that involved the drawing upon earlier traditions. Hence, the reference to "tribes of Israel" in verse 1 and the awareness of territorial borders throughout this subunit contribute to the transformation of a historical ideal into a vivid future hope.

The King's Entry into Jerusalem, 9:9–10

This second literary subunit of chapter 9 contains some of the most memorable lines in all of Hebrew Scripture in its portrayal of the future king's entering Jerusalem and of the character of the future age that will be ushered in. The two verses are at the center of the chapter and constitute the centerpiece of the entire poem from a theological, as well as a literary, point of view. The placement of these verses after the opening unit, which depicts the restored land of Israel, and before the final verses, which concern the restored people of Israel, suggests that the entire piece is carefully crafted: the restored royal figure is the lynchpin of the restored land and people.

Throughout the NOTES we have indicated where the hand of an editor or redactor may be discerned. One such instance is the phrase that ends the first subunit ("for now I am watching with my eyes") and explicitly ties the language of chapter 9 to First Zechariah. Similarly, the final verse (v 17) of the third subunit evokes the language of First Zechariah. It would seem, therefore, that chapter 9 consists of a series of eschatological oracles, some of which may have existed earlier, that have been assembled by a prophet or a prophetic circle. Many of the subtleties we have pointed to in the NOTES suggest the involvement of a highly skilled editor or redactor (or committee of such persons), who has organized these oracles into the highly crafted canonical chapter 9. Verses 9–10 may not seem to follow readily after the oracles of verses 1–8 concerning land restoration; yet in their central position, they suit the aim of the entire piece superbly. The final organizer of the whole of chapter 9—who may or may not be the same as the organizer of all of Second Zechariah—stands firmly in prophetic tradition by being aware of the political circumstances shaping events around him and, at the same time, drawing upon traditional authoritative texts.

The depiction of a royal figure in 9:9 is more than a mere calling forth of a familiar theme. It is a statement of ideology that lies at the very core of the message of Second Zechariah. The New Testament has appropriated verse 9 to depict Jesus' triumphal return to Jerusalem (Matt 21:5–9; John 12:14–15), where the peace-loving messiah, riding on a donkey, is welcomed. For the author of the original Hebrew oracle, the processional aspect was deeply imbedded in Near Eastern royal tradition attending moments of great significance. One such moment was almost certainly the accession of the new ruler and the expectation of political stability that accompanied such an event. Because of the eschatological setting of Zech 9:9, however, it is obvious that the momentous occasion is projected into the future. The figure described is none other than a king, in biblical terms most surely a Davidic descendant. But the tone of this passage is both triumphal and pacific, standing in marked contrast to the general tone of verses 1–8 and 11–16 and yet complementary to the message of those passages framing verses 9–12. God will actively, and even violently, restore Israel's land and people; but the polity once established, under instituted royal rule, will be at peace.

What is the message of this centerpiece oracle, which at first glance seems to stand out from its context in tone and content? The message is in harmony with the passages in First Zechariah (e.g., 3:8; 4:6; 6:12; etc.) depicting a future righteous king. The future vision of First Zechariah is thus compatible with that of Second Zechariah, both here and in chapter 12, where the frequent reference to Davidic leadership also is consistent with the tone expressed here, despite the fact that the failures of Davidic leadership do not go unnoticed (12:7, 8, 10, 12 and 13:1; see NOTES and COMMENT below).

The character of the future Davidic king is carefully spelled out in a tight series of descriptive terms, which draw upon imagery that is deeply rooted in earlier prophetic statements and also partakes of common Near Eastern themes. The first quality, righteousness, is particularly apt in light of other biblical depictions of the ideal king (see NOTE to "righteous"). To be sure, "a righteous king" would be one who acts in a proper way, a way that God would favor and that his subjects would respect. At the same time, the term "righteous" conveys the legitimacy of the one who is to rule: the righteous one is the legitimate, or right, one. A second characteristic of the king is that he is "saved." The Niphal or passive participle of the verb "to save" has been challenged by most commentators, who would rather see an active "savior" figure in the righteous king, one who would bring victory or deliverance to the people through his power and deeds. But an active "savior" requires a textual emendation, which seems unnecessary (see NOTE to "saved"); the meaning here in verse 9 is clear enough. Just as the people will be "rescued" and "saved" by Yahweh (see 9:16 and 10:6), so will the one of royal descent be saved by Yahweh. In this chapter Yahweh alone, or Yahweh through Judah and Ephraim, intervenes to rescue and restore Israel. But never does Yahweh act through a militant king. Although the existence of such a figure might be assumed, the text does not mention him.

Still another characteristic of the future king is humility. The translation "humble" has also met with much resistance, critics wanting to understand the root to mean "afflicted," thereby bringing this figure into closer alignment with the Second Isaiah's suffering servant. The inclination to do so is not unwarranted, as we shall explain below. Yet the quality of humility accords with the eschatological tone of the passage and with the vision of restored monastic rule. This quality, along with other seemingly atypical features of a monarchic ruler, also serves to bridge the gap between ruler and ruled. The king, in essence, occupies a relationship of dominance and of unequal access to resources and material benefits. By having the future king be "humble," the text helps this figure transcend the normal disparity and inequity that characterize the relations of dominance inherent in kingship. The future ruler will in some basic ways be identified with and no different from those who consent to come under his rule.

Yet, as king, he will have the resources and power to dominate the nations and to establish worldwide stability and peace while still remaining "humble" or submissive in his relationship to the ultimate sovereign, Yahweh.

The final characteristic of the future ruler is presented in the set of animal terms used to depict his royal mount. The three terms help to sustain the notion of an elite figure as being, nonetheless, one of the people. This king will not ride the typical equine of a triumphant royal figure. The substitution of a donkey for a horse, although the donkey has clear royalist associations in Near Eastern literature where it is mentioned as an animal on which the king rides, is an additional sign that military might is toned down in this passage—emphatically so—by a listing of nonmilitary beasts of burden. Equines enjoy great visibility in the visions of First Zechariah, and the horse or horse and chariot would be the expected royal form of transport. Yet not mentioning the horse, and thus avoiding its associations with violent domination, perhaps contributes to the image of a royal figure who will not exploit those over whom he rules. They can identify with him and thus can fully support him.

At the same time, the question remains as to why this kind of eschatology serves as the vehicle for prophetic expression in the time when this document or collection of oracles we call Second Zechariah was promulgated. Whether such a date is the end of the sixth century or mid-fifth century B.C.E., Persian rule remained dominant throughout this period; the people of Yehud thus had no choice but to speak in such tones. The fortunes of Yehud as a subprovince of the empire and of the Jewish people as a whole were entirely dependent upon Persian toleration and a continuation of the policy of allowing home rule. Whether before or after the satrapal revolts of 460–450 B.C.E., the rationale for expressing future royalist hopes in peaceful language seems clear. The possibility of a royal political leader in Yehud with the capacity to regain land and people being remote, God becomes the "activist" and the restored monarchic figure rules in peace.

The political situation of the mid-fifth century in another way can be associated with the humble status of the restored king, with the fact that he rides lowly beasts of burden, and with the idea that he too needs to be saved. The eschatological focus, as we point out below in our COMMENT to verses 11–17, provides a perspective to this chapter that is particularly sensitive to the Judean Exile. Whether this chapter emerges from Babylon itself cannot be determined, but the language of verses 11–17 is strikingly similar to that of a community in exile. Consequently, the depiction of a future leader should be seen as an important, if not typical, element in one of the ways exiled peoples cope with their fate. For such peoples, the composition of literature in which a hero figure plays a prominent role is a characteristic survival mechanism (see D. L. Smith 1989: 84–88, 153–73).

When the social setting allows for no real possibility of a hero's achieving what the folkloristic imagination of the exiles hope for, the character of the hero becomes far less antagonistic. The hero, in a sense, becomes passive; his fate is similar to that of his community. Thus the powerless and humble status of the exiles is projected onto the royal figure. In the mid-fifth century, when Persian fortifications of its eastern provinces were established, the hope of both Yehudites and exiles for indigenous leadership exercising full political power must have evaporated. The hope for the future, as in that instance, thus becomes eschatologized. At the same time, the eschatological ruler himself appears dependent on transcendent powers for salvation. The royal figure himself must be saved; and he warrants this treatment because, like the second, third, or fourth generation captive community, he has been subjected innocently to the trials of exile (from his throne and/or from his land) and thus is a righteous individual to whom kingship rightly belongs according to the eschatological ideal. In this sense, the images of humbleness and restoration associated with the royal figure of Zech 9:9 are like certain features of the servant motif of Second Isaiah. The social relevance of both figures should not be viewed apart from the perspective of the folklore of hope that emerges from powerless diaspora or colonial settings. The psychosocial function of a humble and afflicted ruler is effective to the extent that the people can identify with the one who will be their leader.

At first glance, the second verse (v 10) of this second subunit seems to be closer to the other two subunits than it is to verse 9 because of its military terminology. Although the language seems to be harsh, however, the verse in fact proclaims the elimination of war in the rule of the future king. The vehicles of war appear, in contrast to the humbleness of mounts in verse 9, but the chariot and horse along with the "bow of war" are mentioned because of their imminent removal from Ephraim and Jerusalem, i.e., from all Israel. The removal of the implements of war and of the enemies that wield them signifies dramatically that the new regime will be radically different from all previous ones—political power will exist without coercive violence. The restored ruler will surely have the ability to dominate militarily, with Yahweh fighting for him, but that ability will no longer need to be activated. The hope for peace and stability that characterize new regions will this time be actualized.

The establishment of peace is an essential component of biblical eschatology and is often associated with a Davidic figure who is called "prince of peace," whose reign will witness the end of military might and violence (see Isa 9:6–7) or whose rule will stretch to the ends of the earth (Mic 5:4 [NRSV 5:3]; cf. Ps 72:7–8). The Book of Jonah too, if it be assigned to this period, with its benign attitude to Nineveh and its people, is as articulate a statement as any on the theme of peace. In proclaiming "peace to the nations," Second Zechariah expresses an important theme of prophetic eschatology, which is the climax of First Zechariah (8:18–23); according to Zech 8:19, when "truth and peace" are established in Yehud, then and only then will other nations of the world acknowledge Yahweh's sovereignty. Similarly in Second Zechariah, without "righteousness" (see NOTE at 9:9) there can be no peace.

The statement that the just ruler's dominion will extend "from sea to sea" and "from the river to the ends of the earth" involves universalistic language almost identical to that of Ps 72:8. The text is exactly the same except for the verb, which in the Psalter is *rdh*, that is, "to have dominion over." In this text, however, it is *mšl*, "to rule over," a verb used exclusively with David, Solomon, and Hezekiah, the greatest of Israel's kings and those whose realms extended beyond the traditional borders of Judah. This subtle shift in the text underscores the expectation that the future Davidide will, like his most illustrious predecessors, extend Yahweh's sovereignty far beyond Israel. Although violence may be involved in restoring Israel's territory (vv 1–8) and people (vv 11–17), this conclusion to the centerpiece oracle proclaims that peace will thereby be established.

These two verses are eclectic in the best sense. The author has drawn from the language and imagery of the earlier prophets and the psalms, thus indicating the authority of those materials. Yet he has adjusted traditional language and imagery to suit his own message in the postexilic age. Second Zechariah, or those responsible for putting chapters 9–14 into their present canonical form, has created a work that is in the mainstream of biblical prophecy and at the same time at the end of that line. As a purely poetic statement, it is the very last of such presentations. The reworking of older materials, especially prophetic materials, was a sign that the authority of those utterances was sufficiently great to impact on prophetic creativity. As one of the final statements of prophetic poetry, it is surely one of the finest. Verses 9–10 stand as eloquent testimony to the prophetic genius of that day.

Restoration of the People Through Yahweh's Intervention, 9:11–17

This third subunit of Zechariah 9 complements the message of the first subunit (vv 1–8). Whereas the central unit (vv 9–10) portrays a future king ruling in peace over all Israel and extending his sovereignty throughout the world, the other two parts of this chapter depict what God will do to achieve the restoration that will accompany the king's return to the holy city. That restoration has two dimensions: the greater land of Israel itself will be reclaimed, as the first eight verses of the chapter set forth, and the people themselves will be released from their captivity and returned to Zion.

In the seven verses that make up the third subunit, there is a progression in terms of content that begins with an introduction of the captive status of the exiles (vv 11–12), continues with an account of God's intervention through historical and cosmic forces to secure the release of the people (vv 13–15a, b), and then concludes with a portrayal of the prosperity and safety of those brought back from captivity (vv 15c, d–17). In terms of grammar, this subunit might be divided somewhat differently: verses 11–13, all of which have Yahweh in the first person and use the second-person feminine singular for the people; verses 14–16, with Yahweh in the third person and, for the most part, the people as "them" in the third-person masculine plural; and verse 17 as a sort of epilogue. Still, the shifts in person for Yahweh and in reference to the people could equally be construed as linking, or providing transitions for, these first two sections as divided in the first way suggested. In either case, verse 17 connects quite well with the preceding material.

However it may be divided, this subunit with its three sections brings together a seemingly disparate set of images—imprisonment, Yahweh as warrior, divine theophany, the people as sheep, and a beatific view of ultimate fecundity. Yet the very contrast among these images in itself serves a purpose. For what contrast could be greater than that of the people being near death, that is, the social or cultural death that threatens when a group is alienated from its homeland, and the restoration of that people to its land and the establishment of a condition of great prosperity? The whole transformation is nothing less than a social resurrection, which would be beyond the capability of normal human political activity. Enormous power is required, and only the greatest power of all—Yahweh of Hosts (v 15)—can bring it about.

The specific historical context that may have given rise to such a sweeping view of restoration is difficult to reconstruct. However, comparative sociological analysis does suggest that the theme of divine intervention in the folkloristic tradition of captive peoples is a concomitant of a social setting lacking the possibility of self-generated escape. As we have suggested above, the mid-fifth century seems to have had the features that would give rise to this sort of oracular portrayal of rescue. At that time, renewed Persian military activity in Palestine cut off any possibility of Yehud's achieving true political independence. The use of "stronghold" in verse 12 (see NOTE) apparently refers to that activity, and the reference to Greeks in verse 13 (see NOTE) likewise reflects the Greco-Persian wars of this era.

At the same time, inasmuch as Ezra and Nehemiah were both products of a diaspora community that continued in Babylon despite the significant returns of the late sixth century, it was clear that the Judeans still in Babylon, generations after their ancestors had been carried out of Judah, were entrenched in their land of captivity. Whether they stayed of their own accord or through Persian reluctance to allow a mass return is a moot point. The prophet sees a population of dispersed Israelites in need of restoration, whether they were held captive by their own intransigence or by the imperial policies of their captors.

The innocence of the exiles, like that of the "righteous" king (v 9) who will rule over them in Zion, is asserted by the twofold use of the term "prisoners," in verses 11 and 12, as well as by the concept of the double restoration of what the exiles had left behind in their homeland. "Prisoner" is a key image. As we explain in the NOTES, prisons were not used for punitive restraint in Israel and the ancient Near East. Rather, they held people accused of some misdeed or crime, of which they might be found innocent. Surely that would be the case for the exiles as prisoners beyond the generation of those who had been carried into captivity because of their sins in disobeying God and the covenant, according to Deuteronomic and prophetic perspectives on the end of Judean independence. Those still in Babylon were like prisoners, innocent of wrongdoing and so deserving of double compensation for their suffering. Zechariah 9:12 is to be compared to Isa 61:7—"because their shame was double, they shall possess a double portion."

The "waterless pit" phrase, which accompanies "prisoner" in verse 11b, likewise contributes to the image of helpless victims. Only external forces—in this case Yahweh's intervention—can bring about removal from such a prison. This vocabulary is specific to the condition of exile. At the same time, it provides recollection of the first great departure from bondage, the Exodus from Egypt. The association of blood with covenant (v 11) occurs elsewhere only in Exod 24:5ff., in reference to the Sinai event that followed the deliverance from Egypt. In addition, the "waterless pit" image is found in the Joseph story, which itself may be a product of exilic hero-literature developments, but which in its Pentateuchal form prefigures the Israelite imprisonment in the land of the Nile. The announcement that God will set prisoners free (v 11) is the equivalent of the language of Exod 5:1–2, in which Moses calls upon Pharaoh to "let my people go." But now, as at the Exodus, only Yahweh's might can effect the release. In recalling the Exodus, Second Zechariah resembles Second Isaiah, who interpreted events of the late sixth century, when Cyrus proclaimed that the people could return to their ancestral homeland, as a second great entry to the Promised Land.

The central part of this last subunit of Zechariah 9 portrays the way in which the impossible becomes a reality, albeit an eschatological one. God's infinite power is activated on behalf of the exiles, and the language of military might expresses Yahweh's intervention. The prophet here draws upon ancient mythic materials that depict divine forces as warriors, replete with weaponry. The rhetorical effect of the warrior metaphor operating in poetic language is immense, as well it must be to convince the downtrodden or imprisoned that their status can be reversed.

The metaphor is advanced in two stages, first with Yahweh using Israel itself as the means of the divine exercise of power—Judah and Ephraim together are likened to God's bow and sword (v 13). But then Yahweh directly takes action, as expressed by the theophanous appearance, marked with the unmistakable accompaniment of lightning and trumpet blasts (i.e., thunder?), the visual and aural components of southern storms (v 14). This language of theophany, like the warrior imagery, also draws upon ancient biblical themes, in this case the deity emerging from a southern sanctuary, perhaps Sinai itself. The terminology of theophany is meshed with that of warfare: lightning represents arrows, and the noise is that of trumpet blasts, which were sounded as a call for war or for armies to advance. The Song of Deborah in Judges 5 also fits this schema: the Song evokes the Sinai experiences and emphasizes the role of Yahweh and of Israel, together bringing about victory. The oracular language of Zechariah 9 thus draws upon ancient imagery that was apparently still current in the postexilic period, certainly in its earlier biblical manifestation, and perhaps also in the pagan world around the people of Yahweh.

Yahweh's presence in behalf of the people has been aroused by the need for God to rescue those who are hopelessly imprisoned, and who thereby gain hope ("prisoners of hope," v 12) by acknowledging that God can accomplish what humans cannot. But divine presence involves more than military matters, more than rescue and protection. As the prophecies of both Haggai and First Zechariah repeatedly claim, God's presence among the people involves the restoration of fertility. God provides for the people even beyond bare subsistence; Yahweh's concern for the people will mean plentitude.

This dimension of Yahweh's presence takes over from the aspect of divine power in verse 15b and continues to the end of the chapter. Not only will the Israelites be empowered to vanquish their enemies, they will also have ample to drink and to eat. Agricultural bounty appears in both verses 15 and 17. In the former, the similes of satiety—drinking to the state of merriment, and fullness like that of the basins (presumably used for grain offerings; see NOTE) at the corners of the altar—continue the poetic structure of the verse. Under Yahweh's aegis, the people will be able to protect themselves and to prosper; these two aspects of life are linked together by the arrangement of the poetic lines.

Although Yahweh's role in establishing security and sustenance for the people is clearly central, there are also allusions to the human leadership that will be present. The mention of "basin" and "altar" (v 15), terms for sacral equipment, implies a functioning temple cultus. That cultus signifies Yahweh's abode on earth and also implies a functioning priesthood. Similarly, "gemstones" and "crown" (v 16) are terms that have both priestly and royal connotations (see NOTES to these words), the latter providing reference to the royal figure of verses 9–10.

As the warrior metaphor gives way, at the end of chapter 9, to the depiction of fecundity, another symbolic category is introduced, that of sheep and shepherds. In this case (v 16), God is the shepherd and the people are the flocks. This imagery, derived from the pastoral component of the Israelite economy, appears frequently in the Bible and certainly constitutes an important part of Second Zechariah's rhetorical repertoire. Introduced at this point in the Zechariah 9–14 corpus, it adumbrates the elaboration of sheep/shepherd language, especially in chapters 10 and 11 (cf. also 13:7).

Just as the comparison of the people to sheep anticipates themes of the succeeding chapters, so too does the language of agrarian fecundity connect with prophetic material yet to come. The verse immediately following, 10:1, portrays the abundance of grain provided by Yahweh, with the God-given lightning and storms now having an agricultural, rather than military, function.

Not only do certain rhetorical and thematic aspects of 9:11–14 link with materials in subsequent sections of Second Zechariah, but the central focus of this subunit also recurs in the next chapter. Here the concern for the restoration of the exiled "prisoners" does not specify which dispersed Israelites are involved, although it seems that those in the Babylonian dispersion are the ones being rescued. Be that as it may, the situation of those exiled long before the Persian conquest of Babylon by Cyrus in 539–38 B.C.E. is a special and separate issue. All of the next chapter is dedicated to the status, rescue, and restoration of those people who, voluntarily or through the imperial demographic manipulation of the Assyrians, had been separated from their homeland in the Northern

Kingdom since the eighth century. The northerners—Ephraim, or the House of Joseph—are a special case; the attention given to them in chapter 10 is a continuation and narrowing of the general portrayal of restoration of land, king, and people that chapter 9 so eloquently sets forth.

ZECHARIAH 10

◆

Yahweh Empowers Judah and Rescues Ephraim

10 ¹Ask of Yahweh rain at the time of the spring-rains,
  of Yahweh, the lightning maker;
and rainstorms may he give to them,
  to each one grain in the field.

²For the teraphim have spoken deception,
  and the diviners have seen falsity.
They speak worthless dreams
  and give vain comfort.
Therefore they have set forth like sheep;
  they're humble without a shepherd.
³My anger has flared against the shepherds,
  and I will attend to the he-goats.
For Yahweh of Hosts has attended to his flock, the House of Judah,
  and will make them like his mighty horse in battle.
⁴From them will come the cornerstone,
  from them the tent peg,
  from them the bow of war,
  from them every overseer—together.
⁵They will be like heroes in battle,
  trampling in muddy places.
They'll fight because Yahweh is with them;
  they will confound those mounted on horses.
⁶I will make the House of Judah mighty,
  the House of Joseph I will save.
I will restore them because I had compassion on them;
  for they will be as though I had not rejected them.
For I am Yahweh their God,
  and I will respond to them.
⁷Ephraim will be like a hero;
  their heart rejoices as with wine.
Their children will see and rejoice—
  let their heart exult in Yahweh.

[8]I will whistle to them and gather them in,
>   for I have redeemed them.
> They will multiply as before.
> [9]Though I sowed them among the peoples,
>   in remote places they'll remember me.
> They'll give life[a] to their children,
>   and they will return.
> [10]I will bring them back from the land of Egypt;
>   and from Assyria I will gather them.
> To the land of Gilead and to Lebanon I will bring them,
>   till no room is found for them.
> [11]He will traverse the sea of stress,
>   he will smite the rolling sea,
>   and all the depths of the stream will dry up.
> The splendor of Assyria will be brought low,
>   and the scepter of Egypt will pass away.
> [12]I will make them mighty in Yahweh;
>   in his name they will go about—utterance of Yahweh.

NOTES

10:1. *Ask of Yahweh*. The author of this initial section (vv 1–2) of Zechariah 10 calls upon the Israelites to request ("ask"—*š'l* in the plural imperative) of Yahweh rains in their seasons. The exhortation (cf. the designation *Mahnwort*, "admonition," in Horst and Robinson 1964: 249) to "ask of Yahweh rain," while introducing a section with a distinct message and style, also connects thematically with the concluding verse (v 17) of chapter 9, which proclaims that in the eschatological era (see NOTE to "on that day," 9:16), "grain will make the young men flourish, and new wine the maidens" (see NOTES to 9:17, especially "Grain . . . new wine"). For there to be sufficient grain and wine for people to flourish, there had to be sufficient water, that is, rain; and the rains had to come at the appropriate times for crops to ripen (see NOTE below in this verse to "rain . . . spring-rains"). Thus the last verse of chapter 9 presents a condition that will be the result of what is described in verse 1 of chapter 10. In a sense, the two verses dovetail, because 10:1 sets forth the conditions—ample and appropriately timed rainfall—that produce the fertility described in 9:17 as well as at the end of 10:1.

Not only does the first verse of this chapter provide a link with the previous one, but its first words—"Ask of Yahweh"—also constitute an anticipation, by way of contrast with the next verse (10:2) of this chapter, where the turning to various mantic functionaries or devices—"teraphim," "diviners" (see NOTES below)—is shown to be useless or worse. The verb *š'l*, "to ask," has a wide range of usages, including to indicate petitions to the deity. In 1 Kgs 3:10–11, it appears in the context of Solomon's request of Yahweh for a dynastic successor,

___
[a]Reading the Piel *wĕḥîyyû*.

and in Isa 30:2 it is used in reference to the Israelites' failing to seek God's counsel. In this technical sense, it overlaps somewhat with *bqš*, "to seek," (cf. Isa 65:1) as a term for the consulting of a deity or oracle in a cultic context. Noteworthy in this aspect are 1 Sam 23:2 and 4, in which David inquires of Yahweh about a projected military offensive, and, especially, 1 Sam 30:7–8, in which David performs a similar act, this time explicitly with the aid of the priest Abiathar and the ephod.

Thus, in urging the people to seek the benefits of the natural world through Yahweh, the prophet is adumbrating the critique of the modes of contacting divinity as set forth in the next verse. It is noteworthy that the exhortation is to address Yahweh directly. There is no notion of intermediaries, be they professional prophets (soothsayers or diviners of some sort) or "true prophets." Indeed, the former are ruled out by the message of the next verse, and the latter are also eschewed in that true prophets are those whose oracular statements come forth unsolicited.

At this point, the question of whom the prophet is addressing in this exhortation must be considered. We are not told directly. However, insofar as this chapter is to be viewed as a unity (see our discussion in the Introduction above and in COMMENT below), there is a certain justification to taking into account the identifiable focus of the second half of this chapter, namely the exiled northerners (see below, NOTE to "teraphim," 10:2), in specifying those to whom this message is addressed. Thus it can be suggested that the prophet directed his words to the dispersed population of the Northern Kingdom. It should also be noted, however, that the meteorological and agricultural conditions of this verse are apparently Palestinian and would not necessarily obtain in all the places to which northerners were exiled. Hence the audience would be Palestinian. The poet is thus drawing upon traditional language appropriate for exhorting Judahites and weaving it into a poem that ultimately involves the restoration of all to the land exhibiting the climatic characteristics underlying verse 1.

The exhortation to ask Yahweh for the conditions of material well-being initiates a chapter containing literary and thematic forms that have aroused much scholarly discussion. P. D. Hanson (1975) and Mason (1973) in particular have made considerable contributions to the analysis of Zechariah 10, and their views are explained in our Introduction. At this point, we simply indicate that their views, each of which have merit, are not necessarily antithetical; many elements of both perspectives help our understanding of this complex chapter.

Our translation reflects the punctuation of the MT, which places the major division in the verse at the *athnach* after "lightning maker." With additional subdivisions after *malqôš* ("spring-rains") and *lāhem* ("to them"), the verse is a double bicolon or quatrain, reasonably balanced in syllable count and accent. This four-line division involves two major verbs: the opening imperative *šʾl* ("ask") and *ytn* ("may he give"), to be taken in the jussive sense (see NOTE below in this verse). By following the MT, the participial construction with the second

"Yahweh" is best understood as an address to the deity by the title "lightning maker" (see NOTE below in this verse for a discussion of this designation).

rain . . . spring-rains. The MT presents two terms for rain: *māṭār* and *malqôš*. The LXX has a third term, usually translated "autumn rains" or "early rains" for *yôreh*, which is frequently restored in some English translations (e.g., NEB) and by some exegetes (e.g., P. D. Hanson 1975). Those who supply "early rains" are no doubt influenced by Deut 11:14, which contains all three terms for rain as well as "time" or "season": "I will give rain *(mṭr)* for your land in its time *(ʿt)*, the early rain *(ywrh)* and the later rain *(mlqš)*." Other prophetic passages also contain all three terms: Jer 5:24 (which uses *gšm* rather than *mṭr* for "rain") and Joel 2:23; cf. Hos 6:3.

Although "rain" (either *gšm* or *mṭr*) is a common term in the Hebrew Bible, the words for the early and late seasonal rains are in comparison rather rare. Sometimes the latter are paired, as in the passages cited above; elsewhere they can occur alone. "Early rain" occurs by itself only in Ps 84:7 (NRSV 84:6), where no other terms for rain are found. "Spring-rains" appears in Job 29:23 where it is a focusing of *mṭr*, in Jer 3:3 where it is parallel to "showers" *(rbbym)*, and in Prov 16:15 where there is no other term for rain. Of the instances in which "spring-rains" occurs without "autumn-rains," this passage in Zechariah is the only one that otherwise has a full complement of the terms used in the paradigmatic text in Deuteronomy (11:14). Thus one wonders whether the omission of "autumn-rains" is intentional; the fact that the LXX restores it indicates that the expectation would be to include it, although it may simply be that LXX has been influenced by Deut 11:14. If the author has purposefully used "spring-rains" alone, the reasons for doing so may be purely poetic. However, the fact that this verse continues its meteorological language with a reference to lightning (or thunderbolts; see NOTE below to "lightning maker") may help resolve the omission. Severe storms, accompanied by thunder and lightning, were more apt to result from the convectional conditions that marked the onset of the rainy season in October (Baly 1963: 34). Thus the fall of early rains, rather than the spring-rains, would have been those associated with violent thunderstorms.

The need for rain in ancient Palestine, and the way in which the Bible equates the granting or withholding of rain with God's blessing or curse, is the result of related aspects of ancient life. First, Israelites practiced rainfall agriculture (Borowski 1987), in which the success of their crops was dependent on seasonal rain rather than on water from springs, lakes, or rivers. Second, the situation of Palestine is a very precarious one with respect to the dependability of rainfall as a source of water for farming, and so is subject to periodic droughts (Hopkins 1985: 84–91), which were interpreted as the result of divine wrath.

The rainy season, with the spring-rains marking its ending, usually begins in October at about the time of Sukkoth, the Feast of Booths. (Note that Zech 14:17 proclaims that the rain will be withheld for anyone failing to celebrate Sukkoth properly.) It continues then, sporadically, throughout the winter months and ends at about the time of Pesah, the Passover festival. The ancient cropping pattern was sensitively geared to these climatic conditions, and the hope for rain was actually hope that the rains would come in that overall period, although there were special needs for rain at the beginning and end of the rainy season (see next NOTE). Indeed, to this very day, Jewish liturgy involves prayers for rain only between Sukkoth and Pesah. However, special prayers for moisture from dew, which sustains certain crops during the dry season, are recited during the summer months, from Shabuot (Pentecost) to Sukkoth (cf. the theme of dew shortage in Hag 1:10, in reference to a crisis in late August, 520 B.C.E., just before the fall harvest and thus a critical time in a dry-farming system; see Meyers and Meyers 1987: 30–31).

time. The opening exhortation of chapter 10 involves not only asking for rains but also requesting that they come at the appropriate time of year. That aspect of the need for rain was as critical as the need for moisture itself. The rainy season, although lasting for roughly half the year, did not include rain falling continuously during the winter months. Rather, there were three periods of rainfall—the early fall-rains *(ywrh)*, the sporadic rain from November through March, and the late rains *(mlqš)* of April/May (see previous NOTE for a discussion of these terms). A delay of even a week or so of either the first or third period of rainfall could spell disaster for the potential harvest (Baly 1957: 48, 52). Furthermore, especially in the spring, the timing of the late rains with respect to the sirocco or *ḥamsin*, the hot, dry desert winds that typically come during the two periods of seasonal transition, in early winter or late summer— there being really only two seasons in Palestine—was critical. If the sirocco comes too soon in the spring after the onset of the spring-rains, it will destroy the emerging buds (Hareuveni 1980: 37); hence the imagery of the devastating east wind, as in Ezek 17:10. The extreme anxiety attending the timing of each stage of the rainfall, and the conception of divine might in reference to the granting of rain at the right time, are a function of the precarious balance of agricultural patterns and meteorological conditions, a balance all too often not present.

lightning maker. As indicated in the first NOTE to this verse, ʿōśeh ḥăzîzîm is a participial construction, describing Yahweh. This second use of "Yahweh" is thus an address to the deity using one of his titles: "lightning maker." Such a designation is probably analogous to the Greco-Roman title of "Thunderbolt Thrower" for Zeus/Jupiter and may go back to the language used for Canaanite Baal as god of lightning and thunder, that is, the storm god who brings rains. Yahweh certainly partakes of storm-god imagery, as the narrative of the contest between Elijah and the prophets of Baal at Mt. Carmel suggests. There, Yahweh's "fire" from heaven (= lightning?) ultimately results in a storm and "great rains" (1 Kgs 18:38, 45).

Like the following expression ("rainstorms"; see next NOTE), "lightning" is an unusual word. Although in English translation it conjures up familiar enough images, the word in Hebrew would have been less well known than *brq*, which occurs more frequently, including once in Second Zechariah (9:14), where it is used in a simile to indicate the brightness or swiftness of Yahweh's arrow. The term used here with the participial *ʿōśeh* is the plural of *ḥăzîz*, which can also mean "thunderbolt," and seems to be more directly related to the meteorological phenomena it represents than is *brq*, which tends to be used more metaphorically. However, *ḥăzîz* appears elsewhere only in Job (28:26; 38:25), where it expresses divine control over the natural components of the cosmos, as a way of emphasizing to Job that God is unquestionably in control of all the world and that the vastness of divine power means that a human may not be able to comprehend all that God does. Thus the metaphorical aspect of the term in those passages, and perhaps also here, is in keeping with the storm-god epithet "lightning maker" (see also, above, NOTE to "like lightning," 9:14).

The language expressing "lightning" or "thunderbolts," apropos of the discussion above in the NOTE to "rain . . . spring-rains," can also be associated with the autumnal rains of the Near East, when the global air currents move in patterns that produce violent electrical storms. Thus, although the technical term for "fall-rain" is unexpectedly absent from this verse, the October downpours may well be represented by this word indicating lightning and/or thunder.

rainstorms. Although composed of two fairly common words for rain (*mṭr* and *gšm*; see NOTE above to "rain . . . spring-rain" in this verse), "rainstorms" here is an unusual construct chain: *mĕṭar-gešem*. Like "lightning" (see previous NOTE), it occurs only here and in Job 37:6, where it intensifies the idea of rain, which God provides, as a way of underscoring God's absolute control of the natural realm. Similarly here, the doubling of the term for "rain" serves to emphasize the idea of the abundance of water and so to acknowledge the might of God in providing rain, and thus life, to the people. The relationship of this phrase along with "lightning" to the elevated language of God's cosmic activity in Job indicates the presence of a similar awareness of God's global realm and the mythic nature of divine activity in the cosmos. These notions are suitably part of the divine-warrior imagery of verses 3–12, which form the complement to the introductory materials of 10:1–2.

to them. Some would emend "to them" *(lhm)* to "bread *(lḥm)* to everyone," as first suggested by Duhm (1910) and now preserved in the apparatus of *BHS*. The MT is perfectly sensible, however, and means that God will provide "for everyone." The real problem is the shift here to the third-person masculine plural pronoun from the second-person plural used in verse 1 ("ask," second-person masc. pl.). The poet never does return to the second-person masculine plural until the imperative at the beginning of the next chapter. Although it is not always possible to understand such frequent and seemingly awkward shifts, it may be best to see this third-person usage as dominant in chapter 10, with the second-person masculine plural of verse 1 serving to align the opening of this chapter with that of the next.

to each one. The Hebrew seems repetitive, but "to each one" *(lĕʾîš)* serves to clarify who the "them" are—namely, everyone. If the community of Israel will direct its prayers to Yahweh, then God will provide sustenance for all: give each and everyone "grain in the field."

grain in the field. This expression is intended to convey the general result of

Israel's request for seasonal rains, namely, that grass will in fact grow in the field, i.e., that the natural world will flourish. The use here of terminology that echoes the language of the second creation story in Genesis (2:5 and 3:18) means that this phrase can denote plant life in general and need not be understood literally, that is, as indicating only grass. The Hebrew for "grain" is ʿēśeb, which may also be translated "herb" or "herbage." In the first Genesis reference (2:5), it is part of a construct and lacks the preposition "in" before "field." As for its meaning, ʿēśeb, which is in parallel with the rather rare word for "bush," denotes grain, the epitome of a cultivated plant. That is, unlike "bush of the field," which denotes all nonanimal growing things, "grain of the field" represents field crops, plants that are grown for consumption by both domesticated animals and people, plants that are the essence of life for agriculturalists (C. L. Meyers 1988: 83). This meaning is also present in Gen 3:18 where the male, in being banished from the paradisiacal Garden of Eden, is informed that only by arduous labor will he be able to eat the "grain of the field," which represents all plant foodstuffs produced through agricultural activity.

This nuanced meaning suits quite well the context of Zech 10:1, where the fervent plea for rains at certain times of the year is the concomitant of the knowledge that such rains are essential for the cropping pattern in Palestine (see above, NOTES to "rain . . . spring-rains" and "time"), whereby human subsistence is achieved.

Note, however, that Deut 11:14, the classic biblical statement (cited above in NOTE to "rain . . . spring-rains") about God's sending the specific rains at their appointed times, appears to connect the "grain of the field" with what livestock consume: "I will give you grain in your fields for your livestock." That statement comes immediately after God's promise that with the giving of appropriate rain, people will have "grain (dgn), wine, and oil," the staples of Palestine's basic tripartite agrarian scheme. However, that result of the granting of timely rain is omitted in Zech 10:1, although at least two elements of it— grain and wine—appear in 9:17. Consequently, in the elliptical poetry of 10:1, "grain in the field" represents what is grown for both humans as well as animals, as the statement that these plants are for "each one" clearly indicates. Nonetheless, although Zechariah goes his own way in adapting the Deuteronomic blessing, the covenant context of that blessing must surely hover in the background: God's bestowing rain, and thus subsistence, on the people is not an automatic reward or response to human request, but rather comes as the result of obedience to God's word.

2. *teraphim*. This is the first of the categories of religious or prophetic divination upon which verse 2 focuses. A variety of exegetical problems surround the way these figures are portrayed. Do the teraphim and diviners (see NOTE below) represent legitimate Israelite prophetic activity of the nonclassical variety? Or is the prophet referring to the work of non-Israelite divination? Or is the language portraying these questionable prophetic practices really meant to be a condemnation of idolatry or of the worship of gods other than Yahweh? Inextricably related to these questions is the matter of the identity of those to

whom the results of the diviners' activities are being addressed. Who are the ones who go about like lost, leaderless sheep at the end of this verse? Finally, is the prophet referring to a condition of problematic divination that occurred in the distant past or is he addressing a more recent situation?

It is not clear, as with so much in Second Zechariah, that a definitive answer can be provided for any of these questions. However, clarifying any one of these issues can, to a certain extent, provide the possibility of resolving one or more of the others. Our sense of the overall context and direction of Zechariah 10 is helpful in addressing the last of the questions mentioned above, namely the identity of those to whom the diviners are offering the patently unhelpful messages described in the second bicolon of this line. In our NOTE below to "they have set forth" we explain that this last bicolon apparently refers to exiles, to leaderless people, and that the exiles of particular concern to Second Zechariah, especially in this chapter, are those who have been dispersed to lands other than Babylon, that is, those carried away from their homeland with the collapse of the Northern Kingdom. If this be the case, then at least we can suggest that the setting for this verse is the diaspora, chiefly the non-Babylonian one.

In this context, the role of the teraphim (Heb. *tĕrāpîm*) can now be evaluated. Teraphim were apparently cult objects of some sort, as indicated by the famous story of Rachel and the teraphim (Gen 31:19, 30–35) and by the story of the household shrine of Micah (Judg 17:5). In addition to these well-known passages, teraphim as objects, probably somewhat smaller than life-size, figure in another prominent tale, that of Michal's deception in 1 Sam 19:11–17. Altogether, the word "teraphim" appears in fifteen different texts, many of them presenting no additional clues as to the identity of such objects. Thus, although much scholarly attention has been given to these relatively obscure objects and the puzzling practices associated with them, the actual appearance and function of teraphim remain somewhat elusive.

Most translations, following an opinion widely held in scholarly treatments, render "teraphim" in some of its biblical occurrences as "idol" (NRSV), "household idol" (NJPS), or "household gods" (NEB). These translations, which imply some sort of idolatrous cultic activity, do not necessarily account for all the uses of the term. Nor do they deal satisfactorily with the acceptance with which they are presented in at least some of the texts. Moreover, while they may convey an idea of the physical form of the teraphim, they contribute nothing toward an understanding of their function.

Consequently, another possible reading of "teraphim" should be entertained, as recently proposed and carefully defended by van der Toorn (1990), although suggested by several other scholars over the last century. This alternate reading is based on an analysis, first, of all the biblical texts as well as associated ones—those dealing with the ephod, for example—that offer clues about its appearance and use. In addition, extrabiblical data, which are of some limited value, are reviewed. Such data provide relevant phenomenological information about the use of such statuettes, although an investigation of terms in cuneiform literature that have a putative etymological connection to "teraphim" are not particularly helpful. The result of this renewed investigation of the teraphim problem is the conclusion that, rather than denoting small statues meant to represent either Yahweh or some other deity, the term "teraphim" more likely designates ancestor statuettes or figurines.

Teraphim thus were probably symbolic representations of humans—of deceased ancestors—who may have held quasi-divine or godlike status by virtue of how they were approached by the descendants who revered them, but who nonetheless were not regarded as deities. Particularly helpful in establishing such an understanding is the way in which the account of Josiah's reform alters the Deuteronomic listing of the practices of other peoples to be repudiated by Israel. In Deut 18:11, the text denounces (1) someone who casts spells, (2) a person who consults an ancestor (*ʾôb*) or familiar spirit (together these may be a hendiadys for "ancestral spirit"), and (3) one who asks (i.e., seeks oracles from) the dead. In 2 Kgs 23:24, a similar sequence substitutes "teraphim" where Deuteronomy has "the dead." The overall context of associated terms in both cases is necromancy, or communication with the dead in order that their living descendants receive some help or guidance in making a decision. Consulting deceased ancestors is thus a form of prophetic activity.

Identifying teraphim as ancestor statuettes helps in comprehending why their presence in the households of Laban, David, and Micah arouses no condemnation. Similarly, Hos 3:4 does not condemn teraphim as such. Perhaps ancestor worship, if not consultation, operated phenomenologically in much the way that saints figure in postbiblical Western religion, in which shrines and statues of revered human figures have a place in religious practice and beliefs but are not considered threats to the monotheistic idea (van der Toorn 1990: 216). That Deuteronomic law and Josiah condemn teraphim and many other divinatory practices merely means that, like other aspects of Israelite/Judean cult proscribed in the Deuteronomic reform, they were a normal part of religious behavior until the seventh century. Presumably the exiled Israelites, not subjected to the Deuteronomic reform in quite the same way as the Judeans, continued in their diaspora homes the practices forbidden by Josiah. The condemnation of teraphim in 1 Sam 15:23 is not so much a categorical repudiation as it is a concern about practices, including the bringing of sacrifices and offerings, that distract people from obeying Yahweh's word.

If teraphim functioned as part of necromantic practices, which were surely acceptable among northern Israelites at the time of their dispersal, their continued use would have found a congenial setting particularly in Assyria. Of all the data available from cuneiform texts that bear upon the phenomenology involved in teraphim as ancestor figurines, the evidence from ancient Assyria is most relevant. Necromancy was apparently quite rare in ancient Babylonia (Finkel 1983–84), but the existence of an ancestor cult together with necromancy is attested in Old Assyria and well into the first millennium in neo-Assyrian times, according to the texts adduced by van der Toorn (1990: 217–19; see also his analysis of relevant texts from Nuzi and Emar).

In sum, the mention of teraphim as ancestor figures here is quite appropriate. It suits a context involving exiled northerners, who are the special concern of this chapter of Second Zechariah. Moreover, in dealing negatively (see next NOTE) with the advice received from teraphim as symbols of ancestors, that is, from former generations, the prophets may be alluding to decisions of the exiled Israelites that were quite different from those made by many Judeans by the fifth century, namely, to return to their homeland. At the same time, the notion that prophetic activity based on the words of ancestors rather than Yahweh is futile and false, is related to the recurrent allusion to the notorious problem of false prophecy that beset Israelite prophets. Jeremiah in particular reflects the struggle with deceiving prophets; hence it is no wonder that Second Zechariah, who was greatly influenced by Jeremiah, among other earlier prophets, was sensitive to the tension between true and false prophets (see below, NOTE to "Shepherd," 11:4).

have spoken deception. The verb is in the perfect tense and indicates actions that took place in the past. As such, it can refer to past events that continue to have an effect (GKC §106.k), as the shift to the imperfect of the same verb in the next poetic line also suggests (see below, NOTES to "have seen" and "speak"). The verb *dbr* has the general meaning "to speak" and is commonly used in prophetic literature to express God's speaking to humans, i.e., the oracular word of Yahweh. Its oracular connotations are surely behind its usage here, where it indicates what the revered ancestors have communicated to their descendants (see preceding NOTE).

The use of "deception" (ʾāwen) to specify what the deceased generations have said seems to have been influenced by 1 Sam 15:23, where ʾāwen and "teraphim" are paired (and where "divination" also appears, as it does here; see next NOTE). The exact nuance of ʾāwen is difficult to establish, in part because neither the noun nor its verbal root (ʾwn) is attested in another Semitic language and also because of the great variety of terms or ideas that are used in parallel with ʾāwen. Thus, although it can mean "violence" or "intentional harm" or "iniquity" at one end of its semantic spectrum, it is also related to emptiness, nothingness, worthlessness, or vanity at the other end. This Zechariah passage may well represent a transition to the latter aspect of its semantic range, because it occurs here in association with both worthlessness and vanity (see NOTES below in this verse). Hence the deception cited in Zech 10:2 is not necessarily that of evildoers bent on harming others; rather, leaning toward the nothingness that appears in parallel bicola in the next line, it involves self-deception or unintentional deception (Bernhardt 1974: 142). Yet the end result is essentially the same: a prophetic activity functions in a way that is the antithesis of true prophecy, which provides Yahweh's word.

The teraphim give information that misleads, just as do the "diviners," whose message is a false one (see below, NOTE to "falsity," *šeqer*), perhaps because it is precisely the misleading message of the teraphim. Both ʾāwen and *šeqer* are used to characterize the nature of the oracles and visions being communicated. They are almost adjectival, as if this line asserts that the

187

teraphim have spoken deceitfully, though perhaps not intentionally so, and that the diviners have had false visions. The immediate effect of the erroneous directives produced by prophetic activity is supplied by the two bicola of the next line. Although we are not told what those deceptive (and false) directives are, we are told of two kinds of results in the next two lines: (1) what it feels like for the recipients of these directives and (2) how it affects their status. On both counts, the intervention of Yahweh and the Judean agents, as described in the rest of this chapter, is the necessary consequence.

diviners. The term "diviners," a participial form of the verb *qsm*, "to practice divination," seems to be a more general term than "teraphim" (see NOTE above) of the preceding bicolon. It apparently refers to practitioners or professionals who provide answers to questions about the present or future to those who seek their advice; it indicates a mode of predicting activity. The means by which diviners engage in such activity are not specified; presumably various mantic devices could be employed, or the meaning of natural events or signs might be interpreted. Indeed, consulting teraphim might even be an activity practiced by diviners (see Ezek 21:26 [NRSV 21:21]), in which case the diviners of this line are those who interpret or communicate the misguided message of the teraphim of the previous line. Decision making is the motivation behind any process of divination (see Prov 16:10). Israelites, like all peoples, felt the need to understand God's will before proceeding with important personal or communal matters. In this sense, divination is a form of popular prophecy.

Biblical texts depict foreign nations or individuals engaged in divination (e.g., Num 22:7; 23:23; 1 Sam 6:2; Isa 2:6) as often as they mention divination within Israel. Most of the references to divination castigate the people for believing what diviners tell them rather than seeking God's word directly (e.g., Mic 3:6 [NRSV 3:7], 11; Ezek 13:6). In this sense, they are false prophets. That is, what they advise those who seek their help is not from God and thus cannot be deemed reliable. The fact that "falsity" (*šqr*) is frequently associated with "diviners" (as in Jer 14:14; 27:8–9; 29:9–10; see below, NOTE to "falsity" in this verse) reveals the attitude of the literary prophets toward those practitioners. Second Zechariah, in this negative depiction of diviners, shares the language used by other prophetic voices. The presence of the word "deception" ("lies"), as well as "speak," "see" (*hzh*), and "dreams" (*hlm*) in this verse, along with "diviners," links the prophet with his predecessors, especially Jeremiah, who also brings all these terms together (in 14:14; see Mason 1973: 93–95).

Although the prophetic castigation of diviners and other false prophets is prominent, the reasons given for the repudiation of such practices is that God's true word is not obtained by such means. These practices in and of themselves are not anywhere directly forbidden except in Deut 18:10–11, which links them to the prophetic activities of foreigners and for that reason proclaims them unacceptable in Israel. The language of Deuteronomy is virtually the same as that of 2 Kgs 17:17, which asserts that the destruction of all but the tribe of Judah (v 18) is the result of, among many other wrongdoings, the people's recourse to "divination." In other words, as a condemned activity, divination is linked to the Northern Kingdom and to its dispersion by the Assyrians.

Thus, because it was a prophetic technique practiced by foreigners, and because it is connected with the life-style of the Israelites rather than the Judeans, "divination" here in reference to the exiled Israelites is a highly suitable choice of a word to indicate that these people have been misguided. Its suitability is further enhanced in light of the fact that, at least in one text, divination is connected with necromancy. In the story of the medium of Endor *(ba'alat-'ôb)*, Saul asks this professional to "consult" (using the verb *qsm*) an ancestral spirit, namely Samuel. It may be that in these parallel statements in the first line of 10:2, the idea of a specific kind of prophetic activity, represented by teraphim as the consulting of past generations, is then expanded by the designation of a larger category, divination, of which necromancy is a prime example. This shift, which involves increasing the scope of the fruitless attempts to make good decisions, serves to intensify the negative aspects of such activity and hence serves the prophet's intention to highlight the misguided behavior of the Israelites. In this way, he prefigures the true leadership and right decisions, imposed from without by none other than Yahweh through the action of the Judean warriors. At the same time, in calling attention to the counterproductive work of diviners as false prophets, he anticipates the direct expression of the tension between true and false prophecy that appears in the enigmatic shepherd narrative of chapter 11 and in the condemnation of false prophets in chapter 13.

have seen. As a loanword from Aramaic, where the verb *ḥzh*, "to see," can refer to the natural sight of the eyes, in Hebrew its meaning is primarily, as here, in reference to supernatural vision of various kinds and, hence, to prophetic activity (Jepsen 1980: 280–90). When the verb or its nominal form is used in association with a prophet, the verb means "to have a vision" and the noun indicates "vision" or "revelation." It is thus part of the technical vocabulary of prophecy and as such is one of a series of terms that cluster in this verse (see NOTES to "teraphim" and "diviners" above). Like its parallel in the first half of this line, the verb is in the perfect tense and so reflects past activities. Both verbs may refer to events in the distant past, which led to Israel's exile at the hands of the Assyrians. Yet the switch to the imperfect for both verbs of the next line, which contributes further information about the problems involved in the use of teraphim and divination, seems to suggest that the unhelpful results of such decision-making techniques continue into the prophet's present. What the diviners "see" turns out to be false (see next NOTE), hence the need for divine intervention that will result in the restoration of the northern exiles.

falsity. The noun *šeqer*, although it can also mean "deception," does not necessarily imply intentional deception or lying on the part of those who utter or "see" (see previous NOTE) falsity. Rather, what the diviners (see NOTE above in this verse) offer to those who seek their services turns out to be bad advice, and thus the effect is one of the diviners' having deceived their clients. Just what that bad advice was, and when it was given, is difficult to determine. However, based on the sequence of verbal tenses (see NOTES to all verbs in this verse) and on the consequence that God will have to intervene to change the situation, the false advice, or even deception, may have been related to the northern exiles' retaining their dispersed status.

The association of *šeqer* with the verb *ḥzh* ("to see") is especially prominent in Jeremiah, where it occurs thirteen times, including the verse cited above, Jer 14:14, where other words found in this passage ("speak," "divination") are also used. Although Second Zechariah may well be drawing upon the language of Jeremiah, it is important to note that he is not quoting him exactly; the terms may be the same, but they are arranged differently. In addition, Jeremiah specifies the content of the falsity—that Judah will be spared destruction by sword and famine—whereas Zechariah leaves it to his audience to infer the content of the false divination. Indeed, Second Zechariah's concept of the "falsity" provided by prophetic figures is probably more inclusive than that of Jeremiah. His retrospective scope is larger than that of his influential predecessor—he sees the falsity of idolatrous prophets as well as of those wrongly claiming to provide Yahweh's word (see NOTES to 13:2–6, especially to "you have spoken falsity" in 13:3). Moreover, the use of *šeqer* is linked to the appearance of *šāwʾ* ("worthless") in the next line (cf. the strong use of these two words in the third and ninth commandments of the Decalogue, Exod 20:5, 16; although the parallel list of commandments in Deuteronomy uses *šāwʾ* in both places), thus contributing to the interweaving of all the parts of this verse and hence to the inclusivity of this prophet's concern with all manner of nonlegitimate prophetic activity.

speak. The verb *dbr* here repeats the verb of the first bicolon of the preceding line, where it refers to the prophetic or oracular result of the use of teraphim (see first two NOTES to this verse). This time, however, the tense of the verb has been changed to the imperfect. Rather than indicating a redundancy by a later hand (Mitchell 1912: 287), the shift in tenses may be a deliberate touch. It conveys the idea that the misguidance of prophetic functionaries, which began in the past, presumably at the time of the Assyrian conquest, continues into the prophet's present, when the condition of a leaderless and lowly people, as set forth in the third line of this verse (see NOTES below to "they're humble" and "without a shepherd"), obtains. "Speak" thus initiates a poetic line that, rather than repeating the ideas of the first line of this verse, specifies the immediate results of the pronouncement that are false and that deceive. If the parallel structure of these first two lines of verse 2 is followed, then the results of each of the two prophetic activities presented in the first line are given in the second. However, because "diviners" may simply represent a larger category of prophetic practices that would include teraphim, then the two bicola of this second line would present the sad results of all such prophecy that operates indirectly through mediums or devices, rather than by inquiring directly of Yahweh. In any case, it is clear that this line·does not repeat the thoughts of the first line of verse 2; it expands them by depicting one stage in the immediate results of prophecy that misleads.

Having said that the shift in tenses may be deliberate, we would also point out that in the elevated style of passages such as this one, the interweaving of perfect and imperfect is a poetic way of connecting all the thoughts or actions of the series of poetic lines. Rather than meaning that some actions are past and others are future or present, the intertwining of tenses is a poetic way of preserving the ongoing existence of something, in this case the presence of an array of divinatory practices that are counter to true prophecy and Yahwistic ideals. The linkage of *šqr*, "falsity," and *šāwᵓ*, "worthless," of lines b and c of this verse contributes to the interconnections of tense and terminology of the whole verse, but especially of these two lines.

worthless dreams. "Dreams" (from the verbal root *ḥlm*, "to dream") may indirectly allude to another sort of prophetic activity, namely, dream interpretation; or they may refer to the dreams that the people themselves are having and as they themselves understand them. The Bible rarely, if ever, depicts an Israelite in need of a professional dream interpreter; the dreams, even the symbolic ones, experienced by the Israelites are self-explanatory (Bergman, Ottosson, and Botterweck 1980: 430). Note that Jer 27:9 and 29:8, despite the versional and scholarly attempts to make these verses refer to professional dreamers or the dreams that professional dreamers have, really refer to the indirect mode of divine revelation that constitutes any person's dreams, without need of mediating professionals. In this verse, however, even if the dreams are those of dead Israelites, i.e., the ancestors consulted in the attempts of Israelites to make decisions about their lives, the meaning of the dreams may come via the "diviners" who interpret teraphim and dreams but do so wrongly and provide empty comfort (see next NOTE). And the dreams thereby revealed defy normal expectations—that the dreams will come from the divine realm and offer information about the future. In this case, the dreams are empty, portray nothing, provide no clue. How disappointing for people uncertain as to how to conduct themselves to acquire no clue from a common phenomenon of human mental activity!

The dreams are without value, i.e., "worthless." Although *šāwᵓ* can mean "emptiness" and thus lies within the semantic field of *hebel*, "vain," in the next bicolon (see NOTE below), the fact that it is used here with "dreams" mitigates the possibility that it is a simple parallel of *hebel*, because dreams by definition have content or there would be no dream at all, and because parallel words or phrases usually have subtle differences of meaning. The ancestral dreams give no worthwhile information to the exiled Israelites; only inquiring directly of Yahweh would yield meaningful information. And worse, because of the link between *šāwᵓ* and *šeqer*, the "worthless" dreams are condemned for leading to iniquity or involving falsity.

and give vain comfort. These four English words translate two Hebrew words: the verb *nḥm* in the Piel, meaning "to comfort, console, give comfort," and the noun *hebel*. The Hebrew has no conjunction, perhaps resulting from haplography with the preceding word, *ydbrw*, which ends in *waw*. Perhaps the most famous biblical use of *nḥm* is in Isa 40:1, 2, where the prophet touchingly proclaims "comfort, comfort my people" to the exiles. Indeed, such consolation is what exiles, torn from their homeland, seek. The diviners (see NOTE above) provide no such encouragement or compassion for the exiles, as the presence of *hebel* indicates. That noun, which originally meant "breath" or "vapor," is more often used as here in the abstract or figurative sense. Furthermore, as in Job 21:34, where it also appears with *nhm* in the Piel, it is used adverbially. It expresses the fact that the comfort proffered by the diviners (see NOTE above) is meaningless; it negates an expectation in an emotion-laden way (Seybold 1978: 316). The diviners are failing in what they purport to do. Surely, then, they cannot speak Yahweh's message.

they have set forth. Many commentators regard this term, from the root *ns*ᶜ ("to depart, set out, journey") as inappropriate to the context. Thus it is variously emended to the root *nw*ᶜ ("to wander"), *nt*ᶜ ("be broken," in the Niphal), *nws* ("to flee"), or *s*ᶜ*r* ("to be scattered," in the Niphal). The difficulty in understanding what the verb means is related to the matter of identifying its subject. Theoretically, the verb could be indicating further action on the part of those represented by the last-mentioned noun, namely, the "diviners." However, this line is introduced by "therefore," an adverbial form composed of *kēn* ("thus," "so") preceded by *ᶜal* ("upon"). This particular combination tends to introduce a fact, rather than prophetic declaration as does the related combination *lākēn* (*BDB*: 487). In this case, it indicates the consequences of a given condition, namely, the futile and misleading communication of prophetic practitioners. The verb is in the perfect tense, corresponding to the verb tenses of the first line of this verse, which introduces the subject of prophetic activity that misleads.

Because this passage disparages such activity, it is unlikely that the sad fate of its practitioners is of concern to the prophets. The only other possible referent is then those who are affected by the misguidance of the diviners and teraphim, namely, the exiles who have sought their help. In this case, *ns*ᶜ, which signifies a deliberate departure, may well apply, as we have suggested above in the first note to this verse (cf. COMMENT), to the exiles from the Northern Kingdom. Unlike those later exiled to Babylon, many of whom returned to Zion, the northerners apparently were not so motivated or directed. Thus, although they may have felt motivated to escape from their status as exiles—a status akin to slavery in many ways (see NOTES to "your prisoners" and "hope," 9:11–12, and D. L. Smith 1989: 38–41)—their movements were undirected. The comparison with "sheep" is appropriate here (see next NOTE). We have no record of any attempts to return on the part of exiled northerners. Such actions are certainly not beyond the realm of possibility, however, inasmuch as the idea of returning to the homeland is a typical concomitant of forced exile. Hence, this may be an allusion to an attempted return. It could, however, equally be a projection by the prophet, who assumed that, just as many Babylonian exiles sought to return to Zion, so too would exiles to Assyria and elsewhere have sought to depart the regions in which they had been forcibly settled.

sheep. Although it is difficult to determine the subject of this simile, our discussion in the preceding NOTE suggests that the exiled Israelites are the ones who have set out (from the places to which they had been exiled by the

Assyrians), only to move like sheep. In this case, the sheep simile is amplified by the second part of this line, which indicates that they have no shepherd, i.e., no leader (see last NOTE to this verse for a discussion of the shepherd's identity). Hence, their departure is for naught. Sheep without leadership can hardly survive, let alone reach a destination. The prophet here may be drawing upon the language of 1 Kings 22, which uses the imagery of sheep without a shepherd (v 17) in relationship to the ill effects of questionably prophetic activity.

The comparison to sheep grows naturally out of Israel's familiarity with stock raising, because the keeping of small herd animals, especially sheep and goats, was an integral component of the agrarian subsistence base of ancient Israel (see below, NOTE to "the shepherds," in v 3). The word translated "sheep" here is *ṣōʾn*, which in fact can also represent goats, or at least a "flock" consisting of both goats and sheep (see Gen 27:9). As common as the word is in denoting actual animals, it is also frequently used in figurative language as a simile or metaphor for a group of dependent people, usually Israelites. Both Ezekiel and Jeremiah make extensive use of this imagery; Second Zechariah also frequently mentions sheep and/or shepherds in reference to some aspect of Israel's corporate existence and/or its leadership (see, e.g., Zech 9:16 above and virtually all of chapter 11 below). The presence of "sheep" at this point in chapter 10 not only echoes the simile in chapter 9 and anticipates the extended comparison in chapter 11 but also provides a connection to the rest of this chapter, which heralds the ultimate rescue of leaderless or misled sheep.

they're humble. Here the verbal tense is imperfect, corresponding to the verbs of the second line of this verse. Just as "set forth" (see previous NOTE) corresponds to the verbs of the first line and indicates the consequence of the prophetic misdirection, this verb describes the resulting conditions. Again, as with "set forth," many commentators choose to emend, notably to *nwʿ*, "to wander," despite the support of the versions for the MT. However, the root *ʿnh* is particularly suitable here. For one thing, it echoes one of the words used to describe the royal figure of Zech 9:9 (see NOTE there to "humble"). In so doing, it resonates with the humble condition, if not affliction, that characterizes the social and political status of exiles, or of any people dominated by others. It is no accident that this verb (in the Piel) is used in the Covenant Code (Exod 22:21–22) to refer to the condition of disenfranchised elements of society—resident aliens, widows, orphans. The marginal status of these landless groups made them vulnerable, and they were not to be exploited. Similarly, the various adjectival and nominal forms derived from this verbal root refer to the individuals or groups at the bottom of any socioeconomic or political hierarchy.

The status of being "humble" thus denotes exactly the condition of those in exile vis à vis the imperial power that held them in their alienated state. Although the conditions of the transplanted northerners are even less visible to us than are those that characterized the Babylonian exiles, it does not really matter that their social and economic status cannot be recaptured. So many centuries after the deportations, it is unlikely that the activists of Second Zechariah's day themselves had access to such information. What is more likely is that the experiences of the Babylonian exiles are being projected, no doubt with some measure of validity, upon the lives of those dispersed when Samaria fell to the Assyrians. If the Judeans in Babylon experienced the humiliation and powerlessness attendant upon their minority and landless status, then that is the condition the prophet assumed would have obtained for the Israelites in exile.

without a shepherd. As we indicate in our NOTE to "the shepherds" in the next verse, the metaphoric usage of this term can signify a variety of individuals or groups. It is found in several different parts of Second Zechariah, and its meaning differs from place to place. In this instance, partly because of the way it refers to human leadership in the next verse and partly in anticipation of the way "shepherd" stands for prophets in Zechariah 11 (see, inter alia, NOTE to "Shepherd," 11:4), the singular noun apparently refers to a true prophet who, as in Jer 23:4, would be a legitimate leader and protector of the flocks. A case might be made for "shepherd" representing a political leader, of which the exiles are deprived in their alienated condition far away from their homeland. Yet in light of the content of the first two lines of this verse, which deal with false prophecy, this last line might also be a reference to their lack of a true shepherd or prophet. After all, necromancy and divination, whatever their shortcomings, had as their goal the procurement of God's word, a message from the deity. But the attempt to make contact with the divine will has proved to be futile. As a result, the people endure their marginal status ("humble"; see previous NOTE) without the prophetic leadership that, in communicating God's true word, could make a difference in their lost or "humble" status.

3. *My anger has flared against.* The verb *ḥrh*, "to burn" is a common word, appearing nearly a hundred times, in the Hebrew Bible. Nearly all of these occurrences are in the Qal, with *ʾap* ("nose"), either explicitly or implied, as the subject. The resulting idiom, *ḥārâ ʾap*, literally means someone's "anger (nose) burned hot," i.e., that someone was very angry, or someone's anger was kindled. Several things can be said about this kind of anger (see Freedman, Lundblom, and Botterweck 1986). First, it is extremely intense, as compared with that expressed by other words for "anger" in the Hebrew Bible. Second, although this idiom is sometimes used to express human anger, God is most often the subject of *ḥrh*, with the derivative noun being used only in referring to Yahweh. Third, the divine anger expressed by this idiom is, with only two exceptions (both dealing with God's cosmic ire against the nations), directed at Israelites, either corporately or as individuals. This last point is of some significance for our interpretation of "shepherds," which is the object of God's wrath in this verse (see next NOTE). If God's anger is almost always kindled against Israelites, it is unlikely that "shepherds" in this context should be understood as representing foreign rulers.

This phrase is normally used with the preposition *b*, "against," or *l* or *ʾl*, meaning "for." Its appearance here with *ʿl* is rare, occurring elsewhere only in Job 19:11. Perhaps the preposition *ʿl* is employed here because of its common usage with the verb *pqd* ("attend"), which appears in the next bicolon: "I will attend (*pqd*) to (*ʿl*) . . ."

The abrupt change here to the first-person singular for Yahweh begins a new idea—divine response—and adumbrates the use of the first person for Yahweh below in verses 6ff. (see first NOTE to 6). There is a frequent shift between first and third person for Yahweh in this chapter.

the shepherds. The term *rō'eh*, "shepherd," is actually the participial form of the verb *r'h* meaning "to pasture," "tend," "graze," hence the substantive meaning "shepherd" or "herdsman." Its frequent and varied usage in the Hebrew Bible is the result of a pastoral component being such an integral part of the Israelite subsistence economy. Such was the case throughout much of the ancient Near East (Thomson 1955: 406–18), and the imagery of shepherds and flocks is ubiquitous in the art and literature of many Semitic peoples. Thus it is not surprising that Yahweh is depicted as a "shepherd"—such a tradition going back to the Exodus event itself and especially influencing the prophets of the Exile, Jeremiah, Second Isaiah, and Ezekiel (Freedman 1980: 285). The shepherd image was also frequently used for human rulers or leaders of Israel (e.g., 1 Kgs 22:17; Isa 63:11; Jer 2:8; 3:15; Ezek 34:2², 5, 7, 8², 9, 10, 12; Nah 3:18; Zech 11:3, 8, 5, 16², 17; 13:7²; etc.) and of foreign nations (as Cyrus; Isa 44:28). Ultimately it became a metaphor for future leaders of Israel (Ezek 34:23; 37:24; Mic 5:3 [NRSV 5:4]). Clearly, its most frequent usage in the Bible to connote leadership or to express the future restoration of a royal ruler is in Jeremiah, Ezekiel, and Second Zechariah. Brouwer (1949) suggests that the clustering of the shepherd references in these prophets is the result of Mesopotamian influence during the Exile and later, but the ubiquity of pastoralism in the Palestinian economy precludes the need to look for outside influence. Rather, the decline of urbanism in the sixth and fifth centuries in Palestine may itself have caused pastoralism to be more visible and hence more accessible as a literary image.

P. D. Hanson (1975: 329–31) argues that "shepherds" here refers specifically to the Davidic governor and his officials in the late sixth century. In support of this assertion he cites the common designation of shepherd and flock for a king and his people in both Egypt and Mesopotamia, as well as Israel (1 Kgs 22:17; Isa 44:28; Jer 6:3). Moreover, he claims that the plural "shepherds" in Jer 23:1f. and Ezek 34:2 refers to the civil officials as a whole, and he cites Ezek 37:24 as indicating that "shepherd" was in fact the Davidic governor. The language of Ezek 37:24, however, is not at all decisive on this matter: "My servant (*'ebed*) David shall be prince (*nāśî'*) over them; and they shall have one shepherd (*rō'eh*) . . ." It is quite possible, given the use of the imperfect (future) tense at the end of verse 23 and at the end of verse 24, that the Ezekiel reference is simply to the prospect of a future royal Davidic restoration and not an endorsement of the diarchy. It is also not clear that the role of "prince" was intended to be the same as "king" (*melek*). In any case, reading into the Zech 10:3 usage an attack specifically on the Davidic governor seems unjustified.

What is clear is that the context here is negative, that the image of "shepherd" surely is an appropriate characterization of some sort of leadership, and that this adversative sense carries over to the next bicolon, dealing with the "he-goats." Beyond that, the possibility that this negative characterization of leadership figures may refer to false prophecy, as well as to royal or civil officials, is compelling. There are several reasons for this. One is the prophet's critique of misleading prophetic figures in the preceding verse (see NOTES there to "tera-phim," "have spoken deception," "diviners," and "falsity"). Another is the recurring evidence in Zechariah 9–14 of this prophet's sense of the ongoing tension between true and false prophecy; in particular, see Zechariah 11 (see NOTES and COMMENT) and 13:2–6 (see NOTES and COMMENT). And, in the extended treatment of the struggle with worthless prophetic leadership in the shepherd narrative of chapter 11, "shepherds" there may represent prophets.

I will attend to. The idiom *pqd ʿl* can mean either "to take care of" in a positive sense (Jer 23:2; 2 Kgs 9:34) or the more negative "to visit upon, punish" (Amos 3:2, 14; Hos 1:4; 2:15 [NRSV 2:13]; Isa 10:12; Jer 9:24 [NRSV 9:25]; 11:22; etc.). The negative meaning is called for here because of the context as well as the parallelism with verse 3a. In addition, *pqd* is used twice in this verse, as it is in the striking parallel in Jer 23:2, where both usages are negative. Moreover, the first-person imperfect of the verb picks up on the first-person suffix with "anger" of verse 3a. The substitution of *ʾet* (after the verb *pqd*) for *ʿal* in its second use in this verse reinforces the shift in meaning there away from the negative to its more positive aspects (see below, NOTE to "has attended to").

he-goats. The term *ʿattûd* has been carefully chosen. Elsewhere in the Bible, it is variously used to represent leadership (Isa 14:9; Ezek 34:17) or to denote sacrificial victims (Isa 1:11; Num 7:17; Ps 66:15; 50:9, 13); it can also be used figuratively of princes and people for Yahweh's great eschatological slaughter/ sacrifice (Isa 34:6; Jer 51:40). The use of animal terminology for human leaders is a long-standing tradition (cf. Exod 15:15, inter alia), also occurring in Ugaritic imagery (see P. D. Miller 1970). The behavior of an *ʿattûd* as an animal within a herd of goats is reflected in Jer 50:8, where "he-goats" are the ones that lead the flock. This function of he-goats within a herd undoubtedly underlies the metaphoric use of the term for human leadership. Note that in Isa 14:9 "he-goats" (usually translated "rulers") appears in parallel with "kings." The two terms are not synonymous in the Isaiah passage. Rather, together they constitute the royal hierarchy (made up of the kings and bureaucrats) of the nations that have held Israel captive. It is significant that *ʿattûd* occurs only in the plural in the Hebrew Bible, thereby assuring that its figurative use to denote leadership does not mean the unitary rule of a monarch, or of God, but only the second tier of leadership. Therefore, if God can "attend to the he-goats" as well as to the problematic "shepherds" (see NOTE above in this verse), the flock Israel will surely be provided with the leadership it needs. As for the possible historical background of the "he-goats" as leaders, it is as difficult, as for "shepherds," to identify a specific group of historical personages or particular political officers with this term.

If we eschew connecting shepherds or he-goats with specific historical individuals, can something nonetheless be said about the historical context? Several features of the he-goat metaphor and its context in chapter 10 deserve mention. First, beginning with divine-warrior terminology in verse 3b and continuing with the explicit mention of restoration to the land in verses 6, 8, 9, 10, and 11, this chapter has a demonstrable interest in the exiled community. Thus, it may be that the leadership here alluded to in verse 3a is the diaspora leadership, people who have, like he-goats, emerged from the flock but not through appointment. Conceivably, they have not used the full potential of their positions to encourage those still in exile to return to the land of Israel, to the province of Yehud. "He-goats" thus could refer to the presence of a leadership cadre that was far less positive or active in bringing about a return to the homeland than was the leadership group in the time of the first return during the governorship of Sheshbazzar, or even in the time of Zerubbabel. Even then, despite the presence of leaders urging a return to Yehud, many Judeans stayed behind in Mesopotamia (Meyers and Meyers 1987: 340, 368); and clearly some opposed the idea of leaving Babylon. This certainly would have been the case for the dispersion of the Northern Kingdom, for which there is no record of a return.

Second, the two verses cited above (Isa 14:9 and Jer 50:8) in our discussion of the meaning of "he-goats" belong to passages dealing with the Babylonian Exile. The Jeremiah text in particular is relevant in that it urges the "he-goats," as grass-roots leaders of the "flock" (= exiles), to flee from the land of the Chaldeans. Although the data just cited relate to the Babylonian Exile, such references to inadequate leadership in the diaspora need hardly be limited to the Babylonian exiles. Indeed, since the language below in 10:6–7 specifies Joseph and Ephraim (see NOTES below) and in verses 10 and 11 signifies a wide dispersion, the condemnation of leadership may in fact be directed mainly toward that of the northern tribes.

Having called the leaders, probably of the northern exiles, to task in the first part of verse 3, the prophet abruptly changes both the tone and content in the rest of the verse, which emphasizes Yahweh's actions with respect to the House of Judah. However, although the ensuing message differs, the language used is connected with that of the first part of the verse as well as with that of the military imagery that follows in verses 4–12.

Yahweh of Hosts. This expression occurs disproportionately often in the Haggai–Zechariah–Malachi corpus, with these three biblical books accounting for more than one-third of the total biblical usages. This configuration cannot be easily explained; but it surely can be related, at least for Haggai and Zechariah 1–8, to the theophanic tradition of God enthroned in the Temple in Jerusalem (Meyers and Meyers 1987: 18–19; cf. Mettinger 1982). However, the military aspect of "Hosts" (= armies) should not be overlooked, and the subsequent military might to be exhibited by the leaders of Judah on behalf of God makes this divine title particularly suitable at this point (see NOTE to "like heroes" in 10:5 for another aspect of this imagery in relationship to divine power).

has attended to. The transition to God's positive activity from the negative message of the first half of this verse, with God being angry with the leadership of the exiles (see preceding NOTES), is effected through a subtle shift in language. The verb *pqd* ("to attend") is repeated; but the accusative marker *'et* is substituted here for the adversative preposition *'al*, "against" (see NOTE above to "I will attend to" in this verse). The same difference in the use of prepositions occurs in Jer 23:2, to which this passage apparently alludes.

The use of the perfect tense of the verb helps to affirm that Yahweh's actions on behalf of the people have already begun. God now takes the role of shepherd in attending to, which in this case really means "appointing," his flock, namely the Judeans, to the task of rescuing the rest of the dispersion. The Judean restoration, although not complete, was nonetheless significant and hence could be seen as an accomplished event to mark the next task, that of securing the return of all Israel.

As in Jer 23:2, "attend" appears twice in this verse. Both usages are negative in Jeremiah. The prophet here is drawing on that language but changes it, for the intent of the second use, "attended", in this verse is positive.

his flock. The pastoral imagery begun in the first half of the verses is sustained through the employment of the term *'ēder*, which can also be translated "herd" and which here, as in, e.g., Isa 40:11 and Jer 13:17, is figurative language pointing to the exiled Judeans as God's flock. The imagery is quite similar to Zech 9:16, which may refer to all exiles, in comparing Yahweh's people to sheep (see NOTE to "his people will be like sheep," 9:16).

House of Judah. Reference to the people of Judah by this expression is quite frequent in the Hebrew Bible. In Zech 8:13, it is paired with "House of Israel" to indicate all Israel, thus indicating that it refers to the Southern Kingdom rather than the major component of the Southern Kingdom, namely, the tribe of Judah. Similarly, in Zech 8:15, the fate of "the House of Judah" is tied to that of its capital, Jerusalem. The Southern Kingdom is singled out here as the flock of Yahweh that has already been looked after and so is about to be given a role in God's ongoing redemptive scheme. If this chapter in general is concerned with the restoration of the broader dispersion rather than with the Babylonian Exile of the Judeans, then this could well represent the perspective of the restoration of much of the latter, that is, those in Babylon, by the end of the several waves of return. The restored Judeans then are to be instrumental in securing the return of the rest of Israel.

like his mighty horse. Literally "like the horse of his splendor" or "like his magnificent steed." The war horse is a vivid symbol of military power (see NOTE to "chariot . . . horse" in 9:10). The exalted role of the horse is intensified here by its connection with the language in the succeeding verses of military victory through Yahweh's presence. "Horse in battle" thus anticipates the divine-warrior imagery of much of the rest of this chapter.

This metaphorical use of military language is surely eschatological. No one who lived in the Persian period would assign such power and might to Judah, even with her restored population. The political and economic status of Yehud in these times was well known; the province was tiny, poor, had little power or autonomy, and was completely dependent upon Persian imperial policies for its existence. Metaphors of power, therefore, are being appropriated to express confidence in the eschatological future and the effective leadership that will emerge from Judah in that day (see NOTES to v 4 below).

The hope for proper royal leadership is implicit in the unusual way in which "mighty horse" is expressed in Hebrew. The word for "horse" is the familiar *sûs*. The word for "mighty," however, is *hôd*, also translated "majesty" (see NOTE to "bear royal majesty," at Zech 6:13, in Meyers and Meyers 1987: 358). These words occur together elsewhere only at Job 39:19–20 ("Do you give the horse its strength? . . . The majesty of its snorting is terrible"). The term for "majesty" or "mighty," *hôd*, has a decidedly royal nuance and even appears in divine-warrior contexts (Warmuth 1978: 352–56). Thus there may be an allusion here to a future Davidide who one day will ride a powerful horse and rule from Judah from strength.

in battle. The last word of verse 3, "battle," also links it to the military language in the succeeding verses. Specifically, it anticipates "battle" in verse 5 (see NOTE below) and "bow of war" in verse 4, where "war" renders the same Hebrew word *milḥāmâ*, as here. In addition, it echoes a preceding passage of Second Zechariah: 9:10, also "bow of war" and *milḥāmâ* in Hebrew (see NOTE to "bow of war," 9:10). The idea that an empowered Judah will do battle must surely represent an eschatological future. Judah's might will be dependent on divine intervention—on the ultimate power of Yahweh—in order to become the instrument of securing the restoration of all Israel.

4. *From them.* The preposition "from" carries the third-person masculine singular suffix, which refers to "House of Judah" in verse 3. Because *bêt* ("house") is masculine singular and a construct, each of the four occurrences of the preposition plus object in this verse refers back to it. "House of Judah" is collective and so implies many individuals; thus we translate the suffix in the plural even though it is singular in Hebrew. The repetition of "from" with the singular suffix has the effect of emphasizing that those who will come from the "House of Judah" will become the instruments of the divine redemption that is set forth in the succeeding verses. God is about to rescue the homeless Israelites, a task requiring extraordinary might. The language of this verse and those that follow is full of military imagery, which conveys God's power in effecting the monumental reversal of the historical condition of political and social alienation of the exiled northerners (see NOTES to "teraphim" and "without a shepherd" in 10:2).

will come. The verb governing all four nouns ("cornerstone," "tent peg," "bow," and "overseer") actually appears only once in the Hebrew, before the last in the series, "every overseer." The verb *yṣ'*, with the preposition *m(n)* ("from"), means "to come from" or "to go forth from." Perhaps the verb comes at the end, before "overseer," to emphasize the rather dramatic shift in meaning that characterizes each of the four terms in this verse, especially the last one, "overseer" (see NOTE to that word below, and NOTE to Zech 9:8, "oppressor").

The delay of the verb, although rare in English, is not so unusual in Hebrew. It is a literary device that can be called "reverse gapping" to indicate that the verb applies to all of the units. The use of one verb for all of the units would be ordinary if the verb came first but is unusual because it is last. Whatever the reasons may be for its position in Hebrew, for the sake of clarity in our translation we have placed the verb at the head of the list, with each succeeding "from them" being governed by the same verb.

the cornerstone. It seems odd that the first of the four terms to be listed as emerging from "the House of Judah" is *pinnâ*. Its first and most frequently attested meaning is "corner," normally an architectural designation (e.g., Exod 27:2; 38:2; 1 Kgs 7:30, 34; Ezek 43:20; 45:19; 2 Chron 28:24; etc.). At times this word refers specifically to the wall of Jerusalem (2 Kgs 14:13; 2 Chron 25:23; 26:15). Most significantly, it can designate a "cornerstone" (Jer 51:26; Job 38:6; Ps 118:22; Isa 28:16), which is evocative of "the premier stone" of Zech 4:7 *(hāᶜeben hārōʾšâ)*, that is, the foundation stone that was laid on just before the rebuilding of the Temple of Zerubbabel (Meyers and Meyers 1987: 246–48).

All those architectural meanings lie behind the metaphoric usage in this verse. "Cornerstone" can signify an officer or chief insofar as a leader is the essential support for the group being led, in much the same way that the corner or wall is the foundation of a building's superstructure and, thus, of that building's ability to stand. In Judg 20:2 the term *pinnâ* denotes all the "chiefs of the people" who assembled at Mizpeh, and in 1 Sam 14:38 it is a term for the "leaders" of the people who come to address the king. In Isa 19:13, it is used with irony in reference to foreign leaders, who as "cornerstones" led the people of Egypt astray. Note that the next term, "tent peg" (see next NOTE), also has a technical, structural aspect that at the same time represents a leadership position.

The occurrence of *pinnâ* in Psalm 118, a song of thanksgiving and deliverance, seems particularly relevant to this Zechariah passage. Mason (1973: 114–15) contends that in Ps 118:22, *pinnâ* provides a wordplay on "stone"—the stone the builders reject is the cornerstone, that is, the chief leader or king *(rōʾš pinnâ)*! He also argues that verses 19–21 of Psalm 118 bear some similarity to Zech 9:9, especially in the use of "righteous" and "salvation." In addition, he notes that the "cornerstone" of Ps 118:22 and of Zech 10:4 is identified by later Christian and Jewish tradition as "messiah." Because of all these links and in view of the fact that the next item ("tent peg") in this series also has an association with royal messianism by virtue of the way it is used in Isa 22:23ff., the selection of the somewhat unusual term *pinnâ* ("cornerstone") as the first item becomes comprehensible. Its figurative meaning, representing a chief or leader—probably the royal leader, an eschatological Davidide—is appropriate not only to the immediate context of this verse, where "House of Judah" (10:3) is the source of the cornerstone/leader (king?), but also to the expectation of a future royal ruler that appears in Zech 9:9 (see NOTES to that verse and also COMMENT to Zechariah 9) and at several points in First Zechariah. Judah is to provide the cornerstone. Those who will carry out God's redemptive acts will thus emerge from Judah, and the first of these will be the leader, the cornerstone or foundation upon which the success of the enterprise will rest. This leader may well be the royal ruler.

tent peg. The architectural imagery (see preceding NOTE) continues in the second item of this series with the use of *yātēd* to connote another aspect of future leadership coming forth from the House of Judah. The nuances of *yātēd*, beyond its literal meaning of "tent peg," are difficult to convey in English. We retain its literal sense in the translation because that suits the military language that prevails in this chapter. Only in our discussion of the term can its subtleties, and the inner biblical exegesis that underlies it in the Hebrew, become apparent.

"Tent peg" clearly partakes of the technical vocabulary of buildings or shelters and, as such, is widely used in the Hebrew Bible. It is the term for the wooden peg or pin that holds the cords or material of a tent securely fastened to the ground on which it is pitched. Yael drives such a tent peg into Sisera's temple (Judg 4:21, 22; 5:26) within a military context, in which Sisera was seeking refuge from battle in Yael's tent. Also in Judges (16:14), Delilah uses a tent peg to braid the locks of Samson's hair. The term is also frequently used in the Tabernacle texts of Exodus in reference to the tent pegs used in setting up the temporary dwelling of Yahweh in the wilderness (e.g., Exod 27:19; 35:18; 38:31; 39:40; Num 3:37; 4:32). This technical aspect underlies the imagery of "tent peg" as used in this verse. From Judah comes the device that will provide mooring—what it takes to establish security for the people wherever they may be.

The imagery, however, extends beyond what the technical aspects of the term provide; it also has royal associations, as does "cornerstone" (= ruler; see previous NOTE). A passage in Isaiah (22:15–25) provides the basis for this aspect of the term. It refers to an incident involving Eliakim son of Hilkiah, who was in charge of the royal palace in the days of King Hezekiah (2 Kgs 18:18ff.). He achieved his position as a replacement for one Shebna, whom God accuses, according to Isaiah's reporting of Yahweh's words, of improper activities in constructing a royal tomb in the City of David (Isa 22:15–19). Eliakim is accorded special authority, with robes and insignia of office, as "a father to the inhabitants of Jerusalem and to the House of Judah" (v 21). Furthermore, according to the prophet, God will "place on his shoulder the key to the house of David (v 22) . . . and fasten him as a tent peg in a secure place, and he will become a throne of honor to his ancestral houses" (v 23). In this Isaiah passage, the association of "tent peg" with Hilkiah accord him the place of next-in-control to none other than the king. In addition, Hilkiah is called Yahweh's "servant" (*ᶜebed*), a term often designating royal leadership in close relationship with Yahweh (as in Ezek 34:23, 37:24, and Ps 78:70–71, where David is also called a shepherd; see also Hag 2:23 and Meyers and Meyers 1987: 68–69).

One other biblical text further expands the connotations that "tent peg" may have in this passage and its postexilic setting. In a retrospection on Israel's recent past and a reflection on the present state of affairs, Ezra is quoted as saying that Yahweh has shown his people favor and has "given us a tent peg in his holy place, in order that our God may brighten our eyes and grant us a little sustenance in our slavery. . . . Yet God has not forsaken us in our slavery, but has extended to us his steadfast love before the kings of Persia, to give us new life to set up the House of our God, to repair its ruins, and to give us a wall in Judea and Jerusalem" (Ezra 9:8–9). This remarkable text, which probably dates to the second half of the fifth century B.C.E., after the rebuilding of the walls of Jerusalem, probably postdates Second Zechariah. If Zechariah has enlisted Isa 22:23 in using "tent peg" as a way of alluding to the future existence of an official who will accompany or secure the rule of a Davidide, Ezra 9:8 has in turn drawn upon Zech 10:4 to express the long-standing policy in Yehud of accepting Persian rule in the interim but at the same time reaffirming in eschatological language Israel's age-old preoccupation with Davidic rule. Indirectly, and with the ironic twist of a double entendre—"a tent peg in his holy place," which must surely be a reference to the tent pegs of sacred architecture but which may also be an allusion to the rule of a governor and/or high priest in Yehud until Ezra's days and beyond—Ezra's language suggests that the present state of leadership may signify the possibility of the restoration of royal power as part of Yehud's eschatological future. It should also be noted that the granting of a "tent peg" ameliorates the condition of domination ("servitude" or "slavery") that characterizes Yehud's lack of autonomy, just as the humble or downtrodden exiles will be rescued through the "tent peg" of Zech 10:4.

bow of war. This phrase, which occurs above in Zech 9:10 (see NOTE to "bow of war" in that verse) and is alluded to in 9:13 (see NOTE to "bent . . . to me" in that verse), serves to link chapters 9 and 10. It has a straightforward military meaning, the bow of war being an item of weaponry. That the House of Judah will one day have such an implement signals its future autonomy, because the ability to field an army is a sine qua non of political independence. The quintessential long-range weapon in the arsenal of Near Eastern warfare thus represents the ability of the House of Judah to exert its power and thereby restore to their homeland all those still scattered (see below, vv 8–10).

It seems unlikely that this military term represents the future king himself, as several commentators have suggested (as noted by Mason 1973: 118–19). Unlike the first two items of this verse, "cornerstone" and "tent peg," which are material objects with allusions to leadership roles, and unlike the last item, which is a direct reference to leadership positions, "bow of war" apparently operates only at the level of an object. Hence, exegetes would like to assign to this term too a human referent, as it has in 2 Sam 1:18 and 22. There are, however, no clues to such a referent, particularly not to a specifically royal figure. Yet the prominence of the war bow conveys the existence of a military striking force, which could not exist without the national autonomy for which a restored monarchy is the political paradigm. Although the bow need not represent a messianic ruler, it does represent the power, symbolized by military language, of the House of Judah in its role as God's instrument of redemption. Judah (Yehud) could hardly take on this role under the conditions of the postexilic period, as the reference to the situation of servitude, or "slavery," in Ezra 9:8–9 (see previous NOTE) vis à vis the Persians indicates. Thus it is the future age that will mean power for the House of Judah.

every overseer. The use of the term "overseer" (*nôgēś*) with "every" (*kol*) is notable because of its use in Zech 9:8 with another nuance (see NOTE to "oppressor"). As noted in that connection, because of the association with the bondage of Israel in Egypt, *nôgēś* is normally equated with the term "taskmaster" (Exod 3:7; 5:6, 10, 13, 14) or "oppressor." Indeed, that meaning of the term clearly is intended in 9:8, where Yahweh's Temple is to be protected; the Hebrew idiom there is quite explicit: "An oppressor will not overrun (*yaʿăbōr*) them again."

In this verse the verb that governs all four subjects is *yṣ'*, "to come from" or "to go forth" (see NOTE above to "will come" in this verse). The word translated "oppressor" has a different nuance when the verb changes, just as in the preceding verse the verb "attend" changed its meaning as the preposition changed to the accusative marker (see NOTE to "attend" in 10:3). The meaning of *nôgēś* in this verse also relates to people exerting power, but now the power is viewed positively. The key to understanding this shift is in Isa 60:17, where *nôgēś* is used in parallel with *pĕquddâ*, a noun from the same root as "to attend to." The text at Isa 60:17 reads: "I will make peace your overseer (*pĕquddâ*) and Righteousness your taskmaster (*nôgēś*)." The meaning there is obviously positive.

What, then, is the meaning here? Why do we render *nôgēś* "overseer"? Clearly, as we have pointed out, the overall context is positive. The overseer, like the cornerstone, tent peg, and bow (see NOTES to these words) will come from the House of Judah to do God's battle in securing safety and restoration for Israel. The overseer will be part of the second tier of leadership, the ones who see to it that the forces of the House of Judah carry out what God intends them to do. As we observed in our NOTE to "oppressor" in 9:8, the verbal root *ngś* means "to exact from" (as Deut 15:2, 3; 2 Kgs 23:35). Although perhaps an unusual word to represent future Judean leadership, it provides an ironic twist to the notion of oppression in 9:8. At the same time, it perhaps hints that the House of Judah will itself achieve dominance over others, as it will have to do in this eschatological scheme in order to secure the release of those still in exile in Assyria and Egypt (see below, v 10). Just as overlords exact tribute or labor from those they dominate, the House of Judah will now produce overseers who exact freedom for the oppressed exiles. In so doing they will, in a sense, become oppressors of the nations that hold Israel captive.

"Overseer" is the last in a collection of four terms that indicate the way in which Yahweh will bring forth from the House of Judah the tools to achieve the emancipation of the exiles. The terms are hardly straightforward, and on a literal level alone they seem confusing. Yet they all draw upon allusions to terms within this prophetic book as well as to passages in earlier biblical texts (see COMMENT, below, to this chapter).

together. The appearance of *yḥdw*, "together," at the end of this verse in the MT arrangement has occasioned many suggestions for emendation. The most popular one is to simply transfer it to the beginning of verse 5, in place of "they will be" (*whyw*). Similarly, the perfect *waw*-consecutive of the verb "to be" is repointed as the imperfect "they will be" (*yhyw* from *whyw*) and read "together they will be." However, the MT has correctly placed "together" (third-person plural) at the end of verse 4, indicating that the Masoretes understood "together" as describing the verb "will come" and thus referring, as does the verb, to all four subjects of this verse. The adverb *yḥd* thus summarizes the four items working in unity in verse 4 (cf. a similar construction in Jer 31:8).

5. *They will be.* Depending on how one divides verses 4 and 5, *whyw* (*waw* plus the perfect) might be read as the imperfect *yhyw*. Because we have understood "together" as coming at the end of verse 4 (see preceding NOTE), we find the present MT acceptable and read a *waw* consecutive. Moving "together" to the beginning of verse 5 would require an emendation of *hyh* to the imperfect.

like heroes. Those who come forth from Judah to carry out God's mission are compared to "warriors." The Hebrew noun *gibbôrîm*, from the root *gbr*, "to be strong, mighty," involves the doubling of the middle radical and so is an intensive form. Used frequently in military contexts, it thus represents warriors who were particularly strong, courageous, and successful, more so than would be ordinary soldiers (Kosmala 1975: 373). This meaning underlies the designation of King David's elite group of warriors, recruited especially (perhaps because they were taller or stronger or better trained) from the Cherethites and Pelethites (2 Sam 10:7; 23:16; 1 Kgs 1:8, 10). Indeed, David himself may have been considered such a hero, considering his extraordinary military exploits (see 2 Sam 8:1–14; 22:32–46).

This military aspect of "heroes" certainly is appropriate to the context of this verse and of this chapter, which announces God's actions, via the House of Judah, to rescue all those still dispersed. However, another dimension of the Hebrew *gibbôrîm* adds to the rich imagery of the term. Sometimes God's agents, who carry out divine orders, are called "heroes" or "powerful heroes" (Ps 103:20; Joel 4:11 [NRSV 3:11]). This attribute of military might or power is even associated with Yahweh, in some ways the hero par excellence, as in Ps 24:7–10, which describes Yahweh as the king of glory, with heavenly hosts (= armies), strong and mighty (*gibbôr*) in battle.

Thus the use of "heroes" as a simile for the Judeans who will do God's will associates them with the special qualities of uncommon strength or power, along with a direct relationship to Yahweh. These attributes together epitomize the function of the divine-warrior language of this chapter. The language is figurative, suggesting that Yahweh's ultimate purpose cannot be achieved by normal means but only by superhuman power. Comparing the leaders who emerge from Judah (see NOTES in previous verse to "cornerstone," "tent peg," and "overseer") to "heroes" endows them with the extraordinary qualities that allow them to participate in Yahweh's saving deeds. It also anticipates the use of the verb *gbr* at the beginning of the next verse (10:6; see NOTE to "I will make . . . mighty"), where it similarly expresses the role of the House of Judah. The importance of the term "heroes" is further enhanced by its linkage with "battle," the two words together forming an envelope around related material (see next NOTE).

The concept of heroes as part of the means for the redemption of Israel contributes to the way the eschatological idea develops among those living under the domination of a political power (see D. L. Smith 1989: 85). When that power seems too entrenched to be vanquished by ordinary means, the defeat of former enemies and the freeing of the oppressed can come only from superhuman efforts, from Yahweh along with the earthly representatives of divine power.

in battle. The syntax of the Hebrew is very complex, with the text of this line reading literally "like heroes trampling in muddy places in battle." Many exegetes consider "in battle" a gloss. However, *kgbrym* ("like heroes") in Hebrew precedes "trampling in muddy places"; and *bmlḥmh* ("in battle") follows those words. The result is an envelope around relevant material, a formation found elsewhere in Hebrew poetry (cf. Isa 10:5). That is, instead of having parallel construct chains, the second pair is split and surrounds the other material. Such syntax is indicative of the poetic nature of this section of Second Zechariah.

The use of "battle" is appropriate here, picking up the military language of the preceding two verses, especially the "bow of war" (= battle)" of verse 4 and "in battle" (i.e., in war) of verse 3. The word for "battle," *mlḥmh*, thus comes in each of these three verses. Its repetition helps establish the military imagery that presents Yahweh as the champion of Judah's forces, which carry out the divine battle plan.

trampling. The relatively rare verb *bws*, "to tread, trample," is most frequently associated with war on warriors (e.g., Isa 14:25; 63:6) in the sense of "vanquish," although, in a somewhat extended sense, it can mean "to desecrate" (as Isa 63:18). This graphic verb, which clearly goes with the following phrase "in muddy places," is unusual in this passage in that it does not have a direct object. Normally, the verb expresses the trampling of a certain enemy or commodity (e.g., Ps 108:14 [NRSV 108–13]; Jer 12:10; Isa 14:19). The choice of the verb thus has the effect of creating the expectation of a wartime violence (see next NOTE).

in muddy places. This expression is identical to "mud of the streets" of 9:3 and hence constitutes one of many lexical connections between chapters 9 and 10. The classic scriptural antecedents of this phrase (see NOTE to "mud of the streets," 9:3) are Ps 18:43 (NRSV 18:42) and 2 Sam 22:43, where David's victory over his enemies is described as making them like "dust" (ʿpr) and "mud of the streets" (kĕṭîṭ ḥûṣôt). The verbs in both those texts imply that the enemy has been decisively and utterly vanquished. Here the idea of "muddy places" conjures up the idea of trouncing the enemy.

they'll fight. This is the fourth and final occurrence of the root "to fight" (*lḥm*) in three verses ("in battle," vv 3, 5; "bow of war," v 4) and its only use as a verb. The shift to the verb perhaps signals an escalation in rhetoric. Although verses 3 and 4 announce that Yahweh is empowering the House of Judah to carry out the redemptive plan, verse 5 at last has the warriors carrying out their mission, which they are able to do specifically because, as the rest of this bicolon tells us, Yahweh is in fact with them (see next NOTE).

Yahweh is with them. The success of the future leadership rests ultimately with Yahweh. Although the idea of Yahweh's presence being *the* source of power is at the very core of biblical thought, its usage in this military setting has already been accomplished in the third part of chapter 9: verse 14, "Yahweh will appear above them"; in verse 15, "Yahweh of Hosts will protect them"; in verse 16, "Yahweh their God will rescue them" (see NOTES to these clauses). The appearance of Yahweh in 10:5 intensifies the idea of the enabling presence of Yahweh. Indeed, it is a culmination of the description of the preparation of Judah to do God's will. Hereafter, in the next five verses, God speaks in the first person, thereby emphasizing that however heroic and well armed and highly motivated Judah may become, Yahweh is the one who secures freedom and restoration for the dispersed Israelites.

Although Yahweh is mentioned by name here, it is in the context of God's announcing what will come forth from Judah, consequent to the flaring of divine anger against the "shepherds," i.e., the existing leadership (see NOTE to "the shepherds," 10:3). The use of the divine name does not necessarily indicate that someone other than God is the speaker, as it is possible for God to name "Yahweh" in the context of oracular speech. Such may indeed be the case in 10:7 below. Thus the use of the first person in the subsequent verses may not actually indicate a shift in speakers.

The phrase "with them" or "with us" is characteristically found in the heroic tradition of Israel, when God's presence makes victory possible despite overwhelming odds (e.g., Judg 6:12, 13, 16; see Levine 1968).

will confound. The Hiphil of *bwš* is identical in form to that used at 9:5 and 10:11, each time with a slightly different nuance. The other occurrences probably derive from *ybš*, "to make dry." Although the nuances are different, the very repetition of the word serves, as do other words in these two chapters, to connect chapters 9 and 10. Its meaning here, "to confound," is a military one and is directed at the soldiers on horses. For a possible confusion in the roots of this verb see Joel 1:10, 11, 12, 17—verse 11 most closely reflects the meaning here.

those mounted on horses. As we have pointed out above (see NOTE to "like his mighty horse" in v 3) the symbol par excellence of military power in antiquity was the horse and rider. Unlike a donkey or "ass" (see NOTES to 9:9), the horse is frequently associated with military activities. Confounding the cavalry (see previous NOTE) is tantamount to securing the defeat of the enemy, i.e., achieving victory. The future leaders of the House of Judah therefore will successfully challenge those in power—"those mounted on horses"—and will bring them to accept a nation that will possess power, sovereignty, and autonomy. These features of such a rule are incorporated into the terms that introduce the future leaders of Judah in verse 4 (see NOTES above), terms that in Hebrew mean more than any English translation can convey. Although the struggle is set in the eschatological future, what it will accomplish is clear: a transformation of Israel from a powerless people to a nation that once again possesses the ability to carry out God's will, beginning with the restoration to their homeland of all the dispersed northerners.

6. *I will make . . . mighty.* These four English words translate the first Hebrew word of v 6, *wĕgibbartî*; in fact, an additional word, a prefatory

conjunction ("and" or "thus") might also be included, since the word begins with the *"waw"* connector. The subject of the verb is now the first-person singular (cf. first NOTE to v 3), here and in most of the rest of the chapter. God evidently is also the subject in verse 3. Elsewhere, although there are references to Yahweh (as in vv 3 and 7), it is not clear who is speaking; perhaps God is indicating self by using the divine name. In any case, the first person here and in the next few verses emphasizes what God will accomplish now that certain Judeans have been activated to serve as God's agents.

The House of Judah as a whole is to be made mighty. The Piel of the verb *gbr* is an intensive form, indicating unusual or extraordinary strength. Indeed, the noun form of the Piel verb, which appears in verse 5 (see NOTE above) calls the new leaders of Judah "heroes," people who possess superhuman power and who act in close relationship to God's transcendent might. The verb here ascribes a similar role to Judah in its entirety. However, the Piel does not have intensive force here. Rather, it is causative, like the Hiphil, indicating that Yahweh has made someone else strong.

House of Judah. That is, the Southern Kingdom; see NOTE to this phrase in 10:3. In Hebrew, the syntax of this bicolon resembles that of English, with the direct object, "House of Judah," following the verb. However, this order is reversed in the second bicolon, so that "House of Joseph" immediately follows "House of Judah" and precedes the verb of which it is the object. This reversal serves to juxtapose Judah with Joseph, i.e., the Southern and Northern Kingdoms, so that the central part of this poetic line features all Israel. The actions of part of Israel will rescue the other part, for they are two parts of a whole: God's people.

House of Joseph. Hebrew *bêt yôsēp*, "House of Joseph," represents the Northern Kingdom, which consisted of ten tribes, just as "House of Judah" (see previous NOTE and also NOTE to this phrase in 10:3; cf. "Judah" in 9:13), which consisted of two tribes, represents the Southern Kingdom. The leading tribe in each of these nation-states stands for the whole in a kind of geopolitical synecdoche. For the north, Joseph actually represents two tribes, Ephraim and Manasseh, which together occupied the highland core of the Kingdom of Israel and thus most of its population and resources, and, by extension, the whole Northern Kingdom. Indeed, Ephraim alone, as the strategically and historically more important of the Joseph tribes (cf. Gen 48:19, where Jacob accords priority to Ephraim over Manasseh), itself sometimes stands for all the northern tribes (see NOTES to "Ephraim," in 9:13 above and 10:7 below). In any case, it is clear that these two tribal names represent the two kingdoms, as they do elsewhere in prophecy (as in Amos, so Andersen and Freedman 1989: 109, 111, with respect to Joseph). Hence their syntactical juxtaposition in this poetic line (see previous NOTE) signifies all Israel, as composed of two parts, each of which will be involved in its own way in God's redemptive plan.

The pairing of Judah and Joseph make this verse a transitional one. Verses 3–5 concern Judah and its new role in God's scheme, and verses 7–12 lay forth the welcome results of God's plan, with Judah's new independent and powerful status as agent. Here in verse 6, presenting the role of Judah in reversing the fortunes of Israel effects the shift from the focus on the southern tribes to the northern ones.

save. The essence of the verb *yšʿ* involves liberation, setting free or placing into freedom whoever is the object of this verb. It is to be one of the functions of the royal figure of Zech 9:9 (see NOTE at that verse to "saved"). In its Hiphil form, it refers frequently and almost exclusively either to the actions of God in saving or redeeming the people or an individual (such as David [2 Sam 8:6, 14] or God's servant [Ps 86:2, 16]), or to the deeds of Israel in battle. Both these aspects of "saving" are present in the context where God's might, which will bring about the emancipation of the northern tribes from their status as exiles, is activated through the agency of the Judeans, whose leaders are exactly such "heroes" (see NOTES to "like heroes," 10:5, and to "I will make mighty [= heroic]" above in this verse), together with the northerners themselves.

In the Deuteronomic history and preexilic prophets, the verb "to save" almost always indicates deliverance from enemies who threaten Israel's existence in a military and political sense. Yet in exilic and postexilic prophecy, it signifies the redemption of Israel from exile. In Jeremiah, Yahweh's saving the people, the "remnant of Israel," means bringing them back from the ends of the earth (see Jer 31:7–10, specifically in reference to the Northern Kingdom, Ephraim). First Zechariah (8:7) proclaims that Yahweh will save the people from wherever they are, east or west, and bring them back to Zion. Second Isaiah declares that God will signal to the nations and secure the release of Israel's sons and daughters; i.e., God will save Israel's children (Isa 49:23–25). Although the verb, especially its participial form (*môšîʿa*, "the one who saves" and hence "savior"), ultimately comes to have a moral sense, indicating the deliverance from sin (as perhaps Ezek 37:23) or at least from impurity (Ezek 36:29), such instances are rare and controversial in the Hebrew Bible. By and large, "to save" is exclusively a military and political concept, involving the rescue of people by extraordinary means. Such people are in great jeopardy, and only the direct intervention of God or the heroic agents of Yahweh can secure their freedom. Consequently, whenever we refer to God's redeeming or saving Israel (or Judah or Joseph), we are restricting the meaning of such terms to the idea of political liberation, of removing people from the domination of foreign powers and restoring them to their own land and polity.

In this verse, the object of God's salvific acts is the House of Joseph, i.e., the Northern Kingdom (see previous NOTE). The prophet is evidently aware that much of Judah, that is, much of the Babylonian Exile, has already been saved from its dispersed condition. Hence it is the exiled remnants of the ten tribes of the kingdom of Israel that need God's intervention to secure their liberation.

I will restore them. Once God has taken the northerners out of their position as exiles, dominated socially and politically by the nations to which they had been dispersed, the next step is to return them to the place where they will be able to live in freedom. The verb *šwb* ("to return, turn back") in the Qal appears several times in First Zechariah, where it is a key word. It emphasizes both the people's return to Yahweh, which should accompany God's restoring them to Zion (in the sixth century), and God's returning to the repentant returnees (Zech 1:3, 4, 6, 16; 8:3; see NOTES to these verses in Meyers and Meyers 1987). This notion of the people's returning to God and God to the people may figure faintly in the use of the verb here. Yet, its Hiphil form is strongly causative. God will cause the exiles to return to their homeland. Through Judah's recovered autonomy, God will secure their release from the quasi-slave status that characterizes peoples detained away from their natal territory (Patterson 1982; cf. COMMENT below).

The form of the verb is *wĕhôšĕbôtîm*, which apparently represents something of a conflation between the Hiphil of *šwb* ("to return") and of *yšb* ("to settle, reinstate"). Although most Hebrew manuscripts have this hybrid or "mongrel" form (Mitchell 1912: 300), some do preserve a form based on *yšb*, as does the LXX; and others have yet another aberrant verb. The similarity of the two roots involved, and the complementarity of their meanings ("to bring back" the exiles implies God's concomitant intention "to resettle" them in their homeland), no doubt underlie the confusion. Note that in verse 10 below, the Hiphil of *šwb* appears in its proper form; similarly, the Vulgate, Peshitta, and Targum all translate that form.

Whatever the original verb, the idea of the exiles returning to their native land is not in doubt. The verb bears the third-person plural suffix "them," which occurs three more times in this verse, twice in verse 8, once each in verses 9 and 12, and three times in verse 10. This repetition underscores the relationship of the people represented by "them" to the action of the verbs of which it is a suffix. Those people are being acted upon; they are passive recipients of God's activity on their behalf. With so many verbs-plus-suffix ("them") occurring, one after another, in these verses, the text conveys the idea of an extremely active deity, carrying out one task and then another, with all this frenetic activity directed specifically to the benefit of "them." The identity of the "them" is undoubtedly the northern tribes, called variously "House of Joseph" in this verse and "Ephraim" in verse 7. This verse is a transition, as discussed above in the NOTE to "House of Joseph," between an exposition of Judah's renewed leadership (vv 3–5) and the resultant rescue of Joseph (7–12), all made possible against overwhelming odds by God's might. In this second line of verse 6, the focus on Joseph has begun; Ephraim is hence the "them."

I had compassion on them. In the midst of the military imagery of the core of this chapter, in verses 3–7, this verb—one Hebrew word rendered by these five English words—stands out in stark contrast. The language of war is masculine language: it speaks of weapons, heroes, cavalry, battles. Yet here is a demonstrative verb, *rḥm* ("to have compassion"), from the noun *reḥem* (or *rāḥam*), which means "womb" and embodies female attributes of caring, of maternal concern for one's children. It is that feeling of God toward Ephraim that is presented as the motivating factor in God's decision to save Joseph and bring him back from the misery of exile. Here, as in Zech 1:12 and more than thirty other instances in the Bible, this female imagery poignantly conveys God's compassionate care for the people. It is interesting that in the handful of instances in which *rḥm* denotes human compassion, it usually refers to the mercy of military conquerors to the vanquished, who are as helpless and as dependent on their captors as are babes in the womb dependent for survival on maternal impulses. In any case, it is clear that divine compassion was bestowed throughout the past and is not something that is just going to happen in the future. In effect, it is God's past and ongoing love and compassion that assures Israel of God's future caring.

The verb has "them" as its suffix, the second of four such forms in this verse and eleven instances in verses 6–12. See the previous NOTE. "Them" signifies the northern tribes.

not rejected them. The verb *znḥ* ("to reject, spurn, exclude") conveys the antithesis of maternal compassion (the utter acceptance of a child by its mother; see preceding NOTE). Just as God is most often the subject of *rḥm* ("to be compassionate"), so too God is most often the subject of this verb. The application of the concept of rejection to the exiled Israelites implies a Deuteronomic judgment. The exiles exist in their difficult and undesirable status of landlessness and oppression not because of the random ability of the Assyrians or others to exert power, but because God had judged the northerners to be no longer fit to claim title to their land—thus the notion of rejection. In the account of the conquest of Samaria, God becomes angry with the Israelites because they have rejected (ʿzb, "left") the Commandments; hence they are removed from their land, i.e., rejected by God (2 Kgs 17:17), inasmuch as title to the land is equated with divine favor. Indeed, "Yahweh rejected (*mʾs*) all the descendants of Israel; he punished them and . . . banished them" (2 Kgs 17:20). Although the verbs for Israel's rejection of God and God's rejection of Israel are different from the one used in this verse, the intent is the same. The condition of exile is the result of God's intention to punish, and thus amenable now to the opposite intention of God, namely, to have compassion. Punishment meant banishment; its antithesis will mean restoration.

"Them" as an object suffix occurs here for the third time in this verse, in which it appears four times, and it is used seven more times in the succeeding verses (see NOTE above to "I will restore them").

For I am Yahweh their God. Many see this and the next phrase as later additions, modeled after Isa 41:17 ("I Yahweh will answer them," i.e., the poor and the afflicted; cf. NOTE to "humble" in v 2). The parallelism of the preceding two lines of this verse certainly does not continue here. However, the poetic quality of this chapter does not adhere to "classical" standards, and the formal variation alone should not disqualify this line from being original to the verse. Second Zechariah in general brings together ideas and language found in earlier prophetic works, and it is impossible to say whether this eclectic tendency comes from the *Urform* of Second Zechariah or from its redactional history. In any case, identifying the ultimate source of the Israelites' rescue as Yahweh is a logical corrective to what the Israelites will empirically observe as Judean power in securing their release.

I will respond to them. Again (see preceding NOTE) the language echoes Isa 41:17. Still, the verb "respond" with a third-person plural suffix also fits the string of such verbs in this and the following verses (see NOTE to "I will restore them" above). Even though Yahweh has punished Israel's apostasy by rejecting her, which in historical terms is equated with the deportations, that fate is not permanent. Centuries after the Assyrian conquest of Samaria, the prophet is aware that there must still be Israelites languishing in lands not their own. Just as the Babylonian exiles had been remembered by God and returned, at least in part, to Zion, so too will the northerners. The prophet assumes that the same longing for homeland, and thus the calling out to God for compassion and restoration, obtains among the exiled Ephraimites. Hence their restoration will be a compassionate response to their asking God to remember and reclaim them.

7. *Ephraim*. Like "House of Joseph" in 10:6 (see NOTE above) the name of the largest and most powerful of the northern tribes represents the Northern Kingdom (see NOTE to "Ephraim . . . Jerusalem," 9:10).

Ephraim appears in this verse apart from mention of the Southern Kingdom. The focus is now, here and in the rest of this chapter, on the remnant of the ten tribes of the Northern Kingdom. The first part of this chapter (vv 1–2) apparently signals to the northerners. Then verses 3–5 announce the role that the Southern Kingdom will play in securing the return of the northern exiles. Verse 6 serves as a transition, mentioning both the House of Judah and the House of Joseph. Finally, with the naming of Ephraim at the beginning of verse 7, the return of the northerners is anticipated.

hero. This is the third time in three verses that the root *gbr* appears: twice as a substantive (here and in v 5; see NOTE above), and once as a Piel verb (v 6; see NOTE). It occurs again in the last verse of this chapter (v 12) as a Piel verb. Although many translations use "warriors" for *gibbôrîm*, that word does not quite signify what "heroes" does, in that warriors can be ordinary military personnel, men who can lose as well as win in combat. "Heroes" conveys the notion of a positive outcome to whatever struggle will have taken place. Hence the idea of rejoicing or celebrating, in the next colon, follows naturally from the comparison of Ephraim to heroes. Whereas the "heroes" of verse 5 were called "heroes in battle," the words "in battle" are not added to "heroes" here. The simile involves not the struggle itself but, rather, the successful result, and the rest of the verse elaborates on the attendant emotions.

their heart rejoices. The verb *śmḥ* ("to be glad, rejoice") is sometimes used with "heart" as its subject, forming an idiom that depicts the intensity of joyful feeling as coming from the heart, that is, from the innermost parts or thoughts of a person. The third-person plural suffix ("their") with "heart" refers to Ephraim (see previous NOTE), which stands collectively for all the northerners. Ephraim is about to experience restoration, and this is the first of a series of three responses to or characteristics of that experience described in this verse. Each of these responses involves a noun with a third-person plural suffix: "their heart" (twice) and "their children." Viewed in light of the frequent use of the verb with third-person plural suffix (see above, NOTE to "I will restore them" in v 6), these terms contribute to the emphasis on Ephraim in Zech 10:6bff.

The interrelatedness of the three responses is achieved by the use of this idiom, "their heart rejoices." It appears here in its entirety. In the next clause only the verb ("rejoice") is used; and in the last clause of this verse, "their heart" is the subject of another verb. The breakup of the idiom serves to carry along its full meaning in the clauses that use only its parts.

with wine. This common beverage of the east Mediterranean world is linked with various emotions or with social and religious functions in the Hebrew Bible. Here, its role in festive occasions and as part of the merriment involved in such celebration serves to emphasize the rejoicing that the previous words ("their heart rejoices") depict. It is possible, because these verses describe the restoration of the exiled northerners, that the prophet is consciously reversing the words of doom addressed to the Northern Kingdom by Hosea. In Hos 9:1, Israel is told *not* to exult, for Ephraim will soon be exiled to Egypt and Assyria (cf. v 10 below), and in exile they will not pour our "drink offerings of wine" to God (Hos 9:4). Although Zech 10:7 is not referring to the cultic use of wine, it does describe the joy of restoration, which would include Ephraim's ability once again to offer sacrifices to Yahweh.

Their children. Not only will Ephraim as a whole rejoice in the forthcoming return to its homeland, but especially will the younger generation be joyful. The children represent the future: they have no future in exile but surely possess one in their ancestral land. A similar thought is expressed below in verse 9 (see NOTE to "They'll give new life to"). Contrast the dismal situation of children in Hos 9:10–17.

see and rejoice. These two verbs together describe the way the upcoming generation will experience the restoration of Ephraim. The verb *rʾh*, "to see," occurs frequently in First Zechariah to introduce the prophet's visions. There, as here, it has no direct object, which is somewhat atypical of this verb. In First Zechariah, the particle "behold" complements "see" as a way of introducing a vision, whereas here a verb indicating the response to what the children perceive completes the clause. Thus, if the appearance of "see" bears any relationship to its use in First Zechariah, it is a contrastive one.

"Rejoice" repeats the verb of the previous bicolon; and although "their heart" and "like wine" are not also repeated, those amplifications of the first use of "rejoice" carry over into this attention to the response of a subset of Ephraim's collective identity. "Their heart" (see next NOTE) does recur in this verse, as part of the next clause, and that also adds to its applicability here.

their heart. The interconnectedness of the second, third, and fourth clauses of this verse describing how Ephraim will respond to its deliverance is achieved by the repetition, in the third and fourth clauses, of each of the two elements ("rejoice" and "their heart") of an idiomatic expression (see NOTE above in this verse) of the second clause. There is some ambiguity about whose heart is being referred to here: it could be that of Ephraim, as in 10:7b; or "children" of 10:7c could be the antecedent. A third possibility, that it refers to both, seems more likely in light of the way the idiom of verse 7b is broken up and used in the two subsequent clauses.

exult. This verb, a jussive from the root *gyl*, is frequently found parallel to and nearly synonymous with "rejoice" (*śmḥ*) as well as with other verbs expressing joyful feelings. The word is entirely associated with poetic texts, inasmuch as it never appears in the Pentateuch or the historical books of the Hebrew Bible. Although it can sometimes refer to moods of rejoicing that accompany secular events, such as harvest time (Isa 16:10) or marriage (Cant 1:4), it more typically conveys a response to God or to some act of God (Barth, Bergman, and Ringgren 1975: 475), as it does here. More specifically, Yahweh's help or deliverance (*yĕšûʿâ*) can inspire such exultation (Ps 9:15 [NRSV 9:14]), as it does here in light of what God announces in verse 6: "I will save" (see NOTE above). Similarly, those who are most vulnerable are the ones to rise to heights that involve exultation, as in Isa 29:19, where "rejoice" (*śmḥ*) and "exult" (*gyl*), the same two verbs that appear in this verse, are used in reference to the response of the poor and humble (cf. NOTE to "they are humble" in 10:2) to the eschatological events that Isaiah sets forth. Of all such sacral uses of *gyl* (cf. 9:9 above), nearly half of them refer directly to Yahweh as the cause for rejoicing, as is the case here. Although the verb is followed here by "in Yahweh," the whole phrase is to be understood elliptically. That is, the exultation in Yahweh is the consequence of what Yahweh will have done, which is what defines who Yahweh is in biblical thought.

8. *I will whistle*. The choice of the root *šrq* ("to hiss at, whistle") to begin a series of utterances that resume the pastoral imagery and announce in the first person God's restorative intentions is unusual and dramatic. Of twenty attestations of this verb, all but this one have a negative or derisive meaning. Jerusalem is a city to be "hissed at" and a horror in the time of its punishment and capture (Jer 19:8; Lam 2:15, 16), as will be Edom (Jer 49:17) and Babylon (Jer 50:13). Tyre is also to be "hissed at" in her coming destruction (Ezek 27:36). Nineveh is described as a city of desolation, and "everyone who passes by it hisses and shakes the fist" (Zeph 2:15). The noun form (*šrqh*) also, in all its occurrences except in Judg 5:16, has the sense of derision, "hissing at" (e.g., Jer 19:8; 25:9; 18; 29:18; 51:37; Mic 6:16; 2 Chron 29:8). In Judges, however, it means the "pipings" or "whistling" to call the sheep (5:16). That is its sense here: God is making the sound that a shepherd makes on a pipe or whistle in order to gather in the scattered flocks.

The shepherd imagery involved in whistling to herd animals thus continues that established in verses 2 and 3. Yahweh's exiled people are like a lost flock without a shepherd (v 2; see NOTE above), for they seek God through mediums and not directly. The shepherd imagery appears again in verse 3a but involves a substantial shift, for it is quite negative, if not pejorative, there. "Shepherds" are now human leaders in Yehud, and they are the object of God's anger. The positive use of this imagery returns in verse 3b (see NOTE to "his flock") and again in this verse. Using a verb that otherwise normally has such a strongly negative connotation helps to draw attention to God's actions and, in its allusions to the derisiveness that whistling (or hissing) can represent, gives an ironic coloration to the word. In taking a familiar word and using it in its more unusual (though perhaps older) sense, Second Zechariah exhibits a literary style that may be typical of postexilic prophecy in general, insofar as late prophecy is acutely aware of the existence of an authoritative, protocanonical literature.

to them. The antecedent of "them" is "Ephraim," the collective term that appears at the beginning of verse 7 (see NOTE above) to designate the northern tribes in exile, also called the "House of Joseph" in this chapter (v 6; see NOTE above). Although verses 3–5 concern the instrumentality of Judah in the divine plan to save Ephraim, verses 6c and following focus on Ephraim. A series of verbs with the third-person plural suffix, indicating actions involving "them" (= Ephraim), and several nouns with the third-person plural suffix all serve, as does this phrase, to point to the helpless and hopeless exiles who will miraculously be rescued by Yahweh (see above, NOTES to "I will restore them," v 6; and "their heart," v 7).

gather them in. The verb *qbṣ* in the Piel is similar to the previous word "whistle" in invoking pastoral imagery. It is frequently used of God as one who "gathers" the flock (e.g., Mic 2:12; 4:6; Zeph 3:19, 20; Jer 31:10; Isa 54:7; 56:8; etc.). In fact, the two verbs are so similar in meaning that P. D. Hanson (1975: 327) deletes "gather" on metrical grounds and preserves the following "for I have redeemed them," which is frequently taken as a gloss and eliminated by other commentators. Such scholars justify keeping "gather" but not "redeem" by analogy to verse 6b, where there is no second verb before "for" *(kî)* as there is here. However, the recurrence of the identical form in verse 10 below favors retention. Indeed, all verbs in the MT of this verse are appropriate. God's whistling to the northern exiles results in their being gathered. Their redemption (see next NOTE) involves two stages: first being alerted to the forthcoming return—"whistle to them"—and then being brought back, i.e., "gathered."

for I have redeemed them. As indicated in the preceding NOTE, P. D. Hanson (1975: 327) retains this phrase, whereas *BHS* has recommended its deletion, presumably on metrical grounds. However, the verb *pdh*, "to redeem," which can also mean "to ransom," has clear associations with the Exodus (Deut 7:8; 13:6 [NRSV 13:5]; Mic 6:4; Ps 78:42; etc.) and is appropriate to the present setting, where God is about to rescue the people once again from a foreign land. Similarly, Second Isaiah, for whom the message of a second exodus is so central, uses *pdh*: "So the redeemed of Yahweh shall return, and come to Zion with singing" (Isa 51:11 = Isa 35:10). That the author of Zechariah 10 has the original Exodus in mind in announcing this new and impending return to Zion is obvious from verse 11 below, where explicit reference to the Nile drying up conjures up the image of Israel's first departure from Egypt.

God's calling out or "whistling" to the exiled flock is followed by an announcement that God will "gather" the exiles in *because (kî)* Yahweh has already "redeemed" them. God has made the prior arrangements that allow for the exiles to be beckoned and collected back to where they belong. The idea of God's ransoming the people is a necessary theological component to the prophetic utterance. It is precisely because God has redeemed them, making it possible for them to return, that they will multiply, i.e., have a future (see next NOTE).

They will multiply as before. The English translation does not do justice to this elegant Hebrew expression, *wĕrābû kĕmô rābû*, which the prophet has coined by using familiar language but varying it to suit the context. The *waw* consecutive with *rābû*, meaning "they will multiply," establishes the future setting of the clause, which is followed by "like" *(kĕmô)* and completed with the perfect *rābû*, "they multiplied." Literally the text reads: "They will multiply as they [once] multiplied." The verb *rbh* ("to multiply, increase") evokes the anticipation of a return from exile, as it does in both Jer 23:3 and Ezek 36:11, where these prophets of the Exile look toward a future when the remnant "will be fruitful and multiply." Such language, in echoing the words of Genesis (1:22, 28; 9:1, 7²; 35:11), envisages a new creation. Second Zechariah also echoes those words, although with an emphasis on how the future population growth has historical precedents. The people will soon increase in numbers, in their homeland, as they had before. In forming a new expression, the author remains in the mainstream of biblical thought: first, by recalling the language of return from exile of his prophetic forebears Jeremiah and Ezekiel; and second, by evoking (along with Jeremiah and Ezekiel) the phraseology of Genesis, in the Primeval History and in God's promise to the patriarchs that they would become a great and populous people, an idea that served polemical purposes in postexilic literature (Tadmor 1987: 15–27). But Second Zechariah adds to this echo of earlier biblical language by acknowledging that the northerners had at one time "multiplied," as God had intended them to do; hence it becomes all the more compelling that they will do so once again.

The concern for an expanded population, although clearly influenced by the traditional language of creation and of patriarchal promise, may at the same time reflect the prophet's awareness of the acute demographic decline of Palestine in the Babylonian and Persian periods. Recent ethnoarchaeological studies have used sophisticated analytic techniques to provide population esti-mates for various epochs in the biblical period. The Persian period is marked by a dearth of royal centers and market towns and by a preponderance of rural estates, tiny villages (57 percent of Persian period settlements are labeled "very small," i.e., with eleven to thirty families per village, and barely 11 percent of the settlements would have had more than sixty families per village; see Carter 1991), and isolated fortresses (Hoglund 1992). Consequently, its population was shockingly small, especially in the Persian I period (539–38 to ca. 450), the end of which is the presumed backdrop for Second Zechariah.

For Yehud itself, an analysis of excavated sites and surveyed areas, with possible undiscovered sites taken into account, yields a figure of approximately ten thousand people in the Persian I period (Carter 1991: 155–61). This figure was reached by calculations using a coefficient of twenty-five people per dunam, which is probably too large a figure given the evidence from recent ethnographic studies of the area that would have constituted Yehud. Hence, the population of

Yehud in the sixth and fifth centuries was probably considerably less than ten thousand—perhaps as few as eight thousand or less. A prophetic vision of a prosperous restored land would thus entail a dramatic reversal in the existing demographic situation. Perhaps it was this bleak reality of the fifth century that influenced Second Zechariah to single out the northern diaspora for special attention. The restoration of all Israel to its former borders, as chapter 9 sets forth, is unimaginable without an enormous increase of population, of both Judeans and Israelites, to fill and secure the historical claim to this territory.

It is interesting to note, with respect to the Persian population of Palestine, one feature of an ideology current in fifth-century Yehud about the original entry to the Promised Land. The historian Hecateus of Abdera, apparently reflecting a Persian-period perspective, states that after leaving Egypt the Jews entered a land that was "at that time utterly uninhabited" (cited in Mendels 1983). Because this assertion is so patently in conflict with the biblical account of the settlement/conquest, one wonders whether the sparse population in Yehud during the second Exodus, i.e., the several waves of return from Babylon, occasioned this blatant tampering with the long-held view of the first Exodus.

9. *I sowed them.* The root zr^c, which means "to plant, sow, scatter seed," is very close to the verb zrh, which means "to winnow, scatter," and is used in Zech 2:2 and 2:4[2], to refer to the exile of Judah among the nations (see Meyers and Meyers 1987: 137–38, 140, 143–44). Hence it is not surprising that many commentators suggest emending the text from *wĕʾezrāʿēm*, "I sowed them," to *wĕʾăzārēm*, "I scattered them" (so *BHS*, etc.), for the context clearly depicts exile. However, the roots zr^c and zrh, although both examples of agricultural terminology used metaphorically, are derived from distinct agrarian procedures, with discrete applicability to the concept of exile. The term zrh, as used by First Zechariah and other prophets (e.g., Ezek 5:2, 10, 12; 6:8) in reference to the Judean Exile, means "to winnow," that is, to throw up (or "scatter") the grain so as to separate the wheat from the chaff. The grain that falls to the ground lies there, waiting to be collected, just as did the dispersed Judeans. Quite different is the sense of zr^c, which involves the idea that the seed distributed by the process of sowing will take root where it falls, i.e., be planted and grow (see Hag 1:6). The use of zr^c thus is far more appropriate for describing the dispersion of the northerners. They were not simply scattered; they were sown, and so they grew in the places to which the Assyrians had deported them. The metaphor of planting is eminently appropriate to the prophet's awareness of the long duration—the rootedness—of Ephraim's exile. The image of planting the northerners also contrasts with the image of scattering the southerners. The latter had, in a relatively short time in comparison with the northerners, been gathered up and, at least in part, returned to Zion, whereas such was not the case for the former.

The MT of the verb zr^c is preceded by the simple waw-conjunctive (*wĕ*), which is perhaps better read as waw-consecutive (*wā*). The verb takes the third-person plural suffix, "them," in reference to the exiles from the Northern Kingdom. Repeatedly in verses 6–12 the verbs take this suffix; and several times nouns have the third-person plural possessive suffix, "their." The overall effect (see NOTE to "I will restore them" in 10:6) is to emphasize Ephraim as the focus of God's redemptive acts.

among the peoples. This phrase and the next one ("in remote places"; see next NOTE) deal with the location of the exiled community, the character of which has been set forth in verse 2 (see NOTES above). The exiles have been sown (*bāʿammîm*) "among the peoples." The plural of *ʿam* ("people") indicates the multiplicity of places to which the northerners, upon whom the second half of Zechariah 10 focuses, had been dispersed. The spread-out resettling of the northerners by the Assyrians, in contrast to the Babylonian policy that brought the exiled Judeans largely to the Babylonian heartland, undoubtedly was one factor in the very different response of the northerners to their exiled status.

The use of *ʿam* recalls its appearance in the final oracle of First Zechariah (8:20–23), where a vivid depiction of the end of days includes "peoples" (v 20) and "many peoples" (v 22) along with "leaders" and "mighty nations" (vv 20, 22) and "nations of all tongues" (v 23; see Meyers and Meyers 1987: 435ff.). The selection here of *ʿammîm* ("peoples") rather than *gôyîm* ("nations") may, as in Zech 8:20 and 22, have been made because the prophet intended to convey a sense of consanguinity or connection with the cultures in which the exiles found themselves. Although we normally would expect Egypt and Assyria (specified in the next verse as the places of the northern diaspora) to be excluded from such a designation, the realities of the Persian era, with imperial domination and the extensive use of Aramaic as the lingua franca, meant the spreading of common cultural forms throughout the areas of Persian hegemony. As we noted in our COMMENT to Zech 8:23, the purview of First Zechariah was such that Jerusalem and Yehud constituted the innermost of several concentric circles. "Peoples" then constituted the next circle, by signifying neighboring groups with some affinity to Yehud. The outermost circle would be "the nations." Given the fact that Persian imperial rule had actually brought that intermediate circle closer through greater communication, a common language, and an administrative infrastructure in the satrapies, we may suppose a similar perspective in Second Zechariah and, hence, the use of "peoples" here rather than "nations." Indeed, the readiness with which the northerners seem to have been incorporated into the cultures of the areas to which they were deported stands in contrast to the behavior of the Judean exiles. Dispersed as they were, mechanisms for national/ ethnic survival among the descendants of the ten northern tribes did not become operant as they did for the Judeans, who were probably fewer and a more concentrated population.

in remote places. This expression modifies the following verb "they'll remember." However, it also provides another piece of information about the nature of the northern diaspora. The preceding "among the peoples" (see NOTE above) connotes the sense of the multitude of groups among which the Israelites had been settled, as well as perhaps their acculturation to those groups. The present phrase, *bammerḥaqqîm*, indicates the geographical diversity of the dispersion of the Northern Kingdom. This form is used infrequently and always carries the nuance of faraway lands (e.g., Isa 8:9; 13:5; 46:11; Jer 4:16; 6:20; etc.). Thus it serves as a meaningful complement to the more cultural-political nuance of "among the peoples." Together they indicate the great obstacles faced by the exiled northerners with respect to the maintaining of identity and, hence, the potential for restoration.

they'll remember me. The obstacles of distance from the homeland and acculturation to local ways can be overcome only by Yahweh's intervention. The idea of remembering God is used to suggest that, despite factors that would pull them further and further away from their ancestral identity, the Israelites can be rescued from geographical and cultural oblivion. The verb *zkr*, "to remember," occurs frequently (sixty-nine times) with God or God's deeds as the object of human mental activity. The many instances of people recalling God most often involve recollections of God's past deeds, as at the Exodus (e.g., Deut 5:15; 16:12; Isa 63:11; cf. 1 Chron 16:12), as a way of inspiring confidence in God's forthcoming salvific acts. The citing of past events and the admonition to remember them are of great significance for the conduct of the present and, hence, for the future condition of the people (cf. Eising 1980: 68). Even more specifically relevant here are the instances in which God as deity is being remembered, usually when those who remember are in a situation of mortal danger, with the remembering of Yahweh tantamount to the belief that God will redeem or rescue those in trouble (as Jonah 2:8 [NRSV 2:7]; see also Isa 46:8).

Along with the idea that people remembering God involves the hope for and acceptance of God's redemptive deeds, the verb *zkr* also evokes the way that verb is used of the Babylonian exiles, whom the prophets exhort never to forget Yahweh despite their removal from Zion (Jer 51:50). This response to exile is perhaps most eloquently expressed by the composer of the famous "rivers of Babylon" psalm (137) in which the remembrance of Zion is tantamount to remembering God.

They'll give life to. The Qal form with *waw*-consecutive that is preserved in the MT, *wĕḥāyû*, is very difficult, especially because it is followed by the accusative marker *ʾet*. The Qal normally means "to live" or "to have life"; it can also mean "to sustain life," usually when followed by *ʿal*. The Vulgate or ancient Latin is alone among the versions in favoring the MT: "They will live with their children" *(vivent cum filiis suis)*. Among recent commentators, Rudolph accepts this view (1976: 193–94). P. D. Hanson simply makes it an imperfect Qal *(yîḥyû)* and translates "their children will survive"; but he has to remove the *ʾet* in order to make sense of the text (1973: 326). The Greek and Syriac, however, support the shift to the Piel by translating "they will raise up their children." The change to the Piel involves only a minor vowel change, from *wĕḥayû* to *wĕḥîyyû*. Indeed, the shift to the Piel, which means "to keep alive, make live," seems justified if one is to retain "children" in its accusative relationship to the verb.

The verbal root *ḥyh* refers, in its basic usage, to survival—life as opposite to death—especially as used of individuals. Here, however, it deals with corporate existence, the life of Ephraim (see NOTE in 10:7), the exiled northerners. Several prophetic texts prefigure this one in their concern for national existence and the linking of that existence to loyalty to Yahweh. If the Israelites do in fact "remember" God (see previous NOTE), then they become eligible for the corporate survival that acknowledgment of Yahweh offers. One particular passage, Amos 5:6 (cf. 5:4) may underlie Second Zechariah's use of "give life." Amos is anticipating the destruction of the "House of Joseph" (5:6; cf. Zech 10:5) and trying to forestall that event by calling up the Ephraimites to seek God and therefore "live" (= survive) as a political or cultural entity. This passage in Zechariah 10 constitutes a reversal of what Amos proclaimed. The House of Joseph had not sought Yahweh and hence, as a sociopolitical entity, had died. But now Ephraim will remember God, and its existence as a people will consequently be revived. The people will now have a future (see next NOTE), whereas for centuries that was not the case; they are about to return to their homeland to reacquire the national identity, the "life," that the return signifies.

their children. It is the next generation that will reap the benefit of the northerners' acknowledgment of Yahweh. Instead of oblivion or death, the exile of the ten tribes of Israel will be terminated and thus Israel will live. More specifically, the children will experience the national identity that their ancestors had largely lost in the widespread diaspora imposed by the Assyrians (see NOTES above in this verse to "among the peoples" and "in remote places"). The jubilation of the children in verse 7 is now comprehensible: they are the ones who are being given life, i.e., national survival.

they will return. The ultimate destiny of the people whom God is calling, gathering, and redeeming (v 7) is return to homeland. The verb *šwb*, found here in the Qal and in the Hiphil above in verse 6 (but see NOTE to "I will restore them") and below in verse 10, is the classic term to express the restoration or return of the exiles. The third-person plural here does not necessarily refer only to the children of the exiles, which seems to be the case because "children" is the nearest noun. Those commentators who take "children" as the subject apparently assume that only the offspring will return. The prophet's perspective, however, is one that stretches over long periods of time. Hence, all exiles— parents and their children—are presumably intended to return. Furthermore, verse 10 surely describes the return of the entire community exiled to Egypt and Assyria.

10. *I will bring them back.* In verse 6 above, at the very point where the prophecies of this chapter begin to focus exclusively on the northern exiles, Yahweh announces his intention to "restore" the House of Joseph. Although the verb there is a conflated form, it is essentially the same as the verb here. Having specified the process of redemption and the effect it will have on the dispersed people, Yahweh now specifies the places from which the people will be recovered and the places to which they will be restored. This shift to geographical specificity is marked by the repetition of the Hiphil of *šwb* ("return"; cf. preceding NOTE), a root that occurs three times in Zech 10:6–12 and so signifies with some intensity the concept of return. The third-person plural suffix ("them") of the verb here, as repeatedly in this section in reference to Ephraim, adds to the attention bestowed upon the northern tribes.

Egypt. This is the first of the two specific places of exile that the prophet mentions, although the general notion that the dispersion was extensive has already been set forth by the use of "among the peoples" and "in remote places" in verse 9 (see NOTES above). Egypt is mentioned again, also with Assyria, in the next verse; see the NOTE to "Assyria . . . Egypt" in verse 11 for a comment on the chiastic arrangement.

Although the preponderance of biblical mentions of Egypt are in reference to the period of bondage and the subsequent deliverance from servitude by Yahweh at the hands of Moses and Aaron, the land of the Nile does continue to play a role in the post-Exodus history of ancient Israel. Passages such as this one, especially when Egypt is paired with Assyria, point to the existence of a population of Israelites in Egypt, probably from the eighth century onward. Zechariah 10:10 is not the only prophetic text that links Egypt with Assyria as places where Israelites will be in residence. Significantly, the eighth-century prophets are the ones who have such a perspective. First Isaiah (e.g., 11:11, 15–16), Hosea (7:11; 11:5, 11; cf. Andersen and Freedman 1980: 469), and Micah (7:12) all recognize that Israelites have gone to Egypt and Assyria—First Isaiah and Micah both anticipate Yahweh's bringing the people away from those lands, whereas Hosea merely mentions these foreign dwelling places as signs of Israel's apostasy.

The existence of northern Israelites in Egypt, and in Assyria, thus seems certain on the basis of such texts. The question remains as to how or why they left their homeland to sojourn in foreign lands. The perspective of Second Zechariah, aware of the deportation practices of both Assyria and Babylonia, perhaps views the Israelites living outside their homeland as remnants of mass deportations, which were a characteristic feature of Assyrian imperial policy of the neo-Assyrian period, beginning with Tiglath-Pileser III. The practice of group deportations had long been used in the international struggles of the ancient world, but the neo-Assyrians made it an integral strategy in their imperialist goals (Oded 1979). As their means of securing the domination of many different groups, it had a profound impact on the political, cultural, and demographic character of the ancient Near East from the eighth century until well into the Persian period.

The biblical texts recounting the Assyrian conquest of Samaria in 722–21 B.C.E. indeed record that Israelites were taken into exile. But that exile was to the east, to Assyria and environs (2 Kgs 17:23; 18:11). Can this citing of Egypt by Second Zechariah be related to the Assyrian Exile? Although Egypt is not specified in the 2 Kings passage or in contemporary Assyrian documents chronicling the conquest and deportation of Samaria, it is possible that the vast rearrangements of populations that the Assyrians practiced did involve the transfer of some Israelites to Egypt. Assyrians, in fact, deported people both to and from Egypt. The documentary evidence (mainly royal inscriptions) for these movements, although quite extensive, is hardly complete. Thus, even though the evidence is indirect, it is quite possible that resettlements by the Assyrians involved the movement of Israelites to Egypt.

However, another explanation for the Egyptian diaspora seems more likely.

Throughout the biblical period, residents of Palestine periodically migrated to Egypt for economic or political reasons, as several episodes in the patriarchal narratives of Genesis indicate (see also 1 Kgs 11:40). By the Babylonian period, it is quite clear that Judeans were going to Egypt (and also to Assyria [Jer 2:18]) to escape what they viewed as impending disaster in Judah. Jeremiah in particular is concerned with those who descended to Egypt (Jer 24:8; 41:17–18; 42; 43; 44). Apparently, the same phenomenon occurred during the final decades of Israelite national existence in the eighth century. The northerners clearly sought diplomatic succor from Egypt (Hos 7:11, 16); and for economic reasons too, they left their homeland (Hos 9:3, 6).

Whether they went willingly or unwillingly, the end result was the same in the view of Second Zechariah. He saw a population of the descendants of Israelites living in foreign lands. The view of a greater Israel put forward in chapter 9 involves an inclusive geopolitical scheme. The prophet anticipates the recovery of territories meant to be inhabited by all Israel, both north and south (see NOTES to "tribes of Israel" in 9:1, and to the various toponyms of 9:1–8). Consequently, the dispersed inhabitants of both north and south must be restored. The Judeans, exiled to Babylon, have partially returned to Zion. Now those left in Egypt (and Assyria) remain to be brought back to Israel. Their condition was one of exile, whether the cause was self-imposed removal or externally imposed banishment.

One final point deserves consideration, namely, the well-known existence of a military colony at Elephantine that consisted of Arameans and/or Jews (see first NOTE to 14:18). In the late sixth and fifth centuries, this colony was in the service of the Persian crown. The composition of its inhabitants is not entirely clear, nor is the period in which they may have migrated to Egypt. The fact that, in the Persian period, the Jews there sometimes called themselves Arameans can perhaps be related to a migration from the Northern Kingdom where Aramaic had become the prevalent language by neo-Assyrian times (Porten 1968: 16–17). In any case, the Jews of Elephantine were in contact with Yehud during the Persian period, and the papyri discovered at Elephantine indicate both cordial and strained relationships between the two communities. Yet, however prominent the Elephantine group may seem because of the archival materials that have survived, they were a rather small group. It seems unlikely, therefore, that this reference to the Egyptian diaspora could refer specifically to the Elephantine colony. Rather, a wide purview for what is meant by "Egypt" seems more appropriate, especially because Egypt is paired with Assyria.

Assyria. The major deportation of Israelites, following the fall of Samaria (722–21 B.C.E.) was clearly to Assyria. But because Assyria is coupled here with Egypt, the population that the prophet sees as needing redemption may have included those who willingly left Israel for Assyria, even before the events of the late eighth century (see previous NOTE). Whether Second Zechariah knew why Israelites were residing in Assyria cannot be determined. Indeed, we cannot be sure that he was personally aware that certain inhabitants of Egypt and Assyria in the Persian period still identified themselves as descendants of people who had left Israel hundreds of years earlier. In fact, it is much more likely that his concern for Israelites in exile derived from his familiarity with existing authoritative literary sources—the protocanon of his day—rather than from direct or indirect contact with exiles in Assyria.

gather them. The verb *qbṣ,* "to gather, collect," is the same as that used above in 10:8 (see NOTE to "gather them in"). Used in the Piel as it is here, it is part of the biblical vocabulary describing Yahweh's restoration of the dispersed people, often represented figuratively as God's flocks. The place "from" *(mn)* which the people are gathered is not always indicated, but in this case, as in many other passages, the source of the ingathered exiles is specified. Usually the place from which the people are taken is the entire dispersion, i.e., from all the places/nations to which they have been scattered (e.g., Isa 11:12; Jer 23:3; 31:8; 32:37; Ezek 11:17; 37:21; Ps 106:47; Neh 1:9). This passage is thus unusual in specifying an individual country, or countries—inasmuch as Egypt and Assyria should really be taken as a pair, linked as they are in a distinct chiasm in verse 10a, with the action of both verbs affecting exiles in both places.

The verb takes a third-person plural suffix, as do many verbs in 10:6–12 (see NOTE above to "I will restore them," 10:6), thereby intensifying the attention to "them," the exiles from Israel.

Gilead. A geographical term, "Gilead" designates the territory east of the Jordan. Sometimes it refers to a limited part of Transjordan, and the biblical texts vary in what areas of the land across the Jordan are assigned to which tribes. However, it can also designate all of Transjordan (see Deut 3:12, 13; Josh 12:2–6; cf. Aharoni 1979: 38–39). That was considered Israelite territory: southern Gilead, south of the Jabbok, inhabited by Reuben and Gad; and northern Gilead, north of the Jabbok, occupied by the half-tribe of Manasseh.

The land itself is rugged and mountainous with only a relatively narrow band of tableland. It was probably densely forested throughout the biblical period and did not have the same resources for development as the land west of the Jordan. Its importance to Israel lay in its strategic features: it served as a buffer against peoples of the east and was the location of the King's Highway, one of the two major north-south arteries of the Levant. Although Gilead, or parts thereof, at times came under the control of the Syrians or others (see 2 Kgs 10:32–33; cf. Amos 1:3), it apparently was part of the Northern Kingdom in the late eighth century, when Tiglath-Pileser III captured various western cities in his campaigns of 733–32 B.C.E. (2 Kgs 15:29). Both its topography and its history indicate its somewhat marginal status vis-à-vis the Northern Kingdom. As such, Gilead (along with Lebanon; see next NOTE) represented relatively empty territory that belonged to the Northern Kingdom and would be filled by Israelites only when they were exceedingly populous, exactly the condition that is specified at the end of this verse.

Lebanon. Derived from the Hebrew word for "white," probably because much of the heights of this area are snowcapped, "Lebanon" refers in the Bible to the chain of mountains that begin in northern Palestine and continue northward for about a hundred miles. The Lebanon was reckoned as part of

Israel (Deut 1:7; 3:25; 11:24; Josh 1:4; 13:5–6; 1 Kgs 9:19). If the coastal areas to the west of the Lebanon range are meant to be included in the designation "Lebanon," then the Phoenician cities there controlled territory that perhaps was considered part of Israel's allotment (see NOTE above to "Tyre and Sidon," 9:2). The mountainous areas of Lebanon themselves were not settled in any significant way until the Roman period. Similarly, the eastern edge of the Lebanon—the Beqaᶜ Valley—has never been very extensively settled. In short, the geographic and historical features of Lebanon are similar to those of Gilead (see previous NOTE): it was considered Israelite; part of it was taken over by outsiders; and most of it was not suitable for agricultural development. Hence, Lebanon was marginal Israelite territory. It would be settled by the northern tribes only when the heartland of Israel, the northern hill country and Galilee, were fully populated, a condition anticipated in the clause that follows.

Together with Gilead, Lebanon thus represents Israelite territory to be populated under optimal conditions, i.e., the eschatological restoration of all Israel. Some would see "Lebanon" as a gloss for metrical and other reasons (as Mitchell 1912: 244, 301; P. D. Hanson 1975: 327). But, as we have seen in our examination of the various geopolitical names in chapter 9 (see NOTES to these names), the toponyms of Second Zechariah have been carefully selected. This instance is no exception; Gilead and Lebanon as a pair are integral to the prophet's concern for the full restoration of the Northern Kingdom. Perhaps the best corroboration of this is found in Jer 22:6, where Yahweh compares wayward Judah to Gilead and Lebanon; Judah will surely become uninhabited, i.e., like those areas that are quintessentially underpopulated. The Jeremiah passage is usually misunderstood, with the metaphoric use of "Gilead" and "Lebanon" being seen as positive. However, the poetic line that follows is introduced by ʾim-lōʾ, which is an emphatic affirmative. Hence Jeremiah views Gilead and Lebanon as uninhabited areas:

> Gilead you are to me, the summit of the Lebanon;
> I will surely make you a wilderness, cities not inhabited.

Second Zechariah uses the same imagery—Lebanon and Gilead as empty wilderness—to anticipate Israel's successful return, i.e., the filling up of even marginal lands.

This geographical term appears below in 11:1 (see NOTE to "O Lebanon!"), also in a poetic context and also without the definite article that accompanies this place name in many other instances in the Hebrew Bible.

bring them. The root *bwʾ*, one of the most frequently used verbs in the Hebrew Bible, represents movement directed toward a particular goal in space and in time (Preuss 1975: 21). In the Qal ("to come") and in the Hiphil ("to bring") as here, it is part of the stereotyped vocabulary used for the coming or bringing of the people into the land that they are to possess. Because of its prominence in the Deuteronomic literature in reference to the Israelite occupation of the Promised Land, it is natural for it to appear in the literature of the exilic and postexilic sources in reference to the second entry into the homeland, i.e., the restoration or return from exile (e.g., Neh 1:9; Ezek 36:24; Jer 31:8). Like the other verbs in these verses (10:6–12) dealing with Israel's repatriation ("restore," v 6; "gather" and "redeem," v 8), the third-person plural suffix ("them") of the verb serves to emphasize Israel's role as object of God's redemptive deeds (see NOTE to "I will restore them," 10:6).

no room is found for them. The Hebrew is idiomatic and elliptical: *wĕlōʾ yimmāṣēʾ lāhem.* The verb *mṣʾ*, in the Niphal, means "will be found," i.e., "will be (found) sufficient" (cf. similar Qal usage in Num 11:22 and Judg 21:14). Its use in reference to territorial matters is established in Josh 17:16, where the Josephites complain that their allotted territory in the hill country "is not sufficient for us" *(lōʾ-yimmāṣēʾ lānû).* The anticipated repopulation of the exiled northerners will be so successful that even areas that normally are only sparsely populated (see NOTES in this verse to "Gilead" and "Lebanon") will overflow.

The prophet's concern for an enormous repopulation of the historical territory of Israel in its fullest extent no doubt draws upon the promises and commands of Genesis. However, it may also be a reflection of the dismal reality of the fifth century, when population in Yehud was apparently at an all-time low since the beginnings of Israel (see above, NOTE to "They will multiply as before," 10:8). Any vision of a restored people claiming its full territorial heritage would have to involve a veritable population explosion, which is exactly what this verse depicts.

11. *He will traverse.* The text of the three parts of this colon is difficult, and many emendations have been suggested. The LXX and Old Latin both have a plural verb, which most modern commentators favor. Reading the plural would allow the previous "them" to be the antecedent, thus avoiding an abrupt shift to a third-person singular, which would presumably have Yahweh as its subject. The shift would be startling, because Yahweh has been speaking in the first person in the preceding verses (vv 6–10). However, the sudden change to the third person for Yahweh would surely have to come in the next clause ("he will smite the rolling sea"), and thus the sudden change in person for Yahweh is not a compelling enough reason to disregard the MT. Indeed, there is a frequent pattern of switch in person in this chapter and in other poetic biblical passages. In this particular instance, God's actions in the preceding verses, presented in the first person, have Israel as the object and the deeds as restorative. Here the enemy waters, representing Israel's captivity, are the object. Perhaps this shift in divine activity to the quasi-mythological reader (see below, NOTE to "he will smite") has prompted the shift to the third person for Yahweh.

Suggested changes to the plural should also be rejected because of the way the first two clauses of this verse provide complementary expressions of divine might in securing the release and return of the dispersed people. The repetition of "sea" surely serves to link 11a and 11b, thus indicating that the verbs are both singular with "he" (= Yahweh) as subject.

The imagery here, of God traversing and smiting the waters so that they all "dry up," i.e., are vanquished (see following NOTES), is drawn from the mythological idea of God's conquering the cosmic waters (see M. S. Smith 1990: 52–55). Martial and cosmological aspects of deity, especially as known in Ugaritic literature, converge in depicting Yahweh's dominion over the watery enemy. A good example is Psalm 74, especially verses 13–17, where Elohim slays the sea monster, lopping off Leviathan's (seven) heads. The text of that psalm perhaps has some lexical congruence with Zech 11:11 in that both passages use the root *ybš* ("to dry up"). In addition, the Exodus tradition of Yahweh's parting the waters so that Israel could cross on dry land became part of the mythic motifs of God's smiting the sea, as it does in Isa 11:15 and certainly in this verse.

sea of stress. The word for "sea," *ym*, usually refers to particular broad bodies of water that we would call seas or lakes (as the Mediterranean, the Sea of Galilee, or the Dead Sea). However, it also can signify broad rivers: the Nile, as it does in Isa 19:5, an oracle against Egypt that also anticipates the drying up of the Nile's waters (see NOTE to "will dry up" below); and the Euphrates, as in Jeremiah's oracle against Babylon, in which Yahweh promises to dry up her sea (Jer 51:36).

The combination of "sea" with "stress" (from *ṣrr*, "to bind, tie up, restrict") is unique to this passage. The metaphoric reference of this phrase may be to the restricted lives of exiles in either Egypt or Mesopotamia. Many exegetes would prefer to emend the text and have it refer only to Egypt: *bym mṣrym*, "the sea of Egypt." It does not seem necessary to do so, however, if we are willing to credit Second Zechariah with creative use of language and if we recognize that each of the tricola of this line concerns a sea. Whatever the nuance of "sea of stress," it is clear that this phrase depicts the enemy, or hostile forces, that Yahweh must battle in order to release the dispersed Israelites.

he will smite. The third-person singular here again (as in "He will traverse") refers to God's actions toward the sea, the rivers of Egypt and Mesopotamia (see previous NOTE). The sea will be destroyed so that the exiles can pass through and return to Israel. Mythological notions of conquering the sea converge with historical allusions to the Exodus. Emending the verb to Hophal (as P. D. Hanson 1975: 327), along with making the first verb in this verse plural, would obviate the need to understand the change in person that this verb would institute and would create a parallel with the next tricolon. Yet such an emendation prevents the reader from recognizing the somewhat different relationship between God and the object of divine activity that the use of the third person may signify (see first NOTE to this verse).

rolling sea. Literally, "sea of waves." The image is of the waters—the rivers of Egypt and Mesopotamia (see NOTE above to "sea of stress")—at their fullest, i.e., the enemies, whether mythic or political, at their most powerful. So depicted, their being dried up, which the third colon of this line envisages, becomes all the more dramatic and all the more effective in attesting to God's saving power. That "sea" refers to rivers here and in the preceding tricolon is further supported by the fact that in Jer 51:42 (cf. 51:55) the destruction of

Babylon is portrayed as the rising of the "sea" (= river) and its "waves" (gallîm, as here) over the wicked city.

The relationship of "rolling" to "sea" in this line is the same as that of "stress" to "sea" in the previous line. In both cases, a somewhat anomalous noun after "sea" describes some feature of the "sea." The first identifies the sea as restrictive and therefore hostile, whereas the second depicts the rolling, serpentlike movement of waves, conjuring up the sinuous movements of the sea serpent. The historical and mythic referents of the sea imagery are thereby brought together in these two phrases.

depths of the stream. This word, mĕṣûlôt in Hebrew, carries with it allusions to the Exodus event, at which time Pharaoh's armies drowned in the "depths" of the eastern deltas (Exod 15:5; cf. Neh 9:11). The watery demise of the Egyptians is contrasted with the dry land God forms in the water, enabling the Israelites to pass through, just as is the case here. Although the combination of depths with "stream" (yĕʾōr) would seem to form a phrase representing only the Nile, because yĕʾōr frequently designates the Nile or, in the plural, the streams that make up its varied waterways in the north, the word can indicate watercourses in general (as Isa 33:21; Job 28:10) or even the Tigris (as Dan 12:5–7; cf. 10:4). The imagery in this first line of verse 11 clearly draws from Exodus language, inasmuch as that event is the paradigm for God's bringing the people to the Promised Land. However, the bodies of water are not in fact named, and all the references to water can be to the great rivers of Mesopotamia as well as to the Nile. The Israelites are dispersed along all these rivers, and it is God's intention to remove them from their exile in both Egypt and Assyria, which is what the preceding verse (see NOTES to "Egypt" and "Assyria") and the next line specify.

will dry up. The Hiphil of ybš, "to be dry, dried up," indicates that the fullest of waters ("rolling sea"; see NOTE above) will be made dry to their very bottoms ("depths of the stream"; see NOTE preceding). Such an act defies nature and hence can be accomplished only by Yahweh. The mythological background of this language has already been suggested (see first NOTE to this verse). The drying of the waters of Egypt at the time of the Exodus is also the clear prototype of the expected removal of Israelites from the "stress" of their captivity. Although the verb "dry up" does not have any special connection to the language of the Exodus, its noun form (yabbāšâ) almost always refers to the "dry land" that Israel traverses at the Exodus and at crossing the Jordan into the Promised Land.

It should be noted that the Hiphil of ybš normally has a waw after the he, as would be expected in a Pe Waw verb. The form of the verb here thus might better suit the Hiphil of bwš ("to be ashamed"). If we take bwš, the passage would have a slightly different nuance, with the seas being "totally ashamed" of their actions. In either case, the Hiphil is intensive, like the Piel, rather than causative; it means that the water "will totally dry up."

splendor . . . scepter. The noun gĕʾôn can refer to political and/or economic power and the resulting material expression of the strength of a nation-state or city-state (see NOTE to "pride," 9:6). It is paired here with šēbeṭ, which literally means "a rod or staff." In a slightly extended sense, however, it denotes a ceremonial object held by the leader of a political group and thus represents the political sovereignty of a group, as it does here (although it can also denote a social unit, as when it stands for a "tribe" of Israel).

"Splendor" and "scepter" together in this line are complementary components of parallel cola. Together they indicate the invincible—save for Yahweh's intervention—political and economic power of the two areas of the ancient world in which the dispersed northerners are located. God will take action against them, as the exiles are leaving their "sea of stress" (see NOTE above in this verse), so that not only will the exiles be restored but also the superpowers will cease to exist, at least in their historical forms. To be sure, neither Egypt nor Assyria had autonomy by the fifth century. The poet is drawing on historical notions and giving those nations symbolic value as oppressors in linking them here. That these two nations appear chiastically in verses 10 and 11 (see next NOTE) contributes to the way they function symbolically.

Assyria . . . Egypt. The two lands in which exiled northerners remained dispersed; see the NOTES to these geopolitical terms used in verse 10.

The order of Assyria and Egypt here is the reverse of that in verse 10. This chiasm shows the close connection between verses 10 and 11 and the way the linkage of these two nations is a cliché representing oppressors of Yahweh's people. Compare, for example, Lam 5:6; Lamentations bemoans the Babylonian conquest but uses "Egypt and Assyria" as representative of past problems.

will be brought low . . . will pass away. In Hebrew, this line opens with one verb ("be brought low") and closes with the other ("will pass away"), thus linking the three complementary pairs that constitute this colon (see NOTES above to "splendor . . . scepter" and "Assyria . . . Egypt"). The common Hebrew verb *yrd* ("go down") is used figuratively in the Bible to describe the political humiliation and death of nations (as Jer 49:16) that have oppressed Israel (Mayer 1990: 319). The nations whose economic and political success ("splendor" and "scepter") is removed are brought low; they can no longer exist as sovereign states. The final word of the verse, the verb *swr*, denotes "removal, departure"; the termination of the imperial existence of both Egypt and Assyria is emphatically announced.

12. *I will make them mighty.* This is the fourth occurrence of the root *gbr* in chapter 10, the second of the Piel form (also in v 6; the noun form "hero[es]" occurs in vv 5 and 7; see NOTES in those verses). As in verse 6 above and in the one other place where it occurs in the Hebrew Bible (in Eccles 10:10), it means "to make strong." Yahweh is the subject of the verb in verse 7; and in verses 5 and 7, Judah and Ephraim respectively are called "heroes." Because "in Yahweh" follows the verb here, there is some ambiguity about the subject of the verb in this verse. However, who else but God could make the returnees strong through Yahweh? The image of exceptional strength is linked here to the presence of Yahweh (see next NOTE), a result that constitutes a response to the exhortation of 10:1, that the people look directly to Yahweh.

The verb bears the third-person masculine plural suffix "them." It is difficult to be sure to whom "them" is referring. It may continue from the previous verses about Ephraim and indicate the northerners. However, inasmuch as this verse is the culmination of the whole chapter, the first part of which is devoted to Judah, it may have a more inclusive intent, involving both Judah and Ephraim as reunited people, now "mighty" together in Yahweh's name.

in Yahweh. As indicated in the preceding NOTE, the returnees will become strong through their new and closer relationship with Yahweh. This verse represents a shift away from the more direct military language of previous verses. "In Yahweh" complements the notion of becoming mighty, and the second half of the verse anticipates that those empowered by Yahweh will walk about bearing the name of the deity. There are very few, if any, other texts in the Bible that ᴄontain the sort of combination featured in the first half of this verse. However, Jer 17:7 (cf. Ps 40:5 [NRSV 40:4]) uses *geber* plus "in Yahweh" to indicate how individuals receive strength by trusting in God: "Blessed is the person *(geber)* who trusts in Yahweh, for Yahweh is his security *(mibṭaḥô)*." Although the idea of deriving strength and support from Yahweh is common throughout the Hebrew Bible, the present text offers a new combination of words for expressing a familiar idea. It echoes and resonates with the preceding military language, yet also moves away from it.

in his name they will go about. The second half of this verse also contains an otherwise unattested combination: the Hithpael of *hlk* ("to walk") plus "in his (God's) name." Indeed, the novelty of this clause apparently seemed unacceptable to the Greek and Latin, both of which read the text as "they will glory *(ythllw)* in his name" (cf. Ps 34:2 [NRSV 34:3]; 105:3). It is common in the Bible "to call upon God's name" or "to answer in his name" or "to swear by his name" or "to swear falsely in the name of." Thus the expression "to go about in God's name" is freighted with theological overtones, yet is a departure from earlier patterns, as an examination of its two components reveals.

The Hithpael of *hlk*, used in First Zechariah in 1:10, 11, and 6:7[3], has the meaning of "totality" and conveys a sense of the vastness of the territory being explored in the equine scouting expedition of the First Vision and in the final vision of the Four Chariots. The verb means that one "goes to and fro"; by the force of the implied merism, one thus "goes everywhere." Elsewhere in the Bible, the most notable use of the Hithpael occurs in Job 2:2, where Satan appears before the Divine Council after having "roamed far and wide" or "to and fro" in all the earth. Another instance is in Gen 3:8, when God appears in the garden in Eden "to patrol" the area, i.e., to indicate that he is watching over the whole place. The meaning intended here is quite similar, i.e., those who bear God's name will travel far and wide or "go about" demonstrating that their God is with them everywhere, not just in what they say (by swearing, calling, or answering in God's name) but also in all their activities—in all their movements.

The combination of the Hithpael of *hlk* plus "in his name" is unique. What does it actually mean "to go about in God's name"? The word *šēm* ("name") occurs ten times in Malachi in association with God and three other times in Second Zechariah, once in reference to idolatry (13:3) and twice in reference to

God (13:9; 14:9). Malachi 1:11 perhaps provides the clearest sense of its postexilic usage: "from the rising of the sun until its setting, my name is great among the nations, and in every place incense is brought to my name as a pure offering; for my name is great among the nations . . ." (the other references in Malachi are 1:6², 14; 2:2, 5; 3:16, 20 [NRSV 4:2]). This passage indicates the two foci of name theology that coexist in the postexilic era. First is the notion that God's name can be made great in all the world, that is, far beyond the borders of the holy land. Perhaps it is the expectation that recognition of God's name—which stands for divine reality—will spread throughout the world in the new times to come, as suits the universalistic perspective of postexilic prophecy (see NOTES and COMMENT to Zech 8:23 in Meyers and Meyers 1987). That is, as in the universal language of First Zechariah, the foreign nations will somehow recognize Yahweh's greatness.

The other relevant focus of postexilic thought is the way it is connected with Pentateuchal ideas, e.g., Exod 20:24 and Deut 12:5, 11, about God's presence in the Tabernacle and Temple. When Malachi speaks of bringing incense to God's name, it is presupposed that the setting is the Temple where God dwells (*škn*). The use of "to dwell" in First Zechariah at 2:14, 15 [NRSV 2:10, 11] and 8:3 demonstrates how that old "tabernacling" language was appropriated in the restoration period. Because the context of chapter 10 presupposes the idea of return to Zion, and given the fact that the verb connotes the broadest context for "walking in God's name," we seem to have a conflation of the two components of Mal 1:11, namely, a tendency toward the universal and at the same time a tendency toward the specific. Such a dynamic undergirds the whole of Second Temple thought and can be viewed as a significant aspect of biblical thought in general.

utterance of Yahweh. Literally, "the utterance of Yahweh." The construction is definite because the absolute, Yahweh, is definite. This formula, *nĕʾûm-Yahweh*, is not used uniformly in Hebrew prophecy. At one extreme, for example, it is found frequently in Jeremiah but only four times in Hosea; and it never appears in Habakkuk or in Jonah. It is primarily a marker indicating that the divine word is transmitted through a prophet. However, it often is used to signify a transition in the text and thus may not be integral to the prophecy with which it is associated. Therefore, its presence can be the work of the prophet, or of an editor or redactor. In the present instance it marks the end of a unit, chapter 10, and thereby separates it from the beginning of chapter 11. Some commentators view 11:1–3 as the concluding verses of chapter 10, but the appearance of the marker "utterance of Yahweh" at the end of chapter 10 weakens that suggestion.

The formula occurs more than thirty times in the Haggai–Zechariah–Malachi corpus: twelve times in Haggai, thirteen times in First Zechariah, seven times in Second Zechariah, and only once in Malachi. Late biblical prophecy is characterized by an increased use of formulas, which apparently are meant to lend greater authority to the prophetic word. The presence of phrases such as "word of Yahweh" (Hag 1:1) and "thus says Yahweh of Hosts" (Zech 8:20) helps the prophet or editor establish that the source of the words is none other than Yahweh and, thus, that the message is legitimate. Although Malachi does not use such formulas as often as the others in the Haggai-to-Malachi group, five different transmission formulas appear in the first two verses of the book: "oracle" (maśśāʾ), "word of Yahweh," and "by the hand of" in verse 1, and "said Yahweh" and "utterance of Yahweh" in verse 2.

COMMENT

With Zechariah 10, the long and intimate relationship between Hebrew poetry and prophecy comes to an end. As we explain in our Introduction, the prose particle count, as an indicator of poetic material, indicates that Zechariah 9 (with 1.4 percent prose particles) should be considered pure poetry. The chapter after this one initiates the elevated prose that is characteristic of the very last works of postexilic prophecy (Zechariah 11 is 20.9 percent prose particles). In between the two is this chapter, with 7.2 percent prose particles. Still poetic, it nonetheless begins to take on more of the features of prose. As such, it is a fitting central unit of Part One (Zechariah 9–11) of Second Zechariah, partaking of the poetic and prose aspects of the chapters that precede and follow it. This unit, as we have explained elsewhere, is introduced, as is the next one (Zechariah 12–14) and then Malachi, by the heading "oracle (maśśāʾ) of the word of Yahweh."

The unity of the chapter seems apparent from this consideration of its poetic character in relationship to the surrounding materials. In addition, it has a thematic unity, its various images dovetailing with each other as well as forming links with the themes and images of chapters 9 and 11. We emphasize this point in light of the fact, as we discuss in the Introduction, that many commentators would see the first two verses, or in some cases the first three verses, as a distinct unit that ought perhaps to be considered part of chapter 9. In addition, at the other end of this chapter, there is a tendency to include with chapter 10 the opening three verses of chapter 11, which are somewhat more poetic than the rest of that chapter and which in some ways continue the imagery of the last verse of chapter 10. Many salient points are offered in justification of such rearrangements, and our overall sense that chapters 9–11 constitute a larger literary unit takes such points into account.

Nonetheless, the chapters as divided by the Masoretic tradition do make sense. They have literary integrity in terms of prose versus poetic character and in terms of thematic development and use of imagery. Hence we look at each of these chapters separately. They are not random collections of eschatological prophecies but, rather, coherent reflections of the prophetic struggle to make sense of a troubling world in light of an intimate awareness of the Israelite heritage. Although the anonymous author remains beyond our reach—as does the process by which this chapter, as well as all the others of Second Zechariah, reached its final form—nonetheless, we assume a degree of historical specificity in the life situation that compelled the prophet to give voice to his contemplation of Israel's destiny. The idea of diverse origin and/or authorship of these materials, we contend, does not sufficiently appreciate the impact, by the postexilic period, of both the long history of Israel and the richness of its authoritative literary production on prophetic sensibilities. If Zechariah 10 seems diverse, in other words, it is because of the various and complex materials upon which it can draw. Indeed, it is a mark of no mean literary skill that the disparate images are brought together as successfully as they are. Images of exile and destruction certainly go back to the eighth century and the fall of Samaria, and these emerge prominently again in the sixth century with the fall of Jerusalem.

It is no wonder then that this prophet, acutely concerned with the reversal of centuries of dispersal, draws upon existing prophetic works and perhaps other authoritative materials that give eloquent voice to the national traumas of the past. The continued dispersion evokes his focus on the hope for return and thus brings about his use of relevant tradition. How much of the language of this chapter and of the rest of Second Zechariah uses preexisting texts and how much is the artful creation of this poet cannot be determined, so integrated into these passages are the echoes of earlier poetry.

The overriding concern of chapter 9 is the eschatological recovery of the Promised Land and the restoration of the exiles to their homeland. Chapter 10 follows directly from these issues with its attention to one particularly trouble-some aspect of the project restoration. In the fifth century, which is the era in which we locate the collection of this material, the exiles in Babylon have retained through a variety of coping strategies, some of which are visible in Second Zechariah and Malachi as well as in other postexilic works, their religioethnic identity. Yet this does not seem to have been the case for the northerners, for the ten tribes that had constituted the Kingdom of Israel. The popular designation "ten lost tribes" is a telling indication of the assumption that many of the people of northern Israel lost their historical connection with *ʿam yiśrāʾēl*, "the people Israel," during the centuries of their dispersion. The prophet is aware of this problem, perhaps made evident to him by the fact that former Judeans were returning to a province named Yehud, which did have some, albeit limited, measure of autonomy. The eschatological vision of Zechariah 10 contemplates the future for all Israel, with different roles for north and south, as befit their distinct postdispersion fates.

The explicit attention to the northern tribes, as a distinct part of the future restoration, is certainly comprehensible in light of the prophet's vision, in chapter 9, of the territorial restoration, which clearly includes lands allotted to those tribes. Yet Zechariah 10 is perhaps overemphatic in its emphasis on the saving and gathering in of the dispersed northerners. As we point out in the NOTES, the frequent repetition of the direct object suffix "them" in the "Ephraim" section (vv 6–12) of chapter 10 underscores the focus of those verses on the House of Joseph (= Ephraim = ten northern tribes) and secures our awareness of the prophet's great interest in Ephraim. The result of the redemption of Ephraim will be its people's extraordinary demographic expansion. Therein may be the clue to the attention devoted to them. The early centuries of Persian rule over Yehud were marked by what was apparently an exceptionally small population in that province. The reader is referred to the last NOTE of verse 8, to the clause "They will multiply as before," for a discussion of the ethnoarchaeological reconstruction of Yehud's population of the sixth and fifth centuries. Suffice it to say here that Yehud was seriously underpopulated at the time of Second Zechariah. This demographic situation may well have contributed to the heightened attention in this chapter to the anticipated restoration and population growth of the northern tribes.

The special concern for the northerners, although strongly developed in verses 6–13, is not immediately apparent in the opening verse of this chapter, which begins with an exhortation. The identity of those being urged to call upon Yahweh, however, is not directly provided. Only retrospectively, having listened to what the prophet has to say as he carries us through the various other images of this chapter, do we realize that the lost Israelites are being addressed. They are not chided for their centuries of neglecting Yahweh; rather, they are simply exhorted to look toward Yahweh as the source of the most fundamental aspects of existence. Yahweh, as the one who controls the cosmos, provides life-giving sustenance, as verse 1 explains. In so doing, this verse connects the opening of the chapter with the concluding sentiments of chapter 9, which proclaims that "grain will make the young men flourish, and new wine the maidens." At the same time, by establishing that Yahweh controls the natural realm, it undergirds the subsequent assertions about Yahweh's control of the fate of those who populate the world, especially the Israelites but also the other peoples.

How is it that the Israelites were so removed from their heritage? Although not castigating them, the prophet attributes their lack of identity, their failure to look toward Zion, to two interrelated aspects of their behavior in exile. First, they are characterized as not having done what they are urged to do here, namely, to seek Yahweh directly. Rather, they had apparently used traditional patterns of popular prophetic activity—consulting ancestors (apparently via the teraphim) and diviners—to cope with the exigencies of life on foreign soil. The vocabulary employed by Second Zechariah to describe this useless and misleading behavior is clearly drawn from the language of earlier prophets, such as Jeremiah, Micah, and Ezekiel. Yet, unlike those other prophets, this passage contains no direct threats against or scoldings of prophets whose activities deceived. Rather, we are presented with the simple sad fact that the Israelites' reliance on false prophetic intermediaries, rather than on Yahweh directly, led them to a situation of hopelessness and a sense of emptiness. It is worth noting that however the prophetic voice may oppose or denigrate necromancy and divination, only in Deuteronomy is such activity proscribed. Could Second Zechariah somehow realize that the northerners were removed from their land and from their political autonomy before Deuteronomic standards of behavior achieved ascendancy? Although Second Zechariah does not directly attack false prophecy here, it is clear that such activity had tragic results. Hence, the attention to diviners and the like in this chapter adumbrates the full-blown invectives against false prophecy in chapters 11 and 13.

Whatever the reason for the Israelites' use of mantic prophecy, the effect was that Yahweh ceased to be seen as their leader. At this point, one of the most persistent literary images of Zechariah 9–11 serves to portray the sad state of affairs among the northerners. The pastoral imagery—more specifically, the metaphoric use of sheep and shepherds for the people and their leaders—emerges in verse 2 to depict the helplessness of people out of touch with their God, lacking in authentic prophetic leadership and effectively abandoned in the foreign lands to which they have been taken. The status of exiled peoples places them at the bottom of the social hierarchy of their new dwelling places. That was certainly the case for the Babylonian exiles, although it may not have been so for the exiled northerners, who were treated differently by the Assyrians than were those removed from Palestine by the Babylonians.

Clearly, the survival of Judeans in Babylon was to some extent the result of the adjustment of leadership patterns to the new social situation and the emergence of an infrastructure of community life that provided continuity with preexilic forms but functioned in altered ways to cope with the conditions of displacement. This apparently did not happen in the north—or if it did, it is invisible to us. In any case, the prophet views the northerners as having lost Yahweh and/or a human king as "shepherd," i.e., ruler, thereby becoming lost to their heritage and homeland.

This is not to say, however, that there was no leadership at all among the northerners. Yahweh's anger was aroused (10:3a, b) against the "shepherds" and the "he-goats" (these terms apparently representing two tiers of human leadership). The suggestion (e.g., as by P. D. Hanson 1975) that the brief representation of Yahweh's anger is part of a stereotypic *rîb*, or court case, against the exiles' leaders, is intriguing. But because the subsequent course of action does not involve dealing with those leaders, the validity of invoking such an image seems less compelling. The prophet's language in verse 3 involves a clever shift. Since God is angry at the leaders, he takes care of ("attends to") a cadre of them, presumably putting them away. But then, God "attends to" another group, the Judeans, who are not lost sheep. They are God's flock and so God can and will use them to carry out the restoration of the lost Israelites, who have no effective leadership. The word translated "attend" is used in two different ways, indicating a negative treatment of northern leaders and then a positive treatment of Judah, from which true and effective leadership will come.

God's attention to Judah coincides in verse 3 with the introduction of military imagery, which echoes the language of chapter 9 and dominates the rest of this chapter. Although the representation of God's people as sheep does not disappear—it surfaces again in verse 10 and is the dominant metaphor of chapter 11—the vocabulary of power exerted through military action supercedes the pastoral imagery. That it does so is a direct result of the hopelessness of the northern dispersal. Normal activity cannot reverse the loss of identity caused by centuries of assimilation into foreign cultures. The northerners have been "sowed" (v 9) in lands not their own; that is, they have been transported to new lands and have taken root there. If they are to be part of all Israel in the future restoration, only divine intervention will bring about such a change in status. The problem Yahweh faces here is different from that in other situations: Yahweh must deal not with Judah's sins or Israel's transgressions, nor with the belligerence or wickedness of a foreign nation; rather, the amorphous dissolution of the exiles from the Northern Kingdom to the lands of their dispersal is the critical issue.

Because the issue Yahweh faces here in the eschatological restoration of all the people to Zion is a departure from earlier crises in the biblical period, the military imagery used to resolve the problem is used somewhat differently in Zechariah 10 than elsewhere in the Bible. Recent scholarship is virtually of a single voice in calling attention to the divine-warrior language of this chapter. Yet we have been restrained in so labeling the various examples of this language because its usage departs in two significant ways from the classic Hebraic use of this hymnic celebration of Yahweh's power, which is derived from Canaanite mythology and is expressed in such archaic poems as Exodus 15 and Judges 5 and in later prophetic echoes of divine-warrior materials, such as Habakkuk 3 and Isaiah 42 and 63.

For one thing, in Zechariah 10 the military language is attached to the Judahites rather than to Yahweh. It is Judah that will become "like his mighty horse in battle" (v 3) or "heroes in battle" (v 5); it is from Judah that the "bow of war" (v 4) will come forth; and it is from Judah that the royal leadership (the "cornerstone" and "tent peg" of v 4; see NOTES to these terms) that will execute God's victory plan will emerge. In other words, Yahweh's people, specifically the Judeans, are empowered in this vision of the future. Even in Zechariah 9, Yahweh is the one to use weapons and sound the battle horn (v 14), or to encamp against the enemy (v 8). But Zechariah 10 represents a shift. Perhaps the partial restoration of the Judahites to Yehud has given the prophet cause to envision them as having an instrumental role, as God's agents, in the ultimate and total restoration of the future age. Only in verse 11 does Yahweh directly engage in aggressive activity, but that is a special case to which we shall return in light of the second way in which Zechariah 10 departs from the classic divine-warrior hymnology.

The very raison d'être for warrior language involves battle against enemy forces. The classic examples of the biblical text invoking the divine-warrior motif involve Yahweh's conquest over Israel's foes: Egyptians and Canaanites in the archaic poems, and later antagonists or generic enemies in the recrudescence of the mythic language in biblical prophecy. However, just as God's involvement is now indirect—Judah wields the weapons of battle—so too is there a change with respect to the enemy. In point of fact, there is no enemy at all. The language of war is present, but not the concomitant language of destruction. Perhaps this shift is best exemplified by the term "trampling" in verse 5. A verb almost exclusively associated with war, and thus with the trodding on some enemy, is used without a direct object. The warriors trample but no victims are involved. The only possible mention of an enemy, also in verse 5, refers to those mounted on horseback, i.e., the opposition's cavalry. But the cavalry is not drowned, destroyed, or otherwise overcome by Yahweh's agents; its riders are simply "confounded," and there is no reason to believe that these vague enemies thereby cease to exist. The overall language lacks the vindictiveness or violence present in classic divine-warrior passages. The only possible exception is in verse 11, which is also apparently the only exception to the fact that Yahweh does not fight directly in this poem.

The special case of verse 11 invokes the idea of the Exodus. Although there may be other allusions in Zechariah 10 to the departure from Egypt, as in the use of "redeem" in verse 8, this verse is explicit in conjuring up the notion of waters that dry up, allowing the people to cross over, dry-shod and in safety. Here God acts directly in striking ("smiting") the rolling seas, which represent both the Reed/Red Sea and the Jordan River, the two bodies of water that the Israelites crossed at the time of Moses and Joshua. However, neither of those bodies of water is named; rather, the language can easily be inclusive of the Mesopotamian rivers that represent Assyrian exile. Verse 11 adapts the language of Egyptian bondage to allow it to indicate the rescue of those dispersed in both Egypt and Assyria, as explicitly set forth in the preceding verse (v 10). Thus waters in general are the object of Yahweh's direct activity. Furthermore, unlike what happened in the Exodus precedent, no horses and chariots drown as the rolling seas are dried up. The enemy is simply water itself—the primordial chaos of the mythic antecedent of this image here representing the oblivion of Israel's lost status in the dispersion. Even the last colon of verse 11, which at first seems to present the destruction of Yahweh's enemies, involves a shift of language.

The damage to Egypt and Assyria is not total, nor is it accomplished directly by Yahweh's deed. One of the verbs is a reflexive form—"will be brought low"— and does not specify how this will happen or by whom; the other states that Egypt's scepter will "pass away." Neither of these verbs is one of violence, and neither specifies the destruction of the nation-state involved. Rather, verse 11 anticipates that the political and economic might that has characterized Egypt and Assyria in recent or distant memory, i.e., in historical time, will be replaced by a new regime in which the imperial dominance of the two superpowers will be terminated. However, that eventuality is subtly distinct from an announcement that either imperial power will be destroyed. In the eschatological future, they will have identity as Egypt or Assyria but without the oppressive qualities of their historical power mongering—without "splendor" or "scepter," i.e., without political and economic power.

The future release of northerners from foreign lands involves the stripping of those lands of the normal attributes of politically and economically successful nation-states. The removal of power from Egypt and Assyria is accompanied by the empowering of both of the Israelite kingdoms. The House of Judah, as we have already noted, becomes the vehicle of Yahweh's supreme might in the divine intervention necessary to release the northerners from distant lands. Twice the root *gbr*, which refers to the heroic might of successful warriors, is used for Judah—as a noun in verse 5 ("heroes in battle") and as a Piel verb in verse 6 ("make the House of Judah mighty"). The prophet uses this root twice more in chapter 11, but he changes the people so characterized from the Judeans to the Israelites, i.e., Ephraim. The noun is used first, as it is for Judah, in verse 7 ("Ephraim will be like a hero"); then at the end of the six verses (6–12) focusing on Ephraim, in verse 12 the Piel verb again appears to portray Ephraim's newfound strength ("I will make them mighty in Yahweh"), although in that case the object of the verb may be more inclusive, involving both Judah and Ephraim as the culmination of this chapter's concern with restoration.

There can be no question that the empowerment of the northerners, however it may be effected by Yahweh through the instrumentality of the southerners, involves the Ephraimites' rediscovery of their God. If they are urged at the outset to call upon Yahweh, it is clear by the end that they will have acceded to this exhortation. At the outset of these six "Ephraim verses," there is an assertion that God is responding to them, which implies that they are somehow calling out to Yahweh. In verse 7 they (and/or their children) are exulting in Yahweh. And in verse 9 they are remembering their God. The concluding statement of verse 12, that they will be "mighty in Yahweh" and walk about "in his name," is the culmination of these indications that Ephraim and probably Judah, too, will have returned to Yahweh's fold. This is tantamount to saying that they will have responded positively to what is asked of them in the first verse of the chapter, i.e., that they look directly to Yahweh for life's sustenance. They will indeed be revivified (cf. v 9, "They'll give life to their children"), in terms of both physical and spiritual existence, by the time Yahweh's intervention will have come to pass.

The saving of the Ephraimites will involve their departure from "remote places" (v 9) where they have been settled among various peoples (v 9). The completion of their removal from foreign lands will be their resettlement in the Promised Land, which will have been restored to Israelite control, under peaceful royal rule according to Zechariah 9. So successful will be the repatriation that even the most marginal of the traditional territories of all Israel will be overflowing (v 10). The elegant Hebrew at the end of verse 8 describing the northerners' repopulation of their homeland ("They will multiply as before") evokes the language of creation and of God's promise to Abraham, and the language of human fertility in the land that will be theirs as the ultimate sign of divine presence and blessing.

ZECHARIAH 11

♦

Opening Oracle: The Cry of Trees, Shepherds, and Lions

11 ¹Open your doors, O Lebanon!
    Let fire consume your cedars.
²Wail, O cypress! for the cedar has fallen,
    the mighty ones destroyed.
Wail, O oaks of Bashan! for the dense forest[a] is brought low.
³Hark: the wail of the shepherds,
    for their wealth is destroyed.
Hark: the roar of the lions,
    for the pride of the Jordan is destroyed.

The Shepherd Narrative

⁴Thus spoke Yahweh my God, "Shepherd the flock to be slaughtered. ⁵Those who buy them will slaughter them, and they will not be held guilty; and those who sell them will say,[b] 'Blessed is Yahweh, for I have become rich.' For their shepherd will not pity them. ⁶For I will not again pity the inhabitants of the land"—utterance of Yahweh. "I will indeed deliver every person to the hand of his neighbor and to the hand of his king; they will crush the land and I will not rescue [any] from their hand."

⁷So I shepherded the flock to be slaughtered, for the merchants[c] of the flock. I took for myself two staffs: one I called Delight and the other I called Bonds. Thus I shepherded the flock. ⁸I got rid of the three shepherds in one month; for I became impatient with them and also they felt loathing toward me. ⁹Then I said, "I will not shepherd you. Whoever is to die shall die. Whoever is to be destroyed shall be destroyed. And whoever is left shall devour each other's flesh."

¹⁰Then I took my staff Delight, and severed it, to break my covenant, which I made with all the peoples. ¹¹And so it was broken on that day. The merchants[c] of the flock, who were watching over me, thus knew that this was the word of Yahweh. ¹²Then I said to them, "If this seems good to you, give me my wage; but if not, withhold it." So they weighed out my wage, thirty pieces of silver. ¹³Then Yahweh said to me, "Cast it into the treasury,[d]" this worthy sum at which

---

[a]Reading the Kethib *habbāṣûr* as a passive participle.
[b]Reading plural *yᵓmrw*.
[c]Reading with the LXX.
[d]Reading with the Peshitta and Targum.

237

I was valued by them. So I took the thirty pieces of silver, and I cast it into the treasury,[e] at the House of Yahweh.

[14]Then I severed my second staff, Bonds, to break the kinship between Judah and Israel.

[15]Then Yahweh said to me, "Again, take for yourself the gear of a foolish shepherd. [16]For I will indeed raise up a shepherd in the land:

> Those to be destroyed he will not attend to,
>> the one who wanders[f] he will not seek;
>> the injured one he will not heal,
>> the one who stands firm he will not sustain.
> But the flesh of the fatted he will devour,
>> and their hooves he will tear off."

Woe Oracle to the Worthless Shepherd

[17]Woe O worthless shepherd,
>> the one who abandons the flock!
> May a sword be against his arm,
>> and against his right eye.
> His arm will surely wither,
>> and his right eye will surely go blind.

NOTES

11:1. *Open your doors.* These are the opening words of a brief poetic section (vv 1–3) that introduces chapter 11, the last section of Part One of Second Zechariah, and provides continuity of theme and image with chapters 9 and 10. The apostrophic beginning calls upon "Lebanon" (see next NOTE; cf. 10:10), using the singular imperative *pĕtaḥ* (from *ptḥ*, "to open"), to open itself, specifically, to open its "doors" (plural of *delet*, "door"). These two words (like "close" and "door") are frequently found in combination.

The act of opening (or closing) doors relates to the function of boundaries, the division between external space and internal space, between the unknown and thus dangerous or threatening without, and the known and thus safe and ordered space within. The door, like its analogues "gate" (*šaʿar*) and "opening" (*petaḥ*), is thus a vulnerable liminal zone, standing at the threshold between two realms. Hence it would take a considerable sense of trust for a person to open wide his or her gates on command. Doors are by nature closed in biblical usage (Baumann 1978: 232). It takes initiative to reverse that status. The command here is intended to provide that initiative, otherwise Lebanon will not simply be open to whatever might enter.

[e]Reading with the Peshitta, Targum, and one Kennicott manuscript.
[f]Reading with the LXX and the Peshitta.

If this opening imperative at all evokes the imperative of Ps 24:7, "Lift up your head, O gates," then the command here is certainly an ironic one. In contrast to the psalm, in which Yahweh's presence will enter when the gates are swung open, the opening of the doors in this passage will spell disaster for Lebanon. Because the result is so negative, some are wont to call this poetic section a taunt against an enemy of Israel (e.g., Wolff 1964, in reference to passages such as Isa 14:4–20 and Jer 6:1–5). However, that label does not accurately or adequately describe the convergence of images that this opening introduces, especially because Lebanon is hardly a classic foe. Nor does this command represent the beginning of a dirge. Although it calls upon the "cypress" and "oak" to "wail" and notes the "wail" and "roar" of "shepherds" and "lions" (see NOTES below to all these words in vv 2–3), it is not itself a poem lamenting what has happened, even though it does involve in an ironic sense, the grief of the trees, shepherds, and lions affected. On the contrary: the destruction of Lebanon's natural vegetation allows for God's eschatological plan to be effected (see NOTES to 10:11).

O Lebanon! The command to open one's territory, that which is protected by the door but which can be entered if the door is opened (see previous NOTE), is directed to Lebanon. Our NOTE to this geographical term in 10:10 explains that this was marginal territory in biblical antiquity—heavily forested and greatly underpopulated. It is not clear that the Phoenician coast was considered part of the Lebanon, which seems to designate the mountain chain parallel to the coast. What is certain is that the Lebanon was renowned for its great forests, especially its stands of cedars and cypresses, which are precisely the two kinds of trees associated with the Lebanon in this verse and the next (see NOTES to "cedars" and "O Cypress!").

"Lebanon," which occurs more than seventy times in the Hebrew Bible, is usually preceded by the definite article in Hebrew. In this verse and in 10:10, as in a number of other late poetic passages, the article is omitted.

Let fire consume. By opening its doors Lebanon will meet with disaster. This phrase uses the verb *ʾkl* ("to eat, consume") in the Qal; the same phrase, with the verb in the Hiphil, is used to describe the future destruction of Tyre in 9:4 (for a discussion of this idiom, see NOTE in 9:4 to "She will be consumed by fire"), which may indicate that the Phoenician coastal cities are perhaps to be included in "Lebanon." Such language of destruction (cf. especially Amos 1:4, 7, 10) is so common that it would be difficult to make a case for including Phoenicia in the Lebanon purely on the basis of this common use of "consume by fire" to indicate the devastation of both Tyre and the cedars. There was certainly a connection between Tyre and the Lebanon forests on an economic level if not a geographic one, because the prosperity of Tyre was linked to its role in trading the great cedar timbers of the Lebanon mountains to Egypt, to Palestine, and to eastern areas as well. Yet the burning of cedars is not an image that suits the overthrow of the Phoenician cities. Rather, the idea of burning cedars may be a literal description of land clearing (see next NOTE).

cedars. This common word for an important botanical species (*Cedrus libani;*

Hebrew, ʾerez) has given rise to all sorts of speculation about its meaning in this context. Such speculation is based on the assumption that "cedars" is used symbolically here—that the destruction of these trees is really meant to portray the destruction of certain people or groups of people. Although this assumption may have merit and will be considered below, it would be a mistake to jump immediately to a consideration of the symbolic aspect of the arboreal imagery without first examining its role on a literal level. As we point out in several NOTES to 10:10 (e.g., "Gilead," "Lebanon," and "no room is found for them"), the eschatological vision of chapter 10 involves the full restoration of the remnant of the ten northern tribes. The result will be a demographic expansion of such magnitude that previously marginal territories—the densely wooded uplands of the Lebanon and Gilead—will become densely populated. That future condition would, of course, involve the deforestation of those areas. Thus verses 1–3 of this chapter spell out in vivid detail the destruction of the natural vegetation, notably the cedars of Lebanon, that is a necessary accompaniment to the dramatic increase of human occupation that will mark the future age.

The idea of cedars (and probably the oaks of the next verse too) being burned by fire certainly partakes of the general idiom of destruction (see previous NOTE and 9:4). Prophetic passages such as Amos 1 and 2 repeatedly use fire imagery to indicate the eschatological destruction of Israel's enemies. However, in those texts the fire is directed at the walls and strongholds of a series of political foes. Here, the Lebanese forests, either literally or symbolically (see below), are probably not foes; and it is worth considering that the destructive fire has additional or separate implications, perhaps alluding to a technique for the clearing of land. Although axes and adzes were undoubtedly also employed, the burning of trees was commonly used as a remarkably efficient way of deforestation, particularly if large tracts of land had to be emptied of vegetation in a short period of time, as would be the case at the time of the eschatological population surge in the areas peripheral to Israel.

The idea of willful destruction of large stands of an economically and ecologically valuable commodity such as cedars may be repugnant to us, but such issues would not have been of concern for the prophetic author of this passage. Particularly if the wealth of Phoenicia, which was in part based on its access to cedars as a marketable product of the Lebanon, was about to be cast into the sea (Zech 9:4), then the burning of the cedars would hardly have been seen as faulty management of resources. On the contrary, it was obviously viewed as a way to open up resources, i.e., potential agricultural lands and/or space for new towns, villages, and cities. Indeed, in some ecological zones, the burning of forest trees is more than a labor-saving device; it actually helps provide nutrients for crops and rid the area of insects that would harm agricultural growth (Peoples and Bailey 1988: 54–55). This benefit is probably more applicable to the tropical areas of the Jordan Valley than to the cooler highlands of the Lebanon. Nonetheless, it helps us realize that deforestation would not have had the same negative connotation for the ancients that it has today.

The issue that remains, despite the clear meaning of the cedars on a literal level, is whether these trees also operate on a symbolic level and represent human leaders. Biblical narrative provides a reason for entertaining such a possibility in the account of Jotham's Fable. This poetic section of Judges 9 (vv 8–15) serves as a critique of Abimelech's illegal claim to be king. In that passage, a potential king is portrayed first as an olive tree, then as a fig tree, then as a grapevine, and finally as a bramble. None of the fruit-bearing trees will agree to cease their productive role, and hence they decline the offer of kingship (Judg 9:9, 11, 13). Yet they suggest that the nonproductive bramble reign over all the other trees. In taking on the office of king, the bramble invites all the others to take refuge in his shade, i.e., to acknowledge his protective power. If they will not or do not, the bramble says that fire will come forth from him and "consume the cedars of Lebanon."

It is noteworthy that in the fable itself, the cedar is the only one of the botanical species mentioned that is *not* personified. This fact makes us pause in our willingness to assign a specific metaphoric value to the cedars in this case. Jotham's use of cedars seems simply to be saying that dire consequences will befall everyone if Abimelech is not accepted: the unthinkable will come to pass in the burning of even the mighty Lebanon cedars. In the verses that follow (Judg 9:16–21), Jotham asserts that treachery in making Abimelech king will result in internecine warfare between the local rulers of Shechem and Beth-millo and in a clash between those rulers ("lords") and Abimelech. Jotham describes these possibilities as fire coming out from the various lords to consume Abimelech, and vice versa. However, it is notoriously difficult to align these projected conflicts with the tree metaphor of the fable itself. Even if it were possible to see Judges 9 as referring to "cedars" as leaders to be "consumed by fire," it is difficult to see how, in the Zechariah 11 passage, the cedars might represent leaders in the Lebanon who would resist Israelite expansion and so be themselves destroyed. The Lebanon was virtually unsettled, and leaders with the status of "cedars" would hardly have existed.

The emphasis in these verses on the forested areas of Lebanon, Bashan, and then the Jordan Valley seem to preclude the possibility that the settled areas of the Phoenician coast, which did have leaders that might be destroyed, should be included in what "Lebanon" designates. But even if Tyre and Sidon were to be accounted as part of the Lebanon, it is significant that Tyre (and Sidon) as a whole, and not just her leaders, is "consumed by fire" in Zechariah 9 (v 4). This fate is quite different from that of the Philistine cities whose leaders alone are to be destroyed (see 9:5 and NOTES to this verse).

Hence we are not convinced, on the basis of the Jotham material or the connection with Tyre, that "cedars" here in verse 2, "oaks" and "dense forest" in verse 2, and "pride of the Jordan" in verse 3 are operating at a level other than the literal one. Yet having said all this, we note that the shepherd imagery in the rest of chapter 11 (vv 4–17) is unmistakably metaphoric, although the identification of the referents of the images is difficult to ascertain. Second Zechariah has already, in chapters 9 and 10, shown prominent use of metaphoric language. Moreover, the tree imagery of verses 1–3 does seem to portray a hierarchy (cedars, cypress, oaks, forest), albeit with no readily identifiable political identity. In addition, we recall the prominent use of tree imagery in First Zechariah, most notably the lampstand vision (4:1ff., esp. v 14), and the monarchic "branch" and "shoot" imagery of 3:8 and 6:12. Because of the many connections between First and Second Zechariah, it would be unlikely for tree imagery to lack metaphoric value in Second Zechariah.

In light of all this, we would point to one passage in Ezekiel that may provide the necessary backdrop for a metaphoric meaning of the tree images of 11:1–3. In Ezekiel 31, Assyria is called a "cedar of Lebanon" (v 3) as a way of saying that it had achieved great imperial power. That is, like the cedar, Assyria towered above all other peoples; all other nations were overshadowed by its beautiful and well-watered foliage (vv 3–9). Yet even the seemingly invincible cedar—Assyria— will be destroyed; it will be cut down by nations empowered by Yahweh to do so. Although the notion of destroying the cedars by fire is not part of the metaphoric use of "cedar of Lebanon" in Ezekiel 31, the idea of even the mightiest of trees, i.e., seemingly invincible empires, being destroyed may underlie the appearance of "cedars" here. The ultimate restoration of Israel cannot be envisioned without the reversal of the political fortunes of any superpower, i.e., cedar, that dominates God's people. If this be the case, the other trees would represent less powerful polities, dependent on the superpower for whatever autonomy they may hold. Thus their future too would be in jeopardy; they would indeed "wail."

The use of "cedars" to represent the supreme political power(s) of the ancient world certainly emerges naturally enough from the qualities of the cedar, which is the largest and one of the longest-lived trees in the Mediterranean world. Its wood was greatly prized for the construction of monumental buildings (such as the Jerusalem Temple) and for the masts of ships. Cedar planks were not only strong, long, and straight; they were also fragrant and durable—greatly resistant to decay. No wonder that they might represent an imperial power that seems to have it all, that controls all the natural and human resources of the known world. A similar positive sense underlies Second Zechariah's use of "trees" representing "all the peoples" consumed by fire in 12:6.

Why then would "cedars" be plural here? It would seem that the prophet may face only one empire, Persia, as the superpower of the day. That plural form may be the prophet's way of making this metaphor more than an allusion to a specific polity of his day. After all, this imagery develops the eschatology of the end of chapter 10. Thus it may transcend historical specificity and simply represent all superpowers, present or in the distant past or in the future, whose imperial rule will come to an end in the new age. Such an extended chronological purview is in keeping with the way the shepherd narrative (11:4–16) incorporates past, present, and future in a complex and dense portrayal of the problems of prophetic leadership (see NOTES and COMMENT to these verses).

2. *Wail.* The verb *yll* always occurs in the Hiphil and is appropriate to oracles of destruction. Its basic meaning denotes the wailing that is heard in a lament or in the face of catastrophe (Baumann 1990: 82). It is frequently found, as it is here, with the root *šdd*, "to destroy" (cf. Isa 23:1, 14; Jer 25:36; 48:20;

49:3; Joel 1:10–11). The root *yll* appears twice more in this set of three verses: the imperative plural occurs in the second half of this verse, and the noun form at the beginning of verse 3. Indeed, the four poetic lines that constitute verses 2 and 3 each begin with a command or exclamation that is based on sound: "wail" in 11:2a and b; "hark" in 11:3a and b.

The root *yll* is often used to announce a judgment or threat of judgment against foreign nations (e.g., Jer 25:34, 36; Isa 23:1, 6, 14; etc.) or against Israel herself (e.g., Isa 65:13–15; Hos 7:13–15). These alternatives—that "wail" announces a threat either to Israel or to the nations—are those proposed in the scholarly literature on the meaning of verses 1–3. However, the occasion for the "wailing" or screaming is the destruction of the cedars of Lebanon, which seem to stand for neither the many nations nor Israel (see previous NOTES). The smaller and less stately cypress tree is called upon, along with the scrub oak, to respond to the loss of the cedars.

The idea that trees will wail and respond to the call of "hark" contributes to the way this oracle gives human attributes to nonhuman characters. Thus, although neither the trees nor the lions (v 3) speak, and although there is no narrative line, the very idea of flora and fauna acting as humans gives these verses a fablelike quality (cf. the discussion in NOTE to "cedars," v 1). Some aspects of the dynamics of a fable are present.

O cypress! The cypress tree, (*Cupressus sempervirens*) is a tall evergreen that grows abundantly in the Lebanon and is often confused with the juniper (*Juniperus excelsa*) or with a type of pine (Mitchell 1912: 296). It is renowned for its full and lush foliage and its stateliness. Sometimes it is cited in parallel with cedar (e.g., Ps 104:17) and at least once with myrtle (Isa 6:13), which is also known for its thick foliage (see Zech 1:8 and NOTE to "myrtles" in Meyers and Meyers 1987: 111). Like the cedar, the cypress tree was prized as a building material for the Temple (1 Kgs 5:22, 24 [NRSV 5:8, 10]; 6:34; 2 Chron 2:7 [NRSV 2:8]; etc.), ships (Ezek 27:5), and some musical instruments (2 Sam 6:5; 1 Chron 13:8). The cypress is the second species in a series of three that are featured in verses 1 and 2—the third being the "oaks" of verse 2b, below. Together they form a cluster of arboreal images that climaxes in the general term "dense forest" of verse 2b (see NOTE below) and perhaps also in "pride of the Jordan" (v 3).

Although the cypress tree was one of the most important in the economy and in the aesthetic sensibility of the peoples of the ancient Near East, it was not quite the peer of the cedar. Admired for its foliage and its timber, it nonetheless is not credited with the extraordinary height or grandeur of the cedar. The following phrase, "mighty ones," is used in reference to "cedars" and so sets them apart from other important kinds of trees, such as the cypress or (in the next line) the oak.

cedar. Here the noun appears in the singular, whereas in verse 1, "cedars" is plural. Yet the next bicolon refers to cedars as "mighty ones," also plural. Hence the general idea of multiple cedars is sustained. See NOTE to "cedars" in 11:1 for a discussion of the cedar's literal and metaphoric identity.

has fallen. In agreement with the singular "cedar" in this bicolon, the verb is singular. But, just as the parallel noun in the next bicolon (see previous NOTE) is plural, so too is the verb "destroyed" that is parallel to this one. There is movement from the actual toppling of the tree (the result of the "fire" of v 1; see NOTE) to the state of destruction that then characterizes the burnt and felled cedars. Note, however, that the change from plural to singular to plural is continued in the use of the collective singular "forest" and the accompanying singular verb "brought low" in the next line. This movement may be related to what is described above in our NOTE to "cedars" in 11:1. The metaphoric value of this tree perhaps lies in its representing the one imperial power familiar to the prophet and, at the same time, all past or future superpowers that will lose their dominion in the eschatological age. The shift back and forth between singular and plural uses the power of language to move the audience from the familiar—the present political scene—to the abstract and general.

mighty ones. In the Hebrew text, "mighty ones" is preceded by the relative *ʾăšer*, which need not be translated; cf. GKC §156. The word *ʾaddîr*, as either a noun or an adjective, means "mighty, majestic, powerful" and in this sense can refer to rulers or nations (e.g., Ezek 32:18) or even to Yahweh (Isa 33:21). However, it also can denote a majestic aspect of the natural world, such as waters, a vine, or a tree; Ezekiel (17:23) refers specifically to a "mighty cedar." The word thus provides a suitable double meaning, indicating the towering political entity as well as the enormous tree that "cedars" represents (see NOTE to "cedars," v 1). It also anticipates the use of the related noun *ʾadderet* ("might, glory, wealth") in verse 3 (see NOTE to "their wealth").

Note also that the phrase "mighty ones of the flock" (*ʾaddîrê haṣṣōʾn*) appears in Jer 25:34–35, which is part of a poetic passage (25:34–38) that seems to have provided much of the imagery of both Zech 11:1–3 and 11:4–17. The idea of wailing shepherds and destroyed pasturage, along with the use of sheep and shepherds to represent various aspects of ancient Israel, are developed in both sections of Zechariah 11. Verse 34 of Jeremiah 25 is a good example of the confluence of images that emerge prominently in Zechariah 11:

> *Wail*, you *shepherds*, and cry out;
> > roll in ashes, you *mighty ones* of the *flock*;
> For the days of your slaughter have come—and your dispersion,
> > and you shall *fall* like a choice vessel.
> > > > (Italics are the authors'.)

Whatever the specific reference of "slaughter" or "dispersion" may be, it is striking to see so many of the words and phrases of the Jeremiah passage echoed and developed anew in Second Zechariah.

destroyed. The Pual of *šdd*, which is used again in verse 3a with "their wealth," means "to devastate, destroy" and usually involves the idea of violence, although it is used in Joel (1:10) in reference to crops, the destruction of which comes about by drought. Normally, the verb indicates the destruction of cities, places, or dwellings. Because it is such an expressive and intense verb, it here conveys emphatically the great extent of the devastation accompanying the collapse of the "mighty ones," whether trees or political powers. The two bicola of this line involve a progression: the toppling of the trees results in the condition of devastation.

O oaks of Bashan! This second line of verse 2, like the preceding one, is an apostrophe to trees—first the cypress trees, now the oaks. Like the cypress, the oaks are being called upon to "wail" (see first NOTE to v 2) because of the destruction of the "cedars." That is, the oaks themselves are not specified as being destroyed. Rather, it is the loss of the "dense forest" (see next NOTE) that the oaks ought to bewail. The parallelism of these two lines means that the attention of the cypress trees and oaks is being directed in both cases to trees labeled successively as "cedar," "mighty ones," and "dense forest" and all apparently designating the cedars. These are the trees that will be destroyed for the eschatological resettlement of Israel, and they also probably symbolize the demise of the existing world order (see NOTE to "cedars" in v 1).

The oak, like the cedar and the cypress, is another large tree that is part of the natural forestation of mountainous areas of Syria-Palestine. Various species of this wide-spreading tree are found in the Levant. The connection in this verse of "oak" (*ʾallôn*) with Bashan, the plateau and heights (Jebel Druze) of Transjordan extending from south Syria to the hills of Gilead, thus represents the particular variety that grows in northern Transjordan (cf. the "Tabor oaks" of the Cisjordan highlands).

If the world order (= "cedars" as imperial power) is destroyed, the somewhat less prominent powers of the world—cypress and oak—must respond. They must be exhorted to wail, presumably because their natural reaction might hardly be one of lament. But note that neither cypress nor oaks are themselves destroyed: will they then, as lesser political powers, exist autonomously as perhaps they rightfully should?

the dense forest. This is a very difficult expression and the Masoretes, in the form of Qere, have suggested emending the text to read *yaʿar habbāṣîr*, i.e., "forest of vintage," possibly having in mind the text of Jer 48:32, in which the vineyards may be identified with the land of Moab. However, the Qal passive participle of *bṣr* ("to make inaccessible, fortify, enclose") is what is intended here. Of thirty-eight occurrences of the verb, twenty-five are passive participles. In the present instance, such a verb is appropriate to portray a forest so thick that it is inaccessible, as if it were "fortified."

The absence of the definite article before "forest" in the Hebrew is expected in this construct chain, which makes both nouns definite; hence the Greek supplies it. Compare several parallels in First Zechariah: "the Holy Land" (2:16 [NRSV 2:12]), "the Holy Mountain" (8:3), and "the City of Truth" (8:3).

The idea of a dense, virtually impregnable forest as a representation of the great cedar stands of the Lebanon, suits the double imagery (see NOTE to "cedars," v 1) of this passage. Those forests are so vast and mighty that the idea they could disappear is almost beyond belief. Thus the eschatological image of a populous Lebanon, which would have to involve extensive deforestation, clearly reverses the present world order in terms of the vegetation of the Lebanon. Similarly, on a symbolic level, the current imperial power (or powers) would seem well established and impregnable. Hence the idea of the future age bringing about the demise of such a power likewise turns human expectations upside down. Again, the double eschatological thrust of the tree imagery is well expressed.

brought low. The appearance of the verb *yrd* ("to go down") with "forest" or "trees" is rare, although Isa 32:19 depicts the future age as one of people living at peace, apparently with all forests having disappeared (the text is difficult: "will wail when the forest comes down"). That imagery fits this context, which, at one level, depicts the Lebanon forest as disappearing to make way for the restored Israelites (see NOTE to "cedars," v 1).

The verb is singular, referring to the collective singular "dense forest." There is a back-and-forth shift between the plural and singular of the various nouns and verbs referring to cedars in this verse. See our discussion of how this shift fits the imagery in NOTE to "has fallen" in this verse.

3. *Hark*. This use of *qôl* (literally, "voice"), plus the genitive at the beginning of a sentence is relatively rare (GKC §146.b). In such a case, "voice" is taken as an exclamation (as in Gen 4:10; Isa 13:4; 66:6; Mic 6:9; etc.). Both lines of verse 3 begin with this construction, which serves to focus attention on the sounds— wailing and roaring—of those affected by the loss of the forest. Whereas verses 1 and 2 open with imperatives, addressed to Lebanon, the cypress, and the oak, the beginning of the two poetic lines of verse 3 shifts to the exclamatory mode, thrusting the agonized response of those dependent on the forest into the consciousness of the prophet's audience.

wail of the shepherds. In verse 2 the cypress and oak trees were called upon to "wail" (see NOTE above) for the fallen cedars. Now it is the "wailing" of the shepherds that is presented (cf. Jer 25:34, 36). Unlike the cypress and oaks of verse 2, however, the shepherds of this line and the lions of the next are not called upon to wail at the loss of the cedar(s); they instinctively or naturally do so. As indicated in our NOTE to "the shepherds" in 10:3 (see also NOTE to "without a shepherd" in 10:2), the shepherd image is deeply rooted in Israel's agricultural heritage. Although the prophets regularly use such language metaphorically, with "shepherd" representing some sort of leadership, it is often difficult to identify the prophetic image with specific circumstances. Indeed, if our understanding of "cedars" (see NOTE in v 1) has any merit, then we would follow through and suggest that "shepherds," and "lions" below, here represent the lowest tier of leadership, the bureaucrats whose livelihood is cut off by the fall of imperial power.

But even this possible understanding may be pushing the imagery beyond what it is meant to do. Perhaps it is best to reemphasize the literal level of the meaning of these verses and emphasize that shepherds will lose their pasturage if all of the forested areas become agricultural lands. The eschatological vision (see NOTES to 10:10) involves an enormous settlement of formerly marginal lands, which were virtually uninhabited except for the occasional shepherd and the indigenous wildlife—the "lion" of the next line. Without the forests, the "wealth" (see next NOTE) or livelihood of shepherds is in jeopardy; they would have good cause to wail.

their wealth. The noun ʾ*adderet* with the third-person plural masculine suffix can mean "cloak" or "mantle," as it does in Zech 13:4, 1 Kgs 19:13³, or Gen 25:25. It can also mean "glory" or "magnificence" as it does in Ezek 17:8, where the vine is described as a "vine of magnificence," i.e., a plush vine. Because this sense of the root is so rarely found in its use as a noun, caution must be exercised in assigning such a meaning. In this case, however, because of the occurrence of the adjective ʾ*addîr* ("majestic, mighty") in verse 2a (see above, NOTE to "mighty ones"), a wordplay is operating here, justifying the translation of "glory" or "wealth."

As explained in the previous NOTE, the "wealth" of the shepherds, at least at a literal level, is associated with the eschatological restoration of all Israel, in great numbers, to even the most peripheral areas of the promised land (see 10:10). The concomitant deforestation is what is depriving shepherds of their pasturage.

is destroyed. This is the second of three occurrences in the opening poem of the Pual *šdd* (see NOTES to vv 2a and 3b). The loss that is lamented here is represented by the subject of this bicolon, "their wealth." As indicated in the preceding NOTE, that wealth is the mountainous pasturage that would be given over to new settlers in the future time when the exiles of the northern tribes return. The root *šdd* conveys a strong sense of loss by destruction, so the impact anticipated by such shifts in population and, perhaps, the preceding eschatological cataclysm, is devastating. This emphasis on the loss of the natural vegetation, although repugnant to our ecologically sensitive present, must be seen as a positive statement for those who see population growth and agricultural development as desiderata.

Hark. See the first NOTE to this verse.

roar of the lions. The verb *šʾg* ("to roar") and the derived noun (*šaʾăgâ*) can indicate the cry of an animal, as here (cf. Judg 14:5); it is also commonly used in a figurative sense: to describe the noise of invaders (e.g., Jer 2:15), of wicked rulers (e.g., Ezek 22:25), of humans in distress (Ps 32:3), or even of Yahweh's thunderous theophany (Jer 25:30; Amos 1:2; Joel 4:16 [NRSV 3:16]). Whether it has a metaphoric meaning in this verse, along with its literal sense, is difficult to determine. Unlike "shepherds" (see above, NOTE to "wail of the shepherds" in this verse), which is frequently metaphoric in prophetic language, "lion" is not used quite so explicitly in that way. Just as the shepherds' survival is at stake because of the loss of their pasturelands (see NOTES that mention "wealth" and "destroyed"), so too are the lions in jeopardy because their ecological niches will be destroyed (see next NOTE).

pride of the Jordan. This technical phrase is used for the jungle or thicket found on both banks of the central and southern parts of the Lower Jordan River before deforestation. The narrow strip of land at the bottom of the Rift Valley, characterized by a tropical ecosystem, was quite distinct from the barren wilderness and seasonal pasturelands that bordered it. Willows, cane, poplar, reeds, oleander, and tamarisks grew there; it was a place in which lions and other wild animals made their coverts (see Jer 12:5; 49:9; 50:44). The word "pride" (gāʾôn) links this verse with the end of Zech 10:11, where "splendor [gāʾôn] of Assyria" (see NOTE) is mentioned as one of the places from which the northern exiles (see other NOTES to 10:10–11) will return. Although the English word "pride" tends to suggest self-esteem more than anything else, in Hebrew its meaning is much closer to "majesty" (e.g., Isa 4:2) or "place of excellence" (Isa 60:15). The Jordan's "thicket" or "pride" would have been an area of dense tropical beauty, in striking contrast to the gray, barren terrain of most of the Jordan Valley floor. To this day, it teems with wildlife and thick undergrowth where it has not been violated by armies or hydrologists. Nowhere else in the Bible is a dense forest called "pride," probably because the "pride of the Jordan" is a unique region, its lush vegetation and variety of fauna representing an extreme contrast to the burning desolation on either side (see Har-El 1984).

What, then, is the prophet's intent in announcing that the "pride of the Jordan is destroyed"? First, there is a geographic aspect to the designation, inasmuch as the Jordan River obviously runs between the Sea of Galilee in the north and the Dead Sea in the south. East of the river in the south lies Moab; northeast of the river lie Bashan and Gilead, precisely those areas of focus in Zech 10:10–11 and 11:1–2. As the exiles return in greater and greater numbers, just as the empty pasturelands of Bashan will be disturbed so too will even the wilds of the thicket of the Jordan River. The idea is that eschatological development will disrupt the natural habitat of even those areas of the Promised Land least likely to be used for human habitation, areas fit more for animals than for people. Thus the destruction of the Jordan River's vegetation and wildlife is a signal that the old era has ended and the new one has arrived.

is destroyed. This is the third and final use of the Pual of *šdd* in this opening section of chapter 11 (see NOTES that mention "destroyed" in v 2 and earlier in this verse).

4. *Thus spoke Yahweh my God.* This clause, which introduces the shepherd/flock section of chapter 11, is unusual if not unique. Indeed, the Syriac and the Kennicott manuscripts sense a change from familiar introductory formulas and read "to me" (ʾly) instead of "my God" (ʾlhy). In an examination of the various formulas that are used to introduce divine oracles or to conclude them, it is clear that the basic "Thus spoke Yahweh" (e.g., Jer 6:16; Isa 49:8; Amos 1:3, 6, 9, 11; etc.), which is probably part of an ancient messenger formula, is at times amplified by the addition of one or more epithets or names for God. Perhaps the most common such expression is "Thus spoke Yahweh of Hosts" (kōh ʾāmar YHWH ṣĕbāʾôt), which occurs frequently—more than twenty-five times—in the Haggai–Zechariah–Malachi corpus, as well as elsewhere in prophetic contexts. Another common embellishment involves the addition of "Adonai"—"Thus spoke Adonai Yahweh" (kōh ʾāmar ʾadōnāy YHWH)—especially by prophets who tend to emphasize God's omnipotence and majesty (e.g., Amos [3:11],

Isaiah [30:15], and Ezekiel [17:3]; cf. Eissfeldt 1964: 78). Sometimes these epithets were even combined, to further indicate divine might and glory (e.g., Isa 3:15). However, although "Yahweh" is frequently combined with *ʾelōhîm* ("God"), with or without a suffix on the latter, the two terms never appear together, except in this verse, as part of the formulaic expressions that introduce oracular statements with "Thus spoke Yahweh."

If these two terms, "Yahweh" and *ʾelōhîm*, are uniquely brought together here, then the suffix used in this formula with *ʾelōhîm* likewise is clearly unexpected. Its appearance with *ʾelōhîm* may, in fact, underlie the unusual combination. It has long been noticed that *ʾelōhîm* can appear with a variety of suffixes and that the first-person singular, *ʾĕlōhāy* or "my God," can have different nuances of meaning (Eissfeldt 1947).

Those categories of meaning have been described by Mason (1973: 139–42), among others, as basically falling into two main areas. First, in certain texts presenting a worshiper in a context of prayer or devotion, "my God" expresses the close relationship between the individual and God. Not surprisingly, many such instances can be found in Psalms (e.g., 38: 22f. [NRSV 38:21f.]; 22:12 [NRSV 22:11]; 31:15 [NRSV 31:14]), as well as in the prayers of prominent persons such as David, Solomon, Ezra, and Nehemiah. A second major category involves the distinction between the God of Israel and other gods, as when Balaam says "my God" (Num 22:18) or when David or Solomon use the term when addressing non-Israelites (2 Sam 24:24; 1 Kgs 5:18f. [NRSV 5:4f.]; see also Ruth's use of "my God" in 1:16).

Both of these nuances of "my God" may be relevant to understanding its use in Zechariah 11. Clearly, the prophetic speaker is claiming a personal, individual relationship with Yahweh. Whether the prophet also intends to dissociate Yahweh from other deities is less clear. The imperial setting of fifth-century Yehud, with the gods of the dominant political power visibly close at hand, may make this aspect of the "my God" terminology relevant. Yet even if that is not the case, there is one further biblical precedent for this personal language with reference to God that needs to be considered. The special relationship between Yahweh and Moses is epitomized in Moses' claim (Deut 4:5) that he has transmitted to the people everything that "Yahweh my God" has commanded him to do. A somewhat different sentiment is found in the Deuteronomic passage about prophecy (Deut 18:15–22), which quotes a statement concerning the almost intolerably close relationship of the people with Yahweh ("If I hear the voice of Yahweh my God anymore . . . I will die" [v 16]).

These Deuteronomic texts reflecting the tension between true and false prophets seem especially relevant to this section of Zechariah 11 and the related material in Zechariah 13. The prophet in this chapter is about to describe his sense of being called by God to be a "shepherd" or prophet (see next NOTE) in Israel. As we explain in the various NOTES to 11:5ff., the message of broken covenant and divided nation is a retrospective one, describing the devastation that has befallen God's people (the "flock") throughout the monarchic era. That those events have in fact taken place, as many a prophetic voice had warned they might, serves to legitimate the prophetic voice that had offered such messages. By identifying with those messages, and by here asserting a similar close relationship to God such as Moses paradigmatically represents, the prophet legitimates the hopeful message he has delivered in chapters 9 through 11:1–3 and in the rest of Second Zechariah (see our COMMENT for further discussion of the function of 11:4–17). Coming at a time near the ending of a form of Hebraic prophecy that had existed for hundreds of years, Zechariah's self-understanding as a prophet apparently brought him in conflict with others claiming a prophetic voice. That he uses this unexpected, and thus startling, variant on the traditional formulaic language of Hebrew prophecy can be understood as his emphatic claim to be part of the Mosaic model that included an intimate relationship with Yahweh, his being compelled by God to speak the oracular words that follow as well as those already uttered.

Shepherd. God's command is directed to the prophet, who has interjected himself into the scenario to follow by virtue of the unusual form of the opening formula, in which the introductory statement includes the expression "my god" (see previous NOTE). The ensuing complex series of divine commands and prophetic responses, centering on symbolic actions involving two staffs, functions through the imagery of shepherd and flock. The prophet follows through on the implications of this imagery, which appears in this very first word of the passage, where the verb rʿh, "to pasture, tend, graze," begins God's directions to the prophet.

From the outset of this section, the prophet is represented by the shepherd metaphor. The idea of caring for dependent animals lends itself readily to figurative meaning; hence the metaphoric use of "shepherd"—as God, as a ruler—is virtually as common in the Bible as the literal use of such terminology. Pastoral language has already figured in Second Zechariah in 9:16 and 10:2–3 (see NOTES to pastoral terms in those verses), and the verse just before this one reintroduces the shepherd in a statement that operates on both a literal and a figurative level (see NOTE to "wail of the shepherds") while providing a transition from the poetic introduction (vv 1–3) of chapter 11 to the shepherd narrative of verses 4–17. In addition, the shepherd image appears again in Second Zechariah, most notably in the first part of the oracle of 13:7–9 (see below, NOTES to 13:7), which is a kind of sequel to the passage presently under consideration. Although the referent of "shepherd" can vary, in this case and throughout the narrative of chapter 11, it seems to represent "prophet" as much as "political leader."

The identification of the prophet here with the role of shepherd is perhaps unique in the Hebrew Bible. To be sure, Moses, as the prototypical prophet, is given a distinctive role as shepherd. From David onward, however, the shepherd motif is attached to political leaders, both Israelite and foreign. Hence it is striking that this prophet claims the shepherd image. Perhaps it is because of the postexilic setting here that the motif is opened to include nonroyal leaders. It is also to be noted that in Second Zechariah's eschatological view of restored Davidic rule, the shepherd imagery is not invoked—quite unlike the way both

Jeremiah and Ezekiel use the shepherd figure. Thus, although it is unusual for a prophet to identify with the shepherd role, such a shift can perhaps be understood as part of the general way in which this prophetic work uses traditional language and ideas but reworks them to its own purposes.

This shepherd narrative draws on prophetic tradition in two significant ways. The first is in the actual use of shepherd imagery which, as we have previously noted, is prominent in the figurative language of the Bible. Perhaps one of the most extended instances of the shepherd theme is in Ezekiel 34, which is a polemic against the shepherds as the leaders (probably kings) of Israel who have not fulfilled their responsibilities. God as ultimate shepherd will thus intervene, restore a Davidic shepherd, and establish a covenant. Although there are identifiable similarities between Ezekiel 34 (and Jeremiah 23) and Zechariah 11, the overall thrust of the latter is virtually opposite that of the former. As we have already suggested, and as we explore further below in COMMENT, the grim picture presented by this chapter bespeaks a retrospective angle of vision rather than a view toward a hopeful future. That view is presented earlier in chapters 9 and 10, and the vision of devastation explains why such a hopeful perspective is in order.

The second major way in which this narrative depends on prophetic tradition, again especially on Ezekiel (37:15–23), is through its focus on symbolic prophetic actions. This is discussed below in our NOTES to "two staffs," "Delight," and "Bonds" in verse 7 (cf. NOTES to those words in vv 10 and 14), as well as in our NOTES to verses 12 and 13, which recount the casting of prophetic wages to the treasury.

Jeremiah 23 also contains shepherd imagery, and there too, as in Ezekiel, the context is a diatribe against evil kings. Yet it is interesting to note that Jeremiah's condemnation of evil kings is juxtaposed with a lengthy series of oracles against false prophets, who have been complicitous with the ruling establishment and who likewise will be destroyed. Perhaps this juxtaposition has provided the prophet of Second Zechariah with the linkage leading to his unusual identification of prophet with shepherd.

Additional insight into the conceptual or metaphoric nuance of the shepherd imagery involves the way the verb "to shepherd" is used. This opening verb is in the imperative, but because it is introduced by the oracular formula indicating Yahweh's past speaking to the prophet, the time when this is meant to have been said can surely also be in the past. Indeed, when the prophet's response to Yahweh's imperative begins in verse 7 (below), the same verb ("to shepherd") is used, with the *waw* consecutive, to indicate a past action on the part of the prophet. In short, despite the way in which scholarly exegesis has characteristically sought to find contemporary historical experience refracted, albeit very unclearly, in the shepherd narrative, the language itself does not demand such a chronology of present plus future; and we do not feel constrained to understand it in that way.

One final point concerns the imperative form of the verb. This is typically how Yahweh's charge to a prophet appears, following the introductory formula.

Yahweh is hereby commissioning the prophet to say and/or do certain things. This introductory charge thus opens an extended directive (vv 4b–6); it is then followed by the prophet's response (vv 7–14), which includes a subsidiary directive from Yahweh. Then, a final charge from God appears in verses 15–16.

flock to be slaughtered. This phrase reads, literally, "flock of the slaughter (ruin)," although the feminine noun substantive *hărēgâ* (from *hrg*, "to slaughter, destroy, ruin") may be understood as the equivalent of a Niphal infinitive of purpose (see GKC §128.2.i). Most modern translators have understood the term in that way. However, the LXX renders "feed (= shepherd) the sheep of the slaughter," which may be more faithful to the original.

The rare expression "flock of the slaughter" (i.e., the doomed sheep), occurs again below in verse 7, which describes the prophet carrying out God's command. This particular form, without "flock," appears elsewhere only in Jeremiah. In Jer 12:3, the prophet asserts that the wicked among the people should be removed: "Pull them out like sheep to be slaughtered (*lĕṭibḥâ*)/and set them apart for the day of slaughter (*hărēgâ*)." In Jer 7:32 and 19:6, *hărēgâ* appears in reference to Gehennah as the "Valley of Slaughter," i.e., the place where children were sacrificed to Moloch.

At this point, our translation "slaughtered" deserves comment. "Slaughter" does not necessarily mean that the entire flock will be destroyed. It is clear from the rest of this passage that some sheep are survivors, and the lexical range of the verb allows for the possibility that *hrg* here means that the total flock is "ruined," not butchered. Several considerations point in that direction. First, the basic usage of *hrg* in Hebrew is for the killing or slaughtering of *persons*. There is a varied vocabulary for the slaughtering of animals for food and/or for sacrifice, and *hrg* is not part of that terminology. Indeed, there is only one instance in which *hrg* does not have a personal object; in Isa 22:13 it denotes the killing of oxen for a feast in parallel with a reference to the slaying of sheep, using the expected verb *šḥṭ*, and thus constituting usage that is meant to vary the expected terminology. Two other possible uses with animals depict the ones to be slaughtered as other than ordinary animals: the Leviathan (cosmic enemy) of Isa 27:1; and the animal that has lain with a human (Lev 20:15 and 16), who has perversely partaken of humanity as the human has partaken of bestiality, so that both shall die. Thus, on closer examination, the use of *hrg* to mean "butchering" or "slaughtering" with sheep is not clearly attested.

Second, the somewhat extended idea of "ruined," that is, of devastation that does not necessarily involve death, may be supported by the evidence from cognate languages. As common as the verb is in the Bible, the root does not appear in the typical cognates of Hebrew—Akkadian, Ugaritic, and Aramaic. Rather, it is found elsewhere chiefly in Old South Arabic and probably in a few difficult Moabite texts. The semantic range in Old South Arabic is instructive. Although it generally has precisely the same meaning—the killing of enemies—as in Hebrew, it is also well attested with a somewhat less violent nuance: the taking away (*hrg*) of booty or profit in battle, thus ruining the enemy in an economic sense (Fuhs 1978: 448) but not involving slaughter.

Third, in several instances, texts having *hrg* usually understood as "slaughter" make more sense if a weaker verb is used, inasmuch as total death is not the result. For example, in Lam 3:43, God is said to "ruin" people "without pity"; some have died, to be sure, but others are taken away and scattered "among the people." And in Hos 9:13, Ephraim is told to take his children to "slaughter," the result of which is that some die in infancy or even before birth, and others are cast away from home (9:15) to become "wanderers among the nations" (9:17).

For these reasons, it seems best to understand what happens to the flocks here as something other than absolute total butchering. There is destruction, to be sure, but not all of it is lethal. This imagery of devastation rather than annihilation fits the metaphoric thrust of the verses to follow, in which different parts of the flock (i.e., different segments of all Israel) suffer different fates. Further, in its retrospective view, it reflects the varying fate of Israel and Judah at the hands of their conquerors.

5. *Those who buy them.* Introduced by the relative ʾšr, the participial substantive has a feminine-plural suffix ("them"), as does the verb that completes the first clause of this verse (see next NOTE). The gender of the suffix derives from its reference to "flock" of the previous verse, which is a feminine noun. Because "flock" is used collectively to represent all the members of the group of animals (i.e., all the people), the suffix is legitimately plural even though "flock" is singular.

The entire narrative sequence of verses 4–16 is fraught with interpretive difficulties, and this verse is perhaps the most complex of all. The problems begin with speculation about the identity of those presented as the ones who buy or sell God's flock, i.e., the people. The result of their dealing is clearly negative. The metaphor does not need to be pushed too far to see that some sheep are slaughtered and others exploited in some other way. But it is impossible on the terms of the verse itself to say who the perpetrators of such devastation might be. In other places where the butchering of sheep is used metaphorically for Israel's destruction, as in Ps 44:12, 23 (NRSV 44:11, 22), the actions of Israel's conquerors, in slaying the people or in carrying them off to foreign lands, is implied by the presence of ill-treated sheep. Indeed, Yahweh is the one who sells the people for a pittance (Ps 44:13 [NRSV 44:12]). But here those who wreak havoc with the flock appear to be more internal forces—neither foreign imperial powers nor Yahweh. Thus, in light of the fact that the entire narrative has a retrospective quality and because of the "staff" imagery below (see NOTES to vv 7, 10, 14), which seems to reflect matters internal to Israel, our sense is that "those who buy" and "those who sell" represent any Israelites whose behavior has violated the covenant.

More specifically, inasmuch as buying or selling possessions implies some measure of control over those things (i.e., people), the buyers and sellers must surely be those who have some control over people's lives. In other words, these vague figures must be individuals with some sort of leadership role. But can those leaders be specified? Many suggestions have been made, indicating the lack of direct information provided by the material at hand. Perhaps the words relating to sheep dealers are meant to be vague, so that they can in fact refer to anyone—whether king, priest, elder, sage, or prophet—who takes advantage of a position of power. We want to stress, however, the inclusion of prophet in this list of those with public community roles. Much of this narrative in chapter 11, from the opening formula with its unique claim for prophetic authority to the overt indictment and castigation of certain prophetic figures in verses 15–16 (and in the poetic oracle of v 17) and again in 13:2–3, seems to involve a tension between the true prophets of Yahweh, with whom the anonymous prophet known as Second Zechariah strongly identifies, and the false prophets who have led the people astray. Thus, the way false prophets have perpetrated the dissolution of the people must surely be part of, if not dominate, the notion of corrupt leadership that underlies the imagery of "those who buy . . . and sell."

will slaughter them. For a discussion of the term "slaughter" *(hrg)*, see the last NOTE of verse 4. The verb has a final *nun*, which is not a suffix, but rather is the archaic energic *nun* attached to the Qal imperfect. However, a suffix must be understood; it is possible that the original form included a suffix, which later was lost. The present form may be the result of an ellipsis.

In this context, "will slaughter them" means that people who have power over others will use that power for ill instead of good. Rather than exercise social, religious, or political responsibility, they will exploit their positions of authority.

they will not be held guilty. The verb *ʾšm* can mean "to commit an offense" or "to be guilty," but both those possible nuances are implicit in the action already specified—the ruin or devastation of the flock. What is intended here is the state of affairs that compounds the misdeeds of those in power, namely, that society does not condemn them, or hold them guilty, for misleading the people. This sense of *ʾšm* is well attested, chiefly in prophetic texts (e.g., Hos 5:15; 10:2; Jer 2:3). The issue here is not only that people in leadership positions are abusing their authority but also that they are not held accountable for the damage they do. This bespeaks a kind of internal corruption akin to what Ezekiel condemns in preexilic Jerusalem: Jerusalem is to be "held guilty" for the blood it has shed (22:4), by which is meant the abuse of office by "the princes of Israel in you [Jerusalem], everyone according to his power (22:6, NRSV)" to the detriment of those lacking power, notably disenfranchised segments of society (the resident alien, the poor, and the widow [22:7]), as well as those who suffer through the dishonesty, lewdness, and otherwise abominable deeds perpetrated by their fellow citizens (Ezek 22:8–13). We also note the Chronicler's exhortation to officials (certain Levites, priests, and heads of families) who act in judicial capacities to act fairly lest they incur guilt for miscarriage of justice (2 Chron 19:8–10).

These passages in Ezekiel and Chronicles attest to the wide range of officialdom whose members might be held guilty for wrongful behavior in their capacity as community leaders. Thus the vagueness of the metaphoric intention of "those who buy," which we have pointed out in the NOTE to that phrase, indeed seems to be related to the fact that those in the upper echelons of the political, social, religious, and economic hierarchies that characterized society in the monarchic state were all to be held guilty for corrupt behavior. That behavior, as explained below, is in fundamental violation of the covenant and must be considered the cause for the prophetic act representing the dissolution of the covenant (11:10).

We note that the prophet is not among those held accountable in the Ezekiel and Chronicles passages. However, that omission is not to be taken as an indication that this verse would not include prophets among those who abuse power. As we suggested in the first NOTE to this verse, the fact that specific attention is given in Zechariah 11 to the misuse of prophetic authority provides good reason to suppose that the false prophets were among those leaders who were the referents of this symbolic language.

those who sell them. The verb "sell," like "buy" and "slaughter" (see NOTES in this verse), has the third-person feminine plural suffix, referring to "flock" (feminine singular) as a collection of many animals. The question of who these sellers might represent in the metaphoric scheme of this chapter is no more easily answered than the question of who "those who buy them" might be. In that the former term is no more self-revealing than the latter, we refer the reader to the NOTE to "Those who buy them" (above) for an exploration of the possibilities. In addition, because the matter of accountability provides supplementary allusions to the acquirers, the previous NOTE includes further discussion of the identity of all these despicable characters.

The use of imagery rooted in the language of economic transactions is noteworthy. One wonders whether there is some subconscious critique of a market economy at work here. If buying and selling goods is a merismic construction representing the totality of economic dealings, then on a literal level the message is that such activity cannot have a positive outcome; whatever happens, the flock comes to ruin.

will say. The Hebrew text has the singular imperfect verb. However, the subject of the verb is surely the preceding plural particle ("those who sell them"); hence the MT singular may be the result of the loss of the plural ending, perhaps because the quoted statement (see next NOTE) refers to the speaker in the first-person singular ("I have become rich"). The Versions (LXX, Vulg, Syr, and Targ) all read the plural *yᵓmrw*.

Blessed is Yahweh, for I have become rich. This quotation of the words of the sellers (see previous NOTE) is the structural equivalent of "will not be held guilty," in reference to those who acquire sheep. Just as the latter are guilty but are not condemned as such, so the former have done wrong in their selling but do not see their acts as wrong. On the contrary, monetary gain is seen as a mark of divine favor.

Such a conclusion is not at all foreign to the prophetic and covenantal viewpoint of the Bible: prosperity is bestowed by God upon those who adhere to the covenant and obey God's word. Yet that perspective does woeful damage to the overall well-being of society and creates the great existential questions about

255

the prosperity of the wicked with which biblical wisdom struggles. Indeed, even the prophets addressed that horrifying anomaly of the increase of wealth by those who have forsaken Yahweh in deed and in belief. Hosea, for example, castigates Ephraim for claiming, "I am rich; I have acquired wealth for myself. All of my gain will not be found in me as sin" (12:9 [NRSV 12:8]). The meaning of those words of the eighth-century prophet of Israel is echoed, albeit through a very different literary genre, in Second Zechariah's ironic quotation of the self-satisfied sellers. All those who benefit from having control over others may claim divine favor, as those in power are wont to do; but such a stance ultimately results in thoroughgoing internal corruption, which must surely bring about the collapse of the system. The whole society will inevitably suffer from disobedience to the covenant by those who are in authority.

The two parts of this quotation deserve comment. The first is a blessing formula, "Blessed is Yahweh." The Qal participle of *brk* ("to bless") followed by a proper name is a special way in which this root occurs in the Hebrew Bible. The present example of this formula consists of only two words, *bārûk* and *yhwh*: "Blessed are you, O Yahweh." This short formula, which often functions in a way analogous to *ʾārûr* ("cursed"), indicates the existence of an intimate relationship between the speaker and the one named in the formula. For this reason, it is particularly suited as an acknowledgment of God's covenant with Israel (Scharbert 1975: 284–86).

In late biblical texts, this sort of benediction can refer to Yahweh's acts on behalf of Israel or, as in this instance, Yahweh's beneficence to the individual. Whether or not we agree that Yahweh lies behind the prosperity of the "sellers" in this verse, it is clear that these individuals attribute their success to divine blessing. The prophetic perspective in this chapter would also see Yahweh's will behind the transactions of those who buy and sell, even though the reasons—to bring about the ultimate dissolution of a corrupt society and disobedient people—for God's allowing this temporary prosperity are not related to the moral stature and covenant fidelity of those reciting the formula. The presence of covenant language, in the form of the expression of blessing in this first part of the narrative of chapter 11, is significant in light of the symbolic breaking of covenant that occurs in verse 10 (see NOTES below).

The second part of this quotation ("I have become rich") is one word in Hebrew. The MT reads *waʿšir*, which is probably a defective spelling of the Hiphil, *waʾaʿšir*, with syncope of the *aleph* (see GKC §19.k; cf. Qere and thirty Kennicott manuscripts). The verb is preceded by the connector *waw*, which has circumstantial force here (Mitchell 1912: 312), introducing the situation that gives rise to the formula "Blessed is Yahweh."

The idea of gaining riches at the expense of others, in violation of God's covenant, is also found in Jer 5:27, where it exemplifies the kind of situation that God must terminate. The conclusion of Jeremiah 5 is interesting from the perspective of this chapter of Zechariah in that the sorry state of affairs in the land is equated with the undue influence of false prophecy, the latter being one of the issues that is motivating the author of this narrative.

For their shepherd. Several textual problems are found in the Hebrew text of these words. The plural noun has a masculine plural suffix, which is at odds with the other feminine plural suffixes in this verse: "buy them," "ruin them," and "sell them" (see NOTES above). If the masculine stands, it might thus refer to the buyers and sellers, who presumably are male. However, the sense of the verse is that "their" refers to the members of the flock, in which case the final *mem* of the suffix ought to be read as a final *nun*, as it is by many LXX manuscripts. As P. D. Hanson points out (1975: 340), the orthography of these two letters would have been very similar at the time. Another possibility derives from the fact that in late Biblical Hebrew the masculine plural form sometimes displaces the feminine plural; such may be the case here.

Another textual problem concerns the matter of the number of the verb here. The major versions (Targ, Vulg, LXX, and Syr) translate all the verbs in verse 5 in the plural, and we have already suggested emending "will say" (see NOTE above) to the plural. However, the situation is even more complicated because some manuscripts have transcribed a singular form of "their shepherd" (P. D. Hanson 1975: 340; Mitchell 1912: 312), whereas the MT is probably "their shepherds," whatever the gender of the suffix. The occurrence of *rᶜhw* in verse 6, probably to be read as "his shepherd" rather than "his neighbor," has added to the confusion. Reading the noun as a singular, as do some manuscripts, fits the singular verb ("will not pity").

Again, the metaphoric referent of "shepherd" is problematic. We refer the reader to the NOTE above in verse 4 to "Shepherd" (as a verb). The use of "shepherd" in this verse seems to be an ironic contrast between the guidance provided by true shepherds (i.e., real prophets of Yahweh) and the ultimately fatal leadership of false prophets or misguided leaders. However, because Second Zechariah here has been charged by Yahweh to "shepherd" the people, whose ruin is inevitable, he too as true prophet is put in the unwelcome position of leading the flock to its doom. This is clearly what he does in breaking the two staffs in the symbolic action yet to come (see below, vv 7–10). This whole section of Second Zechariah is reminiscent of the agony of preexilic prophets, especially Jeremiah, who felt compelled to act against their own feelings. Hence, this assertion that a shepherd does not pity the flock—just as God now does not—may well apply to the prophet's tragic predicament. In this sense, the true prophet may seem no different from the awful "foolish shepherd" of verse 15 (see NOTE below).

will not pity them. The verb *ḥml* means "to be sorry for, have compassion on" in the sense of both emotional response and actions. In three-fourths of its usages, as in this verse and the next, it has a negative force; that is, it indicates that someone will not feel sorry for someone else. This is particularly true in prophecy. Because the preexilic prophets frequently portray a dismal future in which the people will be punished for disobeying God's word, they use this word to describe the lack of compassion that will exist for the people. Because God is the one who will bring about the resulting destruction, Yahweh is frequently the subject of the verb (Tsevat 1980b: 471). In this verse, the "shepherd" (see previous NOTE) is the subject. But the shepherd is clearly doing Yahweh's bidding, inasmuch as the very next verse proclaims that it is Yahweh who "will not again pity," and therefore not spare from impending devastation, the people of the land.

6. *For I will not again pity*. This statement is introduced with *kî* ("for"); and the second part of the verse, after the interruption of the "oracle of Yahweh" formula, begins with "behold" or "indeed" *(hinnēh)*. These two words together are repeated at the beginning of verse 16 below, where a similarly horrible portrait of destruction is offered. The *kî . . . hinnēh* combination thus appears at the conclusion of Yahweh's initial oracular statement (vv 4–6) of the shepherd narrative and again, as an inclusio, as part of the third and final oracular statement of the narrative (vv 15–16).

For this reason alone, verse 6 should be viewed as an original part of the sequence of presentations of Yahweh's words to the prophet. In terms of content, too, this verse is integral to the first oracular statement in that the charge to the shepherd (i.e., the true prophet, "Second Zechariah" or whoever is reporting here) becomes meaningful by virtue of what God says in this verse. Although some commentators (e.g., Chary 1969; Elliger 1975; Gelin 1951) see this verse as a later gloss, because it is so negative toward all the people and not just the leaders, that generality of God's intent to destroy is precisely what verse 4 is asserting—that the "flock" (= all the people) in its entirety will be affected by the corruption throughout the land.

For the meaning of "pity," see the previous NOTE. The addition of "again" (Hebrew *ʿôd*) implies that Yahweh in the past has felt sorry for the people and so has spared them. That emotion with its concomitant positive action—sparing the people—will not this time be part of God's response to what the people are doing.

inhabitants of the land. The verbal root *(yšb)* of the word for "inhabitants" *(yōšĕbîm)* can, in a small set of usages in the Bible, denote leadership (see Meyers and Meyers 1987: 437; cf. above, NOTE to "not be ruled" in Zech 9:5). However, in this case the more common meaning—"those who dwell, inhabitants"—is to be understood because the next clause, connected with this one by the *kî-hinnēh* construction (see previous NOTE), involves the destruction of everyone.

The participial form lends itself to the formation of phrases that indicate the occupants of a particular place, e.g., "inhabitants of the cities," "inhabitants of Jerusalem," i.e., "inhabitants of X (toponym)." Within this group, "inhabitants of the land" is very common. In Pentateuchal sources and in Joshua–Judges, along with later texts (e.g., Neh 9:24; 1 Chron 11:4) that refer to the early history of Israel, this phrase denotes the non-Israelite occupants of the Promised Land. They are the ones who are to be displaced by the arrival of the Israelites, as in Exod 23:31 ("I will set your borders from the Red Sea to the sea of the Philistines, and from the wilderness to the Euphrates; for I will hand over to you all the inhabitants of the land"; cf. Num 33:52, 55; Josh 2:9, 24; Judg 1:32, 33). Ironically, this same phrase is used by the preexilic prophets to depict the impending doom they envisage for their people. Israel will lose the right to dwell in its land because of its own sins, and the Israelites in turn will now be cast out of their dwelling places whether by death or dispersal. Such a fate is proclaimed, using this phrase, once each in Isaiah (24:6), Hosea (4:1), and Zephaniah (1:18). But it is Jeremiah who uses it most often (in 1:14; 6:12; 10:18; 13:13; 25:29; cf. 25:30) and who sometimes uses "inhabitants of Jerusalem" or "of this city" to represent all the people. Furthermore, for Jeremiah, it is a fully inclusive term; all segments of society—young and old, male and female, husband and wife, kings and priests and prophets—will be destroyed. Such a depiction of God's punitive measures is similar to Second Zechariah's portrayal of the full annihilation of the people in this verse and verse 16 and in the image of the broken covenant in verse 10.

utterance of Yahweh. For the distribution of this formula, which is common in certain prophets such as Jeremiah, Amos, and Haggai–Zechariah (thirty occurrences) and rare or nonexistent in others, see the NOTE to this phrase at 10:12. The frequency of formulaic attribution to Yahweh of prophetic words is a general feature of late biblical prophecy and its attempts to claim authority for its message.

I will indeed deliver. The interjection *hinnēh* (literally, "behold," but used here for emphasis, hence "indeed") is paired with "For" (*kî*; see first NOTE to this verse) at the beginning of this verse. The terms together serve to integrate the message of the first clause of verse 6 with that which follows the oracular formula, "utterance of Yahweh." In addition, combined with the participle of the verb, *hinnēh* usually points to an incipient future if not to events already set in motion (Andersen and Freedman 1989: 588). In this case, with the prophet "hearing" an oracle of times gone by, the imminence has already been effected (see below, first NOTE to 11:16).

The Hiphil of *mṣ'* is commonly used to mean "cause to go out, send out, or drive out," which can thereby mean "deliver," with persons or groups of persons as object. In this sense, it may be viewed as an auxiliary, with people then in some way affected by having been delivered (e.g., Gen 38:24, in which Tamar is brought out to be killed; see Preuss 1990: 236). The presence of the Hiphil of *mṣ'* further contributes to the ironic tone of this section of Zechariah 11, for a significant portion of this form is used to indicate God's deliverance of Israel from bondage. Here it functions to herald a reversal of that celebrated event in Israel's past. See above, our NOTE to "inhabitants of the land" for a similar instance of reversal. The pervading mood of Zech 11:4–15 involves the contrast between the best of God's relationship with Israel (as signified by the terms "Delight" and "Bonds" in v 7; see NOTES) with the worst—breaking the relationship and destroying all. Thus the ironic allusions to reversals contribute to the mood of radical change.

every person to the hand of his neighbor. The first part of this phrase consists of two words, the collective noun *'ādām*, meaning "human," and the term *'iš*, which can also mean "people" in general but usually refers to an individual, especially a male. Together here, they emphasize the inclusive nature of the fate described; God will deliver each person (all people) to his neighbor. However, the word *ʾādām* in fact links with more than just *ʾiš*, because the latter is a variation of a stock phrase ("each person/man to his neighbor") consisting of *ʾiš* and *rēʿēhû*, "his neighbor." The phrase is used to denote social stability as evidenced by harmonious interpersonal relations and reciprocity (see Zech 3:10). As with much of the language in Zechariah 11, terms used elsewhere in a positive sense (see, e.g., previous NOTE) are here turned around. Each person will become victim rather than friend of his neighbor.

The word for "his neighbor" (*rēʿēhû*) is emended by some, through a simple change in vocalization, to *rōʿēhû*, "his shepherd." The justification for such a change is that "shepherd" would suit the imagery of this chapter and would fit better, if shepherd represents a ruler, with the parallel phrase involving "king." However, although "neighbor" may represent a wordplay on "shepherd," we see no reason to emend, because "person to his neighbor" is a common expression and because the whole passage is depicting the corruption throughout society, not simply among the leadership. To read "shepherd" would be to lose the irony of the phraseology linked with harmony here conveying its opposite.

The phrase "to the hand of" represents the power or agency of the person or persons who are the object of the expression, over those who are the object of the preceding verb. Thus "every person" will become subjected to his neighbor's control, in this case for ill rather than for good, as the next clause makes clear.

his king. Although we translate *malkô* as "his king," we point out a suggestion made by Feigin (1925: 203–6). In looking at the difficult phrase in Eccles 5:8 (*mlk lśdh nᶜbd* [NRSV 5:9]) and comparing it to *lugal a-šág-ga-ge* ("the owner of the field") in Sumerian, he proposes that *mlk* sometimes means "possessor" rather than "king." Such a reading would certainly fit the context of this passage, in which the exploitation of people by those many who have authority, not by just the king, is the issue. Still, the presence of "king" suits the retrospective nature of this narrative, in which the prophet blurs chronological distinctions between past events, present conditions, and future expectations.

they will crush. The subject of this verb must be both the "neighbors" and "the king," i.e., everyone. The verb *ktt*, which is not found very often, means "to beat, to crush fine (by beating)." In an extended sense, as here, it depicts enemies destroying each other (2 Chron 15:6; Deut 1:44).

the land. Although it might be expected to have humans as object of the verb, the use of "land" (*ʾereṣ*) is appropriate because of the integral relationship between the existence of Israel as a people/nation and their claim to a national territory. Because a reference to the "inhabitants of the land" appears earlier in this verse (see NOTE above), "land" alone here can be viewed as part of that phrase standing for the whole.

I will not rescue [any] from their hand. That is, God will not intervene and come to the aid of anyone; all are in each other's power. The verb, Hiphil of *nṣl*, is used with "from their hand, power" (*mydm*) nearly sixty times in the Bible to indicate rescue from an enemy. The paradigmatic examples concern God's saving Israel from Egypt (e.g., Exod 3:8: "I have come to rescue them from the Egyptians"; and many other instances) or other enemies. Similarly, biblical prophecy—notably Jeremiah—uses the phrase to anticipate God's present or eschatological rescue of the beleaguered or exiled people (e.g., Jer 15:21; 20:13; 42:11; cf. Ezek 34:27, in the shepherd narrative). In this passage, however, the classic function of the phrase is reversed—God emphatically will not intervene to keep the people from self-destruction. Once more in Zechariah 11 (cf. NOTES above in this verse to "every person to the hand of his neighbor" and "I will indeed deliver"), traditional language is used to convey the opposite of what it usually means.

7. *So I shepherded the flock. . . . Thus I shepherded the flock.* This twofold use of the verb "to shepherd" plus the *waw* consecutive, followed by "flock," begins the prophet's account of his response to God's mandate of verses 4–6. Although Second Zechariah is not the only prophet to have received a command from God or to have performed a symbolic action, the reporting of the actual carrying out of the divine word is not necessarily typical of the narratives of prophetic actions. Furthermore, the repetition of the prophet's response makes that response all the more striking. How then should we understand this double reporting? To begin with, it is most obvious in providing linkage between the prophet's account of what he has done and the divine command to do it. Given the prophetic self-consciousness present in the phrasing of "Thus spoke Yahweh my God" in verse 4 (see NOTE above) and the apparent need to assert the authority of his message, the emphasis on his carrying out the message can be seen as a further indication of his claim to be a true spokesman of Yahweh. At the same time, the use of "shepherded the flock" both at the beginning and at the end of this verse encapsulates the announcement of the symbolic action involving two staffs. The prophet initiates his reporting of that episode within the context of the overall shepherd imagery, with the account of those actions thus being enmeshed in the overarching symbolic framework of this chapter. Finally, the double reporting serves to sustain the symbolic theme by twice mentioning "shepherd." These two uses of the verb *rʿh* ("to shepherd") contribute to a total of ten times that the verb or its noun form is used in Zechariah 11; the repetition of this root provides the shepherd imagery that ties the whole chapter together.

to be slaughtered. See the NOTE at verse 4 ("flock to be slaughtered") for an explanation of our translation. The word encompasses the range of negative consequences that befall the flock, God's people, because of the widespread corruption (see NOTES to vv 5 and 6).

merchants of the flock. The Hebrew reads "afflicted ones of the flock" (*ʿăniyê-haṣṣōʾn*), which might emphasize the unfortunate state of the Israelites being punished for their evil deeds, inasmuch as the root *ʿnh*, as we explain in our NOTE to "humble" at 9:9, can mean either "to be afflicted" or "to be lowly, humble." However, the Greek reads *lknʿnyy*, i.e., "in/at Canaan," or "to the Canaanites/merchants"; that is, it reads the two words in the MT as a single word, here and in verse 11. Canaan is frequently a euphemism for "trader" in the Hebrew Bible (as in Hos 12:8 [NRSV 12:7]; Prov 31:24; Job 40:30 [NRSV

41:6]; Zeph 1:11; Ezek 17:4). The Greek translation has influenced many modern renderings, e.g., NRSV, "sheep merchant"; and R. L. Smith (in Word Biblical Commentary; 1984: 268) "sheep dealer." Surely "merchants" makes the most sense here, because it indicates exactly what the prophet/shepherd is instructed to do in verses 4–6. That is, he shepherds them to the slaughter, which is effected by the merchants (the buyers and sellers of v 5). Although it is difficult to understand why the Hebrew divided the word, the versional reading gets rid of an awkward text and also fits precisely the prophetic actions of this narrative. In any case, "merchants" represents the "buyers" and "sellers," who are probably any Israelite leaders in positions of power or control over others; see the first NOTE to verse 5.

I took for myself. The verb *lqḥ*, "to take," has not only a direct object ("two staffs"; see next NOTE) but also an indirect object, *lamed* plus a personal pronoun used in the dative sense. This seems to signal a high degree of personal involvement, by the prophet, with the objects and acts that are part of the symbolism of the two staffs. The prophet on his own initiative takes these objects and, as becomes apparent in verses 10 and 14 below, acts upon them almost as if he were Yahweh carrying out the actual deed represented by the symbolic act (see first NOTE to 11:10).

two staffs. The symbolic action enclosed in the prophet's announcement that he did what God commanded ("I shepherded the flock"; see first NOTE to v 7) begins without a specific directive from Yahweh. The "staff" or "two staffs" (*šnê maqlôt*) is an implement that can be used when walking (e.g., Gen 32:11 [NRSV 32:10]; Exod 12:11; Num 22:27; Ezek 39:9), or it can be a symbolic almond rod (Jer 1:11) or a diviner's tool (Hos 4:12); but it can also be a shepherd's crook (Gen 30:37). Given the nature of this narrative sequence in 11:4–16, the shepherd connection seems most likely.

The idea of *two* staffs involved in a symbolic prophetic action bears striking similarities to the account of two sticks (the term being *ʿēṣ*) in Ezek 37:15–23. In that passage, Ezekiel is instructed to take a stick inscribed "for Judah and the Israelites associated with it" and join it to another stick labeled "for Joseph (the stick of Ephraim) and all the house of Israel associated with it." The result of the symbolic action in Ezekiel is the formation of one stick (37:19), which represents the reunification of north and south, of Judah and Ephraim. And, according to the last statement of the Ezekiel passage, it also represents God's covenant with Israel. The word "covenant" does not appear, but a formula that represents the new covenant, because it is the same as the statement found in Jeremiah's depiction of the future covenant (Jer 31:33), concludes the Ezekiel stick narrative: "Then they shall be my people, and I will be their God."

The Ezekiel sticks thus represent unity between the divided kingdoms and also covenant. Those are precisely the two concepts being portrayed in Second Zechariah's grasping of two rods. However, the meaning of the two items in Ezekiel is completely reversed in Zechariah 11, where the prophet's use of the two staffs bespeaks the termination, not the formation, of unity and covenant. Instead of two sticks becoming one, they are each fragmented. The dramatic shift in what exists in earlier prophecy is thus conveyed both by the prophet's action, in breaking the rod, and by the very language of this narrative (see, e.g., NOTES above to "inhabitants of the land," "I will indeed deliver," and "every person to the hand of his neighbor," all in v 6).

I called. The process of labeling the two staffs involves verbal designation. Hebrew *qr* means "call" or "name," the process of calling out names being the act of naming (as in God's naming features of the cosmos in the Genesis 1 creation story—Gen 1:5, 8, 10). This verbal naming of the staffs is significantly different from that in the related Ezekiel passage (see previous NOTE), in which the sticks are labeled by their being inscribed. It is difficult to determine whether there is any conscious distinction involved in the prophet's saying the names rather than writing them. Could it be that the written label bespeaks permanence more than the pronounced label? Because the staffs were to be broken, their identity thereupon would become irrelevant; in contrast, the inscribed sticks of the Ezekiel pericope are joined and represent an everlasting condition ("Never again" will they be separated or defile themselves [37:22–23]).

Delight. The word *nōʿam* defies finding a translation into English that adequately conveys its meaning here. The Greek renders it "Beauty." Various English versions offer "Favor" (*NRSV, NJPS, NEB*), "Pleasant," "Pleasantness," "Goodwill" (Jerome Bible), "Grace," and "Harmony." The very variety of renderings indicates the problem in representing the abstraction and the symbolic value of the Hebrew term.

Examining its semantic range is not particularly enlightening. As a noun, it is attested only here (and in v 10); in Ps 27:4, where it stands for the splendor of Yahweh for one who lives in God's presence; in Ps 90:17, where it indicates divine favor that will be bestowed upon those who serve God; and in several Proverbs passages, where God's words are said to be "ways of pleasantness" (Prov 3:17; cf. 15:26; 16:24).

The adjectival form of *nʿm* is used to describe the "lovely" relationship between David and Jonathan (2 Sam 1:23), the attractiveness of knowledge as if it were wealth (Prov 24:4), the pleasantness of speech (Prov 23:8), the fulfillment of a life well lived (Job 36:11), or even the beautiful music that a lyre can produce (Ps 81:3 [*NRSV,* 81:2]). Perhaps the two most significant readings are the famous line in Ps 133:1 about beautiful human relationships—"How good and wonderful it is for kinfolk to live together!"—and the verse in Ps 16:11 indicating eternal pleasantness for one who follows the right path and exists in God's presence. Both these passages relate to what the staff symbolizes, i.e., the covenant, as is made explicit below in verse 10.

Beyond these two passages, the variety of positive images associated with *nʿm*—music, wealth, love, wisdom—in itself contributes to the broad scope of positive sensations associated with the word. Although they cannot all be reduced to a single English word, the overwhelming sense of that which is positive in life, especially the experience of God's presence and of harmonious relationships, is contained in *nōʿam*. Again, anticipating how the destruction of this staff called Delight will be interpreted in verse 10, those positive attributes are surely part of the prophet's understanding of what covenant implies (cf. NOTES to v 10).

Bonds. The prophet names the second staff *ḥōbĕlîm* ("Bonds"), an active participle from *ḥbl*, "to bind" or "to take on pledge." The derivative noun *ḥebel* denotes a cord, band, or length of cord used for measuring. The cord as a measure underlies the sense of allotted territory that it can also have (Josh 17:5, 14, etc.). Finally, in a single instance, it has a more abstract meaning of "band" or "group" of people—the band of professional prophets of 1 Sam 10:5–10.

As with *nōʿam*, for "Delight," this term is difficult to express in English, and many different proposals exist in the translations and commentaries—"Unity," "Concord," "Couplers," "Bonds," "Union." The Greek preserves a literal reading with "line" (and "even line" in v 14). However, those suggestions, among which we include our own, that attempt to capture the symbolic value of "rope" seem more appropriate. Indeed, the imagery of the "Bonds" staff is apparent from the description of what the breaking of it signifies according to verse 14, namely, the dissolution of the relationship between Israel and Judah. Consequently, the unbroken staff surely represents what binds the two parts of all Israel together, hence our rendering "Bonds." Furthermore, as Mason points out (1973: 157–58), the root *ḥbl* involves the idea of pledging as well as binding. Thus "Bonds" implies the mutual obligations of the two parties tied together and thus intensifies the tragedy of that unity's being torn asunder.

8. *I got rid of.* This is the Hiphil imperfect plus *waw* consecutive of the root *kḥd* with the *yodh* missing, although many Hebrew manuscripts preserve it. It anticipates the Niphal usage of the same root in verse 9, where it means "to destroy." In either conjugation, the root involves severe action. The use of the *waw* consecutive here helps to establish the completed nature of the action. The same is true for the verbs of the previous verse. Although this verbal form implies past action, it cannot signify how distant that past is. Nonetheless, it does contribute to the sense that this narrative describes past, rather than future, events.

the three shepherds. The existing literature on this verse, especially the discussions of this phrase, can be summarized by the statement that verse 8 is "the most enigmatic in the whole Old Testament" (Baldwin 1972: 181). More than a half-century earlier, Mitchell (1912: 306) wrote that there were forty proposed identifications of the shepherds. Prophets, kings, high priests, nations, peoples, and sundry leaders from the eighth to the second century B.C.E. have been proposed as "the three shepherds." R. L. Smith, in resisting the temptation to follow the urge to identify the shepherds with practical figures, characterizes this prophecy as an allegory (1984: 270), adopting the rather idiosyncratic view of A. F. Kirkpatrick (1915: 467), who wrote that no precise identification could be made but that "the three shepherds" were "part of the furniture of the allegory, and their removal by the prophet within a month is intended to signify God's intention to deal promptly and effectually with the oppressors of His people, whoever they may be."

Commentators have been correct in pointing out that three is a significant number, one that plays a special role in ancient Near Eastern number symbolism. As the smallest complete number, it represents wholeness or totality (Pope 1962: 564; Farbridge 1970: 100, 113). It thus could well represent all the many shepherds, i.e., all the people in positions of power who are being held accountable for the decay of Israelite society. It is not surprising, therefore, that the research for three specific historical individuals or incidents that supposedly lie behind the three-shepherd figure leads to a misleading and misconstrued interpretation of this passage. "Three shepherds" is deliberately vague and, thereby, inclusive.

Although we are convinced that specific personages are not to be connected to these shepherds, we do entertain the possibility that they represent a specific type of leader. As we have repeatedly noted, "shepherd" is a common image in biblical prophecy and can signify various aspects of human or divine leadership (see NOTE to "wail of the shepherds," 10:3). Perhaps it most often represents God, who has a pastoral relationship to the people ("flock," "sheep"); but it surely also designates humans, including prophets, as is the case in this chapter, where the prophet is told to "shepherd the flock" and thus act in the role of shepherd. Because of the content of verses 15–16 below, in which Second Zechariah present false prophets as shepherds (see NOTE to "a foolish shepherd" in v 15; see also "worthless shepherd" of v 17), and in light of the attack on false prophets in 13:2–6, it seems possible that the three shepherds here are the false prophets with whom the prophet of these chapters is struggling. That Second Zechariah is at pains to establish his prophetic authority (see NOTE to v 4, "Thus spoke Yahweh my God") can be attributed in part to the enduring difficulty in distinguishing true prophecy from false.

Does the prophet here mean to reflect on his own difficulties in establishing prophetic authority or to allude to past confrontations? The text does not tell us, and we suggest that these are not mutually exclusive circumstances. In any case, the idea of getting rid of shepherds (= false prophets) is part of the process of having God's will correctly known by the people so that they will comprehend the true meaning of what takes place in the world in the past, present, and future.

in one month. That is, in a short time. The designation of a single month need not be construed as a literal designation of a specific period of lapsed time, because it is unlikely that this verse refers to historical events or people (see previous NOTE).

I became impatient. Literally, "my soul grew short." The idea of impatience is expressed by the use of the Qal verb *qṣr* ("to be short, impatient") plus *nepeš* ("soul"), in that order. It also anticipates the phrase that follows in its use of *nepeš* before the verb *bḥl* ("to feel loathing"). Reversing the word order produces a chiastic arrangement of the second half of the verse (verb/noun, noun/verb).

they felt loathing. The MT verb *bḥl* is a hapax legomenon; its meaning is not at all clear. The Greek has "their soul cried out," which is also reflected in the Syriac translation. A popular emendation is the substitution of the somewhat more common root *gᶜl*, which occurs twelve times in the Bible and which has a similar meaning in the intransitive form but mostly with a covenantal connotation (Fuhs 1978: 45–48). When intransitive it is followed by *b* and also occurs with *nepeš*, as in Jer 14:19. Usually when it takes an object, the verb means "to consider someone or something as dung or filth." An apparently separate root, as well as a hapax legomenon, *bḥl* as a Pual appears in Prov 20:21 with the meaning "gotten by greed," which would make no sense here. In light of the unconvincing alternatives, we accept the MT. Despite its difficulties, the intention of the term to express a negative evaluation of the shepherds seems clear. Unquestionably, great tension exists between the prophet and the other three, probably prophetic, figures.

9. *Then I said.* The prophet's own reported speech appears for the first time, introduced by the *waw* consecutive plus the imperfect of *ʾmr*, "to speak," as is the second reported speech in this narrative in verse 12. This shift to the prophet's reported speech may mark the point where he feels he has done his duty and thus surrenders his mandate to shepherd the people.

I will not shepherd you. This is the seventh time that the root *rʿh*, "to shepherd," occurs in this chapter (see first NOTE to v 7 above), which is replete with shepherd imagery. It first appears in verbal form in verse 4, in the imperative (see NOTE above), and twice in verse 7 as an imperfect with *waw* consecutive. It occurs here as an imperfect and initiates a short reported speech of the prophet. Coming after the statement regarding the removal of "the three shepherds" in verse 8 (see NOTE above), which may allude to the past and present tension between true and false prophets, the shift to an internal quotation and to the future mode lends a sense of reality to the harshly negative statements that follow.

The question of who is represented by "you," the object of the verb "to shepherd," is a vexing one. Presumably, because it is a kind of reprise of God's command in verse 4 "to shepherd the flock," the refusal to do so must involve that same flock, i.e., the sheep who represent all the people. But why now does the prophet balk? The answer must be that his task is futile and meaningless. It has apparently been made so by the internal corruption of the flock and by the failure of any with authority to intervene. Seemingly among the worst such offenders are the professional and/or false prophets. In the long shepherd narrative of Ezekiel 34, the bad shepherds are the kings, who have exploited their office and have not taken proper care of their "flock," which is now utterly lost; but one day a true Davidic shepherd/ruler will change all that. In stark contrast, this narrative does not have a positive outcome. We attribute this fact (see COMMENT) to its retrospective character, whereby it recalls and thus tries to understand the horrible destruction and dispersion of the people in the past. In so doing, the prophetic self-consciousness of Second Zechariah plays a prominent role. Insofar as he identifies with the plight of true prophets of the past, of whom Jeremiah is a prime example, he is painfully aware of the reality that such true shepherds could not transform society and forestall its demise. Thus why should they have acted as shepherds? Should they not have refused, given the ineffectiveness of their oracles, to be shepherds to the hopelessly doomed people as this verse suggests?

Whoever is to die shall die. This is the first of three clauses depicting the awful fate of the flock. Each part of the bleak threefold picture is expressed in striking Hebrew phraseology composed of the present participle plus the imperfect of the same verb or, in the third clause, a different verb. In this first clause, the Hebrew, using the root *mwt* ("to die") reads literally "the one who is dying will die." This series of clauses involving the repetition of verbal roots is somewhat reminiscent of Jer 15:2, ("those [destined] for pestilence to pestilence,/ those for the sword to the sword,/ those for famine to famine,/ and those for captivity to captivity"), except that in Jeremiah there are four clauses and the repetition involves substantives rather than verbs. Still, the overall effect is quite similar: a dramatic expression of utter destruction. This negative assessment of the fate of the flock is an apt prelude to the conclusion in the next verse (and in v 14) of the two-staff imagery that was introduced in verse 7 (see NOTES to "two staffs," "Delight," "Bonds") and that represents dire consequences for what the staffs symbolize. The verbs in all three clauses are feminine, which suits the imagery of "flock," a feminine noun. However, in the preceding clause, the suffix "you" ("I will not shepherd you") is second-person masculine plural. The shift from masculine to feminine may reflect the prophet's blurring of people and animal metaphors.

Whoever is to be destroyed shall be destroyed. The same construction as in the first clause in this series (see previous NOTE) is formed with the Niphal of *kḥd*, which also appears below in verse 16. The same root is found in the Hiphil at the beginning of verse 8 (see NOTE to "I got rid of"). The Niphal usage is fairly rare (cf. Job 4:7; 15:28; 22:20; Exod 9:15), but it seems clear that its intent is much the same as that of the more common Piel and Hiphil. It involves the ruin of whoever is involved, whether it be by physical annihilation or by being torn away from wherever one belongs.

whoever is left shall devour. This third clause in the series (see two previous NOTES) differs in using two distinct verbs: "Whoever is left" is the feminine plural participle of the Niphal of *šʾr*, "to remain"; and "devour" is the feminine plural imperfect of *ʾkl*, "to eat, consume."

each other's flesh. The feminine is used here also (see previous NOTE), again continuing the imagery of "flock" (a feminine noun). The word translated "each other's" is *rĕʿûtâ* (literally, "of her neighbor"), which is similar to "of his neighbor" in verse 6. Perhaps the two uses of "neighbor" meaning "each other," one masculine and one feminine, together are meant to connote the totality of the population, i.e., all women and all men. In Exod 11:2, the people comprise "every man" and "every woman," each making a request of his or her neighbor. In any case, the sentiment in verses 6 and 9 is the same: people are destroying each other (cf. v 16 below). But here the imagery is much more graphic. People come under the control of their neighbors in verse 6; here they devour each other's bodies. This vivid and horrible metaphor (but cf. the apparently literal cannibalism in Jer 19:9) of internal corruption and consequent doom completes the prophet's quoted words.

10. *Then I took my staff Delight*. The prophet here resumes the symbolic action involving two staffs that was initiated in the midst of his response in verse 7 to God's command to shepherd the flock. As we have pointed out (see NOTES to "two staffs" and "Delight" in 11:7), the description of the prophet taking this action does not include a specific directive that he do so, in contrast, e.g., with the Ezekiel two-stick passage, in which God tells the prophet what to do (Ezek 37:15ff.). In this case, the prophet seems to be identifying so strongly with what he feels is divine intention that the division between divine command and the following prophetic response is blurred. Thus the possessive pronoun with "Delight"—"my staff"—links the prophet with the very staff that also, in its symbolic function in this verse, is God's (see below, NOTE to "my covenant").

severed. The root *gdᶜ*, "to cut, hew, hew off/down" describes the physical act involved in taking something that is supposed to be whole and cutting it into pieces. Indeed, the verb *šbr* ("to break") is often used in parallel with *gdᶜ* (e.g., Jer 48:25, "Moab's horn is cut, and his arm is broken"). Although this verb can be used figuratively, it is not anywhere connected with covenant terminology. Thus it represents the physical breaking of the two staffs. If anything, its graphic meaning is more suitable to the severing of Bonds (v 14), which divides into two parts, than of Delight. Yet because Delight represents the covenant, severing it makes it ineffectual, just as cutting the Asherim or other idols removes their efficacy (Deut 7:5; 12:3; 2 Chron 14:2 [NRSV 14:3]; 31:1).

break. This is the first of three terms that are part of Israel's covenant language. This Hiphil verb, from the root *prr*, is the biblical word used to express the breaking of a covenant agreement. Most often it concerns Israel's violation of its covenant with Yahweh (e.g., Deut 31:16, 20; Lev 26:15; Ezek 44:7; Gen 17:14; Isa 24:5), although it is also found in passages describing people abrogating covenants with other people (as Isa 33:8; 1 Kgs 15:19 = 2 Chron 16:3). Aside from this passage, in only three other places does it refer to Yahweh's breaking of the covenant with Israel—in Judg 2:1; Lev 26:44; and Jer 14:21. In the Judges and Leviticus texts, God is proclaiming that the covenant with Israel will never be broken. Assuming that this Zechariah text concerns that very same covenant (see next two NOTES), can it really be telling us that God will have broken that which we are told elsewhere can never be broken?

To answer this question, we must keep in mind, as several passages in Jeremiah and Ezekiel seem to indicate, that the events of the sixth century—the destruction of Jerusalem, the devastation of Judah and the exile of many Judeans—were understood to mean that the covenant was broken. This view can be observed from two perspectives. The first is a consideration of what happens to the Mosaic covenant as the result of the destruction. The second derives from the implication of God's breaking the covenant for the emergence of the idea of a new covenant.

Let us first look at how the status of the covenant might have been perceived in terms of the destructive events of the sixth century. The verse in Jeremiah that mentions God's breaking the covenant, like those in the Judges and Leviticus texts cited above, also has "break the covenant" with a negative. However, instead of saying that God will never break the covenant agreement, the Jeremiah passage (14:21) is a plea to Yahweh, given the iniquity of the people, *not* to break the covenant. Striking down Judah and bringing terror to all (Jer 14:19) are seen as signs that God could very well be abrogating the age-old agreement with Israel. Ezekiel is even more direct: "Yes, thus says the Lord God: I will deal with you as you have done, you who have hated the oath, breaking the covenant" (Ezek 16:59). The implication is clearly that Israel's sins have been so profound as to destroy the covenant and that God will respond in kind. Thus, although no verse in the Hebrew Bible other than Zech 11:10 directly refers to God as the revoker of the covenant, these two prophets of the exilic period indirectly make such a claim.

Yet, for both Ezekiel and Jeremiah, the idea that Yahweh might abrogate the Mosaic covenant is inextricably linked with the idea of a new covenant. Indeed, the very notion that God will make a new covenant, or the covenant anew, implies that the covenantal relationship of the past is being superseded. This is, in a sense, tantamount to the previous covenant's being broken—not only by the iniquities of the people but also by God in dealing with a people so recalcitrant that only by beginning anew can the covenant relationship truly work. In Ezek 16:60, following the verse cited above, God asserts that in remembering the former covenant, an "everlasting covenant" will now be made. Similarly, Jeremiah describes the "new covenant" as one that will differ from the Sinai covenant, thus implying that the Sinai covenant as such is no longer in effect, at least in its original arrangement (Jer 31:31–34). The new covenant will be the same as the old one but will be constructed in such a way that the people will no longer be able to violate its terms. It will be written on the hearts of the people, so that they will automatically obey its stipulations.

my covenant. The idiomatic expression that links "to break" (see previous NOTE) with "covenant" uses the first-person singular possessive pronoun in two of the other three places in which the idiom is used for the termination of Yahweh's covenant with Israel (Judg 2:1 and Lev 26:44); and in the third text, in which the people are speaking to God, it is "your" covenant that is mentioned. This verse presents, therefore, the peculiar problem of the prophet speaking and thus giving the impression that it is the prophet's covenant that is at stake. However, because we have no evidence of true prophets making covenants with anyone, let alone "with all the peoples" (see NOTE below), the possibility that the prophet is talking about any sort of personal covenant agreement must be ruled out. What seems to be the case is that in his role as prophet, he identifies so completely with God's will and words that the tradition of God's making and/ or breaking "my covenant" has been interiorized by Second Zechariah. Hence, in describing his symbolic action—breaking a staff that symbolizes the cove- nant—he is speaking as if he were God breaking that covenant in historical actuality, which is the way the prophets of the Exile (Jeremiah and Ezekiel), who have great influence on him, have viewed the devastation of the Babylonian conquest.

Thus, although some (e.g., *BHS*) would emend the text here to read "covenant of Yahweh which he made" for "my covenant which I made," there seems to be enough justification, because of the unique role the prophet is assuming here, for retaining the MT. Second Zechariah is caught up in the horror of the past events that have brought about the need for the eschatological intervention and restoration depicted in chapters 9 and 10. In his unparalleled claim for prophetic authority at the outset of this shepherd narrative, he set the mood of his agonizingly close relationship to God (see first NOTE to 11:4). Similarly, in claiming the staffs as his (see NOTE to "I took for myself," 11:7, and first NOTE to this verse), the action involving the staffs merges in his thinking with the divine action represented by what he does. Hence, in saying that he took up his staff in order to break "my covenant," he surely means to be speaking as if he were God announcing the inevitable termination of the historical agreement between Yahweh and Israel. It is precisely Second Zechariah's retrospective view, looking at the seemingly hopeless dispersion and dissolution of the people over the past centuries, yet subscribing to the idea of a new covenant and an eschatological restoration, that allows him to do what no other prophetic figure had dared—to proclaim explicitly the breaking of the historical covenant.

which I made. This is the prophet speaking, as if he were God (see previous NOTE). As God's spokesperson his individual identity as shepherd converges with God's metaphoric role as Israel's shepherd. The word translated "made" is literally "cut" and is part of Israel's covenant vocabulary (cf. Meyers and Meyers 1987: 52).

with all the peoples. The plural of "people" (*ʿam*) is unexpected here, for the phrase "all the peoples" typically signifies the larger group of ethnic or national groups out of which Yahweh had chosen Israel to be God's people (e.g., Deut 7:6, 14; 10:15; 14:2); or sometimes it refers to the general population of non-Israelites (1 Chron 16:24; 1 Kgs 5:14 [NRSV 4:34]; Esth 1:16; 3:8; Hab 2:5), especially those among whom Israel had been scattered in exile. This last group figures prominently in the next chapter of Zechariah.

The unexpected plural "peoples" can be accounted for in several ways, which may not be mutually exclusive. For one thing, although it is not common, the components of Israel are sometimes referred to as *ʿammîm*, "peoples." In Genesis, Judah's ascendancy over his brothers is described in terms of the expected obedience "of the peoples" (i.e., his brothers) to him (Gen 49:10). Similarly, Jacob recounts God's promise to make him fruitful so that he will become a "company *(qhl)* of peoples" (Gen 48:4); and in Isaac's blessing to Jacob, the promise that all his brothers and cousins will serve him is equated with the idea that "peoples" will serve him (Gen 27:29). Another example involves a prophet who apparently, like Second Zechariah, was poignantly aware of the tension between true and false prophecy: Micaiah, in proclaiming the veracity of his warning to the king of Israel, addressed all around him, presumably all Judeans and/or Israelites, as "Hear, all you peoples" (*ʿmym klm* in 1 Kgs 22:28; this citation, a direct quotation of Mic 1:2, suggests a possible confusion between Micah and Micaiah, or else indicates a common form of prophetic address). Finally, in Isa 3:13, Yahweh is depicted as entering into judgment with the leaders of the people—"he stands to judge the peoples."

These precedents for referring to the components of all Israel as "peoples" may have affected this passage in its position just before the oracles of restoration in Zech 12:1–6. Numerous times in those verses, the nations from which Yahweh will rescue Judah and Jerusalem are designated as "all the peoples." That is, the clustering of that phraseology in the next chapter in reference to foreign nations perhaps led to its unusual though not unprecedented use for the peoples of all Israel in this passage. In any case, the variation in meaning that the term *ʿam* can have (see discussion in Meyers and Meyers 1987: 435–36) should be reason enough for caution in assuming that "all the peoples" here might mean non-Israelite nations. Because there is no indication of God's having made such a pact, and because there are good reasons for seeing "all the peoples" as unusual but understandable in this instance, this phrase as a reference to the various groups that constituted all Israel makes sense as it stands (cf. Otzen 1964: *ad loc.*).

11. *And so it was broken.* The *waw* consecutive with the Hophal of *prr* affirms that the staff/covenant was in fact broken. See the NOTE to "break" in verse 10.

on that day. Although this phrase often indicates the eschatological future, it can also be a simple time indicator. Or it can partake of both meanings—it can refer to a specific moment in time that is inevitably connected to an eventual and expected outcome in the eschatological future (Meyers and Meyers 1987: 212). Such may be the case in this verse, in which the symbolic breaking of the staff represents God's foreclosure of the historical agreement with Israel but not the final termination of Israel's relationship with God; an eschatological saving of all the people is the focus of the chapters of Second Zechariah surrounding this one.

the merchants of the flock. The MT has "afflicted ones." For this reading, see the NOTE to this phrase above in 11:7.

who were watching over me. The symbolic action has an audience, all the "merchants," i.e. leaders, to whom its meaning is directed. The separate pronominal object of the verb, "me," may be yet another indication of prophetic self-consciousness, along with the unique emphasis on the oracle coming from "my God" (see first NOTE to v 4) and on the symbolic staffs being his (see NOTES to "I took for myself," v 7, and to "then I took my staff" and "my second staff, Bonds" vv 10 and 14).

The similarity of *hšmrym*, "those who were watching over," to the word for Samaritans, *hšmrwnym*, has led some commentators to suggest an allusion here to that group and thus to tensions between Yehudites and Samaritans in the postexilic period (e.g., Coggins 1975: 11; P. D. Hanson 1975: 340ff.). However, as we explain in various NOTES and in our COMMENT, we do not see this

271

enigmatic shepherd narrative as a veiled presentation of tensions among specific historical groups or personages.

knew that this was the word of Yahweh. The assertion that the prophet's action was acknowledged by his audience to be a valid symbol of God's will is part of the dynamics of prophetic activity in the ancient world. In some passages describing the tension between true and false prophecy, there are clues that true prophets viewed the coming to pass of conditions described in prophetic speech as verification of their prophetic authority. The passage cited above, in our NOTE to "with all the peoples" (v 10), refers to the prophet Micaiah (or Micah?) and his last words to the "peoples." Here we call attention to what Micaiah was announcing to the peoples: if what he has proclaimed does not happen, then God will not have spoken through him.

The relevance of Micaiah's statement is what it shows about the authentication of prophecy (cf. NOTE to "prophets" in 13:4). In this verse in Second Zechariah, there is a similar dynamic at work. The breaking of the staff/covenant merges in the strange syntax of verse 10, which has the prophet severing the staff identified with God breaking the covenant. Thus the prophet's deed and the act it represents become one, so that the "merchants" (leaders) must acknowledge the veracity of God's word through the prophet.

"Word of Yahweh" is a technical term for prophetic revelation. As part of the vocabulary involved in the transmission of authoritative messages from God, it usually announces an oracular statement (see Meyers and Meyers 1987: 7). However, the nature of prophetic revelation is extended in this instance to actions that constitute a message from God as much as do actual words.

12. *If this seems good to you.* Literally, "if it is good in your eyes." This familiar idiom expresses someone's subjective evaluation of an event, of a person's conduct, of words that have been uttered, or of news that has been announced. As such, the expression may be a set formula of approval (Höver-Johag 1986: 308). Indeed, when it is used with "Yahweh" (as "good in the eyes of Yahweh") it seems to relate to covenant approval—that is, Yahweh would find a given event or behavior to be in accordance with covenant standards. Given its conventional usage, the prophet's reciting of this formula to the "merchants of the flock" (see NOTES to that phrase in vv 7 and 11) carries considerable irony.

The prophet has just carried out the first of two symbolic acts involving his two staffs; and the severing of the second, although it is not reported until verse 14, is surely anticipated in this section, dealing with the interaction between the prophet and the people affected by the symbolic actions, that comes between the two acts of staff breaking. The prophet's audience should not be pleased with the symbolic action—the breaking of Delight—nor with the explanation of what that means, i.e., the termination of the covenant. Yet they apparently acknowledge that the action comes from Yahweh.

It is possible to see such approval as an acceptance of the authenticity of the prophet's act rather than of the meaning of the act (as in v 6 above). Verse 11, which asserts that the "merchants" acknowledged that the symbolic breaking of the covenant was truly God's word (see previous NOTE), anticipates these words of approval. Thus the approval is actually an acknowledgment of the veracity of the prophet's words and deeds, as being truly the will of Yahweh, rather than an approval of the content of the words and deeds—covenant breaking—which might not be so readily accepted. Indeed, because the rest of the prophet's statement involves the payment of wages (see next NOTE), which is part of the process of popular acceptance of what is perceived to be an authentic message from God, the approval expressed by the idiom clearly reflects the fact that the symbolic act is valid.

However, can the acceptance of the authenticity of the act be separated from its content? It seems unlikely, in which case the acquiescence of the leaders ("merchants") to the doom represented by the breaking of Delight means an acceptance of the inevitability of the end of the covenant. Such a response comports with the retrospective thrust of this passage. The historical covenant in fact has been severed, many people are suffering as a result, and the whole episode of traumatic national destruction is the authentication of Yahweh's word through the earlier prophets writ large. In short, usual categories of past, present, and future are transcended in this prophetic action: the leaders or officials, who will pay the prophet, are the very ones who witnessed the breaking of Delight/ covenant. Here they confirm the terrible decree by participation in a symbolic acceptance of it.

give me my wage. The prophet's demand for payment for his prophetic act continues the irony and probably reflects ongoing tension between true and false prophecy. The people called upon to pay are certainly not taken aback by what is asked of them, inasmuch as they proceed to measure out payment (see NOTES below to "weighed out" and "thirty pieces of silver"). The idea of paying for prophetic oracles was an integral part of ancient Near Eastern life. Professional prophets and priestly prophets, often working together in bands or guilds (1 Sam 10:10), presumably earned their living by consulting Yahweh through various special techniques or devices. Although the existence of such groups or individuals seems quite acceptable in many biblical texts (e.g., the priest of Micah, who gave oracles for his keep [Judg 18:4–5]), these "popular prophets," who earned their living by soothsaying, were in many ways the antithesis of true prophets. True prophets did not seek to prophesy or to earn a living by doing so, although it is conceivable that some may have been paid for their pronouncements. Consider Amos' eloquent rejection of Amaziah's criticism of him ("O seer, go, flee away to the land of Judah, earn your bread there, and prophesy at Bethel" [Amos 7:12–13]) and his vigorous defense of his own nonprophetic source of income as a "herdsman and dresser of sycamore trees" (7:14; cf. NOTE below, in 13:5, to "I am a tiller of the soil").

It is well known that popular, or professional, prophets continued to exist during the postexilic era. Our understanding of much of Second Zechariah as reflecting the ongoing tension between "true" and other prophets depends on the assumption that such other prophets were active in the Persian period. Many of those prophets became employed as Temple singers and musicians (2 Chron 20:13–23; 34:30; see Blenkinsopp 1983: 254–55). Presumably they also continued in their "prophetic" roles. The willingness of the people here to remit wages earned clearly suggests that they were accustomed to doing so. Although it is difficult to assert that it was the conscious intention of popular prophets to deceive and mislead their clients, there no doubt was an irresistible tendency for such professionals to announce only what would seem favorable (see 1 Kgs 22:13, 18, in which the four hundred prophets speak favorably to the king, whereas Micaiah, the true prophet, prophesies disaster) and thus be assured of receiving payment for their prophetic efforts. Popular or professional prophecy, it would seem, could not be critical, could not chastise people for disobeying the covenant, which is precisely what true prophecy involved.

In light of all this, how can we understand this obvious instance of a true prophet's accepting payment? From all that has been said about this passage, it is clear that its rhetorical power comes in great measure from the way it turns familiar language or practices into meaning the opposite of what they normally mean. In other words, the whole shepherd narrative uses irony repeatedly and to great advantage in its attempt to deal with the great traumas that have befallen the people. Perhaps, then, this is the greatest irony of all—a true prophet being paid for a message of doom. The assessment of this act, however, cannot rest on the fact of payment alone. It is only the first of two actions that form the wage-payment section (vv 11–13) of Zechariah 11. The disbursement of the silver pieces (see NOTE in this verse to "thirty pieces of silver") to the prophet is then followed, in verse 13, by another action; the silver is, in a way, returned to Yahweh, which may serve to abrogate the apparent slipping of the true prophet into the ways of the "foolish" (see NOTE in v 15) or "worthless" (see NOTE in v 17) prophets/shepherds.

As we indicated in the previous NOTE, this symbolic action of wage paying in verses 11–13 comes between the severing of Delight (v 10) and the severing of Bonds (v 14). Because of its position between the two verses describing the breaking of staffs, there has been a tendency to view verses 11–13 as later interpolation (e.g., Mason 1973: 160–65). However, the texture of Second Zechariah is so complex that such logic seems inappropriate in evaluating this passage or any of the six chapters of Second Zechariah. Rather than see the wage-payment account as a later addition, one can view it as a symbolic action subordinate to the dominant action relating to the two staffs. The latter acts and their meanings apply retrospectively to Israel and Judah; but the role of prophecy—in having been unable to forestall the destruction of the kingdom and the covenant, in part because of the way popular or "false" prophets were heeded instead of the true prophets—is of ongoing concern. Hence the subsidiary action of verses 11–13 theoretically extends the prophet's purview from the destruction of the past, to the tension of the present, as a way of ensuring that the expected eschatological resolution will not be jeopardized by the misleading words of prophets who do not speak Yahweh's words and who have agendas other than delivering God's message to the people. Such agendas, expressed largely in the negative, are spelled out in verse 16 (see NOTES) in yet another symbolic action interwoven into the overall shepherd theme of chapter 11.

The word for "wage," *śākār* (from the verb *śkr*, "to hire"), is used for the payment given to various workers who perform a service: servants, soldiers, and even animals. That it is not found elsewhere in reference to wages paid to a prophet is not surprising because that aspect of popular prophecy is not directly mentioned. However, the verbal form is in fact used once in reference to payment for prophetic work: the narrative about the priest-prophet of Micah includes the information that Micah has "hired" this professional (Judg 18:4).

but if not, withhold it. Because we have already been told that the prophet's audience has acknowledged the authenticity of his act, it would seem that the previous statement, "If this seems good to you, give me my wage" (see two previous NOTES), would suffice. Yet because that statement may involve formulaic language, then perhaps the present statement offering an alternative response is simply part of a complete recitation of what a prophet says upon completing his contracted task. However, it would not seem to be good business for a professional to offer his clients the possibility of nonpayment. Thus the appearance of the nonpayment option must indicate the prophet's surety that he has truly given God's word and that the people know he has. Hence the added option, which clearly will not be chosen, contributes to the rhetorical focus on the fact of a true prophet receiving wages.

weighed out. Each piece of silver is carefully weighed out for the payment of the wage (cf. Exod 22:16 [NRSV 22:17]; 1 Kgs 20:39; Jer 32:10; Isa 55:2). The root *šql*, "to weigh," comes to signify a measure or specific weight, *šeqel*, as in Amos 8:5, and can refer to bronze (1 Sam 17:5), silver (Exod 21:32), or gold (Josh 7:21). The noun form may also represent an actual kind of currency (Neh 5:15; 10:33 [NRSV 10:32]), as in "silver shekels," or a denomination of currency, as in "half-shekel" (Exod 30:13[2], 15; etc.).

my wage. To accentuate the fact that the payment of thirty silver pieces is for a wage to the prophet, the author of the passage has made it absolutely unmistakable through the use of the accusative marker *ʾt* before *śěkārî,* "my wage," a term that appeared earlier in this verse (cf. the use of term in Zech 8:10[2] and Mal 3:5).

thirty pieces of silver. This phrase occurs in apposition to "my wage" (see previous NOTE) and literally reads "thirty of silver," i.e., "thirty pieces of silver." Virtually all commentaries point out that such a sum of money is that which is due a slave owner in the event that an ox gores a male or female slave (Exod 21:32). The language in Exodus is even more specific: the sum is "silver, thirty shekels worth." Commentators also suggest that it is a paltry sum because of the putative sarcastic reference to it in verse 13 (see NOTE to "this worthy sum"). A similar price was paid by the prophet Hosea for the adulteress (Hos 3:2), half in cash (fifteen shekels of silver) and half in kind (a homer of barley and a measure of wine).

However, it should be noted that silver was more valuable than gold until sometime in the Achaemenid period, after 500 B.C.E., when it became more plentiful, so that when the two are paired together silver usually appears first (Meyers and Meyers 1987: 348; see also NOTE to "she has piled up silver" in

9:3). During the Persian period new sources of silver increased to the point where silver came more and more to be used as a basis for evaluating coinage and hence was used in coins in relatively pure form and in alloy. The language here reflects the awareness of such matters, and the sum need not be regarded as paltry if it can be compared even remotely to the value of a slave. Obviously, if one presupposes that the shepherd/prophet is really a king or another leader of high rank, then the sum paid out would truly be regarded as too small. Because we have rejected this line of interpretation we merely conclude that the prophet's fee itself is appropriate; whether it is appropriate at all for him to receive a suitable fee is a separate issue (see the discussion above in NOTE to "give me my wage").

13. *Then Yahweh said to me.* This formula occurs twice in the shepherd narrative, here and in verse 15, thereby interweaving part of the "payment" section (vv 11–13), which is at the core of the "two-staffs" narrative, with the final symbolic action of chapter 11, the "foolish shepherd" passage of verses 15–16. In terms of the literary structure, it is also parallel to the opening formula in verse 4 (see above, NOTE to "Thus spoke Yahweh my God"), though in form and content the formula in verse 4 is unique. Nonetheless, in each case the formula is followed by a command and, ultimately, with a symbolic action. Only verses 1–3 and the concluding poetic piece, verse 17, fall outside these oracular structures (see COMMENT). The appearance of "Yahweh said" formulas lends a prophetic and oracular character to the shepherd narrative as a whole, whereas the opening and closing poetic sections, as examples of oracular poetry, frame the series of symbolic actions that constitute the narrative. The formula here and in verse 14 include "to me." This prepositional phrase is one of a number of instances in Zechariah 11 in which the God–prophet connection receives emphasis (see, e.g., first NOTE to v 10 above).

Cast it. The verb is the Hiphil of *šlk* ("to throw, cast"), with a masculine singular suffix referring to the prophet's wage, followed by *ʾel*, "into." This verbal form is common and does not, despite what many contend (e.g., Mitchell 1912: 313), have a negative connotation or imply contempt. The combination of *šlk* with the act of depositing money in a chest appears in 2 Chron 24:10, in which the act is in response to the call of King Joash to restore the House of Yahweh (2 Chron 24:4–6). This Chronicles passage is instructive in understanding the present one, which may in fact be elliptical, thereby giving the impression that the casting of the silver pieces was done with some sort of negative gesture. But "to cast" when used with the Temple "treasury," as it is here and in 2 Chronicles 24, probably means "to put into a receptacle at the treasury." Indeed, such an ellipsis may underlie the textual confusion surrounding the next word, which seems to indicate some sort of combination—of both a container and the Temple treasury (see next NOTE).

into the treasury. The Hebrew text reads *ʾel hayyôṣēr*, literally, "to the potter," but is best rendered "into the treasury," even though in this case a "potter" may be a Temple functionary who deals with donations of precious metal; see the discussion below. The Temple context is assured because of the additional phrase "House of Yahweh" before the second use of "to the treasury" at the end of this verse (see NOTE below).

The word *yôṣēr* as "potter" is problematic. Among the Versions, the Syriac and Targum have *ʾôṣār*, "treasury," as does Kennicott Manuscript 530 (Saebø 1969: 79), for *yôṣēr* in its second appearance in this verse. Such an emendation, which we accept in both instances, supposes that a *yodh* has been confused with an *aleph*, a possible scribal error. Because four of the five letters of "potter" and "treasury" are the same, the reading of the more appropriate "treasury" is compelling.

The Greek text reads *chōneutērion*, "melting furnace," a word used to translate *ʾēš mĕṣārēp* ("refiner's fire") of Mal 3:2 or *yôṣēq* ("smelter") of 1 Kgs 8:51. Saebø (1969: 82) posits that one of these terms, probably *yôṣēq* (or perhaps *sôrep*), may underlie the MT of Zech 11:12, *yōṣēr*. He suggests that the MT is a *Kompromissform* (compromise form), a combination of *yôṣēq* ("furnace" or "smelter") and *ʾôṣār* ("treasury"), derived from two early variants in the history of the transmission of the text. Saebø's proposal is based on text-critical and grammatical considerations. Although compelling in some ways, the idea of "smelter" being involved at one stage in the development of the MT is somewhat difficult to maintain.

However, some information provided by C. C. Torrey (1936) in his understanding of the word *yôṣēr*, meaning "potter," may be relevant. First let us consider the noun *yôṣēr*, which is derived from the root *yṣr* ("to fashion, form"). This verb gives rise to the image of God as potter, because it is part of the Genesis narrative describing God fashioning the first human in Eden (Gen 2:7, 8). Similarly, many texts depict a human potter forming vessels from clay (e.g., Isa 29:16; 41:25; Jer 18:4[2], 6[2], etc.). However, "potter" seems to make little sense in this context.

Torrey (1936: 256) retains *yôṣēr* but provides an intriguing suggestion about its meaning by pointing out that this term does not always mean someone who makes something out of clay, but can also involve metalwork. He cites Isa 44:9–11 and Hab 2:18 in this regard, as well as the golden calf incident in Exodus (32:2–4, 24; cf. Saebø 1969: 80–81). Torrey also refers to a practice, believed to have existed in the Persian period at the time of Darius I, in which metal was melted down and stored in earthen jars, which would then be broken when the metal was needed (so Herodotus 111.96). If such a practice underlies the use of *yôṣēr* as "metalworker" rather than "potter," it would refer to a Persian-period artisan or official, attached to the Temple, who had charge of collected metal melted down and then later reshaped for other purposes.

It is difficult to know whether Torrey's suggestion, which seems in a different way to give a reading similar to that of Saebø, is valid; that is, both scholars, but for different reasons, claim that metalwork is involved in the appearance of the unexpected *yôṣēr*. Although their suggestions are ingenious, they may be unnecessarily complicated and contorted. Thus we prefer to emend the text, assuming scribal error, as do some versions. We also mention here the widely accepted suggestion (Mitchell [1912: 313] lists more than five works holding to such a view) that the original reading was *hayôṣār*, an Aramaism for *haᵓôṣār*.

At this point the New Testament allusion to this verse deserves mention. In Matt 27:3–10, the chief priests apparently reject "the thirty pieces of silver" returned by Judas for "the treasury." Judas responds by "throwing down" the pieces of silver in the "Temple" and then committing suicide. Thereupon the priests decide that the silver should not go into the Temple treasury and instead use it to buy the "potter's field" for the burial of foreigners. The Gospel attributes this story to the fulfillment of Jeremiah's prophecy (Matt 27:9), although some traditions name Isaiah and some name Zechariah. Clearly, Zechariah is to be preferred, given the many points of contact between elements of the Matthew passage and Zech 11:13. What is of interest in the problem of *yôṣēr* is that the Matthew story assumes that both "potter" and "treasury" are part of the Zecharianic account. Again, a combined or double meaning seems to lie behind the Gospel. Also of note is the negative aspect of the Matthew story. The tendency of many modern commentators to see the prophet's casting down of the silver in Second Zechariah as a contemptuous deed may be the result of a subconscious influence of the well-known acts of Judas.

What should not be overlooked in this discussion of *yôṣēr* is that the prophet's action involves making a contribution to the Temple. In addition to the obvious and large-scale collection of offerings-in-kind, monetary funds were also brought to the Temple. The term *ᵓôṣār* is used with *bêt* ("house") in Neh 10:39 (cf. Dan 1:2) in reference to the Temple treasury (i.e., storerooms). In addition, *ᵓôṣār* alone is well attested as a designation for the Temple stores, particularly where silver and gold, as well as bronze items, were kept (e.g., 1 Kgs 7:51; 15:18[2]; 1 Chron 9:26; 26:20[2], 22, 24, 26, etc.). Such texts are among the many indications that the Temple should not be viewed narrowly as a religious institution. Much recent social scientific discussion of the Israelite Temple shows it to have played highly significant political and economic roles in national life, as did ancient Near Eastern temples in general (see, e.g., C. L. Meyers 1983a, 1987, 1992; Lipiński 1979; Lundquist 1984).

this worthy sum. Here the prophet resumes speaking, with a parenthetical statement about the "it" that Yahweh tells him to cast into the treasury. In adding this statement, he apparently wants to emphasize that his services had been adjudged as worth the thirty pieces of silver.

The phrase "this worthy sum," in the Hebrew, is unusual. It consists of two elements. The first is the word represented by "worthy": *ᵓeder*, or "glory, magnificence," which is to be related to "mighty ones" and "wealth" in 11:2 and 3 above (see NOTES to those terms) and also to "hairy mantle" in 13:4 (see NOTE below). As a segholate noun, *ᵓeder* is probably unique, unless we accept the MT of Mic 2:8 as original, instead of emending it to *ᵓaderet* as do BDB and BHS. Moreover, the use of the genitive of the noun instead of the corresponding adjective is atypical. The second word is *yĕqār*, which means "price, cost, preciousness." The two terms together provide *ᵓeder hayĕqār*, a combination that can be compared to the "holy land" of Zech 2:16 [*NRSV* 2:12] and "City of Truth" and "Holy Mountain" at Zech 8:3.

Commentators and translators offer "princely sum" or "noble sum," among other suggestions. Like the "worthy sum" of our translation, the implication is that the wages paid to the prophet were more than adequate, "thirty pieces of silver" (see above, NOTE in this verse) apparently being more than a respectable amount. Although the munificence of the payment is important here, so too is the very fact of remuneration awarded to a true prophet. Such an apparent departure from what we know about the nonprofessionalism of Yahweh's true spokespersons constitutes yet another example of the reversal of accepted or conventional language or actions that characterize the shepherd narrative (see various NOTES to 11:4ff.). Thus the mention of a "worthy sum" is not meant to be sarcastic in itself but rather to contribute to the overall reversal and, hence, rhetorical irony of this chapter.

at which I was valued. The MT has the first person, *yāqartî*; the prophet has resumed speaking. The root *yqr*, "to be precious, valued" is the same as that used to describe the sum of money to be paid the prophet (see previous NOTE) and thus provides an effective play on words, thereby calling greater attention to the fact that the people are evaluating and paying a prophet.

by them. The antecedent, as for "to them" in verse 12, is the group watching over the prophet: the merchants of the flock, i.e., the leaders.

thirty pieces of silver. See above, the NOTE in verse 12.

I cast it. That is, the prophet took the wage of "thirty pieces of silver" and deposited it in the "treasury." The root *šlk* (see above, NOTE to "Cast it") in the Hiphil does not have the pejorative sense usually assigned to it by commentators (see above, NOTE to "into the treasury" in this verse for an exploration of how the negative reading of the prophet's act may have arisen).

into the treasury, at the House of Yahweh. We have already expanded on the question of *yôṣēr* ("potter") at the beginning of this verse (see NOTE to "into the treasury"); we explain there why we have decided to emend the MT in both instances in this verse to *ʾôṣār*. Here the Hebrew text, which attaches the phrase "House of Yahweh" to it, reinforces our decision to emend to "treasury." The four words together read like a formal title: *bêt yhwh ʾel-haʾôṣār*, literally, "the House of Yahweh at the treasury." The importance of this alignment of *ʾôṣār* with "Temple" ("House of Yahweh") cannot be overstated.

The designation "House of Yahweh" is the normal Hebrew expression for the Temple in Jerusalem (see Meyers and Meyers 1987: 21–23 and 40). Although the Temple was a cultic institution in which God's presence was believed to have resided, and in which sacrifices were presented, its function was far broader. As we indicate in the first NOTE to "treasury," near the beginning of verse 13, the Temple in Israel and in the ancient Near East was also intimately connected to the formation and administration of the state. In First Temple times, palace and temple together constituted the administrative core of the realm. In postexilic times, with a monarchy no longer in existence, the administrative importance of the House of Yahweh, if anything, increased. The prophets Haggai and First

Zechariah are concerned with the consequences of such a change in circumstances, which augmented the political and economic function of the Temple. Priestly revenues in kind replaced royal revenues in producing national stockpiles. The Second Temple therefore constituted the necessary central administrative institution in Judean society. It provided a framework for the Yehudites to deal with their kinfolk in diaspora lands and to interact with the Persian royal authorities who had permitted the Temple to be rebuilt and had even allotted funds for that purpose.

Thus it is not at all unexpected to have this text linking the treasury and the Temple. Moreover, in view of the absence of kingship, it is not surprising to find the prophet himself performing a symbolic act at or near the Temple. Although the decline in prophecy in the postexilic period has been attributed, among other reasons, to the fact that the postexilic prophets were too closely associated with the Temple establishment (P. D. Hanson 1975: 12–16 and passim), Second Zechariah's presence here at the Temple can hardly be construed as compromising prophetic standards of justice, truth, and cultic obligation. Furthermore, in carrying out his symbolic act in this sacred locale, Second Zechariah stands in the tradition of many of his prophetic precursors, whose words and deeds took place in the Temple or in its vicinity (e.g., Jer 7:2; 20:2ff.; 24:1ff.; 26:2ff.; 28:5; 35:2–4; Amos 7:13; Isaiah 6; cf. Ezekiel 40–48).

14. *Then I severed.* See above, in verse 10, the NOTE to "severed." The *waw* consecutive with the verb *gd⁽*, as with "took" in verse 10, continues the prophetic action involving two staffs initiated in verse 7. The prophetic action involving the staffs is thus interspersed in the shepherd narrative in verses 7 through 14. Some critics would see the interruption in the "staffs" narrative as an indication of later insertion. However, we have suggested (see NOTE to "severed" and COMMENT) that the accounts of the various prophetic acts are intentionally interwoven to provide a complex fabric of metaphor and so address the profound concerns of the prophet's people about their past history as it impinges on the veracity of what he sees as the prospects for the future (as related in chapters 9 and 10 and then in chapters 13–16).

my second staff, Bonds. See the NOTES to "two staffs" and "Bonds" in verse 7 and the first NOTE in verse 10. Again we emphasize that the possessive pronoun "my" contributes to the sense of the prophet's intimate connection with what God has done as symbolized by what he is doing with the staffs, each in its turn.

to break. See the NOTE to this word in verse 10.

kinship. The Hebrew noun ʾaḥăwâ is a hapax legomenon that is clearly an abstraction based on the kinship term ʾāḥ, "brother." In many instances the meaning of ʾāḥ can be broader than simply "a person's blood brother": it can denote someone from the same country or group, a kinsperson, a companion (Ringgren 1974a: 188, 190). In such cases it is not gender-specific to males. Consequently, in this text in which the Bonds are broken between two nations, each of which contains a population of both males and females, it seems better to use the gender-neutral and entirely appropriate term "kinship" rather than the usual "brotherhood" (*NJPS, NEB, RSV, JB*; but cf. *NRSV*, "family ties").

The breaking of "kinship" serves as an explanation for the prophet's symbolic act of severing his second staff, which he had named "Bonds." The kinship to which this refers is, as the following phrase "between Judah and Israel" (see next NOTE) makes clear, the historical and original national unity among all the Israelite tribal groups. Thus the breaking of the close ties between the groups that formed the United Kingdom in the days of Solomon and David can refer only to the traumatic breakup of that nation-state, with its imperial dimensions, into the two smaller and less powerful states, Judah and Israel.

between Judah and Israel. These two terms here denote the two kingdoms into which the United Monarchy of David and Solomon split many centuries earlier. Like other terms in chapters 9 and 10 (e.g., "Ephraim" and "Jerusalem" [= Judah], 9:10; "Judah" and "Ephraim," 9:13; "House of Judah" and "House of Joseph," 10:6), these two geopolitical terms are grounded in the understanding of all Israel as a kinship-based unity consisting of the twelve tribes that were formed from the eponymous ancestry of the twelve sons of Jacob. Thus the representation of the division of the United Monarchy into the Northern (Israel) and Southern (Judah) Kingdoms is appropriately expressed by the idea that the "kinship" (see previous NOTE) uniting all the tribal groups was thereby severed.

Many centuries after the breakup of the Davidic kingdom, that event continues to represent one of the major traumas in Israel's historical consciousness. In the formation of the great historical record of Israel and Judah that constitutes the Books of Samuel, Kings, and Chronicles, the less than a century of the United Monarchy's existence is given disproportionate attention; significantly more historiographic material is included in these works for the 98 years of Saul, David, and Solomon than for the 200 (Israel) and 335 (Judah) years of the separate kingdoms—eighty-seven chapters as opposed to sixty-three chapters. This kind of difference, appearing in work achieving its final form in the exilic and postexilic periods, signifies that the first century of Israelite existence as a nation-state was viewed retrospectively as the ideal. Hence prophetic eschatology of these periods, which looks ahead to the reestablishment of Davidic rule, simultaneously views the monarchic renewal as involving *all* Israel, north and south. Consequently, if this chapter of Second Zechariah represents a retrospective view of what led to the disruption and dispersal that will come to an end in the glorious future, the two major events that constitute the national trauma are the breaking of the covenant, which is how the events of the sixth century are conceived (see NOTES to v 10), and the breaking of the United Monarchy at the end of the tenth century.

15. *Then Yahweh said to me.* This formula is identical to that which begins verse 13, and it is similar in form and function to the formula that opens verse 4 (see NOTES above). In each instance Yahweh's words to the prophet concern a symbolic action that the prophet is instructed to perform. In the present instance, the donning of "the gear a foolish shepherd" is the mandated action. However,

in this case—unlike the two previous ones—the formula and directives are not followed by a description of the prophetic response (see COMMENT).

These three formulaic introductions to God's directives are interspersed in the narrative of verses 4–16, which is preceded by a poetic introduction (vv 1–3) and followed by a poetic conclusion (v 17), which form an inclusio to the entire shepherd narrative of the chapter.

Again. The Hebrew ʿôd introduces Yahweh's final directive to the prophet. In expressing continuance, it serves to connect the series of prophetic actions of this chapter.

take for yourself. The verb is the imperative of lqḥ ("to take") followed by l ("to") plus the second-person pronominal suffix. Because an accusative ("gear") follows, the l plus pronoun serves as a dative.

gear. The word kĕlî, indicating "garb" or special clothing, is unusual in that it normally means "article," "utensil," or "vessel." It can, however, refer to clothing as it does in the stipulation about cross-dressing in Deut 22:5, where a woman is constrained from wearing a man's garment (kĕlî-geber) and a man from wearing women's apparel (śimlat ʾiššâ). Similarly, the Levitical discussion of contaminated clothing repeatedly refers to garments made of skin as kĕlî-ʿôr (Lev 13:49, 52–59).

This use of kĕlî to indicate the clothing of the shepherd is thus in keeping with other biblical texts. It also is appropriate in that it anticipates another reference to the shepherd's clothing—the "hairy mantle" of 13:4 (see NOTE below). Thus it does not seem necessary to accept, as do many commentators, the readings of some of the ancient versions, which understood "gear" differently. The Greek, Latin, and Syriac all read a plural for kĕlî, no doubt understanding it to refer to a shepherd's implements, such as a pouch, staff, and pipe (see 1 Sam 17:40; Judg 5:16).

Our translation, "gear," is intended to be inclusive, inasmuch as that English word can denote both clothing and equipment. If the "worthless shepherd" using this "gear" is indeed meant to represent false prophets (see next NOTE), then this word might represent clothing that was somehow associated with guilds of professional prophets. That such people wore distinctive dress is nowhere directly indicated, although it is not impossible, because in the ancient world clothing in general, or certain items thereof, often signified rank, status, or occupation. Indeed, the "mantle" associated with Elijah and Elisha may be a reference to a certain garment associated with prophets. At the same time, if this is referring to false prophets, it may denote the mantic devices used in at least some aspects of professional prophecy. Still, considering the fact that this term appears as part of God's instruction to carry out a symbolic action, it may not specify anything at all about prophetic garb or equipment but may simply denote shepherd's apparel. That is, God is telling the prophet to take up the gear of a shepherd, one who happens to represent shepherds who do not act responsibly toward their flocks. Thus the term would convey the shepherd imagery at its literal, rather than symbolic, level.

a foolish shepherd. With this phrase the shepherd imagery of chapter 11 is resumed and is sustained through the rest of the narrative (in v 16) and in the oracular conclusion (v 17), where the shepherd is called "worthless" (see NOTE below). The overall perspective continues the retrospective view that characterizes the whole shepherd narrative in that it mocks the destructiveness of bad leadership, including the false prophets of past generations, whose actions are viewed as having served personal self-interest rather than Yahweh's will. In this sense, the retrospective aspect no doubt emerges from the prophet's own self-consciousness as a spokesperson for God whose words are in conflict with other prophetic voices of his own day (cf. above, NOTE to "the three shepherds" in v 8). It also merges into the future-oriented portrayal of the shepherd of verse 16 (see next NOTE), where his deeds are the opposite of what a true prophet of Yahweh would do. This final symbolic action, therefore, involves giving dramatic visibility to the object of the divine critique of verse 16.

The adjective "foolish," from the noun *ĕwîl* ("fool"), is part of the Bible's wisdom vocabulary; it refers to behavior that is contrary to and the opposite of "wise" behavior (e.g., Prov 1:7; 14:29; 24:9). However, it also occurs several times in biblical prophecy. Perhaps the most significant of the prophetic usages is found in Hos 9:7, which apparently quotes Israelites as saying "the prophet is a fool" and a madman. The text of Hosea is difficult but seems to consist of mockery, in which the people refuse to heed the true prophet, calling him a fool. The meaning of "fool" in reference to prophecy is further comprehensible in light of Jer 4:22, in which foolish people are those who do not know Yahweh and consequently perform evil deeds. Both those texts help us understand the irony involved in Second Zechariah's use of the term to denote a shepherd who is the opposite of what one should be: he does not know Yahweh and hence his deeds are evil. Exactly such is the behavior of prophets who speak only their own thoughts and not those of God—their deeds too are reprehensible, as verse 16 demonstrates in considerable detail (see NOTES below).

16. *For I will indeed raise up.* Yahweh's final words to the prophet are introduced by *kî* ("for") plus the Hiphil participle of *qwm* plus *hinnēh* ("behold, indeed"). This announcement formula, which is nearly identical to that in First Zechariah concerning the expected Davidic scion (3:8) and to the one above in verse 6 (see first NOTE to that verse), indicates something that is about to happen. The negative aspects of the shepherd to be raised up are anticipated by the image of the "foolish shepherd" of the previous verse (see NOTE above), by the catalog of negative characteristics that complete this verse, and by the oracle concerning the "worthless shepherd" in the next verse (see NOTE below). The identity of this shepherd is linked with the shepherd imagery that dominates this chapter, expresses the bad leadership of the past, and reflects the tension between true and false prophets, which must surely derive from the prophet's own experience. It underlies his retrospective view of traumatic experiences in Israel's history (see previous NOTE and NOTE to "the three shepherds" in v 8), and it inevitably affects its anticipation of the future. The nonlegitimate prophets with whom he must have been struggling, in his mind if not also in reality, will

ultimately have to answer for their misuse of prophetic function, according to verse 17 and to 13:4–6.

Up to this point, the prophet has been reliving and reexpressing the struggles of his predecessors, such as Jeremiah and Ezekiel, with whom he identifies. Now, with the foolish shepherd, the prophet acts out and acknowledges his awareness of prophetic figures who abuse their roles in his own day. What is striking about the language here is that the pronouncement formula, used to proclaim what God is doing or is about to do, is coupled with the negative assessment of "foolish shepherd" as false prophecy. Perhaps this combination serves to authenticate Second Zechariah's struggle, making the prophetic figures of whom he is critical nonetheless part of God's plan, a plan that will ultimately result in the abolishment of such despicable individuals, according to verse 17 and 13:2–6 (cf. 10:3a).

a shepherd. The scholarly literature is preoccupied with relating this shepherd to historical figures. For most Jewish commentators, this shepherd is identified as Herod the Great, the wicked king who ruled Judah from 37–34 B.C.E. (Cohen 1948: 3, 7). Others have posited that Ptolemy IV, who came to power in 222 B.C.E., is represented by this figure (Mitchell 1912: 315). Similarly, various despised leaders in Jewish history, such as Alcimus the high priest of the early Maccabean era in 164 B.C.E., have been proposed as real figures represented by the shepherd.

Such suggestions ignore the way the shepherd imagery of this chapter (and of 10:3; see NOTE there to "the shepherds") represents prophetic as well as civil or royal leadership, and the retrospective nature of much of the shepherd narrative. As we have repeatedly pointed out in various NOTES to this chapter (see also COMMENT), much of the extraordinary difficulty that biblical scholars have experienced in dealing with this chapter arises from just such a tendency to link all its shepherd figures with real people and to think in terms of normal chronological sequence. Our approach differs from such traditional ones, and hence our understanding of "shepherd" eschews attempts to link this figure with a historical personage. Rather, the shepherd imagery extends the prophet's own self-consciousness, his sense of being part of an ongoing prophetic tradition— from past times, to the present, and into the future. That tradition inevitably involved struggles with prophets who did not know or heed Yahweh's word (see NOTES to the various uses of "shepherd," as a verb or noun, in vv 4, 5, 7, 8, 16, 17).

in the land. Although this phrase is not specific, it probably refers to the land of Israel, the inheritance of Yahweh's people.

he will not attend to . . . their hooves he will tear off. The structure of the remaining six clauses of this verse is carefully crafted in the Hebrew. Indeed, the Hebrew text gives the impression of a wisdomlike list of sayings depicting negative features. The form of these clauses has poetic characteristics, despite the high prose-particle count. The balance between the various parts is striking, and the consistency of syllable count (see following chart) has a rhythmic quality and can hardly be accidental. The vocabulary as well as the sentence structure, especially the parallelism, are not typical of ordinary prose. Furthermore, the absence of either the object marker *ʾet* or a preposition before the objects of the verb is an indication that this verse is highly stylized. The only prose indicator is the definite article; and of all prose indicators, this is the one most likely to occur in poetry, even early poetry such as the Song of Deborah and David's Lament. Although English translations of these clauses inevitably must begin with the verb, the Hebrew in each instance begins with the noun or noun substantive, which in three instances is the participle. In sum, these lines exhibit features of poetic language perhaps best characterized as prophetic discourse (see Andersen and Freedman 1980: 62). The structure of this passage is indicated in the following chart:

Clause		*Syllables*
1. *hannikḥādôt*	lōʾ-yipqōd	7
2. *hannaʿar*	lōʾ-yĕbaqqēš	6
3. *wĕhannišberet*	lōʾ yĕrappēʾ	8
4. *hanniṣṣābâ*	lōʾ yĕkalkēl	8
5. *ûbĕśar habbrîʾâ*	yōʾkal	9
6. *ûparsêhen*	yĕpārēq	7

Note that the first four clauses, which appear with the negative *lōʾ*, consist of two kinds of materials. Clauses 1 and 3 deal with the failure of the shepherd with respect to his responsibility to those of the flock who are in need, whereas clauses 2 and 4 concern the relationship between the shepherd and certain individuals, apparently leaders of the flock. These two themes alternate, telling us how such shepherds fail in their responsibility to the sheep (people), directly and indirectly, by not remonstrating against leaders who could, but do not, make a difference in society, and by not supporting those who can. The rhetorical effect of these four "no clauses" is heightened by the recurring *nun* as the first letter of the four objects of the verb. Then clauses 5 and 6 provide the climax, graphically presenting the way in which such a shepherd exploits his situation.

All the verbs in this sequence are imperfect (future), indicating that the despicable behavior is still happening. Yet the language is drawn from past indictments, notably by Ezekiel, and so the time frame should not be conceived of as limited to the future. We also note that all the substantives alluding to various elements of society are feminine, to sustain the sheep metaphor, inasmuch as "sheep" is a feminine noun.

To understand the function of these clauses, which list a series of despicable deeds on the part of the foolish shepherd, it is important to recognize that in tone and style these six clauses are strikingly similar to the six clauses in Ezek 34:16 that describe the ultimate purpose of the "good shepherd" or true prophet. The first four clauses in the Ezekiel passage all begin with the object marker *ʾet*; and they balance evenly in terms of syllable count, as the following chart indicates:

Clause		Syllables	Translation
ʾet-hāʾōbedet	ʾăbaqqēš	8	I will seek the lost,
wĕʾet-hanniddaḥat	ʾāšîb	8	and I will bring back the strayed ones,
wĕlaništbberet	ʾeḥĕbōš	8	and I will bind up those who are injured,
wĕʾet-haḥôlâ	ʾăḥazzēq	8	and I will strengthen the weak.

The remaining two clauses in Ezekiel 34 are similar in content to those in the Zechariah verse but are more complex in literary structure. Nonetheless, the overall marked similarity between the form and content of the two passages reinforces the idea that the Zechariah passage is modeled after Ezekiel, but with the opposite intent. Instead of depicting the qualities of the good shepherd, none other than Yahweh, Zech 11:16 presents the behavioral characteristics of the "foolish shepherd." The connection between Zech 11:16 and Ezekiel is evident in Ezek 34:4 as well as in 34:16. In 34:4, there is another listing—a negative one—of the outrageous behavior of the shepherds. The similarity in language to some of the words in the Zechariah catalog of misdeeds is noted below. Here it is sufficient to note the negative formulation of the listing. Zechariah, in drawing on the imagery of Ezekiel 34, is using the way his predecessor condemned earlier leadership—probably royal leadership, because the awful shepherds are ultimately to be replaced by a Davidide (34:23)—to lay out the horrendous behavior of the foolish shepherd, the prophet who speaks for himself and not for God (see NOTES to "a shepherd" in this verse and "a foolish shepherd" in the previous verse).

Those to be destroyed. This is a Niphal participle from the root *kḥd* ("to destroy"), which is found above—once in verse 8 and twice in verse 9 (see NOTES in these verses). The presence of the Niphal singular in verse 9 has led some commentators to read the singular here. However, the plural poses no problems. What is difficult is the change in how "those to be destroyed" are to be treated. In verses 8 and 9, the true shepherd, representing prophets of the past, acknowledges that God intends to destroy the corrupt society and thus goes along with the destruction. But here the failure to attend to those facing destruction is depicted as the deed of a foolish shepherd, a false prophet or other bad leader. The difference is that this indictment, which does not hold the view that all will again be destroyed, belongs to the eschatological future. Hence the flock, in trouble and "injured" (see NOTE below), will then be in need of succor from its shepherd; and the failure to give it will contribute to the condemnable nature of the foolish, worthless shepherd.

he will not attend to. The verb here is *pqd*, which is discussed at length in our NOTES to "I will attend to" and "has attended to" in 10:3. As we observed, the use of *ʾet* (the accusative marker) or the preposition *ʿal* ("concerning") with *pqd* affects its meaning—the former being positive and the latter negative. Neither of these particles is present here, given the poetrylike quality of this verse (see previous NOTE). The context here, however, makes it clear, inasmuch as it is being negated by *lōʾ* ("not"), that *pqd* is positive. The shepherd is accused of not doing what he is expected to do, namely, attend to or heed the needs of the flock.

the one who wanders. The MT has *na'ar*, which usually means "youth" or "young man." It occurs in Zech 2:8 [NRSV 2:4] with the meaning of "official" (Meyers and Meyers 1987: 153–54), and it may originally have designated young functionaries in the service of a priest (Eli [1 Sam 2:13, 15]) or prophet (Elisha [1 Kgs 18:43]). However, Ziba, *na'ar* to Saul (2 Sam 9:9–10), serves as custodian of Saul's property but is clearly not a young man (Avigad 1987: 205).

As straightforward as the Hebrew seems, it disrupts the parallelism of these four lines. The other three all deal with the failure of the metaphoric foolish shepherd to care for those for whom he is responsible, and it would be expected for this line to function in the same way. Furthermore, the absence of a participle here, if one keeps the MT, disrupts the pattern of the other three lines, because the preceding one and the two following all have participles. In addition, the verb here, *bqš* ("to seek"), which in the related Ezekiel passage is linked with "lost ones" (*h'bdt*), is a term quite different from "official." For all these reasons, an emendation seems justified.

One possibility is that the original text may have been a Niphal participle from the root *n'r*, "to shake," which would refer to those who are badly shaken up and thus in need of being sought so they can be helped. However, a better emendation (see Mitchell 1912: 319), one reflecting many manuscripts of the Greek and Syriac, restores a participle of *nw'*, "to wander." The idea of "the one who wanders" goes well with the verb "to seek"—"the one who wanders he will not seek." This emendation provides necessary coherence to the vocabulary of this line and to the general meaning of all the clauses of this passage.

The first participle is plural, but this and the next two are singular. The singular forms are probably meant to be inclusive and distributive, representing all in each category presented in the parallel lines of this section.

he will not seek. The Piel of *bqš* ("to seek") can mean "to make a request of" in a legal sense, as in Mal 2:7 (see Meyers and Meyers 1987: 55; E. M. Meyers 1983; cf. the use of *š'l* in Hag 2:11), or in terms of seeking God; it can also be used figuratively (cf. Zech 6:7; 12:9). But here it indicates seeking in a literal sense. Those being sought are those who have wandered off (see previous NOTE), as in the related verse in Ezekiel, where the "lost ones" are sought (Ezek 34:4).

the injured one he will not heal. One would normally expect the verb "to heal" (*rp'*) in the Piel to appear with the word "sick" (*ḥôleh*), as it does in Ezek 34:4, a verse that has influenced this one (see above, NOTE to "He will not attend to . . . their hooves he will tear off"). The word for "injured" here is *nišberet*, the Niphal participle of *šbr*, which occurs in Ezek 34:4 with the verb *ḥbš*, "to bind up." The same combination of *ḥbš* and *nišberet* occurs again in Ezek 34:16 (cf. Isa 61:1); but *ḥôleh* occurs there together with the Piel of the root *ḥzq*, i.e., "I will strengthen the sick." "To heal the injured" thus is a novel combination that draws from the language of the shepherd passage in Ezekiel 34, which has played an influential role in shaping this verse and this chapter.

the one who stands firm he will not sustain. Although this fourth clause is problematic, the meaning of the verb, the Pilpel *klkl*, is not in doubt. Probably derived from the root *kwl*, it means "to support, nourish" and is well attested (e.g., Gen 45:11; 50:21; 2 Sam 19:33, 34; 20:3; Neh 9:21).

The difficulty concerns the object of the verb and is evident in the variety of translations that have been proposed. The word rendered "the one who stands firm," *hanniṣṣābâ*, is the feminine singular Niphal participle of *nṣb*, which means "to stand, be stationed, stand up, be firm." This word apparently has a positive connotation and is taken that way by the versions. The Greek (*holoklēros*), along with the Syriac and Latin, reads "that which is whole," hence "healthy" (see NRSV and the discussion in Rudolph 1976: 203). In other words, the foolish will not only fail to deal with serious problems besetting the flock, as laid out in the first three clauses of this passage, but will also fail to maintain the good condition of those without problems.

All this having been said, we point out that the vagueness of the term has led others to emend. The NJB, for example, takes the root to be *ṣbh*, i.e., "to swell up," and translates "who will not support the swollen." Others propose *hannaḥălâ*, "the diseased," "the sickly" (e.g., NEB), or "the frail" (NJPS).

But. Taking the *waw* in an adversative sense, which is supported by the dropping of the negative particle *lōʾ*.

flesh. The word *bĕśar* ("flesh") echoes its earlier use in verse 9, and the meaning here is very similar. The graphic image of someone tearing apart and gluttonously consuming animal flesh here contributes to the prophet's estimation of the gross misuse of power.

the fatted he will devour. The Hebrew is absolutely clear in the use of the feminine singular, though many translations favor the plural under the influence of the Greek, which has "choice ones," apparently taking the root to be *brr* rather than *brʾ*. The adjective *bārîʾ*, meaning "fat" or "fatted," may refer to either cattle (Gen 41:2, 4, 5, 7, 18, 20; 1 Kgs 5:3 [NRSV 4:23]) or sheep, as here and in Ezek 34:3, 20.

To eat (*ʾkl*) the flesh of "the fatted," in view of the similar language in Ezekiel, indicates that the reprehensible prophet or leader is like the shepherds who prey upon the fat sheep of the flock, leaving nothing for the poor, having no time to heal the sick, etc. (Ezek 34:3–6). As a result, the flocks were scattered over the face of the earth (Ezek 34:6), only to be rescued by God, the true shepherd (Ezek 34:11). In the context of Second Zechariah's condemnation of false prophecy here and in chapter 13, this metaphor may attack a continuing problem of prophecy—the fact that false prophets took advantage of their flock, i.e., the people, taking fees and getting rich for speaking what pleased their clients rather than what was God's word—as well as the irresponsibility of corrupt political leaders.

This apparent meaning may be accompanied by one that is less visible to the modern reader. That is, there is evidence from Mari that certain prophetic actions involved the tearing asunder of a live sheep. In one such instance, the prophet ate (*akālum*) the raw flesh in view of the city elders and interpreted this vulgar performance through a wordplay: the *eating* of the flesh represents a pestilence (*ukultum*) that will appear in the land (see ARM 26.1–2 [1988]:

434ff., and the discussion in Malamat 1991). The Mari material seems relevant here in support of the idea that the "shepherd" of this chapter represents prophetic activity. In addition, the idea that eating a sheep's flesh may signal pestilence is interesting to consider in light of the emphasis on plague, which eats the victim's flesh, in chapter 14 (vv 12–15; cf. Num 17:10 [NRSV 16:45], in which God, as prelude to a plague, warns, "I will consume them," the verb being ʾkl, "to eat"; see also Num 11:1 and 25:11, in which "consume" [ʾkl], is used in reference to plague.)

their hooves. The noun *parsâ* ("hoof") is feminine and occurs here as a plural, *parsēhen*, because a herd animal obviously has four legs. The antecedent of the third-person feminine plural suffix is "fatted," a singular form but perhaps a collective. The meaning appears to be idiomatic, that is, "he will eat the flesh of the fatted one completely, leaving nothing over" (so Rudolph 1976: 203), a meaning that is supported by the Targum and Syriac. In other words, the greed of the shepherd is so great that he consumes virtually everything in sight, leaving no leftovers. There may also be a meaning related to symbolic actions; see the previous NOTE. The grisly image of eating raw flesh completes the six clauses that catalog intolerable behavior on the part of anyone with a responsibility toward others.

17. *Woe.* The Hebrew *hôy* is a common prophetic interjection, found in all of the three Major Prophets (Isaiah, Jeremiah, and Ezekiel) and in six of the Twelve Minor Prophets (see Meyers and Meyers 1987: 162–63). It is used once in the Former Prophets (1 Kgs 13:30), where it introduces a statement concerning a prophet. The expression is usually translated "woe!" or "alas!" although we have translated it "hey!" in Zech 2:10, where it does not seem to introduce a prophetic lament but rather to summon the attention of the exiles so that they might return to Zion. Normally, however, it introduces a lamentation, an oracle of doom, or an exhortation (Clifford 1966; Gerstenberger 1962; Janzen 1972; Zobel 1978). In such cases *hôy* is sometimes followed by a preposition and always by a noun. This standard construction identifies the group or classes of people to be alerted by the interjection. The statement then goes on to describe the action of the group that has been cited; it is usually an evil deed toward Yahweh that has occasioned the "woe" that will come upon the perpetrators of the deed.

"Woe" here opens a poetic conclusion to the whole of chapter 11, which begins with the introductory poetic oracle of verses 1–3. In literary form, the interjection pattern most closely resembles the use of "Hark" in 11:3 (see NOTE above), in which a single word is followed by a construct. The use of an interjection again here, also involving a shepherd as does 11:3, echoes the introductory verses and contributes to the way verses 1–3 and 17 serve to frame the shepherd narrative of verses 4–16.

It is probably not accidental that the sole use of *hôy*, other than in the Latter Prophets (Isaiah, Jeremiah, Ezekiel, and the Book of the Twelve [Minor Prophets]), occurs in the story of the confrontation between Jeroboam and the man of God at the altar at Bethel in 1 Kings 13. That complex narrative also involves the withering of a hand (1 Kgs 13:4-6; cf. "wither" below in this verse) and the fatal tension between the man of God, who is not labeled a prophet in the narrative, and an "old prophet" of Bethel (1 Kgs 13:11). The latter figure, who calls the man of God a prophet like himself is in fact a deceitful prophet; the result of his interaction with the man of God is that man's death—he is led to partake of food and drink, on his way home from Bethel, against God's command.

The similarity between the 1 Kings narrative and this woe oracle of 11:17 contributes to our understanding the shepherd metaphor. Throughout the narrative of 11:4–16, "shepherd" may represent "prophet" as well as other leaders, inasmuch as Second Zechariah is called upon to act the shepherd role. Second Zechariah is the good shepherd, i.e., true prophet, of verses 4–14; and the "foolish shepherd" of verses 15 and 16 is the "worthless shepherd" (see NOTE below), who is presented in language that echoes the story of the deceitful prophet of 1 Kings. In addition, the link between Second Zechariah and 1 Kings contributes to our assertion that Zechariah 11 has a dominant retrospective quality. Ezekiel is the only other prophet who exclaims, "Woe, O shepherds"; but he intends evil kings as the referent. However, Ezekiel does use the woe construction directly for false prophecy: "Woe to the senseless prophets" (cf. the "worthless shepherd" of Second Zechariah and next NOTE).

worthless shepherd. The difficult grammar of this expression and the following phrase, "the one who abandons the flock!" (see next NOTE) has caused much confusion. The *ḥireq yodh (î)* ending on "shepherd" is probably the sign of the obsolete genitive case ending, otherwise known as the *î compaginis* (cf. Gen 49:11; Deut 33:16; etc.), no longer understood by those who preserved the MT (GKC §90.3k[a]). Hence the *î* is not the first-person suffix here, or following the next noun, as so many claim (e.g., NRSV). Nor should it be emended to the plural construct as apparently the Greek does, i.e., "vain shepherds" or "worthless shepherds" *(rōʿē hāʾĕlîl)*. The use of the obsolete genitive case ending is unexpected because the word is in the nominative or vocative.

The term rendered "worthless" *(ʾĕlîl)* is a substantive that occurs in this form in the singular only here and in Isa 10:10 (cf. singular *ʾĕlîl* in Job 13:4 and perhaps Jer 14:14). In neither instance should the text be emended as is frequently suggested (Preuss 1974: 285). By analogy to "foolish shepherd" in verse 15 (see NOTE above), a common suggestion is to substitute *ʾawîlî* for *ʾĕlîl.* Rudolph (1976: 202; cf. GKC §128.w) contends that *ʾĕlîl* actually functions as a genitive substantive, so that "worthless shepherd" would literally read "shepherd of worthlessness."

This possibility merits serious consideration, for it accommodates the old case ending and suits the overall context of the woe oracle. The word *ʾĕlîl* in its plural usages always contrasts Yahweh's might and majesty with the powerlessness and emptiness of idols (Preuss 1974: 207). Thus its presence with respect to a shepherd (prophet) connotes the uselessness of such a shepherd (perhaps a false prophet; see previous NOTE) in comparison with a true prophet, who speaks the word of Yahweh. Such a "worthless shepherd" indeed deserves the "woe" directed to him.

the one who abandons the flock! As indicated in the previous NOTE, the *î* (*ḥireq yodh*) at the end of ʿ*zb* ("to leave, wander") is the *î compaginis*, the sign of an obsolete genitive case ending. The participle of the verb thus serves as a substantive, and with "flock" would read literally "the abandoner of the flock," in apposition to "worthless shepherd."

The image of a shepherd leaving his flock draws, as does much of this chapter, upon Ezekiel 34. Second Zechariah transforms the Ezekiel image by structuring it as a diatribe. Furthermore, Ezekiel perceived the scattering of the flock, that is, the dispersal of God's people, as the result of faulty royal leadership, because the overthrow of these terrible shepherds ultimately would involve the restoration of a Davidide (Ezek 34:23). Such imagery is surely present in Second Zechariah. At the same time, because he plays the role of shepherd, the imagery here may be extended to prophecy. The worthless shepherds are false prophets who habitually, in their self-centered behavior, fail to serve the people. In the past, and in the present of Second Zechariah's own day, false prophecy inhibited the speedy realization of God's will.

sword. The eschatological thrust begun in verse 16 (see NOTE to "For I will indeed raise up") finds its culmination in the predictive words setting forth the fate of the "worthless shepherd" (see NOTE above), who represents false prophecy. The use of "sword" introduces a note of violence to the ultimate removal of deceitful prophets, just as does the apostrophe to the "'sword'" called upon to slay the shepherd in 13:7 (see NOTE to "O sword").

The sword in this verse appears apart from any mention of who is wielding it. Because of this, and because of certain prophetic passages with a similar use of "sword" to bring about the destruction of any people interfering with God's plan for Israel (e.g., Jer 50:33–37; Ezek 21:8–17; 30:4; Hos 11:6), the sword can be none other than Yahweh's sword (cf. the phrase "sword of Yahweh," Jer 47:6; see also passages such as Amos 4:10; 9:1; Ezek 30:24; Zeph 2:12). Thus it is Yahweh who will ultimately put an end to false prophecy.

arm . . . right eye. These two body parts together symbolize the shepherd's autonomy, that is, his ability to do whatever it is that he does in the world. As a part of the body, the arm (Hebrew *zĕrôʿa*) is often used in the Bible metaphorically. Deriving originally from the warrior's use of his arm as the source of military might, "arm" stands for military power (e.g., Ezek 30:21) and, by extension, power in general, including physical power (e.g., Jer 17:5; Job 26:2).

"Eye" also has metaphoric value. By representing the ability to see and thus to know, it can indicate someone's mental and even spiritual faculties (e.g., Isa 44:18; 65:16). It is not surprising, therefore, that "eye" is part of many idiomatic expressions in Hebrew. "Right" is often coupled with a body part, notably the hand or arm as a way of indicating the most powerful or useful hand or arm (e.g., Ps 44:3) and thus emphasizing the strength of the one whose hand is mentioned. Like "arm," "eye" can also denote military prowess; cf. the "right eye" of 1 Sam 11:2, in which the people of Jabesh-Gilead were required by the

Ammonites to sacrifice their right eyes and thus provoke a rescue operation on the part of Saul (see a discussion of the Greek and Qumran expansion of this passage by McCarter 1980: 198–99). Thus the use of "eye" with "right" is a way of intensifying the idea of the mental qualities that "eye" represents as well as enhancing its connotation of power.

The presence of "eye" in this passage is just one other instance of Second Zechariah's use of a word that runs through First Zechariah, often in reference to that true prophet's visionary experience. See Zech 9:1, 8 and 12:4 (and NOTES to those verses).

Together, "arm" and "right eye" represent the shepherd's physical and mental abilities. Operating on both the literal and figurative levels, those terms stand for all that he can do in the world. Consequently, removing the use of arm and eye, which is what happens in this oracle, makes the shepherd powerless and unable to function.

will surely wither. The infinitive absolute of the verb appears here before the imperfect of the same verb (*ybš*, "to be dry, withered"). This double verbal form serves to intensify the verbal idea and is usually rendered in English, as here, by an adverb ("surely") that places extra emphasis on the verb; the classic biblical example of this arrangement is Gen 2:17, "You will surely die" *(môt tāmût).* The image of the withering arm expands the imagery above, the arm made powerless by the sword, just as the image of the blinded eye in the next clause continues the image of the eye put out by the sword in the previous line.

As we pointed out in our NOTE to "Woe" at the beginning of this verse, the notion of a hand withering up is to be related to the story of the "man of God" in 1 Kings 13. Indeed, although the verb "to wither" occurs often enough in reference to the drying up of nature (e.g., Isa 19:5; Amos 4:7; Jer 23:10), this passage and those in 1 Kings are the only ones in which an arm is said to wither. Such withering, whether of natural elements or of a person's extremity, is to be attributed to Yahweh's negative judgment. In this case, the worthless shepherd will be rendered ineffectual by Yahweh's action (see previous NOTE for a discussion of the figurative meaning of "arm").

his right eye. The placement of the pronominal suffix "his" after "right" rather than "eye" (*ʿên yĕmînô*), which has undoubtedly been influenced by the form of the same phrase in the previous line, causes no particular problem. For the meaning of this expression, see the NOTE above in this verse.

will surely go blind. As in "surely wither" in the preceding bicolon (see NOTE above), the infinitive absolute plus imperfect emphasizes the verbal idea. The root *khh* means "to grow dim" and is used in several other instances to refer to the loss of eyesight. Along with losing the use of his right arm, the "worthless shepherd" becomes blind, thereby becoming an essentially nonfunctioning individual (see NOTE above to "arm . . . right eye"). This graphic imagery represents Yahweh's inevitable intervention to render ineffectual the false prophets (see above, NOTE in this verse to "worthless shepherd") who have continually interfered with the role of true prophets. Second Zechariah's concern for the problem of false prophecy and his anticipation of its obliteration underlie chapter 11 (see COMMENT) and is addressed explicitly in chapter 13.

COMMENT

Long regarded by commentators as one of the most difficult passages in all of Hebrew Scripture, Zechariah 11 has an overall structure that is almost deceptively simple and straightforward. It opens with a poetic oracle (vv 1–3) bemoaning the destruction of certain forested areas; and it closes with another poetic oracle (v 17), a chant of woe for the shepherd who fails in his responsibilities. These oracles surround an extended prose passage, with verse 16 being a poetic transition to the concluding verse. They thereby frame the narrative of verses 4–16 with respect to the simplest matter of structure. In addition, the oracles provide the overall mood of the chapter, which is among the most gloomy and negative in Hebrew prophecy. They both also involve the presence of shepherd imagery, which is the dominant literary vehicle for the complex messages of the whole chapter.

Although the organization of the chapter is clear, the overall mood painfully visible, and the symbolic figures familiar enough, the underlying meaning of and motivation for Zechariah 11 pose seemingly insoluble difficulties. Indeed, the enormous variety of scholarly claims or interpretations signifies the problematic nature of the material; any number of thorny exegetical questions frustrate attempts to make sense of them.

Among the most prominent of these questions are the following:

Why, after the resoundingly hopeful mood of chapters 9 and 10, does this horrifying picture of strife and destruction present itself? Is it a later interpolation, unrelated to the preceding oracles?

What, or whom, does the shepherd (and shepherds) represent? If this is such a familiar biblical image, why is it so difficult to unravel?

What is the historical context for this gloomy depiction of strife and failed leadership? Or is that a legitimate question at all?

Does the narrative, mainly prose, of verses 4–16 constitute an example of any literary genre or genres, the identification of which will contribute to penetrating its message? Or does the very attempt to sort out literary types actually obscure the underlying meaning?

It would be presumptuous to claim that we can satisfactorily resolve all the issues represented by such questions. Nonetheless, as the reader who has negotiated at least some of the NOTES to this chapter will have discovered, our approach diverges fundamentally from that of virtually all the scholarship that has tackled Zechariah 11. We have been able to follow a different tack not because we have access to any new materials that were unavailable to our erudite predecessors. Rather, we have tended to examine these materials from a somewhat different angle of vision. In the series of questions above, except perhaps the first one, the second interrogative in each set of queries represents a fresh way of considering the material and has helped us to comprehend what has for so long mystified students of late biblical prophecy.

Opening Oracle: The Cry of Trees, Shepherds, and Lions, 11:1-3.

The three verses that constitute this poetic beginning to chapter 11 accomplish several important introductory tasks. For one thing, they provide a link with the preceding materials. The very mention of "Lebanon" echoes the presence of that toponym in 10:10, where Lebanon along with Gilead signify the relatively uninhabited territory that will be filled to overflowing in the great return of the exiles that chapters 9 and 10 anticipate. The low population of Lebanon is integrally related to its ecological characteristics—mountainous and densely wooded. Viewing Lebanon as, one day, being densely populated against great environmental odds thus serves well the eschatological thrust of the prophetic view. It also provides the imagery that opens chapter 11. Although the demographic surge is a concomitant of restoration, it will mean the end of the great forests of those areas. Consequently, it is those forests that are called upon to mourn.

The wailing of trees, and even of shepherds and lions, however, is in a sense a mockery of lament. Do trees really mourn each other? The destruction of the forests is in fact the creating of inhabitable land, a result that is the subject of rejoicing in the previous chapter. Thus, at least on a literal level, the fablelike specter of inanimate trees wailing at the demise of the forest creates a mood change. The hopeful tone of the preceding verses gives way now to cries of pain.

This bemoaning of loss is set forth in a series of poetic lines that convey reversals. The mightiest of all trees, the cedars, are destroyed (vv 1, 2); the lofty forest is "brought low" (v 2); the pasturage on which shepherds, since time immemorial, could rely is gone (v 3); and even the perennially luxuriant Jordan jungle is eradicated (v 3). This series of reversals, in addition to the negative mood of mourning, also anticipates what is to come in the shepherd narrative of verses 4-16, in which again and again the prophet reverses expectations or images in order to achieve his rhetorical purposes.

The question remains, however, with respect to the fablelike image of flora and fauna lamenting as if they were people, as to whether these figures represent something other than themselves. Do the trees, for example, as many have suggested, represent certain foreign leaders whose threatening presence is being destroyed? The idea of Assyria and Egypt becoming ineffectual, which appears at the end of chapter 10, understandably raises the possibility that such is the case, as does the presence of such representations in other biblical passages, such as Jotham's parable in Judges 9. In addition, this chapter is so thoroughly dominated by the use of symbolic language that it would be difficult to claim that all the shepherd language operates as metaphor whereas the tree figures are to be taken only literally.

To acknowledge the symbolic role of the trees, however, does not thereby necessitate assigning to them specific historical referents, either individuals or nation-states. Rather, the trees can be understood in terms of the hierarchical ordering that they present. The cedars are supreme; they are "mighty" (v 2), as are political entities or even Yahweh. The eschatological future thus involves the toppling of the world order—the empires that control the political scene at any given moment, past, present, or future. If the cedars fall, then lesser entities— cypress and oak—will inescapably be affected. The tree imagery thus has a double eschatological import: the deforestation of marginal territories to accommodate the restoration of Israel, and the destruction of political systems to accommodate the worldwide rule of Yahweh from Jerusalem. The threefold use of the word "destroyed" in verses 2–3 emphasizes devastation in a more inclusive way than do any of the military images interspersed through chapters 9 and 10.

Although the word for "destroy" *(šdd)* does not appear again in chapter 11, its multiple presence in verses 1–3 conceptually anticipates the repeated scenes of destruction in the narrative that follows. As for specific linkages of vocabulary between the introductory oracle and the succeeding sections of this chapter, the figure of the shepherd stands out. The word for "shepherd" *(rʿh)*, as both verb and noun, occurs repeatedly in the narrative of verses 4–16 and serves as the major image, from which a series of prophetic actions and interactions emanate; and the shepherd appears once more in the concluding poetic oracle of verse 17. The concept of shepherding and the figure of the shepherd together provide the unifying thread that holds together the entire chapter.

No one can doubt the centrality of shepherd/shepherding in verses 4–16 or question the focal role of the shepherd figure in verse 17. But what about its role in this introductory section? The shepherds who wail do not appear until the last of the three verses, and they certainly seem much less prominent than the arboreal imagery of the first two verses and, less directly, of the last bicolon of the second line of verse 3 (where "pride of the Jordan" refers to the thick undergrowth in the Rift Valley). Furthermore, the fablelike quality of these three verses means that the reader expects to meet animals or trees, not humans. Although the floral and faunal actors do not actually speak, nor is there a tale being told—both usual features of fables—there is an assigning of humanlike qualities to these nonhuman actors. The wailing of the various trees and the roaring of the lions imply human emotional response, and thus these verses can be said to partake of the dynamics of the fable.

In view of the quasi-fable nature of these verses, the appearance of shepherds is a disruption. It is vaguely out of character with the rest of the active images. Placed between trees and beast, the shepherds wail as do the trees and respond to "hark" as do the lions. In the movement of the oracle, they function as do nonhumans. Yet their identity as humans cannot be questioned; there is no textual or versional hint that some other animal might have once been placed where "shepherds" appears in verse 3. Consequently, this unexpected insertion of human actors must be purposeful: it introduces an image that, as we have already asserted, dominates all of Zechariah 11.

The Shepherd Narrative, 11:4–16.

This section begins in verse 4 with an apparently typical clause, such as is common in biblical prophecy to introduce a statement of Yahweh to the prophetic messenger; and the ensuing statement, or at least that part of it that appears in verse 4, seems clear enough. Yet neither of these two parts of verse 4 is as simple as it might seem at first glance; the complexity of each part is representative of the vexatious problems that have, virtually since the beginning of exegetical tradition in the early centuries C.E., beset those who have sought to fathom the message of this narrative.

The introductory clause, as we have explained in the NOTES, does in fact present a formulaic introduction to an oracular statement. Yet it does so in a doubly unique way—in the particular combination of divine names (Yahweh plus ʾĕlōhîm, "God") following "Thus spoke," and in the use of the first-person singular possessive suffix "my" with "God." These two departures from the conventional ways in which Yahweh's words are introduced call bold attention, at the very outset of the shepherd passage, to salient aspects of this narrative and of the prophet's role in the ensuing actions.

The combination of divine names heightens the authority of the person to whom Yahweh is speaking. Throughout the history of biblical prophecy, the understanding that a prophet's words came from a transcendent source, Yahweh, constituted the sine qua non of true prophetic speech. Although the dynamics of establishing such credibility remain somewhat elusive to us and probably varied over time and under different circumstances in biblical antiquity, there is no doubt that formulaic introduction to oracular speech served to authenticate the divine message. Whereas the use of pairs of divine names and/or epithets is indeed characteristic of the literary way in which prophecy is validated, this particular ordering is unparalleled. As a departure from conventional language while preserving the overall formulaic nature of the introduction, "Yahweh" plus "God" serves to signal the divine authority of the message. Similarly, "my God," although hardly a unique expression, appears nowhere else within the range of stereotypical phrases that introduce oracles.

Thus the first clause of verse 4 is both familiar and different. In a few simple words, the prophet here captures what in many ways is his essence—he stands in the tradition of biblical prophecy, perhaps more overtly than does any other prophet in his utilization of language, images, and themes of earlier biblical prophecy. Yet his appreciation of such aspects of his predecessors' literary productions is never a slavish borrowing. He imbues them with his own characteristic message, which emerges from his own existential predicament as a transmitter of the divine will to the world of humans.

By calling attention to the divine authority behind the statements to come, and by interposing "my" in the citing of the source of his message, the prophetic narrator reveals his heightened self-consciousness as a prophet. Because of these signals, both here and at scattered points below, the audience is alerted to a tension that runs through the ensuing narrative. Why must the prophet assert his special relationship with Yahweh in this manner? Why does he interject the personal into the oracular formula? Our understanding of this phenomenon is somewhat dependent on what is to come, both in this chapter and in chapter 13. Using those materials to come to illuminate this initial clause in turn helps us to follow the complexities ahead. This process of using cross-exegesis may appear circular; yet there are ample allusions in the text along the way to substantiate what emerges from such an endeavor—that the prophet was constantly struggling, either internally or in actual confrontations, to establish his credibility over against other prophetic figures to whom we shall refer by the Bible's own terminology for such problematic individuals—those who speak falsely in Yahweh's name (13:3; cf. Deut 13:2–6 [NRSV 13:4–5]; Ezekiel 13), i.e., false prophets. It is no accident that one of the earlier prophets upon whom Second Zechariah shows great dependence is Jeremiah, the very prophet whose materials are replete with the mention of opposition to or even confrontations with other so-called prophets (e.g., Jer 14:13–16; Jeremiah 23, which includes in vv 9–40 an extended series of oracles against prophets).

Whether Second Zechariah's struggle was an internal one, in which he scrutinized his own apostolic compulsion over against others he saw making such claims, or whether he actually experienced opposition from and publicly condemned others, cannot be determined from the evidence in the writings attributed to him or his followers. Nonetheless, the indubitable existence of such others in his own day, along with his consciousness of their presence in the past, together are the determining forces behind the shape and content of this narrative.

Thus, in considering the nature of verses 4–16, it is difficult to separate the literary form of the narrative from its content. Exploring aspects of its genre will provide entré into the materials and will mean dealing with its messages.

Many would call it an allegory (e.g., Childs 1979: 480; Caquot 1985), a designation not without merit in light of the way certain of the narrative principals—beasts, humans, inanimate objects—have a symbolic meaning, and what happens to them bears a message. Yet the label "allegory" does not allow for the way in which the oracular language ("Thus said Yahweh," "oracle of Yahweh," "Then Yahweh said," etc.) is intrinsic to the narrative; nor does it acknowledge the fact that the narrator = prophet = shepherd is interwoven into the accounting of the symbolic events as well as into the actual performance of those events. These two features of the narrative provide a complexity that the typology of allegory cannot accommodate. In addition, the symbolic value of the characters and the actions are unevenly revealed: some are directly named and hence indirectly interpreted, such as the two staffs of verses 7, 10, and 14; but the identity of others, including the central figures, the shepherd/shepherds, is frustratingly obscure without recourse to the context of the entire prophetic work (Zechariah 9–14).

Another common interpretative strategy calls this section a parable (e.g., Mitchell 1912: 303; Dentan 1956). Its adherents tend to be using the modern notion of what a parable is rather than the biblical tradition, in which "parable" is more accurately understood by the wider term "metaphor" (Crossan 1985: 747). If a parable is thus a very short story with double meaning, the fact that it has double meaning—a literal as well as a symbolic one—is the only characteristic of a parable truly exhibited by this passage. The brevity of the passage as a whole cannot be maintained, nor can its narrativity in a technical sense. It is too fragmented for such categories; that is, it contains too many subunits, or, better, interwoven components. Although one could perhaps label one of the subunits a parable, those parts of the whole do not stand alone—they are interlocking pieces of the whole passage. Thus, calling the whole a parable precludes acknowledging its diverse elements and imposes the concept of a brief tale upon a complex narrative; and calling it a series of parables would not account for the intricate way in which each part bears its own message, but only in the context of its being integrated into or determining the thrust of other segments of the narrative.

The suggestion (e.g., P. D. Hanson 1975: 337–41) that it is a commissioning narrative, or, rather, two of them if verses 15–16 are considered a subsequent such commission, is useful in relating the materials of verses 4–16 to similar calls (e.g., Jer 27:2; Isa 20:2; Ezek 24:16) by Yahweh instructing prophets to take some sort of action. This passage surely involves such calls, and the actions evoked have the requisite double meanings. Yet not all of the actions of verses 4–16 are evoked by divine commission; hence to call it that means to oversimplify the complexity of language and image. This category, like the others, has merit, notably in calling attention to the symbolism of word, deed, character, or object; but it does not capture the overweaving and interweaving of the component parts.

If none of these designations is fully satisfactory, can any others be more successfully applied? Those who have worked through some of our NOTES will have come across several terms we have used in dealing with this material. In the NOTES and in this very discussion the term "narrative" is used to refer to the largely prose material that constitutes these thirteen verses. The word may indicate a special kind of prose, with a succession of events being communicated to an audience (Longman 1987: 76), and in that sense the contents of verses 4–16 surely are narrative materials. Even that understanding may be too narrow, however, since the succession of events ought perhaps to be linked in a way that those of this passage are not. Rather, the word "narrative" is used in the NOTES and in this discussion in as loose a way as possible. It indicates a discrete passage that has some sort of theme or thread running through it and which, in addition to its purely formal separation as prose from what precedes and follows it, is distinct from the surrounding materials by having its own particular focus. By labeling it "shepherd narrative," the word "shepherd" supplies the identifying focus, the motif whereby its surface as well as deep meanings are conveyed.

Another designation figures in our discussion in the NOTES, viz., symbolic action, or prophetic action, or even symbolic prophetic action. These expressions denote the subunits alluded to in the preceding discussion of "commissioning narrative." They designate what the prophet does, or says he does (see below), so as to convey an abstract message that is signified by a physical activity. These terms are used not so much to indicate a formal literary type, because the patterning or organization of the series of actions is hardly regular or consistent, either internally in this narrative or in relation to other examples of prophetic symbolic action. Rather, they should be taken at their most literal level: they depict something that a prophet does in order to provide a message other than what is involved in what is done, i.e., to use the principle of partial similarity to communicate an abstract idea.

Prophetic symbolic actions are, in a sense, pragmatic metaphors. They rely on the comparative value of one activity, which is easily visualized and grasped, in making another one comprehensible. The persistently symbolic nature of the interlocking characters, objects, and deeds of verses 4–16 is both the key to their richness and the cause of their obscurity. Metaphors are not explained. They rely on the audience's frame of reference being reasonably congruent with that of the author. The drawing of an interpretive meaning is inextricably related to the social and historical context of interpretation (Ricoeur 1977). The inherent vagueness of symbolic language is what makes it succeed in leading to the recognition of what it signifies, for it requires processing by the reader and thus provides a sense of accomplishment when the connections are made. But if the designing author's mind and creative energies are too divergent from those of the audience, the association may be troublesomely imperfect.

One further literary strategy recurs throughout the narrative and deserves special mention. The prophet again and again uses irony to convey his message. If irony implies double-edged meaning—that things are not what they seem to be, or that conventional words are made to have an opposite effect—then the prophet exploits such rhetoric in manifold ways in verses 4–16. He does so through the irony of language, as we point out in our NOTES along the way. And he does so through the dramatic irony involved in the symbolic prophetic actions. The prophet is an actor in a scene being observed by an audience, whether real people witnessing the prophet or the literary audience of the narrative's readership/listenership. Either audience has the necessary distance from the action to appreciate its twists. We know, for example, that Second Zechariah is the true prophet. Yet he accepts a wage; hence we cannot help feeling astonishment and shock, such emotions heightening our interest in trying to understand this reversal and alerting us to possible resolutions and their meaning.

To extract several salient points from the discussion thus far, let us emphasize the following: (1) the inapplicability of commonly used genre categories, and thus the fluidity of genre (rather than rejecting all such categories, we learn from each of them some critical aspects of the material); (2) the overarching symbolic qualities of all the subunits and features of the narrative; and (3) the double-edged aspect of rhetorical strategies as well as of symbolic features. All of these factors operating simultaneously contribute to the extraordinary complexity of the shepherd narrative.

In making sense of a narrative with such complex features, the concept of composite artistry (Alter 1981: 131–54) is helpful. Although it may disrupt contemporary notions of logical coherence, a text such as this has its own properties and its own purposes. It is helpful to consider it something of a montage of actions and images, of deeds and doers. Indeed, such complex texts, as contemporary analysts of biblical literature are discovering, need not be a patchwork of different authorial hands and epochs but may in their very complexity convey an essential message. Our hesitancy to accept traditional suggestions of glosses, interpolations, duplications, and emendations thus stems not only from respect for the MT but also from acknowledgment of the fact that complex literary structures from a world so separated from ours in time, language, and social organization may well speak with a logic at times different from ours.

Perhaps the matter of chronological ordering gives us the most difficulty in penetrating a complex text, which can violate our most instinctive Western sense of how a narrative should proceed and what the signals of sequence might be. For this particular narrative, it is our contention that it defies our contemporary chronological expectations. The almost universal scholarly assumption about this passage is that the various symbolic actions of the shepherd are for the most part not eschatological or future oriented but, rather, are historical, that is, symbolic allusions to political events of the prophet's lifetime—hence the profusion of suggestions about who the referents are. The profusion in itself indicates that this approach may be wrongheaded. We reject the notion of explicit political referents to events of the prophet's day, but we also do not believe the narrative to be completely future oriented. Instead, as various of the NOTES have indicated, this narrative derives its creative momentum from the prophet's looking to the past in light of his present.

This judgment derives from several features. The first involves some characteristics of the narrative that have already been mentioned, namely, the prophet's sensitivity to the tension between true and false prophecy, a tension he undoubtedly experienced and sought to deal with in terms of his sensitivity to what his influential predecessors had themselves experienced. That is, the author's acute prophetic self-understanding within the tradition of Hebraic apostolic prophecy involves a looking back and is visible in his repeated adaptation of earlier prophetic language and imagery, especially those of Ezekiel and Jeremiah.

The second feature involves the larger context of chapter 11, coming as it does after the overwhelmingly positive tone of chapters 9 and 10. However, the abrupt shift in mood need not be taken as a sign of disjunction; rather, it is a key to the symbolic meaning of the various prophetic actions of chapter 11. Let us try to recapture the predicament of the prophet's audience of Yehudites and/or exiles upon hearing, generations after the dispersal and destruction, that (1) Israel and Judah will come together and (2) the greater land of Israel will be populated to the full and beyond. The necessity for these two aspects of restoration to be effected stems from the essence of biblical religion involving a people covenanted with God to establish autonomous existence in a physical locale. Neither of these conditions obtains in the prophet's day. Why is that so?

If his audience is to find compelling his projection of the future, it will have to be reminded of the reason that such a future of restoration and reunification should be expected.

The shepherd narrative provides just such an explanation with its retrospective view. Because the prophet identifies so strongly with his predecessors, he hears Yahweh's instructions to them as being also to him: to "shepherd the flock to be slaughtered" (v 4b) is to be a prophet to a hopelessly corrupt society, where, no matter what a leader might do or say, the inevitable culmination of the wrongful deeds of too many is the ruin of all (see especially vv 5, 6, 7, 9). The repetitious language of destruction is the recounting of God's allowing the people to be conquered and scattered because of their evil ways. Its horrifying detail, of people tearing at each other, conveys the simple yet salient fact that Yahweh has empowered the nations to terminate both Israel and Judah because of their internal flaws in disobeying the covenant.

The third feature involves the one symbolic action for which no leaps of interpretive ingenuity are necessary. The message of the two staffs (vv 7, 10, 14) pertains to the historical schism between north and south and to the breaking of the Mosaic covenant implicit in the fact of destruction and exile. The text itself supplies the explanation, but critics have been unwilling to see these two pivotal events of Israelite history as underlying the tone of gloom throughout this narrative. Yet the very way the staff symbolism is spread out in the narrative, penetrating the shepherding action of verses 4–8 and surrounding the treasury incident of verses 11–13, constitutes a structural involvement with those two other symbolic actions that is the key to its conceptual involvement, i.e., recapitulating past horrors that have led to the need for restoration. Only the last of the symbolic actions, regarding the foolish shepherd of verses 15–16, stands outside this structure. But this is rightly so, because those verses move out of the past and into the prophet's present struggles in witnessing the continued presence of poor leaders and false prophets. The existence of such figures in the past prevented God's true prophets from averting disaster; the prophets of Yahweh had no choice but to acknowledge impending doom while the false prophets with less troublesome messages were acclaimed.

To recapitulate briefly, chapters 9 and 10 proclaim a positive future, and chapter 11 explains why such a vision is necessary. In so doing, the expected chronological ordering of past-present-future is violated. However, such reordering in fact is not atypical of biblical thinking, especially in preexilic prophecy. Insofar as prophecy sees the future in terms of present conditions and in light of past events, it is no wonder that this sense of the connectedness of events far removed from each other in chronology can often mean the bringing together of such events in a text in accord with the prophet's train of thought—in which all these forces merge—rather than in accord with historical sequence. The effect, in this particular case in Second Zechariah 9–11, is not unlike that of Tom Stoppard's play *Artist Descending a Staircase*, in which the first scene depicts the present life and struggle of an elderly artist and subsequent scenes depict him at earlier stages in life, thereby illuminating and explaining how the dynamics of life in the older years are inextricably linked to features of the younger years. The analogy of medieval drama, which also reorders historical chronology, may likewise be useful.

Much of the preceding discussion of verses 4–16 has involved recognizing that the passage is a complex one, certainly in its reordering of the time sequence with respect to the preceding text, and in terms of its literary structure. At this point, the character of the shepherd narrative as a composition involving a series of symbolic actions deserves specific attention. We have already referred to these actions, but now we list them to show more explicitly how they achieve the quality of montage in forming a whole while yet remaining distinct:

Action	Verses	Yahweh Comments*	Prophet Acts*
Shepherd the flock	4–6, 7	X	XXX
Taking and breaking staffs	7, 10, 14	—	X
Wages cast to the Temple	11–13	X	X
Wearing gear of foolish shepherd	15–16	X	—

*The Xs in these two columns indicate that Yahweh commissions the action, and whether the prophet carries it out.

The overlapping of the first three subunits is clear from the verse listing of this chart; only the fourth stands somewhat apart, as befitting its distinct chronological orientation. The actions do not conform to the pattern of all being commissioned by Yahweh and all eliciting a response. Yet there is balance in that only one action is not commanded, and only one lacks the description of a response. This pattern epitomizes the prophet's agonizing predicament. On one hand, he is bound to respond to Yahweh's word, and hence he is an extension of the divine will (recall the unique connection between Yahweh and the prophet in the introductory formula of v 4). Yet, on the other hand, he is an autonomous being, initiating behavior which he nonetheless sees as consonant with God's will (recall what the first NOTE in v 10 and second NOTE in v 14 point out about the unusual use of "my" before the two staffs as an indication of the prophet's identifying with the God-given nation and covenant that the staffs represent).

This juxtaposition of actions, actors, beasts, and objects, and the harsh picture of the past couched in language making it seem current, create a complexity to which the modern reader is unaccustomed, except perhaps in certain works of fiction (as by Faulkner or Joyce) that have a reputation of being notoriously complicated and thus difficult for the average reader to understand. But the fact that our mental processes have been conditioned to respond to different kinds of texts should not prevent us from acknowledging that at least some ancient biblical writings, although confusing to later minds, make sense in terms of their own literary strategies. Let us push that point even further with respect to prophecy. Prophetic experience, by which we mean the prophet's awareness of an intensely close relationship with God and a concomitant extraordinary clarity and conviction about God's intentions, is by nature intensely private and personal. Yet, in terms of biblical prophecy, the prophetic experience becomes also public as the prophet succumbs to the compulsion to expose his innermost thoughts to an audience. This very personal aspect of prophecy means that the complexity of human mental processes is brought rather directly into public view. It is no wonder, then, that prophetic materials can be so complex. The metaphorical elusiveness of verses 4–16, then, is a function of the prophet's inner struggles as much as of our distance from his world.

The matter of audience is particularly problematic with respect to the shepherd narrative, which is presented as oracle—as words to be proclaimed— and which also contains symbolic actions to be performed. Most works of biblical prophecy give us scant clues as to where and to whom the oracles were recited and before whom the deeds were performed. Second Zechariah is no exception. We are left wondering whether the prophet in fact actually did what the text relates. If our assertion about the retrospective character of most of verses 4–16 is correct, then it is possible that the actions involved were the prophet's mental activities, no less real for being so, but communicated externally only through this verbal account rather than through actual enactment. Surely the first action—shepherding the flock—underlies the subsequent ones and does not seem to be something that lends itself to replication in actual deed, even though the prophet reports, at least three times (in vv 7, 8, 9), that he has carried out God's charge. He can claim that, because it has happened in the past. Interestingly, only the fourth action, of verses 15–16, which apparently brings us into the prophet's present, is the one that lacks a description of its taking place. If the "foolish shepherd" indeed represents the irresponsible prophetic figures of his own day, as well as corrupt leaders of the past—people who serve themselves rather than Yahweh—the prophet hardly needs to enact their presence. The harsh reality is that despite all the trauma in Israel's national life, such people have not been eradicated. The need for divine intervention thus has not yet disappeared.

Woe Oracle to the Worthless Shepherd, 11:17.

Because the last two verses of the preceding section portray a reality of ongoing prophetism that interferes with God's plan, it is only fitting that this chapter conclude with an oracle that responds to such a reality. After all the gloom and horror of the shepherd narrative, the woe oracle provides the reassurance that those seen as responsible for at least some of the ills in society, or at least for failing to help remedy those ills, will lose their power. In deft poetic lines, the oracle proclaims the physical and mental impotence that is sure to overtake the shepherd who does not care for his flock.

This verse thus provides a glimmer of hope that relieves the gloom of the preceding section. At the same time, in both meaning and form, it connects with the first three verses and thus, as we have indicated in our discussion of those verses, serves to frame the shepherd narrative. The destruction of Lebanon's forests, it is to be recalled, was to be part of the anticipated full restoration of all Judah and Israel. It will surely involve a reordering of world powers. But, as the last verse indicates, it will also require internal change so that there will no longer be threats within Israel to its relationship with Yahweh.

PART TWO

ZECHARIAH 12–14

◆

PART TWO

ZECHARIAH 12–14

ZECHARIAH 12

♦

Introduction: Yahweh as Creator (12:1)

12 ¹An oracle: the word of Yahweh concerning Israel—utterance of
Yahweh,
The one who stretched out the heavens and founded the earth,
Who fashioned the breath of humankind within.

Oracles Concerning the Nations and Judah (12:2–11)

²"Behold, I am making Jerusalem a cup of reeling for all the peoples around,
for [they] will be in the siege against Judah, and against Jerusalem. ³On that day
I will make Jerusalem a burdensome stone for all the peoples. All who carry it
will surely cut themselves, for all the nations of the earth will be gathered against
her. ⁴On that day"—utterance of Yahweh—"I will smite every horse with panic
and its rider with wildness. But on the House of Judah I will open my eyes,
while every horse of the peoples I will smite with blindness. ⁵Then the clans of
Judah will say in their hearts: 'There is strength for the leaders[a] of Jerusalem in
Yahweh of Hosts their God.' ⁶On that day, I will make the clans of Judah like a
fire pot amid trees and like a fire torch amid sheaves. Then they will consume,
on the right and on the left, all the peoples around. Jerusalem will dwell again
in her place, in Jerusalem."

⁷Yahweh will save the tents of Judah first, so that the glory of the house of
David and the glory of the leaders[b] of Jerusalem will not be greater than Judah's.
⁸On that day, Yahweh will protect the leaders[b] of Jerusalem so that the weak one
among them on that day will be like David, and the house of David will be like
God, like the Angel of Yahweh before them.

⁹"On that day I will seek to annihilate all the nations that come against
Jerusalem. ¹⁰Then I will pour out on the house of David and on the leaders[b] of
Jerusalem a spirit of favor and supplication, so that they will look to me
concerning the one they have stabbed."

They will mourn for him as one mourns for the only child and grieve for

[a]Reading *lĕyōšĕbê* with the Targum and one Hebrew manuscript.
[b]Reading plural with the major versions and several Hebrew manuscripts.

him as one grieves for the firstborn. ¹¹On that day the mourning in Jerusalem will be as great as the mourning of Hadad-Rimmon in the plain of Megiddo.

Catalog of Mourners (12:12–14)

¹²The land shall mourn, all the families by themselves:
    The family of the house of David by themselves,
        and their women by themselves;
    The family of the house of Nathan by themselves,
        and their women by themselves;
¹³The family of the house of Levi by themselves,
        and their women by themselves;
    The family of the Shimeites by themselves,
        and their women by themselves;
¹⁴All the remaining families, all the families by themselves,
        and their women by themselves.

NOTES

12:1 *An oracle.* This is the second of three occurrences of *maśśāʾ* (for a discussion of the meaning and use of the term, see first NOTE to 9:1) in the Haggai–Zechariah–Malachi corpus. Its final use, in Mal 1:1, suggests that a redactor of the Book of the Twelve or of the Haggai–Zechariah–Malachi component of the Minor Prophets has placed the term at these key points to provide for Second Zechariah and Malachi a structure composed of three units (Zechariah 9–11; 12–14; Malachi 1–3). However, each formulaic introduction varies slightly from the others. At Zech 9:1 the preposition *b* is used with "oracle." In this verse we have the preposition *ʿal*, and in Mal 1:1 it is *ʾel*. In addition, only here does the introduction end with the redundant formula, "utterance of Yahweh" (see NOTE below). This phrase adds to the legitimation of the sayings and may reflect the point of view of whoever assembled the oracles in their present order.

The placement of the *athnach* under "Israel" indicates that the Masoretes understood the opening formula to end there. "Utterance of Yahweh," from their point of view, goes with the second half of the verse, leaving "An oracle," with "the word of Yahweh" in apposition, as a heading. Such a division between the *maśśāʾ* formula and a secondary formula also occurs in Mal 1:1, where "by the hand of Malachi" (or "my messenger") appears after the *athnach*.

the word of Yahweh. The Masoretic notation understands this phrase to be a construct chain following "An oracle." Although it is similar to "word of Yahweh" in Zech 9:1 (see NOTE above), the poetic character of 9:1 means that it functions as part of the title or superscription and as part of the opening poetic line. Here, the prose character of the opening allows all of verse 1a to stand on its own.

concerning Israel. The use of the preposition *ʿal* meaning "concerning" occurs twice elsewhere in the Haggai–Zechariah–Malachi corpus—in Hag 1:5 and 7. Some manuscripts read *ʾel* ("to") here, which is what Mal 1:1 has; but there are no grounds for accepting such a reading as original. The preposition indicates to whom the ensuing oracle will be directed; and it can have either positive or negative implications, depending on the content of the oracle. In this case it is positive, because all that follows is to Israel's benefit.

The use of "Israel" is somewhat surprising, inasmuch as the rest of this chapter (as well as chapter 14 and, to a lesser extent, chapter 13) is concerned with Judah and Jerusalem. Chapters 9–11 refer explicitly to "Israel," but nowhere else in chapters 12–14, except for this verse, does that designation appear. Consequently, it is difficult to discern what is meant by "Israel." The possibilities, as we see them, are as follows:

1. "Israel" is a postexilic term for Judah (Cohen 1948: 318).

2. "Israel" refers to the Southern Kingdom, Judah and Benjamin, in keeping with the way it is used in Chronicles (so Mason 1973: 191). The Chronicler refers to "Israel" in expressing faith in the Southern Kingdom, with its Temple, its capital in Jerusalem, and its Davidic monarchy. This rather specialized use of "Israel" would mean that such a community represented the true Israel.

3. "Israel" can be used, as it is in 11:14, to indicate the Northern Kingdom in its political form prior to 722 B.C.E. Note, however, that in chapters 9 and 10 the people of the Northern Kingdom are referred to as "Ephraim" (9:10, 13; 10:7) or "House of Joseph" (10:6).

4. "Israel" can be used in an inclusive sense, to refer to all the people of Yahweh.

Although it is difficult to reach a decision about which of these options is most likely to be correct, we prefer the fourth one for several reasons. To begin with, the collective appears at the beginning of chapter 9, which refers to Yahweh as the god of all the tribes of Israel. Similarly, Mal 1:1 (cf. Mal 1:5), as noted above, has Yahweh's word coming "to Israel"; given the overall inclusive thrust of Malachi, and especially the reminder at the end of the book in 3:22 (*NRSV* 4:4) that Moses' teaching is for "all Israel," the Malachi usage is an inclusive one. With the formulaic language of 9:1, 12:1, and Mal 1:1 linking together the three parts of Second Zechariah–Malachi, and with 9:9 and Mal 1:1 both using "Israel" in a collective sense, it stands to reason that 12:1 also has that intent.

Another factor is the general pattern of usage in Hebrew prophecy. Aside from Hosea and Amos, both of whom are frequently, although not exclusively, concerned with the Northern Kingdom, the biblical prophets tend to use "Israel" in its collective sense (see the statistics provided by Zobel 1990: 401–4) much more often than as the name of the Northern Kingdom. Ezekiel, e.g., refers to all Israel by the term "Israel" more than 160 times and to the Northern Kingdom only 5 times (Ezek 9:9; 25:3; 27:17; 37:16, 19). Furthermore, in Ezekiel and in other exilic and postexilic prophets, the use of "Israel" for the northerners is almost always paired with some designation or other, usually "Judah," of the

Southern Kingdom. "Israel" standing alone for the northerners is virtually nonexistent.

In addition, aside from Hebrew prophecy, the use of "Israel" for the Southern Kingdom is extremely rare. In all of Hebrew Scripture, it appears no more than 17 times in such a sense, in contrast to the more than 1,000 times it serves as a comprehensive designation for Yahweh's people. Even in Chronicles, where four of the references to Judah as "Israel" occur, the term appears far more frequently (167 times) in reference to all Israel, even if this means the postexilic community is continued for the time only in Yehud, a fact that weakens the claims of both Mason and Cohen. Indeed, the Chronicler's interest in the totality and continuity of Israel leads him to use emphatic and inclusive language, such as "all Israel," and "all the assembly of Israel."

This discussion, by the way, does not take into account phrases such as "sons of Israel," "house of Israel," "God of Israel," etc., in which the name "Israel" appears. If the hundreds and hundreds of such expressions are taken into account, the preponderance of "Israel" as a comprehensive term becomes all the more striking.

Perhaps the main argument against "Israel" meaning all Israel in Zech 12:1 is the fact, as noted above, that the rest of Second Zechariah focuses on Judah and Jerusalem. It is our view, in light of these considerations, that the subsequent focus on those components of all Israel is precisely the reason that "Israel" collectively is meant in the formulaic introduction. The prophet is operating from the belief that the Southern Kingdom and its Davidic monarchy are the key to the eschatological restoration of all Israel as depicted in chapters 9 and 10. Having established the inclusiveness of the restoration, he then considers how the ruler from the house of David will reemerge. Chapters 12–14, in a sense, expand the brief royalist passage of 9:9–10. Because the Northern Kingdom broke with the Davidic dynasty, it lost its place as an integral part of the process of restoration, which Second Zechariah herein presents, but not as the result of that process, which will be inclusive, as previously indicated in chapters 9 and 10. That the ensuing oracle is uttered "concerning Israel" is the formulaic way for the prophet, or his redactors, to connect the conceptualization of all Israel restored with the role of Judah and Jerusalem as central to the restorative process.

utterance of Yahweh. If one takes this oracular expression as an introduction to verse 1b, as some do (Rudolph 1976: 217), it would be one of only a very few such instances in the Bible (e.g., Isa 1:24; 56:8; Ps 110:1). Much more frequently "utterance of Yahweh" occurs within the broader matrix of an oracle. Such examples abound in the Haggai–Zechariah–Malachi corpus (Hag 1:13; 2:4, 14, 17, 23; Zech 1:4; 2:9, 10², 14 [NRSV 2:4, 6, 10]; 8:17; 10:12; 11:6; 12:4; 13:8; Mal 1:2) and frequently in other books. Its placement here following the title to chapters 12–14 means that it either completes the title, thereby ending it with yet another formula of legitimation, or begins the next half of the verse by lending it the stamp of authority. Because the Masoretes have placed the athnach after "Israel," they apparently felt it belonged with the beginning of verse 1b. In any case, the addition of the formula is consistent with the tendency in late biblical prophecy to add formulas legitimating the words of the prophet and may or may not be the result of editorial activity.

who stretched out the heavens. This phrase, which consists of a present participle plus a noun, is the first in a series of three such phrases, all beginning with participles, that constitute verse 1b. Each of the participles should be construed as referring to past time, with their cosmological content requiring such an understanding. Indeed, the image of Yahweh as creator is the underlying element of all three components of verse 1b. This series begins with the creation of heaven and earth and culminates with the fashioning of humankind, as does the P account of creation (Gen 1:1ff., 26ff.). However, in alluding to the fashioning of the breath of humankind, it reflects the J creation story (Gen 2:7ff.). From the perspective of the canonical tradition, the author of this verse provides evidence of the composite tradition of the MT of Genesis, where the P account is followed by that of J.

The character of verse 1b is so distinctive that it has been called a "hymn fragment" (R. L. Smith 1984: 275) or a doxology (Mason 1973: 192; 1977: 115). The juxtaposition of the two verbal roots *nṭh* ("to stretch") and *ysd* ("to found") occurs numerous times in the Bible but seems to have especially close ties to Isa 51:13, 16. Verbal and thematic similarities also link this verse to Isa 42:5, 44:24, 45:12, and to Amos 4:13 and 9:6 (cf. also Jer 10:12; 51:15; Amos 5:8; Ps 18:10 [NRSV 18:19]; 104:2; Job 9:8).

The first phrase, concerning "heaven," and the second, concerning "earth," together represent the basic ancient Near Eastern bipartite view of the universe. The stereotyped pairing of "heaven" and "earth" expresses a totality, i.e., the entire cosmos. Egyptian literature has many examples of this antithetical pair (e.g., Khnum as creator god is "the potter who made heaven and earth"), and in Akkadian *šamû u erṣetu* ("heaven and earth") equals the entire universe (Ottosson 1974: 390–91). These two opposites function as a partial merism, representing the most important parts of the universe and thus all that lies in between. Both water and the underworld were probably seen as existing apart from heaven and earth, yet the latter pair represents enough of the universe to indicate its totality. Many biblical texts, from the creation story (Gen 1:1; 2:4) onward (e.g., Gen 14:19, 22; Ps 89:12 [NRSV 89:11]; Isa 66:1), reflect this bipartite perspective of the cosmos.

In using these stylized and familiar expressions, the author or editor of this passage is accomplishing several things. First, he is providing an introduction to the oracular materials that follow, much as verses 1–3 of chapter 11 serve to introduce that chapter. Second, he is lending a global significance to the fate of Judah and Jerusalem, thus adumbrating the involvement of all the nations in the passages below (especially vv 2, 3–4, 6, 9). Third, by affirming Yahweh's cosmic creative deeds, he is affirming Yahweh's universal power, without which the supranational scheme of this chapter would not evolve. Fourth, the reminder of the beginning-times creativity of Yahweh is the symmetrical antecedent in the natural world of the anticipated activity of Yahweh in establishing a new creation in the future for all the humankind that came into being at the beginning.

founded the earth. Although the participial construction *ysd* ("to found") plus "earth" occurs elsewhere only in Isa 51:13, the combination of these two words is very common, especially in texts in which creation themes figure prominently (as in Job 38:4; Ps 24:2; 78:69; 104:5; Prov 3:19; cf. Amos 9:6). The root *ysd* is also used in connection with the foundation ceremonies of ancient temples, as in Hag 2:18 and Zech 4:9; 8:9 (see Meyers and Meyers 1987: 63–64). This is the second in a series of three phrases (see two previous NOTES and next one) that form this introductory statement and give it its elevated "hymnic" style. It is certainly no coincidence that the first two phrases of verse 1b ("The one who stretched out the heavens and founded the earth"), which are an antithetical pair reflecting the whole of the cosmos, together contain ten syllables and are balanced by ten syllables in the third phrase ("Who fashioned the breath of humankind within"), even though the latter consists of a single participial construction with modifiers.

fashioned the breath of humankind within. This third phrase, in terms of poetic structure, forms the second half of verse 1b in that it balances perfectly the first half (or first two phrases) with its ten syllables. It also sustains the cosmic imagery with its reference to the first creation in language that explicitly evokes the words of Gen 2:7, where God "fashions" the first human out of the clay of the earth and blows the first breath of life into that first earthling. Although this verse draws upon the Eden tale, however, it also diverges significantly. Both Genesis and Zechariah use the verb "to fashion" (*ysr*), which conjures up the image of a potter working with a lump of clay and modeling it to suit his or her tastes. But "the breath of humankind" (*rûaḥ-ʾādām*) of Zechariah 12 differs from "the breath of life" (*nišmat ḥayyîm*) of Gen 2:7. Moreover, the addition of "within" (*běqirbô*, literally, "within him," with the pronominal suffix referring to "humankind") is a departure from the Genesis material. The Zechariah author perhaps includes it to emphasize the individuality of God's relationship with people, in consonance with the trend of postexilic prophecy. "Within" emphasizes that God breathed the first breath into the very corporeal existence of the first individual, who is the archetypal representative of all subsequent human beings (see C. L. Meyers 1988: 80–81).

"Humankind" is used here to translate *ʾādām*, unlike the other versions that render "man" (e.g., RSV, NEB), in recognition of the gender-inclusive nature of that word in many biblical contexts (C. L. Meyers 1988: 81–82; cf. NRSV, "human spirit," and Harrelson 1990).

Technically, because "heavens . . . earth" is stereotyped language representing the totality of the created world, there is no need to specify one aspect of that world. But the Bible holds humanity in a special place—hence, e.g., the extra creation story dealing with humanity, and this phrase concerning the origins of humankind.

The assertion of divine power through the example of God's cosmic creativity (see NOTE above in this verse to "who stretched out the heavens") is intensified by this reminder that human existence is directly dependent on God's creative deeds. From heavens, to earth, and now to humanity, this single line of elevated prose provides the backdrop for the oracular claims Yahweh will make in this chapter concerning God's people and all peoples, i.e., all the "humankind" represented in this introductory verse.

2. *Behold*. In other contexts (e.g., 11:6, 16) we have translated *hinnēh* as "indeed" to emphasize the accompanying verb. In such cases, the *hinnēh* statement is consequential to some previously stated condition. Here, following the formulaic introduction of 12:1, it begins the substance of what Yahweh is about to do. The heralding aspect of "behold" thus seems appropriate in this context. Such use of "behold" with the participle is frequent in the earlier prophets and always indicates future time, i.e., *futurum instans*.

Jerusalem. This is the first of eleven mentions of Jerusalem in verses 2–11. Only verse 4 lacks the name of the holy city. The centrality of Jerusalem in the series of oracular statements—by Yahweh and by the prophet (vv 7–8)–that forms the core of this chapter is thus expressed not only by the content of the oracles but also by the frequent repetition of the city's name. The concern for the restoration of Judah and Israel in chapters 9 and 10 does not involve such a focus on Jerusalem. In those two chapters, only the subunit of 9:9–10 mentions Jerusalem. Even there, the first use of "Jerusalem" is really a stylized reference to the city's population as witness, and the second use probably represents Judah rather than the capital city itself (see NOTE to "Ephraim . . . Jerusalem" [9:10]). Thus this chapter, as also chapter 14, provides an intense and detailed focus on Jerusalem as central to God's plans for the future.

cup of reeling. This second object of the verb consists of two words in a construct chain in the Hebrew, *sap-raˁal*. Although *sap* can sometimes mean "threshold," it also denotes a small container or vessel—a goblet or basin. The latter meaning is certainly the primary one here. Yet the symbolic implications of "cup" are more typically provided in phrases using the word *kôs* (e.g., Ps 23:5; Jer 16:7; Isa 51:17, 22) rather than *sap*. Thus it is possible that *sap* serves as a double entendre; like "stone" (see NOTE to "a burdensome stone" in v 3), it is an architectural feature that will involve unexpected difficulty—the stone being a burden and the threshold causing stumbling ("reeling") rather than passage from one zone to another (see C. L. Meyers 1986). However, it should be acknowledged that nothing in the semantic range of the verb *rˁl*, a hapax legomenon known more from its several derived noun forms and from its Aramaic cognate than from the verb itself, offers support for the association of "threshold" with some sort of faltering step.

The meaning of *raˁal*, which is found once in the Hebrew Bible as the "reeling" or staggering characteristic of an intoxicated state and thus as the result of drinking, finds support in the way the related noun, *tarˁēlâ* ("reeling"), is used. Twice in Isaiah 51 (vv 17, 22) it appears with "cup" (*kôs*) to signify a "cup of reeling" in parallel with a "cup" (*kôs*) of "wrath." The potent contents of such a cup, on the more literal level, are indicated by the "wine of reeling" (*yayin tarˁēlâ*) of Ps 60:5 (NRSV 60:3). But even in Psalm 60, a more figurative aspect to the staggering caused by imbibing wine is present; the parallel line of 60:3 depicts people suffering difficult things, a situation equated with the drinking of the "wine of reeling."

"Cup of reeling" thus presents a negative image, which builds on the everyday meaning of "cup" as a vessel that holds a portion or a measure of something that an individual will consume. This common object lends itself to figurative meaning, a cup of something respresents a quantity of something set aside for a person or, in extended usage, for a group. Sometimes the cup containing an allotted amount has positive connotations, as in the cup of abundance in Ps 23:5 or of salvation in Ps 116:13 or of consolation in Jer 16:7. But more often, as here, drinking from certain cups brings negative results. In addition to the divine wrath cited in Isaiah 51 (cf. Hab 2:15), there is the cup that signifies divine punishment (Jer 49:12; Lam 4:21; Ps 75:9 [NRSV 75:8]) and that brings horror and desolation (Ezek 23:31–33 [NRSV 23:32–34]).

Of all the places in which the cup imagery appears, Jeremiah 25 is perhaps most relevant to Zechariah 12. In Jer 25:15–31, the prophet is commanded by Yahweh to give a "cup of the wine of wrath" to "all the nations" to whom God sends the prophet. All of these doomed nations will get drunk and vomit and fall (25:27), that is, be visited with the utter disaster of divine punishment (25:29, 30–31). The list of nations begins with Jerusalem, the cities of Judah and the king, and the princes. It then continues with Egyptians, Uzites, Philistines, Moabites, Sodomites, Ammonites, Babylonians, Tyrians, Sidonians, Arabians, Medians, and others—peoples near and far are included among "all the nations." Thus, although the concept of drinking from the cup that represents divine judgment against the guilty is common to Jeremiah 25 and Zechariah 12, the perspective of Second Zechariah differs radically from that of Jeremiah. Jerusalem and Judah are not about to drink of the fateful cup; rather, the other peoples (cf. next NOTE) will find that Jerusalem itself represents the cup of judgment.

all the peoples. This phrase can sometimes mean just the components of Israel (see NOTE to "with all the peoples" in 11:10). Such is not the case here, however, with Judah and Jerusalem being the entities in jeopardy because of the advances of others. In other cases, the term "peoples" (ʿammîm) seems to represent groups foreign to Israel but somehow closer at hand than more distant groups, which might be termed "nations" (gôyîm; see Meyers and Meyers 1987: 435–37). The fact that "all the peoples" is followed by "around" might seem to support such an understanding.

Nevertheless, other factors would suggest that "peoples" here is a very broad and inclusive term. Because of the way this "cup of reeling" verse relates to Jeremiah 25 (see previous NOTE), where the groups affected by drinking of the cup of judgment are listed in great detail, it can be concluded that "all the peoples" serves as a collective designation for all those included in Jeremiah's geopolitical catalog. Furthermore, although "all the peoples" is repeated in the next verse, in which "burdensome stone" (see NOTE below) is the metaphor for Jerusalem in relationship to other entities, this section of Zechariah 12 is summarized in the second half of verse 3. There, "all the nations" are those who are threatening Jerusalem and who must consequently find Jerusalem to be a "cup of reeling" and a "burdensome stone."

Looking at verses 2 and 3 together leads us to view "all the peoples" and "all the nations" as a pair, meant to denote all possible populations of the world. "Peoples" tends to be a cultural or social term with implications of ethnicity, whereas "nations" connotes political or territorial affiliation (see Clements and Botterweck 1975). Having these two terms in proximity here makes them complementary: together they represent all other human beings, grouped ethnically and/or politically. Still, the way the two terms are used in chapter 14 makes them seem virtually interchangeable here; see especially 14:2 and 12, as well as verses 3, 14, and 16.

Although this image of a "cup of reeling" being drunk by hostile nations is dependent to some extent, as we have noted above, on Jeremiah 25, it departs in significant ways. For one thing, (see previous NOTE) there is a shift in the status of Jerusalem—Jeremiah included it among those to be judged and punished, whereas for Second Zechariah it becomes the instrument of divine activity against those who besiege God's people. Another aspect is the generality with which Second Zechariah presents the hostile groups. Jeremiah, rooted in agonizing awareness of the volatile international political situation of his day, lists the groups to drink of the fateful cup with great specificity. In so doing, he also sustains the personal or individual aspect of the cup image, the cup being an individual's portion, for he has the kings of all the countries and city-states of the ancient world drinking from the "cup of the wine of wrath." Second Zechariah, by making the cup itself be symbolized by Jerusalem, depersonalizes the imagery and has "all the peoples," and not their rulers, being affected by that fateful cup. This global and more abstract use of the cup imagery bespeaks a perspective governed less by historical reality and more by eschatological expectation than that of Jeremiah.

for [they] will be in the siege. Although the MT is somewhat awkward, it is perfectly comprehensible. The Greek and Syriac versions are very close to the MT but have no preposition before "siege" (māṣôr). The Latin and Aramaic Targum have no equivalent to *ʿal* ("against") before the following word ("Judah") but retain the preposition before "siege." The editor of *BHS* thus calls the MT a conflate or a *textus mixtus*. Assuming that the Greek and Syriac readings are more supportive of the MT than are the Latin and Aramaic, we need only justify the syntax of the Hebrew. The presence of *b*, or "in," before "siege" thus presents no problem at all and, in fact, supports our understanding of the text.

The singular verb *yhyh* takes "all (the peoples)" as its antecedent; and although the verb usually agrees with the genitive noun after the singular *kl* when the noun is feminine or plural, there are numerous exceptions (e.g., Isa 64:10; Prov 16:2; see GKC §146.c). Thus, although the verb is singular, perhaps under the influence of the singular *kl*, it refers back to *ʿammîm*. The use of *gam* after the *athnach* serves to intensify the clause as a whole (GKC §153).

Many translators and commentators have experienced difficulty in comprehending this text and have frequently ended up adopting a translation that does not agree with the rest of the passage; see, for example, the Revised Version (Mitchell 1912: 321). Hanson ultimately adopts a translation that agrees with his view of inner dissension in Judah: "Also Judah will be in the siege against Jerusalem," although freely admitting that this reading derives from an interpretive perspective (P. D. Hanson 1975: 361).

The term *māṣôr* is used in 9:3 for a kind of "siege work" or "bulwark" (see first NOTE to that verse). But it can also, as here (cf. Ezek 4:1–7, which describes a siege of Jerusalem), represent the state of siege to which a city is subjected by a hostile force.

against Judah, and against Jerusalem. Here Judah is mentioned for the first time in chapter 12. Although not so prominent a *Leitwort* (theme word) as is "Jerusalem" in 12:1–11, "Judah" nonetheless figures prominently, being mentioned six times in verses 2–7. The scope of Zechariah 9–11 is inclusive, with Judah and Ephraim both figuring, in terms of the historical past and the projected future, in God's plan for the people. Here the focus seems to narrow, in that only Jerusalem and Judah are mentioned. This omission of Ephraim or Israel (but cf. v 1, NOTE to "concerning Israel") may not necessarily be an intentional exclusion. It may, rather, result from the fact that Jerusalem is the central city in biblical tradition and so must be central in eschatological projection, and from the fact that only Yehud (partly equivalent to Judah) still exists in Second Zechariah's day and thus provides the only surviving model and basis for the anticipated Davidic restoration (cf. NOTE to "House of Judah" in 12:4). In addition, the Davidic line, for centuries prior to its loss of power in 587 B.C.E., had ceased to be the regnal authority in the Northern Kingdom.

3. *On that day.* This stereotyped phrase (Hebrew *bayyôm hahûʾ*) is one of several such phrases (cf. "in those days," "in that time," etc.) that represent the "day of Yahweh" as a day of God's judgment upon Israel and/or other nations. Although such language usually indicates historical time and the anticipated calamities of the political world in preexilic prophecy, the Exile marks a turning point in the use of these terms. In postexilic prophecy, "on that day" and similar phrases tend to have an eschatological character. They announce the final disaster and accompanying deliverance that will come to all the world in temporal existence but as ultimate resolution of the world's problems (cf. Meyers and Meyers 1987: 67, 212–13).

Zechariah 12–14 and the Book of Joel are particularly replete with terms signifying the approaching day of Yahweh. Joel varies the terminology ("day of Yahweh," 1:15; "day of darkness," 2:2; "afterward," 3:1 [NRSV 2:28]; "in those days and at that time," 4:1 [NRSV 3:1]; "in that day," 4:18 [NRSV 3:18]), but for Second Zechariah the one phrase "on that day" recurs again and again. In chapter 12 it is used *seven* times; it appears three times in chapter 13; and in chapter 14 it again is found *seven* times, one of those times being in the final words of the whole prophetic book (cf. also the use of "one day" [v 7] and "day of Yahweh" [v 1] in chapter 14). Nowhere else in Hebrew prophecy is there such an oft-repeated invocation of stereotyped terminology heralding God's final judgment of all the world.

a burdensome stone. The metaphor of Jerusalem as a stone of burden is just as unusual as that in verse 2, where Jerusalem is presented as a "cup of reeling" (see NOTE above). The phrase *ʾeben maʿămāsâ*, literally, "stone of burden," is composed of the construct of "stone" plus the only biblical occurrence of the feminine noun "burden" or "load." The latter comes from the root *ʿms* ("to load," "carry a load, bear a load"), which occurs nine times, all in association with beasts and their loads (Gen 44:13; Isa 46:3; Neh 13:15) or to describe the efforts of "loading up" or "bearing up" (e.g., 1 Kgs 12:11 = 2 Chron 10:11; Ps 68:20 [NRSV 68:19]; Neh 4:11 [NRSV 4:10]). This unambiguous meaning of the verbal root along with the following statement about the injury to be incurred by those who "carry" or bear (see NOTE below; the same verb is used: *ʿms*) the symbolic stone indicate the negative connotations of the imagery. Thus the suggestion (as by Mitchell 1912: 322–23; Mason 1973: 209; and others) that this metaphor derives from the Greek sport of weight lifting posits a somewhat far-fetched association. Such a connection derives from an assumption that this text is Maccabean, a date we reject. Thus, the idea of this image referring to a weight-lifting contest cannot be defended with respect either to date or to the nuances of the words employed.

The prophet's choice of a "stone" metaphor can perhaps be explained in part by his wish to link this oracle with materials in First Zechariah, where stones figure prominently in several of the visions. In each instance the stones of Zechariah 1–8 have positive connotations: the "engraved stone" set before Joshua the priest in 3:9, the "premier stone" of the Temple of Zerubbabel in 4:7, the "tin stone" of 4:10, and the "lead stone" of the Ephah vision in 5:8 (see Meyers and Meyers 1987: *ad loc.*; cf. "gemstones of a crown" in 9:16 above). These are all positive instances of stone imagery and involve reference to the Temple, which is at the physical and spiritual core of Jerusalem. Similarly, Isa 28:16 sees in Jerusalem a stone, a foundation block laid with "justice" and "righteousness" (v 17). Isaiah 34:11, generally attributed to Second Isaiah, puts an ironic twist on the measuring line and stone (i.e., plummet, or plumb weight) used to lay Jerusalem's stone: the line becomes one of "confusion" and the stone one of "chaos." This last image, then, is similar to Second Zechariah's use of "stone." Jerusalem as a precious stone will cause enormous difficulty (see NOTE below in this verse to "will surely cut themselves") to those who attempt to control her.

all the peoples. This is probably an inclusive phrase to indicate all peoples except for the Israelites—those in Jerusalem and Judah. See the NOTE to this phrase in 12:2. Although chapters 9 and 10 communicate an awareness of Israelites (both northerners and southerners) living in the diaspora, the terminology of chapter 12 is much more polarized and less nuanced—Jerusalem (and Judah) representing all Israel, on one hand (see NOTE in 12:1 to "concerning Israel"), and "all the nations" or "all the nations of the earth" (see NOTE below in this verse) representing the rest of the world, on the other hand.

All who carry it. "All" translates *kōl*, again a singular collective, as is "all" in "all the peoples." The participle of the verb *ʿms* ("to bear, carry" a load) continues the imagery of "burdensome stone," in which the noun "burden," derived from this verb, is used in construct with "stone." The idea of foreign peoples bearing or carrying Jerusalem can only mean that foreigners have taken Jerusalem (= Israel) into their political orbit and denied it the autonomy that Yahweh intends for it. Lifting Jerusalem, a gemstone of a city, will thus become a disadvantage to those who have done so, just as drinking of a cup will cause fateful disequilibrium rather than the pleasure that the contents of a goblet usually provide. Jerusalem will bring harm (see next NOTE) rather than glory.

will surely cut themselves. The infinitive absolute with the Niphal imperfect of *śrṭ* constitutes a double verbal form to intensify the action that the verb represents, hence our adverb "surely." Just what that action is, however, is difficult to determine, inasmuch as the verb appears elsewhere only in Lev 21:5. In the Leviticus passage, it occurs with a noun form used as a cognate accusative: "they shall not lacerate themselves [with lacerations]" (cf. Lev 19:28). The verb clearly refers to an injury to the skin or flesh rather than to a strain incurred by lifting a heavy load. Indeed, its cognate in Akkadian, *šarāṭu(m)* (AH 3: 1186) apparently denotes battle wounds.

Jerusalem in this case is therefore a sharp or jagged stone; carrying it will result in severe flesh wounds. The image of Jerusalem as a "burdensome stone" (see NOTE above in this verse) is thus a mixed metaphor with an ironic twist. Jerusalem is a gemstone, the very foundation stone of the universe, but all who try to make it their own will find it too heavy a load and one that will inflict damage on whoever attempts to bear it.

all the nations of the earth. As indicated above in our NOTE to "all the peoples" (12:2), the term for nations, *gôyîm*, nearly always has a political meaning. The element of consanguinity paramount in "peoples" is not necessarily absent from "nations." However, the idea of political organization and attendant territorial domain seems to dominate the semantic range of the latter term. This would especially be true wherever "nation" might refer to an imperial power consisting of various ethnic groups. The fact that "all the nations" here follows close upon two mentions of "all the peoples" and is itself followed by "of the earth" indicates that this clustering of expressions is meant to be fully inclusive of all the peoples of the world. The entire population of the world is herein viewed as being opposed (see next NOTE) to the independent and central role of Jerusalem in the cosmic scheme of God's plan. A similar perspective appears below in 14:16, which mentions "all the nations" in reference to those who had threatened Jerusalem; see also 14:2.

will be gathered against her. The Niphal of the common verb *ʾsp*, "to gather, collect," denotes the collectivity of all the world in opposition to God's people, represented in political terms by "her" = Jerusalem. This verb is often used, when it indicates the gathering of people (as opposed to animals or commodities), to denote especially the mounting of forces for armed conflict (see, e.g., Josh 10:5; Judg 11:20; 1 Sam 17:1). Sometimes the verb is followed by *ʿal* ("against"), as it is here (cf. Gen 34:30), to indicate the object of the hostile amassing of forces, although other prepositions, such as *ʾel*, are also used. An example of the latter is the very similar expression used in Zech 14:2—"I will gather all the nations to Jerusalem, for war" (see NOTES to these words below); and Zech 14:16 mentions "all the nations that had come against Jerusalem" (see NOTES below).

4. *On that day.* This phrase, which occurs seven times in chapter 12, serves to highlight the eschatological character of these oracles (see first NOTE to 12:3).

utterance of Yahweh. This oracular formula sometimes follows directly the phrase "on that day," as in Hag 2:20 and Zech 13:2, thereby emphasizing the authoritative source for the ensuing announcement about the future (see NOTE to "utterance of Yahweh" in 12:1).

I will smite. Yahweh is speaking and so is directly involved in the military action that this verse anticipates. The image of Yahweh as warrior, which figured prominently in chapters 9 and 10, reappears in the language of this chapter. God's action is both direct and indirect—God deals with the enemy and also empowers Judah to do so (see next verse). Yahweh first weakens the enemy, but it is God's people that deliver the mortal blows.

The verb "smite," from the root *nkh*, is a common word referring to general physical attack and, frequently, to the military destruction of an individual, an army, or a territory. It means more than just "to strike" an enemy; it implies the defeat of the foe. When it is used, as it often is, to describe God's intervention against an enemy, the means of Yahweh's smiting, if they can be determined in any given passage, are different than when human soldiers are involved. Yahweh smites with physical afflictions visited upon the foes. The parade example of this is God's use of plagues against the Egyptians (e.g., Exod 7:25; 9:15; 12:13; cf. 1 Sam 5:6, 9); but it also is found in God's warning to Israelites (as in Num 14:12) and in the covenant verses of Deuteronomy (28:22, 27, 28, 35). All such instances involve the idea that whatever happens to humans can be attributed to God, and that if disease or disability strikes, God is responsible.

This Deuteronomic use of "smite" is especially relevant here because Deut 28:28 includes three other words ("panic," "wildness," and "blindness"; see NOTES below) that also appear in this verse. That is, Zech 12:4 is drawing directly on Pentateuchal language. The text in Deuteronomy (28:28), itself derived from ancient prototypes, proclaims that covenant disobedience will be cursed: "Yahweh will smite you with wildness, blindness, and panic." In reusing an authoritative curse formula, Second Zechariah has worked it into material of a totally different genre. Its new oracular setting represents an example of generic transformation—in this case, of curses into oracles—one of the many ways in which Second Zechariah among other biblical authors participates in the ongoing exegetical tradition in ancient Israel (Fishbane 1985: 500–1).

The use of "smite" here, with horses and riders, draws upon earlier biblical usages but constitutes something of a mixed metaphor. The direct effect is on specific military targets, not on a more generalized foe. Yet the "weapons" are not military; Yahweh uses a physical affliction, "blindness" (see last NOTE to this verse), and psychological ones, "panic" and "wildness" (see NOTES below in this verse), against those threatening God's people.

horse. The horse (*sûs*) is the animal most often associated with warfare in the Hebrew Bible and in the ancient world. Horses (with riders or chariots) appear prominently in the visions of First Zechariah (1:8; 6:2–3, 6–7) and figure in the military language of Second Zechariah in 9:10 (see NOTE to "chariot . . . horse"). However, the horses (and chariots) of First Zechariah are vehicles of divine surveillance (see Meyers and Meyers 1987: 113–14; 320–22), and the horse (and chariot) of Zech 9:10 represent the war machine of God's people, which will be obviated when the peaceful rule of the future ruler of 9:9 is instituted. Here the horse is that of the enemies of Jerusalem and Judah—those "gathered against" Jerusalem (see last NOTE to 10:3). Thus, although the basic military aspect of horses is sustained in this passage, thereby providing links with First Zechariah and the first part of Second Zechariah, the prophet here uses it to denote the might of enemies rather than the omniscience of God or the strength of Jerusalem.

with panic. This word (*timmāhôn*) is unusual in the way it is used here. Nowhere else in the Bible is the noun, which occurs elsewhere only once, or its verbal root (*tmh*) found in reference to animals. The verb means "to be astounded, dumbfounded." The English phrase describing a horse being overcome with panic may not seem strange, for it conjures up the idea of horses rearing up in fright and throwing their riders. However, the Hebrew is unusual and thereby heightens the dramatic effect of Yahweh's involvement in this military scenario.

It is hardly a coincidence that the only other use of this noun comes in the covenant curses of Deuteronomy, where the verb "to smite" (cf. NOTE above in this verse to "I will smite") appears, as do the nouns "blindness" and "wildness" (see NOTES below), these words also appearing in this verse. The Deuteronomy text (28:28) depicts the terrible fate of Israel should it disobey the covenant, whereas this passage directs such disaster upon the nations that surround Israel. The threat to Jerusalem's existence is no longer internal, i.e., its own misdeeds, but rather lies in the machinations of external forces. Thus, although it seems unusual to have "panic" used of an animal, the animal really represents the vast human enemy, the nations of the earth.

Second Zechariah here draws upon the Deuteronomy text, in which a sinful Israel would be struck with "wildness," "blindness," and "panic," in that order. He changes the order and metes out each of these afflictions to a different victim: horse, rider, horse of the peoples. But the victims are really the same, varying symbols of the whole, i.e., all those threatening God's people. The prophet has used familiar language to purposes diametrically opposite to those of its earlier biblical context.

its rider. "Rider" is paired with "horses" (see NOTE above in this verse); and together they denote the military might, and thus the threat to Jerusalem, of all external political powers (see NOTES to "all the peoples" in 12:2 and "all the nations of the earth" in 12:3).

wildness. This is the third of four words in this verse that appear also in Deut 28:28 (see above, NOTES to "I will smite" and "with panic" and NOTE below to "smite with blindness"). The punishments to be inflicted on Israel in the covenant curses of Deuteronomy are here to overtake Israel's foes. The stereo-typed curse language is broken up—with panic, wildness, and blindness affecting different parts of the whole (the enemy)—and reordered, but the divinely sent devastation to affect those interfering with God's will is resoundingly clear. Indeed, rearranging and expanding the Deuteronomic language make God's punitive deeds all the more dramatic.

In addition to its appearance in Deuteronomy, "wildness" (*šiggāʿôn*) occurs elsewhere only in 2 Kgs 9:20, where it is preceded, as here, by the preposition "with" (*b*) and where it refers to the manner of Jehu's horsemanship as he conspired against Joram. Jehu is said to ride a horse "like a maniac" (NRSV), i.e., "with wildness." Like panic, wildness descending upon a horseman will make him an ineffectual threat. The ultimate destruction of the enemy will be in Judah's hands; Yahweh here prepares the way by rendering the enemy helpless.

House of Judah. References to the Southern Kingdom that place "house" before its name are common in the Hebrew Bible. In Zech 8:13, such a phrase is paired with "House of Israel," the two expressions together representing all Israel (cf. 8:15, 19). In Second Zechariah, it appears in chapter 10 in verses 3 and 6; in the latter instance it is paired with "House of Joseph," the two phrases denoting all Israel (see NOTES to "House of Judah" and "House of Joseph" in 10:6). Thus the term consistently refers to the Southern Kingdom. However, in the absence here of the typical pairing with a term representing the Northern Kingdom, it is possible that it becomes more inclusive and represents all Israel (cf. NOTE to "concerning Israel" in 12:1). Moreover, because "house of . . ." can be dynastic language, as it surely is below in verse 7 (see NOTE to "house of David") and because the legitimacy of the Northern Kingdom with its non-Davidic dynasty was open to question, the use of "House of Judah" may be intended to represent the restoration of legitimate dynastic (i.e., southern) rule over the north as well as the south. Further, the eschatological aspect of Zechariah 12, insofar as it continues the inclusive messages of chapters 9–11, would suggest a similar scope (cf. NOTE to "against Judah, and against Jerusalem" in 12:2).

I will open my eyes. The grammar and syntax of this clause are not unusual, but the idea of opening one's eyes in the sense of watching out for someone (cf. NRSV, "keep a watchful eye on") is apparently unique. The prophet, however, uses such innovative language in part to establish continuity with First Zechariah, as well as with the "eye" or "blindness" imagery elsewhere in Second Zechariah. "Eye" occurs some twenty-two times in the Haggai–Zechariah–Malachi corpus—including the "open eye" of Zech 2:12 (NRSV 2:8; see Meyers and Meyers 1987: 162), the many visionary introductions of Zechariah 1–8 (as 2:1 [NRSV 1:18]; 2:5 [NRSV 2:1]; 5:1, 5; 6:1), and the "eyes of Yahweh" of 5:8. In Second Zechariah, "eye" figures in "the eye of the people" in 9:1 (see NOTE to that phrase) and in 9:8, where God is said to be watching Israel "with my eyes" (see NOTE). That latter verse is perhaps closest in meaning to this one, for both depict Yahweh as looking at the people with an eye (sic) to taking care of them or seeing (sic) to their welfare. The notion of God's open eyes also contrasts effectively with the "blindness" that will be the downfall of Israel's enemies (see below, NOTE to "smite with blindness") as well as the blindness that will incapacitate the "right eye" of false prophets in Zech 11:17 (see NOTE to "arm . . . right eye"). In any case, God's watching the people is a positive action and stands in contrast with God's negative acts—smiting—in the preceding and following clauses.

every horse of the peoples. The phrase "all the peoples," which occurs twice in verse 2 (see NOTES above), is broken up here so that "all" ("every") comes before "horse." The effect is that these words refer to all those who are threats to God's people while yet involving the specific military imagery—the horse and rider (see NOTES above)—of this verse. In other words, "horse" stands for the whole group: horses and riders. This phrase begins a statement that parallels, although in tighter language, the first clause of the verse. The first clause had two objects ("horse" and "rider") and two conditions affecting them ("panic" and "wildness"); here we have just "horse of the peoples" and "blindness."

smite with blindness. The first verb of this verse is repeated, and here the smiting produces "blindness." As pointed out above (see NOTES to "I will smite," "with panic," and "wildness"), these words are derived from the covenant curse of Deut 28:28. "Blindness" stands alone in this last clause of verse 4 (see previous NOTE), either as an intensification of the panic and wildness already presented or perhaps as a metaphoric depiction of the incapacitation that will characterize God's enemies (cf. NOTES to "arm . . . right eye" and "will surely go blind" in 11:17). Either way, the notion of blindness, as the final characteristic of the people who are the enemies of the House of Judah, contrasts dramatically and effectively with the visual acuity of Yahweh looking out for the "House of Judah" as expressed by "I will open my eyes" (see NOTE above).

5. *clans of Judah.* In chapter 9, the singular (*ʾallūp*) of the term used here in the plural has the meaning "clan" (see NOTE in 9:7 to "like a clan in Judah"), for it seems there to be a social unit (as in Gen 36:15, 17, 19 and 1 Chron 1:51ff.). This passage is similar, except that the military aspect of the word here comes to the fore, even though that may be its most archaic sense (cf. Gottwald 1979: 277–78). The use of *ʾallūpê*, a plural in construct with Judah, to denote social units fits the contextual sense of both this verse and the next one, where it appears again. The Judean clans represent the fighting forces, drawn from all the populace, under the leadership ("rulers"; see NOTE below in this verse) of Jerusalem. The clans, mustered for battle, can feel confident because they recognize ("say in their hearts") that Yahweh has empowered their commanders. Similarly, in the next verse, the clans, as the combined fighting force of Judah, overcome the entire enemy—"all the peoples around."

say in their hearts. This idiom (*ʾmr blbm*) means "to say to oneself," that is, to think that something is so or, even more forcefully, to believe, or to be convinced of something (e.g., Isa 47:8, 10). Usually it refers to something people believe erroneously (as Deut 8:17; Isa 14:13), whereas here it denotes something that can surely be believed.

There is strength. The word *ʾamṣâ* ("strength") has evoked much scholarly discussion as to whether it comes from *ʾmṣ*, "to be strong or bold." The preferable option is to read it as a feminine noun meaning "strength," which is a hapax legomenon. A masculine form, *ʾōmeṣ*, occurs only once, in Job 17:9. The adjective occurs in Zech 6:3, 7, where it refers to the "mighty" horses and hence represents another instance of a term or root used one way in First Zechariah and another way in Second Zechariah. Here it is the horses that are stricken with "panic" and "blindness" and the "leaders of Jerusalem" who are mighty, or who have "strength."

Another possible interpretation that retains the MT is this: "The leaders of Jerusalem are my strength. . . ." This is the view of the medieval commentator Rashi, who, however, understood *yôšĕbîm* ("leaders") to be "inhabitants" (see following NOTE to "for the leaders of Jerusalem"). The NRSV translates in a similar way: "the inhabitants of Jerusalem have strength. . . ." The problem with such renderings is that they do not take into account that the word is masculine and plural.

The reading adopted here was first proposed by Mitchell (1912: 328) and later supported by G. R. Driver (1938: 403), although neither of them renders *yôšĕbîm* as "leaders." It does require a slight emendation: removing the *yodh* from *lî* and moving the *lamedh* to *yôšĕbê*, which yields *lyšby yrwšlm*, "for the leaders of Jerusalem." As indicated in the textual note to the Translation, such an emendation is supported by the Targum. In addition, all the versions support a similar reading of this word in verses 7 and 8 below, and in verse 8 a resumptive plural further points to an original plural (see NOTE to "leaders of Jerusalem" in v 8). For a much more radical approach to this problem, see P. D. Hanson (1975: 357).

The "strength" accorded to the "leaders" (see next NOTE) comes from Yahweh, who first weakens the foe by bringing "wildness," "panic," and "blindness" (see NOTES above) and now empowers the leadership of the Judean forces so that they will decimate them.

for the leaders of Jerusalem. As indicated in the preceding NOTE, we have slightly emended the text in order to respect the MT "strength." Most translators have understood the plural noun *yôšĕbîm* as "inhabitants," not as "leaders." This technical usage of the word has been accepted by Gottwald (1979: 512–34) and others for a small but significant number of passages in the Hebrew Bible. It has this same sense in Zech 8:20 (see Meyers and Meyers 1987: 437); cf. the use of *yšb* ("to rule") as a verb in 9:5 and 6 (see NOTE to "not be ruled" in 9:5). In all these passages it indicates community leaders and normally occurs in the plural.

"Leaders of Jerusalem" is probably an inclusive term for the royal bureaucracy, with its authority extending not just in the city of Jerusalem itself but over all the territory for which Jerusalem is the capital. Thus, although "leaders" is coupled with "Jerusalem," the extent of the leaders' rule goes beyond the capital city. The term applies to the period of monarchic rule before the Exile but not to the exilic and postexilic periods, when kingship and its associated governance structures ceased to exist. Hence the use of "leaders of Jerusalem" and "house of David" in this context involves language of past political organization being projected upon the eschatological future (see NOTE below to "house of David . . . leaders of Jerusalem," in v 10, for a fuller discussion of "leaders" in this late prophetic context).

These officials here are those who are empowered by Yahweh (see previous NOTE) to lead the national fighting force ("clans of Judah"; see NOTE above in this verse) to victory over all the peoples/nations gathered against Jerusalem (12:1). It is only fitting for Jerusalem's leaders to receive strength from God for this task, because it is the plight of Jerusalem that in verse 1 stands for the beleaguerment of all.

Yahweh of Hosts their God. This is the fullest designation of Yahweh that exists in the Bible, and it occurs only one other time in the Haggai–Zechariah–Malachi corpus—in Hag 1:14. The addition of the appellative "their God" is not unusual at all and frequently follows "Yahweh" directly as it does in Hag 1:12[2], or in Zech 6:15 with the second-person suffix, and with various suffixes in Zech 9:16; 10:6; 11:4; 13:9; 14:5; and in Mal 2:16.

The addition of the appellative here, as in other cases, has the effect of emphasizing the covenantal connection which the "leaders of Jerusalem" enjoy. Ringgren (1974c: 277–78) has pointed out that the origin of the appellative "God" (*ʾĕlōhîm*) plus the pronominal suffix lies in the concept of the ancient allotment of Israel to Yahweh (Deut 32:8–9). This full nomenclature for God adds considerable strength and authority to the utterance and places the welfare of Judean leadership within the larger context of Deuteronomic law and sanction (Meyers and Meyers 1987: 45).

6. *On that day.* This is the third of seven repetitions of this eschatological formula in chapter 12; see the first NOTE to verse 3.

clans of Judah. See the NOTE to this phrase in verse 5. Yahweh has weakened the enemy by smiting it with "panic," "wildness," and "blindness" (see NOTES to these terms in v 4); now the people themselves will destroy "all the peoples" and enable Jerusalem to be restored to its rightful place. Yahweh's people are here represented by the "clans of Judah," archaic terminology for the social components, serving a military function, of the tribal units.

like a fire pot. The word for pot is *kîyôr*; such vessels are used exclusively in cultic contexts in the Hebrew Bible—as part of the bronze laver in the courtyard of the tabernacle (Exod 30:18, etc.), as vessels for cooking sacrifices (1 Sam 2:14), as components of the ten elaborate bronze stands in the courtyard of the Temple (1 Kgs 7:30, 38, etc.), and, apparently, as some sort of platform on which Solomon stood (according to 2 Chron 6:13) before the altar in the Temple courtyard in making his Temple dedication speech. All these cultic associations notwithstanding, *kîyôr* undoubtedly originated as a mundane vessel; its use with "fire" (*ʾēš*) may mean that it was a container used for live coals, to carry them from a burning fire or hearth to another place where one wished to ignite a fire.

Nonetheless, the cultic aspect may simultaneously be present here, in that the resulting conflagration is clearly intended to be one for which Yahweh is responsible.

"Fire" together with "consume" (see NOTE below) is a common idiom used to describe the devastation of war (see NOTE to "she will be consumed by fire" in 9:4). When it is linked with Yahweh, even indirectly as in this case, it involves the idea of divine judgment and punishment being sent against targets in the human realm. Usually, such targets are specific dynasties, cities, or lands (e.g., Amos 1:4, 7, 10, 12, 14; 2:2, 5; Jer 17:27; 49:27; Hos 8:14; cf. Andersen and Freedman 1989: 239–42). Here the language lacks such historical-political moorings. In targeting "all the peoples around," a note of global destruction is sounded as befits the eschatological thrust of this chapter. The figurative language of fire is used here with "trees" to represent the destruction of all the peoples. In using this image, Second Zechariah echoes the language of 11:1, where fire consumes "cedars," which apparently represent the imperial powers of the ancient world (see NOTE to "cedar" in 11:2).

In presenting the Judean forces under divine aegis as a source of destructive fire against all those surrounding Jerusalem (cf. the language of v 3, where all the nations are gathered against Jerusalem), the prophet here develops the imagery of First Zechariah: in the second vision, in 2:9 (NRSV 2:5), Yahweh claims to be the "wall of fire" protecting Jerusalem so that the city "will be inhabited." That very notion—of Jerusalem being inhabited—is the concluding idea of this verse (see NOTE below to "Jerusalem will dwell").

amid trees . . . sheaves. The quasi-poetic nature of the prose is evident in the use of two parallel images to convey the idea of the total and inevitable destruction of the enemy. The notion of fire consuming trees functions on a literal level to conjure up the idea of the dangers of forest fire, especially hazardous in the dry season in Near Eastern lands, when a single untended spark can cause widespread and uncontrollable damage. Fire is thus inherently dangerous, and conflagration is inevitable if the fire is set in a forest. The trees (cf. NOTE to "cedars" in 11:1) and sheaves here signify the political threats to Jerusalem, i.e., to all Israel. Judah's fighting forces thus become the source of destructive fire that "will consume all the peoples."

The use of "sheaves" here heightens the sense of danger and imminence. Although the word *ʿāmîr* is singular in the Hebrew, it represents a row (or bundle) of grain. It thus has a collective connotation that legitimates the plural rendering. Although found elsewhere only in Amos 2:13, Mic 4:12, and Jer 9:21 (NRSV 9:22), it is clear that the word denotes grain that has already been cut. Thus, although living trees may not normally burst into flames, sheaves of cut wheat or barley would indeed be inflammable. Used together with "fire torch" (see next NOTE), which involves flames more directly than does "fire pot," this second part of the conflagration imagery intensifies the danger to Israel's enemies introduced by the first part ("fire pot amid trees").

fire torch. The word *lappîd* ("torch") is used here with "fire" (*ʾēš*) and in conjunction with "fire pot"—all symbols of great danger to everyone who comes in contact with these instruments of potential destruction. Although not weapons or destructive in themselves, it is their contact with flammable materials that makes them dangerous. That lit torches can serve military purposes is evident from the story of Samson, who ties torches to the tails of foxes, lights the torches, and sends the foxes into the standing grain (i.e., the uncut grain) of the Philistines (Judg 15:4–5). How much more flammable, then, is the cut grain or "sheaves" (see previous NOTE) of this passage!

consume. On the imagery and meaning of "consume," especially in conjunction with "fire," see the NOTE above in this verse to "like a fire pot" and the NOTE to "she will be consumed by fire" in 9:4. The stereotyped phrase "consume with fire" is broken up in this passage. "Fire" appears twice, with "pot" and with "torch," where "trees" and "sheaves" are the symbolic targets of the fire, i.e., the fighting forces represented by "clans of Judah" (see NOTES to all these words, above in this verse). Now the verb itself has as its object the real target of the destructive conflagration. As with the use of Deut 28:28 in verse 4 (see NOTES to "panic," "wildness," and "blindness"), the prophet uses familiar terminology but expands or reorders it to amplify its meaning. He draws on existing literary materials but does not slavishly copy them; authoritative expressions lend authority to his prophetic message while yielding to the freshness of their new literary shape.

on the right and on the left. The words for "right" (*yāmîn*) and "left" (*śĕmôʾl*) are found together quite frequently in the Hebrew Bible (and also in Ugaritic: *ymn* with *šmʾl*, *KTU*, 1.2.I.40; 1.23, 63f.). When the two terms come together, "right" almost invariably, as here, precedes "left." The pair constitutes a merism—they represent two opposite directions and thus everything in between. They thus mean "everywhere," or totality (cf. Isa 54:3; Ezek 21:21 [NRSV 21:16]), in much the same way that "sea to sea" in 9:10 (see NOTE to that phrase) represents geographic totality.

all the peoples around. See the NOTES to "all the peoples," in 12:2 and 3 for an indication of the inclusiveness of this phrase (cf. NOTE to "all the nations of the earth" in 12:3). In this instance, the addition of *sābîb* ("around") contributes to the sense of Jerusalem's vulnerability, in that the holy city is depicted as surrounded by enemies—all the peoples are "in the siege" against her and are "gathered against her" (see NOTES to these phrases in vv 2 and 3).

Jerusalem will dwell. Although many translations have "Jerusalem will be inhabited," such a rendering is actually a paraphrase and does not do justice to the powerful image of Jerusalem personified as a woman, a metaphor used frequently and effectively by many biblical prophets and poets. One of the best examples is Lam 1:1–2, which depicts Jerusalem as a widow—bereft, weeping, lonely. In v 1, she is said to be dwelling alone, an image that would not work if *yšb* there would be translated "is inhabited." In this case, the verb is accompanied by "in her place," which uses the feminine suffix and thus contributes to the female imagery for Jerusalem.

These words replicate the beginning of an oracle delivered by the angel-who-speaks-with-me, one of the prominent visionary figures in First Zechariah, in

Zech 2:8 (*NRSV* 2:4); and they appear again in Second Zechariah in 14:10 ("will dwell in her place") and 11 (see NOTES to these passages). In the Zech 2:8 passage, the nature of that inhabitation is set forth, along with the protective "wall of fire" that will encircle Jerusalem (cf. NOTE above in this verse to "like a fire pot"). That passage uses the term "in her midst" and "within her" to indicate the specificity of Jerusalem itself being the scene of eschatological flourishing (see Meyers and Meyers 1987: 154–61). In this verse, "in her place" seems to be the equivalent of those terms; and in 14:11 "in security" (see NOTE) follows "will dwell." The overall effect is that of Second Zechariah drawing upon earlier language, but breaking up the sequence of that language and varying it in his own way. This literary modus operandi seems to be characteristic of Second Zechariah in general and of this chapter in particular (see, e.g., NOTE to "consume," above in this verse, and NOTE to "with panic" in v 4.

in Jerusalem. The name of Jerusalem is repeated here, not in needless redundancy but rather to emphasize its centrality in the scheme just described, where it is dramatically rescued and restored. Verses 2–6 constitute a distinct sequence within this chapter, in describing Jerusalem's role in becoming an instrument of her own salvation, but with Yahweh weakening the enemy and the clans of Judah finishing the job. Because the first verse of this section, verse 2, contains two mentions of Jerusalem, the double use of "Jerusalem" again in this verse, which concludes the section, constitutes an inclusio. "Jerusalem" now has appeared six times in this chapter, and it will occur five more times— once each in the next five verses (cf. NOTE to the first "Jerusalem" in v 2 above), which form the next section of the prose materials of chapter 12. The preposition *bĕ* here may be a *bet essentiae*, serving to reinforce the subject: "even Jerusalem."

7. *Yahweh will save.* The verb *yšᶜ*, here in the Hiphil, means "saving" or "delivering" from external evil or enemies. The noun form "savior" (*môšîaᶜ*) is thus frequently used for God, as the one who saves or delivers the people; see our NOTE to "saved" in 9:9, where the Niphal form is discussed in relationship to the Hiphil. The word is so often used to indicate rescue from a military threat that the Niphal is sometimes translated "victorious." Such a military aspect to the term is present here, given the language of destruction and warfare in the previous section, verses 2–6.

The subject of the verb, still "Yahweh" as in the preceding verses, changes somewhat abruptly from the first person to the third person. This verse and the next one now describe God's activities. The change indicates the beginning of a new subunit of the oracular materials of chapter 12, with the double use of "Jerusalem" in the preceding verse (see previous NOTE) marking the end of the section composed of verses 2–6. Although those verses focus on the struggle between Judah/Jerusalem and all the nations or peoples of the world that constitute a threat to its existence, and then on the Judean victory through Yahweh's agency, the next section (vv 7–11) is directed more toward internal affairs: Jerusalem, its leadership, and the house of David.

tents of Judah. This use of "tent" (*ʾōhel*) with "Judah" is unique in the Bible, although the combination of "tent" with the name of a tribe or group may be a poetic way of referring to that group (e.g., "tents of Edom," Ps 83:7 [NRSV 83:6]; "tents of Kedar," Ps 120:5; "tent of daughter of Zion," Lam 2:4, as a term for "Jerusalem"). It is not clear that the use of "tent" is to be taken as a sign of nomadic or seminomadic existence (see Gottwald 1979: 440–41); even the famous references to the tents of Jacob (Jer 30:18; Mal 2:12) are not archaic allusions to patriarchal pastoral nomadism. Rather, the term for one kind of less substantial dwelling functions as an alternate word designating a habitation or home (cf. Ps 132:3 and Judg 19:9, where "go to your tents" is translated "go home" by NRSV), especially in the case of Yahweh's dwelling place on earth, the "tent of meeting," which is conceived of as God's house (cf. Ps 27:4 and 5).

These statements about the general use of "tent" to signify habitation or, with a proper name, inhabitants can be augmented in this case by noting two other aspects of the term. One is its military use: in 1 Sam 17:54 and Jer 37:10 it designates the field dwelling of soldiers. Inasmuch as the "clans of Judah," which represent its fighting forces (see NOTE to this phrase in 12:5), are the ones to do battle with the enemy, it is their "tents," representing both Judah as a people as well as the military nuance suiting this context, that Yahweh will save. The second aspect derives from the fact that David's royal dwelling is known as the "tent of David" in Isa 16:5. Because this verse points toward a favoring of Judah, the use of such a term may be a way of highlighting Judah's role over against that of the house of David. Finally, there are two instances in which the dwellings of Israelites in tension with the royal house are called "tents" (1 Kgs 12:16 [= 2 Chron 10:16]; 2 Sam 20:1). The way this verse establishes that the role of the people should not be eclipsed by the leadership may reflect that ancient saying and reverse its meaning: the tents of Judah are now part of its privileged place, not part of the rejected place of certain Israelites.

first. Determining the precise meaning of this temporal indicator is difficult. The MT has *bāri'šōnâ*, which is the word rendered here. However, many versions (LXX, Syr, Vulg, and Targ) support a reading that has *k* before *b*: *kbr'šnh*, "as at first." Accepting the versional text (as does Mitchell 1912: 325) would mean understanding it as a reference to an early part of David's reign, before he and his entourage became dominant. However, such an allusion to a subtle distinction of the period of Davidic chieftainship is unlikely. The MT reading is thus to be preferred, although it opens the possibility for scholars, notably P. D. Hanson (1975: 354ff.), to use this verse as a proof-text for the supposition that Zechariah 12, 13:1–6, and other parts of Second Zechariah reflect a bitter rivalry, in the prophet's own day, between the Jerusalem leadership and the rest of the people.

Yet, as we explain in our COMMENT to this chapter, this apparent assertion of the primacy of the Judeans over the royal house and bureaucracy does not necessarily have to represent an internal struggle during the prophet's day. Rather, it is evidence of the restructuring, decentralizing, and democratization that inevitably arose with loss of political autonomy and domination by an imperial power, such as characterize the external structuring of Yehud in the postexilic period. Just as the monarchic rule of the Davidides of the First Temple period left its formative impact on the eschatological vision of virtually all the biblical prophets, so the postmonarchic realities of restructured indigenous leadership left its impact on the postexilic prophets. In First Zechariah, for example, the dyarchic vision of chapter 4 (see especially 4:14; cf. Meyers and Meyers 1987: 258–59, 275–77) surely anticipated the future joint rules of king and priest (6:12–13; Meyers and Meyers 1987: 370–73). Here, Second Zechariah's future scenario involves a reduction in royal power (cf. 9:9, NOTES to "saved," "humble," and "riding on an ass") and a concomitant rise in prominence of the populace of Judah.

glory . . . glory. The term *tip'ārâ* ("beauty, glory") can refer to fine garments (Isa 3:18; 52:1) or priestly garb (Exod 28:2,40), or even to Yahweh's splendor (e.g., Ps 71:8; 1 Chron 29:11; Isa 63:14). However, the aspect of its semantic range most relevant here is its use to express divine approval of the royal claim to Jerusalem. The familiar expression "crown of glory" (*'ăṭeret tip'eret*) signifies both royal power and the Davidic claim to it (Isa 62:3; Jer 13:18; Ezek 16:12; 23:42; cf. Zech 6:11 and NOTE to "crowns" in Meyers and Meyers 1987: 349–51). Thus the "glory of the house of David" (see next NOTE) and "of the leaders of Jerusalem" (see NOTE below) represent the traditional claims of the monarchy and its bureaucracy. As legitimate as the "glory" of king and courtiers has been, historically speaking and eschatologically anticipated, the experience of exile and domination has changed that notion, so that the people themselves will not be overshadowed by the future rulers in the new age.

house of David. This is the first of five explicit mentions of the Davidic line in this chapter (see vv 8², 10, 12). The fate of all Judah, indeed of all Israel (see NOTE to "concerning Israel" in v 1 above), is tied to the hope that one day a Davidic ruler will usher in a new age of peace for all Israel and humanity (E. M. Meyers: forthcoming; and see above, NOTE to "your king" in 9:9). Such an idea lies at the very core of biblical eschatology and is an essential theme of First Zechariah (see especially Zech 3:8–10; 4:6–10; 6:9–14). That it continues in Second Zechariah shows the strong links of Zechariah 9–14 with chapters 1–8 as well as with earlier Hebrew prophecy and its concepts of a future Davidide.

Here, however, the prophet asserts that the restoration of the house of David would not mean a return to the full-blown sociopolitical prominence and dominance, in terms of internal community life, that it held in the centuries of preexilic monarchic rule. As we suggest in the previous NOTE, this shift in relationships between royal power and the populace must surely reflect the changing dynamics of community structure and leadership during the centuries of exilic and postexilic survival. The question remains as to whether the fate of the actual Davidic line, the descendants of the last reigning king of Judah, is in any way connected to this perspective depicting a somewhat diminished place for the Davidides vis-à-vis the rest of the people. If these oracles do in fact date from the period between the apparent disappearance of the last Davidide (Shelomith; see chart 2 in Introduction and discussion in Meyers and Meyers 1987: 12–13) and before the installation of Nehemiah or Ezra as strong leaders, the loss of a national focus of political leadership may have colored the shadings of royal vs. Judean prominence in the future age (cf. our discussion below in COMMENT).

leaders of Jerusalem. See the NOTES to this phrase in verses 5 and 10. The MT has a singular reading, *yōšeb*, whereas the major Versions (LXX, Vulg, Syr, and Targ) preserve a plural construct, *yōšĕbê*. For textual and contextual reasons, the latter is preferred. The COMMENT to this chapter includes a discussion of the sociopolitical reality that may underlie the vision of king and Jerusalemite leaders not exceeding the glory of the "tents of Judah" (see also preceding two NOTES).

8. *On that day*. This is the fourth occurrence of this eschatological formula in verses 2–11 (cf. first NOTE to v 3). Although the acts of Yahweh are here and in verse 7 described in the third person rather than the first person, the occurrence of this thematic phrase provides continuity with the rest of the chapter.

Yahweh will protect. Again, the subject here (cf. first NOTE to v 7) is Yahweh. Verses 7 and 8, unlike the preceding five verses and the following three, describe Yahweh's anticipated deeds in the future age in the third person. As indicated above in our NOTE to "will protect them" in 9:15, the verb *gnn* ("to defend, protect") occurs only eight times in the Hebrew Bible and its meaning is quite straightforward. The subject is always Yahweh (e.g., Isa 31:5[2]; 37:35; 38:6) and the object is either Jerusalem (as 2 Kgs 20:6; 19:34) or God's people (Zech 9:15). This verse, in a sense, combines the two kinds of objects of divine protection— Jerusalem and people—in its specifying "leaders of Jerusalem." The idea of divine protection over Jerusalem (or the people it represents) links this verse with the idea of the inviolability of Zion, which appears strongly in First Isaiah. Here it is coupled with the Davidide tradition, although the premier place of the eschatological ruler, especially as it is expressed in this verse (see last two NOTES in this verse), is tempered with the prominence of Judah in v 7 (see NOTE to "first") and by the strange image of the royal family and bureaucracy immersed in profound mourning.

leaders of Jerusalem. For the third time (cf. vv 5, 7), we read the construct plural as do the major versions. This emendation receives added support here by the addition of "among them" (*bāhem*) as a resumptive that can only refer to plural "leaders." The meaning of *yōšĕbê* as "leaders" is discussed in the NOTES to this term in 12:5 and 10.

the weak one. This term is a Niphal participle (*hannikšāl*) from the root *kšl* ("to stumble, totter, stagger"); it indicates a condition of being "weak" or "feeble." The idea that God empowers the weak and the weary is at the core of the message of Second Isaiah (e.g., Isa 40:30–31), yet its use here in reference to leaders of Jerusalem seems unexpected. However, this startling notion is part of a striking comparison that likens the least effectual of the leaders to David, who himself is part of a dynasty comparable to none other than God or the Angel of Yahweh (see NOTE below to "like the Angel of Yahweh"). Although the glory of the king and the courtiers may not be greater than that of the people (see NOTES in v 7 to "first" and "glory . . . glory"), the accessibility of the

Davidides and their bureaucracy to God, and the intimacy that characterizes the image of God's special relationship with the house of David, are dramatically sustained in this verse.

There may be an additional allusion at work here in the prophet's choice of the root *kšl* to refer to a segment of the Jerusalem leadership. That word is found frequently in Jeremiah in various contexts. Among the Jeremianic usages are two verses that refer explicitly to those who were persecuting the prophet; they indicate that God will ultimately cause such individuals to "stumble" or "totter," that is, to be weakened in their efforts to oppose the prophet (see Jer 18:23; 20:11). These passages are direct references to the officers who have taken Jeremiah into custody and who seek to take his life. Those royal bureaucrats who will become the "weak" ones, according to the Jeremianic oracles, will, in the eschatological vision of Zech 10:8, have a totally different status—they will be like David, who did (for the most part) heed Yahweh's word as delivered through the prophetic voice. In this sense, the comparison of such elements to David, and of David to God, is perhaps a way of proclaiming that the historical opposition to Yahweh's prophets will be utterly reversed in the future age of Davidic restoration.

on that day. Yet again (see first NOTE to this verse and to v 3) in this verse, the eschatological note of this chronological formula is sounded, thereby establishing the future time of the ensuing remarkable comparisons. The editor of *BHS* would like to delete this occurrence of the phrase; but without it, the total of its seven usages—probably a symbolic and intentional number—in verses 2–11 would be lost.

like David. The figure of King David, the most prominent individual in the historical writings of the Hebrew Bible, is an apt one through which to demonstrate the protective power of Yahweh. If God is defending even an ineffectual member of the Jerusalem leadership (see NOTE above in this verse to "the weak one"), then that person will be as strong as if he were the premier king of Israel, the paradigmatic dynastic figure and the symbol of future royal rule. This verse, like the ones preceding and following it, assumes that Davidic rule will be part of the eschatological scheme. This heightened emphasis on the future Davidic ruler may be conversely related to developments in the prophet's own day, during which the surviving, disempowered descendant(s) of the royal family apparently disappeared from public life and, perhaps, from existence (see COMMENT to this chapter).

the house of David will be like God. If the comparison of a lesser member of the Jerusalem leadership to David is unexpected, this clause surely presents a stunningly bold idea. The comparison of any human, even the most exalted one, to God (*ʾĕlōhîm*), understandably created difficulties for the ancient translators, who felt uncomfortable with such extraordinary treatment of the Davidic house. The Targum, for example, translates here: "the house of David shall be like princes and shall flourish like kings." The Septuagint reads: "the house of David will be like the house of God." Mason (1973: 227) correctly turns to the Book of Exodus for help in understanding this unusual, if not unique, expression. When Moses complains that he is unable to speak properly God's words, God reassures him that Aaron will be his stand-in: "He shall speak for you to the people; and he shall be a mouth for you, and you shall be to him *as* God" (Exod 4:16; italics are the authors').

Although the preposition "as" in Exodus is *l* and in Zechariah "like" is *k*, the purpose of the text in Exodus may be relevant. It shows that the roles of Moses and Aaron are complementary and fall under God's aegis—Aaron too is to be a spokesman for God. Similarly, the author of the text in Second Zechariah is perhaps conveying the idea that leaders of Yehud/Judah must stand as complementary or supportive with respect to the house of David. In the future age Jerusalem's leadership will be at one with its king and its God. Even so, this comparison reflects the postexilic tendency to idealize and exaggerate the Davidides. It may complicate the idea of the incomparability of God; yet it comports well with the theology of the Chronicler, who spares no effort in praising the house of David. Although Freedman sees the Chronicler's history (1 and 2 Chronicles plus Ezra 1–3) as a work completed by the end of the sixth century (1990: 325), we suggest, on the basis of texts such as this, that it is better placed in a period when the Davidic house is no longer a factor in contemporary history but rather an idealized object of eschatological speculation and praise.

like the Angel of Yahweh. The phrase "Angel of Yahweh" echoes the language of Haggai (1:13) and First Zechariah (1:11, 12; 3:1, 5, 6) and anticipates Malachi (2:7; 3:1). In so doing it participates in the general biblical concept of the existence of divine beings possessing some of the characteristics of Yahweh yet appearing in human form as messengers (see Meyers and Meyers 1987: 114, 183). The phrase appears only this once in Second Zechariah and could well be the mark of a redactor or compiler of the Book of Zechariah. Such a person might also be the one who redacted or influenced the redactor of the Book of Malachi. However, this second comparison could surely be part of the original oracular statement, with the following "before them" (see next NOTE) apparently including both "God" and "Angel."

The use of a double comparison—to God and to the Angel of Yahweh—may be another example of the repetitive divine terminology discussed above (see NOTE to "Yahweh of Hosts their God" in v 5). Because of the extraordinary hope and praise attached to the house of David, it would not be surprising to find such an emphasis here on the special place of the Davidic line. To say that it will be both "like God" and "like the Angel of Yahweh" not only intensifies the level of expectation and elevates the degree of praise but also, in the reference to "Angel," places these prophetic words squarely into the mainstream of the Haggai–Zechariah–Malachi corpus.

This comparison of the Davidic dynasty to the Angel of Yahweh may draw upon the language of 2 Sam 14:17, in which the wise woman of Tekoa likens David to the "angel of God" (cf. the variant in Greek Lucan, which has "angel of Yahweh," as here). As elsewhere, the prophet appropriates language from the past to delineate the future. A historical statement about a reigning king of the house of David, in fact David himself, is projected into an eschatological future.

Thus, this seemingly extravagant comparison of the Davidides to the deity has precedent in Scripture. Such use of earlier texts is very much in keeping with the style and strategy of the author.

before them. The idea of the "Angel of Yahweh" (see previous NOTE) being "before them" (*lipnêhem*) does not really add to the comparison and may thus be an allusion to the Exodus account, in which God or the Angel goes "before" the Israelites to guide them day and night (Exod 13:21; 14:19). The language in Exodus, however, presents "Yahweh" and the "Angel of God" as before the people. If Second Zechariah is drawing upon these two verses in Exodus, he is reversing the designations, for he uses "God" and "Angel of Yahweh." The military context of the Exodus passages and this one, and the need for divine protection mentioned in both, provide some justification for the sense that the prophet here has drawn upon the Exodus texts.

9. *On that day.* For the sixth time, this eschatological expression appears in the oracular materials of chapter 12. See the first NOTE to verse 3 for a discussion of this phrase.

seek to annihilate. The verb *bqš* ("to seek") followed by *l* ("to") plus the infinitive construct of another verb, in this case the Hiphil of *šmd* ("to annihilate"), serves to intensify the intention to carry out the deed represented by the second verb. Usually, such a combination expresses a negative intention (Wagner 1975: 233), often involving the taking of human life, as is the case here (cf. 1 Sam 19:10; 20:1; 22:3).

The Hiphil of *šmd* denotes severe devastation: annihilation or extermination. Its appearance here is akin to many other prophetic and other examples of its use, notably in reference to Yahweh's destruction of one or another of the enemies of Israel (e.g., Deut 2:21; Josh 9:24; Isa 13:9; Amos 2:9). Here the enemy is nothing less than "all the nations" (see next NOTE and NOTE to "all the nations of the earth" in v 3).

all the nations. Virtually interchangeable in Zechariah 12 with "all the peoples," this phrase denotes the enemies who threaten Israel or, more specifically in this chapter, Jerusalem as the center and symbol of all Israel. For further discussion, see the NOTE to "all the nations of the earth" in verse 3; cf. 14:2.

come against. The verb *bw³* ("to come") with *ʿal* ("against"), as the verb of action, constitutes a next stage in the aggression of "all the nations" against Jerusalem. In verse 3 above, those nations "are gathered" against her; now they are in motion, making Yahweh's destructive acts imminent indeed.

10. *pour out.* When the verb *špk* ("to pour, pour out") is used figuratively with "Yahweh" as subject, it usually has a negative object—Yahweh pours out anger or contempt (e.g., Hos 5:10; Jer 10:25) upon those who defy God's will. Here, however, such imagery is turned around; the opposite of divine anger will come upon the Davidic house and leaders: "favor and supplication" (see NOTES below).

house of David . . . leaders of Jerusalem. The fact that both these groups (the dynastic family and the Jerusalem bureaucrats; see NOTES to these phrases in vv 5 and 7) will receive the "spirit of favor and supplication" from Yahweh indicates that both are involved in the enigmatic stabbing incident of this verse (see NOTE below to "they have stabbed"). That both groups then also mourn is likewise indicated (see "They will mourn"). In short, the royal family and the officials under royal patronage together are implicated in the stabbing. If the identity of those represented by these two phrases is related to those who mourn, as suggested not only by this verse but also the next one, as well as by the Catalog of Mourners in verses 12–14, then the Davidides plus the leaders of Jerusalem are a rather comprehensive group, including the royal family, priestly families, and perhaps even prophetic or military families (see below, NOTE to "house of Nathan" in v 12). Although these oracles are generally eschatological in their terminology and in their anticipation of universal destruction and the attendant restoration of Zion—all under Yahweh's direct aegis—this verse, with its stabbing, seems to introduce a peculiar note of historical specificity to this set of oracles (but see the discussion in COMMENT to this chapter). Thus the rather inclusive nature of the implicated groups is significant.

The range of officials represented by "leaders" is informed by two features: the terms with which it is paired elsewhere in the Hebrew Bible as well as in this chapter, and the negative evidence provided by the omission of leadership terms in this chapter. To begin with the latter point, it is important to note that there are many biblical terms for a considerable variety of officials and leaders, both appointed ones and those emerging from the social units of ancient Israel. In the postexilic period, there are additions to and changes in leadership terminology and roles, in keeping with the appearance of new kinds of leaders (e.g., *peḥâ*, "governor"; see Meyers and Meyers 1987: 13–16) and the shifts in the way existing positions of leadership were able to continue their roles (as in the way the *rōš*, "head," apparently assumes, in postexilic times, the functions held by the *zāqēn*, "elder," before the Exile; see D. L. Smith 1989: 96–99, and Rost 1938: 62–69). Among all the terms used in the postexilic period (in addition to *rōš*, see, e.g., *ḥōrîm, śar, sĕgānîm*; Neh 2:16; 4:10 [NRSV 4:16]; 5:7; 12:31; etc.), none is part of the language of Second Zechariah in these eschatological visions, in which the prophet is depicting the future using terms from the past.

The second feature of the participle construct "leaders" (*yôšĕbē*) is that it is nearly always coupled with mention of royal rulers, as is the case here, in the use of the verbal form in Zech 9:5 and 6 (see NOTE to "not be ruled" in 9:5), and in many of the other texts where the specialized use of this word is found (e.g., Lam 4:12 and Amos 1:5, 8; see the detailed discussion in Gottwald 1979: 511–34). The relationship to royal rule is, of course, implicit in the root of the verb, *yšb* ("to sit"), often meaning "to be enthroned." Although we agree with Gottwald that the scope of "leader" is certainly greater than that of kingship itself, we define that range as all those whose official positions are dependent on royal sponsorship. Such positions would vary but might include military personnel, royal bureaucrats, perhaps judges appointed by the crown, and even priestly personnel under royal patronage. Hence, with the removal of monarchic rule in Yehud after 587 B.C.E., all such classes of ruling officials were de facto removed from power. Surely at least some continued to exist and keep alive the concept of the offices formerly held, but presumably all positions intrinsically dependent on royal patronage would cease in reality, their functions to be filled by other internal Yehudite bureaucrats or by officials operating under imperial sponsorship. Yet insofar as prophetic eschatology kept alive and enhanced the idea of the eventual return of monarchic rule, so too it sustained the expectation that the accompanying royal bureaucracy would reemerge. Furthermore, just as the king and all the courtiers would enjoy universal dominion over and peace with other peoples or nations, so too would they hold office with an absence of the internal tensions and struggles that had characterized monarchic rule for much of its centuries-long existence. This part of Zechariah 12, then, deals with the last eruption of internal—as well as external—violence before the final age of peace.

spirit. When the Hebrew word *rûaḥ*, in its sense of "spirit" (rather than "wind" or "breath"), is used in construct with another term, it often indicates a particular temperament or disposition toward some sort of emotion or behavior (e.g., jealousy, in Num 5:14; justice, in Isa 28:6). Such is the case in this verse, in which the Davidic family and Jerusalem bureaucracy are overcome, evidently because of their culpability in some misdeed (see previous NOTE and NOTE below to "they have stabbed"), by feelings of "favor" and "supplication" poured out on them by Yahweh (see next two NOTES).

favor. The noun *ḥēn* appears dozens of times in the Hebrew Bible, most often as part of the idiomatic expression "find favor in one's eyes" (e.g., Gen 39:4; Exod 33:12; Num 32:5; Judg 6:17; etc.). The idea of favoring someone is thus prominent in the usages of *ḥēn*: it denotes a positive attitude by someone toward someone else. This instance marks a departure from the typical way the term is used. Furthermore, it differs from all the other examples that fall outside the "find favor in one's eyes" idiom. The verb used here to denote the bestowing of "favor" is "to pour" (*špk*; see NOTE above) rather than the more usual "to give" (*ntn*). In addition, *ḥēn* is infrequently paired with another term, and when it does occur together with a related noun, that noun is nowhere else the one present here ("supplication"; see next NOTE).

This unique usage of "favor" is apparently evoked by an unparalleled set of circumstances. Although Yahweh typically bestows favor, here the recipients do not receive "favor" itself but rather the ability to be themselves positively disposed toward another party. In other words, the horror of a deed perpetrated through negative feelings of anger, jealousy, fear—whatever would cause some people to stab another—will now be mitigated by the emergence of a different, positive disposition: "favor." There seems, however, to be no accountability in terms of justice for a crime of assault (or murder); rather, an internal change comes over those responsible for the terrible act. They now become able to show favor, and this is accompanied by a simultaneous asking for favor—the "supplication" of the accompanying term.

supplication. "Favor" (see previous NOTE), which is *ḥēn* in Hebrew, is uniquely paired here with another substantive derived from the same verbal root (*ḥnn*, "to be gracious, show favor"). This term, *taḥănûnîm*, is found only in the plural and denotes requests for favor, i.e., "supplications," made either to persons (as Prov 18:22) or to God (commonly in Psalms, as 28:2, 6; 86:6; see also Jer 3:21 and 31:20). Such requests can be for help, but they also can be pleas for forgiveness (as Ps 130:2; 2 Chron 6:21; Dan 9:3, 17), which would be the appropriate sense here. Such a plea is not directed toward Yahweh, inasmuch as it is Yahweh who provides the royal family and leadership with the motivation ("spirit"; see NOTE above in this verse) for supplication, that is, motivation to ask forgiveness, as well as to act favorably toward a certain one or ones ("the one they have stabbed" and/or his group). Thus the "supplication," like the "favor," is directed toward human(s). Both these dispositions represent a reversal of previous feelings, and they are instigated by Yahweh alongside the military-political reversals—enemy nations being overcome by the victim Jerusalem—that are anticipated in these eschatological oracles. To render this word "compassion," as does the RSV and NEB is to miss the subtlety of its use here.

they will look. The root *nbṭ* ("to look") is used mainly in the Hiphil, as it is here (*hibîṭû*). Although it can refer literally to the act of observing or glaring at something, it is often used figuratively to indicate the directing of attention toward someone or something, in which case it is often followed, as it is in this verse (see next NOTE), by *ʾel* ("to"). When humans in the Bible are described as looking toward someone, it is often as not Yahweh (or divine words or deeds) to whom they look (e.g., Isa 22:11; Ps 119:6, 15). Thus this verb in the plural expresses the idea that, now being favorably inclined toward and asking forgiveness from the one(s) whom they had previously treated with violence (see NOTES below to "concerning the one" and "they have stabbed"), the authority figures in Jerusalem ("house of David . . . leaders of Jerusalem"; see NOTE above in this verse) recognize Yahweh as the source of their new disposition and pay attention to God and the divine will. The *waw* consecutive before the verb places the action in the expected future and gives it a sense of being a result of previous conditions or events, hence our rendering "so that" before the verb.

Although the Davidic house and the Jerusalem bureaucracy are surely the antecedents of this verb, other authors, notably traditional Jewish commentators (see Cohen 1948: 321) take the "nations" of verse 9 as the ones here looking to God and thus mourning the Judeans who would have died in defense of their country and beliefs. In such a reading, which we find unacceptable, the stabbed one becomes a martyred messianic figure.

to me. The MT reading of *ʾēlāy*, first-person singular, is supported in all the major versions. It is a reading, however, that enjoys little higher critical support because it seems to contradict the third-person references to the "stabbed one" that follow in this verse. The most common emendation, therefore, is to change *ʾly* to the third person, *ʾlyw* ('to him"), a reading that is supported in John 19:37 and Rev 1:7, where this text is quoted, and in a number of the Kennicott manuscripts (so Mitchell 1912: 334–35). A defective third-person spelling (*ʾlw*) would allow for a simple *yodh/waw* confusion. Another emendation suggests repointing to *ʾēlēy*, as in Job 3:22, and omitting the *ʾet* that follows. Still another proposal involves omitting ʾet and reading simply ʾel-ʾăšer, with the sense of "whither" (so GKC §138.e).

However, we find no reason to depart from the MT, which has overwhelming versional support. Indeed, the God-given change of disposition on the part of the traditional Jerusalem leadership (see NOTES above in this verse to "house of David . . . leaders of Jerusalem," "favor," and "supplication") certainly is consonant with the result of those people now looking to God as the source of their change of heart regarding what they have done. Following upon that, they show great remorse: the theme of "mourning" now comes to the fore in this verse and the rest of this oracular section (vv 10–11) and in the subsequent Catalog of Mourners (vv 12–14).

concerning the one. As indicated in the preceding NOTE, the interpretation of this phrase, ʾet ʾăšer, cannot be separated from the reading of "to me." For the latter, our translation again reflects the MT. The accusative marker ʾet indicates that the ensuing clause refers to the one who has fallen and is followed appropriately by the relative pronoun, which functions like a demonstrative, not unlike that in Mic 6:1 (GKC §138.e). The syntax is difficult, to be sure, and other translators would simply substitute "because" for ʾet ʾăšer, an approach adopted by the Targums and subsequent Jewish commentators, who see the nations turning to God because they were responsible for the martyrdom of the "stabbed" one (see above, NOTE to "they will look"). The solution of the *NRSV* is rather ingenious—"to me" is rendered as "the one whom" for a smooth "when they look on the one whom they have pierced"—but does not accurately reflect the MT. Nothing seems to be gained, exegetically speaking, by removing Yahweh as the one to whom the leaders will now direct their attention.

Keeping "to me" (ʾly), which refers to Yahweh, and not emending, makes it difficult to understand the following ʾet ʾăšer, because ʾēt is the sign of the direct object. The result would mean looking at both the one they stabbed and at Yahweh, who could not be the one stabbed. At least one commentator (R. L. Smith 1984: 276) does suggest that Yahweh has been metaphorically stabbed, i.e., by the people's attitudes of rebelliousness. Yet this seems far-fetched in view of the content of the rest of the verse. Even Gesenius regards the text as unintelligible (GKC §138.e [and] n. 1) and suggests emending ʾēt here to ʾel and dropping the preceding word (ʾly, "to me"), thus reading "they will look where they have stabbed" (cf. Ruth 1:16). None of these suggestions is compelling, and our retention of the MT is admittedly strained. Still, we keep it and understand that the Davidides and leaders are looking to Yahweh and at the same time to the stabbed one, with these two acts of looking being connected and with "concerning" constituting a guess at how they are connected.

they have stabbed. The single Hebrew word dāqārû, from the root dqr ("to stab, wound, pierce"), is surely one of the major interpretive cruxes in Second Zechariah, if not in all of prophecy. The outpourings of scholarly discussion do not center on the actual meaning of the word but rather on the identity of the one stabbed, the identity of those who commit this act of violence, the meaning of such an act, the relationship—if any—of this deed to general historical reality, and the possible allusion of this text to a specific political event. Mason gives a brief summary of the range of opinions (1973: 234–40 and notes), as do Saebø (1969: 96–103) and Rudolph (1976: 223–25); see also P. D. Hanson (1975: 354–67).

Let us first establish that the root *dqr* does not mean "to kill" but rather "to stab, pierce, wound" with a thrusting weapon, notably a sword (e.g., Lam 4:9; Isa 13:15; 1 Sam 31:4 = 1 Chron 10:4). In several instances it is clear that the victim of such an attack died (as in Num 25:8 and Judg 9:54, in addition to the references just cited). But the very addition of another term (as "and he died") indicates that although death would be expected because sword thrusts generally inflicted mortal wounds, this would not be necessarily or always the case. Indeed, Jer 37:10 mentions "wounded" soldiers who remain in their "tents" (cf. NOTE to "tents of Judah" in v 7); and Jer 51:4 may also indicate serious but nonfatal battle wounds.

The question of whether the "stabbed" one in this verse has in fact died thus must remain open. That the perpetrators of the stabbing are not held accountable in terms of being themselves subject to the death penalty may indicate that the stabbing in this instance was serious but nonfatal. This leads to the possibility that the image of confrontation, of violent opposition, is what is intended here in a somewhat more figurative sense. Still, the next image is that of mourning; here it is likely that death is involved but that divine favor toward the future Davidides and other leaders precludes the ultimate penalty.

We have already asserted, in our NOTES above to "house of David . . . leaders of Jerusalem" and "they will look," that the ones who are doing the stabbing are members of the royal bureaucracy—the royal house and all the officials coming under royal patronage. Who is it, then, whom they are attacking? We eschew political specificity here despite the temptation to read it that way, as do so many commentators and critics. Just as we have opposed the identification of the fate of various geopolitical entities in chapter 9 with certain recorded historical events (see, e.g., NOTE to "Hadrach," 9:1, and COMMENT to chapter 9), and just as we have insisted that the complex shepherd narrative of chapter 11 does not involve reference to specific events contemporary to the prophet's ministry (see, e.g., NOTE to "the three shepherds" in 11:8, and COMMENT to chapter 11), so we propose that the presence of "they have stabbed" does not have to indicate a specific act of violence in the prophet's day.

However, it is still incumbent upon us to suggest who the target(s) of such violence might be. The inclusive nature, in terms of the preexilic monarchic organization of Judah, of the ones who do the stabbing militates against the suggestion (as by P. D. Hanson 1975: 363–67) that this passage reflects factional tension in postexilic Yehud. For one thing, as our NOTE to "house of David . . . leaders of Jerusalem" explains, that terminology does not indicate any group holding power in the Second Temple period, although, of course, descendants of the preexilic royal bureaucracy were surely still present and so identified. But those implicated in this verse apparently included "hierocratic elements," inasmuch as the Levites and Shimeites are among those listed in the Catalog of

Mourners (see below, v 13 and various NOTES to that verse) who repent of their violent act, as well as the royal house and perhaps military officials (see NOTE to "house of Nathan" in v 12). Indeed, the wide range of leadership involved in this act seems to preclude any of the many suggestions as to specific groups in conflict that have been proffered.

Yet there is one remaining group, or rather series of individuals, who were habitually in conflict with virtually all establishment figures, i.e., with any or all of the full royal bureaucracy represented by "house of David" and "leaders of Jerusalem." We refer now to the true prophets of Yahweh. We propose that true prophecy is what is under attack in this verse. We do so for the previously stated reasons, which would seem to eliminate the other suggestions proposed in the scholarly literature. In addition, several other points should be taken into account.

First, a leading issue in much of Second Zechariah is the tension between true and false prophecy (see COMMENT to chapter 11). The prophet, in identifying with preexilic prophetic figures, especially Jeremiah, is acutely aware of how those in power—the royal bureaucracy in the preexilic period—brought suffering to prophets as the result of their compulsion to speak Yahweh's word. That suffering often included physical danger if not death, a possible fate of which Jeremiah was quite clearly aware (Jer 26:7, 11, 15, 16, etc.), especially because he knew that a similar fate had previously threatened Micah of Moreshah (Jer 26:18) and had indeed befallen Uriah ben Shemaiah of Kiriath-jearim. The latter was killed, with a sword, by King Jehoiakim through the instigation of "all his warriors and all the officials," i.e., the royal bureaucracy (Jer 26:20–23).

Second, the same word—"stab"—is found once more in Second Zechariah, in the next chapter. Although not used for an attack on true prophets, it depicts a legitimate confrontation with false prophets, whereby those who prophesy falsely in God's name will immediately be recognized for what they are by those who know them most intimately, and then they will be stabbed (see NOTE to "Then . . . will stab him" in 13:3). Because the case of Uriah demonstrates that swords were used against accused prophets, which are the weapons most likely to cause the stab wounds indicated by *dqr*, the use of "stab" may have come to denote all violent acts against prophetic figures, whether mortal or not.

Third, the retrospective nature of much of Second Zechariah must be taken into account. This prophet is keenly aware of centuries of Israelite history and tradition. He cites or alludes to the division of the monarchy (11:7, 14; see NOTES to "Bonds," v 7, and "kinship," v 14), the exile of the northerners (10:10; see NOTES to "Egypt" and "Assyria"), and the fall of Judah (11:10; see NOTE to "break"). Furthermore, as we have explained above, the perpetrators of the stabbing are those who held power before the Exile. This too may thus be a retrospective reflection of the historical struggle between prophecy and the ruling establishment, a struggle that will come to an end in the future age described here.

Fourth, the relationship of Second Zechariah to First Zechariah is also significant. In various NOTES (cf. Introduction) we have called attention to the way Zechariah 9–14 picks up on the language of Zechariah 1–8 and how it echoes certain themes or images of the earlier work. Despite their great differences, there are also unmistakable points of contact between the two. First Zechariah devotes a discrete section—the oracular introduction (1:1–6) that constitutes Part One of the tripartite organization of Zechariah 1–8 (see Meyers and Meyers 1987: 87–104)—to a retrospection involving preexilic prophets. Verses 4–6 in particular refer to divine anger directed toward "your ancestors," who ignored messages from God delivered through prophetic voices. Although First Zechariah does not specify any acts of violence committed against those prophets, he does mention their mortality along with the portentous refusal of the Judeans to attend to the prophetic message. Thus Second Zechariah follows his immediate predecessor in this consciousness of the failure of preexilic society with respect to the prophetic message.

Having said all this, we nonetheless would add that the prophet here is not simply indulging in historical sentimentality. The very fact that this stabbing holds such a powerful position in chapter 12, with the subsequent mourning developed through a series of similes and a subsequent Catalog of Mourners, suggests that the prophet is motivated by what he is experiencing in his own day, both personally and as a member of Yehudite society. As we have suggested elsewhere, the recurrent theme of the tension between prophetic groups—true and false prophets—surely indicates the prophet's direct and probably difficult involvement in the ongoing struggle. Here and in 13:2–6 he sees it resolved: those who attempted to thwart prophecy in the past are remorseful and mourn their wrongdoings, and any future false prophets that arise will be cut down at their roots, so to speak—by their own parents.

The difficulty Second Zechariah must have experienced because of his prophetic role is also connected with the larger world in which he lived. After all, why would there have been prophetic tensions at all if there were not disagreements about how Yahweh intended the people to manage their affairs, as individuals and especially in a corporate sense? Prophets expressed what they understood to be Yahweh's will in the unsettled days of Persian domination. We explore this further in our COMMENT to this chapter. Suffice it to say here that both Persia's tightening of its control over western provinces in the fifth century and the disappearance of Davidides from the Persian-appointed local Yehudite governorship must have contributed anew to concerns about national restoration and recovery of independence with a monarchic ruler in Jerusalem.

It is worth reflecting again on the semblance of specificity in this verse. Although we have argued against accepting the action described therein as an allusion to a single, real event, the fact is that precious little is known about Yehudite history of the fifth century. Perhaps some traumatic event, for which we do not have any evidence now and probably never will, did occur. But in the absence of such evidence, we have deemed it necessary to seek other ways to comprehend the vivid and powerful language of this part of chapter 12.

They will mourn. The verbal root *spd* ("to mourn, wail") appears four times in verses 10 and 11, and a fifth occurrence in verse 12 carries the idea of mourning throughout the Catalog of Mourners of verses 12–14. This repetition of the word for "mourning," accompanied by three powerful images portraying the intensity of grief (mourning for an only child, a firstborn, and perhaps a dying god) emphasizes the dramatic change in disposition that will overcome the royal establishment (see all the previous NOTES in this verse). Just as the external threat to Judah and Jerusalem will finally be removed according to the oracular statements of verses 2–9, so too will the internal threat—the failure of the royal rulers to listen to God's word as presented by the prophetic conscience of the nation—to the ideal kingdom be removed in the future age. All those who have done violence to God's word (by assaulting prophets) will now feel positive (with "favor") toward prophetic figures, will ask forgiveness ("supplication") and will greatly mourn all the evil they have done in failing to heed God's spokespersons and in attempting to suppress them.

In the ancient world, as they are in many cultures even today, rites of mourning could be very elaborate. Often there were public expressions of mourning. Certainly, events of national trauma led to the emergence of fixed days of community fasting and mourning, such as for the destruction of the Temple (2 Kgs 25:8–9; Jer 52:12ff.) and the assassination of Gedaliah, whom Nebuchadnezzar had appointed over Judah as governor after the fall of Jerusalem (2 Kgs 25:25; Jer 41:1ff.; see Meyers and Meyers 1987: 388–94). Indeed, the idea of national mourning may be drawn from the Gedaliah experience. Even though it is not clear that this projected mourning will be of such a national character, it clearly has national implications in that those who are depicted here as mourning all have national stature. The efficacy of this grieving on the part of the royal bureaucracy and ruling family is demonstrated by the first verse of the next chapter, which implies that the "sin" and "impurity" (see NOTES to "for cleansing [sin]" and "defilement" in 13:1) will be washed away.

for him. Namely, the "one they have stabbed." See above, the NOTE to "they have stabbed."

for the only child. This is the first of three powerful images that convey the idea of just how intense the mourning for the stabbed one (see NOTE above to "they have stabbed") will be. The word *yāḥîd* means "the only one," but because it is parallel here to "firstborn" (see NOTE below in this verse), it seems certain that it means an only child. Such an understanding is supported by the evidence of the most famous passage in which this term appears—the story of the binding of Isaac in Genesis 22. In that remarkable tale, the awful consequences that would result from Abraham's carrying out the sacrifice of Isaac in obedience to God's command are given dramatic poignancy by the repetition (Gen 22:2, 12, 16) of *yāḥîd* in reference to Isaac. Not only is Isaac the only child of Abraham; he is also the covenant incarnate. Without Isaac, as the audience listening to or reading this tale well knows, there will be no great nation descending from Abraham nor a claim to the Promised Land. The two aspects of the divine promise to Abraham will be null and void, and Yahweh will be discredited.

The dramatic force of "only child" in the Isaac story emerges from the concerns of a society in which property is transferred within family lineages. Thus even in circumstances less fraught with national significance, the loss of a sole offspring causes severe problems with respect to family landholdings and to the care of elderly parents which normally rests with their children. Thus the loss of an only child places a severe strain on a variety of social and economic circumstances and is indeed a cause for intense mourning. As difficult as is the loss of any child, the death of an only child stands to cause an exceptional depth of mourning.

The association between "mourning" and "only child" is attested in Amos 8:10 and in Jer 6:26 in the expression "to make mourning as for an only child" (ʾēbel yāḥîd). In Jeremiah the root spd ("to mourn") occurs in a parallel phrase together with mrr ("to grieve"; see next NOTE); in Amos only the root mrr is present, along with ʾēbel yāḥîd. From such passages it becomes clear that the idea of mourning for an only child is familiar in language expressing extraordinary grief.

grieve. The major versions read the third-person plural. However, the MT wĕhāmēr looks like a singular but is perfectly acceptable as an infinitive absolute, which can be used with plural subjects (cf. Amos 4:4–5, where there is a series of plural imperative forms with one exception, wĕqaṭṭēr, which looks like a singular but is really an infinitive absolute used as a legitimate substitute for the plural imperative).

The root mrr usually means "to be bitter," and its association with grief or grieving is apt. We have indicated in the preceding NOTE its attestation in Jer 6:26 as a noun ("mourning of bitterness") and in Amos 8:10 as an adjective ("a bitter day"). The sense of bitterness that is conveyed here and in the following infinitive absolute ("as one grieves") may be related to the way the Piel of mrr is used; in at least one case (Isa 22:4) it appears with weeping—to be bitter to the point of tears, which is how the NRSV understands it ("to weep bitterly").

With the root for "mourn" (spd) appearing five times and the one for "grieve" occurring twice, a total of seven terms for these emotions occur: the remorse is total.

firstborn. The word bĕkôr is parallel with "only child" and is a variant within the theme of loss that would cause extraordinary mourning and grief. The loss of an only child is paired with that of a "firstborn" (see NOTE above in this verse). They are complementary ideas and together express the great intensity with which the "house of David" and the "rulers of Jerusalem" (see NOTE above in this verse) express sorrow over their act of violence (see NOTE to "they have stabbed").

11. *On that day.* The final (seventh) occurrence of this eschatological formula in Zechariah 12. See the first NOTE to 12:3 for a discussion of this expression.

in Jerusalem. This is the last time that the name "Jerusalem" occurs in this chapter (see NOTE to "Jerusalem" in v 2). The constant repetition (eleven times) of this word in verses 2–11 establishes a central theme in this chapter, which depicts the eschatological future of Jerusalem—representing Zion, Judah, and all Israel—in the context of the rest of the world, and the future of Jerusalem as the setting of the royal leadership that will be restored to power. Yahweh is the source of the oracles that describe these two aspects of Jerusalem, and Yahweh is also directly involved in the events that will produce the restoration of autonomy to the nation and sovereignty to the royal bureaucracy.

Hadad-Rimmon. This proper name, which occurs only here in the Bible, is composed of two elements: Hadad, the West Semitic storm god identified with Baal in the Ugaritic texts from Ras Shamra; and Rimmon, apparently a variant of Ramman (see Greenfield 1976) and another name for Hadad (see 2 Kgs 5:18, which mentions a temple to Rimmon, where the Aramaean general Naaman wants to worship Yahweh). The root *rmm* in West Semitic (cf. Isa 33:3) is associated with storms, and Rimmon can thus mean "thunderer." However, the root *rmm* cannot be separated from the similar root *rwm*, which means "to be high, elevated, exalted." Such a meaning, for a place name, may be just as likely.

Although Rimmon is also used as the name of three different places in the Bible, none of these would qualify as being in the "plain of Megiddo." Hence the possibility that one or both of these terms is a toponym seems remote (but cf. next NOTE). Rather, the association of this name with extreme mourning, which is what this verse accomplishes in providing the kind of three comparisons that indicate the intensity of grief to be displayed by the "house of David . . . rulers of Jerusalem" (see NOTE in v 10), it may be understood as a reflection of one aspect of the cult of Baal, or Hadad-Rimmon. From the Ras Shamra texts, four major annual festivals can be identified in the cult of Baal. One of these, the Festival of Mourning (AOAT 16, 195f., 200f.; cf. Gaster 1961: 604, 609–10, 687), was probably related to the idea of the dying god and involved rites of mourning by the worshipers of Haddu-Baal. Moreover, the god Ramman is not known to have had any mourning rites associated with him; only by his connections with Haddu-Baal, and because of this reference in Zechariah, can such rites be suggested for this deity.

It is thus compelling, given our knowledge about mourning customs associated with Baal and Rimmon, to accept this name pair as a reference to such customs. However, because this name is known nowhere else and because the plain of Megiddo has another connection with mourning, the possibility that another allusion is present, instead of or in addition to this one, must not be excluded (see next NOTE).

plain of Megiddo. If the previous NOTE is correct in identifying Hadad-Rimmon as the name of a Northwest Semitic deity for whom a mourning festival was annually held, then this term apparently denotes a cult center in the Esdraelon valley in which such a festival was held.

However, there is no other evidence for such a Canaanite cult center existing there; hence the possibility must be considered that mourning in the "plain of Megiddo" (*biqʿat mĕgiddôn*) provides a historical rather than, or in addition to, a cultic allusion. It was at Megiddo that Josiah was killed by Pharaoh Neco in 609 B.C.E., according to 2 Kgs 23:29–30. In the Chronicler's version of that national trauma, the 2 Kings citation of "at Megiddo" as the locale of Josiah's death is expanded to "the plain of Megiddo" (*biqʿat měgiddô* [2 Chron 35:22]). In addition, the Chronicler tells us (2 Chron 35:24–25) that the burial of Josiah in Jerusalem becomes the occasion of an outpouring of mourning—"all Judah and Jerusalem mourned for Josiah"—and of lamenting by both the "singing men and singing women." Furthermore, that extraordinary outburst of grief over the dead king became an occasion for annual mourning—"to this day . . . a custom in Israel."

With the Chronicler's activity taking place in the postexilic period, perhaps very close to the time of the work of Second Zechariah, it seems certain that this annual mourning custom would have been familiar to the prophet. The fact that Zech 12:12–14 makes special mention of women mourning also fits the Chronicles description of the Josiah laments. Thus the connection with this highly unusual annual ceremony associated with a Judean king, the last one ever to have done "what was right in Yahweh's eyes" (2 Kgs 22:2), seems too prominent an example of extraordinary mourning to be excluded from the frame of reference known to the prophet's audience and hence informing their understanding of this statement. To be sure, the mourning for Josiah takes place in Jerusalem, not in the vicinity of Megiddo; but the deed that occasioned this custom did originate in "the plain of Megiddo" and so this conflation of deed and response need not pose a problem.

If "plain of Megiddo" is in fact a reference to the Josiah event, then Hadad-Rimmon would probably be a tiny, otherwise unnamed village or geographical feature in the Megiddo plains. Both elements are used to form compound names, and so their appearing together as a toponym is not impossible. Nor does the lack of such a name in the biblical onomasticon constitute a reason for suggesting such a place did not exist. Furthermore, the absence of ʿal before Hadad-Rimmon, which would be expected if one were to be mourning "over" Hadad-Rimmon, suggests that this term is a subjective genitive and not an objective genitive.

In sum, although it is difficult, if not impossible, to know whether "Hadad-Rimmon in the plain of Megiddo" refers to a Canaanite festival renowned for its mourning rites or to a unique Israelite custom of national grieving for a righteous Judean king, the latter possibility seems more compelling. Yet perhaps both possibilities would have struck a familiar note with the prophet's audience. They would have well understood his point: the mourning that will take place in the eschatological remorse of the royal establishment will be unique in its intensity and in its ongoing nature. For, unlike the mourning for an "only child" or a "firstborn" (see above, NOTES to these terms in v 10), the mourning of verse 11, whether for a Syrian deity or for an exalted king, is an annual occasion for the expression of grief. Thus all the comparisons together give a sense of the intensity and the ongoing nature of the mourning; the royal bureaucracy will have fully turned away from whatever negative acts had been part of their grief.

12. *The land shall mourn.* The idea of "the land" (*hāʾāreṣ*) mourning is an unusual personification, although there are a few other examples of "earth" as the subject of some action—e.g., "earth" (*ʾereṣ*) in Gen 1:11f. produces vegeta-

tion, and the "land (*ʾereṣ*) in Lev 20:22 "vomits" up those who disobey God's statutes and ordinances. One other striking example of the earth doing something is found in Isa 26:19, where the "earth" (*ʾereṣ*) brings forth shades (i.e., those long dead). In this case, as in several other instances, "land" may refer to the underworld, the earth in which the dead are buried (as Jonah 2:7 [NRSV 2:6]; Ps 22:30 [NRSV 22:29]; cf. Ugaritic, *yrdm ʾrṣ*). Thus "land" in this verse is probably not an inclusive term for all Israel or all Judah. The word for "land" can be used in many specialized ways (see Ottosson 1974; cf. Hag 1:10; Zech 1:11; 3:9; 5:3, 6; and see NOTES to "land" in these verses in Meyers and Meyers 1987); in this case, with its unusual personification of the term, the earth that receives the dead itself is said to mourn. Such a concept adds to the intensity of the mourning that the comparisons of verses 10 and 11 have already indicated (see NOTES to these verses) and that this very Catalog of Mourners sustains.

all the families. The word for "families" appears twice in succession without an intervening particle. This doubling expresses the idea of entirety (GKC §123.c)—the families without exception will be mourning. The repetition also sets the literary tone of these two verses, which is characterized by the formulaic repetition of certain words and phrases. "Families" is the first of these, followed by "themselves," "house," and "women."

"Families" (*mišpaḥôt*) represents the secondary level of social organization in ancient Israel—smaller than a tribe but larger than the "family household" or extended family (Gottwald 1979: 257–84). Thus the translation "family" is somewhat misleading, for this entity really consisted of a group of families (each known as the *bêt ʾāb*), linked together because they traced their genealogies to a common ancestor and/or because they inhabited a common geographical area (R. R. Wilson 1985). Thus it may technically be preferable to call such groups "clans" or "phratries," but such terms impart a sense of anthropological jargon that is not appropriate to the Hebrew text. Furthermore, because the families here are clearly larger units than the various lineages ("house of . . .") that are mentioned, there seems to be no possibility that "family" in verses 12–14 would be taken as a term for a nuclear or extended household group.

The use of "families" twice in the plural here is mirrored by the last part of verse 14, where the same plural word is also repeated. Thus these words form part of an inclusio that begins and ends this Catalog of Mourners. Because "the land shall mourn" precedes the words that form the framework of these verses, it thus serves as a title or a more abstract and general announcement of all the specific sets of mourners that are listed in these verses.

themselves. The Hebrew *lĕbād* means "alone, separate, apart" and is used to indicate something people do by themselves. Although it often takes a suffix, it can stand alone as it does in these two verses in reference to the families that are mourning. The word "families" is found both in the plural, at the beginning and end of this catalog, and in the singular elsewhere. Thus *lĕbād* might be translated "themselves" here and at the end, and "itself" everywhere else. Because "family" is a collective term for many individuals, however, and because *lĕbād* is repeated in exactly that form, without suffix, throughout verses 12–14, the uniform translation "themselves" seems to best represent the Hebrew.

The addition of "themselves," meaning "they alone," after each use of "family" or "families" underscores that all the members of these groups of royalty and the Jerusalem establishment (see NOTE in v 10 to "house of David . . . leaders of Jerusalem") will participate in the mourning for past misdeeds (see NOTE to "they have stabbed" in v 10) that will characterize the restored royal rule in the future age.

house of David. This is the first of the four lineages that form the Catalog of Mourners: David, Nathan, Levi, and Shimei. It is also the one that is easiest to understand. Just as elsewhere in this chapter and throughout the Bible, "house of David" refers to the royal lineage. In the case of David, therefore, the "house of David" might also be referred to as the dynastic family. Either way, the idea is that a group of people are linked together by their common descent from the named ancestor. That the royal house itself is mentioned first in this listing befits its position at the top of the administrative hierarchy both of preexilic times and of the projected future age.

their women by themselves. The separate mention of the women as mourners is not a sign of mourners being separated by sex within families (as claimed by R. L. Smith 1984: 277). Rather, it is a reflection of a specialized role held by women in ancient Israel and in the ancient Near East. That women functioned as professional keeners is evident in biblical texts (e.g., Jer 9:16–25 [NRSV 9:17–26]; Ezek 32:16; 2 Chron 35:25) and in monumental and textual remains from ancient Egypt (e.g., ANEP: n.638, n.640) and the Semitic world (see, e.g., Ahiram's sarcophagus, ANEP: n.457, n.459).

family . . . themselves . . . women . . . themselves. See the NOTES above in this verse.

house of Nathan. "Nathan" is a proper name used for seven or eight different individuals in the Hebrew Bible, although nowhere else is this name preceded by "house of." Clearly the most prominent Nathan is the prophet who lived at the time of King David, interacted frequently with him, and did not hesitate to confront the ruler and chastise him for breaches of moral standards (as in the Bath Sheba incident of 2 Samuel 11–12). Thus it is tempting to see here the name "Nathan" as a symbol of prophecy. The interpretation we have given above to the difficult "they have stabbed" (see NOTE in v 10) would seem to preclude such an identification. Those who stab are in conflict with prophetic figures such as Nathan who truly represent Yahweh's will; hence Nathanites would not be among those to mourn prophet(s) slain by the royal establishment. Furthermore, although prophets surely had children, there is not a single case in the Hebrew Bible of any prophet's being identified as the son of a known prophet. Prophets have no dynastic significance, in total contrast to kings and priests, who are classic dynasts.

Another possible candidate for what is represented by "house of Nathan" can be considered. The fact that several of the other Nathans mentioned in the Bible are associated with military figures in Davidic service may be relevant, especially because one of them was a member of the "Thirty" that formed David's elite military guard (2 Sam 23:8–39; see especially v 36, and cf. 1 Chron 11:38). Perhaps Nathan's family continued its prominent role in the military service of the king. Still, it should not go unnoticed that one of David's sons was called Nathan (2 Sam 5:14; 1 Chron 3:5; 14:4) and that this collateral line evidently survived for quite some time, inasmuch as it is recorded as being in the Jesus-David lineage presented in the Lucan genealogy (Luke 3:31).

Also in support of the possibility that "house of Nathan" designates a royal line is the fact that Gedaliah's assassin, Ishmael, is the son of a man called Netaniah, one of the longer forms of the theophoric name of which "Nathan" is hypocoristic (see Jer 40:8, 14, 15; 41:9; 2 Kgs 22:23, 25). Netaniah could well have been a member of the royal family who felt that Gedaliah, in accepting the governorship, was collaborating with the enemy. The mourning linked with the assassination of Gedaliah in First Zechariah (cf. Meyers and Meyers 1987: 388) may well be what lies behind this reference to the house of Nathan. If so, it would constitute another connection between First and Second Zechariah. Furthermore, although we suggest that the stabbing here alludes to the attack on true prophets, it is also worth considering that this chapter appropriates the emotional and ritual response to the traumatic events of the preterun period.

Another fact to be considered is that 12:12, which has the David and Nathan lineages, is set next to 12:13, which appears to have two priestly lineages. Thus, if the Nathan group is in fact a royal lineage, we would have a balanced arrangement, with two pairs of two each: David and Nathan representing royal dynastic families, and Shimei and Levi representing priestly ones.

13. *family . . . themselves . . . women . . . themselves.* See the NOTES to these terms in verse 12.

house of Levi. Unlike the other names in this catalog, "Levi" can represent a tribe rather than a subdivision thereof. Consequently, it seems likely that "house of Levi" is not here meant to be the equivalent of the tribe of Levi, which was viewed as being the landless group that was dispersed to serve as priests in the midst of all the other tribes (e.g., Josh 18:7; Deut 18:1). The actual history of "Levites" as a comprehensive term for priests or to designate a part of the priesthood distinct from the "priests" or the Zadokites is very complex. In the late preexilic period the Levites evidently held subordinate positions in the priestly hierarchy; but after the Exile the Levitical faction, represented by the Aaronides (Jehozadak and then Joshua; see Hag 1:1 and Meyers and Meyers 1987: 16–17), becomes prominent.

It is difficult to know which aspects of the "house of Levi" the term represents in this context, especially because it is not certain whether, in the fifth century, the prophet would have been able to sort out the varying priestly traditions stretching back over many centuries. Perhaps, then, it reflects his own day and the Levitical line that was in place in the Second Temple and assumed to be continuous with that of earlier days. What should be emphasized, however, is that although the priesthood may have had a degree of autonomy, the classic texts delineating the organization of David's reign depict priestly officials, including David's own sons, as being part of a kind of cabinet answerable to the king (2 Sam 2:15–18). It should also be recognized that priestly figures were not simply ritual officiants but had a wider range of administrative responsibilities within the sacral royal capital, including economic functions, teaching, judging, etc. (Deut 17:9; 33:10; see also Zech 3:7 and NOTES to that verse in Meyers and Meyers 1987: 194–97). Thus the "house of Levi" here represents some aspect of sacral national leadership based in Jerusalem under the aegis of the royal house.

family . . . themselves . . . women . . . themselves. See the NOTES to these terms above in v 12.

Shimeites. This proper name, unlike the other three names in these two verses, is not preceded by "house of." Perhaps it is intentionally different. On the other hand, the frequent repetition of several words in verses 12–14 may have caused an omission; indeed, several major versions (Syr, Targ) and two Kennicott manuscripts supply "house of." The Greek and Symmachus have "family of Simeon." In addition to lacking "house of" (*byt*), this proper name differs from the others in the Catalog of Mourners by virtue of being preceded by the definite article. Therefore, it occurs with a gentilic ending, meaning "the Shimeites."

"Shimei" appears forty-three times as a personal name in the Hebrew Bible in reference to at least fifteen different individuals; but only here and in Num 3:21 does it occur with the gentilic ending to denote a group of people associated with Shimei. The collective sense, judging from the Numbers reference as well as several other passages (Exod 6:17; 1 Chron 6:2 [NRSV 6:17]; 23:7, 9, 10[2]), refers to descendants of Gershom in the tribe of Levi. The simplest reading here would be to see "house of Levi" as not representing all priestly lines, and thus "Shimeites" referring to a subsidiary Levitical lineage with a traditional function in that part of the Jerusalem bureaucracy linked to the Temple. The fact that many of the other persons named Shimei are Levites (as in 1 Chron 25:3; 2 Chron 29:14; Ezra 10:23; 2 Chron 31:12–13) would support such a supposition. In addition, the parallelism of the pair Levi and Shimei with the preceding pair David and Nathan, in which "house of Nathan" may be a subsidiary Davidic line (see NOTE above to "house of Nathan" in v 12), strongly suggests such a relationship between "house of Levi" and "the Shimeites."

14. *All the remaining families.* This inclusive phrase is not meant to denote all the people of Israel, Judah, or Jerusalem. Rather, insofar as this Catalog of Mourners expands on the identity of "house of David . . . leaders of Jerusalem" (see NOTE in v 10), who committed the violent act(s) for which they all will mourn, the phrase represents all the other lineages in the royal bureaucracy not covered specifically by the four major groups listed in verses 12 and 13.

all the families. The plural *mišpaḥôt* is doubled here to represent entirety; cf. the NOTE to this phrase in verse 12. In repeating the phrase, along with "themselves," this verse echoes what appears near the beginning of verse 12, thus forming the concluding end of an inclusio. Just as "all the families by themselves" does not come at the very beginning of the catalog in verse 12, so does it not appear at the very end of verse 14, but comes before one more expression ("and their women by themselves"), which concludes the catalog.

COMMENT

The structure of this chapter bears some resemblance to that of the previous one. It begins with a quasi-poetic introduction; and it ends with a distinct unit, verses 12–14, that is not exactly poetic but yet, in being highly repetitive, stands apart from the narrative verses that precede it. In between the introductory and concluding sections is a long series of oracular statements in verses 2–11. All of these statements are given an eschatological coloring by the frequent use of the phrase "on that day." Interspersed throughout verses 2–11, this chronological formula appears seven times, intensifying the authority of the prophetic proclamations concerning future events that constitute the messages of this chapter.

The central oracular section of Zechariah 12, although treated as one unit in our arrangement of the translation, in fact has two major points of interest. The first is the future status of Yahweh's people with respect to the nations all around. This will involve divine action against those nations; and the cosmic might of Yahweh, as expressed in the opening hymnic fragment of verse 1, establishes God's ability to deal with the world beyond Israel. The second concerns internal matters. Historical tensions within Judah have precluded the people's full obedience to Yahweh's word. Those tensions must be resolved in the future age and thus are just as critical in the eschatological scheme as are relations with the powers of the external world; hence Yahweh will bring about the necessary changes. The concluding Catalog of Mourners (vv 12–14) echoes and emphasizes the theme of contrition and grief that the final oracular statements set forth.

Introduction: Yahweh as Creator, 12:1.

As we point out in our NOTES, verse 1 begins with a series of oracular terms or formulas. The first of these, "oracle," is found elsewhere in Second Zechariah only at the beginning of chapter 9. In addition, it opens the Book of Malachi. This set of three occurrences in Second Zechariah and Malachi suggests that Zechariah 9–11, 12–14, and Malachi 1–3 were seen as three subunits of the second half of the Haggai–Zechariah–Malachi corpus at some point near or at the end of their redactional history. Still, each of the three occurrences is distinct in terms of the associated prepositions used, thus indicating how each use of the introductory word "oracle" is sensitively keyed to the ensuing materials.

In addition to providing an introduction to chapters 12–14, as well as to this chapter, "oracle" functions as one of a string of terms, each of which is commonly used in Hebrew prophecy to introduce oracular statements. What is not so usual is the clustering of a group of such terms. "Oracle," "word of Yahweh," and "utterance of Yahweh" come together here to intensify the notion that God is the source of the messages proclaimed in the succeeding oracles. This intensification in the claim for divine authority can be seen in two ways.

First, it fits the general tendency in postexilic prophecy for formulas legitimating prophetic words to be strung together. It is difficult to know exactly why this happens, but it may somehow be related to the gradual fading and ultimate cessation of authentic prophetic figures in the centuries after the Exile. Perhaps the populace is more skeptical of words introduced as God's will, as well they should be in light of the oracular perspectives on prophecy in chapter 13. Consequently, prophetic figures such as Second Zechariah must counter such reticence to accept the validity of their prophecies with additional assertions of the legitimacy of their messages.

The second function of the clustering of oracular formulas here is related to the specific content of the oracles themselves. The scope of the first part of this chapter is universal; it involves Yahweh's power not only over God's people but also over all the nations or peoples of the world. The fact that what Yahweh is about to do is so inclusive calls for an assertion that Yahweh, the God of Israel, is indeed the source of global events. The same can be said for the second part of this chapter. It is precisely the internal leadership of Israel that has been so resistant, over the centuries of royal rule, to accept God's word expressed through the prophetic voice. Hence this postexilic depiction of the future age must be intensely insistent on the validity of that word in proclaiming a radical change in the attitudes of the leaders of the people in the future.

The hymnic language of verse 1 is labeled a doxology by some in recognition of the fact that such language, particularly as it appears in Psalms or in the prophecies of Second Isaiah, functions to praise God for all that God's presence in the world means for humankind. Such praise, however, is not explicit in this context. Rather, the specific content of the words used elsewhere as praise are directly relevant to the ensuing materials. As we have suggested in considering the string of formulas that open this verse, the oracular statements of this chapter involve the concept of Yahweh's universal dominion and of God's power to effect internal changes. Both these future activities depend on extraordinary divine might. What better evidence could be provided of God's ability to carry out what verses 2–11 describe than a statement about God's cosmic control! Thus is the audience reminded that Yahweh is the one responsible for the very existence of the entire world, with "heavens" and "earth" together signifying the totality of the created realm. Then, lest anyone forget where humanity stands within the scheme of creation, the second hymnic line singles out human life as entirely dependent on God's direct creative deeds.

Yet these words exalting divine power do more than that. They serve to identify the deity. They are a cosmological equivalent to the historical identification of the deity in such covenant passages as Gen 15:7 and Exod 20:2. The use of similar language in Jer 33:2 is significant in this regard. In Jeremiah, Yahweh as creator is involved, and the text uses the same sort of "call" and "answer" sequence that characterizes the covenant restoration passage of Zech 13:9 (see NOTES to "they will call . . . answer them" and "That is my people"

. . . "Yahweh is my God"). Hence the hymnic words can be related to covenant language. In that way they lend additional authority to the divine actions to be described, actions that will vindicate the stipulations of God's covenants with Israel and with the house of David.

This single verse, with its formulaic language heralding prophetic oracles and with its snippet of a hymn exalting divine power, thus prepares the way for the extraordinary claims for a reordered world, externally and internally, that will mark the future age. It begins with the reordering of Israel. Although the oracles themselves deal with Judah and Jerusalem, a focus that fits the postexilic date of the prophecies, which presumably originate within Yehud, the result of all that will take place will involve radical changes for all Israel. The phrase "concerning Israel" brings the message of this chapter into alignment with the attention to northerners as well as southerners that is present in chapters 9 and 10.

Oracles Concerning the Nations and Judah, 12:2–11.

The heart of this chapter is a series of oracular pronouncements, most in the form of direct quotations of divine speech, dealing with the status of Judah: (1) its relationship to other political powers in the world, which constitute a serious threat to Judah's autonomy and well-being, and (2) its internal organization, the dynamics of which must be altered in order for the eschatological vision of this and other chapters of Second Zechariah to be realized. Both of these aspects of Judah's future are couched in political language. Thus, although the repeated chronological formulas ("on that day"; "behold, I am . . .") project the events of this chapter into an eschatological setting, scholarly interest in Zechariah 12 has been characterized by attempts to identify specific political scenarios with supposed allusions to contemporary historical reality. Such attempts produce a predictably broad range of hypothetical reconstructions, especially in the discussion evoked by the enigmatic stabbing incident mentioned in verse 10.

We concur with the notion that the world as it existed in the prophet's own day must have had a determinative influence on the oracular statements of this chapter. Indeed, we will begin our consideration of these materials by examining the sociopolitical dynamics of the Persian period, especially what can be discerned about the fifth century, as a probable backdrop to the oracles and as factors that stimulated their utterance. The very frame of reference of these oracles, in their frequent citations of Judah and Jerusalem, bespeaks the purview of one who is situated within the political continuation—Yehud—of the last existing Israelite polity (Judah), despite the wider implications for the oracles proclaimed by the introductory doxology.

Yet we hesitate to endorse the idea that establishing historical specificity, that is, relating some of the concrete language of verses 2–11 to events purported to have occurred in the prophet's day, is a legitimate approach. We are skeptical of such an approach for several reasons. One is quite pragmatic: there is a serious shortage of reliable data from this dark age of Yehudite history. The widely and wildly divergent theories about possible historical situations underlying some of the verses in this chapter signal the relative lack of information available from other sources to provide a sense of the internal leadership patterns or tensions in fifth-century Yehud. With respect to external matters—Persian control over the provinces—the political realities are somewhat more accessible, even though much speculation remains about how Yehud itself fared within the spectrum of policies that characterized imperial rule in the postexilic era.

However, our reluctance to find historical specificity in the language of this chapter arises from a consideration of certain aspects of that language. The concept of *all* the nations or peoples of the world coming up against Judah expands the reality of the domination of Yehud, in which only one political power is involved. The inclusiveness draws as much upon Judah's historical past, in which a seemingly unending succession of nations sought to conquer the tiny Judean state, as it does upon the present. Similarly, the references to the "house of David" and the "leaders of Jerusalem," which depict the royal bureaucracy ensconced in Jerusalem (see especially our NOTES to those terms in v 7), draw from the preexilic political organization of the nation-state. As with other aspects of Second Zechariah (see COMMENT to chapter 11) and of biblical prophecy, the eschatological vision is future oriented while drawing on past experience. Yet present experience also appears in the formation of such eschatological oracles, and the recent past may be reflected in allusions to the assassination of Gedaliah. Still, the question remains as to the sociopolitical circumstances that impacted on Yehud and this prophet, giving rise to the vivid portrayal in Zechariah 12 of future events. Because the oracles themselves first address Judah's viability in the face of surrounding threats, and then deal with internal dynamics, each of these issues must be considered separately.

To begin with, the very eschatological cast of the vision of a transformed world order constitutes a response to reality in which there seems to be little hope for redress of conditions deemed unacceptable. Sociological analysis of peoples struggling to maintain identity while subjected to some measure of denial of autonomy shows varying kinds of responses (B. R. Wilson 1973: 22–25). These tend to be ideological rather than political, given the inherent powerlessness of those who feel compelled to respond in any way possible to such intolerable situations. Typically, such ideologies involve the idea that human agency alone cannot alter the status quo; rather, some sort of supernatural intervention must take place, usually involving the destruction of formidable obstacles to the restoration of a group's autonomy.

Because such a perspective is unmistakable in the prophecies of Second Zechariah, especially in 12:2–6 (and v 9), the likelihood that these oracles emerge from a situation in which a window of hope has opened, in which a glimmer of possible independence from Persian rule has appeared, would be remote indeed. The theoretical basis of this supposition seems to be borne out by what can be discerned about Yehud's status from nonbiblical sources for the Persian period. In particular, recent demographic and territorial studies of Yehud and Jerusalem in the Persian period, based on archaeological materials, survey data, and ethnoarchaeological analogies (Carter 1990; 1991), show that both those geopolitical entities were far more modest in size and population than had been hitherto supposed. Indeed, most biblical scholars dealing with the postexilic period who bother to consider such factors in their work tend to operate under erroneous impressions of what constitutes Yehud in the Persian period.

The fact of the matter (cf. discussion in Introduction) is that during the Persian period Yehud was barely 1,700 sq. km. (about 660 sq. mi.) in size, that is, about the size of Rhode Island. The extent of Jerusalem itself was barely more than 15 dunams, or perhaps close to 20 dunams (about 4 to 5 acres) if one includes some tiny satellite settlements in the immediate vicinity. With the sophisticated methods of population estimation now available, it can be calculated that Jerusalem—because part of its area was given over to public use (Temple, administrative complex, and perhaps a market district)—could not have had a population of much more than 400 souls. It was not until the end of the fifth century or even the beginning of the fourth, presumably after the time of Zechariah, that the city expanded to its maximum Persian-period size of 50 to 60 dunams, with a population of between 1,250 and 1,500 persons. The population of Yehud shows a similar pattern, with the number and size of settlements remaining quite small until the appearance of a noticeable number of new settlements in the last part of the era of Persian hegemony. For a discussion of these demographic factors, see our Introduction and the study by Carter (1991: 109–20).

In addition to Yehud's weakness, owing to its tiny population and probably a variable contributing to this demographic picture, was its relatively depressed economic situation for much of the Persian period. Between the devastation and depopulation caused by the Babylonian conquest and Exile on the one hand and the tribute or taxes extracted by the Persians on the other, settlements in the marginally productive Judean hills were slow to reestablish their economic potential, however limited that may have been, given the modest carrying capacity of most of the distinct environmental niches that constituted the territory of Yehud.

With this demographic and economic situation, Yehud hardly had the resources to break away from the might of Persian imperial domination. One cannot imagine any increased measure of autonomy accruing to Yehud unless it had been granted by the Persians themselves. The great unlikelihood of such a development is clear, considering the fact that, rather than easing control over the western provinces in the fifth century, the Persians sought to strengthen their presence in response to military threats from the west where the Greeks, in the form of action by the Delian League, supported the Egyptian satrapal revolt of 459 B.C.E. The archaeological record (see Hoglund 1989 and 1992) shows a midcentury upsurge in Persian fortresses in Yehud and neighboring provinces. Such fortresses would not only have helped protect Persian holdings from Greek incursions but would also have served as an added deterrent to any insurrections that might be contemplated by local populations.

The two images of Jerusalem in Zech 12:2–4 are remarkably congruent with the situation in postexilic Yehud, perhaps in the fifth century. Jerusalem is a cup (v 2) held in the hands of the dominant powers. Such powers grasp Jerusalem, to drink from her, because the idea of a cup held for drinking is that it contains abundance, that it even signifies life; thus Jerusalem's meager resources, its very life, was in the hands of superpowers. Similarly, the idea of Jerusalem as a stone may emerge from its role as part of the stone-built fortress system defending the imperial interests of the ancient world. Together these images suggest that, economically and strategically, Jerusalem as symbol of the nation of which it should be capital was, in fact, in the power of others.

What happens to both cup and stone is instructive. The meaning of these images is reversed. The cup, representing abundance and economic well-being accruing to those who hold it, instead has the opposite effect: it impairs the ability to function of those who hold it. Similarly, the constructive connotation of stones is turned upside down: Jerusalem will be the cause of injury, not strength, for those who purport to hold her. In both cases, the reversal is achieved through divine intervention and not through historical process. The powerlessness of Yehud can be overcome only through the direct deeds of Yahweh. Even more than in chapters 9 and 10, which likewise portray Yahweh's actions on behalf of the people through military imagery, Yahweh here is directly involved. Rather than empowering the House of Judah to fight the enemy, Yahweh here takes charge, turning the "cup" and "stone" from benign, if not positive, objects to instruments of destruction, and bringing about the ability to sustain sovereignty through military domination over the enemy by smiting its striking forces with "panic," "wildness," and "blindness" (v 4).

The implication of this direct divine activity is the utter helplessness of God's people to carry out any such resistance to dominance on their own. Once having initiated these actions against Israel's besiegers, however, God empowers the people themselves, through the royal leadership of Jerusalem (v 5) to complete the struggle. The last oracle of these verses concerned with "all the nations" conveys a vivid sense of the people acting on their own. True, Yahweh is involved: by making the Judean forces like "fire pots" and "fire torches." But those beneficial technological devices are used for destruction; and in describing their destructiveness the prophet has "clans" of Judah as subject of an active verb—"they will consume" all who threaten them (v 6). The Judeans thus become agents of their own restoration. Jerusalem too assumes its rightful status, as agent of its own destiny; it will flourish as the focus of the eschatological vision of Judean emancipation and as the locale of Zion, the center of the universe.

The future saving of the people by Yahweh from the domination of external forces and the consequent empowering of indigenous leadership having been established, the second major concern of these oracles of Second Zechariah comes to the fore in verses 7–11 and, through the continuing and emphasizing of what is expressed in these verses, in the Catalog of Mourners of verses 12–14.

Before looking closely at what these eschatological passages have to say about future Judean leadership, we must first consider the political situation within

Yehud in the fifth century. Clearly, the postexilic organization of the remnant of the former Judean kingdom, in having lost dynastic rule and political autonomy, differed radically from the preexilic state. The Davidic line had been severed, and a dyarchic structure involving high priest and governor managed the internal affairs of the tiny province. Indeed, as we suggested in our NOTES and COMMENTS to various passages of First Zechariah, especially 3:8ff., 4:6ff., and 6:9ff. (Meyers and Meyers 1987: *ad loc.*), political pragmatism led the prophet, and presumably the priestly and gubernatorial figures to whom he delivered Yahweh's oracles, to accept and promulgate this partial self-rule within the Persian empire. Such cooperation with the Persian authorities, who themselves had a vested interest in seeing Yehud manage its own affairs, led to the successful completion of the Temple-building project that helped to preserve the identity and sense of community of Yahweh's people following the trauma of exile.

The willingness of prophet and people to accede to such conditions reflects the complex behavioral dynamics of a group forcibly brought under the control of a dominant polity. If survival and identity are seen as goals integrally related to each other, certainly accommodations to the superior might of the conqueror was inevitable. At the same time, the shrewd imperial policy of the Persians enabled provincial acceptance of Persian rule to proceed relatively smoothly. Permission for, if not also active support of, temple restoration projects in Yehud and elsewhere in the empire certainly encouraged the cooperation of subject peoples. Similarly, the use of local dynastic figures as nonroyal governors contributed to the stability and docility of subject populations.

This last feature of Persian policy meant that for about the first half-century of Persian control of Yehud, the governorship (*peḥâ* = governor; see Meyers and Meyers 1987: 9–16) of Yehud was in the hands of a Davidide: first Sheshbazzar, then Zerubbabel (from 520 to ca. 510), and then Elnathan via his *ʾamâ* (handmaid? see E. M. Meyers 1985) from 510 to about 490. However, apparently at some point early in the fifth century, despite the fact that descendants of the Davidic family seemed still to exist, the Davidic share in the governorship of Yehud came to an end (see chart 2 in Introduction and NOTE to "your king" in Zech 9:9). It is impossible to determine the cause of such a fate, although many have speculated about it, to a great extent on the basis of seeing in 12:10 an allusion to an internal power struggle, perhaps one that ended with the death of a pretender to the throne and/or governorship.

We look at that passage quite differently (see NOTES to 12:10, and discussion below) and instead claim that there is not a shred of hard evidence to lend credence to the idea that a Davidide was slain, although the language of stabbing and mourning may be drawn from the Gedaliah incident and its aftermath. The disappearance of royal figures from a position of leadership may just as easily, and perhaps more logically, be comprehended as an astute move by the Persian authorities to have local rule securely fixed in the hands of nonroyal individuals. Such leaders would not symbolize so directly the lost independence of the province nor hold out the dream of reestablishing full local autonomy for Yehud as a dynastic state. The existence of a dynastic figure as governor clearly, at the outset of Persian rule, was efficacious in securing compliance and cooperation. Yet, as the decades wore on, the presence of a Davidide having only limited, and nonroyal, power in Yehud may have become too bitter a pill to swallow, particularly as other forms of community life resumed stability and as traditional sources focusing on the rule of Davidides gained authoritative status.

However it may have come about, the result was that, about a decade into the fifth century, governors with a connection to the house of David were a thing of the past. The appointment of Nehemiah as governor in 445 B.C.E., as documented in the Book of Nehemiah, shows a very different Persian strategy in appointing a governor (or *peḥâ*). Nehemiah was a functionary in the Persian court and, as such, would have been a loyal imperial subject when sent to be an official in his ancestral homeland. Although his immediate predecessors did not leave a similar record, the Nehemiah strategy may have already been in operation. That is, the termination of Davidides as governors is comprehensible as a way to appoint governors whose loyalty to Persia could be better monitored.

The cessation of participation by the house of David in the internal administration of Yehud took place precisely during the period, somewhere in the first half or middle of the fifth century, to which Second Zechariah or its compilation may tentatively be assigned. Thus, just as the intensification of eschatological depiction of Judean independence and even universal dominance represents a reversal of the political reality, so too would this emphasis on the house of David arise from a historical situation in which just the opposite condition—the deemphasis of Davidic potential—obtained.

It must be recognized that the reversal of historical reality that characterizes the eschatological picture of Second Zechariah does not involve the projection of a future that will simply be a restoration of past conditions. Certainly the prophet is strongly influenced by his reading of the past as he sets forth in bold language a vision of the future. Yet that future is never a straightforward replication of historical circumstances. The past is held sacred but is not uniformly idealized; its shortcomings are altogether too apparent in the traditional sources, prophetic and Deuteronomic, which apparently informed the prophet's understanding of the centuries of monarchic rule in Israel. Thus the prophet's portrayal of the future involves significant departures from what had existed in Israel's past.

Israel's relationships with other peoples are quite dramatically altered in Second Zechariah's eschatological scenario. Not only is there a return to autonomy, but there is also a clear sense of Israel becoming central in all the world. This is not worked out explicitly in Zechariah 12, except in terms of Judah's God-given ability to establish and maintain independence despite onslaughts from without. But it is clearly present elsewhere in Second Zechariah (e.g., 9:2, 10; 10:11; 14:8–9, 16), and it is a resounding theme in the oracles at the end of First Zechariah (8:20–23).

A revisionist perspective on the internal dynamics of the restored monarchy is an important, if not central, message conveyed by the attention to the house of David and the Jerusalem leadership in 12:7–11, as well as in verses 12–14. However, these changes are more subtly expressed than are the alterations in the view of Israel's status in the world. Perhaps because the idea of a Davidic monarchy was so firmly entrenched and absolutely accepted in Israelite belief, with Yahweh's promise in 2 Sam 7:8–16 of eternal Davidic rule apparently never questioned, any future view of the restored dynasty that included significant change might be construed as critical of the sacred idea of kingship as the requisite mode of political organization.

Nonetheless, Second Zechariah offers a vision of renewed ascendancy of the "house of David" and "rulers of Jerusalem" that has two significant differences. The first of these is the apparent lessening of the wide powers that had been exercised by the royal bureaucracy in the preexilic period. Although the inviolability of Davidic rule was never questioned, Deuteronomic and prophetic literature is often highly critical of actions taken by the crown and many kings are portrayed as little better than oriental despots. Thus a critique of the exercise of royal powers was already firmly part of prophetic expression among Second Zechariah's predecessors.

In addition, the years of exile and then partially restored national existence, i.e., at least a century of community life without royal leadership and subject to the rule of an imperial power, inevitably meant a reordering of leadership modes. Indeed, changes in leadership patterns by peoples deprived of their previous autonomy and self-determination is a critical survival mechanism for such dominated groups (D. L. Smith 1989: 73–74, 78–80). In the altered terminology present in biblical sources for various community officials, there are clear indications that internal self-governance, as opposed to the externally validated rule of the Persian-appointed governor and other officials, underwent structural shifts to accommodate the exigencies of external imperial control. Many of these shifts were no doubt made in the exiled communities, those physically removed to Mesopotamia, where discontinuities were even greater than for those not uprooted from ancestral holdings, and then brought back by returning exiles and eventually aligned with adjustments made by those who had remained in Yehud.

Whatever the exact forms of such restructuring may have been, it can surely be characterized as a decentralizing and, in a sense, a democratizing process, in that it represented, among other things, a response to the absence of the strong central royal figure of a monarchy. To some extent, priestly rule and ecclesiastical hierarchies emerged to fill the gap left by the absence of a king and royal bureaucracy. But at the same time, and especially among exiles without access to the Temple, grass-roots forms of leadership and community organization helped sustain the identity and group life of a people, distinct from the defining parameters of a nation-state. Some would even suggest, on the basis of careful examination of postexilic sources, the formation of a self-consciously communitarian structure ("citizen-Temple-community"; see Weinberg 1973; 1974).

These critical and transformative shifts in group structure and leadership are surely reflected in the dramatic statement of verse 7 that the "tents of Judah," i.e., the people themselves, will be the first to be rescued by Yahweh, for they are no less important than are the traditional splendors of the royal bureaucracy. As we explain in the NOTES to that verse, this reordering of the expected priorities of dynastic restoration reflects an accommodation to the decentralizing and democratizing adaptations that occurred in the many decades following the Babylonian conquest of Judah.

The second difference in internal matters in the prophet's vision of restored Davidic rule is depicted in startling but, at least to us readers in the twentieth century, enigmatic language. In our NOTES to verse 10, especially to "they have stabbed," we have suggested that this reference to an act of violence by members of the royal bureaucracy, although it may appropriate language deriving from the Gedaliah incident, concerns their historical tension with prophetic figures. Such tension actually involved two sets of relationships—between prophets of Yahweh and the national leadership, and between prophets of Yahweh and other ("false") prophetic figures who were frequently heeded while "true" prophets were ignored or were even in risk of their lives. The rivalry and tension between true and false prophets (see COMMENT and various NOTES to chapters 11 and 13) are undoubtedly of great concern to Second Zechariah. But that concern is not simply a matter of which prophetic group will hold the attention and gain the credence of the general populace. Rather, it involves what in many ways is a more fundamental issue—whether those in power, the national leaders, will adhere to God's word as communicated by the eloquent but often unwelcome voices of true prophecy.

Within the space of only one verse (v 10), although elaborating on them in verse 11 and in the Catalog of Mourners of verses 12–14, the prophet envisions sweeping changes in historical royal attitudes to prophetic figures. Only God's intervention, as for Judah's political ascendancy, can bring about this radical change in the attitudes of leadership to the bearers of God's word. Verse 10 sets forth four distinct features of the new mode.

First, the Jerusalem leadership will undergo a radical change of disposition. In their very character as human beings, the king and leaders will show "favor" (ḥēn), that is, react positively, presumably to those to whom they had previously not been so disposed.

Second, the leaders will not only have changed their attitude to such others, but they will also ask them for forgiveness. This attitude of "supplication" makes sense only if there are past misdeeds about which they are showing remorse.

Third, they will look to God for ultimate forgiveness about whatever violence they have perpetrated in the past. If persons have endured bodily harm and, probably, death at the hands of the royal establishment, then those who have so suffered clearly are not present to be the objects of pleas for forgiveness. Only Yahweh can respond to this new "spirit" that will come upon the house of David and its officials.

The final and perhaps most important feature, in terms of the attention given to this change in the quality of royal leadership, is the idea of the utter remorse of those who had acted wrongly toward prophetic figures. The admission of guilt and the accompanying great dismay find expression in the metaphors of mourning that appear at the end of verse 10, in verse 11, and in the concluding section of this chapter, verses 12–14. Not one, not two, but three striking comparisons are offered to characterize the completeness and intensity of the mourning that the ruling elite will experience. The efficaciousness of this outpouring of grief is assumed in this chapter but is then specified by the concept of purification in the opening verse of the next chapter (13:1; see NOTES).

All these extraordinary shifts in the very personhood or disposition of the royal bureaucracy constitute the radical change, accompanying the strong sense of continuity with the past, in Second Zechariah's vision of the restored house of David. In the oracular statements concerning national renewal amid hostile nations in verses 2–6, the language of Judah's restored power vividly depicts the full restoration of Zion. Here, in verses 7–11, equally compelling language asserts the new role of the Davidides. The very intensity of the images in both cases bespeaks both the difficulty, given conditions in the prophet's own world, in imagining that such a future might be realized and the unswerving expectation that it will come to pass because Yahweh has the will and the power, as the creator of the cosmos, to bring it about.

Catalog of Mourners, 12:12–14.

This concluding section of chapter 12 echoes and extends the notion of intense grief that the three comparisons of verses 10 and 11 have already portrayed. Indeed, so poignant and powerful are those three comparisons that one wonders why these additional and apparently repetitive materials about mourning have been included. The function of these verses may be, although it hardly seems necessary, to give further emphasis to what may have seemed unbelievable to the prophet's audience, namely, that the traditional power structure could undergo such a full change of heart. At the same time, and probably more central to their function, these verses serve to clarify what is meant by "house of David" and "leaders of Jerusalem."

A preexilic audience presumably would have known exactly who was represented by this terminology for the political power structures. Yet a century or more after those structures ceased to function, Second Zechariah's contemporaries would have been unsure of what these terms, or at least the second one, meant. Consequently, the prophet here lists four lineages—probably two royal ones and two priestly groups—to provide greater specificity about the future leadership of God's people.

In analyzing the three lineages other than the Davidic one (see NOTES to "house of Nathan," "house of Levi," and "Shimeites"), it is not easy to determine exactly which aspect of bureaucratic power may be indicated by a particular group. Furthermore, it is not clear whether the power structure represented by the four groups—two royal lineages and two priestly ones—is meant to recapture preexilic realities or instead to depict a future that takes present circumstances into account. The prominence of priestly participation leads us to suspect that the latter possibility is the more likely one. Insofar as priestly figures assumed a greater role in postexilic affairs than they had in internal governance during the monarchy, the attention given in this catalog to priestly families may signify the broadened administrative powers of the priesthood in the restoration period (see Meyers and Meyers 1987: 180–82; 194–201).

Despite the attention this catalog attracts, with its listing of specific names, as a repository of information about lineages and eschatological governance, other features of the catalog should not be overlooked. For example, it begins with the statement that the "land" shall mourn, and it includes the sevenfold use of "families" as it sets forth the groups that will grieve. These components add a strong note of inclusiveness to the theme of mourning. Not only will the royal family and Jerusalem leadership experience a change of disposition as well as intense remorse and grief over what has happened in the past; but, because, in a sense, everyone was involved in the failure of leadership, everyone will mourn the historical misdeeds that led to the conquest of the nation and to the exile of many of its people. The frequent repetition of "themselves," actually a singular word in Hebrew, further emphasizes the distributive mourning response. The four designated families are involved, but so is the land and everyone else, individually, as it were. The grief of the leadership is not carried out on behalf of all the rest—all others themselves will respond.

Finally, mourning itself remains a prominent theme of the catalog. The word for "mourning" is the very first word in the Hebrew text of verse 12 and thereby introduces and sets the tone for this concluding section of chapter 12. Beyond that, the phrase "and their women by themselves," which comes after each of the four lineages and then after the summary lineage ("the remaining families"), is really a further expression of mourning behavior. Although this fact would not be readily apparent to a modern reader, unaware of the special role of women in the ancient Near East with respect to funerary customs, the prophet's audience would have heard in the refrain mentioning women a reference to the skilled activities of women as professional mourners. The attention to women mourners as a refrain to each item in the catalog is thus a powerful reminder of the historical misdeeds of the nation's leadership.

ZECHARIAH 13

◆

Oracle: Cleansing of the Leadership

13 [1]"On that day a fountain will be opened for the house of David and the leaders of Jerusalem, for cleansing [sin] and for [cleansing] defilement."

Oracles on the End of False Prophecy

[2]"On that day"—utterance of Yahweh of Hosts—"I will cut off the names of the idols from the land, so that they shall not be mentioned again; and I will also remove the prophets and the spirit of impurity from the land. [3]If anyone still prophesies, his father and his mother who bore him will say to him, 'You will not live, for you have spoken falsity in the name of Yahweh.' Then his father and his mother who bore him will stab him when he prophesies.

[4]"On that day, the prophets will be ashamed, each one of his vision when he prophesies. They will not put on a hairy mantle in order to deceive. [5]Rather, he will say, 'I am not a prophet. I am a tiller of the soil, for the soil has been my possession[a] since my youth.' [6]If someone says to him, 'What are these bruises between your shoulders?' he will say 'I was bruised in the house of my friends.' "

Devastation for Many, Survival for Some

[7]O sword, arise against my shepherd,
>   against one intimate with me—utterance of Yahweh of Hosts.
Slay the shepherd, that the flock may be scattered;
>   I will turn my hand against the least.[b]
[8]And in all the land—utterance of Yahweh—
>   two parts in it will be cut off and perish,
>   and the third will remain in it.
[9]Then I will bring the third to the fire;
>   I will refine them as one refines silver,
>   and I will assay them as one assays gold.
They will call upon my name,
>   and I will answer them;
>   I will say, "That is my people,"
>   and they will say, "Yahweh is my God."

[a]Emending to *ʾadāmâ qinyānî*.
[b]Reading *šĕ'îrîm* with the Septuagint and Vulgate.

361

NOTES

13:1. *On that day.* The eschatological formula that punctuates the narrative of chapter 12, appearing seven times in the oracular statements of verses 2–11 (see NOTE to this phrase in 12:3), provides the opening words of chapter 13. The first phrase of this chapter thus immediately links it to the previous one. This connection is appropriate in terms of the content of the first verse, which continues and, in a sense, concludes the second part of the oracular statements of 12:2–11 concerning the future renewal of the royal house and its administrative adjuncts ("the house of David and the leaders of Jerusalem"). At the same time, the verse introduces the oracular statements of 13:2–6, which themselves relate to the matter of leadership—prophetic leadership—in the future age. As a bridge between the materials of these two chapters, it thus constitutes a small subunit, the first of three, of chapter 13. Still, its rightful place at the opening of chapter 13 (and not at the end of 12:1, where *BHS* puts it) is indicated by the punctuation of the MT and by the medieval scribes' notation.

Although the phrase "on that day" is found ten times in these two chapters (plus seven times more in chapter 14, where the exact same formula, with the imperfect of *hyh* instead of the perfect with *waw* consecutive, occurs in v 20), there are slight variations in the way it is used with the accompanying verb for which it provides a chronological indicator. In this case, the verbal combination is distinct (see NOTE below to "will be opened") and so serves to set off the ensuing statement in a way appropriate to a verse that bridges these two chapters.

fountain. The noun *māqôr* signifies a spring or fountain of water, although in several instances it can function more figuratively as a liquid "flow," as from the eye (Jer 8:23 [NRSV 9:1]) or as menstrual or postpartum blood (Lev 20:18; 12:7). In its meaning of "fountain," it is frequently paired with "waters of life" (e.g., Jer 2:13; 17:13) or, elliptically, with "life" (as frequently in Proverbs: 10:11; 13:14; etc.). As such, it is part of the cosmic language associating Yahweh with the source of life and creativity. The waters of life are among the images associated with Zion as the center of the universe and thus the focus of the Temple and the divine presence (see Meyers and Meyers 1992). Although *māqôr* is not repeated, the same concept of cosmic waters appears in the next chapter, which mentions the "living waters" (v 8; see NOTE) that will spread out from Jerusalem in the eschatological future when Yahweh's universal sovereignty is established (cf. Ezek 47:1–12).

The purifying aspect of the cosmic waters represented by the term "fountain" is unique to this verse. However, the flowing water implicit in "fountain" is linked with both terms—"cleansing [sin]" and "defilement" (see NOTES below in this verse)—used here to designate what will be figuratively rinsed away from the monarchy and the Jerusalem leadership by the fountain. The fact that Second Zechariah uses the concept of purification drawn from certain priestly Pentateuchal texts (Num 8:7; 19:9–31; 31:23) and connects it with a word found in other authoritative sources—prophecy and Proverbs—is another of the many examples of this prophet's creative use of traditional language. He breaks up idiomatic or stereotyped phrases to create a fresh idiom that nonetheless resonates with traditional modes.

It is worth noting that, although the vocabulary differs, the connection between kingship and the cosmic waters of Jerusalem is present in the narrative of Solomon's accession to the throne. At David's urging and under the supervision of the chief priest, court prophet, and other officials, Solomon is anointed king at Gihon (1 Kgs 1:32–40, 45). The spring at Gihon, on the east side of the City of David and just south of the Temple Mount, was Jerusalem's major and closest water supply. It is no wonder then that it was endowed with sacred and sacramental qualities. Likewise, it is hardly a coincidence that one of the four rivers of the cosmic garden at Eden is the Gihon (Gen 2:13). The linkage of the Jerusalem spring with the rivers of Paradise is part of the conception of Zion as the cosmic mountain, which partakes of the features of Eden as primal paradise (so Levenson 1985: 130–31, who refutes the analysis of Speiser 1967). Thus the eschatological restoration of monarchy involves not only the cleansing properties of the Jerusalem fountain but perhaps also the image of anointing associated with the cosmic waters of the holy city.

will be opened. The Niphal of *pth*, "to open," follows the imperfect of *hyh* ("to be"). The verb *hyh* functions in an important auxiliary sense: because *niptāḥ*, a participle, does not provide any chronological information, and because the temporal situation is important for the meaning of this verse, the imperfect *yihyeh* provides the essential future orientation. In so doing, it also serves as a variant to the way "on that day" is associated with verbal forms elsewhere in the ten instances in which that phrase is used in Zechariah 12 and 13. In some cases the finite verb comes directly after the eschatological formula (12:4, 6, 8, 11); in other cases *hyh* appears in the perfect with *waw* consecutive (*wĕhāyâ* in 12:3, 9 and 13:2, 4). Only here (and in 14:20) is *hyh* an imperfect with participle. This subtle variant serves to highlight the function of the verse as an introduction to the issues of chapter 13, which are linked to those of chapter 12, and at the same time it reemphasizes the future orientation of all these oracles.

The use of the finite verb (here the imperfect of *hyh*) with the participle (of *pth*) is an important characteristic of Late Hebrew prose (see Hill 1982 and Polzin 1976); indeed, such a construction prevails in Mishnaic Hebrew. The occurrence of this feature in Second Zechariah is one indication, among others (see Introduction), that its compilation or redaction, if not its composition, is postexilic.

The idea of a fountain being "opened" to cleanse or wash away evil is perhaps most prominent in the flood story of Genesis. Although the word used for "fountain of the great deep" in Gen 7:11 is not the same as the word for "fountain" in this verse (see previous NOTE), the imagery here, of water from primeval or cosmic water sources, is related to that of the windows of heaven being "opened" (*niptāḥû* [Gen 7:11; cf. Isa 24:18]) so that waters could pour forth to remove violence from the earth. More specifically, water served to remove the pollution caused by the widespread wrongdoing of the antediluvian era (cf. Frymer-Kensky 1977: 153–54).

the house of David and the leaders of Jerusalem. These phrases signify the dynastic rulers and royal bureaucracy, probably including priestly officials, of monarchic (preexilic) Israel. See the NOTE to these terms in 12:10 and the COMMENT to chapter 12.

for cleansing [sin]. The MT of "for cleansing [sin]" is pointed as a construct, *lĕḥaṭṭaʾt*, which would be a very improbable form before *waw* (cf. GKC §130.2). Thus it makes sense to repoint it, with BHS, as an absolute *lĕḥaṭṭāʾt*. The doubling of the *tet* in the MT indicates that the feminine noun is derived from the Piel, which Milgrom (1971; 1976a; 1981; 1983: 67; 1991a: 253–61; 1991b) has convincingly demonstrated is a Piel privative that conveys the notion of purging or purifying from uncleanness. Such an understanding is based not only on linguistic considerations but also on the fact that *ḥaṭṭāʾt* sometimes occurs in contexts unrelated to sin (e.g., installation of a new altar [Lev 8:14–15]) in which the *ḥaṭṭāʾt* sacrifice serves to purify but does not itself remove sin. Such arguments are persuasive, but do they imply that the purification offering is not related to the removal of sin? Milgrom would argue that committing sins makes one ritually impure and thus in need of purification but that the sin itself cannot be ritually removed. Although this aspect of the *ḥaṭṭāʾt* does not fit every case (see Anderson 1992: 879–80), it helps in general to understand *ḥaṭṭāʾt*.

The connection here with waters via the image of "fountain" (see NOTE above) and with the terminology associated with "defilement" (see next NOTE) supports the idea of *ḥaṭṭāʾt* as denoting cleansing or purifying. The NRSV translates the term freely as "to cleanse them from sin," which automatically includes the "sin" aspect, which may or may not be present. Other translations such as "for purging" (NJPS) and "for purification" (Soncino Bible; Cohen 1948: 323), exclude the "sin" connection. We have chosen to focus on the purification role of the *ḥaṭṭāʾt* by translating "cleansing." However, we supply "sin" in brackets to indicate that the term may not be entirely free from the nuance of sin while alerting the reader to the fact that the Hebrew consists of only one word. The fact that the next word is "for defilement" (= "for [cleansing] defilement) may mean that we really have an hendiadys here, perhaps "for the cleansing of the defilement of sin." Yet we have refrained from so translating because even if it is only the defilement of sin that is being washed away, the fact of having sinned is too prominent an aspect of this verse and of its ritual background to be relegated to a phrase modifying "defilement."

In the retention of the dimension of sin usually implicit in *ḥaṭṭāʾt*, the broader implications of that term are also retained. "Sin" involves, though not exclusively, misdeeds and the realm of morality. Although sins are committed by people against their fellow humans, whether willingly or unintentionally, they are nonetheless construed as sins against Yahweh. Hence most occurrences of this noun imply offenses to God, which is surely true here. This being the case, the idea of wrongful deeds being eradicated or purged by a purification or water ritual would seem to go against Israelite concepts of sin, because the

Israelites believed that wrong acts could not be obviated by ritual and that those committing such acts would have to be answerable for them. To cite the example of the flood story mentioned above (see NOTE to "will be opened" in this verse), the waters surely wash away the pollution caused by human corruption; but they also destroy all the human life implicated in God's assessment of the wickedness on earth. The Exile was viewed in similar terms as a purgation for sin (see Ezek 7:23; 8:17; 12:19; 45:9; cf. Frymer-Kensky 1983: 409–12).

The notion of cleansing from sin accompanied by a punitive experience is apparently absent from this verse, in which the Davidides and their royal entourage are depicted as becoming purified by the "fountain" itself. Why the difference? Several factors must be taken into account. The first is the emphatically eschatological setting in which there is a suspension of the logic in and ordering of human affairs that otherwise prevail. The Deuteronomic and priestly perspective on sin and culpability in some sense may be obviated in the eschatological restoration of Davidic rule.

A second consideration is the emphasis in the preceding verses in chapter 12 on the admission of misdeeds and the subsequent intense remorse. This remorse, as expressed in extraordinary outpourings of grief and mourning, surely indicates that the sins of the "house of David and the leaders of Jerusalem" (see previous NOTE) will have been directly confronted. Indeed, the fact that the royal family and bureaucrats will have undergone a radical change of disposition, through divine action (see NOTES to "spirit," "favor," and "supplication" in 12:10), can perhaps be viewed as part of the expiation process. Similarly, the mourning behavior is part of becoming answerable for sins and then eligible for the contamination of sin to be cleansed or washed away. The remorse is necessary but not sufficient for the purging of sins.

Third, the purification here is effected by waters, not by the animal offerings normally connected with the *ḥaṭṭāʾt*. This feature is more closely associated with the removal of the defilement than the next term implies. These waters, however, are not ordinary ritual waters that are used to cope with the impurity of certain states of defilement. Rather, the cosmic waters of the "fountain" represent the availability of the metaphysical waters of life. The supernatural powers of such waters, along with the eschatological setting already noted, would indicate that the cleansing could indeed be very inclusive—certainly of ritual defilement but also of more serious problems, perhaps even sin itself if not only the impurity caused by sin.

A fourth factor is the reality that, in a sense, punishment has already taken place in the loss of monarchic rule, when the Davidides and the national leadership were exiled and/or displaced from their customary positions, held for the nearly half-millennium of Judean statehood.

The association of waters with the purification from "sin," apart from "defilement," occurs only in Num 8:7. That passage prescribes the treatment for purifying the Levites so that they will be able to enter sacred space, that is, "do the service of Yahweh" (Num 8:11). They both offer a sin-offering and are physically cleansed by the "waters of (cleansing from) sin" and by being shaved and dressed in clean clothes. This full purification apparently is meant to cover all aspects of uncleanness, both moral and ritual. Such uncleanness would make a priestly figure ineligible to perform his function, a condition that underlies First Zechariah's description of the investiture of the high priest Joshua in 3:1–10 (see Meyers and Meyers 1987: 187–94, 218–22).

The "waters of (cleansing from) sin" in the Numbers text are replaced here, as indicated above, by the cosmic waters of the fountain that will be open in the future. The effect will be the same: the removal of the collective and defiling impurity of all the officials, both royal and priestly (see NOTES in 12:13 to "house of Levi" and "Shimeites"), who will resume office in their special roles with respect to Yahweh at the time of the restoration of God's people to autonomous existence in their land in the eschatological age.

[cleansing] defilement. The second term used by the prophet here is niddâ, which refers to the impurity or contamination resulting from contact with a polluting substance. As for the preceding noun, "cleansing," this term is preceded by l; both terms thus are the objects of what the "fountains" do. Because the language here is highly elliptical, we add "cleansing" in brackets as we do for "sin" in relation to the preceding term, to supply the full meaning and to provide intelligible English.

The word niddâ is used specifically and virtually exclusively in the Hebrew Bible in reference to the state of defilement involved in menstrual flow (Lev 12:2; 15:19, 20, 24, 25³, 26², 33; 18:19; Ezek 18:6) or in touching a corpse (Num 19:9, 13, 20, 21²; 31:23). Occasionally it is used figuratively (as in 2 Chron 29:5; Ezra 9:11; cf. Ezek 36:17, 25) to indicate the defiling effects of idolatry (cf. abolition of "idols" in next verse, Zech 13:2). Although this passage may also provide an instance of its figurative use, in combination with "sin" this term provides a comprehensive conception of the state of pollution, caused by both moral wrongdoing and contaminating activity, that will be removed by the cosmic fountain in the future age.

Unlike sin, "defilement" can be removed by ritual means. Furthermore, although it needs to be treated, it is not normally seen as dangerous unless it is brought into the sacred sphere (the Temple and its precincts). The exception to this is the defilement that comes from contact with a corpse; for that kind of niddâ, the treatment involves the mê niddâ ḥaṭṭāʾt, which means, approximately, "waters of sin-cleansing from defilement." This phrase is found only in Num 19:9; but mê niddâ, literally, "waters of defilement" (Num 19:13, 20 and 21), and, probably, simply "water" (Num 19:18), are most likely elliptical for the full phrase. A similar phrase and the elliptical "waters" alone occur also in Num 31:23 in reference to the purification after the incident at Beth Baal Peor, which involved both transgression (killing and idolatry?) and contamination (cf. the connection of this passage to purification by fire, both here and in v 9 below; see NOTES at v 9 to "I will bring" and "fire . . . refine").

Thus the evidence from these priestly sources provides further information about the linkage between "sin" and "defilement" under exceptional circumstances. Certainly the present context, in terms of both the persons involved and the eschatological setting, constitutes an extraordinary situation. Consequently, the claim of 13:1, through the use of these comprehensive technical terms, is that total purification from any and all sins or defiling actions committed by all royal officials will be achieved. The prophet has drawn terminology from Pentateuchal sources, but the "waters" of the Numbers passages has been replaced with the cosmic "fountain opened by Yahweh." Thus familiar language has been reworked to provide the continuity amid innovation that enables this passage to achieve its effect of assuring that the past deeds of the restored rulers and bureaucrats have been duly admitted (12:10), mourned (12:10–14), and now washed away.

One final point: the use of these various terms in 13:1 brings us into a semantic field that includes the word *ṭāmēʾ* (from *ṭmʾ*), "unclean." That word, although not itself present in 13:1, appears in some of the passages cited above (e.g., Numbers 19; Leviticus 12; Ezekiel 36) that contain one or the other, or both, of the priestly terms of this verse. Thus the use of *ṭmʾ* in "spirit of impurity" in the next verse (see NOTE below) is adumbrated in the language of this one.

2. *On that day.* This eschatological formula appears here for the second time in chapter 13. See above, the first NOTE to 13:1 and to 12:3, for a discussion of its meaning and its role in these chapters of Second Zechariah.

utterance of Yahweh of Hosts. Only in this verse and below in verse 7 does this particular version of the formula signifying an oracular statement appear in Second Zechariah. Both "thus said Yahweh of Hosts" (or, alternately, "Yahweh of Hosts said") and "utterance of Yahweh of Hosts" are found frequently in Hebrew prophecy, no less so in the Haggai–Zechariah–Malachi corpus. Indeed, the addition of the epithet "of Hosts" to the basic "thus said Yahweh" formula is disproportionately common in these prophetic books, while absent from Ezekiel and virtually nonexistent in the Chronicler's work (see Meyers and Meyers 1987: 12–19 for a discussion of this anomalous situation). Yet for Second Zechariah the stereotyped formulas involving "Yahweh of Hosts" are somewhat less prominent: the "Yahweh of Hosts said/spoke" formula is absent from Zechariah 9–14, and "Yahweh of Hosts" with "utterance" (*nĕʾum*) appears, as mentioned above, only here and in verse 7. However, it should be noted that the epithet "of Hosts" with "Yahweh" within the narratives or poetic lines of Second Zechariah does occur sporadically—in 9:15; 10:3; 12:5; and 14:16, 17, 21.

I will cut off. The verb *krt* is a common word meaning "to cut, cut off" (see its usage above in 9:6, 10). A somewhat specialized nuance of the verb involves its use for people being cut off from something by Yahweh. Frequently, priestly texts describe a penalty for some infraction as cutting the wrongdoer off "from" (*min*) the community (*ʿam*, "people"; so Lev 7:20ff.; Num 9:13). Such technical, cultic language is used figuratively in many prophetic texts (e.g., Isa 9:14; Amos 1:5, 8) for the removal of persons or elements that are disruptive of the covenant between Yahweh and Israel. Whether the cutting off implies death or a kind of excommunication is not always clear, although execution is probably always involved. But in either kind of absolute removal, the effect is the same: the influence and activity of whatever is so cut off will thereby be permanently terminated (cf. Andersen and Freedman 1989: 252).

"Cut off," however, has another dimension. As a supplement or enhancement to the capital punishment of the guilty party, it means the "cutting off" or killing of the members of the criminal's entire family or lineage. Consider the fate of Achan, who is stoned to death along with his sons and daughters for his sins (Josh 7:1–26; 22:20). Another example is the fate of Saul and his family; not only is he killed by enemy action, but all his family also suffers untimely death, thus showing that God intended to "cut off" Saul's dynasty. Thus, egregious transgression, which is surely what the idolatry in this context involves, can be eliminated only by doing away with the immediate family, to the third or fourth generation if any are still alive (cf. the old credal statement in Exod 34:6–7).

The objects of Yahweh's cutting off, the "names" of "idols" (see next two NOTES), represent the insidious and destructive presence of threats to Yahweh's sole and absolute sovereignty over the people. Saying they are to be cut off surely means that they will be destroyed. Yahweh thus becomes the agent of removing this threat of idolatry, which, according to the Deuteronomic and prophetic perspective, is the cause, at least in part, of destruction and exile. The use of *krt* in the Book of Nahum is particularly interesting in this respect. Nahum 1:14 describes the cutting off of "carved" and "cast" images and the death of those who use them. One of the phrases used to express the end of idolaters is "your name shall no longer be perpetuated" (cf. Zeph 1:4). Thus destruction surely is meted out to those who worship false gods. The idols themselves presumably cannot be put to death, inasmuch as from the perspective of these prophets they do not represent true divinity. Yet their cultic symbols—their names or images—can indeed be obliterated.

The cutting off of the names of idols is closely associated here, in the next part of this verse, with the removal of false prophets. The term "false" or "falsity" does not appear until verse 3 (see NOTE to "you have spoken falsity"); but the notion of prophets whose messages do not come from Yahweh, who thus must be removed in the future age, is here linked with idolatry.

We discuss below (see NOTE to "idols") the relationship of this verse to Ezekiel 14 (vv 3–8). The similarity of vocabulary involves words for defilement and prophecy in relationship to idolatry, although Ezekiel uses his own idiosyncratic term for "idols." However, he does insist that prophets speaking in the name of idols will be "cut off" (the verb is *krt*, as in this verse) from the people (Ezek 14:8). Indeed, such deceived prophets will be "destroyed" from Israel. The word for destruction, from the root *šmd*, seems to imply death. Similarly, Deut 13:1–5 proclaims death to prophets who lead people into the service of other gods; such behavior is nothing short of treasonous and must be purged from the midst of the people (cf. NOTES below in v 3 to "father and mother who bore him," "you will not live," and "Then . . . will stab him").

names. "Names" are the nuance of a person or thing in Semitic thought. Hence the existence of the name is tantamount to the existence of what it designates. This is perhaps most dramatically obvious in the first creation story of Genesis, in which Yahweh brings various aspects of the created order into existence by divine fiat. By saying, "Let these be X," the feature represented by X comes into being. Calling upon the name of a deity thus is an acknowledgment of that deity's existence. Conversely, removing a name—or cutting it off as in this case (see previous NOTE)—is tantamount to denying the existence and potency of the deity represented by the name (cf. NOTE below to "mentioned again" in this verse).

The use of "name" with "to cut off" occurs several other times in the Hebrew Bible. In each case, the implication is clear—cutting off names means destruction or nonexistence (e.g., Josh 7:9; Isa 14:22; 48:19), and having an "everlasting name" means that those with such a name will endure, will never be cut off (Isa 56:5; cf. Ruth 4:10).

idols. The word for "idol" is *ʿāṣāb*, which occurs only in the plural (*ʿăṣabbîm*) in the Hebrew Bible, as in this case. Several prophets prior to Second Zechariah employ this term in reference to the idolatrous behavior of the people in making images, probably cast of metal—of silver and/or gold (Hos 4:17; 8:4; 13:2; 14:8; Mic 1:7). Those prophetic castigations of idolatry refer to the faithlessness of the Israelites (the people of the Northern Kingdom). Only in 2 Chron 24:18 does *ʿăṣabbîm* refer to the worship of "idols" (and asherim) by the leaders of Jerusalem and Judah. Elsewhere in prophecy, and in psalms and historical sources, the *ʿăṣabbîm* are the idols of foreign nations, the impotent silver and gold images of impotent gods (e.g., Isa 46:1; Jer 50:2; 1 Sam 31:9; Ps 115:4; 135:15).

In Psalm 106, however, which contains a catalog of past sins of all Israelites going back to the worship of the golden calf at Horeb, the people are castigated for having offered sacrifices to Canaanite idols, thus causing the land to be polluted and themselves to become impure (Ps 106:36–39). That Psalms passage is relevant to this one in the sense that idolatry causes general pollution of the land, for here the idolatry in "the land" is at issue (see next NOTE). In addition, the impurity that idolatry causes is indicated by the verb *ṭmʾ*, just as the impurity here—resulting from false prophecy but probably also from idolatry (see NOTES below in this verse to "the prophets" and "spirit of impurity"—causes contamination. The Psalms passage refers to all preexilic idolatrous behavior, and perhaps the similarity of vocabulary to this verse indicates that Second Zechariah here has in mind those historical examples of national iniquity.

It is worth noting at this point that the association of idolatry, prophets, and impurity appears prominently in Ezekiel, notably in chapter 14. Ezekiel, however, uses the term *gillûlîm*, a term found almost exclusively in Ezekiel or in Deuteronomic literature closely linked with Ezekiel (Preuss 1978: 1). Second Zechariah, in using a term found in preexilic prophets, links the sins of idolatry to earlier periods as well as to the late preexilic period (and perhaps also the exilic age) that concerns Ezekiel. At the same time, although not ignoring the cultic implications, mainly impurity, of idolatry, the author of Zechariah 13 is looking beyond the priestly perspective that seems to determine Ezekiel's emphasis on the connection between uncleanness and the historical struggle between Yahwism and idolatry. Ezekiel 14 in particular is relevant to Zech 13:1-2, for there the prophet refers to idolatry (*gillûlîm*; 14:3, 4, 5, 6, 7), to those who seek out "prophets" attached to idols (14:7, 9), to the cutting off of such prophets (14:8, using the root *krt*; cf. the parallel destroying of such prophets, using the root *šmd*, in 14:9), and to the defilement (using the root *ṭmʾ*, 14:11) caused by the integrally linked transgressions of idolatry and idolatrous prophets. Second Zechariah, as often in 9-14, seems well aware of Ezekiel's language and viewpoints. He reworks Ezekiel's material, or draws from it, to express his own divergent perspectives.

from the land. The word for "land" here is *ʾereṣ*, the same term as in Ps 106:38 (see previous NOTE), which proclaims the polluting effect on the land of Israel's involvement in the service of Canaanite "idols." The land here is surely the land of Israel, the entire territory of God's people. The use of this phrase in association with idolatry is echoed in the second part of this verse, which concerns the removal of false prophecy "from the land."

mentioned again. Because Hos 2:19 (NRSV 2:17) reads, "I will remove the Baals' names from her mouth,/and they will not again be mentioned by their names," some manuscripts supply "names" again here. Second Zechariah and Hosea clearly share the notion that removing names (cf. NOTES above in this verse to "I will cut off," "names," and "idols") is tantamount to removing the idols that have been so damaging in compromising Israelite loyalty to Yahweh alone. But Second Zechariah, as is so often the case, is elliptical here and does not repeat in full the language from which he draws.

The term for "mention" is *zkr* in Hebrew, which is almost always translated "remember." When used with "name," however, it seems to be related to Akkadian *zakāru(m)* in its meaning of "to speak, say, name." The phrase *zikrum ša sumīya* apparently means the mention or pronouncing of a deity's name, i.e., the acknowledgment of that deity's existence and power. Thus, not mentioning the god's name is like cutting the name off: it denies the very reality of the idol or deity so designated.

and I will also remove. The adverb *gam*, "also," sets off the second major clause of this verse and introduces the two direct objects of "remove": "prophets" and "spirit of impurity." The verb is the Hiphil of *ʿbr* ("to pass over, pass on") and means "to cause to pass on," i.e., "to take away, remove." The Hiphil usage frequently involves the disposal of some negative quality (e.g., Eccles 11:10), as is certainly the case here. One reference in Kings to things to be removed involves idolatrous practices and is certainly relevant to this verse. In 1 Kgs 15:12, Asa put away the *qĕdēšîm* (illicit male temple functionaries) and removed idols (*gillûlîm*; see NOTE to "idols" above in this verse); he took all these idolatrous items or individuals away "from the land." The Kings passage uses the verb *ʿbr* with *qĕdēšîm*, whereas the parallel Chronicles text (2 Chron 15:8) specifies that Asa took away the idols (the word is *šiqqûṣîm*) and uses the Hiphil of *ʿbr*. Thus Second Zechariah's assertion that Yahweh will remove the prophets and "the spirit of impurity" (see next NOTE), which are clearly a result of idolatry, involves language that is somewhat closer to that of the Chronicler than to that of the Deuteronomist.

the prophets. The fate of the prophets is linked to that of the idols, given Second Zechariah's dependence here on Ezekiel's castigation of idolatry and prophecy and his assertion of the state of impurity that results (see NOTES above to "I will cut off" and "idols"). Thus this mention of doomed prophets may be a reference to prophetic figures who operated within the cults of Canaanite or other foreign deities represented by the term "idols." However, this part of Zechariah 13 is equally, if not more, concerned with another sort of prophecy, namely, that which falsely claims Yahweh as its source (see various NOTES to next verse). Indeed, our examination of "spirit of impurity" (see next NOTE), the other object of the verb "remove" in this clause, reveals that such impurity can result from false claims of Yahweh's word as well as from prophesying in the names of other gods. Thus "prophets" here may be an inclusive term for both kinds of prophets, all of whom will be expunged from Israel in the future age (cf. Deuteronomy 18, especially v 20).

This merging of the two different kinds of unacceptable prophecy may be a result of Second Zechariah's postexilic perspective. Many of the oracles of Zechariah 9–14 (see especially chapter 11 and 12:10, and NOTES and COMMENTS) are retrospective in character, and the condemnation of idolatry in this passage may refer to preexilic iniquity, in which case the condemnation of prophecy may also involve preexilic Judean or Israelite prophets serving Canaanite deities. It is difficult to know whether idolatry and associated prophets of other gods continued to be a serious issue in the postexilic period. However, the claims of prophetic figures to be speaking Yahweh's word, although certainly a major issue in the preexilic period, surely continues to vex Yehudite society and true prophets. Second Zechariah repeatedly and in various ways shows signs of the struggle to make Yahweh's word available over and against other claimants to prophetic voice.

Nonetheless, because of the use of "remove" (see NOTE above to "I will also remove") with "prophets" and its close association with the taking away of idolatrous elements, there seems to be a primacy, though perhaps not an exclusivity, to the connection of "prophets" with idolatry. Those other iniquitous prophetic figures, who speak falsely in Yahweh's name, are penalized with death (see NOTE to "you will not live" in v 3).

spirit of impurity. This phrase, along with "prophets," is the object of the verb "remove" (see previous NOTE and NOTE above to "I will remove"); these two objects are closely linked in expressing that which will be taken away from the land. Yet they are also related to the historical problem of idolatry, insofar as this verse, as we have already suggested, draws upon the language of Ezekiel 14, which condemns idolatry and the prophets connected with the service of idols. The existence of such conditions, diametrically opposed to the basic tenets of Yahwism, creates for Ezekiel a state of defilement in the "house of Israel" (14:11). Ezekiel's term for "defilement" uses the same root (*tmᵓ*) as does "impurity" here. That word, although commonly used for ritual impurity in many priestly passages (e.g., the lists of unclean animals in Leviticus 11; cf. Deuteronomy 14; or the defiling effect of corpses in Numbers 19; cf. NOTE above in v 1 on "defilement"), is also used metaphorically to describe the serious effects of idolatry and sin. Apostasy from Yahweh is paramount among the conditions that cause general impurity. Ezekiel repeatedly asserts—not only in chapter 14 but throughout his prophecies (e.g., 20:7, 18, 31; 22:3f.; 23:2, 13–17; 36:18, 25; 37:23)—that idolatry, as a form of apostasy from Yahweh, causes uncleanness.

In this verse, the feminine noun *ṭumʾâ* (from the root *ṭmʾ*) represents the uncleanness, or "impurity," that results from idolatrous practices. Just as the verbal form can represent ritual as well as moral impurity, so too does this noun denote the unclean state of those who have sinned. It is just such impurity that, historically, led to the destruction and exile, according to prophetic interpretation, especially by Ezekiel (Ezek 22:15; 24:13; 39:24). Ezekiel 36:25 goes on to envision the removal of that uncleanness: the people will be brought back from exile, and the impurity of their idolatry will be washed away with clean water. Similarly, in this verse, God's eschatological removal of impurity is related to the cosmic, cleansing waters of v 1 ("fountain"; see NOTE above).

Despite the frequency with which the verb *ṭmʾ* and its noun form appear in the Bible, only here is it coupled with *rûaḥ*, a word that can mean "breath" (e.g., Gen 6:17) or "wind" (Gen 8:1, etc.). But it can also denote something more difficult to pinpoint, an atmosphere or "spirit" often associated with some quality such as anger, jealousy, or, as here, impurity. In such cases, "spirit" comes close to *nepeš* in indicating the vital essence of something or someone (as above in Zech 12:1, which celebrates Yahweh as the creator of the human essence, "breath of humankind"). Again, a passage from Ezekiel is instructive. In Ezek 13:2–3, the prophet condemns "senseless prophets" who claim to have Yahweh's word but who, in fact, are doing nothing but prophesying out of "their own imagination" (*millibbām*) and following "their own spirit" (*rûḥām*). The association between "spirit" and false prophecy is close to what "spirit of impurity" of Zech 13:2 entails, because the impurity here is brought about by idolatry and false prophecy. Thus, although "spirit of impurity" in English gives the notion of some abstract quality disembodied from human life, it seems rather to be an elliptical phrase, denoting the unclean state that prophets bring upon themselves when they do not speak Yahweh's message.

Such an understanding of "spirit of impurity" is borne out by the way another phrase using "spirit" functions in the story of Micaiah and Ahab, which we have already cited several times in our discussion of chapter 11 (see NOTES to "with all the peoples," 11:10, and "knew that this was the word of Yahweh," 11:11). Micaiah tells the king that Yahweh revealed to him how Ahab would be deceived into setting forth on a military campaign that would result in his death. This feat would be accomplished by the presence of a "spirit of falsity" (*rûaḥ šeqer*; NRSV "lying spirit") in the mouths of all the prophets (1 Kgs 22:21–23). The same word for "falsity" appears in the next verse (see NOTE to "you have spoken falsity") in reference to prophets speaking lies in Yahweh's name. Thus "spirit of impurity" here denotes the result of the false words spoken in Yahweh's name as well as idolatrous prophecy.

from the land. See the NOTE to this phrase above in this verse. Its repetition achieves a certain balance: the idolatry that permeated the land will come to an end in the future age; so too will the uncleanness caused by prophecy drawing upon a spirit other than that of Yahweh, an impurity that likewise contaminated the land.

The emphasis here on removing idolatry, false prophecy, and impurity from the land is continued in verse 8, where the destruction of two-thirds of the land (or its inhabitants) is stipulated. It seems awkward there to have "land" stand for "people"; perhaps the desire to echo the language of this verse underlies the lexical choice in verse 9 (see NOTE in v 8 to "in all the land").

3. *If anyone still prophesies.* This clause introduces a scenario of what will happen if anyone sets out to prophesy, that prophecy being false, as the quoted speech of the parents indicates ("you have spoken falsity in the name of Yahweh"). The structure of this clause, with *kî* as the relative conjunction, is similar to that of some of the casuistic laws of the various Pentateuchal legal sections (e.g., Exod 21:14, 18; 23:4; Lev 1:2; 13:2; Deut 15:7; 18:6). Such case laws often begin with *ʾim* ("if"), but *kî* (meaning "if" or "when") also is found, usually to signify a case more likely to occur. Consequently, its use here involves this assumption that instances of false prophecy will continue to occur until the eschatological future. After the introductory conjunction, the case is then developed by three clauses beginning with *waw* consecutives: this first one states the problem, the second presents spoken parental response, and the third records parental action.

The chief exegetical problem posed by this clause, and indeed by this entire verse as well as the next two verses, is how the false prophecy of verses 3–6 is related to that of verse 2. If all prophets are removed from the land, how can such a case as this still exist? In our various NOTES to verse 2 (see especially "the prophets" and "spirit of impurity"), we drew attention to the strong connection of the language of that verse to other biblical materials dealing with the sins of idolatry and the uncleanness that results. Thus, although the possibility that the term "prophets" of the previous verse does not have to exclude the type this verse is concerned with—those who prophesy falsely in Yahweh's name—verse 2 clearly focuses on idolatrous prophets. Such figures are "removed" from the land, a fate that does not necessarily mean death; whereas here the false Yahwistic prophets will indeed be put to death.

his father and mother who bore him. The responsibility for dealing with a false prophet is placed upon the biological parents of such an individual (see COMMENT for a discussion of this striking exception to divine action in Second Zechariah's eschatological vision). That both parents are involved in this response and action, presented as a legal matter (see previous NOTE), is characteristic of Israelite household management and its jural-legal functions. Children are enjoined to obey mother as well as father (Exod 20:12; Deut 5:16; cf. Lev 19:3); and opposition to parents involves the death penalty (Exod 21:15,

17), from which there seems to be no recourse to an extrafamilial judicial body, although the community elders perform the actual execution (Deut 21:18–21). This jural-legal function of both parents was evidently a departure from other Semitic bodies of law (as Hammurabi n.195 in *ANET*: 175; cf. discussion in C. L. Meyers 1988: 154–57) and was a fundamental feature of Israelite family dynamics.

The responsibility of parents to deal with offspring who prophesy "falsity" (see NOTE to "you have spoken falsity" below in this verse) is nowhere stipulated in biblical law. But persons who encourage idolatry are to be put to death even by close relatives (see Deut 13:6–9), although the death penalty in that case, as for that of disobedient children, involves stoning, not stabbing (see NOTE to "Then . . . will stab him" below in this verse). However, the issues of false prophecy and idolatrous prophecy are not necessarily distinct (see previous NOTE and various NOTES to v 2), as Deuteronomic law makes clear in stipulating death for any prophet "who speaks in the name of other gods, or who presumes to speak in my [Yahweh's] name a word that I have not commanded the prophet to speak" (Deut 18:20). Consequently, the various legal traditions do provide ample precedent for the exercise of parental authority in dealing with offspring who disrupt the stability of either the household unit or the entire community.

The notion that parents will take legal responsibility for offspring who defy Yahweh is clearly and sufficiently expressed by "his father and his mother." Thus the addition of "who bore him," both here and in the next sentence (see NOTE below), adds a note of great poignancy to this situation and acknowledges the human tragedy involved in such a case, wherein the parents as source of a child's life are also the instruments of his death.

You will not live. The shocking scenario of parents condemning one of their own children to death is intensified by the use of quoted speech. We hear the words the parents speak in addressing their sinful offspring, and the first part of the quotation is the stark announcement of the death penalty. However, the death sentence is uttered in a reversal of the way it appears in the two texts cited above (see previous NOTE) concerning the death penalty, parents, and prophets. Those texts proclaim that close relations must do away with those who cause idolatry and that idolatrous and false prophets must be eradicated. In both those instances, the guilty party's fate is expressed by what will be done to him or her: "that prophet will die" (Deut 18:20) and "you shall surely kill them" (Deut 13:9). In contrast, the sentence here is expressed somewhat less directly, perhaps to ameliorate the harsh and extraordinary circumstances whereby parents are called upon to execute their own children. Such use of "not live" as a way of expressing the punishment of death is not unique to this verse, although it is not a common expression (cf. Gen 31:32; Exod 19:13; 2 Kgs 10:19). If it in any way lessens the impact of parents killing children, the last clause in this verse (about the parents stabbing their prophetic son) brings the shocking reality to the fore.

you have spoken falsity. The use of *dbr* ("to speak") for the oracular word of Yahweh is discussed in the NOTE to "have spoken deception" in 10:2. In that verse, "spoken" is used with "deception"; and in the parallel bicolon "falsity" (*šeqer*; see NOTE) is the object of the verb "to see." Moreover, *dbr* occurs a second time in 10:2, in reference to the dream interpretation that misled the Israelites. In using these words, Zech 10:2 (see NOTES), as frequently does Jeremiah, draws upon much Deuteronomic language (Deut 18:10–14) condemning all prophetic activity that derives from practices of other peoples and that consequently provides messages that do not have Yahweh as their source. Zechariah 13:3, although similarly echoing Deuteronomic and prophetic views about false prophecy, does so very elliptically. Presumably this statement about speaking falsity, along with the next phrase ("in the name of Yahweh"; see next NOTE), represents the entire range of behaviors that characterize professional prophets. The next three verses (13:4–6; see NOTES) likewise present aspects of professional prophets. However, there those features are disclaimed by God's true prophets, for whom the label "prophet" should no longer be used.

The prominence of *šeqer* ("falsity") in Jeremiah is noteworthy in its connection to the claims of other prophets, opposed by Jeremiah at the risk of his life, that Judah will be spared destruction. However, the nature of the "falsity" in this verse is not specified. Yet given the reference in the introductory verse to the preexilic governance structure ("house of David" and "leaders of Jerusalem"; see NOTE above) and the connections of this chapter to the allusions in chapter 12 (see especially NOTE to "they have stabbed") to the way the monarchic leaders had listened to the wrong prophets and eliminated the right ones, a similar retrospective view may inform the meaning of "deception" here (see also the connection of "falsity" with "spirit," as pointed out in our NOTE to "spirit of impurity" in 13:2). At the same time, the prophet's own experiences vis-à-vis others trying to influence Yehud's leaders no doubt have motivated this intense diatribe against false prophecy (cf. COMMENT to chapter 12 and to this chapter).

in the name of Yahweh. "Name," as an indication of the essence of that which is so designated (see NOTE to "names" in v 2) is frequently used as a designation of the God of Israel, the so-called Deuteronomic "name theology" being a case in point. Thus the phrase "to speak in/with (*b*) the name of PN [Proper Name]" becomes a stereotyped way to claim the authority of the one whose name is cited. The *locus classicus* for its use in the Hebrew Bible is the passage in Deuteronomy 18 (vv 18–22), cited in the two previous NOTES, which condemns to death prophets who "speak in the name of other gods" or who "speak in my name a word I have not commanded." However, the phrase is not widely found in the Bible in regard to prophetic activity: it is used once with Moses (Exod 5:23), once of David (2 Sam 6:18), once by David (1 Chron 21:19) in reference to past prophets, but elsewhere only in Jeremiah (20:9; 26:16; 29:23; 44:16), who is surely influenced by Deuteronomy 18. This passage in Zechariah likewise echoes the Deuteronomic (and Jeremianic) stance toward false prophecy. Although it refers specifically to wrongful claims to the authority of Yahweh for prophecies offered, Zech 13:3 shares with Deuteronomy 18 the problem of the close alliance of this variety of false prophecy with the idolatrous kind (cf. NOTES in v 2 to "I will cut off" and "idols").

father and . . . mother who bore him. This phrase repeats the language of the second clause of this verse, which identifies the parents of false prophets as the ones who impose the death sentence (see NOTE above in this verse). If that notion is shocking, this one is more so—that parents will carry out the execution. Furthermore, unlike other biblical cases involving parents imposing death upon their offspring (Deut 13:6–10 and 21:18–21; see next NOTE), this one involves no outsiders or members of the community. This case, then, is diametrically opposite to the horrendous one of 12:10, in which the leading public officials stab someone, perhaps a true prophet. Here the false prophets are dealt with and eliminated by the basic unit of society, the family household. Non-Yahwistic prophecy will never again flourish and perpetrate evils if it is rooted out at its source.

Then . . . will stab him. The verb is prefixed by a waw consecutive, as are the verbs of the two preceding clauses of this verse. This, then, is the third and final part of this extraordinary "case of false prophecy" (see first NOTE to v 1).

The verb dqr ("to stab, wound, pierce") and its meaning in Second Zechariah is discussed extensively in our NOTE to "they have stabbed" in 12:10. Much exegetical energy has been devoted to that verse, but we have diverged from the many scholarly proposals by suggesting that the stabbing victim may represent prophetic figures wrongfully injured or put to death by national leaders in the preexilic period. The association of prophecy with the same verb in this verse provided one of several reasons that led us to propose such a possibility. The stabbing here, however, is radically different from the utterly reprehensible act of violence of 12:10. Whereas the slaying or harming of true prophets may be the act castigated in chapter 12, it is the systematic destruction of false prophets that is the act stipulated here.

Because the verb is unambiguous in referring to the use of a thrusting weapon, such as a knife or dagger but more likely a sword, the mode of carrying out the death penalty (see first three NOTES to this verse) for false prophecy differs from that which other biblical sources seem to indicate. Deuteronomy 13:6–10 prescribes stoning for the execution of those individuals—even close relatives—who lead people to idolatry. Similarly, parental action against rebellious children (Deut 21:18–21) involves stoning. However, although those cases are analogous in terms of parents executing children, they lack the specification that false prophecy is at issue; and they also both include community involvement in carrying out the death penalty. Thus they are at significant variance with this case of family juridical action, which is immediate and direct—with no other participants—and which is effected by stabbing.

This mode of execution of prophets is precisely that used in the one case of such an act preserved in biblical sources. Uriah ben Shemaiah was struck down by a sword (Jer 26:23) wielded by the king (Jehoiakim). In an earlier generation, Micah of Moreshet-Gath narrowly escaped a similar fate (Jer 26:18–19), and Jeremiah himself continually fears such a demise. Although "sword" is not mentioned directly in the cases of Micah and Jeremiah, the fact that the Uriah incident is cited would indicate that the possibility of death by the sword of the royal leadership was what struck Jeremiah with such fear and reluctance to prophesy. If some true prophets were executed by the sword or threatened with such a death in the preexilic period, the future age will bring about an utter reversal of those conditions: false prophets will be the ones eradicated, and the process will take place at the grass-roots level, i.e., within the family household, and not by the royal leadership.

when he prophesies. The preposition *b* is attached to the verb. Usually a spatial indication, it occasionally denotes time, as is the case here and in the next verse. The addition of these words (actually only one word in Hebrew) seems to indicate that the death penalty for false prophecy will be executed at the moment of such activity. If so, the inherent privacy of parents interacting with offspring without community involvement (see previous NOTE) is mitigated somewhat in that the essence of prophetic acts involves interaction with those to whom a prophetic message, whether legitimate or not, is being delivered.

4. *On that day.* This is the third and final occurrence of this eschatological formula in Zechariah 13 (see NOTES to this phrase in vv 1 and 2). It is used even more frequently—seven times (in vv 3, 4, 6, 8², 9, 11; see NOTES to these verses)—in chapter 12, and it again punctuates the oracular statements of the next chapter (14:4, 6, 8, 9, 13; see NOTES to these verses).

prophets. The term for "prophet," in both its noun and verbal forms, occurs six times in chapter 13. In all but this instance, it clearly refers to the prophetic activity that is being condemned. Second Zechariah, as this verse and the next one reveal, does not want to give the label "prophet" (*nābîʾ*) to someone who, like himself, utters what Yahweh wants the community and/or its leaders to hear. Thus the prophets in this verse and the next two disclaim that title (see NOTE below to "I am not a prophet") as well as any of the visible markers of professional prophets such as garb ("hairy mantle"; see NOTE in this verse) or physical stigmata ("bruises"; see NOTE in v 6). Yet Second Zechariah nonetheless must label them here for the sake of introducing the dissociation with the professional or popular prophecy that he accuses of falsity.

In traditional biblical texts prophets are known by various titles (e.g., "seer," "man of God," "visionary"; see Orlinsky 1965; R. R. Wilson 1980). Clearly, the term "prophet" is used for legitimate Yahwistic figures, from Samuel (1 Sam 9:9)—or even going back to Moses (Deut 34:10)—through the writing prophets, including Jeremiah and Second Zechariah's immediate predecessors, Haggai and First Zechariah. However, that label was also used for professional prophets, apparently organized in guilds and drawn from lineages, at least in the Second Temple period (1 Chron 25:1–5). And surely any individuals claiming to speak for Yahweh so designated themselves. Second Zechariah's solution to the tension and confusion caused by these disparate figures using a common title is to do away with it—anyone communicating Yahweh's authentic word will not have sought to do so and will thus not bear a label that all too often has identified those who speak without true Yahwistic authority. Indeed, a considerable segment of postexilic prophetic work, perhaps to be called "deuteroprophetic" (Petersen 1977: 13–45), may have denied that classical prophecy continued in their day except insofar as these deuteroprophetic figures sought to reflect on and keep alive the contribution of preexilic prophecy.

will be ashamed. The verb *bwš* ("to be ashamed") is found frequently in the Bible, but only here and in Mic 3:7 is it associated with prophetic behavior. It is often paired with another term, such as *klm* (in the Hophal, "to be confounded, dishonored"; e.g., Jer 14:3; Isa 41:11; Ezek 16:52) or *ḥpr* ("to be abashed, put to shame"; e.g., Jer 15:9; Job 6:20; Ps 71:24). The Micah passage in fact uses *bwš* and *ḥpr* in parallel bicola dealing with false prophecy: "the seers (*ḥōzîm*) shall be ashamed (*bwš*), and the diviners (*qōsmîm*) shall be abashed (*ḥpr*)." The reason for their shame and dismay is that they do not receive Yahweh's word.

If Second Zechariah is drawing on this earlier prophetic language, he is surely equating the behavior of prophets with the seers and diviners who do not speak Yahweh's message (cf. next NOTE and NOTE to "diviners" in 10:2). But, as is often the case when he echoes earlier authoritative traditions, he does so elliptically—here using "prophets" to represent professional figures such as seers and diviners, and using only "ashamed" instead of the pairing of related words for "shame" found in Micah and elsewhere.

each one of his vision. The singular term *ʾîš* ("man, one") is in apposition with the plural "prophets," this shift emphasizing that each individual who uses the trappings of false prophecy will feel dismay or shame about such behavior. The term for "vision," *ḥizāyôn*, is that which "seers" (*ḥōzîm*; see previous NOTE) experience and offer as their message. This noun is an alternate form of the more common *ḥāzôn* (see 2 Sam 7:17, which has one form, and its parallel in 1 Chron 17:15, which has the other). Although both words are used in critiques of false prophecy, visions in and of themselves are not illegal or necessarily non-Yahwistic (in addition to the Samuel/Chronicles passages just cited, see Joel 3:1 [NRSV 2:28] and Ezek 7:26).

when he prophesies. The Niphal infinitive has been incorrectly construed by the Masoretes as a third weak verb ending with *he* rather than with *aleph*; therefore the MT transcribes *bĕhinnāʾbōtô* instead of *behinnābʾô*, which is the form it takes in the previous verse (see NOTE above). Such a confusion is frequently found in Biblical Hebrew and in fact may not be the fault of the scribes but rather the result of an obsolete orthography. In any case, these words are somewhat redundant and so may be seen as the prophet's attempt to intensify the fact that people who say they prophesy are not truly prophets, and that true prophets would be ashamed of such behavior.

They will not put on. This verb resumes the plural; the root *lbš* means "to wear, to be clothed." The connection between professional prophets and a particular kind of clothing (cf. next NOTE) appears in 11:15 in the context of shepherd imagery representing false prophecy (see NOTES to "gear" and "a foolish shepherd" in that verse), although the verb there is *lqḥ* plus *l*, "to take for oneself."

hairy mantle. In our NOTES to "gear" and "a foolish shepherd" in 11:15, we pointed out that, as for many who held public positions or filled certain societal functions, the role of professional prophet was linked with a signifying mode of dress. The designation of such dress in this verse, *ᵓadderet śēʿār*, literally means "cloak of hair."

The word for "mantle" or "cloak" (*ᵓadderet*) can mean "glory" or "wealth" (see NOTE to "their wealth" in 11:3), but it is well attested as a term for a garment (as Josh 7:21, 22). Its most prominent use in that sense is in the description of the garments of Elijah and Elisha (1 Kgs 19:13, 19; 2 Kgs 2:8, 13, 14). That their garments are associated with their roles as prophets is indicated by the way Elisha succeeds Elijah in his prophetic role. When Elijah ascends to heaven, Elisha tears off his clothes and takes up the "mantle" Elijah left behind when he ascended to heaven. That garment had been used for one of Elijah's magical prophetic acts: dividing the waters of the Jordan. Its physical qualities are not specified. However, in another passage in which the term "mantle" itself is not present, Elijah is described as a "hairy man" with a leather belt. The word for "hairy" (*śēʿār*) is the same as the one in this passage. It seems certain that what made Elijah the prophet identifiable was a particular garment, not that he had a hirsute body and wore only a belt. Thus the mantle of the miracle story is undoubtedly a "hairy" one, as is that of the false prophet of this verse. The New Testament certainly understands the Elijah materials that way, for John the Baptist, an Elijah figure as precursor to the messiah (so Mal 3:23–24 [NRSV 4:5–6]), is depicted as dressed in "clothing of camel's hair with a leather belt around his waist" (Matt 3:4).

In short, when used in reference to a prophet's garb, *ᵓadderet*, whether with or without the term "hairy," apparently refers to a special cloak, either one made of animal hair or, more likely, because of the details of the Esau story (see below), a robe made of animal skins with the "hair" or fur intact. Note also that Samuel appears to have distinctive garb; when he is called from the dead, he is recognized by his "robe" (1 Sam 28:14; the word here is *mĕʿîl*).

The phrase "hairy mantle" does appear once elsewhere in the Hebrew Bible. In Gen 25:25, Esau's body is described as being "like a hairy mantle," which apparently means his skin was covered with plentiful body hair so that he looked furry, in contrast to his rival brother who had smooth skin (Gen 27:11). This feature of Esau's appearance adumbrates the grand deception of Genesis 27, by which Jacob procures the birthright when his mother dresses him in animal skins so that his nearly blind father will think that he is Esau, the hairy elder son who should be principal heir to his father's possessions. This story, of course, does not involve prophecy; but then Esau does not wear a prophetic garment—he only appears as if he does. Yet the phrase "hairy mantle" is nonetheless part of the Esau narrative, and the trickery that is also part of that narrative is noteworthy, for it too has an indirect connection with Zechariah 13. The term for the deception in Gen 27:35 is *mirmâ*, from *rmh*, which in Hos 12:1 (NRSV 11:12) occurs in parallel with *kḥš* ("to deceive"), the very word that concludes this "hairy mantle" text in Second Zechariah. Thus the idea of such a garment evokes two major concepts: prophecy and deceit, which together are the essence of "hairy mantle" in this verse (see next NOTE).

to deceive. The verb *kḥš* ("to deceive") in the Piel completes the theme of deception introduced by "hairy mantle" (see previous NOTE). In 1 Kgs 13:18, in the story of the prophet and the man of God that we cited in our discussion of the "worthless shepherd" (= false prophet) of 11:17 (see NOTES to "woe," and "will surely wither" in that verse), there is tension between these two prophetic figures. The one who claims to be a prophet by saying, "I too am a prophet as you are" (1 Kgs 13:18), goes on to deceive (*kiḥēš*) the other, proclaiming that what he said was the word of Yahweh. The fascinating thing about the Kings tale is that the person who self-identifies as a prophet, in claiming to speak Yahweh's word, is in fact one who deceives, hence proving to be a false prophet, whereas the "man of God," who really does prophesy "by the word of Yahweh" (1 Kgs 13:2), is not designated by the title "prophet."

The concept of true prophecy in that tale is remarkably close to that of Second Zechariah: people known as prophets deceive and so are inherently false; only those who make no such claim—either by word or garb or other sign—truly give voice to Yahweh's word. All those who persist in claiming to be prophets are deceitful and will be destroyed (see various NOTES above to vv 2 and 3). A similar notion appears in Ezek 14:9–11, where prophets who deceive (there the root is *pth*, "to deceive, entice," the same root used three times by Micaiah in describing how prophets with a "lying spirit" [*rûaḥ šeqer*] deceive Ahab; see NOTE to "spirit of impurity," above in v 2) are to be destroyed along with all transgressors in Israel.

5. *I am not a prophet.* If a true prophet, or one who continues preexilic classical prophetic tradition, will refuse to wear traditional prophetic apparel as a way of dissociating himself from the falsity and deception of those who wear such garb (see three previous NOTES), here he achieves the same goal by means of a verbal disclaimer. He invokes traditional language, using the same words that one of the very first of the classical prophets used. In Amos 7:14, the prophet responds to Amaziah, the priest of Beth-el, who had accused him of conspiring against King Jeroboam. His stirring reply is among the most well-known prophetic quotations: "I am not a prophet, nor the son of a prophet; I am a herdsman and a dresser of sycamore trees." That is, he claims that he is not a prophet (*nābî*)nor a member of a prophetic guild (*ben nābî*); rather, his social identity is expressed by his agrarian role.

Second Zechariah draws upon the Amos text, quoting the first part of it exactly, omitting the second part, and then substituting a simplified job description (see next NOTE) for the double role that appears in Amos. In so doing, this prophetic work follows a pattern discernible throughout (see Introduction). Second Zechariah appeals to or uses traditional materials but never in a slavish way. The words are used in different configurations, often elliptically, to express the nuances of the perspectives suitable to the postexilic age. In this case, however, despite the differences from Amos 7, the fact that at least part of the Zechariah 13 text is an exact quotation indicates that the message of Amos in dissociating himself from a prophetic profession (see Würthwein 1950) rings true to the view of this postexilic prophet, who speaks out in God's name several hundred years later. Yet Amos clearly played a prophetic role in society (see

Amos 3:3–8), and in citing Amos, the author of Zechariah 13 must likewise be open to the existence of prophetic roles other than the false ones he would eliminate.

I am a tiller of the soil. Whereas Amos (see previous NOTE) identified himself as a "herdsman and a dresser of sycamore trees" in his prophetic disclaimer, Second Zechariah uses a variant occupational designation in his projection of the self-conception of true prophets in the future age. Although the preceding words are a direct quotation from Amos, these words are different as befits the eschatological context. That is, they seem to echo the earliest biblical identification of humans as farmers. This clause (in Hebrew, *ʾîš-ʿōbēd ʾădāmâ ʾānōkî*) draws upon the language of Genesis describing the primeval farmers in the origin of humanity and civilization. In Gen 2:5, 15, the first human "tills" (the root is *ʿbd*) the "soil" (*ʾădāmâ*). In Gen 4:3, Cain is identified as "one who tills the ground" (*ʿōbēd ʾădāmâ*), an occupation taken away from him, to his utter dismay (see 4:13–14), as punishment for fratricide. And Noah, the first viticulturist, is called a "man of the soil" (*ʾîš ʾădāmâ*). These three leading figures in the primeval history of Genesis are the ancestors of all people and, consequently, of all farmers. Thus the quintessential occupation for this eschatological figure who denies he is a prophet is, in apt balance with beginning times, also a farmer.

for the soil has been my possession since my youth. These ten English words translate four Hebrew words; thus this statement balances, in both number of words and number of syllables, the preceding clause (see previous NOTE) that it explains and intensifies. However, the Hebrew text of this clause is corrupt. The emendation proposed by *BHS*, as first suggested by Wellhausen (1898) and as accepted by Mitchell (1912: 340) and others, has considerable merit and is what we read here. That is, the corrupt *ʾādām hiqnanî* (literally, "a man has acquired me") is better understood as *ʾădāmâ qinyānî*, "the soil has been my possession." This change requires only the addition of a *yodh* to the MT, with the misplacement of the *he* on *hiqnanî* apparently being the result of scribal error. The word for "youth" is *nĕʿûrîm*, which is the abstract noun for "youth" and is related to *naʿar* ("young man"; but cf. Meyers and Meyers 1987: 153–54). It indicates the period of time in the life of a person: his or her youthful years, or "youth."

The overall intent of this clause, by stating that that person has been linked with the land since his youth, is to proclaim that he has always been a farmer, not a prophet.

6. *If someone says.* The *waw* before the perfect of the verb *ʾmr* ("to say") introduces an alternate or additional case. That is, verses 4–5 deal with one aspect of false prophecy that will be disclaimed, namely the wearing of special garments signifying professional prophecy (see NOTES to "hairy mantle" and "to deceive" in v 5). Now another example of the behavior of professional prophets that is to be rejected is put forth. Thus the connector (*waw*) can be translated "if" or "and if" (see BDB: 252).

What. The interrogative particle here constitutes the only instance of a question being posed in all of Second Zechariah (see Introduction). Yet even here, it is not part of directly reported dialogue but rather introduces an indirect hypothetical query.

bruises. The question posed to the individual disclaiming the title and trappings of prophecy concerns marks or bruises (*makkôt*; from the root *nkh*, "to strike, smite") on his or her body. Like special clothing (see NOTE to "hairy mantle" in v 5; cf. "gear" in 11:15), certain modes of activity characterized the professional identity of prophetic figures. Dancing, eating or imbibing certain foods or liquids, and chanting were such activities; flagellation or wounding by one's own hand or by that of an associate was apparently another.

One dramatic example of the latter practice involves prophets of a foreign god—in the famous contest between Elijah and the prophets of Baal on Mount Carmel, the Baal prophets "cut themselves, as was their custom, with swords and lances until blood poured out over them" (1 Kgs 18:28) when they failed to receive a revelation from their deity. Perhaps an even more striking example, in terms of its similarity to this passage in Zechariah, is the incident in 1 Kgs 20:35, in which a member of a prophetic guild ("sons of the prophets"; cf. NOTE above to "I am not a prophet" in v 5) says to a colleague, "Hit me!"—the word for hit (*nkh*) being the same root as that found in this verse. The result of blows struck in this specific kind of prophetic flagellation are apparently bruises rather than bleeding cuts, for the root *pṣᶜ* ("to bruise") denotes the wounds in 1 Kgs 20:37 (cf. the same combination of *nkh* and *pṣᶜ* in Cant 5:7 and Prov 20:30); hence we translate "bruises."

Deuteronomy 14:1 contains an unambiguous biblical prohibition against self-laceration. However, it uses the root *gdd* ("to cut"), which is the same verb used of the Baal prophets in the Elijah passage mentioned above, and which also appears in Jeremiah in reference to a funerary custom of self-laceration (Jer 16:6; 41:5; 47:5; cf. Hos 7:14). Because the self-cutting both by the Baal prophets and by mourners apparently involved the flow of blood, the bruising signified by *nkh* would consequently not be included in the behavior prohibited by Deuteronomic law. Indeed, flogging (again, using the root *nkh*) is mandated in Deut 25:2 (cf. Prov 19:29). Thus the negative connotations of bruising activities as practiced by ecstatic or professional prophets (see Petersen 1977: 35, 71), who are condemned by Second Zechariah for not speaking Yahweh's word, are derived from their association with prophets deemd false.

between your shoulders. Literally, "between your hands" (*bên yādēkā*). The idiom is known at Ugarit (*ktp . . . bn ydm*), where "shoulder" is used with "between the hands." A similar expression in 2 Kgs 9:24, "between the shoulders," uses *zĕrôᶜa*, which can mean "arm" or "shoulder." The normal word for "hand" (*yād*), which is used in this instance, is not always sharply differentiated from the anatomical parts with which it is associated: the wrist, arm, or even shoulder (compare the way *regel* can mean "foot" or "leg"; Ginsberg 1978: 131). Thus "hands" here is a kind of synecdoche representing the upper extremities, so that bruises "between the hands" signifies marks on either the chest or back. Because flogging as a punishment (Deut 25:2; cf. previous NOTE) apparently involved striking a person's back (see Prov 19:29, which proclaims that flogging is "for the back of fools"), the likelihood is that the expression "between your shoulders" signifies that the bruises are on the person's back (contra, e.g., NRSV's "on the chest").

This idiom is obscure enough to have been taken literally and associated, by some New Testament scholars, with the nail wounds incurred by Jesus at the crucifixion. Dodd (1953: 65) points out that the New Testament itself does not connect Zech 13:6 with a prophecy of the crucifixion but that later tradition saw in Zechariah's "bruises between the shoulders" a reference to the passion of Jesus.

I was bruised. The person queried about the marks on his back (see two previous NOTES) responds with a denial that they were received through flagellation, presumably of the sort certain members of prophetic guilds practiced, by asserting a different origin for his bruises (*makkôt*). Using the verb *nkh* in the Hophal, he admits to having been "bruised," but the next phrase (see next NOTE) provides an explanation that precludes an association of the marks on his back with any sort of false prophecy.

in the house of my friends. The word rendered "friends" is a Piel plural participle. Elsewhere in the Hebrew Bible it refers to adulterous lovers (Hos 2:7, 9, 12, 14, 15 [NRSV 2:5, 7, 10, 12, 13]; cf. Lam 1:19) or relations with prostitutes (Ezek 23:5, 9, 22), or, more figuratively, to "lovers" (e.g., Jer 22:20, 22; 30:14; Ezek 16:33, 36, 37) as those, rather than Yahweh, with whom Jerusalem or Judah has been intimate. However, it would make no sense to have a person disclaiming the role of false prophet to be admitting to another unacceptable activity. Thus this participle must reflect what another part of the semantic range of the verb *ʾhb* ("to love") denotes, namely, the strong emotional connection betwen friends, even though such human affection is normally conveyed by the Qal participle (e.g., 1 Kgs 5:15 [NRSV 5:1]; Ps 38:12 [NRSV 38:11]; Prov 14:20).

The notion of a true prophet being in the company of "friends" rather than professional colleagues, such as "sons of prophets" (see NOTE to "I am not a prophet" in v 5), is part of the characterization of Jeremiah (Jer 20:4, 6), a Yahwistic prophet with whom Second Zechariah strongly identifies (see NOTE to "they have stabbed" in 12:10). Thus the individual who, like Amos, denies being a prophet, and who also dissociates from the clothing or marks of professional and/or ecstatic prophets, would thus be with friends rather than colleagues. We prefer such an understanding rather than that it might signify parents, who love children and who figure in verse 3 above (see NOTE to "his father and his mother"), as Mitchell (1912: 339) and others assume.

It should not be overlooked, in trying to understand *mĕʾahăbāy* ("my lovers" or "my friends"), that this word is coupled with "house." Whatever has happened has taken place in private space. Thus, whoever the "friends" may be, the fact is that the bruises in question (see NOTES above to "bruises" and "I was bruised") have not taken place in the public locales normally associated with the activity of professional prophets.

In light of all this, it is nonetheless clear that the actual way in which the person received his bruises is not specified. They could have been received in a household accident or in a quarrel with these friends—but we are left wondering, a fact that makes us suspect that this disclaimer is a cover-up. That is, the bruises may in fact be flagellation wounds of a professional prophet who now, in the eschatological future, renounces his profession and thus must find an explanation for the physical signs of his former role. In the other disclaimer of this passage, the former professional simply will not clothe himself in the characteristic apparel of his group and thus can easily prevent being identified as a false prophet. Someone with marks on his body must, as here, resort to another form of denial, namely, claiming an innocent acquisition of the suspicious bruises.

7. *O sword*. The third subunit of Zechariah 13 begins with this apostrophe to an instrument of death and destruction. That the "sword" here is meant as a weapon causing mortal wounds is indicated by its use with the root *nkh* (see NOTE below in this verse to "slay"). In this sense, the imagery here differs from that of 11:17, in which a shepherd is also threatened with a sword. There, however, the "sword" has no associated verb; it is used only against the shepherd's arm and eye, making him ineffectual as a "shepherd" but not inflicting fatal injury (see NOTE in 11:17 to "arm . . . right eye"). This distinction between the fate of the shepherd of this verse and that of 11:17 is one of the considerations that lead us to suggest a different identity for this shepherd (see NOTE below in this verse to "shepherd"). It also constitutes one of our reasons for retaining verses 7–9 in chapter 13 rather than moving them, as do a majority of scholars (e.g., Mitchell 1912: 316ff.; Chary 1969: 194–96; P. D. Hanson 1975: 338–39, 334, 348; Rudolph 1976: 212ff.; Mason 1977: 110; etc.) to a position following 11:17. We are not alone, however, in suggesting that verses 7–9 fit well into their canonical position (see, e.g., Baldwin 1972: 197; R. L. Smith 1984: 281ff.; Saebø 1969: 276ff.; Lacocque 1981: 173, 196).

Although the sword imagery here diverges from that of chapter 11, it is similar (see NOTE to "sword" at 11:17) in that no wielder of the weapon is specified. In such cases, the sword can be none other than the "sword of Yahweh," which functions as an instrument of divine judgment, representing the unequivocal punishment to be inflicted upon those who disobey Yahweh's word. The notion of God's sword as a tool of judgment originates in the idea of Yahweh slaying Israel's political enemies (e.g., Deut 32:41–42) or the "wicked" even within Israel (Ps 17:13; Amos 9:14). In its eschatological thrust, however, particularly in exilic or postexilic sources, it also can reflect the destruction of Yahweh's own people and hence is used in reference to the slaying of Israel's leaders. Ezekiel 21:14–17 (NRSV 21:9–12), for example, depicts Israel's princes along with many others being destroyed by the sword.

arise. The root ʿwr ("to rouse oneself, awake") is not among the many terms used idiomatically with "sword." The verb *qwm* ("to rise"; cf. Amos 7:9) might seem more suitable. However, ʿwr is not inappropriate, especially given the context of apostrophe, of calling to battle (cf. Judg 5:12). Moreover, in its imperative form (ʿûrî), it provides assonance with the object of the word's activity, the shepherd (rōʿî), and thus has literary value in this verse.

against. The preposition ʿal (usually, "upon") has a negative sense when used with verbs indicating some sort of attack, hence our rendering "against." It appears three times in this verse: twice at the beginning to refer to the leader (see next three NOTES) who will be slain, and again at the end to denote the intended victims as the lowest end of the sociopolitical hierarchy, i.e., "the least" (see NOTE below) of the flock.

my shepherd. As in chapter 11, the word "shepherd" is a *crux interpretum*. We refer the reader to our NOTES to "Shepherd" (as a verb) in 11:4, "a foolish shepherd" in 11:15, and "worthless shepherd" in 11:17 for a discussion of the way the shepherd image functions in that chapter to represent prophecy—mainly the false prophecy of past and present times, but also the true prophecy of Second Zechariah. However, this image is hardly restricted to prophecy in earlier biblical materials (see NOTE to "the shepherds," 10:3). Indeed, some of the passages in Jeremiah and Ezekiel that have had a notable influence on the language and themes of Zechariah 9–14 (see Introduction) use the shepherd image to express their views of Israel's leadership. That is, the shepherds in Jeremiah are the past and present Israelite kings, who are to be blamed for the expected destruction and exile, as well as the future monarchs, who will establish just and righteous rule in Judah and Israel (Jer 23:1–6). Likewise, in Ezekiel's famous shepherd passage, the shepherds being condemned are the rulers of Israel, whose harsh and negligent behavior will ultimately be replaced with the benevolent care of David as shepherd (Ezek 34:1–23).

In this instance, the shepherd image seems to follow the usage of Jeremiah and Ezekiel and thus diverge from the way it functions in chapter 11. Rather than representing prophets, here it signifies a ruler. Several factors lead to such a conclusion.

For one thing, the shepherd of verse 7 initiates a third subunit of this chapter. Although the central subunit (vv 2–6) is directly and harshly concerned with false prophets, it nowhere represents them as shepherds. Furthermore, although that subunit begins with Yahweh's announcing the removal of false prophets, it goes on to delineate their removal in terms of internal societal control. The idea of an abstracted sword of judgment slaying prophets is absent. In short, this third subunit does not have direct thematic links with the second one. Rather, it may be seen, along with verse 1, the first subunit, as a frame for the entire chapter. Because verse 1 deals with royal leadership, this concluding section—at least verse 7—resumes that focus. The past situation that will one day be remedied by the cleansing (and restoration) of Davidides is the issue. Israelite kings/shepherds failed to provide just and righteous leadership, and so divine justice effects a violent end to such a regime. The people so ruled will suffer—as this subunit goes on to say; they will be scattered and many will perish—but in the end a new order will prevail for the remnant.

Another consideration is the intimacy attributed to the relationship between Yahweh and the shepherd to be destroyed. The first-person possessive pronoun is used here with "shepherd" and with the phrase used in apposition, "one intimate with me," which involves terminology never used for "prophets."

Furthermore, that very phrase (see next NOTE) indicates a parity between God and shepherd, both being sovereigns of Israel, that would not be applicable to the divine-human relationship for any other set of humans, except perhaps for the community of all Israel, whom God calls "my people" (see last NOTE to v 9).

In addition, the shepherd's demise results in a "scattering of the people/sheep," a concept not part of the shepherd (as prophet) narrative in chapter 11 but prominent in both Jeremiah (23:3) and Ezekiel (34:5, 6, 12, 21) in their presentation of the shepherd/king (see also 1 Kgs 22:17). Furthermore, at least in Ezekiel, the shepherd/ruler image concludes with covenant language similar to the final two clauses of verse 9.

Consequently, it is unlikely that "my shepherd" is the same as the "worthless shepherd" or false prophet of 11:17; nor is he a priestly leader (contra P. D. Hanson 1975: 338–53). Rather, he represents the Davidic line, whose rule comes to a violent end in the sixth century. Whether it alludes to any contemporary officials is considered below in the NOTE to "slay."

In addition, although "shepherd" is singular, and although it refers to a royal ruler, it is probably an inclusive term. These three last verses of chapter 13 reflect the three results of the sixth-century catastrophe—death, exile, and the impoverishment and subjugation of a remnant in the land. As chart 14 in the COMMENT shows, "slay" represents one of the three fates of the Judean population of 587/586. Slaughter was the particular fate of the leadership; the king's sons and officials were killed (Jer 52:10). Furthermore, these last verses form an inclusio with verse 1, which refers to purification of the entire leadership, not only the king.

one intimate with me. This phrase (*geber ʿămîtî* in Hebrew), which literally means "a man, my associate/neighbor," is unique in the Hebrew Bible. The word *ʿămîtî* is found elsewhere only in Leviticus, where it appears eleven times, with second- or third-person possessive suffixes, in several legal contexts concerning relationships between two parties who are neighbors or otherwise closely associated with each other (Lev 5:21[2] [NRSV 6:2[2]]; 18:20; 19:11, 15, 17; 24:19; 25:14[2], 15, 17).

Although *geber* is often rendered by "man," that English word does not properly capture the significance of the Hebrew term. *Geber* is not so exalted as the related *gibbôr* (see NOTES to "like heroes" in 10:5 and "hero" in 10:7); but it is not simply a generic term for males (as *ʾîš*) or people (as *ʾādām*). It contains the connotation of strength, if not virility too in some cases (e.g., Judg 5:30; cf. Rabbinic Hebrew, where it is the word for "penis"). The special quality of *geber* takes on a new and spiritualized meaning, particularly in Psalms, where it denotes an individual who has a particularly close relationship to God (Kosmala 1975: 377–80). This development is perhaps related to a special formula, *nĕʾum haggeber*, "utterance of the *geber*," which is used of Balaam (Num 24:3, 15), David (2 Sam 23:1), and Agur (Prov 30:1). Despite the Proverbs example, the formula indicating divine utterance through someone close to God should be considered part of older biblical literature; its later replacement is the word

geber alone, as a man with an intimate connection to God, especially as used
(fifteen times) in the Book of Job. Still, the fact that the formula is never used
for prophets giving oracles is significant, because the word *geber* in this verse is
in apposition with "shepherd" (see previous NOTE), which is used as a metaphor
for "ruler" rather than for "prophet" as in chapter 11. Moreover, the fact that at
least one ruler—David, the paradigmatic king—is referred to as *geber* is likewise
relevant to this passage, which signifies a ruler.

Putting *geber*, as one close to God, together with *ʿămîtî*, literally "my
neighbor, associate," intensifies the sense of close relationship. The two words
function as a unit to denote "one intimate with me." However, its use here is
highly ironic. A *geber ʿămîtî*, who even more than a *geber* would be one who
would be expected to trust God (Ps 40:5 [NRSV 40:4], cf. Jer 17:7) and do what
is right (Ps 128:1, 4) and thus receive God's blessings, is portrayed as being the
antithesis of such a person. His wrongdoings are not specified; but because the
outcome is death (see NOTES in this verse to "O sword" and "slay") and the
judgment of Yahweh prevails, the shepherd as ruler, as close intimate with God,
is clearly guilty of being the opposite of what such an individual should be.

utterance of Yahweh of Hosts. In Second Zechariah this particular form of
prophetic announcement formula occurs only here and above in verse 2 (see
NOTE above).

Slay. The root *nkh* ("to smite"), when used with "sword," as is the case here
(see NOTE to "O sword" above in this verse), means to inflict mortal wounds (cf.
Jer 21:7). The full idiom would be "to smite with the edge of the sword" (e.g.,
Deut 13:16 [NRSV 13:15], *takkeh lĕpî ḥāreb*; see also Deut 20:13; Josh 11:11,
12, 14). This verse, with its apostrophe to "sword" and its imperative of *nkh*,
uses the phrase elliptically, in that it omits "with the edge of." Indeed, the full
idiom is frequently replaced by the abbreviated "slay by the sword" (cf. "fall by
the sword" instead of the fuller "fall by the edge of the sword") in later biblical
parlance. However, its meaning in this verse—to destroy the shepherd/ruler (see
two previous NOTES)—is unambiguous.

The prophet no doubt is drawing from his knowledge of Israel's tragic history
in portraying the ruler's violent death. The only other prophetic use of this
idiom appears in Jeremiah in his prophecy that King Zedekiah, the last reigning
king of Judah, will be captured by Nebuchadnezzar, who will strike him and all
his retainers and everyone in Jerusalem "with the edge of the sword," sparing no
one (Jer 21:7). This prophecy is not literally realized, in that Zedekiah's sons
and officers are killed whereas he himself is blinded and imprisoned in exile,
according to Jer 52:10–11 (= 2 Kgs 25:6–7). Nonetheless, the royal power of a
Judean king was effectively terminated in that act, and the king's subjects were
concomitantly "scattered" (see NOTE below).

The historical reference of this phrase to the end of monarchic rule seems
clear. The eschatological setting of this oracle, however, has created considerable
discussion about whether its depiction of a violent end to a ruler is meant to be
a critique by the prophet of those in power in his own day, rulers he would
condemn to death. As we have asserted elsewhere, too little is known about the

political dynamics of the fifth century to allow for a response to such a suggestion. Although not insisting that it cannot allude to some tension in the prophet's own day, we remain skeptical that it has such a pointed purpose, especially since the notion of another destruction and exile that would accompany the ruler's demise does not seem warranted by prophetic evaluations of postexilic society. Instead, this image of the slain shepherd and the consequent scattering of the flock is best understood as retrospective language used to anticipate the future age when the suffering and hardships undergone by the scattered flock will at last prove to have been efficacious in the formation of a new order—a renewed covenant with Yahweh (see last NOTE to v 9).

Certainly postbiblical Jewish texts as well as the New Testament understand Zech 13:7 as eschatological. Mark 14:27 cites this passage (cf. Mark 6:34; Matt 9:36), and Jesus' statement that his disciples "will all fall away" may be an allusion to "I will turn my hand against the least" in this verse. And in Qumran materials, Zech 13:7 is quoted, apparently in reference to a messianic figure, the Teacher of Righteousness (Rabin 1954: 31). The connection of this verse with Qumran is also present in the way Qumran literature ascribes messianic qualities to the term *geber* (see NOTE above in this verse to "one intimate with me") and possibly relates it to the Teacher of Righteousness (Kosmala 1969).

shepherd. That is, the ruler; see the NOTE to "my shepherd" above in this verse.

flock. A metaphor for the people, as in the imagery of Jer 23:1–6 and Ezekiel 34 (see also Jer 50:6, 17–20). The use of "flock" (*ṣōʾn*) here is fully inclusive, in contrast to chapter 11, where the word is attached to "to be ruined" (see NOTES to 11:4 and 11:7) and where it is not clear that it represents all the people in each instance.

scattered. The verb *pwṣ* ("to be dispersed, spread, scattered") suits the metaphoric intention of the flock imagery, for it is frequently used to describe the dispersal of Israel among the nations (e.g., Deut 4:27; 28:64; Ezek 11:16, 17; Jer 9:15 [NRSV 9:16]; 13:24; Neh 1:8). This figurative portrayal of all the people as a flock, thrust away from their own pastures, which provide security and sustenance, is also found in other biblical texts (as 1 Kgs 22:17; Ezek 34:5², 6², 12²; Jer 10:21; 23:1, 2). It is to be noted that although the idea of Israel being spread "among the nations" appears in a variety of biblical writings, the metaphoric use of "scattered" is found elsewhere mainly in Ezekiel and Jeremiah, the two prophetic works most influential on Second Zechariah (see Introduction).

I will turn my hand against. The Hiphil of *šwb* ("to turn back, return"), with "hand" and "against" (*ʿal*), is used here and several times elsewhere (Amos 1:8; Isa 1:25; Ps 81:15) in reference to God's judgment. The negative connotation of this language complements the verb "slay," used earlier in reference to the shepherd's fate (see NOTE above). Indeed, the verbs in this verse ("arise against," "slay," "scatter," "turn against") present a rather harsh picture of what will happen to the people and its leadership. That picture, despite its eschatological setting, is derived from the prophet's acute consciousness of Israel's past—its destruction and dispersal (see NOTE to "shepherd" above in this verse).

The idea of God's turning against the people does not, however, mean that they are to be slain or exiled. The third possibility is that they suffer divine punishment right where they are. The idea of this as the third of three possible fates for the wayward people is explained below in our NOTE to "two parts . . . the third" in verse 8. Thus these "least" (see next NOTE) are linked to the "poorest people of the land" (2 Kgs 25:11; Jer 52:16) as those left in their homeland, to be purified and then to reestablish their relationship with Yahweh (see NOTES to v 9). In this sense, the verse in Isaiah (1:25) mentioned above is informative: God proclaims, "I will turn my hand against you." The parallel statement is a metallurgical metaphor not unlike that of verse 9 in Zechariah 13: God will melt away Israel's dross and remove its alloy. Although the technological vocabulary of Zechariah 13 is not the same as in Isaiah 1, the concept of the refinement or purification of those whom God turns against is virtually identical.

the least. As indicated in the note to our Translation, we have followed the ancient Latin and Greek versions and repointed the text to read *ṣĕˁîrîm*, literally, "little ones." That the "little ones" are among the sheep to be scattered is certain from the overall context of this verse and from the twofold use in Jeremiah (49:20; 50:45) of the expression *ṣĕˁîrê haṣṣōˀn*, i.e., "the little ones of the flock," which is figurative for "helpless captives."

The question as to whom this term refers can be answered in light of what the preceding NOTES to this verse consider. The leadership will be destroyed; many will be exiled and all others will suffer, even the least powerful. These "least" may well be those left behind in the land, as our analysis of "I will turn my hand against" in the previous NOTE suggests. That is, society cannot survive if its rulers are corrupt; exile, suffering, and death will affect all. This reading of verse 7 differs from that of some commentators, who identify the shepherd as the evil king of a foreign nation whose own people will one day be dispersed for having oppressed the Israelites (Cohen 1948: 325). For such exegetes "little ones," or the collective "least," would refer to those of lower rank among the bureaucrats of the foreign kings or enemies of Israel. However, in light of the link between the language here and that of Jeremiah and Ezekiel depicting Israel's exile (see various NOTES to this verse), such an understanding seems unwarranted.

8. *in all the land.* This same phrase occurs in First Zechariah in 4:10 and 5:6. Several Greek manuscripts read "in that day," which is incorrect because the preposition "in it" (*bāh: b* with the feminine ending) occurs twice later in the verse in Hebrew after "two portions" and after "will survive." The "it" must have an antecedent, a feminine noun; and feminine "land" (*ˀereṣ*) is surely what "in it" is referring to. However, the reason that the Greek changed this phrase deserves consideration. "Land," in a sense, is inappropriate, because the rest of this verse deals with people, not territory, being divided into three groups. In other words, although "land" as metonym for "people" is reasonable, it is highly

unusual if not unique. Its use in this verse thus may function to connect the description of divine punitive judgment in this verse with the cause of God's decision to punish, namely, the idolatry and impurity and false prophecy in the land of verse 2, where "land" appears twice (see NOTES above).

The term ʾereṣ has a wide range of meanings—from the cosmic (see NOTE to "founded the earth," 12:1) to the particular. In this case the territorial aspect is clear, although the dimensions of the territory are not specified. However, because verse 7 refers to the termination of monarchic rule and the dispersal of the flock (= people), the "land" here would be whatever territory constitutes the "pasture" of the flock, i.e., the sovereign territory of Israel (meaning the Northern and/or Southern Kingdoms) at the time when it was conquered. In an eschatological sense, it would refer to Yehud's territory. As we have indicated repeatedly, both the historical (retrospective) and the future (eschatological) are present in Second Zechariah. These two domains are not mutually exclusive; the former gives shape and substance to the latter.

utterance of Yahweh. This is the third of three occurrences of this formula in chapter 13 (see above, vv 2 and 7). It is also the last of its seven appearances in this prophetic book; other than in this chapter, it is found in 10:12, 11:6, and 12:1 and 4 (see NOTES to these verses). The prominence of this formula in relation to oracular material is most noteworthy in Jeremiah, and it occurs frequently in Haggai–Zechariah (though only once in Malachi). Its appearance twice in this subunit of chapter 13 intensifies the authority of the prophetic word. Painful as the fact of destruction and dispersal may be, such events are the revealed will of Yahweh and thus must be accepted.

two parts . . . the third. The expression *pî-šěnayim,* "two portions," is unusual, because the noun *peh* normally and frequently means "mouth." However, it occasionally means an end or extremity and, as such, introduces a quantitative nuance. Twice elsewhere, in Deut 21:17 and 2 Kgs 2:9, it is used in this way, in both places with "two" as here. Moreover, in both those passages the term "two parts" or "two portions" really signifies a double portion, which is in a sense what is intended here, inasmuch as there is a remaining portion, a "third" that will have a different fate than will the double portion.

The whole of which these three parts are the components is the "land," strictly speaking, because "two parts" is followed by "in it," as is the "third," after the intervening verb "will survive." However, these quantitative words do not refer to territorial divisions but rather to the territory's population, "land" here being a metonym for "people" (cf. NOTE above in this verse to "in all the land"). The elaboration in the next verse of the fate of the third, who are purified and establish a relationship with Yahweh, makes that understanding of land certain.

The idea of a threefold division of society is rooted in both literary tradition and demographic reality. Ezekiel's symbolic action in 5:1–12 involves dividing hair shaven from his face and head into three parts and destroying all three parts (by burning, slaying, and scattering) to symbolize Jerusalem's punishment by pestilence, the sword, and exile. Ezekiel's imagery may in turn derive from

1 Kgs 19:17–18 (so Greenberg 1983: 126), where Jehu's purge involves some killed by Jehu, some by Elisha, and some (seven thousand people) surviving. The connection between the Ezekiel and Kings passages is somewhat loose, in that Jehu's purge involves survival by those innocent of Baal worship, whereas Ezekiel seems to depict total destruction. Even if there are survivors, it will not be because of innocence; but, more probably, the larger world becomes the arena, notified by a few survivors, that testifies to God's punitive justice (see Ezek 12:10 and Greenberg 1983: 140–41).

Zechariah's use of the idea of destruction or punishment affecting parts, i.e., thirds, of the population thus may draw upon Ezekiel, because slaying and scattering, two of Ezekiel's causes of destruction, are part of the scenario of this subunit of Zechariah 13 (see NOTES above in v 7 to "slay" and "scattered," and below in this verse to "will be cut off and perish"). Yet it clearly apportions these three parts in different ways: the two-thirds are killed or removed, and the remaining third also suffers but remains in the land and survives.

The revision of Ezekiel's notion of the differential destruction of the people may be the result of Second Zechariah's perspective well into the postexilic period. The ratio of two-thirds to one-third reveals a rather accurate perception of the effect of the Babylonian conquest of Judah on the population of the land. The conquerors dealt with the Judeans according to a threefold strategy: some were killed in battle (slain), some were carried into exile (scattered), and others were left behind. But because the idea of "two parts" plus a "third" implies the relative equality of the resulting three portions, the notion of two parts plus a third involves more than three different fates: it suggests quantitative parity. Although it is difficult to know whether the number of people exiled and the number killed were about the same, it is possible to discern that the population of Yehud in the Persian period, at least for the first part of it, was roughly a third of what it previously had been at the end of the Iron Age. Extrapolating Shiloh's estimates (1980: 32) for Iron Age Israel to what they would be for Judah at the end of Iron II, and then adjusting them according to more sophisticated methods of population estimation (e.g., Finkelstein 1988; cf. Broshi 1990), gives a population of about 30,000 in the early sixth century. In contrast, Yehud a century later had only somewhat more than 10,000 inhabitants (Carter 1991: 155–62; cf. Introduction and also COMMENT to chapter 12). This radical decline in population as the result of the imperial policy of Babylon as well as the severe economic problems in the ravaged Palestinian landscape of the exilic period, meant that fifth-century Yehud, at least until the time of Ezra and Nehemiah, was a shadow of what Judah was—demographically, politically, economically— at the end of the monarchic period.

The implication of the historical specificity underlying the concept of a threefold fate befalling Israel is that the "third" that survives is the population of Yehud. What the Yehudites must endure (see NOTES to "fire . . . refine" and "assay . . . assays" in v 9) is no less a process of suffering than what happened to the other two-thirds. Yet the permanence of the surviving group in the land allows it to be the core of the restored relationship between Yahweh and the people. These verses in Zechariah 13 are clearly focused on the population that remained in the land (see NOTE to "I will turn my hand against" in v 7).

will be cut off. The verb *krt* ("to cut off, cut down") is paired with "perish" (see next NOTE). The future aspect of the verb is conveyed by the use of *hyh* with the *waw* consecutive at the beginning of this verse. The Niphal is used here to indicate one of the results of God's punitive action against the "flock" (see NOTE in v 7), that is, the people. This verb, when used of people, can mean that the people are destroyed (e.g., Gen 9:11; Isa 29:20; see also the use of this verb in 13:2). However, more often it seems to indicate a living equivalent of death—to be cut off from one's people and/or land. The priestly excommunication texts (e.g., Lev 7:20, 21, 25, 27; Num 9:13; cf. Exod 12:15; 30:33; Num 15:31) proclaim that those who break certain covenant stipulations will be cut off from their people. In either case, the idea is that such people are irrevocably severed from their community, for "cut off" frequently involves the descendants of the guilty party and hence the destruction of his or her posterity (see NOTE to this verb at 13:2). The fact that "cut off" is paired here with "perish" contributes to such an understanding.

The idea of being removed from one's native land and community seems certainly to be the nuance here (and below in 14:2; see NOTE there to "cut off"). As we point out in the previous NOTE, this passage is shaped by reference to the sixth-century destruction of Judah, in which part of the people were slain, others were exiled, and some were allowed to remain in the land (see also our NOTES to "slay," "scattered," "the least" in v 7). The verbs in this verse are related to each of those three fates that befell Yahweh's sinful people. Thus "cut off" here is the equivalent to the scattering of verse 7. This reading of "cut off" is corroborated by Second Zechariah's use of the verb again in 14:2 in parallel with "go into exile"—half of Jerusalem will be exiled, and the rest "will not be cut off," i.e., not exiled.

and perish. The MT lacks *waw* ("and") before the verb, but all the major versions supply it. That it could have fallen out by haplography, because the last letter of "will be cut off" is a *waw*, is certainly possible; and our translation supplies "and" between the verbs. However, the close link between the meaning of the verbs, to the point of omitting the connector, might have been original. The idea that two-thirds of the people were no longer part of the community of Israel is the intent of this statement in verse 8 (see above, NOTE to "two parts . . . the third"), and the distinction between death or exile as the means of removing the two-thirds is not critical. Indeed, it is not clear that the survivors themselves could have enumerated the size of one group over against the other. Thus the two verbs, "cut off" and "perish," are integrally related: together they describe the two-thirds that no longer exist, however that may have happened, as part of Yahweh's people.

The verb *gwᶜ* is frequently paired with other verbs, such as *mwt* ("to die" [Gen 25:8, 17; 35:29]), or used in parallel with *mwt* or *ʾbd* ("to perish"; see Num 17:27, 28 [NRSV 17:12, 13]). The link with *krt* is unique, as befits the special circumstances of this passage in denoting the fate of a majority of the people of preexilic Israel.

remain in it. The root *ytr* ("to be left over, remain over"), when followed with *b* ("in") as here, signifies those who are left in a place. The fate of all the others who have not remained is one of extreme punishment (death or exile); and these too, insofar as they are the equivalent of the "least" of verse 7 (see NOTE above), will suffer from God's punitive actions (see NOTE to "I will turn my hand against" in v 7). The nature of what happens to those who remain after the devastation and exile of two-thirds of the people (see NOTE to "two parts . . . the third" in this verse) is specified in the next verse. A whole extra verse (13:9) is devoted to this remnant; and the noun form (*yeter*) of this verb is used in chapter 14 (v 2) to refer to those who are left in Jerusalem in the vivid eschatological language that characterizes most of that chapter.

The noun form (*yeter*) of this verb appears below in 14:2 (see NOTE to "rest"), where it also refers to that part of the population not killed in wars or taken into exile. Although both the verb and its nominal derivative often have negative connotations—that which is left over being considered of lesser quantity or value (e.g., Exod 23:11; Joel 1:4)—when they refer to those left behind in imperial deportations, a more positive evaluation is present here. See also, for example, Isa 4:3, which asserts that "one who is left (*niš'ār*) in Zion and remains (*nôtār*) in Jerusalem will be called holy."

The prepositional phrase "in it" refers to the "land"—see first NOTE to this verse.

9. *I will bring.* The Hiphil of the verb *bw'* ("to come") is used here with "to the fire." Because Second Zechariah usually is elliptical in his use of stock expressions, one would expect that the second and third clauses of this verse would be sufficient, or that a phrase such as "I will refine with fire" would be sufficient. The question thus arises as to why "bring . . . to the fire" appears here as a separate clause. The answer lies in the fact that those words are very similar to those of Num 31:23, a passage mentioning purification by both fire and water. In expanding the idea of "refiner's fire" (as in Mal 3:2; see NOTE below to "silver . . . gold") by using the verb "to bring," Zech 13:9 echoes the language of Numbers 31, as does Zech 13:1 with respect to purification by water. The result is that the notion of purification of the leaders in verse 1 is subtly linked with the image of the purification of all the remaining people (see next NOTE) of verse 9. For a detailed presentation of the lexical connection between 13:1, 9 and Num 31:23, see our NOTE below in this verse to "fire . . . refine."

the third. That is, the third that remain in the land. These are the survivors of Yahweh's punitive acts of destruction and dispersal (see NOTE in v 8 to "two parts . . . the third"), and they are also represented by the term "least" in verse 7 (see NOTE above). Although they have survived death and dispersal, they are not exempt from divine punishment. The concept of purification presented in this verse constitutes the ordeal of the remaining third to prepare them for becoming God's people once again.

fire . . . refine. The root *srp* in the Qal always means "to smelt," "refine," or even "test"; it is frequently found, as here, together with *bḥn* ("to assay, test"; see below, NOTE to "assay . . . assays"). The phrase "refine with fire" is clearly drawn from the technology of metal refining, in which metals were subjected to high temperatures in a furnace in order to melt away the impurities. Such a process made silver in particular more valuable as tender or for metalwork. The imagery of this process provides vivid expression of the idea of God's judgment of Israel, a process that subjected it to "fire," which is an equivalent of the divine wrath aroused by Israel's disobedience (cf. NOTES to "she will be consumed by fire," 9:4, and "like a fire pot," 12:6).

Several prophetic passages, notably Jer 6:27–30; 9:6; Isa 48:10; Ezek 22:17–22; and Mal 3:2 (cf. Ps 66:10–11; Prov 17:3), make use of this imagery in much the same way as this passage does. What is not specified here—the sins of the people that make them deserving of the ordeal of purification and the judgment of Yahweh in subjecting them to suffering—is implied on the basis of the other prophetic passages, except for Malachi, who also does not rehearse the negative aspects of the refining process.

The fact that neither Second Zechariah nor Malachi, in giving their oracles long after the Exile, emphasized the corruption of the people along with the fiery wrath of Yahweh, probably reflects their different perspective on the efficaciousness of the purification brought about by suffering. For Ezekiel and Jeremiah, the torment of being a remnant, left in the land, bereft of leadership and resources, and with many slain or exiled kin, was viewed as a punishment no less harsh than death or dispersal. But now, in the fifth century, the imagery of metalworking can ignore those aspects and focus on the results of the refining (and testing): the impurity of the people will be gone after such an ordeal, and they will be able to acknowledge anew their covenantal relationship with Yahweh. Their past sinful behavior is the dross that is being removed, leaving them pure.

This purification of the people forms an inclusio with the first verse of this chapter, which depicts the purification of the leadership through the cosmic waters of the "fountain" (see NOTE in v 1). The connection between the purification of the leaders in verse 1 and that of the people in verse 9, even though the vocabulary of purification differs (in v 1: *mqwr lḥṭʾt wlndh*; in v 9: *bʾš wṣrptym*), lies in the way both of these verses are related to the description of the booty taken from Midian in Num 31:23. The Numbers passage presents the process of passing objects through fire (*ybʾ bʾš*), which is similar to "bring . . . to the fire" (*hbʾty . . . bʾš*; cf. NOTE above in this verse to "I will bring"). Both use the root *bwʾ* ("to come," or "to bring" in the Hiphil) and "in fire," and both mention water along with purification and defilement (Zech 13:1 has *mqwr lḥṭʾt wlndh*; Num 31:23 has *bmy ndh ytḥṭʾ*).

silver . . . gold. That "silver" precedes "gold" is significant here, as it is in 9:3 (see NOTES to "she has piled up silver" and "gold"), in that it may reflect the economics of the availability of these two metals. However, at some point in the Persian period, new sources of silver were discovered, making silver more plentiful and thus gold more precious; hence the reverse order of the two metals in Zech 14:14 and Mal 3:3. The value of these metals was related to their states of purity.

Both of these metals feature prominently in Mal 3:2–3, which also uses the imagery of refining silver in fire and then mentions the treatment of gold with a verb different from the one (*bḥn*; see next NOTE) used here:

> For he is like a refiner's fire (*ʾēš mĕṣārēp*)
>> and like the soap of fullers;
> As he sets to refine (*mĕṣārēp*) and purify (*mĕṭahēr*) silver
>> so will he purify (*ṭihēr*) the sons of Levi.
> He will refine them (*ziqqaq*) like silver and like gold,
>> that they will bring offerings to Yahweh with righteousness.

However, unlike the Malachi text, which uses far more extensive technological imagery than this one, Zech 13:9 involves a sequence that becomes clear in our next NOTE. The silver is subjected to the purification that brings about the removal of all its negative qualities (baser metals; this is what the wasting of the land by the conquerors does to the remnant). Then God tests the people.

assay . . . assays. Gold was very difficult, if not impossible, to purify by chemical means. It seems that the ability to do so did not emerge until some time in the Persian period (Lucas 1962: 229, 4–40; but cf. Forbes 1955–64: 7:166). Even then, it was an expensive process, hardly worth the effort. Furthermore, the desirability of purifying gold is questionable, because natural gold, with its impurities, is stronger, harder, and less likely to tear when beaten into leaf than is pure gold. Gold is always workable in its natural state, so the biblical instances of the term *ṣrp* (see NOTE to "fire . . . refine") being used with gold probably indicate the process of heating it to shape it in some way rather than, as for silver, a purification process.

Nonetheless, the idea of purity is attached to gold in the Bible, and indeed there were modes of testing it which involved heating it. Various grades of gold did exist, and determining the quality of gold was related to establishing its value. The image of assaying or testing (*bḥn*) gold symbolizes an appraisal of the worth of the metal in question. The assaying imagery thus develops the refining idea: once put through the fire of judgment and suffering, the people are examined to see whether they are now worthy of reestablishing themselves in a special relationship with Yahweh. As in Mal 3:10, 15, and elsewhere, *bḥn* here means "to put to the test to judge quality," not "to subject to a punitive test or trial" (e.g., Jer 11:20). Thus we have chosen to translate it "assay" rather than "test," because the former conveys more of its technical sense whereas the latter is open to its more extended meanings.

They will call . . . answer them. Two features of the Hebrew of these clauses deserve comment. First, both clauses feature an independent pronoun for the subject, which gives added emphasis to the two parties in this agreement—those who acknowledge Yahweh, and then Yahweh in response. Second, the subject pronoun ("they") of the first clause and the object pronoun ("them") of the second clause are actually singular in the Hebrew. They refer collectively to the one-third that survives and thus are rendered in the plural in our translation. The shift in Hebrew from the plural of the preceding two clauses may be intended to anticipate the singular, collective "people" of the following clause.

The saying of God's name is tantamount to acknowledging God's existence. It reverses the idea of verse 2, which proclaims that divine names will never again be mentioned (see NOTES to "names" and "mentioned again" in v 2). But the divine names of 13:2 are those of idols, and in cutting off their names, Yahweh is making it possible for the people to acknowledge the sole existence of their own God. "Call upon the name of Yahweh" (*qrʾ bšm yhwh*) is used more than twenty times in the Bible. In some texts it seems merely to indicate recognition of Yahweh's existence (as Gen 4:26; 12:8; cf. Jer 10:25), but here it clearly has a more exclusive connotation: that Yahweh is the only God who exists.

The notion of calling upon a divine name undoubtedly originates in supplicatory language. It is a kind of invocation of God's presence prior to addressing a statement to the deity. And it assumes an answer will be forthcoming, as is the case here where God answers the third who have been purified, whereupon they in turn reiterate their relationship to God ("That is my people" and "Yahweh is my God"; see next NOTE).

Indeed, "call" and "answer" (*qrʾ* and *ʿnh*) constitute a pair that reflects the language of worship, supplication, and/or sacrifice. Note that in the contest between Elijah and the prophets of Baal, the contestants "call" upon their god's name, the one who "answers" by fire being the true god (1 Kgs 18:24, 25, 26, 36, 37). Moreover, although the technical terminology of "call" and "answer" is absent, the Temple dedication passage of 1 Kings 8 is phenomenologically connected to this idea; after Solomon's long speech addressed to Yahweh (1 Kgs 8:23), God answers by acknowledging that Solomon's prayer has been heard and is eliciting a response. The language of "call" and "answer" appears explicitly in Isa 65:24, where, in the ideal future age, God answers even before being called. Note too that, in Jer 33:3, Jeremiah is told by God to "call" to him from prison, whereupon God will "answer" him (cf. Mic 3:4, which has "cry" [*zʿq*] with "answer").

"That is my people" . . . *"Yahweh is my God."* These clauses, presented as direct quotations of the people and of God, are part of the covenant formulary expressing the intimate relationship between Yahweh and Israel, as in Exod 6:7 (cf. its negative formulation in Hos 1:9 and its positive echo in Hos 2:25 [NRSV 2:23]). In this usage of the formulas, they appear in a somewhat abbreviated state, in that their full form usually includes a form of the verb "to be" (*hyh*), as in Deut 26:17–18 (cf. Lev 26:12). The Deuteronomy passage uses the infinitive *lihĕyôt*, which serves to emphasize the long-lasting and all-embracing nature of the agreement.

In various prophetic books that draw upon Deuteronomy, variations of the formulaic language appear, such as "I will be their/your God and they/you will be my people" (e.g., Jer 7:23; 31:33; Ezek 37:27) or "you/they will be my people and I will be your/their God" (Jer 11:4; 24:7; Ezek 36:28; Zech 8:8). In addition, an even simpler variation, without the verb "to be," appears a number of times, this being one such example (cf. Hos 2:25 [*NRSV* 2:23]). And there are even more abbreviated allusions to the covenant language, in which only one-half of the formula is explicitly stated (see Ps 100:3; Isa 51:16; Gen 17:6).

The omission of the verb "to be" from the covenant formula apparently characterizes passages that are not completely future oriented (so Bernhardt, Bergman, and Ringgren 1978: 378) and that are not giving a promise of something that will be realized only at some time in the distant future. In this case, although the context is eschatological and the verbs have a future sense, the covenant passage with which chapter 13 ends conveys the idea that the relationship with Yahweh is already under way. The destruction of two parts of the people and the refining of the rest is what the Babylonian destruction initiated. The postexilic era perhaps then was seen as the period of testing, to see whether the refining had brought about the sought-after purity (see three previous NOTES). Thus the restoration of the covenant seems imminent. Note also the singular suffix for "God," the singular (in Hebrew) subject of "will say," and the singular demonstrative pronoun ("That"; Hebrew *hu*ʾ) referring to the people, all of which serve to individualize and personalize the covenant concept. Yahweh is indeed renewing the historical bonds with the "people" Israel, but this time it will involve each person entering into this intimate relationship in his or her own heart (cf. Jer 31:31–34; Ezek 36:26–28).

Second Zechariah is clearly using ancient covenant language. But the particular way in which he expresses it reveals his familiarity with how his prophetic predecessors have developed the concept. At the same time, his own expression of the hope for a lasting and true covenant is given immediacy, even within the eschatological context, by the simple juxtaposition of pronouns and nouns, without intervening verbs. The English cannot quite capture the directness with which God and people are brought together in Second Zechariah's version of the covenant formulary (literally: "my people, that one . . . Yahweh my God").

COMMENT

Considerably shorter than the previous two chapters, chapter 13 yet shares with them a tripartite structure. On thematic grounds, the first verse stands apart from those that follow. And in terms of literary style, the heightened prose, or quasi-poetic form, of the last three verses distinguishes them from the narrative prose of verses 4–6. Yet all these subunits have an eschatological perspective, as signified—though not as often as in chapters 12 and 14—by the formula "on that day" or by the interweaving of retrospective allusions with assertions of future conditions.

Although the three component parts can be set off from each other in terms of theme and form, it is more than an eschatological perspective that brings them together. Verse 1 deals with the royal bureaucracy in Jerusalem, and the retrospective language of the third subunit includes a depiction of the destruction of that leadership, as presented in the image of a shepherd to be slain. The connection between the second subunit, which is apparently quite self-contained in its polemic against prophecy, is more subtle. All three parts concern the removal of impurities. The language that describes that removal is different in each subunit, yet the overall effect is the same. The leadership is cleansed in a fountain in the first subunit; the "spirit of impurity" (v 2) associated with false prophecy is taken away by Yahweh in the second subunit; and the people who survive devastation and exile are purified by a refiner's fire (v 9) in the third subunit.

Although the oracles on the end of prophecy apparently form a discrete section of this chapter, they nonetheless contain some striking lexical connections with the third subunit. The verb "to cut, cut off" is found in both verses 2 and 8: idols are cut off from the land, as are those who worshiped them. Similarly, the "names" of those idols as well as those falsely speaking in Yahweh's "name" (vv 2, 3) serve as a contrast to the valid calling upon Yahweh's "name" in verse 9. And the emphasis on removing sinful elements from the "land" (twice in v 2) is echoed by the description of the three fates to befall all the "land" in verse 2.

Oracle: Cleansing of the Leadership, 13:1.

This verse functions as do the opening verses of several other chapters of Second Zechariah—it serves as a bridge between the materials of the preceding chapter and those of the one it introduces (cf. Zech 11:1–3; 12:1; 14:1–2; Zech 10:1 may also be of this character). The pair of phrases that are the object of purification described in verse 1 figures prominently in chapter 12. The "house of David" and "leaders of Jerusalem" appear in tandem three times in that chapter. As we explain in our NOTE to these phrases in 12:10, these terms denote the royal bureaucracy that held power in Jerusalem from the time of David until the destruction by the Babylonians in 587–86 B.C.E. The loss of political autonomy was a crisis for the Judeans in many ways, and it was made particularly acute by the authoritative divine promise of an eternal Davidic rule as expressed in Nathan's oracle (2 Samuel 7).

The hope for the restoration of monarchic rule may have been tied occasionally to developments in the history of Persian control of Yehud, in which a glimmer of possibility for independence may have been seen by some. However, the reality of Yehudite demographic and economic weakness in contrast to Persian imperial might makes it unlikely that there were ever windows of opportunity for monarchic restoration during the Persian period. Hence, even at the time of First Zechariah, when a Davidide held political office, the prophetic language portraying monarchic rule and national independence is decidedly eschatological (especially Zech 3:8–10 and 6:9–14; see NOTES and COMMENTS in Meyers and Meyers 1987: ad loc.).

Such is certainly the case in Second Zechariah, in which the oracles of 12:7–11 depict Yahweh's intention, after having dealt with the external enemies of Judah and Jerusalem (vv 2–6), to establish the glorious rule of the Davidides and their retainers. However, unlike the idealistic picture of restoration of First Zechariah, as well as that of Jeremiah (e.g., 23:5–6) and Ezekiel (at 34:23–24), Second Zechariah's depiction of the future Davidic rule is tempered by a diminution of royal powers from what they were understood to have been in preexilic reality and by signs of democratization in the power structure (see COMMENT to the second subunit of chapter 12). Such dramatic developments are reinforced by the striking idea that the restored monarchy will not neglect the reasons for its demise—it will recall its sinful ways and have remorse for the misdeeds it has perpetrated. Furthermore, it will mourn profoundly for its reprehensible past (12:10–11 and the Catalog of Mourners in 12:12–14).

This depiction in Zechariah of the eschatological renewal of the royal bureaucracy sets the stage for what verse 1 of chapter 13 portrays. It provides the completion of a sequence by describing the final action that will be necessary to make the royal bureaucracy fit to reclaim power. The ruling elite have experienced defeat, they have admitted guilt, they have mourned for what they have done, and now they are ritually and symbolically cleansed. The corruption that led to the downfall of Judah is identified as idolatrous and immoral behavior—i.e., covenant disobedience—in Hebrew prophecy. Such behavior creates a state of impurity in interlocking moral and ritual spheres, so that the ritual cleansing implied by the waters ("fountain") to be opened in Jerusalem achieves the goal of ridding the future rulers of the impurity caused by all their sins.

The idea of a "fountain" being opened by Yahweh to such ends draws upon imagery of Jerusalem as the sacred center of the universe, where the living waters are part of the quasi-mythic character of Zion's everlasting sanctity. This imagery contributes to the eschatological thrust of the oracle and implies that the cleansing wrought by the cosmic waters will be an ongoing feature of the future age, so that Israel's leadership will never again be impure.

Oracles on the End of False Prophecy, 13:2–6.

The tension between true and false prophets is surely a major feature of Zechariah 9–14 taken as a whole. It figures directly in 10:1–2, it dominates the shepherd narrative of chapter 11, and it lurks beneath the surface of the "stabbing" passage of chapter 12 and thus of the internal affairs of Judah to which the second part of the second subunit of that chapter addresses itself. But nowhere does this tension figure as directly or as explicitly as it does in this passage.

A wide range of issues concerning prophecy emerges in these five verses. The language is fairly straightforward, and it is not difficult to follow the narrative. Yet these oracles evoke some of the most difficult questions about Second Zechariah and about the very nature of prophecy. Clearly, this passage has a strongly negative view of prophetic behavior. But is it a categorical condemnation of all prophets and all prophetic activity? Closely related to that question is the matter of historical specificity that continually arises in relation to many of the oracular passages of Second Zechariah, a question that we have addressed above, especially in the COMMENT to chapter 12.

Basically, our perspective is that the oracles of Second Zechariah do not deal directly or overtly with the prophet's own day but rather draw upon authoritative tradition. Such a view, however, does not preclude the fact that certain conditions in the prophet's immediate context have motivated him to utter these oracles. Still, it is not a simple matter, and indeed may be impossible, to identify the sociopolitical dynamics that have affected the shape of these prophecies.

Second Zechariah's condemnation of prophecy in 13:2 covers the gamut of prophetic offenses that are chronicled in the Deuteronomic history and that are mentioned by his prophetic predecessors. One of these offenses is idolatry, which involves the activities of prophets calling out in the name of gods other than Yahweh. Another is prophecy that claims to be Yahwistic but in fact does not present a true message from the God of Israel but instead poisons the atmosphere of the land—creates a "spirit of impurity." These forms of prophetic misbehavior, together called false prophecy, are not easy to separate from each other in the elliptical language of verse 2. Yet there can be no doubt that both kinds of illicit prophetic activity were considered part of preexilic Israel's sins. Indeed, the idolatry and the lack of heeding God's true word (i.e., the covenant) constituted the sins of all the people, not just the deceptive prophets. Yet, unlike his predecessors, Second Zechariah does not condemn the people for heeding such figures; these verses are directed toward the prophets themselves.

The agency in the removal of the idolatry, the impurity, and the prophets so implicated is none other than Yahweh, according to the first oracular statement (v 2) of this subunit. The claims of this pronouncement are surely retrospective, despite the eschatological formulary. The drastic punitive measure of conquest and exile (a theme that recurs in vv 7–9), if not the earliest attempts at reform by Josiah, surely brought an end, at least for the moment, to the society-wide covenant disobedience that Yahweh could no longer tolerate, according to the Deuteronomic and prophetic worldview.

But Second Zechariah's experience, generations later, has evidently shown that all the aspects of false prophecy that were in preexilic society had not disappeared. The question as to whether idolatrous prophecy continued is difficult to answer, but on the basis of this subunit of Second Zechariah, it seems that the false prophecy mentioned in verses 3–6 involves just those who speak wrongly in Yahweh's name. Thus, after the introduction of verse 2 in which, through Yahweh's agency, idolatry and impurity linked with prophetic behavior are removed, these next verses are characterized by a shift in agency. In verse 3, the families of prophetic figures who might act falsely as true Yahwistic prophets carry out the elimination of those figures; and in verses 4–6, the very individuals who might claim to be Yahwistic prophets themselves disclaim such activity.

This shift of agency represents the changing chronological referents of the prophet. The introductory verse (v 2) of this section, with God removing all aspects of false prophecy, as we have said, is retrospective. At the same time, the language is surely futuristic, probably eschatological; thus there is a prospective component here too. The retrospective element does not exclude the future-oriented grammar and tone of the verse. Both past and future are involved. Verses 4–6 present individuals taking steps to disclaim behavior that might be construed as false prophecy; those verses, as we suggest below, are future oriented. But what about verse 3, which falls between the agency of God and the agency of the individual and in which families are the agents of prophetic control?

The structure of verse 3, in addition to the fact of parental agency, may be the key to understanding its role. This description of parental judgment of a person falsely claiming to speak in God's name is set up as a case. Three clauses present three stages in a judicial process: the problem, the verdict and sentence, the carrying out of the penalty. The idea of familial judiciary activity is not new; Pentateuchal sources in several instances stipulate such grass-roots responsibility for dealing with sinful children. However, given the anecdotal evidence in Jeremiah, it seems that charges against prophetic figures, at least in the late preexilic period, were leveled in bureaucratic settings, by priests, prophets, elders, and others.

Can anything be said, then, about the social setting of family responsibility for jural-legal matters? The evidence is rather indirect, but there is reason to believe that the profound disruption of centuries-old political forms caused by conquest and exile had its effect on the role of the family as it did on other aspects of community life. Both among the exiled groups and among the Yehudites living under Persian control in Palestine, the decentralizing structural adaptations involved an emphasis on familial cohesion and the strengthening of the role of family leaders (D. L. Smith 1989: 74-78; Japhet 1982: 87). Thus one can perhaps see in Second Zechariah's depiction of family-based juridical activity to cope with the age-old problem of professional prophets claiming to be those truly sent by Yahweh, a reflection of the shifting social structures of the postexilic era, although this case may actually be an eschatological projection.

The use of the word "stab," which denotes the parental carrying out of the death sentence, would corroborate our suggestion. That is, it is the same word as that used in 12:10, perhaps in reference to the royal bureaucracy's elimination of prophetic figures who come from Yahweh (see NOTES to that verse). The reappearance of the term in this chapter involves the same kind of ironic reversal that characterizes many passages of Second Zechariah (especially in chapter 11). Instead of the royal leadership taking action, wrongly so, against true prophetic figures, family authorities will act, rightly so, against false prophetic figures. The overall effect of parents executing children may be a chilling one and may not represent the social reality of any period; but its place within a changing order of values and of social arrangements can nonetheless be seen in the way the word for "stab" functions in these two chapters.

The dynamics of coping with false prophecy shift once more in verses 4–6, where the individual takes responsibility for his own actions. The intensity with which he denies any prophetic role that could be construed as false prophecy is achieved in a series of three disclaimers. In one verbal denial of being a prophet, and in two disassociations from the garb or behavior that signify professional prophets, all of whom are false according to Second Zechariah's standards, the individual distances himself from the phenomenon of popular prophecy. If the social control of false prophecy is expressed in the shocking scenario of family jural activity, the ultimate individual responsibility for rooting out such behavior receives emphasis in the threefold nature of the disclaimers and the self-judgment they represent. This view of personal responsibility of achieving the end of false prophecy in the future age is virtually unique in Second Zechariah, whose eschatological language almost uniformly involves divine intervention—God as warrior, a powerful deity, acts directly in the human realm to do what humans cannot do, or else God empowers Judean armies or leaders to do what they could not or would not do on their own.

The function of the individual in the development of Second Zechariah's literary confrontation with false prophecy is set in the eschatological future. The age of the new covenant, as depicted in both Jeremiah and Ezekiel in language upon which Second Zechariah draws, is a time in which all individuals, on their own, will feel part of the covenant and will act—i.e., obey—accordingly. The historical corporate nature of Israel's covenant with Yahweh will not necessarily be replaced; rather, it will be transformed so that every member of the community will participate personally and will truly acknowledge Yahweh's sovereignty.

Each in its own way, these three stages in the critique of prophecy seem to depict a removal of all prophecy. Can this be what Second Zechariah intends? There is no way to be sure. This question taps into the many difficult questions about late biblical prophecy and its relationship to earlier classical prophets (see Introduction). Nonetheless, several points can be made about these five verses with respect to the existence of prophecy. Negating all prophecy in a categorical sense seems to be out of the question, given Second Zechariah's intimate knowledge of and respect for earlier prophetic figures and their literary creations. At the same time, it is also clear that such figures were, in a sense, failures—they had the ear of the leaders of the nation-state, yet they were not able to effect the kind of changes in society that would have staved off the devastation of the sixth century. Furthermore, the intimate relationship between classical prophecy and national monarchic leadership was now precluded by the political reality of the postexilic period.

Thus the negation of prophecy that was non-Yahwistic in origin, which is the obvious reading of these verses, may also have involved a pessimistic view about whether Yahweh's word could any more be mediated through a person called by God to speak in the name of Yahweh. Would Second Zechariah have labeled himself a prophet? We cannot know, nor can we even be sure that he would understand such a query. But that he held himself within the tradition of true prophecy cannot be gainsaid, and he may have been part of a small but growing tradition that did not claim to have the charismatic or "holy spirit" aspect of classical prophecy but yet sought to keep alive and interpret and expound the lessons of those who did (cf. Greenspahn 1989). To avoid any confusion, they may have proclaimed, as these verses seem to, that anyone claiming to be a prophet or exhibiting the trademarks that had for centuries been associated with prophetic practitioners, should not be tolerated within the community.

Prophets fulfilled important social roles (cf. R. R. Wilson 1980; Overholt 1989), and the negation of prophetic legitimacy need not be seen as a denial of the functional role of intermediaries. Cultic activities at one level, being close to popular prophecy, could surely have filled the psychosocial needs that prophetic professionals supplied. And the existence of a corpus of sacred prophetic materials at another level, along with interpreters of such materials, provided an alternative way to sustain prophecy without sustaining prophets. It is no wonder that the next, and last, biblical prophet was called "messenger" rather than "prophet" (Malachi = "my messenger"). By the time of Malachi, the "prophet" had become an interpreter of transmitted, authoritative texts.

Second Zechariah's strong indictments may have been intended to discourage prophetic activity. But his diatribe need not mean that there could not ever again be prophecy. Indeed, Jewish and Christian literature from much later in the Second Temple period freely refers to individuals that they would seem to categorize together with the preexilic giants of prophecy; that is, Jewish tradition did not understand Second Zechariah as announcing the unequivocal cessation of all prophecy.

One must not forget that Second Zechariah is explicit and repetitive in his expectation of the restoration of monarchic rule and of the Davidic house (Zech 9:9; 12:5, 7–10, 12–14). Classical prophecy went hand in hand with royal power (Cross 1969; 1973: 223), albeit to little avail for most of the history of the monarchy, particularly at the end, at least according to the perspective provided by the Hebrew Bible. Hence the restoration of the monarchy cannot be envisioned without the accompaniment of prophecy. And because the new kingdom will not suffer the same flaws as the historical kingdom, the prophets of the future, it is assumed, will be respected members of the Jerusalem leadership.

This seems almost too simple, and perhaps it is. Two features of Second Zechariah's prophecy seem to militate against the likelihood of such a conception. One is what the third and fully eschatological set of circumstances—the self-judgment and the disclaiming of prophetic activity, by individuals—of verses 4–6 implies. In the new order, with everyone bound intimately with Yahweh in covenant, the need for prophets as intermediaries in the classic sense, that is, the need for them to speak out for the obligation to be loyal to Yahweh and to obey the historical covenant, will be obviated. The second feature is a related concept—the future king will be "righteous," "humble," peaceful, etc. (see 9:9–10), and prophetic spokespersons to guide royal leaders will thus be obsolete.

Yet this is all too logical, and the eschatological age, at least at this relatively early period in the postexilic development of views about the future, was hardly one to be mapped out rationally. If anything, the common denominator of eschatological forecasts is their use of literary and social forms taken from past reality. Hence, the unequivocal presence of a monarchic figure as the sine qua non of the ideal future age inevitably must be accompanied by true prophetic individuals. However prominent the religious dimension of the prophetic message may seem to us, the primacy of prophecy's sociopolitical function must not thereby be obscured.

Devastation for Many, Survival for Some, 13:7–9.

The last subunit diverges thematically and stylistically from verses 4–6. It lacks eschatological formulary, although it does include two phrases indicating oracular pronouncement ("utterance of Yahweh of Hosts" in v 7 and "utterance of Yahweh" in v 8). Although it possesses more of the features of prose than of poetry, it reads much less like narrative than does the preceding subunit. There is also a heightened use of parallelism. We have set it off in poetic form in our translation to draw attention to its elevated prose style and to highlight the fact that it does not continue the focus on the nature of prophecy of the preceding section but, rather, turns to a broader subject, the fate of all Israel. However, as we indicated above, the points of lexical contact between these verses and the oracles on prophecy serve to link the second and third subunits of chapter 13; and the attention to leadership connects this last part with verse 1.

Second Zechariah's oracles have been directed toward various factions of ancient Israel. Chapter 9 dealt with the greater land of Israel and with both Judah and Ephraim, as well as the exilic community, probably those in Babylon. Chapter 10 gives special attention to the northerners long ago exiled from their homeland. The purview of chapter 11 is more difficult to specify; its opening verses again seem to depict greater Israel, and the shepherd narrative may be drawn from the experiences of preexilic Judah. Chapter 12 focuses on Judah and Jerusalem, but within a context of all Israel. And chapter 14 is cosmic; it ranges from the center of the universe in Jerusalem to all the nations of the world.

Against this variety of concerns, these vereses are unique in their sympthetic portrayal of the Yehudites who had survived the Babylonian conquest and remained in their land. Although it may not use the expansive language and the warrior imagery that are found in the concern for those who had been taken away from their homeland, in one verse—with the vivid symbolism of metal-working techniques—it gives meaning and value to the experiences of those who were left in Judah after the destruction.

This subunit may be anticipating an eschatological catastrophe, but it draws on demographic realities that reflect the events in Judah in the sixth century. It presents a tripartite scheme that involves the three different fates to which the inhabitants of Judah were subjected. One group met death; another suffered displacement (exile); and the third remained where they were, bereft of leadership and faced with a radical disruption of their economic resources. Verses 7 and 8 achieve a balance in presenting each of these groups, as chart 13 indicates—three terms are used in reference to each of the three groups. But for only one group does the prophet extend his concern; verse 9 examines what happens to the third group, the remnant.

The accuracy of this tripartite division does not lie in suggesting that these three groups were equal in size. Nor does this division adequately reflect the fact that not all leaders were slain—many were in fact exiled. Nor does it indicate that not all the people other than slain leaders or the poorest were sent into exile. It does, however, fairly represent the fact that these three possibilities did affect the people as a whole. And it strikingly reflects the demographic picture of the postexilic period, which saw a reduction in Yehud's population to about one-third of what it had been in the last decades of the preexilic era.

Having sketched broadly the effect of destruction on the people as a whole, the text then focuses on only the third subset, namely, the remnant. Using a sequence of two images from metallurgical technology, it depicts the changes that those in this remaining group must undergo. Although spared from death and exile, they are no less culpable and subject to God's punitive action; they too are impure and cannot remain that way. Thus the hardships of the remnant in the land are viewed as the mechanism that will rid them of their flaws. Just as the technique of silver refining involves subjecting the impure metal to intense fire in order to remove the dross, so will the struggles of those left in Yehud to survive in a war-torn land dominated by a distant superpower constitute a purifying experience.

Will such a process succeed? An affirmative answer is provided by a second metallurgical analogy. The people are assayed, as metal (gold) is tested to determine its quality and thus its value. That this test yields positive results is not directly specified, but the remaining lines of verse 9 provide dramatic testimony to the success of the refinement processes. These purified survivors become the ones to acknowledge Yahweh's special relationship with Israel. In a direct and personal echoing of ancient covenant terminology, the remnant

CHART 13
FATE OF THE THREE GROUPS
OF INHABITANTS OF JUDAH (ZECH 13:7–9)

	First Group	*Second Group*	*Third Group*
Designation	shepherd, 7c	flock, 7c	least, 7c
Action	slay, 7c	scattered, 7c	turn hand against, 7d
Result	perish, 8b	cut off, 8b	remain, 8c
			. . . .
			refine, 9a, b
			test, 9c
			(covenant, 9d–g)

asserts, through the statements of each individual within this third group, that God and people once more partake of the vital and lasting mutuality that is the essence of the covenant arrangement.

The relegation of the reestablishment of the covenant to the seemingly undistinguished remnant that remained in Yehud is striking in light of what is known of the restoration community. The energy and leadership for Yehud's revitalization, however slow and fraught with difficulties the process may have been, was probably provided largely by returning exiles. Indeed, many of the features of emerging postexilic Judaism in Palestine can best be understood as responses of a minority group wrenched from its natal land.

However, the "sons of the Golah," in returning to their ancestral territory, would have found a group that had endured and recovered in its own ways, some of which may have been very much like the coping strategies of the exiles, and some of which may have differed. There were surely grounds for tension between the two groups in all sorts of political, social, religious, and economic matters (see, e.g., P. D. Hanson 1975: 14ff.; Mantel 1973; D. L. Smith 1989: 188–91). That the final verse of chapter 13 apparently accords a prominent place to the contribution of the remnant perhaps reveals a bias toward the group of those left behind. Such a possibility would be compatible with the Deuteronomic influences visible in Second Zechariah, if one gives credence to the theory that the Deuteronomic corpus is the product of tradition-forming activity carried out by the remnant in Judah (Noth 1981; Janssen 1956: 17–18). But most of all, this focus on those remaining in their homeland underscores the continuity of Israel's existence in the land that had been promised to them in the ancestral covenants to the patriarchs and at Sinai. The covenant language with which this chapter closes is explicit in its affirmation of Israel as Yahweh's people. The fact that those who never left the land are the ones to reaffirm the covenant bears the implicit message that the eternal relationship between God and the people is inseparable from their territorial identification with the land of which Jerusalem is center and symbol.

ZECHARIAH 14

◆

Jerusalem's Devastation and Rescue

14 ¹Behold a day of Yahweh is coming:
Your spoil will be divided in your midst,
   ²for I will gather all the nations
   to Jerusalem, for war.
Then the city will be captured,
   the houses will be plundered,
   and the women will be ravished;
Half the city will go into exile,
   but the rest of the people will not be cut off from the city.

³Yahweh will go forth and fight against those nations as when he fights on the day of battle. ⁴His feet will stand, on that day, on the Mount of Olives, which is facing Jerusalem from the east. The Mount of Olives will be split in half from east to west by a very great valley. Half of the mountain will recede northward and half southward. ⁵You will flee [by] the valley of the mountains,[a] for the valley of the mountains will reach to Azel. Thus you shall flee as you fled because of the earthquake in the days of Uzziah, king of Judah. Then Yahweh my God will come; and all the holy ones will be with you.

Jerusalem Restored

⁶It will be on that day: there will no longer[b] be cold[c] or frost.[d] ⁷One day, that will be known to Yahweh, there will be neither day nor night, for at evening time it will be light.

⁸On that day, the living waters will go forth from Jerusalem, half of them to the eastern sea and half of them to the western sea. This will be so in summer and in winter.

[a]Reading *hārîm* for *hāray* ("my mountain").
[b]Reading *ʿôd* for *ʾôr*.
[c]Reading *qorît* for *yĕqārôt*.
[d]Reading *wĕqippāʾôn* with the Qere.

⁹Yahweh will be king over all the earth;
and on that day Yahweh will be one, and his name one.

¹⁰All the land will stretch around like the plain from Geba to Rimmon, south of Jerusalem, which will stand high and dwell in her place—from the Gate of Benjamin to the place of the first gate, to the Corner Gate and the Tower of Hananel to the king's wine presses. ¹¹They will dwell in it, and there never again will be a total destruction. Jerusalem will dwell in security.

The Fate of Jerusalem's Foes

¹²This will be the plague with which Yahweh will smite all the peoples who have waged war against Jerusalem: each one's flesh will rot away[c] while he is standing on his feet; his eyes will rot away in their sockets; and his tongue will rot away in his mouth. ¹³On that day a great panic of Yahweh will be upon them. Everyone will seize his neighbor's hand, and his hand will be raised against his neighbor's hand. ¹⁴Judah also will fight in Jerusalem. The wealth of all the surrounding nations—gold, silver, and garments—will be gathered in great abundance. ¹⁵Such will be the plague on the horse, the mule, the camel, and the ass, and every animal that is in those camps during this plague.

The Future for Jerusalem/Judah and the Nations

¹⁶Then every survivor from all the nations that had come against Jerusalem will go up every year to bow down to King Yahweh of Hosts and to celebrate the Feast of Booths. ¹⁷Should any of the families of the land not go up to Jerusalem to bow down to King Yahweh of Hosts, then there will be no rain for them. ¹⁸And if the family of Egypt does not go up and does not come in, then no [rain will be] for them; there will be the plague with which Yahweh smites the nations that do not go up to celebrate the Feast of Booths. ¹⁹Such will be the sin of Egypt and the sin of all the nations that do not go up to celebrate the Feast of Booths.

²⁰On that day, "Holy to Yahweh" will be on the horse's bells. The pots in the House of Yahweh will be like the basins before the altar. ²¹Every pot in Jerusalem and in Judah will be holy to Yahweh of Hosts. And all who sacrifice will come and take from them and cook in them. No longer will there be a Canaanite in the House of Yahweh of Hosts on that day.

NOTES

14.1. *Behold a day of Yahweh is coming.* This formulaic language introduces the dramatic final chapter of Second Zechariah. The components of this clause

cReading *himmēq* for *hāmēq*.

function in a number of ways to set the tone for the entire chapter. Perhaps most prominent is the use of "behold" and the Qal participle of the verb *bwᵓ* ("to come") along with "day of Yahweh" as a combination of eschatological terms that serve to intensify the notion of the impending events described in the ensuing materials. The eschatological tone is sustained throughout the chapter by the sevenfold use of the familiar expression "on that day" (in vv 4, 6, 8, 9, 13, 20, 21; cf. NOTE to that phrase in 12:3 and elsewhere in chapters 12 and 13), as well as by the use of the related term "one day" (v 7).

The appearance of the phrase "a day of Yahweh" (*yôm laYHWH*) also has its own special significance in the Israelite view of history. The attachment of the divine name to a chronological term presumes a connection between God's activity and the unfolding of history. This phrase occurs uniquely in biblical prophecy. It occurs sixteen times as a genitive phrase ("a day of Yahweh"), without the preposition *l*. Three times (here plus in Isa 2:12 and Ezek 30:3) it appears with *l*—all in texts attributed to prophets from Judah or Yehud—but only in this verse in Second Zechariah is it expanded with the use of *bwᵓ*. There are also some eight other occurrences of "day" plus "Yahweh" with interpolations between those two words, all again in Judean prophets (with the exception of a retrospective instance in Lam 2:22).

The interpretation of this phrase is quite varied (see the convenient summary of von Soden, Bergman, and Saebø 1990: 29–31 and the bibliography on p. 8). The mythological and cultic explanations that were favored earlier in this century are less compelling among more recent scholarly works, P. D. Hanson's (1975: 372ff.) focus on the divine-warrior language of chapter 14 notwithstanding. Rather, scholars recognize that each usage of the term ought to be considered within its own context. Still, the idea of divine intervention in the human sphere and of a future setting for part or all of that intervention seems to characterize every usage of the expression. Because preexilic prophets saw "the day of Yahweh" as imminent, and because the events of exile and destruction were viewed as the "day" already beginning, postexilic prophecy tended to see the "day of Yahweh" as the ongoing or expected completion of what the sixth-century events initiated. Thus the term is fully eschatological, but with its eschatological drama having already begun. Certainly the juxtaposition in Zechariah 14 (and in much of Second Zechariah) of retrospections—past events portrayed in eschatological language—epitomizes the particular postexilic cast to the concept of Yahweh's intervention within time, but at the end-time, to judge Israel and all the nations and to restore Israelite prominence as the exemplary people of Yahweh.

Zechariah's use of the term is thus closest to the way it appears in Joel and Malachi. It is found five times in Joel (1:15; 2:1, 11; 3:4 [NRSV 2:31]; 4:14 [NRSV 3:14]), with one of those instances (2:1) involving, as here, the verb *bwᵓ* ("to come"). Similarly, Mal 3:23 (NRSV 4:5) uses "day of Yahweh," which is associated with an anticipatory *bwᵓ* in 3:19 (NRSV 4:1). In all these prophets, the cataclysmic events of that "day" must necessarily involve the destruction of Israel's enemies, inasmuch as Israel itself has already experienced (and is still experiencing) the punitive effects of divine judgment. Yahweh's mighty and terrible deeds against the nations thus are the essential prelude to the ultimate goal of Israel's full restoration. However, in neither Joel nor Malachi is a consideration of the doom of the nations followed by a view of their subsequent incorporation into Yahweh's kingdom, such as provides the culmination in Zech 14:16–21 of the events of the "day of Yahweh." In this respect, the conclusion of Second Zechariah (vv 16–21, but also especially v 9; see NOTES below), despite its apocalyptic aspects, is similar to the ending of First Zechariah, in which people of all nations acknowledge Yahweh's sovereignty (Zech 8:23; see Meyers and Meyers 1987: 440–42).

We might also note that Malachi includes Yahweh's people among those to suffer, once again, in the final reckoning because of their sins in the postexilic era. Joel apparently lacks such a component to the eschatological judgment (as suits a possible late sixth- or early fifth-century date). Second Zechariah, probably chronologically between these two other prophetic figures, is ambivalent about God's people again deserving punitive action. Surely in this chapter such a component is absent (except perhaps in the concern for cultic matters in vv 20–21); but in his recurrent mention of the damaging effect of false prophecy, Second Zechariah would perhaps concede that the eschatological judgment and punishment of the nations will not bypass Israel entirely.

One final observation about this expression and its incorporation into a "behold"-plus-verb formula concerns the way it functions in this chapter. Not only, as stated above, does it set the eschatological tone for the entire chapter; it also highlights the immediately ensuing material—verses 1b and 2—which are the only first-person (Yahweh as speaker) materials in this concluding chapter of Second Zechariah.

Your spoil. Although the noun *šālal* can indicate "prey" or "plunder" taken through private exploitation (as Isa 10:2), the overwhelming majority of its seventy-five occurrences in the Hebrew Bible refer to the "booty" or "spoil" acquired through military action. Sometimes the type of spoil is indicated: garments or precious metal (Josh 7:21; Judg 8:24), animals (e.g., 1 Sam 30:20), women and textiles (Judg 5:30), or food and clothing (2 Chron 28:15). More often the term is inclusive of all manner of goods, livestock, and humans acquired in war, the humans usually being only women and children because the men would probably have been slain. Deuteronomy 20:14 may be the paradigmatic statement of the Israelite conception of spoil: "You may take as booty the women, the children, the livestock, and everything else in the city, all its spoil (*šēlālâ*)," all the males having been put "to the sword" (Deut 20:13; cf. the harsher conditions in the case of Israelite cities disloyal to Yahweh in Deut 13:12–16). The present case is not so drastic as that in the Deuteronomy text, in that the lives of the people will apparently be spared, with the women being sexually assaulted and the population either exiled or allowed to remain in the captured city; see the NOTES to verse 2.

The idea of Jerusalem (mentioned in v 2) being the object of capture and plunder at first seems to diverge from what is presented in chapter 12, where

Jerusalem is depicted as a "cup of reeling" and a "burdensome stone" (see NOTES in 12:2, 3) to its besiegers. Both of those images imply that Jerusalem is consumed and taken (contra, e.g., Mitchell [1912: 341] who denies that Jerusalem is endangered in that passage), but they lead directly to the downfall of the nations that have come against Jerusalem. Yet, ultimately, in both chapters it is Yahweh's intervention that liberates Jerusalem, the nature of that intervention being more detailed and developed in this chapter than in chapter 12.

divided. The verb *ḥlq* ("to divide, apportion") is used in the Pual to refer to the process of separating into portions that which is obtained through military conquest. The basic meaning of the term derives from the world of socioeconomic apportionment; and it thus conveys the idea that the materials, persons, or animals acquired in battle are due to those who have participated in the conflict and emerged victorious (Tsevat 1980a: 448–49). Thus the response of Yahweh in coming to the aid of Jerusalem is not so much to recover the booty but rather to deal with what caused the plunder of the city in the first place, namely, its having been conquered by other nations. The idea of booty being divided is thus a stylized introductory statement of what the nations have done, with a more detailed description coming in verse 2.

The future time of the action indicated by the verb (perfect with the *waw* consecutive) notwithstanding, the specificity of the details of verses 1b and 2 is surely retrospective, drawn from the experience of the conquest of Jerusalem in the early sixth century. At the same time, the prophet envisages a further onslaught against the city at the dawn of the future age. But clearly he understands that the violation of Jerusalem's integrity has not yet ceased despite the improvement of the early restoration period. Because at least some of the conditions brought about by the Babylonians still obtained in Second Zechariah's day—the continued exile of at least some of the population and the diminished size of the city—the status of Jerusalem in the Persian period could well have been considered a continuation of its conquered status and thus of its need to be rescued by Yahweh's power (see COMMENT for a more detailed consideration of the chronology of Second Zechariah's eschatology). Even Ezekiel's idea of the march of "Gog, of the land of Magog," against a quiet, repeopled Israel "in the latter days" has God intervening before Gog succeeds in taking all the plunder that will have motivated him to attack (Ezekiel 38); thus it is likely that these words of violence against Jerusalem indicate another decimation and dispersion of its inhabitants.

The language describing Jerusalem's destruction, although clearly drawn from the only known example, the events of 587/586 B.C.E., is vague in some respects in its future orientation. Unlike the preexilic prophets, who anticipated doom in specific ways, with reference to who the enemies were, this prophet does not indicate who the opposing forces will be or when this all will happen. Nor does the prophet tell us much about his own people or who their leaders are or will be; and he does not tell us how his people will get from the present, which is not visible at all, to the future. The eschatological nature of these oracles apparently precludes such specificity. However, the prophet is very clear about the sequence and nature of the future events. The rest of this chapter provides such detail, which is drawn from historical experience of attack but introduces a new element, the personal appearance of Yahweh to take charge of the battle. The enemy invades and divides up the vulnerable city Jerusalem; then Yahweh enters the picture.

Thus the image in this verse of Jerusalem being divided up as spoil, along with the first word of the next verse ("I will gather"; see next NOTE), anticipates the ultimate resolution of Jerusalem's predicament. The perpetrators of this violation of Jerusalem themselves will become despoiled with their possessions "gathered" in Jerusalem (v 14). The status of Jerusalem vis-à-vis the nations will be reversed because of Yahweh's intervention.

2. *I will gather.* Commentators have been bothered by the abrupt change to the first person here and have either questioned the authenticity of this verse as a whole, as did Marti (*apud* Mitchell 1912: 344), or have suggested (as does the editor of *BHS*) emending the verb to the third person, taking Yahweh as the subject. However, by understanding the beginning of the quotation to be "Your spoil," i.e., following directly after the opening formula, these difficulties are removed.

The idea of gathering foreign nations to Jerusalem for battle, with Yahweh as agent, is introduced by idiomatic language. The verb *ʾsp* ("to collect, gather") when used with persons or armies and the preposition *ʾel*, literally means "to gather for war." The same expression appears, in almost identical form, in Zechariah 12 (at the end of 12:3), which, as we have pointed out in our NOTE above in verse 1 to "Your spoil," is thematically close to this chapter. In addition, the verb *ʾsp* is used below in verse 14 (see NOTE to "will be gathered"), where it reverses the meaning it has in this verse.

all the nations. Second Zechariah is hardly the first prophet to depict an onslaught of foreign nations against Jerusalem as part of Yahweh's involvement in human affairs. Perhaps most vivid in this respect are the prophecies of Jeremiah, warning of the impending destruction of the city in 587/586 by Nebuchadnezzar (Jer 4:5–8; 25:1–21; etc.). Jeremiah then generalizes the subsequent punishment of Babylon and anticipates the desolation of all the nations that historically have menaced Israel and then "all the kingdoms of the earth" (Jer 25:26). Note also First Zechariah's use of "horns of the nations" as a general statement against all imperial powers that have conquered, and exiled, Judah (Zech 1:20–21; see Meyers and Meyers 1987: 135–38). Second Zechariah, here and in chapter 12, continues in the tradition of viewing Jerusalem (or Judah) as victim of the military superiority of other nations, which themselves eventually will be vanquished as the result of Yahweh's intervention.

Although the author of Zechariah 14 shares with his prophetic predecessors the idea of Jerusalem's succumbing to foreign domination, his perspective on the place of that event in the overall scheme of divine justice and future restoration differs from that of the exilic and early postexilic prophets. That is, his understanding of the world more than a century after the Babylonian conquest has meant a significant reworking of earlier prophecies. Nonetheless, because everything in chapter 14 is set in the future, the preoccupation of this apocalyptic vision is Yahweh's deliverance of the faithful from their suffering at the end of time. The concept of Yahweh's intervention cannot be separated from the idea of tragedy befalling Yahweh's people. We refer the reader to our COMMENT to this chapter for further discussion of the new shape of prophetic eschatology in Second Zechariah.

This use of the phrase "all the nations" is the first of three instances in which it appears in this chapter. The universal scope of Zechariah 14 is thus highlighted. Here the nations are presented in a harsh light, but the dramatic reversals of this chapter entail a radical change in the status of "all the nations" (see NOTE to this phrase at v 16).

to Jerusalem. The preposition *ʾel* ("to") after *ʾsp* ("gather"; see first NOTE to this verse) is part of an idiom depicting an army preparing for war. It indicates the military forces collecting as a fighting unit and marching toward the foe to engage in battle. Thus "to Jerusalem," completing "I will gather," means the movement of the enemy troops *to* this city to fight *against* it; i.e., *ʾel* means "to" and "against."

The focus on Jerusalem in this chapter is adumbrated by the attention it receives in chapter 12. However, there it is coupled with a presentation of Judah's fate, whereas here it stands virtually alone (but note the mention of Judah in 14:14—see first NOTE to v 14—and in 14:21). The intensity of interest in Jerusalem in this chapter derives from its developed depiction of the final stage of the eschatological process. With Yahweh as worldwide sovereign, the earthly home of the divine king—Jerusalem and its Temple (and not the nation-state Judah)—must dominate the vision of all nations acknowledging Yahweh. That is, the very universality that emerges in the fourth subunit of this chapter, with its concomitant focus on Jerusalem at the center of the universe, means that this earlier stage in the eschatological process must also present Jerusalem as the symbolic representation of all Yahweh's people. Rather than excluding Israelites not resident in the holy city, the term "Jerusalem" in a sense expands to include all for whom Zion is the true and historical center of God's earthly domain.

captured. The verb *lkd* ("to capture, seize"), used here in the Niphal, is a standard word to denote the military conquest of a land, city, and/or town. Although the verb can be used in reference to humans, it usually has a figurative sense in such cases: it indicates a person's being trapped or caught (as by God's judgment, e.g., Isa 8:15; Ps 9:16). Still, it occasionally refers to the taking of enemy soldiers (as 2 Sam 8:4 = 1 Chron 18:4), probably as a metonymic way of expressing the domination by force of the polity served by those soldiers.

In this case, the fact of Jerusalem being taken by the "nations" as the composite enemy of the holy city and of God's people is the first of five features of conquest enumerated in this verse, which is an expansion of the general idea of the whole city's being dominated, i.e., being taken as booty as expressed in the introductory clause of 14:1b (see NOTE in that verse).

As a lexical choice to indicate the subordinate position of Jerusalem vis-à-vis its foreign conquerors, "captured" follows in the tradition of Deuteronomic literature in describing various military events in Israelite history. In addition, the presence of this verb in prophetic literature is greatest in Jeremiah, where it appears far more often than in the other prophetic books in which the word appears—once each in Habbakuk and Isaiah, and three times within two verses of Amos (3:3–4, in a metaphor of animals being trapped). Ezekiel never uses it. Second Zechariah here, as often elsewhere, shows the influence of Deuteronomic language and of the concepts and language of Jeremiah (see INTRODUCTION).

plundered. The second feature of the devastation of Jerusalem involves property—the vandalizing and/or looting of people's homes. That is, war causes great economic hardship to the vanquished (cf. Zeph 1:13). This is one of a whole set of acts that constitute the horrors of war from which Second Zechariah is drawing. One of the best examples of that catalog of disasters is the oracle against Babylon in Isaiah 13. There the announcement that their "houses will be plundered" is followed directly, as here (see next NOTE), with the assertion that "their women will be ravished" (Isa 13:16).

The language here, perhaps because it echoes that of Isaiah 13, has several features of the quasi-poetic prose that characterizes the opening verses of chapter 14. First, there is a classic chiasm connecting the second and third cola of this line of verse 2: the verb ("plundered") is followed by the subject ("houses") in standard Hebrew order, only to be followed by the opposite sequence, subject ("women") and then verb ("ravished"), which is the reverse of the normal order. The use of assonance in the Hebrew, the alteration of suffix and prefix forms of the verb, and the agreement of noun endings (even though the nouns are of different genders) also appear in these cola. All of these features are found in Hebrew prose, yet their presence here reflects an archaic and elevated literary style.

women will be ravished. Together with the preceding clause ("the houses will be plundered"; see previous NOTE), this constitutes almost a direct quotation (Isa 13:16) from Isaiah's catalog, in his oracle against Babylon, of the horrors of war. The major difference is that the Isaiah passage has "their" with "houses" and "women," in reference to the Babylonians, whereas this text has the definite article before each of the two nouns, thus diminishing the poetic nature of the Zechariah passage. Still, these first two verses of Zechariah 14 are quasi-poetic, as our arrangement of the Translation suggests, because of the parallelism and the assonance, especially in the first three of the five clauses describing Jerusalem's devastation.

Although there are vivid examples of rape in the Hebrew Bible (e.g., the stories of Dina, in Genesis 34, and the Levite's concubine in Judges 19), those and other instances use different words for what happens to the unfortunate women. The verb used in this verse, *šql*, is found elsewhere only three times in the Bible: in the Isaiah passage mentioned above, Jer 3:2, and Deut 28:30. The latter two instances refer to sexual activity that is not necessarily violent or forceful. This seems to indicate that the treatment of women as the aftermath of war was not conceived of by the ancients as sexual abuse but rather as the transfer of the right of sexual activity with conquered women from their husbands to the military victors. Note, in this respect, that the Qere of the verb in all four instances in which it is found is *škb* ("to lie down"), which is frequently used euphemistically to denote sexual intercourse. Perhaps the Qere uses *škb* simply as a less offensive word.

The idea of the sexual entitlement of warriors to conquered women is rooted in the dynamics of ancient warfare. Men captured in war were perceived to be a greater threat to their captors than were women; thus male POWs were more likely to be killed or mutilated than to be taken into custody (Gelb 1973), although at times groups of males were taken as prisoners of the state and made to serve as forced laborers. In contrast, female survivors, although they too might be carried off en masse as corvée, were likely to serve as human booty, distributed among victorious warriors, who incorporated them into their households. In the latter case, their subordinate political status meant that their male captors were entitled to claim sexual privilege.

In this particular passage, however, *šql* may also function as stylized language for the horrors of war as well as a literal description of what happened to all the women. Because the verse goes on to indicate that half the population of conquered Jerusalem would remain in the city, an assertion that all women were ravished (captured and raped) would be a contradiction unless the statistics about exile refer only to males. That possibility is unlikely, given what is known about Assyrian, Babylonian, and Persian deportation policies. As suggested above, Second Zechariah has selected several components of a long assortment of the awful consequences of war for the vanquished in order to remind his audience of Jerusalem's historical and continuing subordinate status and to depict the cataclysm that will precede Yahweh's future intervention.

Half the city. The fifty-fifty division of the inhabitants of Jerusalem, half being exiled and the rest being left behind (see next two NOTES), need not be seen as conflicting with the statistics provided at the end of the preceding chapter. In Zech 13:8–9, the prophet depicts a threefold fate: one part perishes, one part is exiled, and one part remains (see various NOTES to those verses and also COMMENT to chapter 13).

This verse, in fact, gives much the same information. The city is captured; the goods in its houses and the women are taken as booty (see two previous NOTES). Those three actions represent the military onslaught, with the capture of the city implying death to its armed defenders and the taking of spoil (both material and human) as the concomitant of conquest. Thereafter comes the political resolution of how the conquering power is to maintain its subjugation of the vanquished city. Thus, all those who remain after the military phase will be dealt with by a political apportionment. Zechariah 13 has combined the military actions with the ensuing political ones and has divided the fate of the people into thirds, whereas in this chapter those two aspects of conquest are separated. The end result is the same: some die, and all who survive are divided into two parts—those to be deported and those to be left in the ruined city.

The opening of chapter 14 thus picks up from the concluding section of the preceding chapter. This pattern, an introductory section echoing lexically and/ or thematically the concluding section of the previous chapter, is present in each chapter of this prophetic work except, of course, the first one, inasmuch as chapter 9 does not have an immediate predecessor, and chapter 12, which begins the second of the two parts of Second Zechariah and is somewhat distinct from the materials that it follows (see NOTES to "An oracle" at 9:1 and 12:1).

Although the end of chapter 13 and the opening of this one share certain features, they seem to diverge in their scope. Chapter 13 is far more inclusive in presenting the fate of Israel. That chapter begins with the phrase "house of David and leaders of Jerusalem," which could refer only to Judah, as it apparently does in chapter 12. But its oracles concerning the end of prophecy refer to the "land" (twice in 13:2), which could be broader than Judah. And "all the land" in 13:8 seems to refer to the entire land of Israel, although the postexilic community might understand its eschatological import in terms of Yehud (see first NOTE to 13:8).

In contrast, Zechariah 14 focuses on "the city," i.e., Jerusalem, whose fate in a sense is singled out insofar as it has a special role as Yahweh's city, the locus of the Temple, God's dwelling place on earth. The fact that this chapter concludes with a depiction of Yahweh's universal sovereignty as emanating from Jerusalem and its Temple means that its opening, symmetrically speaking, likewise focuses on Jerusalem. The opening and conclusion, centered on Jerusalem, frame the entire chapter, which presents the interlocking fates of Jerusalem at the center and the nations at the periphery, yet inevitably interacting with each other and affected by each other on "the day of Yahweh" which has already begun (see first NOTE to v 1).

Although this verse minces no words in its depiction of the horrors of war, its fifty-fifty division deals with the political aftermath and does not include the victims of the military phase in its presentation of the total effects of the conquest (as does 13:8–9). This fact should be understood in terms of the demographic dynamics of the postexilic era. The waves of repatriated Judeans, who had endured the humiliation and deprivation of living as a subordinate population in exile, who had restructured their social patterns to preserve their ethnic integrity, and who had intensified certain ritual and cultic behaviors in order to maintain identity, undoubtedly formed a self-identified group in postexilic Yehud. They saw themselves as intimately related to those who had remained in Judah, who had also suffered defeat and deprivation but who had not been wrested from their homeland.

No doubt the survival mechanisms of those left in Judah were comparable in many ways to those of the exiles. Yet after decades of separation, the reunification of the two groups could not have been smooth or easy. If there was any intergroup conflict present in Yehud in the Persian period, the socioeconomic as well as religiopolitical divergence between the returnees and those who had remained in the land would have had to figure prominently (see D. L. Smith 1989: 179–200, who draws especially on the work of Mantel 1973, M. Smith

1971, and Lang 1983). The bifurcation implied here should thus be taken at its face value rather than as a veiled portrayal of a conflict between hierocrats and visionaries (so P. D. Hanson 1975: 373). Indeed, the "half-half" language expresses a consciousness of two groups but has no overtones of tension between them.

into exile. Literally, "in the exile" (*bagôlâ*). The noun *gôlâ* can refer to those taken away into captivity, thereby experiencing natal alienation (as in Zech 6:10; see Meyers and Meyers 1987: 339–40). Alternatively, it denotes the condition and/or place of exile itself. Either way, it reflects the practice of deportation of subject peoples, or parts thereof, by imperial powers seeking to sustain the position of domination achieved by martial activity. It was perfected by the Neo-Assyrians (Oded 1979) and used extensively by the Babylonians and the Persians (Kuhrt 1983). This is the only instance in which this term appears in Second Zechariah (although it does occur in First Zechariah, in 6:10), which is somewhat surprising considering its frequency in Jeremiah and in the Deuteronomic description of the Babylonian conquest. The fact that this specific term is found only once, however, should not obscure the existence of a plenitude of expressions in Second Zechariah referring to the dispersed population of both Israel and Judah (e.g., 9:11–12; 10:8–10; 13:7–9).

the rest. The word *yeter* ("remainder, rest") as a nominal derivative of the root *ytr*, appears above in chapter 13 in much the same sense as does the noun here, that is, referring to that part of Judah's population not taken into exile. See our NOTE to "remain in it," at 13:8, for a consideration of this root with respect to imperial deportation practices. Note also that the root appears once more in this chapter in reference to those among the nations who survive God's punishment (see NOTE to "Every survivor" in 14:16).

cut off. The verb *krt* ("to cut, cut off") is used in 13:8 (see NOTE to "will be cut off") to refer to the deportations of a portion of those surviving the sword of battle. The appearance of the roots *ytr* ("to remain") and *krt* both here and in 13:8 provides a lexical connection that contributes to the linkage between the first subunit of this chapter and the last one of the previous chapter (see NOTE above in this verse to "Half the city").

3. *will go forth.* The verb *yṣʾ* ("to go out") is frequently used as a technical military term; typically it appears with *ṣābāʾ* ("army, war"). But even without "war," it means "to go out to battle" in military contexts such as this one. Here the martial effect is intensified by the following *lḥm*, "to fight" (see next NOTE). It should also be noted that *yṣʾ* is frequently paired with *bwʾ*: the antonyms "go out" and "come back" represent the parameters of a military campaign or, alternatively, of a cultic act (e.g., Num 27:17, 21; see Preuss 1990: 229). This combination, with *yṣʾ* in this verse and *bwʾ* at the end of verse 5 in the expression "Then Yahweh my God will come" (see NOTE to "will come"), thus serves to frame the second part of the first subunit (vv 1–5) of chapter 14.

The use of *yṣʾ* with "Yahweh" as subject partakes of the imagery of holy war. God as the warrior goes out to do battle for the people against their foes (cf. Isa 26:21; 42:13). In exilic and postexilic contexts, this imagery reflects to some degree a sense that the new age is on the verge of beginning if not already under way. That is, Cyrus's edict permitting a return to Judah in 538 B.C.E. and the subsequent restoration of the Temple and its rededication in 516 or 515 B.C.E. were viewed as the initiation of the future age, i.e., a kind of "realized eschatology" (Preuss 1976: 47). Still, the overwhelming sense of powerlessness of both the exiles and those living in Yehud in the fifth century, in the face of Persian imperial domination, made the language of divine might all the more appropriate to this vision of the future. Indeed, unlike chapters 9 and 10, which use military imagery to portray God's might empowering the people to do battle, this passage presents Yahweh acting directly. The cosmic power of God, apart from human messengers, is expressed in the upheaval of the local topography (see, e.g., "will be split in half" in v 4 and NOTE to this term).

fight . . . fights. The Niphal of *lḥm* ("to fight") complements and continues the military nuance of the first verb of this verse, "to go forth" (see previous NOTE). The root *lḥm* appears above in verse 2 in a noun form ("war"), where it represents the actions of the nations against Jerusalem. Here, its twofold use represents the opposite scenario—Yahweh does battle against those nations.

against those nations. Some (e.g., editors of BHS) consider these words an addition. Yet they serve very well to contrast the devastation of Jerusalem at the hands of the "nations" (*gôyîm*; 14:2), of the first subunit, with the dramatic reversal of this subunit, in which nobody other than Yahweh comes forth in opposition to those very "nations" (cf. two previous NOTES).

on the day of battle. The Hebrew word translated "battle," *qĕrāb*, is not a common biblical word. Elsewhere it is used with "day of" only once, in Ps 78:9. It is, however, twice found in parallel with "war" (Job 38:23; Ps 144:1), not unlike the way it appears here with "fight." The introduction of the word "day" in construct with "battle" picks up the eschatological terminology of "a day of Yahweh" of verse 1 (see NOTE above) and of the formula "on that day," which appears seven times in this chapter (see NOTE to "on that day" in vv 4, 6, etc.).

Our understanding of this phrase as a construct chain would mean that there is no definite article before "day," inasmuch as "battle" does not have an article. That is, a literal translation would be "a day of battle." Yet the sense seems to be more specific and definite than that. Perhaps the term *qĕrāb*, because it is so rare, has a special meaning as a technical term for the decisive battle at the end of history. If so, then "battle" is definite, referring to a specific cataclysmic future battle. The construct chain would then be definite, as in the translation we propose.

4. *His feet will stand.* The language with which this verse begins is simple enough, but the image is staggering in its anthropomorphic depiction of Yahweh as a giant astride the heights of Jerusalem. Perhaps it is because of this dramatic scenario that we are presented with Yahweh's "feet" positioned on the Mount of Olives (see NOTE below) rather than with "Yahweh will stand." Still, the direct corporeality of Yahweh rather than the divine action of God in the human sphere is what commands the reader's attention here. God's intervention as a military figure is a frequent theme in the prophecies of Second Zechariah, yet

this is the first instance in which such blatantly anthropomorphic language appears in the service of the military theme.

What are we to make of this graphic depiction of Yahweh as warrior with feet planted on the Mount of Olives? There is an undeniable tendency for anthropomorphic imagery for Yahweh to be avoided in the Bible; it is also clear that this tendency became more marked during the course of Israel's history (M. S. Smith 1990: 100–3), as evidenced in both lexical choices and thematic features. Still, the move away from anthropomorphic imagery was hardlly uniform and complete. Even though both priestly and Deuteronomic traditions use a decreasing number of anthropomorphisms between the eighth and fifth centuries, postexilic works, especially those with priestly and/or apocalpytic tendencies, also draw upon mythic materials that express the divine presence in graphic terms. In this verse, the corporeality of God is the manifestation of God's presence; and in verse 5, it is the "holy ones" as part of Yahweh's heavenly court. Perhaps (as M. S. Smith [1990: 102] speculates) the fact that Canaanite deities ceased to be a threat to Yahwism in the postexilic period meant that the mythic motifs drawn from the old Northwest Semitic cults no longer had to be avoided. Rather, the vivid mythic portrayals of divine activity could serve the purposes of late biblical literature, whether priestly or deuteroprophetic, in underscoring the availability of God's presence and power.

In this particular case, the long Near Eastern tradition, expressed in both literature and iconography, of the deity taking a position with one or both feet planted on the mountain that represents the center of the universe (e.g., *ANEP*: nos. 683–85; see also sources cited in M. S. Smith 1990: 73, n. 86) informs the image of Yahweh astride the Mount of Olives. The motif of the mountain god, the provider of rain (cf. Hag 1:7–11 and NOTES in Meyers and Meyers 1987), anticipates the abundance of water of verse 8, although in the latter text the water comes from cosmic sources below the earth rather than from the heavens (see NOTE to "living waters"). It also adumbrates the rain provided by Yahweh as King in Jerusalem in verse 17 (see NOTE to "there will be no rain for them").

But the heart of the image is the military implication—the vanquishing of the enemy and the rescue of God's people. Indeed, because the whole of the imagery of the next subunit (vv 6–11) revolves around the motif of Jerusalem as the high mountain that connects the realm of God with that of humanity, it is no wonder that Yahweh's place at this nexus of heaven and earth comes graphically to the fore.

Second Zechariah is not unique among biblical prophets in depicting Yahweh in movement on the high places of the earth. Micah 1:2–4 depicts God walking on the mountains, which thereby melt, with great valleys bursting open. Similarly, in Amos 4:13 Yahweh steps on the heights of the earth, and in 9:5 those heights melt away. But in both these prophets' portrayals, Yahweh's earthmoving anthropomorphic activity is directed against Israel. And in both cases, the prophets use general cataclysmic language to present the extraordinary power of Yahweh turned toward punishing the wayward people. In contrast, the specificity of geographic imagery of Zechariah 14 heralds permanent cosmic changes that both coincide with and effect the permanent changes in the human realm of the eschatological age.

on that day. This eschatological formula, which appears seven times in chapter 14, sustains the anticipation of the future presented by the opening words of this chapter, "Behold a day of Yahweh is coming" (see NOTE above). It also continues the frequent usage of the phrase throughout Zechariah 12 and 13 (see NOTES, especially to "on that day" at 12:3 and 13:1).

In this verse, because it seems to interrupt the flow of the sentence and because it does not initiate a clause as it often does elsewhere, this formula is taken by some to be intrusive (so the editors of *BHS*; Mason 1973: 260; etc.). However, its appearance here not only adds to its overall use in this chapter but also echoes the "day" of battle of the previous verse (see NOTE above). Thus it is impossible to know whether the phrase was added in the final redaction of Zechariah or whether it belongs to an earlier stage of composition. Its place within this verse is certainly justifiable in terms of reiterating the eschatological setting for the events depicted in this subunit.

the Mount of Olives. This is the only place in the Hebrew Bible in which this exact term occurs. Undoubtedly, this designation arose because of the abundance of olive trees that grew on the mountain in antiquity. The Mount of Olives, on the east side of the city (cf. next NOTE and biblical references mentioned below), is actually a ridge, approximately two and one-half miles long, running north-south. It is separated from the Temple Mount and the city of Jerusalem by the Kidron Valley, which has always formed the city's eastern boundary. The Kidron begins in a broad valley just north of the present Old City of Jerusalem, near Mea Sherarim, and is called the Valley of Simon the Just, or the Wadi el-Joz in Arabic (Bahat 1990: 12). It continues from there to the east and south, between the city and the intersection of the Mount of Olives with Mount Scopus.

The relationship of the Mount of Olives to the adjacent valley(s) is of significance in attempting to comprehend the nuance of the rest of this verse and its reference to a "very great valley" (see NOTE below). In addition, the fact that the only perennial spring in Jerusalem, the Gihon, is located in the Kidron Valley, just where it meets the western ascent of the Mount of Olives, is to be noted in light of the reference to the "living waters" of Jerusalem (see NOTE in v 8). In 2 Sam 15:30 the Mount of Olives (known as Jebel Tur in Arabic) is referred to as "the ascent of the olives"; it is the place where David stood weeping at the time of Absalom's rebellion, a place where God was worshiped (2 Sam 15:32). It is also apparently the mountain less specifically referred to in Ezek 11:23, where God's "glory" rested east of the city, and in 1 Kgs 11:7 (cf. 1 Kgs 22:43), where high places were built on a mountain east of the city.

The several connotations of this height on the eastern side of Jerusalem are well established by those references. Thus the Mount of Olives as the place where Yahweh's feet are planted (see first NOTE to this verse) is in keeping with the historical sanctity of the site, whether for the worship of Yahweh or of other gods. But the strategic significance of the Mount of Olives is also prominent in its usage here. The Ezekiel passage (11:23) noted above has the Mount of Olives as the last stop on the way to Babylon for God's glory. The "nations" that threaten Jerusalem in this prophet's current experience and historical awareness are those to the east of Jerusalem. A cataclysmic event, effected by God's stance on the Mount of Olives, would therefore be undoubtedly successful in eliminating those nations. Thus the military dimension of God's anthropomorphic rendering is sustained by the specific topographic reference.

which is facing Jerusalem from the east. Although some commentators, such as the editors of *BHS*, suggest that this phrase is superfluous, its presence identifies the location of the Mount of Olives and emphasizes its position east of the city. The latter function seems essential to the combination of sacral and strategic connotations that inform the imagery of verse 4 (see previous NOTE).

The use of the idiom ʿal-pĕnê ("in front of" or "facing") provides information that certainly places the Mount of Olives toward the southern end of the eastern ridge, near Gihon or Water Gate in the time of Nehemiah (Bahat 1990: 36). The same idiom is found in 1 Kgs 11:7, in its reference to a mountain that must be the Mount of Olives but is not named as such.

will be split in half. The repetition of the subject "Mount of Olives" is followed by the root *bqʿ* ("to split, cleave"). Used in the Niphal here, it means "to be cleft, rent open" (cf. the noun form, *biqʿâ*, which means "valley"). The presence of this verb indicates an alteration in the existing geomorphology, and thus the resulting cleft or valley is not to be identified with any existing topographical feature. Yahweh's ultimate intervention in human affairs, in this subunit, involves a final resolution to Jerusalem's centuries-long history of being threatened or subjugated by other nations. Previous chapters presented the imagery of God as warrior; here God's fight against the nations involves a cataclysmic reordering of the natural world in order to achieve security for the people. Similarly, in the next subunit, the created realm is shown to be radically altered so as to provide economic security in the eschatological future (see various NOTES to vv 6–10). In this projected reordering of nature, the eschatological thrust has entered the realm of the apocalyptic.

from east to west. As indicated earlier in our NOTE to "Mount of Olives," both the Kidron Valley and the Mount of Olives are oriented north-south. Hence a split in the mountain ridge necessarily would create a valley (see next NOTE) running east-west.

a very great valley. Not just a small ravine but, rather, an extraordinary rift— *gêʾ gĕdôlâ mĕʾōd*—will emerge as the result of the splitting of the Mount of Olives (see above, NOTES in this verse to "the Mount of Olives" and "will be split in half"). This newly created valley will allow for an unprecedented aspect of the eschatological battle: Yahweh's people will be able to escape (see first NOTE to v 5). As we have already indicated, the very use of the word "split" as well as the overall conception, in the first two subunits of chapter 14, of catastrophe and change in the natural order preclude the possibility that this valley can be identified with an existing feature of the Jerusalem landscape.

Nonetheless, there have been many attempts to relate this prophetic portrayal with the topography of the land around Jerusalem. As mentioned above, the Kidron Valley is parallel to the Mount of Olives and so could not be identified as a valley that splits the mountain. The Kidron turns eastward just south of Jerusalem, and it extends as far as the Dead Sea; but this too would not fit the imagery of Second Zechariah. The remaining candidates are the upper Kidron Valley—the part between the Mount of Olives and the Temple Mount and known as the Valley of Jehoshaphat (King 1991: 30–31) or "Valley of Decision" (see Joel 4:12, 14 [NRSV 3:12, 14])—and the Wadi el-Joz, which is where the Kidron begins just north of the present Old City of Jerusalem. The association of the upper Kidron Valley in Joel, another postexilic prophet, with God's final act of judgment makes it tempting to relate this "very great valley" to the Valley of Jehoshaphat, even though its traditional location moved southwest to the Hinnom Valley, which is now associated with the day of judgment. If any connection exists, it could only be that the suggestion of an east-west valley at right angles to the Mount of Olives provides the possibility in the prophet's eschatological imagining for a major rift to tear the Mount of Olives into two parts, upon which will rest each of Yahweh's feet as God goes forth in the final battle (see NOTES to v 3).

This imagery in Second Zechariah no doubt occasioned the subsequent attention given to the Mount of Olives, especially its western flanks on the edge of the Kidron Valley. The most venerated burial places in Jewish history are located there. These include the elaborate tomb monuments of Hellenistic and Roman times that often commemorate biblical figures, including, appropriately enough, Zechariah, Jehoshaphat, and Absalom (see King 1991: 31), all of whom apparently have some connection with the Mount of Olives. We have just mentioned Jehoshaphat; we refer to Absalom (in 2 Sam 15:30) in our NOTE to "the Mount of Olives," and the association with Zechariah may come from this very verse.

Christian tradition likewise places far more emphasis on the Mount of Olives than does Hebrew Scripture. Jesus is said to have gone there several times, especially in the time just before his passion (see Matt 21:1; 24:3; 26:30; and parallel passages in Mark and Luke; see also Luke 19:37; 21:37; John 8:1; cf. Acts 1:12).

Perhaps most arresting of all the graphic traditions emerging from this verse of Second Zechariah is the lavish fresco on the north wall of the second/third-century C.E. synagogue at Dura Europos. A panel commonly called the Ezekiel panel depicts the cleaving of the Mount of Olives at the end of time. Goodenough (1964: 183) calls this panel the "Mountain of Transition," following the excavator (Kraeling 1940); he connects it with the earthquake of Ezek 37:7 and the several panels depicting the resurrection of the people of Israel in the Valley of the Dry Bones (Ezek 37:1–14).

However, at the top of the so-called Ezekiel panel there are two olive trees flanking a deep cleft, an object called a "castellated citadel" but which is surely an ossuary tumbling down the mountain, as are also pieces of human bodies on the left. Ezekiel imagery is present especially in the idea of resurrection (so

Goodenough 1964: 192; Curtis 1957: 170–72, 178–79), but so is Zechariah imagery (Kraeling 1940). And the fact that the mountain, long since a burial site in the time of Dura Europos, is split in two reflects an interpretation of Zechariah 14 that fits our understanding of the text. That is, despite the various traditions associated with the Mount of Olives and the surrounding valleys, the valley of this oracle is transhistorical. It will result from divine alteration of the created order. It may exaggerate or extend existing land forms, but it will alter forever Jerusalem's topography.

Half of the mountain . . . half. The image of the "Mount of Olives" being "split" (see NOTES above) is developed by the specific language of its being divided in two, i.e., "half . . . half." This further supports our contention that the language of this verse denotes no existing valley east of Jerusalem, because none of the valleys described in our NOTE to "a very great valley" would so evenly divide the Mount of Olives were it to continue eastward from its present location. The idea of a symmetrical division of the ridge east of Jerusalem contributes to the anthropomorphic conceptualization of this verse. If Yahweh is positioned astride the mountain (see first NOTE to v 4), having each foot on a peak of equal size affords stability to the divine figure in the final confrontation with the nations.

In addition to expressing the idea of an even splitting of the mountain ridge east of Jerusalem, the "half . . . half" terminology echoes and ultimately subverts the information provided in verse 2, where "half the city" is taken into exile and the other half left behind. It is precisely that intolerable fate of Jerusalem that Yahweh comes to rectify in verse 3–5, wherein the divine warrior stands astride the Mount of Olives, split in half. With the mountain now divided, the division of the people will come to an end.

will recede. The verb *mwš* normally means "to remove, depart" (see Zech 3:9). In this verse, because of the image of a cataclysmic wrenching apart of the Mount of Olives, we translate it "recede." The significance of this word is that something, usually an inanimate object, moves from a position that is presumably fixed. Thus its being moved constitutes an unanticipated and momentous shift. Such an idea is suitable to the language of natural catastrophe in this verse. If a valley is to appear where none before existed, then either the mountain thereby divided must lose some of its mass at the point where the vale appears, or each half of the mountain must move away from the rift that divides it. The latter is the image presented here, with the verb "recede" indicating the movement of each half of the north-south mountain ridge away from the transverse ("from east to west"; see NOTE above) valley that will separate the two halves (see previous NOTE).

northward . . . southward. These two directional words complete the concept of catastrophe in verse 4. As our various NOTES to this verse have explained, the mountain ridge east of Jerusalem is depicted as being split in two by an extraordinary east-west rift as part of God's intervention to save Jerusalem from its destroyers, "all the nations." This north/south terminology puts the finishing touches on the verbal description of a geomorphological alteration in the topography of Yehud. In some ways it is superfluous, because the idea of the two parts of the Mount of Olives receding, in order that an east-west rift may divide it, presents a sufficiently clear image of this eschatological reshaping of the natural world. Perhaps the insertion of these two directions into the description serves to complement the east/west language used for the valley. All together, all four compass points are represented. The words themselves connote the totality of the world, all of it reorganized by Yahweh, in a new creation, to facilitate the new sociopolitical order presented in the last subunit of this chapter and to complement the altered ecological and geomorphological features, also constituting a kind of new creation, of the second subunit of chapter 14.

5. *You will flee.* The MT as pointed—*nastem*—is very difficult and enigmatic. The textual problem has been created by the threefold repetition of the letters *nstm* in this verse. Many scholars read the Niphal third-person singular perfect from *stm* ("to block, stop"), which is supported by the Septuagint, Symmachus, the Targums, and a few Hebrew manuscripts. Among ancient scholars, both Josephus and Rashi prefer this reading. The Masoretes have understood the verb as the second-person plural Qal from *nws*, "to flee." Their reading, which prevails in most printed editions of the Hebrew Bible, is supported by the Latin and Syriac and is accepted by some of the recent English translations, such as the NRSV, which has "And you shall flee by the valley of the LORD's mountain . . ."

We retain the MT for several reasons. First, the threefold repetition of the verb *wĕnastem*, in the sense of "fleeing," serves the author's emphasis on the concept of the escape of Yahweh's people at this apocalyptic event. Unlike what happened in the past, when the people were besieged and captured, in the future they will escape before Yahweh destroys the enemy. Second, it would be too great a coincidence to have the identical Hebrew letters form totally different words in the same verse. Third, the allusion later in this verse to the earthquake of Uzziah (see NOTE below) makes it clear that panic and flight are very much in the mind of the prophet; thus there would be no reason to suppose that he would not start this verse with the language of flight. Finally, the idea of splitting the Mount of Olives involves the presence of a new topographic feature, a great valley where none before existed. It is precisely because of this that Yahweh's people will have an escape route in the eschatological future, a possibility that did not exist in the historical past.

the valley of the mountains. The MT *gê²-hāray* seems straightforward. Still, most translations and commentaries offer alternative readings for this expression because of the difficulties of the verse as a whole, but especially in view of the suggested emendations to "will be blocked" for "you will flee" (see preceding NOTE), which begins verse 5. Mitchell, for example (1912: 345), emends to "Gihon," i.e., *gîḥôn*, proposing that the perennial spring would have been blocked up. His argument is based on the fact that the verb *stm* in the Niphal, in all but one case in the Bible, is used for the closing of a well or spring. Because of the emphasis on "valley" in verse 4 and "living waters" in verse 8, it is easy to see why some would prefer "Gihon," a spring that is the main feature of Hinnom, the major valley south of Jerusalem and at right angles to the Mount of Olives. However, there is no versional or manuscript support for such an emendation, and the MT is not incomprehensible as it stands.

The same can be said for another popular emendation, which reads *gê*-*hinnōm*, "the Valley of Hinnom," for "valley of my mountains." This suggestion was first proposed by Wellhausen (1898) and has more recently been forcefully articulated by Saebø (1969: 295) and Rudolph (1976: 230). Again, the location of the Hinnom Valley south of Jerusalem, rather than east, mitigates the force of this suggestion. Furthermore, the disruption of the landscape is instrumental in Yahweh's combating the enemies of Israel, not in futher punitive action against Israel. Hence the suggestion of Saebø (following Wellhausen 1898; see also Mason 1973: 65–66) that the Hinnom Valley was "blocked" because it was associated with idolatrous practices and uncleanness is not compelling. A similar desire to associate the beginning of this verse with a polemic against idolatrous worship on the Mount of Olives (Curtis 1957: 140–42), as the Mountain of Destruction of 2 Kgs 23:13, does not take into account the focus of the catastrophe in the heightened eschatology of Zechariah 14.

Thus we see no reason to emend the MT except to read "valley of the mountains" rather than "valley of my mountains." The use of the first-person possessive pronoun can hardly involve a reference to the prophet's mountain. Nor is Yahweh the speaker here, hence a divine claim to the mountain is not in order. Because "valley of the mountains" appears in the next clause, presumably referring to and reiterating the very same valley of this clause, we may assume that the final *mem* has been lost, perhaps by haplography with the following *kap*, inasmuch as these two letters are very similar in early postexilic scripts. Although the Septuagint reflects the MT, both the Aramaic and Syriac read plural *hārîm* rather than *hāray* (with a possessive suffix). An alternative consideration is that this text, in its reflection of some of the imagery of Ezekiel 38, has been influenced by "in all my mountains" of Ezek 38:21, which depicts Yahweh's defeat of Gog, the representative of all Israel's enemies. In that verse Yahweh is clearly the speaker, hence "my" with "mountains."

Aside from the problem of the possessive suffix, the text should not read "Gihon" or "Hinnom." Thus the identity of the valley indicated by the MT is still at issue. Is it the great valley formed by the catastrophe of verse 4, whereby the Mount of Olives is rent asunder (see NOTES to "the Mount of Olives" and other phrases of v 4)? Or does it denote some other topographic feature? We prefer the former possibility, for the Mount of Olives will now consist of two halves with a valley in between. This great valley, which never before existed, will allow Yahweh's people to escape ("flee"), an action never before possible. The final battle will have unprecedented results for the people, as well as the enemy, and for their future existence in restored Jerusalem, as the next section of this chapter sets forth. The geophysical change described here will allow for both a new escape and a new kind of restoration.

valley of the mountains. This phrase repeats the words at the beginning of the verse (where the MT has "valley of my mountains"; but cf. our NOTE and suggested emendation). The repetition of this phrase and the threefold appearance of *nstm* (see first NOTE to this verse and NOTE below to "thus you shall flee as you fled") have both contributed to the textual difficulties of this verse. "Valley" here is defective—the MT has *gê* rather than *gêʾ*, as is usual in biblical texts referring to the Valley of Hinnom (as Josh 15:8; Neh 11:30; 2 Chron 28:3; Jer 7:31–32), which is why the emendation to "Hinnom Valley" is so compelling to many (see NOTE above to "the valley of the mountains").

will reach. The Hiphil of *ngʿ* ("to touch, reach, extend to") is clear enough, but the idea of the verb is completed by the following "to" (*ʾel*) and another word that is difficult to understand (see next NOTE).

to Azel. The syntax and context suggest that "Azel" (*ʾāṣal*) is a place name (see Abel 1936). However, such a location in the Jerusalem area remains unknown or unidentified. Yet the existence of "Beth-Azel" (*bêt-hāʾēṣel*) in Mic 1:11 may be of significance in establishing its validity as a toponym, as may its appearance as a designation for a Benjaminite descendant of Jonathan (in 1 Chron 8:37, 38[2] and 9:43, 44[2]), apparently living in Jerusalem (1 Chron 8:32; 9:38).

Because of the difficulty in locating Azel, and because the LXX has a different reading (*yĕsôd*: either Jasod, a proper name, or "foundation," neither of which is particularly helpful), many (e.g., P. D. Hanson 1975: 369, 371) would emend the text to *ʾeṣlô*, "its side." This suggestion understands *ʾeṣlô* to come from the preposition *ʾeṣel*, meaning "besides" in a substantive sense. It would mean "side" or "flank," with a suffix ("its") now missing owing to haplography with the *waw* of the following verb (*wĕnastem*, "thus you shall flee"). This clause would then read "the valley of the mountains will reach to its side," presumably to the side of the eastern edge of Jerusalem or the Temple Mount. Or, similarly, it is seen as related to *ʾaṣṣîl*, "joining," so that it would read "extend to its joining," i.e., where it reaches the walls/hills of Jerusalem itself.

Such emendations do not necessarily provide better readings, and we prefer to retain the MT and to suppose that a district of Jerusalem on the northeast side, inhabited by Benjaminites who were descendants of Azel, is what the text portrays (cf. "Gate of Benjamin," and NOTE to that phrase in v 10). The "valley of the mountains," presumably the "great valley" (see NOTE above to "a very great valley" in v 4), will run through the Mount of Olives, which is northeast of Jerusalem, and provide an unprecedented escape route for Yahweh's besieged or captured people.

Thus you shall flee as you fled. These are the second and third of three occurrences in this verse of *wnstm*, which we read here as transmitted by the MT, namely, as a second-person plural from *nws* ("to flee, escape"). As we indicated in our first NOTE in this verse, the Latin and Syriac read *nws* in all three places, whereas the Greek (and the Aramaic in the latter two places) reads the Niphal of *stm* ("to block") in all cases. We follow the MT in all three instances. An emended text would read: "Thus it will be blocked as it was blocked because of the earthquake in the days of Uzziah. . . ." Although the knowledge of an eighth-century earthquake is clearly preserved (see next NOTE), there is no evidence for the blockage of a valley at that time. Hence the language here is more likely meant to emphasize the enormous impact of the eschatological catastrophe of verses 4 and 5 and the future splitting of the Mount of Olives to create a "great valley." This valley will provide a way for Yahweh's people, presumably those of the half still left in the city (see v 2) after the enemy's onslaught, to escape before Yahweh brings about the plague (vv 12–14) that will decimate Jerusalem's attackers. Only when the surviving Yehudites manage to flee from the city can Yahweh settle matters with the invading armies.

Escape from Jerusalem, however, has never been easy or even possible because of the geomorphology of the Jerusalem hills and the topography of the Jerusalem area itself. Thus this apocalyptic view of the future involves dramatic changes in existing conditions. The next section of chapter 14 (vv 6–11) shows how those changes will allow for a safe and secure Jerusalem in the new age; these verses indicate that alterations in the topography will facilitate Yahweh's dealing with the enemy while sparing the people of Jerusalem. In this sense, the scenario is strikingly reminiscent of the Exodus event, in which Yahweh changes nature (by parting the Red/Reed Sea) to allow the Israelites to escape while causing the enemy, the Egyptians, to perish (see Exodus 14–15).

The terror and fright that accompany severe earthquakes is the prophet's analogy, and the historical response—fleeing the shaking, trembling earth—represents the human reaction to radical change in the natural order. Apparently, people fled Jerusalem at the time of an earthquake (see next two NOTES), and that is what they must do here in order to vacate Jerusalem so that Yahweh can set a plague upon its enemies.

earthquake. Amos 1:1 also mentions an earthquake in the reign of Uzziah, and Isa 6:4 may have an allusion to it. The use of a natural disaster in the heading of a prophetic book is highly unusual (so Andersen and Freedman 1989: 25, 193–94) and must therefore reflect a major and memorable seismic event, one that had a significant impact on all who experienced it and on subsequent generations as well (see Dever 1992). Earthquakes of varying intensity are hardly rare in Palestine, which lies along the great Rift Valley extending from the upper Jordan River down to the Gulf of Eilat and along East Africa. Invariably, when the occurrence of an earthquake is mentioned in the biblical text, the assumption is that such a disruption of nature is a sign of divine power, often used negatively but also positively: to herald or accompany a theophany (e.g., the Sinai event [Exod 19:18]).

It is no wonder, then, that an eschatological vision such as this section of Zechariah 14, which imagines a radical rearrangement of the geomorphology of the Jerusalem region at the end-time, should refer to the most notable example of the earth's unusual movements in historical times, namely, the great tremors of the mid-eighth century in the days of Uzziah. Other prophets use the imagery of seismic activity to depict the actions of Yahweh in bringing about the restoration of Zion and the desolation of her enemies (e.g., Amos 8:8ff.; 9:1, 5, 9ff.; Joel 3:16–21 [NRSV 4:16–21]). Only Zechariah uses a specific historical analogy. In so doing, this prophet continues a pattern that is visible in many of his oracles, in which past and future are intermingled in his thinking so that the historical details that are vivid in his consciousness provide the outlines for his imaginings of God's ultimate resolution of the destiny of Israel amid the other peoples of the world.

Later Jewish tradition, notably the writings of the first-century historian Josephus, expands upon the references of both Amos and Second Zechariah to the earthquake of about 750 B.C.E. and connects that catastrophe to the Chronicler's account of Uzziah's entrance to the Jerusalem Temple to offer incense (2 Chron 26:16ff.; cf. Cohen 1948: 327). When the priests opposed Uzziah's cultic actions, Uzziah became very angry and then was struck with a horrible skin affliction that remained with him until his death. Josephus records that this presumptuous cultic action resulted in a great rent in the Temple, because "half the mountain broke off from the rest on the west, rolled itself four furlongs, and stood still at the east mountain" (*Antiquities* 9.10.4). This earth movement is said to have taken place at Eroge, which may be a corruption of "Ein Rogel" (so Mitchell 1912: 345) and which apparently shows that Josephus identifies (wrongly) that spring with Gihon. Such a perspective is akin to the way "valley of the mountains" earlier in this verse is read "Valley of Hinnom," the site of Gihon, by some scholars. The Josephus account does not really add to an understanding of a difficult text except to demonstrate that early Jewish "scholarship" of the postbiblical period was perhaps struggling with the same interpretive problems that confront more recent exegetes of Second Zechariah.

Uzziah, king of Judah. King Uzziah, also known as Azariah, ascended to the throne of the Southern Kingdom at the age of sixteen (2 Kgs 15:2). He and his son Jotham were both contemporaries of Jeroboam II, who ruled the Northern Kingdom from 785 to 745 B.C.E. The precise dates of Uzziah's reign are not certain, although it seems clear that Jotham's rule ended in 742.

The Deuteronomic historian presents Uzziah as ruling under the shadow of his more powerful neighbor to the north. In contrast, the Chronicler's account (2 Chron 26:9, 11–15) portrays Uzziah as a more powerful and independent ruler than the brief Kings passage (2 Kgs 15:1–7) would lead us to believe. Indeed, anyone in office for fifty-two years was bound to have achieved some notable accomplishments. According to the Chronicler, these included significant development of the military, both the fighting force and the technological supports for a war machine that was successful against neighboring peoples. In addition, Uzziah apparently strengthened Jerusalem's fortifications, especially at the major gates. The latter accomplishment may have been part of his general military stance, or it may have been in response to a weakening of the walls of the city as the result of the mid-eighth-century earthquake (see previous NOTE; cf. Bright 1981: 258 and Miller and Hayes 1986: 310–11).

The allusion to Uzziah surely, in the first instance, conjures up the image of a disruption of nature that a major seismic movement represents. Yet it also may allude to the defeat of Judah's enemies by a powerful Judean king, an event that will now take place in the future age only by the intervention of Yahweh.

There is, in addition, a certain irony involved in the mention of Uzziah. The strength that he demonstrated was carried too far, in the estimation of the Chronicler, and he suffered a disfiguring skin disease that caused him to be separated from his people. In Second Zechariah Yahweh takes on the military power that Uzziah had held in the eighth century. The earthquake/Uzziah imagery of early biblical texts has been inverted in Zechariah 14 to express the transhistorical might and justice of Yahweh.

Yahweh my God. This expression occurs in nearly identical form in Zech 11:4 (see NOTE to "Thus spoke Yahweh my God"). In 11:4, however, it appears in the context of a traditional messenger formula initiated by "thus spoke." Here it is coupled with "will come" (see next NOTE), which completes the idea begun in the "will go forth" phrase of 14:3 (see first NOTE to that verse).

As in 11:4, the combination of Yahweh and Elohim, the latter with the first-person suffix ("my"), serves to emphasize the prophet's self-proclaimed personal relationship to God. Such a relationship is part of prophetic tradition, perhaps going back to Moses' claim (Deut 4:5) to be conveying to the Israelites all that "Yahweh my God" has charged him to do.

will come. Our NOTE to "will go forth" (14:3) indicates how *bwʾ* ("to come") is often paired with *yṣʾ* ("to go out, go forth") to form a stereotypical expression frequently associated with the description of military campaigns, as in the context of a holy war. Although nearly two verses separate "go forth" from "come," the use of "will come" here does serve to complete the idea, begun at the beginning of verse 3, that Yahweh will do battle with all of Israel's enemies at the end-time. The pair "go forth" (*yṣʾ*) and "come" (*bʾ*) thus forms an envelope around the material in verses 3–5 (cf. the striking example in Hos 8:9–13). The extraordinary catastrophes of nature depicted in the intervening material are thereby presented as part of the martial actions undertaken by Yahweh to bring about Jerusalem's final liberation. The language of human warfare—steeds, bows, swords—that permeates the warrior image of Yahweh in earlier chapters of Second Zechariah (e.g., 9:13, 15; 10:4–5) gives way here to the ultimate weaponry of cosmic upheaval; nothing less than God's control of the natural order is appropriate to God's effecting change in human affairs that have so long resisted being ordered in accordance with the divine will.

By attaching the relatively rare expression "Yahweh my God" (see previous NOTE and also NOTE to this expression in 11:4) to this second element of a familiar pair, the prophet once again exhibits his originality in altering stylized language to suit his own purposes. A similar process can perhaps be seen in the appearance of "holy ones" (see NOTE below) rather than "heavenly hosts," which might be expected in this holy-war context.

all. The MT has "all," but many Hebrew manuscripts as well as the major versions, including Greek, Latin, Syriac, and Aramaic, have *wkl,* "and all."

the holy ones. The MT reading, *qĕdōšîm,* is supported by the Greek and Latin; but the Syriac and Aramaic add the third-person plural suffix (see next NOTE). "Holy ones" can refer to people, in the Hebrew Bible (as Lev 21:7, 8; Num 16:5, 7; 2 Chron 35:3; etc.). Yet it usually refers to God's heavenly colleagues (as Ps 89:6, 8 [*NRSV* 89:5, 7]; Job 5:1; 15:15; Dan 8:13[2]). Such heavenly beings in most cases would be identified in military terms as heavenly "hosts" or "armies" (Deut 33:2; Ps 68:18 [*NRSV* 68:17]; see P. D. Hanson 1975: 375). And indeed, such an aspect of "holy ones" would not be out of the question, given the military language that introduces (see NOTES to 14:3) and concludes (see previous NOTE) these three verses describing Yahweh's attack on Jerusalem's enemies. Note also the military context of Exod 15:11, which uses *qōdeš* rather than *qĕdōšîm*.

This military nuance of "holy ones" is likewise present in the relationship of the term *qdšym* (see Ps 89:6, 8; Job 5:1; 15:15; Dan 8:13[2]) to the angelic beings of Yahweh's heavenly court. These members of the divine retinue, as is clear from the language of First Zechariah (see especially chapter 3 and Meyers and Meyers 1987: 114, 183) are also divine messengers or "angels"—thus the idea of the "angel of Yahweh" as instigator of widespread death in a military encampment (2 Kgs 19:35 = Isa 37:36). The homologizing of "holy ones" and "angels/ messengers" in the visions of Zechariah 1–8 paves the way for the appearance of "holy ones" here to anticipate the destruction (presumably via "angels," which is the theological language often used in the Bible to denote the outbreak of plague) by means of disease that will decimate the enemy, according to the information provided below in the third subunit (especially v 12). "Holy ones" at the end of the first subunit indirectly anticipates the onset of plague at the beginning of the third subunit.

At the same time, a more sacral nuance to "holy ones" may be present (see Mason 1973: 371 and Saebø 1969: 296). That is, "holy ones" is used here rather than "hosts" or "armies," as might be expected in a contest of cosmic conflict, to suggest the purifying role of the heavenly beings whom humans are meant to emulate. The holiness of the heavenly realm will surely and at last become pervasive on earth in the eschatological age. This verse thus adumbrates the cultic language of the last subunit (vv 16–21) of Zechariah 14, where all the nations that had been enemies will participate in the sacral life of Jerusalem (14:16); even the bells on horses (war animals) will be called "Holy to Yahweh" (14:20; see NOTE below). In other words, at the very end of this passage about Yahweh's defeat of Israel's foes by altering the created order, the acceptance of Yahweh's sovereignty by the survivors of those foes is anticipated by the use of a term that emphasizes the sanctity of the heavenly beings that have accompanied Yahweh in the overturning of nature. These "holy ones" do not appear, however, to have marched with Yahweh in battle; rather, they are present as the battle ends to secure the new age for Jerusalem.

with you. The MT has "with you" (feminine singular). All the major versions (LXX, Vulg, Targ, and Syr), as well as many (forty-five) Hebrew manuscripts, read "with him" (*ᶜimmô*) in reference to Yahweh. Most modern commentators accept the reading of the versions and manuscripts over the MT. Note also that the Syriac and Aramaic also put the third-person singular suffix with the previous noun, reading "his holy ones," as does Job 15:15.

However, there are compelling reasons for retaining the MT "with you" in reference to Jerusalem. Verse 5 closes out a section, verses 1–5, that began with an explicit reference to Jerusalem in verse 2 and the anticipatory use of second-person feminine suffixes in verse 1 ("your spoil . . . in your midst," *bqrbk*). Thus it is entirely appropriate for verse 5 to echo the usage in verse 1, mentioning Jerusalem once again through the use of the second-person feminine singular suffix "you." The third-person masculine singular suffix may be the easier reading, as indicated by both the ancient and modern renditions. But emendations obscure the way the more difficult feminine singular suffix contributes to the literary shaping of this first unit of Zechariah 14.

6. *on that day.* This is the second of seven instances in chapter 14 of this eschatological phrase, which appears frequently in Zechariah 12–14 (see especially first NOTES to 12:1 and 14:1 for a discussion of eschatological terminology). The expression here introduces a depiction of the eschatological age in which the natural order of the cosmos itself will be turned upside down. If Jerusalem will be the dominant force in the universe, instead of a puny, ever-dominated, and struggling city in the Palestine highlands, then surely the cosmos itself will undergo an equally dramatic reversal.

"On that day" is preceded by the verb *hyh* ("to be"), as it often is in chapters 12–14. Several Greek manuscripts and the Syriac omit the verb here.

longer. The text is apparently corrupt here. After the verb ("there will not be"), the MT has three words. The first one, *ʾôr*, means "light" and is difficult, for we might expect a term expressing the opposite of "cold" or "frost," the next two words in Hebrew. That "light" is intended seems unlikely, given that the next verse expressly states that the future age will be characterized by the complete presence of "light" (see last NOTE to v 7). However, it is not difficult to see how "light" may have entered the text, inasmuch as it follows *yhyh*, just as does "light" as the last word in verse 7, which echoes the language of Genesis 1. The scribe's eye may have picked up the wrong word (i.e., "light") to place after *yhyh* in verse 6.

The question remains as to whether a pair of words, or even one word, has dropped out. Wellhausen (1898) and many others suggest that *hôm* ("heat") is the missing word. That suggestion derives from the fact that in Gen 8:22, "day" and "night" appear as opposites, as here, along with "cold" and "heat" (*hôm*). Appealing as such a reconstruction is, it falters because of the fact that "cold" here is paired with a like word, and "heat" would not be. Furthermore, the assumption that "heat" would vanish in the future age seems unlikely; whereas cold and frost seem to destroy life, heat has more positive connotations and, like "light" replacing darkness, would be retained in an ideal future.

Consequently, it is our opinion that either *ʾôr* should be deleted completely or that, with Mitchell (1912: 349), we read it as *ʿôd*, almost a homophone of *ʾôr*, in which case, following "there will not be," it would read "there will no longer be." The latter possibility seems more attractive since *lôʾ* ("no") . . . *ʿōd* ("more, longer") is a combination often used for future events that are to be the antithesis of present conditions (e.g., Isa 62:4; Jer 3:16), which is exactly the intention in this verse.

cold or frost. The MT Qere (*yĕqārôt wĕqippā᾽ôn*), literally translated "precious things shall contract (condense)," makes no sense. The Greek, Latin, and Syriac read an abstract and otherwise unattested form of "cold" or "coldness," which involves the deletion of the *yodh*. Similarly, the Qere and all the versions preserve *wĕqippā᾽ôn*, from *qp᾽* ("to congeal"), which is also otherwise unattested but may mean "ice" or "frost," and which involves the change of *yodh* to *waw* in the MT. Considering the difficulty of the received text, the versional readings should be accepted as preserving the original of a corrupt text.

If these emendations are valid, this verse then presents the first of a series of altered conditions that will characterize the future age. The first is a climatic one. The drop in temperature that brings an end to the growing season and appears to cut off life will no longer exist. Certainly, cool weather and the accompanying rainy season were hardly an anathema to Palestinian agriculturalists, and the concept of seasonal weather in the eschatological future remains (see last NOTE to v 8). Yet, if these words ("cold or frost") function as a hendiadys, indicating severe cold that brings frost or ice, then the prospect of a world without such damaging conditions would suit an eschatological ideal. In fact, even if they represent separate though related climatic features, they still point to a critical meteorological variable.

The anticipation of a world without damaging frost and/or cold addresses, as do all the expected changes in this subunit, a feature related to agricultural risk. The meteorological variable of temperature range is at issue in this verse (see Frick 1985: 111–12). The highlands of Palestine, as in Jerusalem, have longer and colder winters than the lowlands, with frequent night frosts. These sustained low temperatures and evening freezes affect crops, especially olives, one of the mainstays of the highland cropping pattern. Indeed, olive trees can endure drought and heat but can be killed by extended frost; or if not killed, the yield of olive trees can be significantly impaired by sustained cold temperature.

Thus "cold or frost" stands as the first of four variables presented in this second subunit of Zechariah 14. All of these features involve environmental conditions relating to agricultural productivity. In combination, the changed conditions constitute a different world—one that is conducive to ease in the agrarian foundation of life in Palestine. The first condition is, rightly, a different climate. If Gen 8:22 proclaims environmental features for historical reality, this verse and the next one present a view that supersedes that reality.

7. *One day.* These words, following the verb *hyh* plus *waw* consecutive, constitute a variation on the more typical eschatological formula "on that day" (see first NOTE to v 6 and first NOTES to 12:1 and 14:1). The variation here is eminently suitable to the content of what this verse presents in terms of the altered environmental conditions of the future age, in which the night and day time markers are terminated. In other words, it combines the two ways in which "day" with the number "one" is used in the Bible—either to note some indefinite future time (as 1 Sam 27:1) or to denote one single day (as Isa 9:13 [NRSV 9:14]). Although "day" appears with various numbers in the Hebrew Bible, including "one," this text may be unique in its intentional ambiguity.

In addition to serving as a variant of an eschatological formula, "one day" (or "day one") evokes the creation, or pre-creation, scene of Gen 1:3–5. This phrase—along with the "day" and "night" pair, the reference to "evening," and the mention of "light," all in this verse (see NOTES below)—draws upon the language of beginning time as expressed in the first creation narrative. The conception of the new creation in the eschatological age thus refers back to the original creation by means of the lexical connection of this verse with Genesis 1. But the new creation will diverge from the first creation according to what appears here and in the following verses. In this verse, the difference is the omnipresence of light. Unlike pre-creation, with total darkness, and unlike the first creation, with alternating light and darkness (day and night), the future age will always be light.

One other aspect of this phrase is worth considering. The heart of this subunit contains a statement announcing the unity of Yahweh and of the divine name. The word "one" appears twice in verse 9: "Yahweh will be one, and his name one" (see NOTE below). This dramatic assertion of the universality and oneness of Yahweh is part of a depiction of a leveling, a new unity, in the natural world and so is adumbrated by the *"one* day" of verse 7.

that will be known to Yahweh. The parenthetical nature of these words have suggested to many that they constitute an interpolation. That may be so, although it is difficult to see what a later hand may have wanted to contribute by adding it. An argument for its originality may be that it supplements the preceding "one day" (see previous NOTE), which is unique as an eschatological expression, by echoing the phrase "to Yahweh" that is part of the eschatological formula introducing this entire chapter (see first NOTE to 14:1). That is, the expected phrase "on that day" changes to "one day" because of the particular content of the new diurnal character of the future age that it anticipates, and because it echoes the language of the first Genesis creation narrative (see previous NOTE). Then a clause including "to Yahweh" follows to pick up the eschatological aspect of "one day."

The idea of God's knowledge is hardly out of place in a depiction of the radical changes to characterize the future age. Divine omniscience can surely be projected into the time to come, insofar as it is Yahweh who announces in prophetic oracles how Israel will be restored and the world order will be different. If that is so for the political world, so too is it true for the natural world. Never before in prophecy has the eschatological age been depicted as so radically other; hence a clause expressing the authenticity of such a depiction by claiming that such a future is within the divine ken is perfectly in order.

neither day nor night. When "day" and "night" are paired as here, they indicate a calendrical period composed of day (= light) plus night (= dark). If the world at pre-creation was without the diurnal pattern of light and darkness that together constituted a recognizable unit of time (so Gen 1:3–5; cf. first NOTE to this verse), the world at the end of time will revert to the pre-creation state, that is, of no shifting between light and darkness. But there will be a crucial difference. At the time of creation, the lack of days meant that darkness

(Gen 1:2) was all-pervasive. In the new kind of time in the future, it is light that will always be present (see next NOTE).

at evening time it will be light. "Evening time" is the part of the diurnal pattern in which darkness is expected. But in the future age that pattern will be transformed into one in which light, the positive antithesis of darkness, is always present (see previous NOTE and first NOTE to this verse). Despite its relationship to the chaos of beginning times, darkness is not a mythic hostile force in the Hebrew Bible. Still, light and darkness are clearly polarized, with darkness having negative attributes. God blesses the light in Genesis 1 (v 4) but not the darkness, and darkness is linked with death, destruction, and evil (Aalen 1974: 157–66). It is no wonder, then, that eschatological language involves the elimination of darkness, which may first prevail as part of the final cataclysm that will precede the establishment of divine light and justice (e.g., Joel 2:1–2; Zeph 1:14–18; Amos 5:18).

The cessation of the daily rhythm implied by the regular sequence of night and day means an end to time as it is known historically. The regular and countable alternation between light and dark provides the basis for marking the passage of time into identifiable units. However, the fact that the future cessation of time markers does not involve a reversion to pre-creation darkness must be related to the radical difference between Urzeit and Endzeit. The former precedes the created order and its culmination in human existence. The latter is the culmination of the created order and human potential. And if human life is to continue as the central feature of the world order in the eschatological age, the world cannot be without light. A world of thriving living beings will be a place of infinite light (cf. Isa 60:1–3, where that light is identified with Yahweh's glory and presence in Zion).

Perpetual light not only presents an aura of divine presence and of positive moral and spiritual qualities, it also, on a more mundane level, speaks to the problems of survival in an agrarian society. The damage to growing things caused by severe coldness is precluded in the first feature of the future age (see last NOTE to 14:6). Now the diminished growth that accompanies the shortening of daylight hours in a diurnal pattern of light and dark is also precluded for the new order at the end of time. The struggle for survival will cease in the ecological-economic sphere as well as in the political arena.

8. *On that day.* This is the third appearance of this eschatological formula in Zechariah 14 (see NOTE to this expression in v 4 and in 12:3 and 13:1; cf. first NOTE to 14:1 for a discussion of eschatological language). Here it introduces the third feature of the radically new natural order of the future age.

living waters. The two Hebrew words *mayim ḥayyîm* consist of the noun "waters" plus a form of *ḥyh* ("to live") that can be either the noun "life" or the plural adjective "living." The latter possibility is preferable in light of the priestly usage (Lev 14:5, 50–52; 15:13; Num 19:17) of "living waters," a term that designates fresh water flowing from natural springs rather than old or stale water, potentially less clean or even contaminated, that has been collected in cisterns. Jeremiah's imagery is instructive in this sense; in 2:13 Yahweh is likened to a "fountain of living water" (*mĕqôr mayim ḥayyîm*; cf. Jer 17:13) in contrast to the dry cisterns (= idolatry?) upon which people have sinfully relied.

The idea of "living water" coming forth from Jerusalem is an expression of the role of Zion as the cosmic center of the universe. The mythic underpinnings of the imagery associated with Jerusalem and the Temple Mount are visible in many parts of the Hebrew Bible, including the depiction of the artistic and architectural symbolism of God's dwelling place in Israel and the many poetic references to Jerusalem as the center of nations (see Clifford 1972; Levenson 1985: 89–184). Zion's role as God's special place on earth meant an identification of the holy city with the Edenic paradigm. Consequently, phenomenological features of the cosmic center and of the paradisiacal garden merge in biblical depictions of Zion.

Prominent among those features is the presence of abundant, fresh waters flowing forth from the Temple in the midst of Jerusalem. The psalmist uses a phrase similar to that of Jer 3:13 in depicting the streams flowing from the Temple, in calling Yahweh the "fountain of life" (*mĕqôr ḥayyîm*, Ps 36:9–10 [NRSV 36:8–9]). This phrase is elliptical for the fuller "fountain of living water" of Jeremiah. The source of these waters is the protological foundation of the world on the primordial waters; hence it is only fitting that those waters flow abundantly, as in this verse, in eschatological time. Just as the future age will revert to beginning-time with respect to the abolition of night and day—except that light will prevail—so now the primordial waters will again be plentiful and available—except that they will be contained and directed (as the rest of this verse explains) rather than chaotically covering everything.

Although we have translated "living waters" in recognition of its fresh, flowing attributes, the connotations of the alternative translation, "waters of life," are also present. The waters flowing from the fountains of the deep, from Zion, are associated with Yahweh's protective and sustaining presence in Jerusalem; they are life-giving waters. They thus constitute the third aspect of the eschatological age favorable to the agrarian ideal of Israel (cf. NOTES to "cold or frost" [v 6], "at evening time it will be light" [v 7], and "like the plain" [v 10]). The "living waters" of Second Zechariah, like the "many waters" of Ezekiel (17:5, 8 and 31:5, 7; see May 1955) will entail great fecundity of the soil.

will go forth. The root *yṣ²* ("to go out, go forth") is commonly used in the Hebrew Bible in reference to the going forth of persons, objects, or things. In relating to the latter group, it often depicts, as here, the movement of a river going forth from a certain source and moving toward a destination. Perhaps the best-known example of this is the portrayal of the "river of Eden," going out (*yōṣē²*) from Eden and becoming the four rivers that water Havilah, Cush, and Assyria (Gen 2:10–14). This beginning-time flow is aptly echoed in the prophetic eschatological visions in Ezekiel (47:1, 8, 12) and Joel (4:18 [NRSV 3:18]) as well as in this text. It is instructive to examine how those two prophets present the flow of waters, because they mention two aspects of the flow that are not explicit in Zechariah 14.

Both Ezekiel and Joel proclaim that the wondrous abundance of water in the future age will originate at the Temple, at the holy center of the universe; for plentiful fresh water is a significant attribute of the symbolic expression of Jerusalem's role as the link between the heavenly and earthly domains (see previous NOTE). Thus, although Second Zechariah mentions Jerusalem rather than the Temple, this is surely a metonymic use of "Jerusalem," especially in light of the last subunit of Zechariah 14, in which the Jerusalem Temple is the focus of the celebratory climax of this chapter. The second explicit aspect of Ezekiel and Joel in their use of *yṣ'* for the flow of waters from Jerusalem is the fructifying quality of the waters. For Ezekiel, despite the salt marshes along the Dead Sea, the water flowing thence from Jerusalem will produce fruit trees on either side, perpetually bearing fruit, precisely because they are watered by the flow from the Jerusalem sanctuary (Ezek 47:12). Joel is somewhat less direct. Still, in announcing that a "fountain" will go forth from the Temple to provide water for the Wadi Shittim, probably located northeast of the Dead Sea (cf. Num 25:1; Josh 2:1; 3:1; Mic 6:5) and hence not a location associated with an abundance of plant life, Joel is indicating that "in that day" even the driest regions will become productive, just as the mountains will "drip wine" and the hills will "flow with water" (Joel 3:18 [*NRSV* 4:18]).

Thus the language of this verse, describing sweet waters that "go forth" from Jerusalem, resonates with the way other biblical texts depict such a flow. The cosmic aspects of the waters are a significant part of the eschatological thrust of this passage. At the same time, the potential for ease of agricultural production represented by ever-flowing fresh waters (see NOTE below to "in summer and in winter") is part of the depiction of a world in which life for the peasantry will no longer involve the constant struggle that the agrarian marginality of Palestine's ecological zones entails.

The idea of streams flowing perpetually takes the intrinsic connection between water and fertility into the transhistorical realm. In Deuteronomic covenant language, the divine blessing upon Israel is expressed as the opening of the heavenly storehouse of waters to provide rain in its season (Deut 28:12). That historical contingency is here replaced with the eschatological prospect of waters always available, without contingency.

half . . . half. The division of the fresh waters flowing from Jerusalem (see two previous NOTES) into two streams is closer to the imagery of Joel, who mentions an eastern and a western sea (2:20; cf. next NOTE), than to that of Ezekiel, who seems to be concerned mainly with the flow of cosmic waters from Jerusalem toward the east (47:3, 8). In envisioning a bifurcation of the waters from Jerusalem at the end of time, the author of Zechariah 14 may be picking up on the notion of the double protological character of waters, with their upper and lower portion (Gen 1:10). Their eschatological character will again evince a division into two. But there will be a difference. The future waters will be readily available throughout the land. Farmers will no longer be dependent on the windows in the heavens to open and allow sufficient water to fall to earth; nor will they be constrained by the availability of springs releasing some of the waters that exist under the earth, according to biblical cosmogony.

At the same time, in a literary sense, the division of waters into two main segments, using the word "half," echoes the division of Jerusalem of verse 2. There the bifurcation was radically and painfully punitive. Here it is fully and forever restorative.

eastern sea . . . western sea. These two phrases undoubtedly refer to two specific bodies of water: the Dead Sea in the east, and the Mediterranean Sea to the west. The two phrases are found individually in reference to their respective seas; "eastern sea" appears once elsewhere (Ezek 47:18), and "western sea" appears twice (Deut 11:24; 34:2). Only in one other text besides this one, Joel 2:20, do they appear in an antonymous arrangement. This perhaps unexpected paucity of usage is somewhat misleading inasmuch as both the Dead Sea and the Mediterranean are represented by other terms, including simply "the sea." However, given the frequency with which geographical boundaries are delineated in the Hebrew Bible and the many times in which the word "seas" is used as part of the vocabulary of cosmic space to denote the extent of the created universe, the relatively rare appearance of "eastern sea" and "western sea" deserves comment.

The fact is that these two terms in opposition are inappropriate as markers of the greater land of Israel, for which the eastern desert as far as the Euphrates typically serves as the eastern or northeastern border, and for which the Mediterranean, called the Great Sea or the Sea of the Philistines, is the unambiguous western limit (as Exod 23:31 and Josh 1:4). With respect to the cosmic aspect of waters representing the universe, the plural "seas" or some combination of "from sea to sea" along with "rivers" (see NOTE to "sea to sea" in 9:10) is used to indicate the entirety of the world. Thus the present combination of terms designates a more specific and limited territory. This territory is that which forms the immediate environs of Jerusalem, as also set forth in verse 10 below, where "all the land" (see NOTE to this phrase, and cf. also NOTES to "Geba" and "Rimmon" in v 10) apparently designates Jerusalem's extent. Furthermore, the east-west orientation of this verse is complemented by the north-south orientation of verse 10.

This whole chapter focuses on Jerusalem as center of the universe, as the locus of Yahweh's sovereignty over all nations, and as the focus of earthly existence for Yahweh's people. Consequently, the imagery throughout chapter 14 contributes to the exalted role of Zion, even if Zion can conceptually represent larger entities, geographically and demographically, than the Temple Mount alone or even the urban extent alone. The Jerusalem of this oracle is a flourishing city, an urban center with a royal-sacral complex and with a hinterland—extending north and south (v 10) as well as east and west (v 8)—that will be transformed.

Historically, the lands surrounding the capital city were hardly able to sustain a major urban settlement. The infertile, poorly watered hills around Jerusalem are not conducive to providing for its prosperity without the contributions of territories beyond its immediate environs (cf. Meyers and Meyers 1987: 160). Thus the eschatological picture of Jerusalem represents a departure from those limitations; it envisions an environmental setting that reverses the natural disadvantages. Abundant waters flowing out to both sides of the Temple, or city (see two previous NOTES), means that Jerusalem and the extended hinterland upon which it ought to be able to depend will no longer lack water resources. The ancient idea of cosmic water flowing from the dwelling place of God (see M. S. Smith 1990: 10 and n. 57) is not absent from this imagery; rather, it is subsumed into the specificity of presenting Jerusalem's eschatological flourishing. Indeed, the reliance of this whole subunit on well-established motifs associating Jerusalem with the cosmic center creates an apparent contradiction between the perennial water of this verse and the contingency of rainfall in verse 17 below (see NOTE to "there will be no rain for them"). Here the specificity of "Jerusalem" is again crucial: the ever-flowing waters, cosmic though they are, serve God's people centered in Jerusalem; for the nations, the availability of water is a separate issue.

This will be so. The verb *yihyeh*, singular masculine imperfect, is omitted by the Peshitta and is rendered as a plural by the Vulgate. However, the LXX preserves the text as it stands, and there is no need to emend.

in summer and in winter. Palestine has basically only two seasons of the year, summer and winter, which are demarcated largely by the presence or absence of rain rather than by temperature gradations. Thus "in summer and in winter" means that the fresh water flowing from Jerusalem (see above in this verse, NOTES to "living waters" and "will go forth") to water its territory (see previous NOTE) will be perennial. No longer will Jerusalem be dependent on the erratic waters of seasonal rainfall.

The notion of the availability of water throughout the year speaks not only to the concern for abundance of water. It also, in the specificity of this phrase mentioning the two seasons of the Palestinian year, reflects the problems of seasonal variation in rainfall (see Frick 1985: 110–11). That is, even a year of abundant rainfall can mean failed crops and famine if the rain does not come "in its season, the early rain and the later rain" (Deut 11:14; cf. Hos 6:3; Jer 5:24; Joel 2:23; and see Zech 10:1 and NOTES to the terms for rain in that verse). If the timing of rains is not right, particularly if they come during the harvest season or if they do not begin until well after the planting season, the effect can be as devastating as if there were no rains at all. Furthermore, if rainstorms are concentrated in too few days, no matter what the annual total rainfall might be, the loss owing to runoff is so high that the value to agriculture of abundant rainfall is significantly diminished. Moreover, if the rains are too heavy, they can be destructive and do more harm than good.

Second Zechariah shares this eschatological view of the year-round availability of water with Ezekiel, whose vision of water flowing eastward from the Temple involves fruit trees on its banks—fruit trees whose leaves never dried up and that bore fresh fruit each month (Ezek 47:12). Both these prophets reverse the reality statement of Deut 11:10–11, which warns the people that their promised land is "not like Egypt," with its readily available Nile water, but rather is "watered by rain from the sky," which all too often is withheld (so Deut 28:23–24).

9. *Yahweh will be king.* Despite the emphasis in 9:9, 12:7–12, and 13:1 on the restoration of monarchic rule in Jerusalem, the context of that rule within a framework of ultimate divine sovereignty over all the world is never forgotten. It comes to the fore in this last chapter of Second Zechariah. The very might that enables Yahweh to vanquish the nations and to bestow upon Jerusalem an exalted role in the universe must inevitably assume its rightful place as the supreme power in the created realm.

The idea of Yahweh as king of the Israelites is found in the antimonarchic passages of 1 Samuel (1 Sam 8:7; 12:12). But most often it appears in poetic contexts—frequently in Psalms (e.g., Ps 5:3 [NRSV 5:2]; 10:16; 47:8; 84:4 [NRSV 84:3]) and in prophecy (as Isa 41:21; 43:15; 44:6; Zeph 3:15; Jer 10:7, 10; 46:18; cf. Mal 1:14). No wonder, then, that it irrupts in the midst of these prose oracles of Second Zechariah in quasi-poetic form. It introduces a liturgical fragment (see COMMENT to this chapter) proclaiming divine kingship, universality, and unity in the eschatological age (see next four NOTES).

all the earth. Although ʾereṣ can signify a discrete territorial entity ("land"), as it does in the next verse (see first NOTE to 14:10), it also can indicate global totality—the earth—as it does here. In Gen 1:26–27, at the beginning-time, humanity is given dominion over "all the earth"; but here it is clear that such mastery ultimately belongs at the end of time to God. The expression "all the earth" is found in First Zechariah with similar scope, although without the eschatological nuance (Zech 1:11 and 6:5; see Meyers and Meyers 1987: 115, 323).

on that day. This eschatological formula appears here for the fourth time in chapter 14. Its frequency in this chapter (see NOTE to this phrase in v 4) and in chapters 12 and 13 (see first NOTES to 12:3 and 13:1) may have been part of what caused the prophet to insert the liturgical fragment of verse 9 (see first NOTE in this verse and also COMMENT to this chapter) into this subunit. Along with the thematic connections of the assertion of divine kingship to the message of this subunit and of the chapter as a whole, the fact that this eschatological formula is part of the fragment makes it fit very well with the style of the end of Second Zechariah.

Yahweh . . . one. The Hebrew of these two words, *yhwh ʾeḥād*, echoes exactly the last two words of the Deuteronomic credo ("Hear O Israel; Yahweh is our God, Yahweh is one" [Deut 6:4]). The presence in this verse of an element of the Deut 6:4 passage is significant for several reasons. First, like the Deuteronomy text, it is part of a passage that has been part of the daily Jewish liturgy since antiquity. Indeed, for that reason and because of the kingship theme of chapter 14, it has been suggested that the present passage is part of an ancient Israelite festival celebrating God's kingship and connected to Sukkoth (see NOTE above in this verse to "Yahweh will be king," NOTE to "Feast of Booths" in v 16, and COMMENT). Second, it constitutes another of the many instances in which

Second Zechariah draws upon Deuteronomic language and/or concepts. Third, although it is related to Deut 6:4, it also diverges.

This last point deserves further comment. The Deuteronomic statement, although becoming integral to postbiblical Jewish liturgy, is not part of the Deuteronomic vocabulary that appears repeatedly in Deuteronomy itself and in Deuteronomic literature. "Yahweh is one" is part of a statement in Deuteronomy that is addressed to Israel and that follows the Decalog's claim that Yahweh is the one God for Israel. Thus the "oneness" of Yahweh in Deuteronomy is the "oneness" or uniqueness of Yahweh for Israel; it refers to the only God to whom Israel's covenant loyalty is due.

This Israelite exclusivity with respect to Yahweh is the penultimate step on the long road to universal Israelite monotheism (see M. S. Smith 1990: 145–60 and Lang 1983, among others). The "Yahweh will be one" expression as it appears in Zechariah 14 is transformed into a universal statement. Linked with the global sovereignty of Yahweh (see two previous NOTES), the unity of Yahweh is thus for the entire world. It is no wonder, then, that in verses 16–19 below, all the nations of the world are expected to acknowledge Yahweh's rule and to participate in a festival that marks the ritual and cultural identity of Israel in its corporate relationship to God.

The idea of one God is not so foreign to the ancient world as it might in fact seem, given the emphasis in Western tradition on the uniqueness of Israelite monotheism. Yet the concept of one God with a claim on all people appears for the first time in Israel, in exilic texts, especially in conjunction with the idea of Yahweh's creation of and control over the natural world (e.g., Isa 40:18–28). Consequently, the statement about Yahweh's uniqueness finds a congenial place in this verse, which is enclosed in a section proclaiming Yahweh's rearrangement of the natural order in the future age.

his name one. Yahweh is represented by the name used to indicate the divine presence. Just as the names of other gods will be removed in the eschatological era (13:2; see NOTE to "names"), so here the name of Israel's God will thereby prevail. The use of the divine name to represent divine reality is a feature of Deuteronomic literature, in which it represents the unseen presence of Yahweh in the Temple as the earthly abode of God (e.g., Deut 12:5, 11; 1 Kgs 8:29). Thus the inclusion of this "name" phrase in the liturgical fragment (see first NOTE to v 9) constitutes an allusion to the Jerusalem Temple. Such an allusion is appropriate to the focus of this chapter on Jerusalem, as the center of the universe, wherein the Temple symbolizes the meeting place between heaven and earth as the essential characteristic of Zion. This indirect reference to the Jerusalem Temple continues the similarly indirect allusions implicit in the cosmic language of this subunit and foreshadows the explicit portrayal of the Temple as center of the world in the last subunit of chapter 14 (vv 16–21; see especially "House of Yahweh," vv 20–21).

10. *All the land.* The Hebrew here is exactly the same as for "all the earth" of verse 9 (see NOTE above). There the scope is global. Here, the word for "land" (*'ereṣ*) is used in its more limited, territorial sense; and the territory

indicated is not all Israel but, rather, the extent of Jerusalem. As we explain in our NOTE to "eastern sea . . . western sea" (v 8), and as is clear from the mention of Jerusalem in verse 8 and of the geographical boundaries presented in this verse (see below, NOTES to "Geba" and "Rimmon"), this subunit is both particular and universal. It deals with one locale, Jerusalem. But that city is hardly an ordinary or typical place. It has mythic and cosmic dimensions as the focus and conduit of Yahweh's involvement with humanity, and thus what happens in and to Jerusalem affects the whole world. Still, the reconfiguration of the city and its environs is what is depicted, however, that may reverberate far beyond its boundaries.

stretch around. Because the verb lacks the connector *waw* before it, the Latin and Syriac along with many commentators restore it in place of the initial *yodh* of *yissôb.* That emendation, however, changes the verb into an unlikely form. Still the text as it stands, even assuming that the absence of "and" is intentional, is difficult because the verb is masculine and its subject, "land," is a feminine noun. But the verb need not be made feminine, as *BHS* suggests, because *'ereṣ* is occasionally masculine; or, more likely, when the verb precedes the subject as here, the uninflected third-person masculine singular is often used even if the subsequent subject is feminine and/or plural (GKC §145.7.a). Thus, we prefer to retain the text as it stands despite the peculiar lack of the connector, which in any case does not affect the English translation.

The verbal root *sbb* means "to surround, go around" and is used to indicate either some sort of movement around something or else the territorial extent marked off by a real or hypothetical circumference. It can also mean "to turn, turn around," again indicating directional movement. It never means "turn" in the sense of change or transformation into something else. Hence the common suggestion (e.g., R. S. Hanson 1975: 369; R. L. Smith 1984: 287; Lacocque 1981: 209–10; Otzen 1964: 269) to translate it "change" or "turn into" seems unnecessary, as does the similarly intended "be leveled" of the *NEB.* Indeed, the territorial nuances of *sbb* are perfectly appropriate, and the notion that the land around Jerusalem will be different in the future age is adequately conveyed by the comparison presented by the next term, "like the plain" (see next NOTE).

like the plain. The word *ʿărābâ* indicates tableland or flatland. Sometimes it is rendered "steppes." This word is frequently used to designate a number of different geographical entities (e.g., the plain east of the Jordan, as in Deut 1:1; or the entire Jordan Valley, as in Deut 1:7), all of which are dry desert areas. Similarly, as a generic term for "plain," it is typically found in parallel with "desert" (*midbār;* e.g., Jer 17:6), thus implying that the flat terrain is dry.

However that may be, the nuance of flatness is the prevailing one in this verse; the aspect of dryness is irrelevant, given the assurance of abundant water provided above in verse 8 (see various NOTES to that verse). In proclaiming that Jerusalem's hinterland (cf. first NOTE to this verse and NOTE to "eastern sea . . . western sea" in v 8) will be flat, this oracle remedies the last remaining agrarian concern of this subunit. The rather marginal character of the territory surrounding Jerusalem with respect to agricultural productivity will be fully reversed in the eschatological age. The rugged contours of the Judean hills, long an anathema to highand plow agriculture (hence the extensive terracing around Jerusalem; see Hopkins 1985: 175), would at last be accommodating to the use of the animal-traction plow.

In addition, steep inclines prevent the accumulation of enriching humus. This keeps the *terra rossa* soils that dominate the hill country from becoming deep and thus as fertile as they might otherwise be (see Frick 1985: 112–15). For this reason too, the leveling of the highlands will mean an enhancement of soil quality.

Climate, diurnal light, water supply, and now terrain all will be completely conducive to transforming Jerusalem's immediate agricultural base, the land from Geba to Rimmon (see next two NOTES), from one providing an insecure bare subsistence to one with the potential for unmitigated perpetual abundance.

Geba. Biblical Geba ("hill") has been identified with Arabic Jeba' since Edward Robinson explored the area just north of Jerusalem on June 4 to 5, 1838. This site, which at about twenty dunams may have been one of the largest towns in Yehud in the postexilic period (see Kallai 1960), is located on the heights to the south of the deep Wadi el Suweinit, or Michmash Pass, just opposite Michmash (Arabic, Mukhmâs); it is situated on the northern edge of the wadi (cf. Isa 10:28–29). A Levitical city within the tribe of Benjamin (Josh 21:17; 1 Chron 6:15 [NRSV 6:60]), Geba figures sporadically in Israelite and Judean history. It was the locale of an encounter with the Philistines (1 Sam 13:3), who evidently had a garrison there (1 Sam 10:5 has Gibeath-Elohim, probably the same as Geba; so Aharoni 1979: 275, 286, 317 [n. 2]). It probably became part of the Northern Kingdom after the division of the Solomonic kingdom, for Asa recovered Benjaminite lands for Judah and fortified Geba and Mizpeh, both on the main route to Jerusalem (1 Kgs 15:22). Moreover, it is cited in tandem with Beersheba in the account of Josiah's reform (2 Kgs 23:8).

The pairing of Geba with Beersheba as dominating the northern and southern boundaries of Judah at its greatest extent brings us to the question of what sort of border, if any, its pairing with Rimmon (see next NOTE) in this text might indicate. Both archaeological survey (Kallai 1960) and biblical texts (Ezra 2:20; Neh 7:30; 11:31) indicate that Geba was among the Benjaminite towns to which exiles returned and which were part of Yehud in the Persian period. The Ezra and Nehemiah texts list other towns in Benjamin, some to the north of Geba, thus indicating that Geba was not the northern boundary of Yehud. Rather, it probably represented the northern extent of Jerusalem's urban control of the hinterland—as far as the deep wadi between Geba and Michmash. Jerusalem and its satellite towns extended to the Wadi el Suweinit, a notion that fits the intent of this entire subunit in depicting a secure and flourishing Jerusalem in the future age (see various NOTES to vv 6–8 above).

Rimmon. Unlike Geba (see previous NOTE), Rimmon (or En-rimmon) is of uncertain location, although some would identify with Khirbet Umm et-Ramamin or Tell Ḥalif (Khirbet Khuweilfeh). Both sites are in the northern Negev. Like Geba, it was apparently not originally part of Judah; it was assigned to Simeon (Josh 19:7; 1 Chron 4:32), yet appears in the list of Judah's towns in Josh 15:32. Surely it was at or near the southern boundary of Judah, and, like Geba, was part of Yehud in the Persian period (Neh 11:29).

The fact that the text of Zech 14:10 adds, after "Rimmon," "south of Jerusalem" (see next NOTE), seems to indicate that the place may not have been well known in the fifth century. In that case it may not be the same as the Rimmon in the northern Negev but rather some other small site, otherwise not mentioned in the Bible nor identified in archaeological survey. The dilemma of identifying Rimmon cannot be solved, but its critical feature—that it is south of Jerusalem—is unambiguous. Thus, with Geba, it forms the full extent of Jerusalem's hinterland (cf. NOTES to "eastern sea . . . western sea" in v 8 and "All the land" in v 10).

This description of Jerusalem's eschatological domain may well derive from the nature of its territorial extent in the Persian period. As such, it is perhaps the equivalent of "Jerusalem and its villages" of First Zechariah (2:8 [NRSV 2:4]), which portrays Jerusalem along with the satellite villages that apparently sprang up around the capital in the Persian period (see Meyers and Meyers 1987: 154–56). No longer the capital of a monarchic state, postexilic Jerusalem could not draw economic resources from the other cities of the realm to the extent that it had in the preexilic period. Thus the lands surrounding Jerusalem had to be developed agriculturally in order to sustain the city, even in its much reduced state, demographically and territorially. That such a task was formidable, i.e., that the highlands surrounding Jerusalem lack agrarian potential and had never before been a significant resource, is clearly reflected in the eschatological visions of First Zechariah and in these oracles of Second Zechariah. Both prophets proclaim a reversal of historical and/or geographic reality, and both envision a populous Jerusalem.

south of Jerusalem. The term south (*negeb*) appears without a preposition as a kind of accusative of location (GKC §118.2.b). As such, it is connected with a noun in the genitive; in this case, the proper noun "Jerusalem." Because such a construction is to be expected, we see no reason to insert a *waw* ("and") before "Jerusalem" and delete the *waw* before the next word so as to begin a new clause with "Jerusalem" (as do some, e.g., the editors of *BHS, NEB,* Chary 1969: 216; Elliger 1975: 177).

See the previous NOTE for a discussion of how this locational expression contributes to the geographic picture of this verse.

which will stand high. The spelling and vocalization (*wĕrāʾămâ*) are difficult. A root *rʾm* is otherwise unattested. Hence it may be that the root is *rwm* ("to be high, lifted up, exalted"), with the letter *aleph* being a vowel letter (Mitchell 1912: 350) as it is in a number of toponyms meaning "heights." For example, "Heights of Gilead" is *rʾmt bglʿd* in Deut 4:43 and *rmt bglʿd* in Josh 21:38. If this be the case, this third-person feminine singular should be pointed *rāʾmāh* (like *rāmâ,* from *rwm*) rather than that which the MT preserves (GKC §72.p).

Because both this verb and the next one are feminine, the subject is

"Jerusalem." The elevated position of the urban center itself, amid the flatlands (see NOTE above to "like the plain" in this verse), is the most distinctive feature of the symbolic role of Jerusalem and its Temple as the cosmic center and mountain of God (cf. "great mountain" of Zech 4:7 and the discussion in Meyers and Meyers 1987: 244–45). Ancient Israel shared the Near Eastern conceptualization of the Temple and its holy city, being the earthly embodiment of the cosmic mountain, as the dwelling place of God or the gods. Jerusalem's elevated location not only enabled it to participate in Near Eastern mythic ideas; it also allowed it to incorporate the Sinai motif—the place of Yahweh's direct and momentous encounter with Israel—into the ideas of the city's special sanctity (cf. Freedman 1981; Levenson 1985).

will . . . dwell in her place. The reestablishment of the holy city is a common eschatological theme. It is found in First Zechariah (2:8 [NRSV 2:4]) and in Zechariah 12 (v 6; see NOTE to "Jerusalem will dwell"), where it appears as it does here together with "in *her* place," thus drawing on the vivid image of Jerusalem personified as a woman. The notion of Jerusalem's restored vitality is so central to the future vision that another verse, 14:11, is added to summarize this subunit and to highlight the expectation that Jerusalem will be fully inhabited once more. Indeed, the verb *yšb* ("to dwell, inhabit") is used three times in verses 10–11.

The focus on Jerusalem's demography in this verse and the next is part of the overall pattern of reversal evident in this subunit. The natural world around Jerusalem will be altered; and integrally related to the environmental changes (see various NOTES to vv 6–8) will be the potential for Jerusalem to sustain a large population. The present woefully small size of the city in the Persian period (see above, COMMENT to chapter 12 and NOTE to "two parts . . . the third" of 13:8), during which it may have numbered fewer than 500 people until well into the fifth century, would certainly have seemed to the prophet a striking contrast to what he knew of the preexilic extent of the city. Given what the rest of this verse tells us about gates, he was probably familiar with its former size. Thus its expansion in future days to a populous urban center would be as miraculous a reversal from an early postexilic perspective as would be the environmental transformation described in the preceding verses.

Both First and Second Zechariah echo earlier prophetic statements about the repopulation of Jerusalem. In this regard, Jeremiah is particularly instructive. In Jer 17:24–27, the idea of the eternal habitation of Jerusalem is embedded in material relating to Jerusalem's gates; and in this verse the anticipation of the city's repopulation is followed by an enumeration of its gates (see rest of NOTES to this verse).

Gate of Benjamin. This is the first of a series of Jerusalem landmarks that form the second half of verse 10. The verse begins by signifying the flat hinterland that will surround Jerusalem in the future age (see first five NOTES to this verse). Then it focuses on Jerusalem, as the premier lofty point in the eschatological landscape (see NOTE to "which will stand high"). Finally, the end of the verse delineates Jerusalem itself.

This gate, along with the other features that follow, apparently belongs to the shape of Jerusalem in the preexilic age. It has been identified with the Sheep Gate (Neh 3:1, 32; 12:39) and perhaps also the Upper Gate (Bahat 1990: 30). Although its precise location is not known, its general placement seems certain. It probably was situated slightly south of the northern extent of the east side of the Temple Mount, near where the present-day Lion's Gate is located, i.e., just on the northern edge of the Temple Mount. Bahat (1990: 36) has shown that location in the time of Nehemiah to be directly north of the Temple itself. Most modern maps of preexilic Jerusalem situate the Gate of Benjamin more or less in this northerly location, although Simons and Dalman have it closer to the eastern wall of the Temple Mount (Bahat 1990: 30–31) or along the edge of the Kidron Valley. This is a relatively important consideration in deciding whether in this text the gate is intended to be the northern or eastern boundary of the city. Because of its location at midpoint and north of the Temple, we suggest it represents the northernmost point in our list (see especially our NOTE below to "Tower of Hananel").

Whatever its exact location, it is clear that the Gate of Benjamin was a fixture of the Jerusalem landscape in the First Temple period, at least from the time of Hezekiah. It was also part of the perimeter of Jerusalem in Nehemiah's day. However, it is not clear that the walled boundaries of the city were in place in the Persian period before Nehemiah, in which case Second Zechariah's frame of reference in mentioning this and other landmarks would have been the memory, record, and/or remnant of the preexilic fortifications. Because several other features in this verse are decidedly preexilic rather than Persian, it seems more likely that this is a retrospective portrayal of Jerusalem rather than a depiction of its fifth-century shape. Indeed, a backward-glancing perspective here would certainly be in keeping with the way this prophet uses historical materials in his eschatological vision (see especially our COMMENT to chapter 11).

place of the first gate. As we suggested in the previous NOTE, the Jerusalem locales specified in this verse may derive from the exceptionally large extent of the capital in the late preexilic period, when the city was the seat of royal dominion as well as the relocation site for many displaced northerners, rather than from the Persian period, when it was a tiny outpost of local jurisdiction in Yehud. Still, this suggestion must remain partly hypothetical in that the location of all of the toponyms in this verse cannot be ascertained.

The "first gate" is a case in point. Because the mention of this gate begins with "place of" (*mĕqôm*), it may not denote an actual named gate; hence our decision to render it with lower-case letters. Such a possibility also arises because the term "first gate" (*šaʿar hāriʾšôn*) does not occur elsewhere in the Bible. Because a First Gate is not otherwise known, the designation "first" may not be a proper name at all but rather an identifying aspect of the gate, equivalent to meaning an earlier gate (no longer in existence?) and/or a major gate.

If this term signifies an older or earlier gate, perhaps it can be identified with the "Old Gate" (*šaʿar hayyĕšānâ*) of Neh 3:6 and 12:39. To confuse matters, explorers and cartographers have called this gate the "Mishneh Gate" (e.g., Simons, *apud* Bahat 1990: 30, Fig. 4), the "Mishneh" being a "second" quarter or district of Jerusalem (2 Kgs 22:14; 2 Chron 34:22; Zeph 1:10; Neh 11:9). Would a gate to the second quarter be called "First Gate"? Bahat (1990: 36) locates "Old Gate" in the time of Nehemiah just below the Tower of Hananel on the west side of the Temple. Paton and Simons (see Figs. 1 and 4 in Bahat 1990: 30) both place "Old Gate" much farther to the west, in the area of the modern Jaffa Gate, which is also the traditional place of the Corner Gate (see next NOTE). However, there is no conclusive evidence for so locating the Old Gate.

In any case, none of the suggestions are compelling. In the absence of any decisive evidence, either textual or archaeological, and given the opinion that these Jerusalem landmarks of verse 10 more or less define the city's perimeter, a point on the east side of the city would be lacking unless this gate denotes an eastern entry. Thus the designation "first gate" may mean an old, if not the oldest, city gate of Jerusalem, at least in the sources available to a fith-century prophet. Because Jerusalem's east flank surmounted the edge of the Kidron Valley, the city spread westward rather than eastward as it grew larger over the centuries after David established his capital on Ophel. Hence, although the western and northern entry or entries to the city may have shifted as the city was enlarged, the eastern edge would have been more or less stable. An old or former or "first" gate could well have been on the east side. It would thus contribute to a depiction of Jerusalem's perimeter, and the phrase "to the place of the first gate" should hardly be eliminated as a gloss (as Mitchell [1912: 350] would have it).

Corner Gate. If the oldest gate is only tentatively located on the east (see previous NOTE), the placement of the "Corner Gate" on the west is fairly secure. This designation occurs in 2 Kgs 14:13, Jer 31:38, and 2 Chron 26:9 as *ša'ar happinnâ*, literally, "gate of the corner." In 2 Chron 25:23 it is found as *ša'ar happôneh*, which is usually emended to agree with 2 Kgs 14:13. The text here has still another reading: *ša'ar happinnîm*, literally, "Gate of the Corners," with the masculine plural ending being used nowhere else in the Bible with the feminine noun *pinnâ*, "corner." Perhaps the *mem* of the next word caused an error in the ending of this word. In any case, whether as a variant or a mistake, there is little doubt that the Hebrew words denote the "Corner Gate."

As indicated in the previous NOTE, this gate is usually located some distance west of the Temple Mount, in the immediate vicinity of today's Jaffa Gate. That would have been its location in the First Temple period (Bahat 1990: 30, Figs. 1 and 4). If so, the intent would have been to delimit the western extent of the city as it existed in preexilic times, as is apparently the case for the Benjamin Gate (cf. next NOTE).

Tower of Hananel. This architectural feature, *migdal ḥănan'ēl* in Hebrew, was apparently a well-known monument in Jerusalem. It is mentioned several times in the Hebrew Bible—in Jer 31:38 and in Neh 3:1 and 12:39. However, no archaeological remains aid in its identification. Its location is thus quite tentative, although there is uniformity in placing it to the northwest of the Temple Mount; the variation comes in how far northwest it may have been situated. Its location at the time of Nehemiah was probably in an area just outside the city walls in the northwest, i.e., to the west of the Gate of Benjamin or "Sheep Gate." Paton and Simons place it considerably farther north in the First Temple period. Dalman and Bahat both locate it at the northwest corner of the Temple Mount in Nehemiah's day (Bahat 1990: 30, 31, 36, and Figs. 1, 2, and 4).

Whatever its exact location, it seems certain that this tower was rather close to the Gate of Benjamin (see NOTE above in this verse) at the north of the Temple Mount area, and thus of the city, in both the preexilic and Persian periods. It apparently represented a familiar orientation point. The landmarks of this verse cannot be expected to provide a neat demarcation of the city's boundaries through reference to a structure near each of the four compass points. Rather, especially if the city walls had not yet been rebuilt or had been only partially restored, the most visible extant architectural remains of greater Jerusalem would be the ones most likely to serve the prophet's purposes in depicting a large and populous city, much bigger than the much-reduced site of the Persian period.

The name Hananel, which means "God is gracious," is not found elsewhere in the Hebrew Bible, although the name Elhanan (ʾel-ḥānān), with the components reversed, is attested. Two of David's chiefs bear this name (see 2 Sam 21:19 = 1 Chron 20:5; 2 Sam 23:24 = 1 Chron 11:26).

the king's wine presses. These are nowhere else mentioned in the Bible but can probably be located just south of the City of David, near the King's Pool (Neh 2:14) and the King's Garden (Neh 3:15). That is, all these features of royal property would be found proximate to each other, between the Siloam Pool and En Rogel, a place that would suit horticultural activity. Although this also is not a secure identification in designating an area in the southern part of the city, it functions as does "first gate" in providing a landmark in a part of the city that would not otherwise be noted in this series of reference to places in Jerusalem. Furthermore, in naming a spot called by a royal term, it signifies a part of Jerusalem that clearly was established in preexilic times, as do the other terms in this listing (see four previous NOTES), which apparently depicts the city at its greatest extent and thus fit for the multitudes that will inhabit it in the future age, when its resources will allow for a demographic surge (see other NOTES to this subunit of Zechariah 14).

If the terms in this listing elude the modern student of Jerusalem, it is only because the contours and architectural features of the city have been altered so many times since the days of Second Zechariah. Sometimes these changes exhibit continuity, of name or location, with the preceding landmarks; but other times they included innovation that obliterated earlier gates or towers. It is no wonder that we cannot possibly know what Second Zechariah saw in the holy city on the eve of its refortification as a city of rather modest proportions in the late fifth century.

11. *They will dwell in it.* This is the second of three times in verses 10–11 that the verb *yšb* ("to dwell, be inhabited") is used to designate the future repopulation of Jerusalem. See our discussion in the NOTES to "will . . . dwell in her place" (14:10) and to "Jerusalem will dwell" in 12:6. The shift to the plural here, as opposed to the other two instances in verses 10–11 that have the singular with "Jerusalem" as subject, has caused some critics to omit this verb or else to emend it to the singular. However, the plural subject can just as easily refer to the multitudes that will live in Jerusalem.

total destruction. The Hebrew word is *ḥērem*, from the verb *ḥrm* (normally used in the Hiphil). The term is difficult to translate. It denotes the awful destruction of war, but tends to have a sacral connotation that often overlaps with its military meaning, whereby the annihilation of an enemy is construed as a sacred act with the booty being dedicated to Yahweh (as Josh 6:19, 24; cf. Lev 27:28). Both the noun and the verb appear most frequently in Deuteronomic passages. Hence it is no surprise to find it part of the vocabulary of Second Zechariah, who often reflects familiarity with the narrative of Genesis through 2 Kings, i.e., the entire Primary History.

This verse is one of only four prophetic passages, all postexilic, in which *ḥērem* occurs (Isa 34:5; 43:28; Mal 3:24 [NRSV 4:6]; cf. 1 Kgs 20:42). Most likely, in these prophetic passages, the word *ḥērem* is used as an "action noun," depicting the extermination that will happen to a people subjected to a *ḥērem*. Such a meaning is distinct from the way it designates the concrete objects that constitute a *ḥērem* in more overtly sacral contexts (see Lohfink 1986: 183–86).

The use of this technical term for the total destruction of a city or people in war introduces a military note in this conclusion to the second subunit of Zechariah 14. The other verses of this section (see various NOTES above to vv 6–8, 10) portray the radical reversals or changes in Jerusalem's environment that will allow the holy city to sustain a thriving population. That is, the unyielding hinterland of Jerusalem will be so altered as to provide bountiful subsistence. But the prosperous endurance of a city is dependent on more than sufficient agrarian resources; it must also have military security. The sword no less than famine was a threat to the ongoing vitality of any geopolitical entity. Thus this summary statement (vv 6–11) dealing with Jerusalem's eschatological landscape includes the assurance of military security to accompany its potential for the material requirements for prosperity. The very last word (see NOTE below to "in security") of this verse reiterates this critical dimension of the future status of Jerusalem. Yahweh will protect, as well as provide for, the inhabitants of the city that is the divine dwelling place on earth.

will dwell. This is the third instance in which the verb *yšb* ("to dwell, be inhabited") is found in 14:10–11 (see first NOTE to this verse and NOTE to "will . . . dwell in her place" [v 10]; see also NOTE to "Jerusalem will dwell" in 12:6).

in security. The root *bṭḥ* ("to feel secure, trust") is often used in a general way in reference to relying on someone (or something). When it indicates something that God promises, utter security is the result. Such is the case here. When Jerusalem is restored in the manner described in the preceding verses, i.e., when it is rendered militarily safe and when it is made capable of sustaining a flourishing population, it will indeed be a safe place.

Thus the use of "in security" (*lābeṭaḥ*) is a fitting conclusion to this subunit, which deals with the age-old problem of subsistence in Jerusalem's hinterlands and of the economic precariousness of the city. But now it can be fully inhabited because of its new ecosystem and because it will not ever be destroyed again. "In security" reiterates the second of these conditions; it repeats what is said earlier in the verse ("there will never again be a total destruction"; see NOTE to "total destruction") and echoes the first subunit's theme of God's protection against enemies while anticipating the similar theme in the next subunit.

The idea of living, lying down, or dwelling "in security" is a recurrent component of the divine promise, particularly as it appears in Deut 12:10, in the archaic poem of Deuteronomy 33 (vv 12 and 28), in the Holiness Code (Lev 25:18, 19; 26:5), in Jeremiah (23:6; 32:37; 33:16) and in Ezekiel (28:26; 34:25–28; 38:8, 14; 39:26). A perusal of these passages shows two relevant aspects of "dwell in security." First, it is used variously for Israel, Jerusalem, and returning exiles; thus its use here for Jerusalem would probably mean a Jerusalem symbolizing all Israel. Second, it is part of covenant language, part of the blessing that will accrue to the people who obey Yahweh. But now, in the end of days, with Israel in a new relationship to God, security along with subsistence will certainly and unconditionally be provided.

12. *plague*. The Hebrew word *maggēpâ*, used here (as cognate accusative of its verbal root *ngp*, "to strike, smite"; see next NOTE), and again twice in verse 15 and once in verse 18, is part of the biblical vocabulary dealing with disease. Throughout the Hebrew Bible, but particularly in prophetic and Deuteronomistic passages, the human suffering and loss of life caused by physical maladies are viewed as divine punishment. Disease is seen as one of the calamities befalling God's people because of their covenant disobedience (as in the covenant curses of Lev 26:16ff. and Deut 28:21ff.). In such cases, the punitive presence of disease is usually part of a long list of misfortunes. Often, however, widespread misfortunes are represented as a tripartite punishment: sword, famine, and pestilence (e.g., in Jer 14:11–12 and many other times in Jeremiah; Ezek 6:11–12; 2 Sam 24:13 = 1 Chron 21:12). This set of three sources of suffering and death undoubtedly represented an interrelated group of circumstances that characterized serious political and economic disruptions in the ancient world. That is, extended periods of warfare, famine, and disease—whether as causes or effects of each other—could bring mighty cities or even larger political bodies to the point of collapse.

As a component of such widespread disruptions of sociopolitical stability, the almost ubiquitous threat of lethal disease is often difficult for us moderns to grasp. But historians have been able to trace the patterns and presence of pestilential disease in the premodern world (see especially McNeill 1976), in which the sporadic outbreak of fatal disease was an ever-present and horrifying reality. Throughout the world, ancient sources that refer to diseases tend to be very much like the biblical sources: such references are likely to appear in the guise of theological language. To be more specific, deaths caused by illness, especially when concentrated in time and in place, are typically recorded as divine punitive action. How else could the ancients (and many moderns as well, considering how the onset of a disease such as AIDS is perceived by some) deal with the otherwise inexplicable and devastating spread of deadly illness?

The word for "plague" in this passage must be seen against such a mind-set. It is one of a modest biblical vocabulary dealing with medical matters. In point of fact, another Hebrew word, *deber*, which is usually translated "pestilence" as in the tripartite list of calamities mentioned above, occurs more frequently than does *maggēpâ*, the word used in this chapter. The former probably refers to the recurrent and devastating outbreaks of endemic disease, whereas the latter, normally rendered "plague" in English, indicates epidemic disease, the abnormal occurrence of acute infectious disease (see the discussion in C. L. Meyers 1988: 64–71). The death rate from epidemic disease can be truly extraordinary. One-third to one-half of the population of Europe is thought to have died from an outbreak of a virulent bubonic infection in the thirteenth century C.E. (McNeill 1976: 166–70). Indeed, epidemic disease was always far more lethal than warfare in premodern times. One striking example is the fact that dysentery claimed the lives of ten times more British soldiers in the Crimean War than did battle wounds.

It is no wonder, then, that *maggēpâ*, the word for epidemic disease, rather than the word for the somewhat less widespread and more differentially lethal endemic disease, should appear in this context. It achieves three purposes. First, it indicates the dramatic, sudden, and almost total effectiveness of a virulent plague in decimating an army (cf. 2 Kgs 19:35, which does not mention disease but uses the theological language—"angel of the Lord"—typical of ancient reporting of disease to describe the miraculous deliverance of Jerusalem, in Hezekiah's day, from the Assyrian war machine). That is, it represents a force, coming from God, potent enough to deal with the amassment of all of Israel's enemies in this final assault. Second, as a lexical choice that stands outside the covenant vocabulary of punishment for Israel, it suits a context involving non-Israelites (contra P. D. Hanson's suggestion [1975: 372ff.], that vv 12–15 are covenant curses). Although this term appears in biblical texts referring to grave loss of Israelite lives, particularly in the wilderness period (e.g., Num 14:37; 17:13–15 [NRSV 16:48–50]; 25:8–9, 18–19), it also denotes the epidemics among two of Israel's traditional enemies, the Egyptians (Exod 9:14) and the Philistines (1 Sam 6:4). Third, although it is enmeshed in the language of divine warfare, it is not the usual term (*deber*) that accompanies death in the military triad of famine, pestilence, and sword. It thus suits the transhistorical nature of this final cataclysm, as something beyond the "ordinary" punitive acts of God.

In using the language of disease in this verse, this chapter of Second Zechariah, as above in the description of geomorphological alteration and in the depiction of many nations coming in war against Jerusalem (see COMMENT), is related to the description of the fate of Gog, as archenemy of Israel, in Ezekiel 38 (and 39). Yet, although there are many points of contact between Zechariah

14 and Ezekiel 38, the former clearly has its own style. The fact that the expectation of disease along with natural calamities in Zechariah 14 involves the use of the word *maggēpâ* ("plague"), whereas Ezek 38:28 has *deber* ("pestilence"), indicates Second Zechariah's divergence from Ezekiel as well as his more intense and focused use of the imagery of pestilential disease.

The language of horrific and lethal disease introduces the third subunit—verses 12–15—of Zechariah 14. Some scholars (e.g., Ackroyd 1962: 655; Mason 1973: 282–83) consider these verses intrusive and suggest that they are a group of sayings that were included by a redactor, inasmuch as they seem to interrupt a presumed flow from the restored Jerusalem of verse 11 to the recognition of Jerusalem's supremacy by the nations beginning in verse 16. Furthermore, even these verses seem to be disparate, with verses 12 and 15 dealing with plague and verses 13 and 14 presenting a separate theme.

It is difficult to evaluate such suggestions, but the canonical ordering and shape of this chapter seem less problematic if a neat and logical progression is not expected. In addition, these verses do complete what the first subunit begins: verses 1–5 depict Yahweh's military stance against Jerusalem's foes, and verses 12–15 reveal the results of God's eschatological reordering of nature. (A similar relationship exists between the second and fourth subunits, vv 6–11 and vv 16–21, and the positive results of God's transforming intervention; see discussion below in COMMENT.) Furthermore, certain thematic and lexical connections between the material in this subunit and that of the others of chapter 14 (e.g., "plague" in vv 12 and 15 and again in v 18) make its placement less disruptive than it might otherwise seem.

smite. The root *ngp* ("to strike, smite") appears in the noun *maggēpâ*, "plague" (see previous NOTE). As a verb, used here and in v 18, it denotes an action, often connected with warfare (e.g., Lev 26:17; Num 14:42; Judg 20:25, 32, 39[2]; 1 Sam 4:2–3), that causes serious harm and usually death, often to great numbers of people. All these features make it an appropriate verb in this passage. Combined with "plague" as a cognate accusative, it intensifies the notion of military activity that involves fatalities and many people. In this case, Yahweh's military role (see first two NOTES to v 3) is carried out through the alteration of the created order (see NOTES to "will be split in half" in v 4), which will trap the approaching enemies, whose forces then will be decimated by the extraordinary devastation of epidemic pestilential disease.

all the peoples. The frequent use (twelve times) of "all" (*kol*) in Zechariah 14 is a mark of its global purview. Here it is linked with *ʿammîm*, "peoples"; compare verses 2, 14, 16, 19, all of which have "all the nations" (*kol haggôyîm*). This divergence from the use of "nations" elsewhere in Zechariah 14 is probably linked to the succeeding depictions of individual suffering. "Nations" is a more abstract and political term, whereas "peoples" as a social and cultural term (see Meyers and Meyers 1987: 435–36) is perhaps closer to the individuals who make up the collective entity "people" and hence more suitable to a verse that specifies the horrors to which persons will be subjected. "Peoples" and "nations" in general are used in somewhat different ways in the Hebrew Bible (see, e.g.,

Clements and Botterweck 1975), although their semantic range involves some overlap. This verse seems to be an instance in which "peoples" is virtually synonymous with the "nations" mentioned elsewhere in chapter 14, especially because verse 16 refers to the "survivors" of "all the nations" (see NOTES below) and verse 18 refers to the "plague" with which Yahweh "smites" the "nations" (see NOTES below). That is, the same population of sufferers or potential sufferers from plague is indicated by "nations" and by "peoples." A similar interchangeability apparently is present in 12:2–3 (see NOTES to "all the peoples" [vv 2 and 3] and "all the nations of the earth" [v 3]).

have waged war. These three English words translate the Hebrew verb *ṣbʾ* ("to wage war, serve"), a root more common in its noun form (*ṣābāʾ*: "army, host, warfare") than as a verb. Indeed, aside from this passage, only in Num 31:7, 42 and in Isa 29:7, 8 does the Qal verb appear in military contexts (cf. the sacral contexts of serving at the sanctuary in Num 4:23; 8:24; Exod 38:8[2]; 1 Sam 2:22). The Numbers 31 passage is particularly relevant because it involves the complete slaughter of the Midianite military forces, along with many of the women and children, and the taking of much booty. Such circumstances are present in God's assault on the nations here: widespread death (see first NOTE in this verse) and extensive booty (see NOTES to "will be gathered" and "wealth" in v 14). As for Isaiah 29, "wage war" is used twice there for the actions of the "multitude of all the nations" in attacking Ariel/Mount Zion, i.e., Jerusalem. In Isaiah those nations wage war on Jerusalem as part of Yahweh's punitive deeds against the wayward people; here the nations themselves are to be punished by Yahweh's destructive intervention for having assaulted a people who should be living in peace in Zion.

The verb ("have waged war") is a perfect and so probably refers back to the attack depicted above in verse 2.

Jerusalem. The focus of chapter 14 on Jerusalem is picked up in this third subunit with the mention here of Jerusalem as the object of the wars waged by many people against the holy city.

each one's flesh. The Hebrew is *bĕśārô*, literally, "his flesh," with the third-person singular masculine suffix referring to the individuals who together constitute "all the peoples" (see above, NOTE to that phrase in this verse). That is, the singular suffix distributively refers to plurals (so GKC §145.5.m; cf. Syr, "their flesh"). However, some translations prefer to use the plural for this and subsequent terms: "their flesh," "their eyes," "their sockets," "their tongues," and "their mouths" (so *NEB; NRSV; NJPS;* R. L. Smith 1984; P. D. Hanson 1975; etc.). The noun *bāśār* can mean the body in its entirety or the fleshy parts of the body as distinct from bone, skin, blood, etc. Because "eyes" and "tongue" are other body parts mentioned here, each signifying a particular function of human beings (sight and speech; see NOTES to these words below), *bāśār* probably represents the flesh but in a somewhat expanded fashion. That is, it stands for the bodily integrity of a healthy living person, an integrity to be completely violated by the awful disease (see NOTE above to "plague" in this verse) that serves to bring about Yahweh's eschatological destruction of Jerusalem's enemies. Describing the violation, or rotting, of the flesh (see next NOTE) is tantamount to portraying an agonizing death.

The use of the word "flesh" for the bodies of Israel's foes operates on another level. It counters the blatant corporeality of Yahweh that appears in verse 4 (see first NOTE to that verse). Many human body parts are anthropomorphically ascribed to Yahweh in the Hebrew Bible, Yahweh's feet being mentioned in this very chapter. But *bāśār* never is used for God or for any heavenly being (Bratsiosis 1975: 330–31). Yahweh thereby retains a highly significant distinction from human life. Humans as flesh are thus the antithesis of God (cf. Isa 31:3) and are fully dependent on God's utterly different and superior qualities. This separation of God from the creatureliness of earthly beings is evidenced in many ways, including the fact that God manifests control over human flesh in the literal sense, that is, over the health or physical condition of bodily flesh (e.g., Exod 4:7; 2 Kgs 4:34; Job 2:5; Ps 38:4 [NRSV 38:3]).

It is precisely the contrast between God and fleshly humans with respect to the well-being of the latter that makes the language of disease in this verse so powerful in underscoring God's omnipotence. God's will is to be established by the way nature is rearranged (vv 4–5, 6–8, 10) and by the way human life is susceptible to God's punitive control. When humans are portrayed as flesh, their weakness as such is implied because of their distinction from Yahweh's non-fleshly vitality. This contrast is given a particularly ironic twist in this verse, in which the dissolution of the enemy's flesh takes place while the individual is "standing on his feet" (see NOTE below in this verse). Yahweh's ability to effect this fatal damage to humans, which derives from God as distinct from the corporeality of humans, comes fast upon the anthropomorphic image of Yahweh in verse 4: "His feet will stand . . ."

will rot away. The MT has this verb (*mqq*) pointed as a Hiphil infinitive absolute and, hence, in apposition with "This" (*zōʾt*, the first word of this verse in Hebrew). However, the verb is used twice more in this verse as a Niphal form and appears nowhere else in the Bible in the Hiphil. Hence it is likely that this is a Niphal infinitive absolute, which would well suit the context conveying the sudden and awful onslaught of disease (Mitchell 1912: 353; cf. GKC §113.4[b] ff.[ε]). Thus we read it with a different pointing (see text note e at the beginning of this chapter) but with no change in the consonantal text: **himmēq* (or *himmaq*), though otherwise unattested for *hāmēq*.

The root *mqq* is found only ten times in the Hebrew Bible. Most of those instances denote the rotting away or decaying of some material, such as some part of the body, as in this verse (cf. the festering of wounds in Ps 38:6 [NRSV 38:5]). Otherwise it is used somewhat figuratively, wherein someone "pines away" because of the suffering brought about by God's punishment for sins (e.g., Ezek 24:23). One instance of the latter (figurative) usage, in Lev 26:39 (two times), is inverted in Zechariah 14. Leviticus has the Israelite survivors of God's punishment languishing (*mqq*) in the land; here the foreign survivors (14:16) of the plague that causes the rotting (*mqq*) of flesh, eyes, and mouth become active participants in the human community that acknowledges Yahweh's sovereignty.

The prophet has reworked a Pentateuchal message to suit this climactic eschato-logical portrayal of a new world order.

while he. The Hebrew has "and he" (*wĕhûʾ*), which can be translated "while he" because of the function of the *waw* in introducing a circumstantial noun-clause (GKC §156.1).

standing on his feet. The dying victim of plague is tragically depicted as having his body eaten away while he occupies a position implying readiness to move. In this case, with Yahweh attacking the invaders of Jerusalem, the image is of an enemy soldier struck down suddenly while doing his duty—standing guard, patrolling the streets, or whatever. That is, someone is dying as he goes about living. The awful predicament of the victim dying "on his feet" is perhaps intensified by the contrast with Yahweh, who has no flesh but nonetheless is depicted in the corporeal language of "his feet will stand" (see NOTE in v 4; and cf. NOTE above in this verse to "each one's flesh"), an image of power and control.

his eyes. Like the suffix of "flesh" (see NOTE above in this verse to "each one's flesh"), the third-person singular suffix of "eyes" is distributive, referring to all the individuals among the peoples subjected here to divine action via epidemic disease (see first NOTE to this verse). If "flesh" represents a person's corporeality and vitality, "eyes" signifies vision and comprehension, and "tongue" (see NOTE below) indicates speech and communication. The totality of what makes someone human will be eroded unto death by the "plague" that Yahweh will inflict upon Jerusalem's enemies. (For the use of "eye" or "eyes" in Second Zechariah and its relation to First Zechariah, see NOTE to "eye of the people" in 9:1; see also the symbolic value of "eye," paired with "arm," in 11:17.)

will rot away. A Niphal form of *mqq*; see the NOTE above in this verse.

in their sockets. The noun *ḥōr* refers to a hole or receptacle in a lid, door, or wall (as 2 Kgs 12:10 [NRSV 12:9]; Cant 3:4; Ezek 8:7). Only here does the word denote the receptacle for an eye, i.e., an eye socket. In several more extended usages, the noun refers to a large hole, cave, or den, which serves as a lair or refuge for animals (Nah 2:13) or people (1 Sam 14:11; 13:6; Job 30:6). In view of the latter set of meanings, a subtle irony emerges: the eye (see previous NOTE) should be safe in its socket, but instead it will rot away as part of the overall lethal progress of the disease (see first NOTE to this verse) in the doomed enemies of Jerusalem.

his tongue. Although "tongue" (Hebrew *lāšôn*) sometimes is found in reference to the function of that part of the human body in drinking or eating (e.g., Judg 7:5; Job 20:12) or in singing (Ps 51:16 [NRSV 51:15]; Isa 35:6), it most often is used in reference to its role as an organ of speech, as here. The tongue is the third and last in a series of references to the body that vividly portray the horrors of pestilential disease (see previous NOTES in this verse). The "flesh" represents the body and its vitality; the eyes connote vision and compre-hension; and now the tongue represents speech and communication, the peculiarly human feature of personhood. This last aspect of human existence will likewise be destroyed. The individuals so affected will thus cease to be humans—they surely will be dead, as humans, even if they have not physically expired.

It is indeed fitting that the tongue figures in this scenario of the demise of Israel's enemies. In the biblical depictions of the tongue as an instrument of speech, it appears far more often as the source of bad speech—of hostility, lying, insolence, falsehood, arrogance, slander, etc.—than of good speech. Hence, on a literary level, it has more negative connotations than positive ones. As the culminating image in this series that portrays the horrible effects of plague, it thus echoes the many instances, scattered throughout the prophetic, psalmodic, and sapiential books of the Bible, of the tongue symbolizing wrongful speech and, hence, reprehensible immorality deserving of divine punishment.

The third-person singular masculine suffix ("his") of "tongue," like that of "flesh" and "eyes" (see NOTES above) is distributive and refers to the tongues of "all the peoples" (see NOTE in this verse) trapped by the cataclysms of nature and the advent of the plague that Yahweh has brought about to end the domination of Jerusalem and its inhabitants by hostile forces.

in his mouth. The Hebrew actually has "their" mouth, correctly understanding the distributive sense of "mouth," of which "his tongue" is the antecedent. However, agreement of number in English demands the singular "his," which is what the Vulgate reads and which is an emendation (*bpyhw*) suggested by many modern commentators.

13. *On that day.* This is the fifth of the seven occurrences of this eschatological formula in Zechariah 14. See our discussion of such language in the first NOTE to 14:1 and in the NOTE to the first instance of this phrase in this chapter in 14:4 (see also its frequent appearance in chapters 11 and 12).

great panic of Yahweh. "Panic" and "Yahweh" are in a construct chain, with "great" as an adjective modifying "panic." The Hebrew word *mĕhûmâ* (from *hmm* or *hwm*, "to murmur, discomfit") is used for a situation of tumult or confusion, often as the result of some act of God's judgment (cf. Ezek 7:7). Perhaps the most striking use of this term in relation to this text is 1 Samuel in which the plague (*maggēpâ* [1 Sam 6:4]) of the "golden tumors," sent by the "hand of Yahweh" (1 Sam 5:6), causes "a very great panic" (1 Sam 5:9) and a "deathly panic" (1 Sam 5:11; or "a panic from Yahweh," according to the Qumran Samuel scroll). The two uses of "panic" in 1 Samuel 5, if one takes the Qumran reading, together provide the full text of the phrase in Zechariah 14.

Beyond this particular parallel with its plague context, the noun *mĕhûmâ*, or its verbal form, is notable as a technical term denoting the chaos and confusion, the "holy terror" (Müller 1978: 419) evoked by Yahweh acting, often militarily, against God's enemy, either Israel herself (Deut 2:15) or the enemies of Israel (as Exod 14:24; Judg 4:15; Josh 10:10; and Deut 7:23, which adds "great" to the noun form as in the Zechariah text). One other Samuel text is notable in this respect; in 1 Sam 14:20, the "panic" of the battle meant that "every sword was against the other." That is, in the unspeakable chaos that characterizes a military rout, people flail in all directions, willy-nilly striking their own compatriots. Exactly this situation is reflected in the following clause, which reads "Everyone will seize his neighbor's hand, and his hand will be raised against his neighbor's hand" (see next NOTE). That is, when God's "hand" intervenes, according to the image of God doing battle (especially 1 Sam 5:6), the soldiers lose all sense of what they are about; and they, or their hands, do the opposite of what they, as warriors, should be doing: they slay each other.

Everyone will seize his neighbor's hand. As pointed out in the previous NOTE, the idea of an attacking army thrown into panic is linked with the consequence of its soldiers fighting against each other in the ensuing chaos and confusion. The scenario of Zechariah 14 is laid out in the first subunit, wherein "all the nations" approach Jerusalem for war, capture the city, decimate its population, and send many of the survivors into exile. Only a final eschatological encounter with the enemy can save Jerusalem and the remnant of its population. This remnant apparently flees (see first NOTE to v 5), and the enemy armies are left in and around the city, where they will be destroyed by Yahweh's extraordinary actions.

Yahweh's intervention involves a horrendous assault on the bodies of the soldiers, through the sudden and pervasive onset of plague, as presented in verse 12 at the beginning of this subunit. Disease in a military environment is hardly a rarity, but here its virulent effect on the individual soldiers is compounded by terror—at the onslaught of plague and perhaps also at the sight of the dramatic shift in topography, the splitting of the Mount of Olives (see NOTES to v 4) that allows Yahweh's people to escape. Together, these signs of Yahweh's involvement in human affairs give rise to inordinate and intense chaos in the enemy camp. This intensity is expressed by the repetitive nature of the end of verse 13: not only does everyone "seize his neighbor's hand," but also everyone's hand is "raised against his neighbor's hand." Both are negative depictions of the "holy terror" evoked by Yahweh's deeds in rescuing Jerusalem and elevating it, literally (see v 10a) and figuratively, to its ordained place in the world order.

The use of the verb "seize" (Hiphil of *ḥzq*, "to be strong, firm") in depicting what the terror-stricken forces do deserves some explanation. Although the term can involve a quite benign grasping of something (e.g., Zech 8:23), it can also involve violence; it indicates the taking hold of someone in a struggle, with an attempt of one person to overpower another (e.g., Deut 25:11). Indeed, in the military setting of 2 Sam 2:16, the grasping of an opponent is preliminary to thrusting a sword into his side and killing him. Inasmuch as the language of "panic" in 1 Sam 14:20 involves soldiers lifting "every sword . . . against the other," the expression here of seizing the neighbor's hand may be elliptical for seizing an opponent in order to (a) disarm him so that (b) the agressor's hand can go against him to kill him (see next NOTE).

The association of the root *ḥzq* with "hand" also perhaps plays on the common expression *bĕyād ḥăzāqâ* ("with a strong hand"), which indicates the powerful activity of Yahweh in human affairs (Exod 3:19; Num 20:20, etc.). God's power is so expressed in military contexts, with God thereby subduing

Israel's enemies. In this passage, Yahweh has already wrought such extraordinary deeds that the enemies themselves exhibit the violent behavior against each other that the root *hzq* together with "hand" connotes.

his hand will be raised against his neighbor's hand. This clause seems somewhat superfluous, inasmuch as the basic idea of internal violence in the chaos of the enemy camp (see two previous NOTES) has already been put forth. However, this whole chapter is one of extremes: of extraordinary divine rearrangement of the natural order and the concomitant changes in human affairs. The preparation for this culminating tragedy within the forces attacking Jerusalem has been twofold: geomorphic shifts (vv 4 and 5) and the outbreak of plague (v 12). The consequent turmoil causes the ultimate irony in the eschatological demise of Israel's enemies—they kill each other. It is no wonder, given all that leads up to this awful moment, that its intrinsic horror and finality are intensified by the somewhat repetitious language.

The raising of one's hand against that of another is conveyed by the verb *ʿlh* with the preposition *ʿal.* Together these words form a technical expression denoting military activity. This terminology appears frequently in the Deuteronomistic accounts of Israel's foes in hostile encounter with God's people (e.g., Judg 6:3; 15:10; 1 Kgs 14:25). How appropriate then, for the enemy to succumb in the final battle to their own internal assaults upon each other.

14. *Judah also will fight in Jerusalem.* There is apparently a discrepancy here in gender between the subject and the verb. "Judah" is normally masculine, whereas the verb is clearly feminine. Whenever "Judah" refers to a person or to the tribe descended from him, it is clearly masculine, as it is also in reference to the Southern Kingdom. However, when the land of Judah is at issue, the noun is feminine, as in Jer 23:6 (= 33:16). Such may be the case here, where the personified land (cf. Lam 1:3) fights with Yahweh to reclaim its capital.

Aside from the matter of the gender of the subject and verb, the first clause of verse 14 is fraught with difficulty. To begin with, many scholars (e.g., editors of *BHS*; P. D. Hanson 1975: 371; Rudolph 1976: 233) consider verse 14a an intrusion. Chapter 14 focuses on Jerusalem and the foreign nations/peoples, and so the mention of Judah is thought to be out of place. However, it should be noted that the final eschatological vision of this chapter, in verse 21, involves the paired participation of Jerusalem and Judah in the sacral acknowledgment of the sovereignty of Yahweh that emanates from the Temple (see second NOTE to v 21). Hence the argument that Judah has no place in the preceding struggle loses some of its force. In addition, the relationship of this chapter to chapter 12 (see last NOTE to 12:2 and first NOTE to 14:2) is relevant; and in 12:2, the siege of Jerusalem by "all the peoples" (as in 14:12) who "gather" against her (12:3 and 14:2) involves both Judah and Jerusalem. As we point out in our NOTE to "to Jerusalem" (14:2) and in our COMMENT below, the role of that city in this chapter is highly symbolic. The cosmic language of the second subunit (see various NOTES) treats Jerusalem as the center of the universe, the site of Yahweh's earthly dwelling, the meeting place between earth and heaven. Jerusalem thus represents all of Yahweh's people in these eschatological oracles, and the political specificity of its role as a provincial or monarchic capital recedes almost entirely.

Yet here the political aspects of Jerusalem emerge briefly. This verse is closest in language and theme to verses 1 and 2; indeed, it reverses the conditions set forth in those verses, the despoiled city now becoming the repository of tribute from all the nations that had perpetrated the sack of Jerusalem. Thus, in this reversal of the historical events reflected in verses 1 and 2, the historical role of Judah as the kingdom of the Davidides and as the nation-state from which Jerusalem draws its earthly raison d'être properly and momentarily surfaces. After all, Jerusalem apart from Judah is unthinkable. Jerusalem's population was Judahite (see Neh 11:4–5) in its core, and its economic viability and even the very existence of its Temple are linked to the Judean/Yehudite hinterland.

Another enormous difficulty remains, however, with respect to the role of Judah in this verse. The text is somewhat ambiguous. Is Judah fighting against Jerusalem in an eschatological struggle so beyond historical possibility that it pits the general populace against its administrative center? Or is Judah involved in the mother of all battles along with Jerusalem, with both being the object of the onslaught by the "surrounding nations"?

The ambiguity of the text is a function of the preposition b before "Jerusalem" and following "will fight." The reading of b as "against" goes back to the Targum and the Vulgate and has been adopted by many modern exegetes, including Wellhausen (1898), Mitchell (1912: 352), P. D. Hanson (1975: 370), and translations (RSV [but not NRSV]; NJB; and Soncino [Cohen 1948]). Such a reading is legitimate, in that b is used almost as often as ʿal after the Niphal of lḥm ("to fight, do battle") with the toponym designating the place being assaulted or besieged. That is, it would not be incorrect to read "Even Judah will fight against Jerusalem." However, whatever the political or sectarian polarities that existed in Judah and/or in Yehud, there is no evidence that any such divisions split Jerusalem from its Judean context. And, as mentioned earlier, Judah (in v 21 and elsewhere in Second Zechariah) is part of the restoration in the prophet's eschatological scheme. Furthermore, the notion of fighting against Jerusalem appears in verse 12 (and in 12:2, 3, 9) with the use of ʿal rather than b (cf. the ʾel of v 2).

For all these reasons, the b is probably not adversative but instead is used in its most basic sense, as an indicator of location, of moving or being in some sphere or region (or time; GKC §119.b). A translation of "in" as "at" (Jerusalem) is thus justifiable; it is supported by the Septuagint and the Syriac and is found in many modern translations (NRSV, NJPS, NEB; see the discussion in Lacocque 1981: 198–99, 211).

One further problem is the very notion of Judah (and Jerusalem) engaged in battle. Throughout this chapter, Yahweh is acting alone, with control of nature and humanity, to effect a reversal in the historical and ongoing pattern of the subjugation of Jerusalem (and Judah) by external forces. The military participation of Judah and Jerusalem as a factor leading to the defeat of the enemy seems precluded by the extraordinary measures of God's activity in this final battle. Yet it must not be forgotten that the miraculous military intervention of Yahweh is never fully removed from the actions of Israel's military forces—as in the Song of Deborah in the recounting of a historical conflict, or in Second Zechariah's depiction in the eschatological oracles of 10:3ff. of the empowerment of Judah (and Ephraim). If the nations will have gathered against Jerusalem, then Jerusalem and its territory Judah are willly-nilly in war against those nations, no matter how weak their ability to resist may be. Furthermore, the notion of Jerusalem and Judah doing battle with their enemies is essential to the immediate consequences portrayed in the second half of the verse, i.e., the acquisition of the spoil of victory in war (see following NOTES).

wealth. The noun *ḥēl* (or *ḥayil*, which also can mean "army") means "riches" or "wealth" in more than thirty instances in the Hebrew Bible. (See its analogous usage in Zech 9:4 and our NOTE there to "slam her wealth into the sea.") The military aspect of this word is especially relevant to the several cases in addition to this verse (Gen 34:29; Num 31:9; Jer 15:13; Mic 4:13; Isa 8:4; 10:14; Ezek 29:19; 30:4) in which "wealth" refers specifically to the booty taken in war. Furthermore, because material riches accrue to humans because of divine beneficence, the spoil of battle, at least when God has brought about victory for Israel, can be viewed as materials given by God. This aspect seems to underlie the elaborate treatment of the spoils in Numbers 31, whereby part of them becomes an offering to Yahweh in response to the generous gift represented by the things acquired from the Midianites.

The actual meaning of *ḥayil* or *ḥēl* as "wealth" seems limited to inanimate movables. The list in Num 31:9 has "wealth" as a category distinct from women, children, cattle, and flocks. Thus the listing of commodities in this verse (see NOTE below to "gold, silver, and garments") properly consists of material items.

The acquisition of these possessions signifies the inversion of the situation set forth at the outset of the chapter, wherein Jerusalem is plundered. However, the spoiling of Jerusalem (see NOTE to "spoil" in v 1) involved the conquest of the city, the violation of the women, the plundering of the homes, and the dispersal of half the population (see NOTES to v 2). Here only the recovery of their "wealth" (presumably goods taken from Jerusalem and/or the cities and towns of Judah) from the attacking armies, is anticipated; there is no general pillage of the enemies. It should also be noted that this taking of "wealth" is the consequence of military victory and not part of the tribute of foreign nations to sovereign Jerusalem as envisioned in Hag 2:6–9 (where "riches," *ḥămūdôt*, is part of the vocabulary of political tribute, of items freely sent; see Meyers and Meyers 1987: 53).

all the surrounding nations. In using "nations," this phrase repeats the terminology of verse 2 (see NOTE to "all the nations"), whereas "all the peoples" appears in verse 12 in this subunit (see NOTE above). The return to the language of verse 2 is especially appropriate, given the fact that the verb in this statement is "will be gathered" (see NOTE below), which uses the same root as the verb in verse 2. However, "all the . . . nations" may be elliptical here, inasmuch as the context involves the forces conquering Jerusalem (see next NOTE). That is, this phrase really signifies the attacking armies of the nations that are Israel's enemies.

gold, silver, and garments. These three items apparently characterize the material booty of inanimate movables acquired by a conquering military force. Such items are collectively called "wealth" (see NOTE above in this verse). The most relevant passage in understanding this one is the account in 2 Kings 7 concerning four Israelite men, afflicted with a skin disease and so ostracized from Samaria during the Aramaean wars. They decide to desert to the Aramaean forces in siege against Samaria. But the Aramaeans had been frightened away, leaving their camp deserted. The four men are thus able to enter the enemy tents, enjoy a meal, and then carry off the wealth that the army had acquired: "silver, gold, and garments" (2 Kgs 7:8). The order of silver and gold differs from this passage, but the identity of the three items constituting plundered wealth is the same.

The ordering of gold before silver is curious here, in that it reverses the sequence of both the Kings parallel and the reference to Tyre as a repository of silver and gold, in that order, in Zech 9:3 (cf. Hag 2:8; Zech 6:11; 13:9). This shift apparently reflects the transitional aspect of the mid-fifth century with respect to the relative value of silver and gold, with silver being more valuable than gold until well into the Persian period (cf. NOTE to "she has piled up silver" in 9:3, and Meyers and Meyers 1987: 348–49). If gold here precedes silver, as it typically does in late biblical texts (Chronicles; Esther; Daniel; see also Mal 3:3), it is perhaps because gold, by the time of the composition of this passage, was more prized than silver.

The listing of clothing (*bĕgādîm*) along with precious metals may seem incongruous. Yet items of apparel ranged from the mundane and utilitarian to the highly decorative and symbolic. Ancient Palestine probably counted textile production as one of its few industries that yielded goods desirable in the international marketplace (Browning 1988: 77). Apparently, by the Iron II period, luxury garments were being manufactured in a number of Palestinian cities. Several Assyrian documents attest to the collection of textile products along with metal objects following campaigns in the Levant. Tiglath-Pileser III, for example, in listing the items received following his advance to the west, includes "linen garments with multicolored trimmings, blue-dyed wool, purple-dyed wool" (*ANET*: 283; cf. *ANET*: 282). Textile goods are consistently the most common items in the tribute lists.

Although tribute and booty are not politically and economically the same, there is certainly an overlap in the commodities involved. Thus Assyrian and Babylonian texts describing tribute from Levantine states reflect the availability and desirability of certain goods. Specially woven and dyed textiles were prominent among them, a fact also evident in the elaborate cultic textiles and garments described in the biblical Tabernacle texts (e.g., Exod 26:1, 31; 28:2–39). Thus the particular combination of textile goods with precious metals in this verse is surely a stereotyped phrase, given its context here and in 2 Kings 7; it represents booty acquired from cities in the Levant. Booty no doubt could include other items, such as objects made of ivory, skins, or fur; but "silver and gold" (or "gold and silver") with "garments" stood for any or all wealth acquired as booty.

The fact that luxury textiles may have been an economic specialty of Iron Age Palestine is, as noted above, surely evident in the Tabernacle texts of Exodus, which depict elaborate cultic textiles and garments in language related to that of the Assyrian texts describing such fabrics acquired from subjugated westerners. In this respect, the contributions of the returning exiles to the work in Jerusalem is of some interest. The people are said to have donated "twenty thousand darics of gold and two thousand minas of silver, and sixty-seven priestly robes" (Neh 7:72). Thus gold, silver, and (cultic) clothing together constitute the wealth of the returnees available for contributions to the rebuilding efforts in Jerusalem.

will be gathered. This verb (from the root *ʾsp*, "to gather") appears above in verse 2; there, as in this verse, the "nations" are also present (see NOTES in v 2 and above in this verse). The use of this word in verse 14 serves the literary craft of the author in effecting a reversal of the situation presented in verses 1 and 2, where the nations "gather" in war against Jerusalem, conquering and looting her in the process. Here the tables are turned. The very booty taken by the nations is to be "gathered" by Judah and Jerusalem, who are now freed from the domination of foreign powers. The irony is a double one: the foes who gathered against Jerusalem (in v 2) now will be themselves despoiled; and because these foes ("all the surrounding nations"; see NOTE above in this verse) are now in Jerusalem, the wealth to be gathered from them may be the very products that Jerusalem herself relinquished. Indeed, the fact that "gold, silver, and garments" (see previous NOTE) is apparently a standardized phrase denoting the goods taken from Palestinian sites means that the wealth being gathered is not wealth characteristic of the indigenous economies of the foreign powers.

Like other aspects of Zechariah 14, the idea of taking booty from those who had despoiled Israel is not novel and can be discerned in other prophetic works. Ezekiel 38 and 39 (and part of Ezekiel 37) in particular are relevant to this chapter. Plunder is mentioned in Ezek 38:12–13 and 39:10. But in the specific language, and even in the goods noted as plunder, the author of Zechariah 14 is quite different from his prophetic predecessors.

in great abundance. The adverbial use of the noun *rōb* ("abundance, greatness") with the preposition *l* to mean "abundantly," in reference to a verb, is characteristic of late biblical Hebrew (e.g., Neh 9:25; 2 Chron 9:9), although it can appear in earlier texts.

15. *plague.* See the first NOTE to verse 12. The return here to the language of plague has led some to suggest that this verse ought to follow verse 12, with verses 13 and 14 being interpolations. Chary (1969: 218), for example, arranges this subunit as follows: verses 12, 15, 13, 14. However, the specifics of epidemic disease that are depicted in verses 12 and 15 can just as easiily be understood as a framework for the content of verses 13 and 14, namely, the awful impact of the epidemic on the enemy and the concomitant positive effects on Jerusalem.

the horse, the mule, the camel, and the ass. The Septuagint translates these animal terms with plurals, because each individual word here is a collective representing all of its class (GKC §126.m). However, the English singular is clear enough in indicating the totality of animals represented by each term. Another grammatical point involves the fact that the connector *waw* ("and") occurs only before the last item in this list. This is somewhat atypical of Hebrew, which tends to have a conjunction before each item (cf. Gen 12:16). The determining factor here may be the sense that all these animals together constitute a type, i.e., the animals of an army traveling great distances from its home territory. These are not livestock but, rather, beasts of burden or, in the case of the horse, animals used for cavalry or for drawing chariots (see NOTES to "chariot . . . horse" in 9:10, "like his mighty horse" in 10:3, and "those mounted on horses" in 10:5). Horses, of course, are the most prominent military animals, and their place as the first of the animals in this list is to be expected. Yet an army could not move without pack animals. Thus this list is a comprehensive presentation of the military equipment consisting of living creatures—animals for attack and for transport—which would be affected no less than humans by the outbreak of pestilential disease in the enemy camp (see first NOTE to v 12).

The inclusion of the "ass" in this list is noteworthy in light of its use in Zech 9:9, where it is the animal upon which the royal figure rides into Jerusalem. There (see NOTE above), as one of several humble beasts of burden, it represents the aspect of humility associated with the restored king. The ass, like any of these animals, could transport either goods or people. But in the movement of large military forces, it was used as a beast of burden for equipment and supplies, with the foot soldiers proceeding, appropriately, on foot. The officers and/or cavalry undoubtedly rode on horseback or perhaps on one of the other animals, all of which could carry humans as well as materials.

That this particular assortment of animals should be viewed in their capacity as beasts of burden is supported by the list in Ezra 2:66–67 (= Neh 7:68) of animals among those returning from exile: horses, mules, camels, and asses. The list has the animals in exactly the same order as in this Zechariah verse. The Ezra text is interesting in the numbers attached there to each animal: the asses are numbered in the thousands (6,720), as compared with 736 horses, 245 mules, and 435 camels. Whether these numbers are correct in their absolute values cannot be ascertained, but they surely depict the abundance of asses, over against other available animals, as beasts of transport.

and every animal. Another *waw* ("and") precedes this noun, as does the modifier "every." Hence "animal" stands apart from the preceding list of four draft animals (see previous NOTE). This word (*běhēmâ*) can mean all living creatures or "beasts" other than humanity (as in Gen 8:1; Exod 8:13–14 [NRSV 8:17–18]; Lev 18:23; Deut 27:21), or it can mean domesticated animals (as opposed to wild animals, as in Gen 1:24–26; 2:20; etc.). A special category of the latter is "cattle," as domesticated by humans and as an important component of the repertory of livestock in the ancient Near East. It may very well be that "cattle" would be a better rendering in this military context, inasmuch as this particular animal may have been the typical kind of livestock to be taken as a food resource for an army on the move (cf. 2 Kgs 3:9). However, because *bĕhēmâ* can be more inclusive, and because there is no way to know whether cattle were the only form of livestock kept by Jerusalem's attackers, "animals"— in the sense of domestic animals used for food rather than transport—seems preferable. In any case, "animal" contributes a category additional to the four draft animals of the preceding list (see previous NOTE).

those camps. That is, the military encampments of the nations that had sent armies to surround and lay siege to Jerusalem (cf. NOTE above in 14:14 to "all the surrounding nations"). From the root *ḥnh* ("to encamp"), the noun *maḥăneh* as a secular word can refer to the temporary settlement of transhumant people (i.e., seminomads), but more frequently in the Bible it designates a military encampment (it also denotes the sacral camps of the Israelites in the wilderness). Such an encampment includes human personnel (soldiers plus support staff), equipment and provisions, and the animals that served as transport and those that were part of the provisions, i.e., livestock that would be slaughtered for food (see two previous NOTES).

this plague. The reference is clearly to the plague (*maggēpâ*) mentioned in verse 12 (see first NOTE to that verse) and at the beginning of this verse. The subunit thus begins—"This will be the plague"—and ends "this plague"—with almost the same words. The theme of plague is effectively established by this inclusio.

These two words are preceded in English by the preposition "during." In the Hebrew, the preposition is *kĕ*, usually translated "like" or "as." Some Hebrew manuscripts substitute *bĕ* ("in") here, but the versions all support the somewhat troublesome MT.

16. *every survivor.* Literally, "everyone who is left over/remains." The term "survivor" is a Niphal participle of *ytr*, a root that occurs two other times in the last two chapters of Second Zechariah. In 13:8 (see NOTE to "remain in it"), it refers to the third of Yahweh's people who survive the destruction of Judah and the exile of many of the people, a fate that befalls the "two parts" that are "cut off and perish." The surviving third is the part that suffers and is thereby purified ("refined," 13:9), thus becoming eligible to be part of the renewed covenant with God. The second instance is the use of the nominal form (*yeter*) in the first subunit of this chapter. In 14:2 (see NOTE to "the rest"), it has a similar meaning to that of the verb of 13:8 in denoting those who survive the destruction of Jerusalem and remain in the city.

The fact that both other occurrences of this term in Second Zechariah refer to Israelite survivors is relevant to its use here to denote foreign survivors. This chapter, as part of the dynamics of its eschatological message, is replete with inversions and reversals. Thus in employing a term that elsewhere indicates the remnant of God's people, the prophet brings the remnant of "all the nations" (see next NOTE) into alignment with Israel. Such is precisely what the rest of this verse proclaims: that all these foreign survivors will do what God's people do, namely, participate in the paramount festival (see NOTE to "Feast of Booths" below) of the Israelite calendar. The prophet could just as easily have used the root *šʾr* here, as in 9:7 where it denotes those Philistines who survive Yahweh's intervention and thus "remain" (see NOTE to "will remain") to become "like a clan in Judah," loyal foreigners assimilated to Judean ways. That root is often used in parallel with *ytr* and is indeed the most common word in this semantic field conveying the idea of "extra, left over" (Kronholm 1990: 484). Both because it is more common and because it has already been used in Second Zechariah in regard to foreigners, the fact that the equivalent root used elsewhere in regard to Israelites in this prophetic work is found here instead helps draw attention to the startling scene it introduces—non-Israelites acting as Israelites.

This notion of reversal—of Yahweh's enemies acting as if they were the survivors of the centuries of assault on Jerusalem—sets the theme for this last subunit of chapter 14 and continues the general themes of upheaval and radical change in nature that characterize the first and second subunits. In particular, this notion continues ideas present in the first and third subunits, which relate the fate of the nations that have attacked Jerusalem.

all the nations. This phrase occurs two other times in chapter 14 (vv 2 and 19; see NOTES), and the related "all the peoples" (v 12; see NOTE) appears once. This terminology bespeaks the universalism that is integral to the eschatological picture so vividly drawn in this chapter. Indeed, the modifier *kol* ("all," "every") is used a dozen times, thereby sounding again and again the note of inclusiveness. The negative aspect of "all the nations" of verse 2, depicted as warring against Jerusalem, is here turned into the same kind of open universalism expressed in the concluding oracles to First Zechariah, where "many peoples and mighty nations" (8:22; see Meyers and Meyers 1987: 439) will acknowledge the supremacy of Yahweh.

The identity of these nations is not specified. But because they are the ones who have attacked Jerusalem (vv 2 and 12), they surely represent Israel's historical enemies, especially the eastern empires that approach Jerusalem from the north-northeast (see NOTE to "the valley of the mountains" in 14:5). Those enemies will have suffered unspeakable devastation through the upheavals of nature (vv 4–5) and the concomitant plague and internal chaos (vv 13–15) evoked by Yahweh's militant response to their treatment of God's people. The fate of the survivors (see previous NOTE) thereby becomes linked to that of the Israelites, who survive similar features of the wars fought against them. The suffering of the nations entitles them and predisposes them, no less than Israel, to the redemptive plan to be effected in the future age.

that had come. The plural participle of *bwʾ* ("to come") agrees in number with the plural "nations" that precedes it, or with the collective "all" that modifies "nations." The time sequence is determined by the perfect of *hyh* ("to be") with the *waw* consecutive that begins the verse and that we translate "then." The past time surely refers to the awful events of verse 2, in which the same "all the nations" appears—gathered for war against Jerusalem—and contrasts with the next verb ("will go up"; see NOTE below), which denotes the positive future acts of those nations.

The negative use of "come" here, to indicate the warlike approach of the nations to Jerusalem, also serves to contrast with the positive use of "come" in verse 21 in reference to all who sacrifice to Yahweh (see NOTES to "will come" and "all who sacrifice"). The language in verse 21 is inclusive, perhaps involving these foreigners as well as Judeans and other local residents of the land (see NOTE to "Canaanite"). Using "come" in this verse, rather than repeating the term "gather (against Jerusalem)" of verse 2 or "waged war (against Jerusalem)" of verse 12, is more than a lexical variation; it is a literary choice to herald the use of "come" for opposite purposes in the last verse of this chapter.

against Jerusalem. Although "Jerusalem" is used repeatedly in this chapter, it stands for more than the tiny postexilic outpost nestled in the Judean hills. Surely it represents Judah, if not all Israel (see NOTES to "Judah also will fight in Jerusalem" in v 14 and "in Jerusalem and in Judah" in v 21). In addition, because the locus of Yahweh's earthly presence is the Jerusalem Temple, war against Jerusalem is tantamount to an attack on God. What an enormous transformation thus emerges in the rest of this verse! All these nations so hostile to Yahweh and the people, in attempting to subjugate them, now themselves acknowledge Yahweh's universal rule and so themselves become subjugated to Yahweh's divine authority (see NOTES to "bow down" and "King Yahweh of Hosts" below).

will go up. The verb, in the plural with *waw* consecutive, is from ⁽*lh*, which means "to go up" and is often used specifically in reference to someone's ascent to Jerusalem. The stereotyped expression "to go up to Jerusalem/the mountain of Yahweh" typically is used in cultic contexts, for example, in speaking of someone going to Jerusalem in order to go to the Temple and participate in formal or ritual community life. In this connection, it should be noted that Psalms 120–134 each bear the title "Song of Ascents" (*šîr hammaᶜălôt*, from ⁽*lh*), perhaps testifying to their use as hymns chanted by pilgrims on their way to Jerusalem to celebrate the three pilgrim festivals: Pesaḥ (Passover), Shabuoth (Pentecost), and Sukkoth (Tabernacles or Booths; see last NOTE in this verse). The act of "going up," without the explicit mention of Jerusalem, signified a trip to Jerusalem with a motivation grounded in the cultic life of the people. Although the idea of going *up* to Jerusalem is rooted in the ancient concept of a sanctuary being on a mountain or high place, once Israel's chief shrine was built in Jerusalem it became common to use this root with "to Jerusalem" or with alternative designations for the holy city (e.g., "to the mountain of Yahweh" [Isa 2:3 = Mic 4:2]; "hill of Yahweh" [Ps 24:3]), with the result that ⁽*lh* alone could represent the entire phrase and signify a trip to Jerusalem and/or its Temple.

Thus "go up" here surely implies going to Jerusalem, and the context of this chapter and its focus on Jerusalem underscores that implication. Furthermore, because this term is part of Israel's cultural life, as expressed in cultic activity, its application here to foreigners, who in this verse are depicted doing what elsewhere in the Bible is ascribed only to Israelites, accentuates this extraordinary reversal in the coming meta-historical scheme. The inclusiveness of this description of eschatological pilgrimage is especially noteworthy in light of the opposite trajectories that characterized life under foreign subjugation in the postexilic period, both in Yehud and in the exilic communities.

every year. The first word in the phrase is *middê*, a composite of the preposition *min* ("from") and the noun *day* ("sufficiency"). Thus a literal rendering would be "from the sufficiency of a year in a year." (See 1 Sam 1:7 and, possibly, Deut 14:22; cf. 2 Sam 21:1 and Neh 10:33 [NRSV 10:34]). This idiom, which can also be paraphrased as "from one year to the next" or "year by year," denotes the regularity of a festival that is part of the sacral calendar.

bow down. The root of this specialized liturgical verb is *ḥwy*: literally, "to bow down," or by extension, "to worship." The form is the Hishtaphal. It is typically followed as here with *l* ("to") plus the object of "worship" (e.g., Jer 7:2; Deut 26:10; see next NOTE). This verb is thus an integral part of the cultic context of this subunit of Zechariah 14. The act of "bowing down," which probably comes from the language of the royal court and of the heavenly court, is the ancient and traditional sign of obeisance or paying homage. It acknowledges the superiority of the one to whom a person genuflects (cf. the stylized openings of many of the Amarna letters: "to the king, my lord . . . seven and seven times I fall at the feet of the king my lord"; *ANET*: 484–90).

This language indicating the eschatological participation of foreigners in acknowledging Yahweh's sovereignty resembles the concluding verses to First Zechariah. The verb "bow down" is not found in Zechariah 8, but other terms, such as "entreat the favor of" and "seek" have cultic implications when used, as in 8:22, with "Yahweh of Hosts in Jerusalem" (see Meyers and Meyers 1987: 433, 439–40 and NOTES to Zech 8:22–23). The participation there of "many peoples and mighty nations" at "happy festivals," the regular annual celebrations (*môʿădîm*) of the Israelite calendar, parallels the annual pilgrimage of "every survivor from all the nations" (see first two NOTES of this verse) portrayed in Zechariah 14. The similarity of universalism in the concluding sections of both First and Second Zechariah is surely an important point of congruence between these two sections of the single canonical work bearing the name Zechariah.

King Yahweh of Hosts. The combination *melek* ("King") plus *YHWH ṣĕbāʾôt* ("Yahweh of Hosts") is unique in the Hebrew Bible, although there are some instances of the close juxtaposition of these terms. Psalm 24:10, e.g., reads "Yahweh of Hosts, he is the King of glory" (cf. "King Yahweh" of Ps 98:6). "Yahweh of Hosts" alone is surely a hallmark of the Haggai–Zechariah–Malachi corpus, in which it accounts for nearly one-third of the occurrences of this title in the Bible (91 of 284 in all; see Meyers and Meyers 1987: 18–19). In Second Zechariah it is used nine times, but only here and in the next verse is it coupled with "King."

The absence of a *patach* under the *lamedh* before "King," which would be expected as a mark of the definite article before the noun, is puzzling. Thus, according to the MT, the phrase reads "King Yahweh of Hosts" rather than with king in apposition, for a reading of "the king, Yahweh of Hosts." As translated here, "King" appears as a title, much like the frequently used title in the historical books for the rulers of Israel and Judah and of foreign lands. However, in the case of the human kings, their names appear before the title "king" (e.g., "King Cyrus of Persia" would literally by "Cyrus king of Persia").

The historical prominence of royal ideology for Yahweh, in which God is regarded as ultimate sovereign over Israel (as in 1 Sam 8:7) and in which God as overlord is party to the covenant, was somewhat compromised, as Samuel warned it would be, by the establishment of monarchic rule in Israel. Thus it might be expected that in the postexilic period, with the absence of royal rule in Yehud, the language of monarchic sovereignty would reemerge. Although "Yahweh of Hosts" is surely, as indicated above, disproportionately frequent in postexilic prophecy, "king" appears in Haggai–Zechariah–Malachi only here (vv 16–17) and in Mal 1:14 ("I am a great king, says Yahweh of Hosts," and "my name is revered among the nations") in relationship to God. Yet these same books, as frequently in Ezra–Nehemiah, use "king" almost reverentially in relationship to the imperial rulers of Persia (Cyrus, Darius, and Artaxerxes).

One might therefore conjecture that there was reluctance in postexilic Yehud to use "king" for a ruler other than the political sovereigns who held power over this province. If so, it is even more significant that this title for God bursts forth in this eschatological section of Zechariah 14. At that point, the very nations whose kings ruled Judah/Yehud will themselves be subjugated, following God's cosmic-military intervention (vv 3–5, 12–15), to Yahweh's rule. With this international or universal purview, the title "king" applied to Yahweh finally becomes essential.

However, it is also important to recognize that the use of "king" in reference to Yahweh, although diminished or absent in historical texts of the monarchy, was probably part of cultic language in ancient Israel. Certain royal psalms herald God as king (especially the Korahite Psalms, 44, 45, 47, 48; cf. Psalms 95, 96, 97, 99 and Jer 10:7–10). Such psalms are often understood as enthronement psalms, perhaps part of the liturgy of a royal enthronement festival celebrating Yahweh's rule, derived from a Mesopotamian prototype (as in Mowinckel 1962; Johnson 1967; but cf. P. D. Hanson 1975: 386–87, who favors a fertility cult of the storm god) and related to the significance of the fall harvest festival or Booths (so Kraus 1966: 186; Harrelson 1968: 90; see next two NOTES).

A complicated set of hypotheses is involved in such suggestions, and fully compelling evidence has not been provided. Yet the association of "king" with liturgical or hymnic, and thus cultic, language seems clear. Hence it may be the cultic context of these verses and of Mal 1:14, in which "king" and "Yahweh of Hosts" are also found in association (although not paired as here), that makes them unique in all of Haggai through Malachi in having the frequent "Yahweh of Hosts" used with "King." Whatever the origin of the combination "King Yahweh of Hosts," whether in political and/or cultic language, its unparalleled expression of Yahweh's universal power and rule perhaps could emerge only in a passage such as this, where the political and cultic spheres unite as the whole world becomes sanctified (see NOTES to vv 20–21) under Yahweh's sovereignty in the future age.

One other point about the cultic overtones of this subunit in relationship to royal language deserves mention. Some suppose there is tension between Yahweh's kingship in this passage and a human king's sovereignty in 9:9–10.

Although both texts are eschatological, the latter passage lacks both the cultic dimension and the extreme eschatology of an altered natural, as well as political, order. Thus Zechariah 9 and 14 are not necessarily competing images but rather reflections of different levels of eschatological transformation. Note also that in some royal psalms (e.g., Psalms 3, 72, 110) the king, although anointed and exalted, is nevertheless clearly subordinate to Yahweh.

celebrate. The root *hgg* means not only "to celebrate" but more specifically "to make a pilgrimage" or "to celebrate a pilgrim feast" (Kedar-Kopfstein 1980b: 202). The historical connection in ancient Israel between celebration and pilgrimage is expressed in the Bible in the command of God through Moses that the Israelites should "hold a festival for me" three times in the course of a year: the feasts of unleavened bread, of the first fruits, and of the ingathering (Exod 23:14–17). These ancient agricultural celebrations involved pilgrimage to a central shrine (see Deut 16:16 for the festivals of unleavened bread, of weeks, and of booths). The biblical injunctions for these feasts, however divergent they may be among the various Pentateuchal texts prescribing them, do not include foreign nations among those commanded to celebrate, although foreigners living within Israel are enjoined to rejoice at these times (e.g., Deut 16:11, 14). Thus this portrayal of the survivors of those who had attacked Jerusalem coming on a pilgrimage (see above, NOTES to this verse) to Jerusalem marks a radical change in the cultic conceptions of the Bible. This is one more instance, among many in this last chapter, of radical transformations in both natural and human life marking the universalism of the eschatological future.

Feast of Booths. The object of the pilgrimage (see above, NOTE to "will go up") of "every survivor" of "all the nations" (see NOTES above) is the participation in a special festival, the Feast of Booths. Called *hag hassūkkôt* in this text and in Lev 23:33–36 (cf. 23:39–42) and Deut 16:13–15 and 31:9–13, it denotes a fall harvest festival, almost certainly to be identified with the "festival of the ingathering" (*hag hā'āsîp*) of Exod 23:16 and 34:22. As a product of the ancient Palestinian agricultural cycle, it was one of three annual celebrations that involved pilgrimage to local shrines and ultimately to Jerusalem. For each of these three yearly events, the agricultural foundations never disappeared but were supplemented by Israelite tendencies toward historicization, whereby each of them was imbued with meanings derived from Israel's historical experience of Exodus (Passover/spring festival), Sinai (Pentecost or Weeks/first fruits), and Wandering (Booths/ingathering). Thus Booths entailed the celebrants reexperiencing the temporary wilderness dwellings in which Israelites lived during their journey from Egypt to the Promised Land (Lev 23:42).

The highlighting of this festival, one of the three yearly Israelite celebrations, at the conclusion of Second Zechariah raises important questions about the cultic calendar of Second Zechariah's day and about the role of Israelite festivals in the universalizing depiction of the future. Why is Sukkoth (Booths) the holiday featured in this passage? Is it meant to stand alone as an all-inclusive festival or would the nations celebrate other festivals too? These questions can be approached by considering the special status of Sukkoth in the postexilic (and later) periods, for this feast apparently occupied a place of prominence among the three agriculturally based pilgrim festivals during the Second Temple era, if not earlier.

Perhaps the most telling sign of preeminence attached to this holiday is the fact that in several biblical passages it is called simply "the feast" (*heḥag*), as if there were none other from which it needed to be distinguished. In 1 Kgs 8:1–2 (= 2 Chron 5:3; cf. the summation in 1 Kgs 8:65 = 2 Chron 7:8, 9) the Deuteronomist relates how the "ark of the covenant of Yahweh" was brought up to Jerusalem at "the feast" that takes place in the month Ethanim, the seventh month, which is when "Booths" occurs, according to Lev 23:34 and Num 29:12. All the assembly of Israel was present, and a great dedicating feast ensued. This special role for the festival of the seventh month may derive from the antiquity of an annual feast at Shiloh called *ḥag-YHWH* (Judg 21:19; cf. Lev 23:39) that involved joyous celebration. Such a festival may also have been the model for the festival of the eighth month instituted by Jeroboam at Bethel in imitation of "the festival" (*heḥag*, 1 Kgs 12:32) that was celebrated in Judah.

The designation "the feast" also appears in Ezek 45:25, which, like Leviticus, gives the seventh-month date for the festival. Similarly, this very same festival is called "a festival to Yahweh" (*ḥag lěYHWH*) in Num 29:12 and "the festival of Yahweh" (*ḥag-YHWH*) in Lev 23:39. In other words, in both priestly and Deuteronomic sources (and in the Chronicler's work), the Feast of Booths/ ingathering is mentioned without an accompanying descriptive term. As "the feast" or "feast to/of Yahweh," it perhaps was *the* feast par excellence in the Israelite calendar (cf. de Vaux 1961: 506).

In addition to this special designation for Booths, the way it is described in the Book of Ezra (from the early restoration period) is of significance. Leaders of the first group of returnees, under the edict of Cyrus, proceeded to put the courtyard altar of the Jerusalem Temple in working order almost immediately. They did this in "the seventh month," apparently in anticipation, to some degree, of the imminent Feast of Booths, which they immediately celebrated "as prescribed" (Ezra 3:1–4). This passage then relates how the returnees made all the regular and freewill sacrifices and celebrated the new moon and "all the sacred festivals of Yahweh" (Ezra 3:5). But only Booths is singled out for specific mention.

This festival's association with the Solomonic Temple dedication ceremony in 1 Kings may well be a cause of its preeminence in the late sixth-century restoration of altar worship. Either one or both of these special roles for Booths may underlie the designation of Booths as "the holiday." In any case, it can hardly be coincidental that in the mid-fifth century Ezra's reading of the Torah to all the people took place during "the festival of the seventh month," which is identified as the time when people should live in "booths" according to "the torah that Yahweh commanded by Moses" (Neh 8:14). This festal assembly was said to be unlike any that had taken place since "the days of Joshua ben Nun" (Neh 8:17), a claim that seems to give Booths an edge over Passover, for which a similar claim was made in the days of Josiah in the seventh century (2 Kgs

23:22 reads "no such Passover had been observed since the days of the judges"; cf. 2 Chron 35:18, which specifies that such celebration had not been held since Samuel's time). Still, the prominence of Booths here need not mean that the other feasts were not known and widely celebrated.

Whether Zechariah 14 predates or postdates the event related in Ezra cannot be determined. Yet it is clear that by some time in the fifth century, if not earlier, Booths was a festival of special significance—associated with the ark of the covenant and with the Torah of Moses. The specific historical explanation of the holiday, in which it was connected to the wilderness wandering, had been supplanted by more abstract and all-encompassing features of Israelite national identity: covenant and Torah. That all the survivors of God's reordering of nature and human affairs in the eschatological age participate in a festival linked to these central aspects of Israelite identity must surely signify that foreigners will in some sense share in that identity.

It is noteworthy that several centuries later, when the Temple was rededicated in Jerusalem as the culmination of the successful Maccabean revolt, the celebration was carried out as if it were the Booths festival, even though the date was in Kislev, several months later (2 Macc 10:5-8). In addition, rabbinic traditions amplify the biblical injunctions for the celebration of Booths to include libation rites (see below, NOTE to "there will be no rain for them"), which may derive from this Zechariah text or possibly reflect another dimension of the fall festival that contributes to its popularity in the Second Temple period, if not before.

The other question raised earlier deserves consideration. Is "Booths" a metonymy for all Israelite feasts (and fasts), and for all Israelite culture? That is, does the fact of international participation in this one festival symbolize such involvement in all? It is tempting to see, in this vivid universalizing portrayal, a sense of the whole world absorbing Israelite culture, i.e., becoming Israelite and part of Yahweh's people. For several reasons, however, this seems unlikely. First, these foreigners are said to "go up every year" (see NOTES above), but no word is said about doing this three times a year, which is a prominent stipulation in the Pentateuchal texts prescribing Israel's feasts. Second, there were other (nonpilgrimage) holidays in Israel's cultic calendar; these are in no way alluded to here and thus seem to be outside the language of "go up" (i.e., pilgrimage) and "every year."

Finally, and perhaps most important, these foreigners from far outside the land of Yahweh's people have a different status than the nearby neighbors dealt with in chapter 9, who somehow become assimilated to Israel's cultural (political-religious) ways. And, although traditional and hostile enemies of Israel, these foreigners are also quite distinct from the internal and paradigmatically dangerous foes of Israel, the enemies within—the Canaanites (see NOTE in v 21)—who must lose their identity, or be destroyed, in order for Israel to be fully restored. The nations of this verse, and of most of this chapter until verse 21, represent the imperial powers that had dominated Israel. In the future Israel's God will dominate them. Their participation in Booths will give them access to

Yahweh's word. They will thus partake of Israel's unique role vis-à-vis Yahweh. But the participation will not extend to all aspects of Israelite culture; the other nations will not dissolve as the Canaanites must.

The idea of other nations coming up to Jerusalem is not new to Zechariah. We have already noted its presence in First Zechariah (8:20–23; see second NOTE to this verse). In Isaiah there are several references to the gathering of the nations to Jerusalem. Isaiah 2:2–4 (= Mic 4:1–4), which we have already cited (see above, NOTE in this verse to "will go up") is one such instance. Another, Isa 56:3–8, has individuals among the foreigners totally accepting Yahweh and following all the precepts of Israel; some will even become Temple servitors (Isa 66:21). But Isaiah 60 is much more in the spirit of Zechariah 8 in relating the recognition and tribute that the nations will bestow upon the City of Yahweh (v 14). None of these texts, however, mentions an annual trip to Jerusalem, nor do they specify participation in a distinct festival or lay out penalties for failure to do so (see NOTES to the next three verses), nor do they single out Egypt (see first NOTE to v 18 and first NOTE to v 19). Clearly Zechariah 14 establishes a unique perspective on the role of foreigners in the eschatological scheme, a perspective that appears in the assertion of medieval Jewish commentators that the ultimate celebration of God's triumph in history will involve Jews and gentiles together and will take place on Sukkoth (Booths; see Cohen 1948: 331).

17. *families of the land*. This is the second of three designations for foreigners enjoined to celebrate Booths (see previous NOTE) in Jerusalem. The first designation appears at the beginning of verse 16 ("every survivor from all the nations"; see NOTE), and the third is "family of Egypt" in verse 18 (see NOTE below). The meaning of the present expression is difficult to understand, especially because this particular construct form—*mišpĕḥôt hāʾāreṣ*—is unique in the Bible. However, a similar combination, *mišpĕḥôt hāʾărāṣôt* in Ezek 20:32 (translated "tribes of the countries" by NRSV but as "families of the lands" by NJPS), is in apposition with *gôyîm* ("nations") and so points to a meaning similar to that which "nations" would indicate. On the basis of the Ezekiel passage, along with "every survivor of all the nations (*gôyîm*)" of the previous verse, the possibility that these are synonymous expressions can be suggested.

Yet the uniqueness of this combination deserves further consideration. The term *mišpāḥâ* normally represents a secondary level of social organization, sometimes called a "clan" or "phratry" (see NOTE to "all the families" in 12:12) and composed of a group of family households (each known as *bêt ʾāb*). The *mišpĕḥôt* themselves then constitute a tribe (*šēbeṭ*). But during the Exile, this apparently ancient terminology for Israelite social structure underwent significant alteration, as attempts were made for the structural adaptations of the exiled Judeans to be brought in line with traditional designations. The result of these shifts was that the term *bêt ʾāb* gave way to *bêt ʾābôt*, with the latter term in the postexilic period representing a group of people much larger than the preexilic family household represented by the former term.

Thus the *bêt ʾābôt* apparently designated a unit similar in size and in organization to the preexilic *mišpāḥâ* (D. L. Smith 1989: 98–117; cf. Weinberg

1973: 400). As the basic large structural unit, the *bêt ʾābôt* could exceed three thousand members. If this is so, and if postexilic sources attempt to contain the new structures in the old nomenclature, then the postexilic use, *mišpāḥâ*, would consequently be shifted to mean something closer in size to what *šēbeṭ* or *maṭṭeh* designated in the traditional terminology. Indeed, the predominance of *maṭṭeh* over *šēbeṭ* as a term for "tribe" in priestly and postexilic sources may reflect some attempt to adjust the terminology to the altered social structures. Be that as it may, with *bêt ʾābôt* reflecting what *mišpāḥâ* had earlier represented, the postexilic use of *mišpĕḥôt* in some cases, such as in this verse, apparently involves the largest grouping of people in any nation.

In light of this shift in reference for *mišpāḥâ*, "families of the land" here would mean, literally, "tribes" of the land. But because "tribes" would not fit the social organization of the empires represented by the "nations" of this chapter, *mišpĕḥôt* in fact means something closer to "peoples" of the land, that is, the groups that constitute an imperial power according to the Yehudite perspective. It is not meant to give precision to this reference to the internal organization of foreign nations but rather to represent them in terms that reflect something other than what the political term *gôyîm* ("nations") involves. This passage moves from the political to the cultic/cultural, so terminology less exclusively political serves the prophet's purpose.

This brings us to the second word of this combination, *ʾereṣ*, a term that exhibits a variety of related meanings. It can stand for "earth" in a cosmic sense as opposed to "heaven" (see NOTE to "who stretched out the heavens" in 12:1); it can mean "land" in the sense of sovereign territory; it can mean "ground," as dirt or soil, in an agricultural sense; and on occasion it can mean "underworld" (Ottosson 1974: 393). It is difficult to determine which of these possibilities best fits this passage. Surely the first and last can be ruled out. But perhaps both of the other two are relevant. That is, the territorial aspect would be in keeping with the political dimension of the related term "nations" that appears in verses 2, 3, 14, 16 (see NOTES above; cf. "peoples" of v 12). At the same time, the agrarian nuance would be relevant to the general depoliticized tone of this last subunit, as well as to the presence of an agricultural feast (Booths; see previous NOTE) and of a reference to the sine qua non of Palestinian farming, rain (see last NOTE in this verse).

Thus "families of the earth," or "peoples of the earth," designates all the "nations" (or the survivors thereof) introduced in previous verses with the exception of Egypt, which is mentioned separately (see first NOTE to v 18). The unique terminology reflects the sociopolitical nomenclature of the postexilic period and is sensitive to the apolitical context of an eschatological cultic event. Furthermore, it reflects the agricultural origins of the festival for which these foreigners are gathered and anticipates the use of rain, or rather its absence, as a punitive measure. As a new expression, *mišpĕḥôt hāʾāreṣ* underscores the new conditions of the future age, which will entail dramatic changes in the familiar structures of historical reality, past and present.

not go up. The verb *ʿlh*, which is in the singular but has a collective sense, echoes that of the previous verse (see NOTE to "will go up"); it is the language of pilgrimage to Jerusalem, especially for a festival. But here the notion is introduced that there may be some residual resistance among the nations—the "families of the earth" (see previous NOTE). Some may be reluctant to reverse their historical role of dominance, in respect to Jerusalem, to one of obeisance to the God whose earthly dwelling is in that city.

bow down. See the NOTE to this verb in verse 16, where the idea of going up (on a pilgrimage; see previous NOTE in v 16) to Jerusalem and bowing down to Yahweh is completed by the information that those pilgrims will "celebrate the Feast of Booths" (see last two NOTES to v 16). Here "bow down" is clearly elliptical; it surely referes to the obeisance paid Yahweh by participating in this highly important annual festival.

King Yahweh of Hosts. See the NOTE to this unique expression in verse 16, where it also occurs.

there will be no rain for them. The failure of some to appear at the Booths festival will mean that they incur a penalty. Rain will be withheld. The withholding of rain is part of the covenant curses of Deuteronomy (28:22–24; cf. Deut 11:14ff.) and Leviticus (Lev 26:19), which portray the desolation of drought, with the earth (*ʾereṣ;* see NOTE to "families of the earth" in v 16) becoming hard as iron. That a punitive measure would follow upon a foreigner's nonappearance at Booths implies an obligation to be there and perhaps is related to the reference to covenant and Torah that is part of the Festival of Booths (see last NOTE to v 16).

More specifically, the withholding of rain is related to the basic agricultural dimension of Booths, the festival at issue here. The fall harvest festival involves the final reaping of the summer's bounty before the onset of the rainy season in mid-October, which is when the seventh month, the biblical date for Booths, would fall. The winter rains were critical for agriculture in Near Eastern lands (although probably not for Egypt; see next NOTE).

Thus, at least by late Second Temple times, prayers for rain became part of the celebration of Sukkoth (Booths; see Cohen 1948: 331). Although it cannot be determined when in the postexilic period such prayers originated, their presence is attested in early rabbinic literature (Taanit 1.1; Tos Sukkot 3.18; Rosh Hashanah 1.3), a fact that would indicate that this custom was already in place in the Hasmonean era if not before. The Mishnah records another connection of water to Sukkoth; it relates that on the Feast of Booths water was drawn from the pool of Siloam and carried in procession to the Temple and poured upon the altar (Rosh Hashanah 4.9; Middot 2.7; cf. Tos Sukkot 3.3(4), 14, 16; John 7:37ff.; see Grigsby 1986: 100–8). Moreover, an early rabbinic source has an interesting explanation or justification for the bringing of a water libation to the Temple on Sukkoth. Water should be brought "so that the rain would be blessed on its account," i.e., so that the winter rains expected after Sukkoth would soon come. The text of Zech 14:17–18 is then cited as a proof-text for this custom and belief (Tos Sukkot 3.18; cf. Goudoever 1961: 34). The agricultural basis of the Feast of Booths clearly reemerges in these traditions, the historicization of the festival in its connection to the wilderness wandering and the association with the ark of the covenant and the Torah notwithstanding.

Both agrarian and covenantal aspects of Booths are probably present in this context. What is striking is that the historical obligation to observe Booths, as incumbent upon all Israel, is here extended to foreigners. Their impulse to go up to Jerusalem is thus not exactly an optional or arbitrary phenomenon. Although this universalistic chapter of Zechariah stops short of involving the whole world in the kind of covenantal relationship that characterizes Israel's relationship with Yahweh (cf. last NOTE to 13:9), it nonetheless envisions the foreign nations somehow partaking of that relationship, at least enough so that the supremacy of Israel's covenant deity cannot be in doubt. The overturning of historical and natural patterns that recurs in this chapter goes so far as to include this partial alteration in the nature of the covenant as a mutual pact between Yahweh and the people chosen, out of all the peoples, to enter into that relationship (e.g., Deut 4:37; 7:7-9; 14:1; 1 Kgs 3:8; Isa 41:8; Ezek 20:5).

A word about the term "for them" is in order. This plural form clearly has the singular subject, the relative ʾšr which means "whichever one" or "any" as we translate it. The subject surely has a collective interest—it means all those who might fail to go up. Thus it is "upon them" (pl.) that the effects of the punitive withholding of rain will fall.

18. *family of Egypt.* In this rather extraordinary scenario of foreigners participating in an Israelite festival and partaking to some extent in Israel's relationship with Yahweh (see previous NOTE and other NOTES to vv 16–17), the Egyptians apparently constitute a special case. The disputed status of the negative (wĕlōʾ ʿălêhem, literally, "not upon them") at the end of this verse contributes to the difficulty in understanding what happens to Egypt (see below, NOTE to "then no [rain will be] for them").

Egypt receives individual treatment here for several reasons, the first of which is related to Egypt's unique climate. If Egypt fails to celebrate Booths, it would be subjected to the withholding of rain as would be other peoples that do not keep this obligation. However, the prophet is well aware that rain is not a factor in Egyptian agricultural productivity; Egypt's traditional fecundity, the place to which Palestinians beset by famine turn (Gen 12:10; 41:52), was a gift of the Nile, not of abundant rainfall. Lack of rainfall would not affect the economy of Egypt the way it would all other areas of the Near East. In lieu of an absence of rain, then plague, which also has a particular association with Egypt (see NOTE to this word below) would be an appropriate, additional punishment. Clearly there is a special treatment, which is expressed in an additional clause, for Egypt with its rainless climate.

Perhaps there is another reason for the special mention of Egypt, namely, the presence of an Israelite community in Egypt. The prophet knows of this presence, as the oracular language of Zech 10:10 makes quite clear. As we explain in our NOTE to "Egypt" in that verse, there was undoubtedly a population of Israelites in Egypt at least from the eighth century onward. The establishment of that community was the result of several factors. The Assyrian policy of mass deportation probably meant that at least some of the population of the Northern Kingdom ended up in Egypt following the fall of Samaria in 722/721 B.C.E. Yet even more credible is that Egypt's historical role as a place of economic refuge continued, with its role as a land of political refuge being added, throughout most of the biblical period. A number of passages in Jeremiah (24:8; 41:17–18; 43; 44; etc.) attest to the presence of refugee Judeans in Egypt by the sixth century. It is probable that there were also northerners who had gone there voluntarily in an earlier period (Hos 7:11; 16; 9:3, 6).

Some important information about one segment of this population of Israelites (both northerners and southerners) in Egypt is provided by the Elephantine materials. These documents reveal the existence of a military community of Aramaic-speaking people, some or most of whom were Jews, in the late sixth and fifth centuries (Porten 1968: 16–17). This military colony maintained close ties with Jerusalem.

Particularly relevant to this Zechariah passage are the data that emerge from one particular Elephantine document, the so-called Passover Papyrus (dated to the fifth year of Darius II, i.e. 419/418 B.C.E.), which is a letter from one Hananiah of Jerusalem to one Jedaniah and the Jewish garrison of Elephantine (Porten 1968: 128–29). This letter enjoins the nonpriestly leaders of the community to keep the Passover by abstaining from work on the fifteenth and twenty-first days of Nisan (the beginning and ending days of that festival) and by locking up all leaven (food forbidden on Passover). Yet the document does not discuss the Passover sacrifice, which was apparently practiced at the temple that served the Elephantine community, although the Jerusalem priesthood frowned on extra-Jerusalem animal offerings (Porten 1968: 133). Thus Hananiah, perhaps Nehemiah's brother (if he is the Hanasi of Neh 1:2) and probably Nehemiah's successor as governor (Neh 7:2; Porten 1968: 130), appears to have tolerated the cultic activity of the colony and allowed the people to celebrate in Egypt what others are enjoined to celebrate only in Jerusalem.

Although the papyrus does not mention Booths, it does attest to the fact that, by the late fifth century, probably not long after the time Second Zechariah takes shape, at least one of the three pilgrim festivals was being celebrated in Egypt—thus without the pilgrimage feature, i.e., without going to Jerusalem (cf. NOTE to "will go up" in v 16). Because this letter deals with a specific issue related to the details of Passover, the absence of any mention of Booths cannot be taken as an indication that the Elephantine community did not celebrate the great fall festival. Indeed, given the special importance of that holiday (see last NOTE to v 16) and the demonstrated adherence of the members of the Elephantine community to the culture of their homeland, there is no reason to doubt that former Judeans and/or Israelites were keeping the Feast of Booths in the late fifth century and probably earlier. Presumably they were doing this, as for the Passover, without going up to Jerusalem. This situation of a Jewish community in Egypt thus may have led the prophet to make sure that, in the eschatological age, the Egyptians should not expect to follow the tradition of the Elephantine community.

Another consideration affecting the special status of Egypt in this passage derives from the international politics of the mid-fifth century. At that period of time, the fortunes of the satrapy of Egypt and the province of Yehud were in some ways linked. As we have described in the Introduction and in several NOTES, there was a satrapal revolt by the Egyptians in 459 B.C.E. In suppressing that uprising, the Persians took measures to secure those parts of the Persian imperial holdings closest to Egypt, namely Yehud and neighboring provinces (see Hoglund 1989 and 1992). The populations of Yehud and Egypt experienced a clampdown by the Persians, for the victorious Persians now took on something of a hard-line policy, in marked contrast to the relative leniency of the earlier decades of Persian rule in the Levant and Egypt (see Meyers and Meyers 1987: xxx–xl). In the eschatological future, the Egyptians would be subjected to a hard-line policy as they were in the prophet's day.

For all these reasons, the special attention to the Egyptians in this verse is comprehensible. The prophet is acutely aware of the past history and the present situation with respect to the interaction of the Egyptians with Yahweh's people. We might add that Second Zechariah's understanding of the Egyptian situation is probably also comprehensive in his use of the singular "family" with respect to Egypt. As we explain in our NOTE to "families of the land" (v 17), that unique expression apparently means "peoples of the land," i.e., nations, and is derived from the altered postexilic biblical nomenclature for social structures. In using the singular for Egypt, its relative cultural unity is thereby expressed. However varied Egypt may have been internally, it nonetheless appeared to outsiders remarkably monolithic and unchanging during its millennia of relatively isolated and self-contained existence.

does not go up and does not come in. The verb for "go up" is ʿlh and refers to pilgrimage to Jerusalem (see NOTE to "will go up" in v 16). The verb for "does not come in" is the Qal participle, with the placement of the accent (bāʾâ) the deciding factor in distinguishing this form from the Qal perfect. There is no serious problem with the text, and the various emendations suggested by commentators are not compelling. This verb augments the idea of "does not go up," a reference to pilgrimage. That is, the not entering no doubt refers to the failure to go into the holy precinct or wherever the holiday festival was held.

then no [rain will be] for them. These words have given rise to a great deal of scholarly discussion and to many suggestions, in the versions and by commentators, for emendation (e.g. Mitchell 1912: 355, 357; Mason 1973: 131; P. D. Hanson 1975: 370–71; R. L. Smith 1984: 291–92; Ackroyd 1962: 655; cf. the omission of the negative in Greek, Syriac, and several Hebrew manuscripts). However, careful attention to the MT shows that the Masoretes have placed a major punctuation break after "them." This break, the *athnach* pause, is never less than the semicolon as an English equivalent. The result is that wĕlō ʿălêhem (literally, "and not upon them") must go with the first part of this verse and not with what comes after. The Masoretes clearly wanted to prevent the reading of these words with the next clause, for such a reading would mean that the Egyptians would not suffer the plague, a meaning that would be just the opposite of what this verse proclaims. Rain not being a suitable punishment for Egypt, something else is needed, and plague would be eminently appropriate (see NOTE below to "the plague . . . smites").

The appearance here of *wlᵓ ᶜlyhm* probably is a deliberate duplication of the same phrase in the preceding verse, with the same meaning intended, namely, that Egypt would be punished, as would the other nations, by the withholding of rain. Thus *wlᵓ ᶜlyhm* is an elliptical repetition of the same words; "and not for them" has the implicit meaning "and no rain will be for them," which is why we supply brackets around the implied words "[rain will be]." Another possible, although less likely, explanation is that "rain will be" (*yihyeh haggāšem*) fell out as the result of haplography (through homoeoteleuton), supposing that the scribe's eye jumped from the *mem* at the end of *ᶜlyhm* to the *mem* at the end of *hgšm*, thereby skipping the last two words. Either way, the meaning would be the same as in the preceding statement: rainfall withheld for violators of the injunction to celebrate Booths.

the plague . . . smites. Here the term for "plague," *maggēpâ*, is the cognate accusative of the verb *ngp*, just as in verse 12 (see NOTES there to "plague" and "smite"). This term for the devastating outbreak of an epidemic disease (as opposed to endemic disease, represented mainly by the biblical *deber*) is used at least once in Exodus to refer to all the "plagues" that Yahweh will send upon the pharaoh and all the people so that they will know Yahweh's incommensurable power (Exod 9:14). Consequently, "plagues" there represents all pestilential disease among the Egyptians subsequently referred to, even though *deber* is used elsewhere in Exodus for the traumatic illnesses to which the Egyptians are subjected (as Exod 5:3 and 9:15; cf. 9:3). "Plague" therefore resonates with the biblical accounting of Egypt's past. The outbreak of plague is presented here as a punishment.

nations. The word is *gôyîm*, as several times above in this chapter (vv 2, 3, 14, 16; see NOTES to this word). Here these foreigners are those who have not learned their lesson from Yahweh's extraordinary intervention and so fail to participate in the festival that would involve their acknowledging Yahweh's sovereignty. Yet such reluctant foreigners, as we have already been told, will be punished with drought (see last NOTE to v 17).

The mention of "nations" in this clause shows that the nations, like Egypt, will suffer a second punishment—not only the withholding of rain but also the devastation of plague. The result is double punishment for both groups. It is as if the author, having specified two actions against Egypt, cannot imagine less than that for other former enemies of Yahweh's people in the eschatological future. Thus although Egypt is treated separately for reasons suggested above (see first NOTE in this verse), the matter of punishment for those not heeding the divine invitation to attend the Feast of Booths involves no favoritism. All peoples had better respond; it will be equally hard for all who refuse to go up to Jerusalem.

19. *sin . . . sin*. The term *ḥaṭṭāᵓt* appears twice here, once in construct with "Egypt" and the second time with "all the nations." The prophet thus continues,

and concludes, the parallel tracks on which he has placed Egypt and other foreigners as two distinct categories of non-Israelites whose fates in the eschatological order diverge (see first NOTE in v 18 and various NOTES to "nations" in this chapter at vv 2, 3, 14, 16, and 18). The word *ḥaṭṭāʾt*, as shown in the NOTE to "for cleansing [sin]" in 13:1, has a range of meanings. There it is part of the vocabulary of sin-offerings and involves the cleansing from sin that certain ritual behaviors effect.

Here, however, as introduced by "Such will be" (*zōʾt tihyeh*), it denotes the behavior, the "sin" or the missing of the mark (which is the basic meaning of the root *ḥṭʾ*), that produces the need for such efficacious ritual acts lest punishment be incurred. It does not refer to the punishment itself (despite the conclusion of *BDB*: 309, which makes this the only place in the Hebrew Bible where it would mean "punishment," and translations such as *NRSV* that accept *BDB*'s analysis). The sin of Egypt, like its punishment, is mentioned separately from that of the other foreigners (see first NOTE to v 18 for a discussion of the reasons for the separate mention of Egypt). This verse is closely related to the preceding ones. Egypt and the nations have both sinned; thus they will both suffer drought and plague (see NOTES to preceding verse).

As we have already pointed out, verses 17–19 give parallel consideration to Egypt and the nations. Yet it should be noted that the nations (referred to as "families of the land," see NOTE above) appear first in verse 17; "the family of Egypt" is then mentioned second, in verse 18. Here the order is reversed—Egypt first, followed by the nations. The result is that this attention to foreigners places Egypt at the center, perhaps another mark of its special place in the eschatological scheme. At the same time, this chiasm binds Egypt and the nations into a single unit: both sin, and both will be doubly punished.

go up . . . Booths. The language here repeats that of v 16 (see NOTES at that verse to "will go up," "celebrate," and "Feast of Booths"), although it is elliptical here, omitting the chronological detail ("every year") and the complementary information about bowing down to Yahweh. Both the first and last verses of this section of the last subunit end with "Feast of Booths," thus forming an inclusion. The response of foreigners to a major national cultural event, operating as an agricultural festival, as well as a marker of an event in Israel's history and a celebration of covenant and Torah, is thereby underscored as the theme of this section. At the same time, it provides a transition to the final verses of this chapter. The Feast of Booths as a cultic event centers on the Temple and Jerusalem, the epicenter of holiness. Thus the holiness theme of verses 20–21 builds on the involvement of foreigners in Jerusalem's holiness in the future age.

20. *On that day*. The last two verses of Zechariah 14 together serve to complete the subunit in which they stand (the fourth subunit of this chapter) and bring both this chapter and all of Second Zechariah to a close. Moreover, in terms of the canonical Book of Zechariah, 14:20–21 forms the conclusion to the entirety of Zechariah. Hence it is noteworthy that verses 20–21 begin and end with the eschatological formula "on that day," these two occurrences of the phrase being the sixth and seventh in this chapter. If much of this prophet's

message has been future directed, the ending of his oracles is emphatically so (for discussion of this formulaic language, see especially the first NOTES to 12:3 and 14:1).

"*Holy to Yahweh.*" The distinction between that which is holy, i.e., that which is associated with the realm of the divine, and that which is mundane or profane, part of everyday life, is fundamental to ancient Israelite thought as to many other religious systems (see Eliade 1961). In the Hebrew Bible, the sanctity of Yahweh is extended to the divine dwelling place and all its paraphernalia. The phrase "holy to Yahweh," not surprisingly, is found largely but not exclusively in priestly texts in the Pentateuch dealing with the Tabernacle, its furnishings, and the sacrificial system. All the products of field and flock brought to the Temple as sacrifice become Yahweh's and are hence considered "holy to Yahweh" (e.g., Lev 23:20; 27:30, 32), as are "dedicated" items taken in battle (Josh 6:19) and precious items sent to the Temple (Ezra 8:28). In these instances the two words (*qōdeš laYHWH*) that are translated "holy to Yahweh" probably form a standard, technical formula used to denote the sanctity of offerings (Haran 1978: 215).

The stereotyped character of the phrase undoubtedly figures in other, extended usages. In several prophetic visions of the future, Jerusalem and even the most profane of its areas become "holy to Yahweh" (Jer 31:39–40); priestly territorial allotments are also considered "holy to Yahweh" (Ezek 48:14). In addition, the spatial dimension of holiness is extended to the temporal in the idea of the sabbath as "holy to Yahweh" (Exod 16:23; 31:15).

Among all the instances, such as the ones just mentioned, in which the phrase "holy to Yahweh" appears, only here and in Exod 28:36 (= 39:30) does it refer to actual words inscribed as a kind of label on an object. In Exodus, these words are to be written like the engraving of a signet on part of the golden diadem set upon the turban of the leading priestly figure, Aaron. As part of one of the most prominent aspects of the high priest's garb, it holds a premier position among the items of greatest sanctity in the elaborate system of graduated holiness that characterizes the sacred precincts of ancient Israel (see Haran 1978: 149–88). This engraved frontlet thus occupies a place of extreme or utmost holiness in the priestly scheme, a role intensified by the way it serves to diffuse or remove any profanity or sin linked to items brought by Israelites to God's precincts: through the inscription "Holy to Yahweh" on his forehead, "Aaron will bear the iniquity of the holy things that the Israelites will sanctify as all their holy donations" (Exod 28:38).

Such a view of the link between priestly holiness and the removal of all the people's sin is alluded to in First Zechariah. Although the inscription "Holy to Yahweh" is not quoted, the words "turban," "iniquity," "engraving," etc., in reference to the garb of the high priest Joshua as he is invested in office in the heavenly court (see Meyers and Meyers 1987: 189–93, 209–12), indicate that the prophetic vision of Zechariah 3 is drawing on the Pentateuchal description of Aaronide garb and its "Holy to Yahweh" element.

This discussion of the phrase "holy to Yahweh" as a designation of the sacral characteristics of materials (and of time) and of its function in removing iniquity provides the information necessary for understanding the imagery of these two verses of Second Zechariah, wherein two items are specified as being "holy to Yahweh." These items are most unlikely ones, in that none of the references to holy items in other biblical texts mention either "horse's bells" or "pots." As we explain in our NOTES to these terms, it is precisely their distance from the sacred realm that makes them appropriate vehicles for the message of these verses. That is, the eschatological age will involve a reversal of temporal reality, with its distinctions between sacred and profane. At that time, even the most profane items will be—as was engraved on Aaron's golden diadem—"Holy to Yahweh."

The choice of horse's bells and pots, however, is not a random selection of everyday items. These two objects have symbolic value relating to warfare and subsistence, the two major themes of this chapter. Warfare is the governing idea of the first and third subunits of Zechariah 14, and concern for agrarian productivity is reflected in the second and fourth subunits.

horse's bells. Some manuscripts have "all" (*kōl*) before "horse's bells" rather than "on." However, the connection of this phrase "Holy to Yahweh" to the details of Aaronic garb (see previous NOTE), where those words are inscribed "on" (*ʿal*) the priest's headpiece, make it likely that this verse intends to indicate a similar inscription "on" these bells. Whether the pots, designated by "every (*kōl*) pot," were likewise inscribed is difficult to determine (see first NOTE to v 21).

The horse is the war animal par excellence in the Hebrew Bible, for it surely was used almost exclusively for military, as opposed to transport, purposes throughout the ancient Near East (see Meyers and Meyers 1987: 113–14; Thompson 1962: 646; and NOTES to "chariot . . . horse" in 9:9 and "like his mighty horse" in 10:3). Because of their association with warfare and with human political power, the Deuteronomist has Moses warning against the Israelite acquisition of horses (Deut 17:14–16), and Samuel repeating the warning (1 Sam 8:11–17). However, although Joshua and David may have heeded such cautionary words (Josh 11:9 and 2 Sam 8:4 mention the disposal of captured horses), later Israelite leaders participated in the acquisition of horses as an essential aspect of political power (1 Kgs 4:26; 2 Chron 9:25, 28; 2 Kgs 14:20; 18:13). The fact that a "Horse Gate" existed in Jerusalem by exilic times (Jer 31:40; 2 Chron 23:15), apparently as an entrance to the royal precincts, indicates the connection of horses to political power.

The horse is thus an apt symbol of all that is antithetical to the conditions of the eschatological age of peace and universal divine sovereignty. As a beast of war and of human political aggression, it represents the antithesis of God's harmonious rule at the end of days. Thus, if it is co-opted into the divine realm by virtue of being emblazoned with the same inscription as is the paraphernalia of the human (Aaron) who comes nearest to God in Yahweh's earthly habitation, it signifies the termination of warfare and power struggles among political states. Then Yahweh will surely reign supreme over all nations.

The word for "bells" (*mĕṣillôt*) is a hapax legomenon, but its meaning is not in doubt. The root *ṣll* ("to tingle, quiver") underlies several words for musical instruments, such as *ṣelṣelîm* and *mĕṣiltayim*, both of which probably refer to "cymbals." If it does not indicate the bells often part of equine trappings, then this term would certainly designate some other metallic band or strip on a horse's trappings, perhaps even on the bridle that stretched across a horse's forehead, just as did the Aaronide headpiece that held the same inscription ("Holy to Yahweh").

Another point of contact with the high priest's apparel (cf. second NOTE to this verse) may lie in the fact that the priest has bells as part of his elaborate garb. The term for "bells" in the description of the priestly garment (*paʿămōnê zāhāb* [Exod 28:33 and 39:25]) is not the same as the one used here (*mĕṣillôt hassûs*), but the appearance of bells on the horse's trappings becomes comprehensible in light of the sacral context of other bells. Although it might seem insulting to compare priests with horses, or the high priest with a horse with bells, the association of priests and bells is worth noting in that it shows how the prophet is making a call for the pervasiveness of sanctity in the eschatological future. Even the bells of a horse will bear the holiness inscription, which is otherwise associated with the high priest himself. Why bells? Because the priest also has bells on his apparel.

pots. The word *sîr*, "pot," apparently designates several kinds of vessels in the Hebrew Bible. It is not certain whether these vessels were all of the same shape but simply used for different purposes. It is equally possible that they were of somewhat different ceramic forms, each used for a different purpose. It is likely that what all the vessels designated *sîr* had in common is that they were used with fire—they were set on hot coals, or they contained coals or ashes. Basically, the biblical use of *sîr* can be divided into two categories: those used in secular contexts and those serving sacral functions.

The term occurs most often to designate a cooking pot, a standard part of the repertoire of Palestinian households since the Bronze Age, if not before (Amiran 1970: 28, 55, 67, 102, 135, 227, 229; cf. Kelso 1948: 11, 27). Produced in various sizes, it was the all-purpose cooking vessel in ancient Israel; water, herbs, spices, vegetables, meat, and/or legumes were combined in such a pot (2 Kgs 4:38–41; cf. Exod 16:3; Ezek 11:3–11; in Ezek 24:3, 6, its use to cook meat is part of the negative imagery comparing Jerusalem to a pot). Both whole vessels and fragments of cooking pots discovered in archaeological excavations are often blackened on the outside, providing evidence of the way they were used to prepare food: the pots were set directly into the coals or else balanced on stones or logs set around the coals (cf. Ps 58:10 [NRSV 58:9]; Ezek 24:11; Eccles 7:6). In addition to referring to a vessel for food preparation, "pot" also can indicate a container used for washing (Ps 108:9 [NRSV 108:10]). As a common household object, the *sîr* lent itself to use in prophetic imagery, perhaps the most famous example being Jeremiah's vision of a pot boiling away from the north (Jer 1:13).

Pots were also used in cultic settings. The Tabernacle texts of Exodus record the presence of bronze "pots," along with shovels, basins, forks, and firepans

(Exod 27:3; 30:3). Within this group of vessels and utensils, the function of the object is designated only for the pots. As part of the appurtenances associated with the "altar of burnt offerings," they were used to carry away the ashes, the remnants of whatever animal was being sacrificed (Lev 6:1-6 [NRSV 6:8-13]). Similar information appears in the Temple text of 1 Kings 7, which describes the bronze work done by Hiram of Tyre for the Temple built by Solomon; "pots" (v 40, reading *sîrôt* for *kîrôt* in many manuscripts, most ancient versions, and the parallel Chronicles text, 2 Chron 4:11; cf. 2 Kgs 25:14 = Jer 52:18, 19) are listed with shovels and basins among the appurtenances of the Temple. These items are not associated with any of the Temple furniture in the Kings account. The reason for this is that they are vessels associated with the bronze altar, and that altar, which must surely have stood in the northeast corner of the Temple courtyard, is strangely absent from the array of courtyard furniture commissioned by Solomon, perhaps because it had already been erected by David (see C. L. Meyers 1992: 359).

In the Zechariah usage, the sacral function of a "pot" is clearly intended. However, in the very next verse the secular aspect appears (see first NOTE to v 21). The twofold use of *sîr* must have been well known to the prophet's audience, so that the playing against each other of the two kinds of pots, each of which has its normal role transformed, is effective in conveying the changed conditions of the eschatological age. The pot as Temple vessel—for it is an object situated in the "House of Yahweh" (see next NOTE)—is among the lowliest of such items. These pots are minor utensils associated with the outer altar, which is the third, or least holy, in the set of three ranks or categories of holiness to which all Tabernacle/Temple materials and furnishings belong. Thus the pots, of all the Temple items, are the ones whose sacral status is lowest and so will be most radically altered by the increase in status involved in being compared to "basins before the altar" (see NOTE below in this verse).

the House of Yahweh. This is the most prominent term in the Hebrew Bible referring to the Jerusalem Temple, although other Yahwistic temples in ancient Israel prior to Josiah's reform may have been so designated. The phrase "the House of Yahweh" (*bēt YHWH*) is first and foremost an architectural designation (see the discussion of the form and function of the temple in Meyers and Meyers 1987: 21-23; cf. C. L. Meyers 1992), but it denotes more than just the Temple building itself. Just as the term *bayit* refers to a dwelling unit as well as its courtyards, furnishings, and implements, among other things (C. L. Meyers 1989: 74), so does the "house" that is God's earthly dwelling include the courtyard(s), furnishings, implements, etc. Indeed, the verse in 1 Kings 7 that mentions the pots made for the Temple concludes with the summary statement that, having "made the pots, the shovels, and the basins, so Hiram completed all the work that he did for King Solomon on the House of Yahweh (*bēt YHWH*)."

Thus the claim that these pots (see previous NOTE) were in the "House of Yahweh" does not mean that they were in the Temple building itself. Rather, they were in the Temple precincts, most likely in the courtyard near the outer altar, for their function was to remove the ashes of the burnt offerings made on that altar. Although these pots are at the bottom of the structure of graduated holiness that characterizes the Temple and everything associated with it, the fact that they are part of the domain of divine holiness is nonetheless clear. The point is that they are to be altered. Just as the objects most mundane and removed from holiness, the "horse's bells" (see NOTE above in this verse), are to become holy, so too are objects already in that category nonetheless subject to transformation in the future age. The pervasiveness of sanctity is such that even items of Yahweh's sacred domain are not exempt from achieving new status.

Although it is found frequently in Haggai and First Zechariah, the use of "the House of Yahweh" here is one of only three references (11:13 and 14:21) to the Temple in Second Zechariah (except for "my House" in 9:8 and the indirect allusions to the sanctity of the Temple in Jerusalem, which is the center of the universe, in 13:1 and 14:8–9; see various NOTES to these verses). Its appearance here need not mean the intrusion of priestly interests into a prophetic work (Zechariah 9–14) that has had little to do with Temple matters. Rather, it is an indication of prophetic recognition that universal holiness will be a major feature of the future age. What better way to convey that notion than to use the images drawn from the epicenter of earthly holiness—God's Temple—to show how holiness extends everywhere from that sacred center!

basins before the altar. This apparently straightforward set of cultic terms is fraught with interpretative difficulty. Unlike "pots," which can clearly be identified as cultic objects, i.e., with bronze vessels that were part of the set of utensils associated with the outer altar of the Temple (see NOTE above in this verse), "basins" (Hebrew *mizrāqîm*; cf. *mizrāqôt*, an alternate plural [e.g., Exod 38:3; Neh 7:70]) can denote cultic items of gold, silver, and bronze (see NOTE to "full like the basin" in 9:15), each of which has a distinct function in Israelite ritual. Futhermore, the term "altar" is ambiguous. Whereas the phrase "corner of the altar" in 9:15 (see NOTE) allows us to identify that altar with the bronze outer altar, inasmuch as "corners" appears only with that altar (Exod 27:2; 38:2; cf. Ezek 43:20; 45:19), this "altar" has no modifier. There were apparently two altars in the Tabernacle and Temple—a small golden incense altar as well as the large, bronze courtyard altar for burnt offerings (the latter does not appear in the 1 Kings Temple text but presumably *was* part of the Temple courtyard furnishings; see C. L. Meyers 1985). Thus the term "altar" alone does not signify which one is meant. The fact that Zech 9:15 almost certainly refers to the courtyard altar does not necessarily mean that this verse refers to the same appurtenance.

Our resolution of these difficulties in this case is contextual. Our NOTES to "Holy to Yahweh" and "horse's bells," two terms mentioned at the beginning of this verse, stress the contrast between the profane world of horses and warfare and the intense sanctity indicated by the phrase "Holy to Yahweh," which was probably an inscription on the headgear of the major priestly figure in ancient Israel. Similarly, our NOTE to "pots," to which these enigmatic altar basins are being compared, emphasizes that these are the most lowly of sacral objects in the hierarchy of sanctity that governs the Temple/Tabernacle structure and all that is used in its ritual. Therefore, the point of mentioning bronze pots used to carry ashes, the dregs of sacrifice, would be to contrast them with vessels of a much more exalted purpose. For that reason, this verse most likely denotes cultic items that were part of the inner furnishings of the Temple rather than part of the set of outer, courtyard appurtenances, because a higher degree of holiness is associated with the inner ones.

The fact that the term "golden" and/or "incense" does not appear with "altar" here does not pose a problem for identifying the altar of this passage with the golden incense altar, for that altar is sometimes designated simply as "the altar," a shortened form of "altar of fragrant incense" (cf. Lev 4:7 and 11). More problematic is the use of "basins" with the incense altar, since such utensils are nowhere mentioned as vessels used exclusively with that appurtenance. Although an elaborate set of golden vessels and tools associated with the golden lampstand and golden table (the other two items of furniture prescribed in the Tabernacle texts for the inner sanctum) are specified, an analogous listing of items used with the golden incense altar is not included in the Pentateuchal account. Furthermore, biblical texts (e.g., 2 Kgs 25:15 and Jer 52:19) mentioning the Temple's utensils are at best ambiguous in their treatment of vessels for the golden incense altar. The Temple texts, if one accepts a chiastic structure for 1 Kgs 7:48–50 (see Hurowitz forthcoming), do seem to have one vessel ("firepans") associated with the incense altar, with "basins" then listed as a vessel for the golden table. Thus, even if there were basins used with the incense altar, they were items shared with the "basins" of the table and probably would have been relatively small vessels.

The difficulty of identifying the "basins" of the incense altar, or any of its putative utensils for that matter, is part of the general set of difficulties surrounding the place of the incense altar in the Tabernacle/Temple cult. The description of that item, one of the three furnishings of the inner sanctum of the Tabernacle, is omitted from the section (Exodus 25) of Exodus containing instructions for the inner furnishings that stood in front of the curtain leading to the holy of holies, the innermost sanctum and holiest place of the entire cultic precinct. The problem of the omission of the incense altar from that passage and its inclusion as an apparent appendix (in Exod 30:1–10) to the prescriptive Tabernacle texts may be more a difficulty of Western ways of viewing an ancient document (so Haran 1978: 228–29) than of an inherent distinction between the incense altar and the other golden furnishings. It is more likely, however, that the incense altar is omitted from the core of the prescriptive texts because its function differs from that of the other items of furniture of the inner sanctum (see C. L. Meyers forthcoming).

The special function of the incense altar, apart from the daily or weekly rituals that were performed with all three of the items of furniture in the inner sanctum, relates to its central location and also, as a concomitant of that position, to the enigmatic "basins" of this passage and various cultic texts elsewhere in the Hebrew Bible. The use of bronze "basins" at the corners of the outer courtyard altar provides the clue to understanding this verse and also the apparent misplacement of the incense altar in the Exodus texts.

It seems that the bronze basins were used for the quantities of blood that were poured at the base of the bronze sacrificial altar in the courtyard, presumably at the corners of that altar (see, e.g., Lev 4:34; cf. Exod 24:6, in which Moses put some blood in vessels and threw [verb, *zrq*] the blood on the altar). Direct information is provided in Leviticus 4 and 5 for this special, nonregular cultic use. The directions of Lev 4:7 and 18 concern offerings made for unintentional sins by a priest or a community. In both cases, a bull was slaughtered in the courtyard and some of its blood was carried *inside* the sanctuary. There the priest first dipped his finger into the blood and sprinkled it seven times in front of the curtain leading to the holy of holies. Then he put some of the blood on the horns of the incense altar. Finally, the rest of the blood was poured out at the base of the courtyard altar.

This series of procedures is noteworthy because it was meant to purge the sanctuary, and by extension the whole sacred precinct, of sin. Similarly, the regular, annual purgation rite (Lev 16:11–19) involved the transfer of blood from the outer altar into the sanctuary and, only in this instance in all of priestly legislature, *into* the holy of holies, the innermost sanctum. The details of this ritual are tantalizingly vague, though they can be reconstructed using biblical evidence along with the information in Misnah Yoma 5:3 (see Levine 1989: 103ff.). Since the incense altar lay in the path the priest would have had to take to perform this rite, it seems probable that the "altar before Yahweh" of Lev 16:12 refers to the golden incense altar, as it surely does in Lev 16:18, which gives instructions for the combined blood of the sacrificed bull (for the sins of the priesthood) and of the he-goat (for the sins of the people) to be smeared on the incense altar's horns and then sprinkled on it seven times.

Both these rites, the one annual event and the occasional or nonregular ones, involved an approach to the innermost sanctum from the outer sanctum. In dealing with a matter of the utmost seriousness, the purgation of the defilement (caused by witting or unwitting sin) that could penetrate the divine dwelling and cause God to withdraw (see Levine 1989: 99 and Milgrom 1991b), vessels ("basins") carried blood from a realm of lesser sanctity—the courtyard— to the one of greatest sanctity. Such vessels were used for a ritual that involved the incense altar in a function *other than* its usual incense-burning role.

These extraordinary circumstances help explain the anomalous location of the incense altar in the Tabernacle texts as well as the confusion about its vessels. They also provide the information that informs the imagery of this passage. The phrase "basins before the altar" of Zech 14:20 alludes to the basins that cross boundaries and that remove all sin. They are thus highly appropriate to the context of this passage, which concerns the transformation of all that is mundane, and theoretically not clean and not allowable in Yahweh's sanctuary, into items as completely and absolutely sacred as are vessels that cross boundaries to approach the utmost sanctity of the innermost space of the sanctuary, in which rests God's unseen presence.

In comparing the least holy "pots" to the "basins before the altar," the simile of Zech 14:20 indicates a change in the essential nature of those pots. A pot used as such a basin is surely a pot radically transformed. Instead of being used for the performance of a menial task, such as taking away ashes, it is instrumental in carrying out a ritual of heightened sanctity. Such will be the eschatological age—when even temple vessels that are already holy by virtue of being part of the furnishings of the "House of Yahweh" (see previous NOTE) have their sanctity vastly intensified.

21. *Every pot*. The NOTE to "pots" in the previous verse explains the different kinds of pot that can be designated by the Hebrew term *sîr*. Although this word in verse 20 clearly refers to the vessels used in the Temple service, because their location in the "House of Yahweh" is specified (see NOTE above), in verse 21 the mundane or secular variety of pot is represented. Because it can mean either a holy or an everyday vessel, the word *sîr* adds to the overall imagery of these two verses, which depict radical changes in familiar items. The pots of God's dwelling place have their sanctity intensified. Something equally transforming must surely occur to their mundane equivalents, and verse 21a describes just what the transformation involves (see NOTES below). Yet the change has already been adumbrated by what happens to the horse's bells in verse 20. They become "Holy to Yahweh," and a similar change is attested here for the pots.

The notion of all mundane pots becoming holy can be linked with some relevant archaeological remains. Several vessels recovered from Iron II strata (at Hazor, Arad, Megiddo, and perhaps Tell Beit Mirsim) bear the inscription *qdš* (see Barkay 1990). This word, either *qādoš* or *qōdeš*, means "holy" or "consecrated." It apparently was used to designate earthenware vessels that were used for certain categories of sacrificial meat. That these deep bowls or kraters were mundane pots in their manufacture is evident from the fact that, in each case, the letters were incised after the vessel was fired. That is, these vessels were not originally intended specifically for sacral use but could be converted to such a function by virtue of the identifying inscription. Furthermore, the fact that the inscriptions are inside the pots and would be covered by any foodstuffs put into them means that the inscriptions identify them as sacral receptacles, regardless of the type of offering they might receive.

In terms of this passage, the inscribed bowls indicate the potential for any pot to become holy, that is, to become intended for sacral comestibles. The difference here is that all pots will become so designated. All food will have the status of sacrifice, and all consumption of food will have a sacral quality.

in Jerusalem and in Judah. The pairing of "Judah" and "Jerusalem" is not a privileging of Judah over the Northern Kingdom but rather the result of Jerusalem's sacred and political centrality, with Judah/Yehud being viewed as an extension of Jerusalem rather than as a separate entity. What happens to Jerusalem and Judah affects all Israel (see NOTES to "concerning Israel" in 12:1 and "against Judah, and against Jerusalem" in 12:2). In the preceding subunit, the special identity of Judah with respect to Jerusalem is expressed in the statement that "Judah also will fight in Jerusalem" (see first NOTE to v 14). In all these cases, "Judah" perhaps functions more as a community of people than as a political unit or as a geographical territory. A similar usage of "Judah" and "Jerusalem" occurs in First Zechariah: "Yahweh will make Judah his inheritance on the Holy Land and will again choose Jerusalem"; Zech 2:16 ([NRSV 2:12]; see Meyers and Meyers 1987: 169–71). There Judah is the entity that exists on "Holy Land," with Jerusalem as its center, a concept not unlike this eschatological portrait of all the land becoming holy (see next NOTE).

holy to Yahweh of Hosts. This phrase repeats the phrase "Holy to Yahweh" of verse 20 (see NOTE above), except that here it is the predicate of a sentence with the verb *hyh* ("to be," with the *waw* consecutive giving it a future meaning), whereas in verse 20 it appears as the subject of the sentence and is something— an inscription—on part of a horse's trappings. Moreover, the epithet "of Hosts" (*şĕbaʾôt*) is added, thus relating this final eschatological image to the language of verses 16 and 17, with their universalism in depicting people from many nations coming to "bow down" (see NOTE in v 16) to "King Yahweh of Hosts" (see the use of "Yahweh of Hosts" as discussed in NOTE to this term in v 16).

At the same time, the idea of everyday cooking pots becoming holy means that all food, and thus sustenance and life itself, will have the status of a sacrificial meal that people share with their deity. That holiness will become all-pervasive among God's people, in contrast to historical reality in which holiness is centered in God's presence and in the physical space and materials associated with God's earthly shrines. Thus the expression of holiness here is the culminating idea of this eschatological statement. The notion that general holiness should be present throughout Israel, by virtue of all people emulating God and adhering to the divine will (as in Exod 19:6 and Deut 7:6), will at last be actualized in the future age (cf. Isa 62:12; Ezek 20:40–41). Furthermore, as the final sentence of this verse makes clear, such pervasive holiness will extend beyond the community represented by Judah and Jerusalem, in that "all who sacrifice" (see next NOTE) will partake of the mundane pots that will now have sacral status.

all who sacrifice. The root *zbḥ* means "to slaughter," that is, to kill an animal. It can simply denote the butchering of an animal, or it can refer to such an act performed as part of a religious ritual. So important was animal, or blood, sacrifice to the Israelite cult that the noun *zebaḥ* derived from this verb means "sacrifice"—usually animal sacrifice, but occasionally sacrifice in general (see especially 2 Chron 7:12; cf. Bergman, Ringgren, and Lang 1980: 12)—and the word for "altar," *mizbēaḥ*, as the "place of slaughter" or the spot where a sacrifice is offered, is also derived from *zbḥ*.

The integral relationship between the slaying of animals and this verb suits well the imagery of the pots with which they are associated in this verse. As explained in our NOTES to "pots" (v 20) and "Every pot" (v 21), the term *sîr* here designates a secular cooking pot, used for preparing stews that usually include meat, although even this everyday pot will become holy in the future age depicted in this chapter.

Thus the verb (used here as a plural participle) represents a confluence of its secular and sacral meanings. It denotes people who are slaughtering animals "in Jerusalem and in Judah" (see NOTE above), i.e., in the community of Israel. But what in historical time would be an act of butchering will in the future be a sacral process, a sacrifice. In some ways, this will be a return to pre-Josianic practice. Before the centralization of the cult, slaughtering of animals in rural shrines apparently had a sacral dimension (Exod 20:24). But the Deuteronomic reform desacralized such practice with its insistence that all sacrificing take place in "the place that Yahweh your God will choose," i.e., at the Jerusalem Temple (Deut 12:4–6, 11), so that the slaughtering of meat in other locales was not considered sacrificial (Deut 12:15).

Because all cooking pots will be "holy to Yahweh of Hosts" (see NOTE above in this verse) in the future age, all slaughtering with the subsequent cooking of food (see NOTE below to "take from them and cook in them") will have the status of sacrifice. The dimension of holiness integral to a sacrificial act thus becomes present at any instance of animal slaughtering. Those "who slaughter," i.e., those who perform the basic act of killing an animal in a locale outside Jerusalem, are automatically participating in a sacred deed usually reserved for a holy precinct. Holiness will be everywhere. Jerusalem's sanctity will be extended throughout the land; Yahweh's home, in a sense, will expand beyond its material reality in Jerusalem (see below, NOTE to "House of Yahweh of Hosts").

will come. The verb "to come" (*bwʾ*) echoes the language of the first subunit. There the verb is used for the eschatological age that "is coming" (see first NOTE to 14:1) and to express that Yahweh "will come" (see NOTE in v 5) in the geomorphological changes that will help bring an end to Jerusalem's subjugated status. On the other hand, in this last subunit, this verb is used in reference to the people who had attacked Jerusalem. They are the ones "that had come" (see NOTE in v 16) against Jerusalem. "Come" there replaces the terms "gather . . . for war" of verse 2 and "waged war" of verse 12. Thus, in this chapter, the verb "come" denotes both Yahweh's coming to save Jerusalem and establish a new order of existence, and the nations coming to fight Jerusalem. Those usages merge in this final statement of the chapter. The nations here will come (cf. "go up" in vv 16 and 17) with positive intent, now that Yahweh will have come with the extraordinary sequence of transforming acts that will create the eschatological era. The very coming of the nations is thereby transformed from a journey with hostile intent to one with the very opposite meaning.

take from them and cook in them. "Them" refers to the pots of Jerusalem and Judah. Although "pot" is singular in verse 21, it appears with "every" and so refers collectively to all pots. And because there are many people coming to sacrifice (the participle denoting these people is plural; see above, NOTE to "all who sacrifice"), there must be many pots in which to prepare the sacral repast. "Them" is preceded by the *min* partitive; thus "from them" means "some of them." The people coming to sacrifice take however many pots they need from the total number of pots in the land, because all will have the condition of holiness necessary for preparing a sacrifice.

The verb translated "cook" is from the root *bšl*, which can mean "to cook" in general (as 2 Sam 13:8), or more specifically "to boil," the latter being the case when the preparation of meat is involved. Which of these aspects of food preparation is intended is less important than the fact that the word can refer to both secular and sacred treatment of comestibles. As such, it is similar to "pots" (see NOTE above in v 20), which can denote containers for everyday use or those that are part of the repertoire of cultic vessels. Indeed, these two terms ("to cook" and "pots") are found together in 2 Chron 35:13, which refers to the preparation of the Passover offerings when Josiah reinstitutes that festival as part of his national political-religious reform.

"Cook" thus allows for the sacred and the profane to merge. This suits the context of verses 20–21, and of this whole chapter, perfectly. What was formerly, at least in preexilic times (see NOTE above to "all who sacrifice"), a desacralized act—namely, slaughtering an animal and eating its meat—will become a sacred act in the future age. The everyday occurrence of food preparation will become holy, with "every pot in Jerusalem and in Judah" (see NOTES above in this verse) now being "holy to Yahweh of Hosts" (see above, NOTE to this phrase).

Neither of the verbs (*lqḥ*, "to take," and *bšl*, "to cook") has a direct object. It is clear, however, that food is what is in the pots. Furthermore, because the contents of the pots have sacrificial status, and because sacrifice typically involves animal sacrifice (see NOTE above to "all who sacrifice"), especially when the word *bšl* is used to specify the technology of food preparation, the food is almost certainly the meat or meat stew that constitutes the people's share of a sacrificial offering.

Canaanite. The Hebrew word is *kĕnaʿănî*. Some translators and communicators render it "trader" (Mitchell 1912: 357; Mason 1977: 133; R. L. Smith 1984: 291; *NRSV*; *NJPS*) or "dealer" (P. D. Hanson 1975: 370). Their reasons for doing so are based on several biblical texts (Hos 12:8 [*NRSV* 12:7]; Zeph 1:11) that use "Canaanite" in contexts that involve mercantile activity. Canaanites, especially those among them associated with Phoenicia and the northern Levantine coast, were renowned for their activities in seafaring and trade. The reputation of Tyre and Sidon (Zech 9:2–3; see NOTES to these cities) as cities rich in silver and gold is related to their favorable location at the intersection of major land and sea routes involving the exchange of goods between various places in three continents. In addition, the New Testament references to people "selling and buying" in the Temple (Matt 21:12–13; Mark 11:15–18; Luke 19:45–46; John 2:13–16), although these passages do not derive from the Zechariah text, have been used to support the idea that "Canaanites" as "traders" is the primary meaning of *kĕnaʿănî* in this verse. Such a meaning for "Canaanites" appears in 11:7, as emended in our translation; see the NOTE at that verse to "merchants of the flock."

Although not ruling out completely the possibility that there is some allusion to merchants in this verse, we deem it highly unlikely. The idea of business transactions taking place in the Temple seems too far afield from the themes and claims of Second Zechariah, especially when the message carried by the use of "Canaanites" as such, which is explained below, would be significantly more appropriate to the context. Similarly, we would rule out attempts to see *kĕna'ănî* as an allusion to some late Second Temple group that was rival to the Jerusalem priesthood, such as the Samaritans (so Horst and Robinson 1964: 260 and Elliger 1975: 178, 186) or some priests jockeying for position during the reign of Antiochus IV (in the second century B.C.E.; so Mason 1973: 292).

Having more or less rejected the idea that *kĕna'ănî* is used euphemistically here, the meaning attached to its literal rendering, "Canaanite," must be explored. The term "Canaan" in the Bible cannot easily be pinned down as a territorial and/or ethnic designation. Although the table of nations in Genesis 10 (v 19) gives specific boundaries for Canaan, other biblical texts are far less precise. Nonetheless, it can be claimed that the Bible typically—in the Penta-teuchal and Deuteronomistic texts in which most references to Canaan and Canaanites occur—refers to these people as inhabitants of the territory that Yahweh is giving to the Israelites. They occupy this role along with a number of other groups inhabiting parts of ancient Palestine, such as the Hittites, Amorites, Perizzites, Girgashites, and Jebusites (e.g., Gen 15:21; Josh 3:10; Judg 3:5), among others.

Although it may be the case that Palestine was inhabited by a complex mosaic of ethnic groups when Israel established a presence in the Levant (see Deut 7:1), it is also true that the term "Canaanite" is often used to denote all such groups, perhaps because the Canaanites were culturally, territorially, and/ or politically dominant. Judges 1:1, for example, raises the question of "who shall go up . . . against the Canaanites," and subsequent verses in Judges (e.g., 1:4) depict struggles against the Canaanites as well as others. Also noteworthy, in a work of the postexilic period, is the use of "Canaanites" at the head of a long list of "peoples of the land" in Neh 9:8, and then the use of "Canaanites" alone, in an analogous passage in Neh 9:24 relating how God had "subdued before them the inhabitants of the land, the Canaanites, and gave them into their hands, with their kings and the peoples of the land." Furthermore, even when a whole list of peoples appears, Canaanites are characteristically first. Thus this term is used synecdochically, with all non-Israelites in Palestine often referred to as Canaanites.

This pattern of usage is accompanied by the fact that the people so designated are almost always presented in a negative light. Biblical references to Canaanites, as representatives of the ongoing threat to the political, religious, and cultural integrity of Israel, are typically hostile. Although we have no explicit reason to believe that Canaanites were a particularly unsavory group of people, they are surely presented as the antithesis of all that was desirable for Israelite national identity. Deuteronomy 20:16–18 is perhaps among the most extreme statements of the tension between Israel and Canaan: all those peoples in the land must be annihilated. The Israelites may make peace with, or kill only the warriors of, enemies outside the land promised to them, but the Canaanites must be obliterated so that they cannot "teach you [the Israelites] to do all the abhorrent things they [the Canaanites] do" (Deut 20:18). The problem of cultural bound-aries between the Israelites and others in the territory they claimed must have been extraordinarily acute to have evoked such heightened anti-Canaanite polemic.

Because Zechariah 14 is replete with presentations of radical reversals of historical and natural reality as the future age dawns, the ultimate reversal would be a change in the status of Canaanites, the paradigmatic and ever-present threat to Israelite integrity and identity. Most other portions of this chapter deal with problems of external threats to survival—the onslaught of the foreign nations— and the continual internal agony over the procurement of sustenance in a marginal environment. But the historical threat to the covenant ideals that Canaanite culture represents is not part of the future vision of this chapter. Nor does it figure in the martial language of chapters 9 and 10, which show Israel and Yahweh ascendant over neighboring imperial powers and inhabitants of the greater land of Israel but does not address the internal Canaanite threat (except perhaps in 13:2, with its references to idolatry and the "spirit of impurity" in the land; see NOTES to that verse).

Whether such a danger of syncretism persisted into the mid-fifth century is impossible to determine. It may well have, although perhaps without the all-pervasiveness of Canaanite inroads that biblical sources report for the preexilic era. Indeed, the attention given to foreign wives in Ezra, Nehemiah, and Malachi is probably not a purely sociological matter but, rather, is related to the problems of religious syncretism involved in intermarriage with non-Yahwistic groups. Thus, in the retrospective consciousness that is so evident in Second Zechariah's portrayal of the future, attention to the historical threat of Canaanite culture to Yahwism would certainly not be out of place. Moreover, "Canaanite" may in fact have become a euphemistic term denoting not "trader" but rather the ever-present danger that the ideals of Yahwism represented in the covenant between God and Israel might be subverted or corrupted by competing influences. In this case, it surely deserves a place in the climax to Second Zechariah's vivid eschatological scene.

That there will no longer be a "Canaanite" in the Temple, which really indicates the larger territory of God's domain and not simply an architectural entity in Jerusalem (see above, NOTE to "in Jerusalem and in Judah"), may be a way of saying, as has so often been said in these last two verses, that traditional boundaries will dissolve in the future age. All the land will partake of Temple holiness. Hence all its inhabitants will become God's people: Canaanites will no longer be in Yahweh's house, because that which defines "Canaanite"—a culture in tension with Yahwism—will no longer exist. Another possibility is that the Canaanites, as enemy par excellence of the Israelites, will finally be completely banished or eliminated, thus no longer posing a threat to the sanctity of Yahweh's people, land, or Temple.

If the former situation obtains, with the Canaanites losing their identity and becoming integrated into the Israelite population of the land, then this transformation would be the most extreme of the universalizing aspects of this last subunit of Zechariah 14 (cf. the universalizing conclusion to First Zechariah in 8:20–23). Peoples or nations outside Jerusalem's territory will acknowledge Yahweh's sovereignty as they come up to Jerusalem to participate in a key celebration (v 16). But they will still retain their national identity, and there is still the possibility that their recognition of Yahweh's kingship will erode. Evidently, as long as they ceased to be a security threat to Yahweh's people, such failings would be dealt with by punishments ("no rain" [v 17]; "plague" [v 18]). Such leeway, however, would be intolerable for the foreign people within Israel's borders. The dynamics of establishing cultural boundaries where territorial ones were blurred had failed historically; the only solution would be the dissolution of "Canaanites" as the discernible other in the landscape of that part of Yahweh's worldwide domain inhabited by Israel.

House of Yahweh of Hosts. This phrase combines the language of verse 20, which has "House of Yahweh" (see NOTE above), and of this verse, which has "Yahweh of Hosts" (see NOTE to "holy to Yahweh of Hosts"). In the joining of these two phrases, the concept of the sacred domain of Yahweh and the heavenly retinue becoming all-pervasive in the eschatological age is heightened, especially given the temporal orientation provided by the concluding words of this book (see next NOTE).

on that day. This formula is used here for the seventh time in Zechariah 14. Because it is not really needed in this sentence, it must have been deliberately added to bring the number of its occurrences up to the right amount, seven. Indeed, it is highly suitable for this eschatological formula to appear here, once more in Second Zechariah, as the final words of this subunit, chapter, and biblical book. From beginning to end, Zechariah 9–14 has been oriented to the future—not to a foreseeable historical shifting of Yehud's fortunes, but rather to a suprahistorical establishment of a radically different order of reality. Despite the historical specificity of much of the literal language and of many of the evocative images, the direction in which that use of language and metaphor consistently looks is the eschatological future. Thus this phrase (discussed throughout, but see especially NOTES in 12:3, 13:1, and 14:1, 4) both echoes and summarizes the dominant tone of this prophet's literary expression of hope for all humankind.

COMMENT

The marked eschatological thrust of Second Zechariah culminates in the astonishing series of end-time images of chapter 14. Whereas the previous depictions of the future by this prophet are focused almost entirely on what will happen to Israelites, Judeans, Jerusalemites, the royal bureaucracies, and the Davidic line, the last chapter builds on the notion that Jerusalem will be restored. That restoration is no small part of the future vision; indeed, the physical well-being and security of the holy city are crucial aspects of the expected world order. Yet bringing the new Jerusalem into being is only a part of the larger redemptive scheme. God's ultimate purpose in rescuing and reestablishing the people in Zion is that the rest of the world will join in the acknowledgment of Yahweh's sovereignty.

That ultimate goal, which will allow for Israel's enduring existence and prosperity, cannot be achieved by the normal course of events in historical time. The prophet's awareness of the history of the past several centuries has led him to conclude that the ancient ideal of a people dwelling securely and autonomously in a land promised to their ancestors by Yahweh will not be realized without earthshaking (!) changes. The conquest of Israel and then Judah by enemies from the north/east may have been efficacious in bringing Yahweh's people to a better understanding of their covenant obligations and thus to a hope for national renewal in their traditional homeland. Yet benign as Persian rule may have seemed in contrast to Assyrian and Babylonian imperial subjugation, Achaemenid policy, especially as it developed in the fifth century, did not include Yehudite independence or Davidic rule. Rather, it involved Persian forts and officers, and it entailed economic drain in the form of tribute to the dominant superpower.

No resolution seemed forthcoming within the foreseeable course of events. As the centuries of Persian control continued, foreign hegemony seemed as strong as ever. Indeed, recent scholarship (see the essays in Sancisi-Weerdenburg 1987) has shown that Achaemenid strength was sustained throughout the fifth century and beyond, in contrast to the previously held view that the mid-fifth century marked the beginning of a period of decay and decadence. Thus the emerging solution for Second Zechariah is the vision of a radically different future. Throughout this chapter, the theme of radical transformation is central. Dealing with the age-old problems of Israel's economic and political vulnerability, it sees the resolution of those problems in the radical changes that God will effect in the world. There will be a new creation. Only then will God's creation of Israel become eternally assured. It will no longer be internally contingent; rather, it will be externally validated.

This message is conveyed in various ways throughout Zechariah 14. The longest chapter of Second Zechariah, its twenty-one verses fall thematically into four subunits. Overall, these subunits form an *abab* structure:

CHART 14
STRUCTURE (*abab*) OF ZECHARIAH 14

1. 5 verses: 1–5	*a*	Warfare/divine rescue begins
2. 6 verses: 6–11	*b*	A new order/economic and political security for Jerusalem
3. 4 verses: 12–15	*a*	Divine rescue culminates/enemies vanquished
4. 6 verses: 16–21	*b*	A new order/inclusive holiness

The first subunit sets the scene, a classic one in Israelite history. Jerusalem's theoretical inviolability is still/again at stake. The cosmic forces set in motion in response to Jerusalem's predicament, however, affect more than just her political survival; the second subunit shows how her entire ecosystem is altered, bringing about a transformation in her economic viability as well as her political destiny.

The third subunit then completes the vivid description of the rescue of Jerusalem. Finally, in the fourth subunit, the components of Jerusalem's agrarian and political security are reworked into the vision of Yahweh's universal sovereignty over a fully sanctified earthly realm.

The theme of transformation is present not only in the explicit language and in the symbolic vehicles of all subunits. It also operates in the way certain words and images are turned upside down in the course of this chapter's discourse. Throughout our NOTES, we indicate how the antonymic shifts in lexical arrangements and in the meaning of familiar tropes brilliantly signify the foundational changes that lie ahead. Biblical eschatology reaches its most developed point in this bold depiction of an altered natural order and the concomitant alteration in the world of human affairs.

The special role of Jerusalem in this complex eschatological vision deserves reiteration and special attention. As we have noted earlier, this chapter differs from the future visions of the other materials collected in Second Zechariah that are specific in their inclusion of the various components of Israel (northerners and southerners, exiles and those left behind) or greater Israel (Philistia, Phoenicia, and even southern Syria). Here, although Judah is mentioned (vv 14 and 21), the focus is clearly on Jerusalem. There is no discussion here of reestablishing borders, returning the dispersed to their homeland, or reuniting the divided nation. Does this Jerusalem-centered perspective negate the participation of all Israel in the eschatological redemption and restoration?

The answer to that question is negative in our estimation. There are several reasons for concluding that the overriding interest in Jerusalem's fate is not meant to exclude any segment of God's people, but rather serves to make the future restoration all-inclusive. For one thing, the canonical position of this chapter is such that it completes and extends, rather than contradicts, what precedes it. Perhaps it is precisely because the various parts of all Israel have already been individually considered in this prophetic anthology that the last chapter can go beyond such factional interests.

A second and related factor is that Jerusalem, although existing in antiquity as an individual city with its own distinct urban configuration and character, is hardly an ordinary place in biblical tradition. The name "Jerusalem" (or one of the related terms—"Zion," "City of David") is found hundreds and hundreds of times in the Hebrew Bible. As the locus of God's earthly dwelling place, Jerusalem is viewed as a site holy to Yahweh and thus the center of the cosmos. It thus signifies, through its particular and intense sanctity, the larger human and territorial configurations that acknowledged its role as the very source of their existence and as the key to their hope for survival, prosperity, and peace. In short, Jerusalem's symbolic value precludes its figuring here as the mere insignificant outpost in the Judean hills that it was in the Persian period, or even as the swollen metropolis that it was at its greatest preexilic extent, when it was attacked by "all the nations" with the awful results that are reflected in the imagery of the first subunit of this chapter.

A third point, which follows from the second one, is the oppositional relationship between Jerusalem as the holy center on the one hand, and all the nations at the perimeter on the other. In a sense, this chapter accomplishes on its own what all the seven-plus-one visions of First Zechariah portray together (see Meyers and Meyers 1987: liv–lviii, and charts 8A and 8B, for a presentation of the structures of Zechariah 1–8). That is, First Zechariah consists of concentric circles of interest: Jerusalem and the Temple are at the center, surrounded by Jerusalem's territory (more or less equal to Yehud), and then by the international setting of foreign nations—all of these surrounded by the encompassing universal dominion of Yahweh. For Zechariah 14, Jerusalem (with its Temple) is the beginning and the end of existence. Its role as symbolic center means that Yahweh "begins" universal dominion from the Temple; thus the eventual recognition by the nations of Yahweh's sovereignty will, as described in the last subunit, ultimately bring the nations to Jerusalem. The focus on Jerusalem, therefore, is surely inclusive of all Israel if this subunit portrays in its final inclusive statements the pilgrimage to Jerusalem of even foreign nations as participants in the national cultic events celebrating God's reign from the holy city.

Jerusalem's Devastation and Rescue, 14:1–5.

The first subunit begins, as do the opening verses of chapters 10, 11, and 13, by echoing the end of the preceding chapter. The presentation of Jerusalem under siege and then conquered, with both its physical and demographic integrity severely violated, recapitulates to a certain extent the material of Zech 13:7–9, in which Yahweh's people and their land suffer devastation. In both chapter 13 and here, some portion of the people survive and remain in their land.

The details involved in the depiction of Jerusalem and/or Judah falling prey to the onslaught of "all the nations" are surely drawn from Israel's historical experience of being conquered by the imperial powers of the mid-first millennia and having some portion of her population carried off into exile. What is different here, and somewhat confusing if not problematic, is the eschatological language. Is there to be yet another wave of imperial aggression against Jerusalem as the future age begins? Although that possibility cannot be ruled out, it is much more likely, as we suggest in our first NOTE to verse 1, that the eschatological perspective of postexilic prophecy views the past destruction and exile as the initial stages of the judgment and then redemption that characterize Yahweh's scheme for dealing with the wayward people. Because, as we have already pointed out, the restoration and return of the late sixth century did not bring into full realization the scenario, found in preexilic and exilic prophecy, of a renewed and autonomous Israel, fifth-century prophecy was compelled to revise the existing prophetic evaluation of destruction and exile vis-à-vis the concept of an ensuing glorious reestablishment of Israel.

Thus the traumatic events of the sixth century became open-ended, incomplete. They were no longer seen as terminating after seventy years, as the prophecies of Jeremiah had projected (Jer 25:11–12) and as First Zechariah had expected (Zech 1:12 and 7:3, 5; see Meyers and Meyers 1987: 117–18). Rather, the continuing foreign domination of Yehud, the ongoing dispersion of many Israelites and Judeans, and the lack of a Davidide in a position of monarchic rule in Jerusalem could not be viewed as congruent with the actualization of the future age of national restoration that was supposed to be the successor to the age of destruction and dispersal. The relatively benign Persian hegemony, although not exactly identified with the radical disruption brought about by Assyrians and Babylonians, was still an impediment to the fulfillment of prophetic expectations.

The successful rebuilding of the Temple was surely viewed (as in the prophecies of Haggai and First Zechariah) as a highly significant sign of Yahweh's renewed presence among the people and of special divine favor for Jerusalem/ Zion. Yet Temple restoration in and of itself did not constitute the full restoration of the city's former glory and power, however idealized those features might seem centuries after the reality of Davidic and Solomonic internationalism. Nor did Yehud's subordinate position within the Achaemenid empire represent an actualization of the anticipated centrality of Zion as the object of international attention and obeisance.

From this perspective, the historical onslaughts against God's people could be viewed as not yet complete, for the essential redemptive consequences had not yet arrived. Persia itself may not have perpetrated the conquest of Jerusalem, the ravishing of its women, the plundering of its dwelling places, and the removal of half the remaining population, but because of its impeding full restoration it too must be included in the generalized indictment of "all the nations" that interfere with Yahweh's plan for the holy city. Thus the language of destruction and dispersal has ongoing application. The city of Second Zechariah's day was still a shadow of its former self, in geographic and demographic size. It could hardly yet be the city of the glorious future age.

The description of destruction in verses 1–2 provides what is basically a replay of the sixth-century events, which are the most relevant historical materials. But here they are transposed into an apocalyptic mode, with the end result to be very different from what happened at the hand of the Babylonians. Because of the relative integrity of the Persian empire, despite the occasional threats to the integrity of its western territories, the prophet sees no immediate danger to Jerusalem and gives no chronological markers to indicate when the final battle will occur. Instead, he relies on traditional prophetic terminology signifying the eschatological future ("on that day," etc.). Yet, ultimately, Israel's enemies will be destroyed; and that destruction will be a response to their conquest of Jerusalem, a future conquest that in a sense continues the conquered status of Jerusalem that has lasted from 587/586 B.C.E. to the prophet's own time.

However, in describing the awful fate of Jerusalem, Zech 14:1–2 is also notable for its absence of rhetoric about Jerusalem's sins. Whereas preexilic and exilic prophets portrayed Jerusalem's fall as the inevitable consequence of idolatry and covenant disloyalty, the thrust of Second Zechariah in relating once more the sorry state of Yahweh's people and chosen city is the impending terrible consequences (subunit three) to the nations for their assault on the city. Of course, the initial result of God's response to Jerusalem's predicament will necessarily be the long and intensely anticipated eternal restoration of Jerusalem (subunit 2). But so different will the world be as the result of this divine intervention that even the nations themselves will experience some sort of restoration (subunit 4). The eschatological emphasis is on an extraordinary transformation that will affect all creation.

It is the fact of a change in the natural order, introduced in the first subunit, that leads inescapably to the conceptualization of a radical alteration in the status of all who inhabit the world: Yahweh's people and the nations as well. As earlier in Zechariah 9–14, and as elsewhere in Hebrew prophecy, Yahweh responds to the helplessness of the people. Their very lack of power in the world calls forth language that conveys Yahweh's might. With power most vividly expressed in terms of the political language of warfare, Yahweh as divine warrior plays a decisive role in the reversal of Jerusalem's reduced and subjugated condition. However, the traditional martial language attached to presentations of Yahweh's actions on behalf of Israel here take on a new dimension.

Certainly the biblical metaphor of Yahweh as warrior is characteristically reticent in projecting upon Yahweh the actual weapons of human assault (Brettler forthcoming). Rather, there is a marked tendency to use images of meteorological phenomena, perhaps related to the language of theophany, to express Yahweh's martial might. That is, God is portrayed as using natural elements to effect political change. Thunder and lightning, the rush of streams, the parting of waters, the sweep of a storm, the eclipse of sun or moon—all these phenomena are linked in biblical conceptualizations of the miraculous power of Yahweh to intervene in human affairs. This propensity for the use of natural imagery rather than the imagery of human warfare perhaps helps the biblical authors to avoid attributing human characteristics, and thus limitations, to Yahweh. For whatever reason, natural imagery abounds in divine warrior passages.

Yet the way the prophet here uses the language of nature in the service of the warrior metaphor for Yahweh takes that imagery to a new mode of divine action and intervention. All the characteristic biblical expressions of Yahweh's martial role, although using images of unusual or exceptional natural events, do not present these phenomena as altering permanently the shape and essence of the material realm as it has existed since the beginning-time of creation, or at least since the second, post-Noahian creation. Not so for Zechariah 14, which introduces images not found in any divine warrior typology in its depiction of fundamental alterations in the natural world.

The prophet depicts the alteration of the geomorphology of Jerusalem's environs in verses 4 and 5 with a distinct sensibility to the military vulnerability of the city and with an eye as to what it would take to transform the superiority of an invading army into one of a force facing inevitable and terrible defeat. The earth movements that will bring about such results involve the splitting of the ridge east of the city, the Mount of Olives, to provide a secure foothold for Yahweh's attack on the enemy camp; the notion of commanding the heights as a strategic advantage is part of the anthropomorphic image of Yahweh astride the eastern ridge. The splitting of the Mount of Olives thus gives Yahweh, as the military aggressor, striking supremacy and stability. At the same time, a great rift is created, thereby allowing for the escape of the remnants of Yahweh's people trapped in Jerusalem; they can flee through this valley, leaving the enemy to suffer the ensuing punitive actions of Yahweh.

The prophet then recalls a historical event to underscore the extraordinary changes that will result; he reminds his audience of the tumult and fear evoked in the eighth-century earthquake when Uzziah was king. Yet the evocation of that event is not meant to be a comparison of past geomorphic changes with future eschatological ones; for the future earth shifts will alter radically and forever Jerusalem's landscape, whereas such extensive changes are not to be understood for the great seismic shock of Uzziah's day. The recollection of the centuries-earlier tremors, rather, is meant to indicate the effect among humans that any such shift in the earth's surface causes. If the earthquake of the eighth century struck terror in the hearts of all who felt it, so much more will the dramatic eschatological changes in the shape of the hills and valleys of Jerusalem penetrate the psyches of those who will witness those changes. In the eighth century people fled because of earthquake; they will do so again in the apocalyptic future because of great earth movements, movements that will assure the safety of Yahweh's people and then the destruction of the enemy.

These extraordinary changes in the natural order, however, cannot be understood only in terms of their military and political efficacy. To be sure, the changes in landscape will directly affect Jerusalem's strategic position and, therefore, her political viability. At the same time, her economic role and viability will be dramatically altered by another series of cosmic changes accompanying those portrayed in verses 4–6. Thus, before specifying the way in which Jerusalem's enemies are to be destroyed, the prophet shifts to a depiction of the radically new meteorological and ecological conditions that will also be established in the future and that will transform Jerusalem's historical marginality into an environment conducive to eternal prosperity.

Jerusalem Restored, 14:6–11

The quest for political autonomy and the hope for national restoration surely dominate this chapter, as they do much of Second Zechariah and, indeed, of postexilic prophecy in general. Yet it must not be overlooked that Israel's survival depended not only on freedom from external oppression or domination but also on the internal productivity of the territory she claimed. Environmental constraints were no less serious than imposed political restraints in determining the ability of Yahweh's people to flourish in their homeland.

Many biblical texts exhibit awareness of the fact that there are serious risk factors involved for a people attempting to establish a secure existence in the highlands of Palestine. The covenant language of blessings and curses in Leviticus (26:4–5, 10 and 26:19–20) and, especially, Deuteronomy (28:4–5, 11–12 and 28:23–24, 38–40) expresses in theological terms the dangers to agriculture in Israel's territory. That is, the failure of crops is viewed as divine punishment for covenant disobedience. Surely the reality of an environment only marginally able to provide subsistence for its population underlies such depictions of horror. That ecological reality is now quite well understood, as the result of recent sophisticated studies of the parameters of agricultural development in the central hill country of Palestine (see especially Hopkins 1985, Frick 1985, and the works cited in both these valuable studies).

On the basis of contemporary analysis of highland ecosystems and through consideration of biblical texts referring, often obliquely but also sometimes quite explicitly, to agricultural failure, it is clear that the heartland of ancient Israel, especially the Jerusalem district, is characterized by conditions that preclude year-by-year predictability and stability in subsistence farming. These conditions include intersecting meteorological and geomorphological features: temperature extremes, shifting growing seasons, wide ranges in annual rainfall, and rugged landforms. These four features all involve such great variability in central Palestine that there is considerable risk for any people attempting to survive, let alone thrive, within the existing environmental parameters. Despite the technological and social mechanisms developed by the highland farmers to cope with the limitations and challenges of the local ecosystems, the agricultural system they developed never fully transcended their vulnerability to the ever-present danger that conditions in a given year or sequence of years would cause shortages that no amount of risk-spreading strategies could forestall.

If the dangers of crop failure lurked in normal times, they were surely exacerbated by the prevailing conditions of postexilic Yehud. Tax payments to the Achaemenid realm cut into yields available for domestic use. Furthermore, the sixth-century decimation of the population posed an additional threat. Mature vineyards and orchards, which require long-term investments of time and energy to be brought to desired levels of productivity, would have been damaged, perhaps to a point beyond recovery, by the ravages of warfare and, more seriously, by the lack of labor to tend and maintain them and the terraces on which they were planted. In short, normal climatic and topographical constraints were no doubt compounded by imperial taxation and by the sparsity of population in Yehud during the first half of the Achaemenid period.

Palestinian farmers thus never escaped a sense of vulnerability with respect to the natural world. Consequently, the eschatological vision of political security in Second Zechariah would have been incomplete, if not meaningless, without an accompanying anticipation of economic security. For a people whose economy was almost entirely based on its agricultural resources, the prospect of a risk-free environment thus would constitute an essential part of the eschatological picture. The second subunit of Zechariah 14 provides exactly that.

The various NOTES to verses 6–8 and 10 demonstrate how the prophet envisions that the critical variables affecting agrarian productivity in the region around Jerusalem (and thus for all Israel) will be dramatically changed in the future age. No longer will the agrarian families, which constituted the majority of the population, need to experience ever-present anxiety about their very survival. All the meteorological and topographical features that could adversely affect their livelihood will be radically altered. All risks will disappear. The dangers of damaging frosts, the constraints of a limited growing season, the specter of insufficient rainfall, and the limitations of the rugged terrain—all these sources of risk, and hence of anxiety and potential suffering and death, will be removed by a new natural order in the end-time.

Together, the new climatic and geomorphological features will result in providing economic security. This will be accomplished by the effect of each of the four individual changes. In addition, the composite environmental picture will create an unparalleled ecological uniformity in the highlands. The central hill country (see C. L. Meyers 1983b for a discussion of Galilee in particular) is notoriously fractured, with the result that it consists of many micro-ecosystems that are quite diverse, despite their overall similarity on a macro-level. As a result of the great variation within a small geographic area, individual producing units needed to make subtle adaptations to the prevailing crop regimens and farming strategies. Even then, and even with the cooperative adjustments that existed at the village or even regional level, the fact remained that there was inevitable and habitual disparity in the productivity of agrarian units occupying neighboring but divergent environmental niches.

The potential consequences of such disparity—socioeconomic hierarchization and social tension—are virtually unavoidable. Thus the leveling out of all environmental variables in the eschatological future not only would provide economic security for all but also would create conditions optimal for social harmony and stability. Resources would be equally and abundantly available to all with the dissolution of the multitude of discrete eco-niches that characterize the Palestinian highlands. The features of the new natural order clearly point toward a new social order, as well as new economic and political ones.

It should not go unnoticed that a new religious order is also implied by the establishment of an environment offering full economic security. As noted above, the very insecurity of the Palestinian environment was incorporated into covenant language: agrarian success is linked to covenant obedience, and failure of field, stable, and even womb is viewed as consequent upon disobedience. The idea of a risk-free environment thus brings with it the concept of a covenant without such contingencies, or of God's people manifesting totally faithful covenant behavior. Either way, a new idea of covenant can be inferred from the new creation, an idea consonant with the concepts of a new covenant in the exilic prophecies of Jeremiah and Ezekiel.

Most of this subunit presents the radical and leveling changes in the environment that will enhance the future age in Jerusalem's hinterland. Yet, in its special urban character, the city itself will retain its distinction from the surrounding territory. The mountainous setting of the city, a critical aspect of its participation in the phenomenology of "sacred center," will not only remain but will be enhanced when all the area around it becomes flattened. Jerusalem's sacral quality will thereby be intensified. This depiction of Jerusalem's elevated position, literally speaking (cf. the well-known depictions of the future Jerusalem in Isa 2:2–4 and Mic 4:1–3), adumbrates its lofty status, in political and cultical terms, as presented in the final subunit of this chapter.

This anticipation of Jerusalem's role in God's universal sovereignty is present not only in the portrayal of its geographical situation but also in the implications of the liturgical fragment embedded in this subunit. Thus far we have treated verses 6–10 as if they dealt entirely with the arrangement of the climate and landscape of Jerusalem. Although this may be true in a very broad sense, it is also the case that the description of Jerusalem's hinterland as it will appear in its radically new form in the eschatological future encompasses a verse (14:9) of a somewhat different character.

Calling the two lines that form verse 9 a liturgical fragment serves to acknowledge the way this verse seems to interrupt the sequence portraying future changes in the natural realm. It stands, somewhat apart, as a text apparently taken from some ceremonial or festival liturgy. Indeed, because of the connection below, in verse 16, between the Feast of Booths and Yahweh's kingship, some scholars postulate that these lines are from an actual Yahwist enthronement festival, which is thought to be part of the annual Feast of Tabernacles (Exod 23:16; 34:22) in the autumn (so Mowinckel 1962: 1:16–92; 2:222–50; Gaster 1961: 442–59).

This hypothesis of a Sukkoth (Booths, or Tabernacles) celebration including a component recognizing Yahweh's royal sovereignty, as manifest in or symbolized by divine control of cosmic waters, is to some extent supported by the specific positioning of the liturgical fragment in this subunit. The liturgical lines come precisely after the specification of the eternal and abundant water source to be provided by the "living waters" of Jerusalem. The new world order will mean an entirely beneficial supply of fresh waters emerging from the cosmic sources below Jerusalem and the Temple. The presence of these purifying waters may be related to Yahweh's universal rule, mythically portrayed in divine control over cosmic waters. If so, the divine sovereignty connected to the Tabernacles celebration of verses 16 and 17 would be present in a refrain appropriately placed after the description of the ever-flowing waters of the future age.

However, that these lines were ever recited at an early Israelite festival cannot be established with certainty. And the concomitant suggestion that such a ceremony included elements of a Babylonian New Year's festival may be pushing the evidence too far (see M. S. Smith 1990: 59). Rather, the explicitly universalistic quality of this verse, as we explain in our NOTES (see especially last NOTE to v 9), could hardly have predated the Exile. Thus it is not impossible that the author of this part of Second Zechariah himself composed these two lines, which were to become an important part of postbiblical Jewish liturgy. They form the conclusion of the *alenu*, a prayer of adoration said at the end of every Jewish worship service since antiquity.

The specific placement of this liturgical fragment within the description of the eschatological Jerusalem is appropriate, as we have suggested, in terms of its connection to the control of waters by Yahweh as king. In addition, the juxtaposition of themes represented by the arrangement of this subunit—divine sovereignty and control of natural phenomena—in other biblical passages dealing with Yahweh as king is noteworthy. Especially in Psalms, Yahweh's role as ruler of all the earth is related to divine control of the natural realm (Ps 29:10; 74:12). Moreover, the very use of cosmic language for Jerusalem along with the metaphor of Yahweh's royal sovereignty appears in Ps 48:1–2 as well as in this chapter of Zechariah.

Thus the irruption of an apparently discrete liturgical fragment into the text of the second subunit is not so disruptive as it might at first seem. It meshes with the message of this section of Zechariah 14. And in its utilization and expansion of an earlier biblical text, in this case a Deuteronomic one (see NOTES to this verse), it exhibits one of the prevalent characteristics of Second Zechariah's prophecy.

Through both the descriptive materials and the lines of prayer, the security of Jerusalem and the sovereignty of Yahweh are proclaimed in verses 6–11. It remains then to elaborate on the fate of Jerusalem's foes—first the bad news, in the third subunit, and ultimately the good news, the positive outcome, in the final subunit.

The Fate of Jerusalem's Foes, 14:12–15.

The first section of Zechariah 14, especially verses 3–5, presents the martial actions of Yahweh on behalf of conquered Jerusalem. Those verses provide us with an image of an anthropomorphic, or rather gigantimorphic, Yahweh astride the twin peaks of the divided Mount of Olives, ready to strike the armies that had attacked and entered Jerusalem as soon as the remnant of Jerusalem's population escapes through the new rift valley east of the city. This third section of Zechariah 14 now describes what will happen to the enemy occupying Jerusalem; it depicts three ways in which the foes are to be destroyed.

First is the epidemic disease, or plague, that will decimate the enemy troops. As we indicate in our NOTES to verse 12, the close quarters of any military encampment create conditions that are ripe for contagious and deadly disease— a plague—to spread like wildfire and cause widespread death and incapacitating illness within a very short period of time. Thus, although Yahweh is depicted as smiting the enemy with plague, the quasi-military language of verse 12a does not imply a discrete martial strike by God against the nations. Rather, plague is an oft-present threat to all closely quartered troops under the premodern conditions of poor sanitation and nutrition and lack of effective medical treatment. Enemies attacking Jerusalem had been so affected historically, as the account of the sudden demise of "one hundred eighty-five thousand" Assyrians who besieged Jerusalem in the days of Hezekiah (2 Kings 18–19; Isaiah 36–37) indicates. All the more deadly would be an outbreak of plague (i.e., a visitation by the "angel of Yahweh" or Yahweh's "holy ones" [v 5]) under the conditions implied in this chapter, with extraordinary earth movements disrupting the existing sewage systems and water sources.

The second consequences for the forces of "all the nations" entrapped by the changes in the natural world of Jerusalem's topography is the psychological state of the enemy troops. Not only will their physical well-being be adversely affected by the ravages of plague; but also will their emotional health be severely impaired, presumably by the threatening effects of death and illness all around, as well as by their being witness to sudden, inexplicable, and dangerous reconfigurations of the very face of the landscape where they are positioned. The resulting chaos and confusion will make the troops their own enemies, for they will turn against each other in the panic that will ensue. The term "panic of Yahweh" (v 13), like the assertion (v 12) that "Yahweh will smite" everyone with disease, need not indicate a discrete action of God against the enemy forces. Both of these are inevitable consequences of God's changes in the landscape described in verses 4–5. Thus, emotionally and physically—i.e., completely—the nations will be affected by the radical earth movements of the future age.

The third result of Yahweh's eschatological intervention in the form of earth-moving changes is even more indirect: it concerns a Jerusalemite/Judean resistance movement (v 14). It hardly seems necessary for Jerusalem/Judah to engage the enemy. Yahweh's actions and the two consequences discussed above apparently will be decisive on their own in vanquishing the attackers. Thus the depiction of Judah and Jerusalem as participants in the cataclysmic battle must have a significance apart from the military efficacy of their involvement.

The key to comprehending their role in this section of Zechariah 14 comes from the overarching theme of transformations—of radical changes in the natural and human realms. At the outset of this chapter, Jerusalem (and, although not explicitly, Judah) is victim. The city is despoiled by the advancing enemy warriors, who violate its property and its peoples (vv 1–2). In the heart of the third subunit we find a complete reversal of that painful predicament. Judah and Jerusalem are no longer victims: they actively do battle, and they collect booty ("wealth") from those who had previously plundered them.

In this reversal of the status of Jerusalem/Judah, however, there are some important distinctions to be made between their behavior and that of the invading enemies. Whereas the destruction of human life and the violation of human (female) bodies to which Jerusalem has been subjected have been done by the nations, the equivalent violence to human persons (but excluding rape or ravishing) in the struggle against Jerusalem will be effected, albeit indirectly, by Yahweh. The plague and panic that destroy the enemy from within will be the result of Yahweh's rearrangement of natural phenomena. The subsequent or concomitant accumulation of wealth, much of which is undoubtedly the reacquisition of its own plundered materials, will represent the Israelite participation in the fray.

Judah and Jerusalem will thus cease to be victims through the act of repossessing their own goods, plus whatever is left by the demise of most of the troops, but not by slaughtering their foes nor by ravishing their women (surely there were female camp followers with these, as with all armies) nor by keeping the survivors from their homeland. Indeed, the next subunit would be virtually meaningless were the remnant of the enemy not repatriated, for it begins with reference to those very survivors (v 16). The empowerment of Judah/Jerusalem involves control over the material wealth of their enemies but excludes violence to their lives. The taking of human life is reserved for divine action and for internal enemy chaos.

The Future for Jerusalem/Judah and the Nations, 14:16–21

The tragic fate that will befall the nations here gives way to a much more positive outcome. Indeed, the suffering of Israel's enemies is depicted as parallel to the suffering of God's own people. That is, there will be a better future for those who survive, and that future will have common elements for both Israel and the nations. The emphasis in this chapter on the ultimate outcome, rather than on the preceding horrors of warfare and plagues, is evident simply from the amount of attention devoted in this chapter to the glorious future. The last section has the same number of verses (six) as the second subunit, which also portrays the positive (for Jerusalem) effects of the eschatological catastrophe, in contrast to five and four verses each for the negative portrayals of the first and third subunits. Yet counting verses, which can vary so widely in length, may not provide the most reliable kind of comparison. Word counts are better indicators of equivalence or emphasis. Thus it is significant that verses 16–21 have more words—more than 20 percent more words—than any of the other subunits. Clearly, the ultimate fate of both Judah/Jerusalem and the nations deserves greater attention than the death and devastation that precedes the final triumph of universal holiness.

If Yahweh as warrior is the primary metaphor of the first and, indirectly, the third subunits of this chapter, Yahweh as king emerges as the dominant trope of the final section. The focus on God's kingship is evident in the repeated (in vv 16 and 17) title "King Yahweh of Hosts," a unique and evocative designation (see NOTE at v 16). It is also expressed in the repetitive language about the nations going up to Jerusalem to bow down to Yahweh. The very term "go up" occurs five times (some of them with the negative) in verses 16–19, and "bow down" is found twice; both expressions contribute to the sense of the nations acknowledging Yahweh's sovereignty.

The emergence of the royal metaphor is, in a sense, an expected development of the intense warrior imagery used for God in this chapter as well as in previous sections of Second Zechariah. Because one of the main roles of a human monarch was to establish and/or sustain an army, and often to command it himself, the aspects of power in military language are, in effect, dependent on royal authority. In other words, the warrior imagery can be considered a submetaphor of monarchic imagery (Brettler forthcoming). In certain psalms, for example, the two metaphors are explicitly interwoven (see Psalms 29 and

47). Thus it is natural and perhaps even necessary that the powerful military image should give way here to the more general and inclusive image, Yahweh's role as king.

The royal metaphor, drawn from the human political arena, is surely among the most prominent examples of the projection of human attributes onto Yahweh. As such, it plays a central role in Israel's attempts to express the nature of its incomparable God through the vehicle of language drawn from human experience (see Brettler 1989). Yet, just as the divine warrior trope exhibits new dimensions in this chapter, in transforming nature, so too does the royal metaphor operate here at a greatly different level. The universality of God's future dominion on the one hand, and the pervasive sanctity of the world so ruled on the other, constitute a dramatically altered and extended use of the concept of Yahweh as king.

There is some question about whether this metaphor of Yahweh as king contradicts the royal language of 9:10, in which the horse (and chariot) are removed from Israel (Ephraim and Jerusalem), but the restored human king reigns in peace "from sea to sea, from the river to the ends of the earth." Certainly the eschatological vision of chapter 14 focuses on Yahweh's universal sovereignty and not on that of a restored Davidide. However, the difference between the two chapters may be one of emphasis rather than contradiction. The removal of horse and chariot from the people is one way to express the apolitical nature of the Israelite rule at the end-time. But even the elevated role of Israel and its king in those days should not supersede that of the divine king Yahweh, whose sovereignty is supreme, who is called King by the other nations, and who is to be worshiped by foreigners at the Feast of Booths.

The universality of God's future rule is made explicit in this chapter in the depiction of all the nations coming to Jerusalem, to the Temple precincts, for a cultic event. The inclusiveness of such a portrayal is rather extraordinary for a postexilic text. The sixth-century conquest of Judah and the subsequent exile of many Judeans only intensifed the age-old problem of boundaries between God's people and other social or political groups. Israel historically, but often unsuc- cessfully, strove to maintain separation between its own cultural patterns and beliefs and those of its neighbors (see Deut 7:1–6). Its own cultic documents stress the ideal of Israelite holiness, in emulation of divine sanctity and in contrast to the detested practices of other nations (e.g., Lev 18:3–5; 20:23–24, 26).

The matter of boundaries becomes especially important in the postexilic period. In fact, much of the priestly legislation aimed at establishing categories of holiness or purity and at structuring ritual behaviors can best be understood sociologically rather than theologically or morally. The latter two categories can give ideological voice to the former, but a functional social dynamic may have primacy. That is, ritual can be understood as a critical means of maintaining boundaries. An exiled or subjugated people, whose identity is threatened by the loss of political autonomy and self-determination, often develops elaborate means to protect its identity; it establishes mechanisms to regulate or retain its socioreligious distinctiveness from the alien majority or surrounding culture (see D. L. Smith 1989: 80–84, 139–51). What has appeared as rigid and formalistic ritual regulations to generations of theological critics can be better understood in terms of the process of cultural distancing and, thus, of survival.

Given such a significant function for cultural, and especially cultic, distinction, it is remarkable to find in this conclusion to Zechariah a situation in which such boundaries are to be transcended. This may be the most radical alteration of all in the series of dramatic shifts presented in Zechariah 14. The remnant of nations, the survivors of those who had advanced against God's people and who had been overwhelmed by Yahweh's cosmic actions aimed at delivering Jerusalem, will acknowledge the supremacy of Yahweh. But this recognition of Yahweh's rule will go beyond the diplomatic or political level. It will involve foreigners joining fully in the pilgrimage to Jerusalem to take part in what was probably the most important festival of the year in the postexilic period (see last NOTE to v 16).

This international participation in a central Israelite festal event surely is a step toward dissolving boundaries rather than maintaining them. It is comprehensible only in a scenario in which Israelite identity, which is defined by its covenant relationship to Yahweh, is no longer in question. Thus the eschatological age will involve a reversal of the historical reality of Israelite failure to maintain its covenant responsibility. The future (new) covenant will not carry the risk of violation—hence Israelite identity will cease to become an issue. Rather, it is the other nations, whose culture will be somewhat subsumed into that of Israel by their acknowledgment of Yahweh and their celebration of the Feast of Booths, whose identity and autonomy will never again be absolute and thus never again stand in opposition to Israelite integrity and existence.

Although the nations will participate in Booths and bow down to Yahweh, they will not entirely forego their distinctions from the Israelites. The contingencies of verses 17–19 indicate that the Egyptians and the others may not always participate as they should. Although their cultural identity may become somewhat blurred and diminished by their obeisance to Yahweh, they clearly are not to be identified with Israel nor to share its special relationship with Yahweh in a new covenant that will preclude any sinful behavior and thus will have no contingencies.

This status of the nations will not be the same for the foreign people of the holy land itself, i.e., the Canaanites. The thorny and persistent issue of boundary maintenance between Israel and Canaan will be overcome in the eschatological future by Canaan recognizing Yahweh and partially acquiring Israelite cultural form. Canaan and Israel were too close—territorially, environmentally, and culturally—for distinction to be sustained. The risk of Israel's falling into Canaanite ways can be resolved either by the ultimate cultural reversal—Canaanites will become Israelites throughout the promised land and in its sacred center in the Jerusalem Temple—or by the total annihilation of Israel's archenemy. The all-pervasive holiness of the future age will pertain to all in the land, Canaanites (if they are still there) and Israelites alike. And because the holiness is that of Yahweh and not of the gods of Canaan, it is the identity of Yahweh's people that will prevail in the land and that will become filled with God's sanctity.

The last two verses of Zechariah 14 focus on this holiness. They do so by heralding two mundane objects that signify the radical transformation of the end-time and that also convey the idea of the dissolution of boundaries in the future age. The horse, the symbol for political power and military might, and of all that interferes with the peace and harmony that are to prevail in the eschatological age, will bear a holy insignia. The Yahwistic nature of that inscription indicates that warfare and contention will cease.

Yet perhaps even more than the image of the holy horses, the appearance of the mundane "pots" of verses 20 and 21 is the key to the radical transformation of the future age. As cooking vessels, they touch the lives of all; food prepared in them is consumed by people throughout the land. Thus by their very ordinariness they bespeak inclusivity. The language used for food preparation— "sacrifice" and "cook"—merges the processes involved in preparing sacral and secular repasts. Thus the inclusivity of a mundane vessel becomes combined with a procedure, actually a reversal of a procedure, that implies sanctity for everything prepared in such a vessel.

In addition to the fact that the processing of food involves the sanctification of all food, and thus of all who eat, i.e. everyone, the pots themselves signify the irrevocable crossing, and thus the obviating, of traditional boundaries between the sacred and the mundane. For the comparison of cooking pots to altar basins means likening them to vessels that, in the cultic scheme of Israel's Torah literature, are the only items that can move from an outer realm of Temple sanctity to an inner one. They are unparalleled in their ability to reach a higher degree of sanctity. Thus they signify a pervasive and vast intensification, even within the holy Jerusalem Temple, of sanctity. The future age will thus transform even the unparalleled and unsurpassed holiness of Yahweh's earthly dwelling place. If that be the case, then surely the surrounding territory can be transformed into sacred space, with all its inhabitants sharing in the incomparable sanctity of the sovereign God.

INDEX OF AUTHORS AND TRANSLATIONS

◆

509

INDEX OF SUBJECTS

◆

INDEX OF HEBREW WORDS

◆

y vocalized

k unvocalized

k vocalized

l unvocalized

š vocalized

šāwʿ 190, 191
šāwpᵓ 191
šālal 410
šālôm 135
šaʿar 238
šaʿar hayyēšānâ 445
šaʿar happinnâ 446
šaʿar happinnîm 446
šaʿar happôneh 446
šaʿar hāriᵓšôn 445
šēᵓāgâ 247
šēbeṭ 94, 226, 471, 472
šēlālâ 410
šēm 228
šēnayim 390
šnê maqlôt 262
šeqel 275
šeqeṣ 114
šeqer 187, 189, 190, 372, 375
šēṭîmû 154
šiggāʿôn 321
šiqqûṣ 114
šiqqûṣîm 370

šîr hammaʿālôt 465
šôpār 150

t unvocalized

tyrwš 161
tmh 320

t vocalized

tāḥîl 108
taḥānûnîm 335
takkeh 387
tarʿēlâ 313
tēmān 152
tēreᵓ 106
tērāpîm 185
tēšēb 109
tihyeh 478
timmāhôn 320
tipᵓārâ 329
tipᵓeret 329
tîrāᵓ 106
tîrôš 160

Index of Other Languages

INDEX OF SCRIPTURAL
REFERENCES

◆

Job

Proverbs